Encyclopedia
of Marriage
and the Family

Editorial Board

Encyclopedia of Marriage and the Family

VOLUME 1

DAVID LEVINSON

Editor in Chief

MACMILLAN LIBRARY REFERENCE USA
SIMON & SCHUSTER MACMILLAN
New York

SIMON & SCHUSTER AND PRENTICE HALL INTERNATIONAL
London   Mexico City   New Delhi   Singapore   Sydney   Toronto

Simon & Schuster Macmillan
866 Third Avenue, New York, NY 10022

PRINTED IN THE UNITED STATES OF AMERICA

printing number
1 2 3 4 5 6 7 8 9 10

LIBRARY OF CONGRESS CATALOGING-IN-PUBLICATION DATA
Encyclopedia of marriage and the family / David Levinson, editor in
    chief.
        p.   cm.
    Includes bibliographical references and index.
    ISBN 0-02-897235-X (set)
    1. Marriage—Encyclopedias.   2. Family—Encyclopedias.
I. Levinson, David, 1947–   .
HQ9.E52   1995
306.8′03—dc20   95-18682
                                                                         CIP

Contents

Editorial and Production Staff

Brian Kinsey
Project Editor

William D. Drennan   Andrea Salvatore
Copy Editors

Mary Grace Butler
Proofreader

AEIOU, Inc.
Indexer

Maureen Frantino
Production Manager

Macmillan Library Reference USA

Gordon Macomber
President

Philip Friedman
Publisher

Elly Dickason
Associate Publisher

Preface

Marriages and families are the most important constants in our lives. Nearly all of us are enmeshed in the intimate relationships of marriage and family, fulfilling the roles of mother, father, husband, wife, daughter, son, brother, sister, grandparent, grandchild, cousin, aunt, and uncle. Many of us have also become stepparents, stepchildren, half-siblings, and ex-spouses. In all societies, marriage and family are basic sociocultural institutions in which the key activities of society—reproduction, child rearing, economic decision making, and the passing of cultural values and customs from one generation to the next—take place. Most people have intense feelings about marriage and family, about their own relations with other family members, and about the roles of marriage and family in society.

As at many other times in history, the late twentieth century is a time of considerable change and turmoil for both marriage and family. Some people say that marriage and family are threatened by the growth of alternative family forms. Others say that marriage and family are evolving into forms appropriate for a society in which individual freedom is cherished, new roles for women and men are emerging, and beliefs about sexuality are being questioned. Another source of confusion is that what prominent people say publicly (and perhaps want to believe) about marriage and family may be at odds with their own lives, and with the lives and experiences of their listeners. Such contradictions are not necessarily signs of social disintegration or political hypocrisy. They may instead reflect something common to life in all societies: tension between the ideal—the way people want things to be—and the real—the way things truly are.

While marriages and families are basic institutions, both for the individuals involved in them and for society as a whole, they are neither simple nor static. Quite to the contrary, marriages and families are varied, complex, and constantly changing. This complexity and this changeability make it difficult to fully know or understand our own marriages and families and even more difficult to understand the roles of marriage and family in society.

I suggested the *Encyclopedia of Marriage and the Family* to Macmillan after several years of teaching about marriage and the family to undergraduates, conducting research on family violence, and at the same time examining and dealing with issues in my own life. It seemed to me that what would help all of us to make more sense of marriage and family in the 1990s was a single publication bringing together and summarizing what we know and pointing out what we do not know. Thus, this work is a compendium of knowledge about marriages, families, and human relationships and about the psychological, cultural, and societal forces that influence them.

This project was developed using a broad, inclusive, and interdisciplinary definition of marriage and the family, and information on topics of interest to a broad range of readers has been included. In selecting topics for coverage, we looked to the following sources for ideas: existing course curricula on marriage and family; high school and college textbooks; scholarly and professional publications; and media coverage of important marriage and family issues. Advisory editors representing the fields of anthropology, gerontology, home economics, law, psychiatry, sexology, and sociology also provided content recommendations.

The final product of this selection process was a list of 169 entries covering the following general topics: marriage and family types, emotions, interpersonal dynamics, economics, health and illness, family law, values and religion, sexual beliefs and behaviors, reproduction, socialization, parenting, and sociocultural influences on marriage and the family. Because the literature on marriage and family includes tens of thousands of journal articles and thousands of books written by sociologists, psychologists, home economists, historians, psychiatrists, social workers, gerontologists, sexologists, attorneys, and others, some topics with a complex and interdisciplinary nature have been handled by including multiple entries with different approaches to the same topic. For example, the entry on divorce is actually a composite of four separate articles: legal aspects, social and economic aspects, emotional aspects, and effects of divorce on the children involved. In all cases, we have encouraged authors not only to write about what is known with some certainty about marriage and the family but also to point out areas where little is known and to discuss significant issues that are subject to alternative or contradictory interpretations.

The *Encyclopedia of Marriage and the Family* is a basic reference source written with the needs of a number of types of readers in mind. For high school students, it will be a trustworthy source of information for discussions and projects in family life, health, and home economics courses. For parents and spouses, it is a guide to the challenges and realities facing marriages and families in the day-to-day contemporary world. For college students, it will serve as a source of substantive material for research papers and as a directory to recent literature on the major topics of marriage and family. For researchers and professionals, it provides an accessible review of knowledge from many disciplines and from various perspectives.

This publication is not a how-to manual; readers are not told how to find the perfect mate, how to discipline their children, how to make a will, or how to care for elderly parents. We are merely presenting a report on the state of marriage and the family, enabling readers to gather information that will help them to think about and analyze their own issues within the broader context of marriage and the family in the 1990s.

There are a number of individuals I want to thank for their contributions to this project. First, Philip Friedman and Elly Dickason at Macmillan Library Reference, who supported the project and first suggested the broad, interdisciplinary approach we have followed. I also want to thank Elly for her careful and thoughtful stewardship and Brian Kinsey, also at Macmillan, for his careful and diligent day-to-day management. Second, I want to acknowledge the vital contribution made by our six advisory editors— Suzanne Frayser, Marilyn Ihinger-Tallman, Rhonda Montgomery, James Ponzetti, Lawrence Rossi, and Mary Moers Wenig—who generously shared their wisdom and played a major role in selecting topics for coverage, recommending contributors, and devoting much time and effort to recruiting these suggested authors. These six editors also carefully reviewed and commented on all articles in their areas of expertise. Third, I want to thank the contributors, who provided the clear, thorough, and thoughtful entries that comprise the *Encyclopedia of Marriage and the Family*. Finally, I want to thank my family—Karen, Tom, and Rachel—for their support and encouragement, and for regularly reminding me of the complexities and joys of marriage and family.

David Levinson

List of Articles

List of Contributors

ALAN C. ACOCK
Oregon State University
Research Methods

GERALD R. ADAMS
University of Guelph
Attractiveness

KATE S. AHMADI
University of Connecticut
Self-Help Groups

RICHARD ALFORD
East Central University, Ada, OK
Naming

A. R. ALLGEIER
Allgeier and Associates, Bowling Green, OH
Sexual Problems

ELAINE A. ANDERSON
University of Maryland
Family Policy

ROSE MARIE ARNHOLD
Fort Hays State University
Polygyny

BARBARA A. ARRIGHI
Northern Kentucky University
Family Values

MARGARET EDWARDS ARCUS
University of British Columbia
Family Life Education

ALICE M. ATKINSON
University of Iowa
Child Care

PHIL BACKLUND
Central Washington University
Communication

HENRY P. BELLUTTA
St. John's Queens Hospital, New York
AIDS

FELIX M. BERARDO
University of Florida
Cohabitation
Widowhood

JERRY J. BIGNER
Colorado State University
Gay and Lesbian Parents

WILLIAM G. BLACK, JR.
United States Air Force
Military Families

EVELYN BLACKWOOD
Purdue University
Sexual Orientation

CARLFRED B. BRODERICK
University of Southern California
Family Systems Theory

GWEN J. BROUDE
Vassar College
Kinship

M. GADRIELLE BROWN
Independent Research Psychologist/Author
Celibacy

TIMOTHY H. BRUBAKER
Miami University
Later-Life Families

BONNIE BULLOUGH
University of Southern California
Birth Control: Sociocultural and Historical
Aspects
Family Planing

VERN L. BULLOUGH
State University of New York (emeritus)
California State University, Northridge
(visiting)
Birth Control: Sociocultural and Historical
Aspects
Family Planning

DANIEL J. CANARY
Pennsylvania State University
Conflict

RODNEY M. CATE
University of Arizona
Mate Selection

F. SCOTT CHRISTOPHER
Arizona State University
Adolescent Sexuality

MARILYN COLEMAN
University of Missouri, Columbia
Remarriage and Children

SCOTT COLTRANE
University of California, Riverside
Division of Labor

RAND D. CONGER
Iowa State University
Unemployment

BROWYN CONRAD
Washington State University
Exchange Theory

STEPHANIE COONTZ
The Evergreen State College
History of the Family

ENID O. COX
University of Denver
Elders

ALICIA CRAFFEY
University of Connecticut Health Center,
Farmington, CT
Genetic Counseling

WILLIAM R. CUPACH
Illinois State University
Conflict

THOM CURTIS
Utah State University
Nonmarital Pregnancy

HOWARD A. DAVIDSON
American Bar Association Center on Children
and the Law
Children's Rights

JOHN DELAMATER
University of Wisconsin, Madison
Sexuality

STEVE DUCK
University of Iowa
Personal Relationships

ELIAS J. DURYEA
University of New Mexico
Sexuality Education

ALICE EICHHOLZ
Vermont College of Norwich University
Genealogy

DAVID M. ENGLISH
University of South Dakota School of Law
Guardianship

NANCY S. ERICKSON
Brooklyn, NY
Child Support

VIRGINIA ERION
Central Washington University
Home Schooling

TONI FALBO
University of Texas, Austin
Only Child

LAURENCE L. FALK
Concordia College (emeritus)
Family Gender Roles

JACQUELINE FAWCETT
University of Pennsylvania School of Nursing
Pregnancy and Birth

BEVERLEY FEHR
University of Winnipeg
Love

GERALD FELDMAN
Farmington Public Schools, Farmington, CT
Truancy

KATHRYN M. FELTEY
University of Akron
Single Parents

RONALD R. FICHTNER
Centers for Disease Control and Prevention, Atlanta
Sexually Transmitted Diseases

BARBARA H. FIESE
Syracuse University
Family Rituals

MARK A. FINE
University of Missouri, Columbia
Stepparenting

DEBORAH L. FORMAN
Whittier Law School
Privacy and Confidentiality

JONATHAN BARRY FORMAN
University of Oklahoma
Entitlements

LAWRENCE H. GANONG
University of Missouri, Columbia
Remarriage and Children

VIKTOR GECAS
Washington State University
Self-Esteem
Symbolic Interactionism

RICHARD J. GELLES
University of Rhode Island
Child Abuse and Neglect: Sociological Aspects
Spouse Abuse and Neglect

IRENE GLASSER
Eastern Connecticut State University
Homeless Families

NORVAL D. GLENN
University of Texas, Austin
Marital Quality

H. WALLACE GODDARD
Auburn University
Parent Education

JUDITH G. GONYEA
Boston University
Middle Age

THEODORE N. GREENSTEIN
North Carolina State University
Substitute Caregivers

GARY L. HANSEN
University of Kentucky
Jealousy

SHIRLEY M. H. HANSON
Oregon Health Sciences University
Fathers

JOHN H. HARVEY
University of Iowa
Attribution in Relationships

RUTH CORDLE HATCH
Omaha, NE
Religion

CINDY HAZAN
Cornell University
Attachment

HONOR S. HEATH
Quinnipiac College School of Law
Bankruptcy

WARREN M. HERN
Boulder Abortion Clinic
University of Colorado
Abortion: Medical and Social Aspects

BARRIE J. HIGHBY
University of Kansas
Rape

SHIRLEY A. HILL
University of Kansas
Chronic Illness

BARBARA A. HIRSHORN
Wayne State University
Intergenerational Relations

JANET SHIBLEY HYDE
University of Wisconsin, Madison
Sexuality

PATRICK HYNES
Connecticut Suicide Education Foundation
Suicide

MARILYN IHINGER-TALLMAN
Washington State University
Marriage Ceremonies
Marriage Definition
Sibling Relationships

MASAKO ISHII-KUNTZ
University of California, Riverside
Mothers

DIANA K. IVY
Central Washington University
Communication

STEVI JACKSON
University of Strathclyde, Glasgow
Childhood

MICHAEL P. JOHNSON
Pennsylvania State University
Commitment

LYNN JOHNSON-MARTIN
Pastoral Counseling Center,
West Hartford, CT
Codependency

WARREN H. JONES
University of Tennessee
Shyness

YOSHINORI KAMO
Louisiana State University
Grandparenthood

RICHARD J. KATES
Hartford Hospital, Hartford, CT
Infertility

KRISTINE M. KELLY
University of Tennessee
Shyness

DIANNE K. KIEREN
University of Alberta
Decision Making and Problem Solving

HARRY H. L. KITANO
University of California, Los Angeles
Ethnicity

DARA KLASSEL
Planned Parenthood Federation of
America, Inc.
Abortion: Legal Aspects

DAVID M. KLEIN
University of Notre Dame
Family Theory

MAXINE J. KLEIN
Hartford Hospital, Hartford CT
Birth Control: Contraceptive Methods
Conception: Medical Aspects

JOAN M. KRAUSKOPF
Ohio State University College of Law
Alimony and Spousal Support

LAWRENCE A. KURDEK
Wright State University
Divorce: Effects on Children

MARY RIEGE LANER
Arizona State University
Singles

ROBERT E. LARZELERE
Father Flanagan's Boys' Home,
Boys Town, NE
Discipline

ANNETTE LAWSON
Aurispa Limited, London
Extramarital Sex

GREGORY C. LEAVITT
Gustavus Adolphus College
Incest Taboo

GREGORY K. LEHNE
The Johns Hopkins University School of
Medicine
Gender Identity

NANCY E. LEVINE
University of California, Los Angeles
Polyandry

DAVID LEVINSON
Human Relations Area Files,
New Haven, CT
Marriage Ceremonies
Marriage Definition

BARBARA W. LEX
McLean Hospital, Belmont, MA
Harvard Medical School
Substance Abuse

CATHERINE M. LINTON
Elmcrest Hospital, Portland, CT
Peer Pressure

AMY LOFQUIST
University of North Carolina, Greensboro
Remarriage

GREGORY LOKEN
Quinnipiac College School of Law
Child Abuse and Neglect: Legal Aspects
Missing Children

EDGAR C. J. LONG
Central Michigan University
Marital Typologies

L. M. LOTHSTEIN
Institute of Living, Hartford, CT
Personality Development

MARGO MAINE
Institute of Living, Hartford, CT
Eating Disorders

JOAN MCCORD
Temple University
Juvenile Delinquency

NORMA L. McCOY
San Francisco State University
Menopause

SARA MCLANAHAN
Princeton University
Poverty

MARYGOLD S. MELLI
University of Wisconsin Law School
Child Custody

ELIZABETH G. MENAGHAN
Ohio State University
Stress

PAMELA K. METZ
University of Denver
Elders

BRENT C. MILLER
Utah State University
Nonmarital Pregnancy

LEIGH MINTURN
University of Colorado
Infanticide

RHONDA J. V. MONTGOMERY
University of Kansas
In-Law Relationships

EARL W. MORRIS
University of Minnesota
Housing

JEYLAN T. MORTIMER
University of Minnesota
Adolescence

JONATHAN D. MIDGETT
University of Virginia
Attractiveness

CAROLE M. MUCHA
Institute of Living, Hartford, CT
Marriage Counseling

CHARLENE L. MUEHLENHARD
University of Kansas
Rape

MARY BETH OFSTEDAL
*National Center for Health Statistics,
Hyattsville, MD*
Demography

J. THOMAS OLDHAM
University of Houston Law Center
Divorce: Legal Aspects

NILS OLSEN
University of Iowa
Attribution in Relationships

LYNN B. OSTERKAMP
University of Kansas
Filial Responsibility

STANLEY PARKER
*Veterans Memorial Medical Center,
Meriden, CT*
Child Abuse and Neglect: Emotional and
Psychological Aspects
Incest

KAY PASLEY
University of North Carolina, Greensboro
Remarriage
Teenage Parenting

JOÄN M. PATTERSON
University of Minnesota
Disabilities

EVE W. PAUL
*Planned Parenthood Federation of
America, Inc.*
Birth Control: Legal Aspects

DANIEL PERLMAN
University of British Columbia
Loneliness

CHRISTOPHER G. PETR
University of Kansas School of Social Welfare
Foster Parenting

JAMES J. PONZETTI, JR.
Central Washington University
Family Stories and Myths

KAREN JEAN PRAGER
University of Texas, Dallas
Intimacy

PAMELA C. REGAN
Albion College
Marital Sex

JOHN K. REMPEL
University of St. Jerome's College
Trust

BARBARA J. RISMAN
North Carolina State University
Dual-Earner Families

DAVID S. ROSETTENSTEIN
Quinnipiac College School of Law
Adoption

SUSAN M. ROSS
University of New Hampshire
Measures of Family Characteristics

LAWRENCE N. ROSSI
*Veterans Memorial Medical Center,
  Meriden, CT*
Psychiatric Disorders

BARBARA R. ROWE
Purdue University
Divorce: Economic Aspects

WILLIAM E. RUSSNER
Bowling Green State University
Social Networks

CAROLYN L. SCHOLZ
*Veterans Memorial Medical Center,
  Meriden, CT
University of Connecticut*
Family Therapy

WARREN F. SCHUMACHER
University of Massachusetts, Amherst
Annulment

MARY C. SENGSTOCK
Wayne State University
Family Violence

DOROTHY G. SINGER
Yale University
Play

JEROME L. SINGER
Yale University
Mass Media

ARLENE SKOLNICK
University of California, Berkeley
Nuclear Family

GARY N. SKOLOFF
Skoloff & Wolfe, Livingston, NJ
Conception: Legal Aspects

WILLIAM L. SMITH
Georgia Southern University
Communes
Utopian Communities

TED SPENCER
*University of Maryland,
  College Park*
Self-Disclosure

SUSAN SPRECHER
Illinois State University
Equity and Close Relationships
Marital Sex

CATHERINE H. STEIN
Bowling Green State University
Social Networks

MURRAY A. STRAUS
University of New Hampshire
Marital Power
Measures of Family Characteristics

DONALD E. STULL
University of Akron
Health and the Family

PEGGY SUDOL
*Thomaston Counseling Associates,
  Thomaston, CT*
Divorce: Emotional and Social
  Aspects

DANETTE JOHNSON SUMERFORD
North Carolina State University
Dual-Earner Families

MAXIMILIANE SZINOVACZ
*Old Dominion University
Max Research Associates, Inc.*
Retirement

IRVING TALLMAN
Washington State University
Exchange Theory

L. EUGENE THOMAS
University of Connecticut
Death and Mourning

MICHAEL CHARLES THORNTON
University of Wisconsin, Madison
Intermarriage

JAMES DIEGO VIGIL
University of Southern California
Gangs

RICHARD A. WAGNER
Smith College
Extended Family
Fictive Kinship

SUZANNE WASON
University of Wisconsin, Madison
Intermarriage

MARY MOERS WENIG
Quinnipiac College School of Law
Inheritance
Marital Property and Community Property

AMY S. WHARTON
Washington State University
Gender
Work and Family

JAMES M. WHITE
University of British Columbia
Family Development Theory

MICHAEL W. WIEDERMAN
University of Kansas Medical Center School of Medicine, Wichita
Sexuality in the Life Cycle

C. PRESTON WILES
Yale Child Study Center
Runaway Children

MARY WINTER
Iowa State University
Housing
Resource Management

ROSALIE S. WOLF
Medical Center of Central Massachusetts, Worcester, MA
Elder Abuse

SHERYL L. SCHEIBLE WOLF
University of New Mexico
Family Law

PAUL H. WRIGHT
University of North Dakota
Friendship

CARRIE L. YODANIS
University of New Hampshire
Marital Power

JOHN G. YOUNGBAUER
University of Kansas
School

JUDITH T. YOUNGER
University of Minnesota Law School
Premarital Agreements

DAVID ZEMKE
Veterans Memorial Medical Center, Meriden, CT
Dysfunctional Family

A

ABORTION

This entry consists of the following two articles:

Medical and Social Aspects
  Warren M. Hern
Legal Aspects
  Dara Klassel

Medical and Social Aspects

Abortion is one of the most difficult, controversial, and painful subjects in modern American society. The principal controversy revolves around the questions of who makes the decision concerning abortion—the individual or the state; under what circumstances it may be done; and who is capable of making the decision. Medical questions such as techniques of abortion are less controversial but are sometimes part of the larger debate.

Abortion is not new in human society; a study by anthropologist George Devereux (1955) showed that more than three hundred contemporary nonindustrial societies practiced abortion. Women have performed abortions on themselves or experienced abortions at the hands of others for thousands of years (Potts, Diggory, and Peel 1977), and abortions continue to occur today in nonindustrialized societies under medically primitive conditions. However, modern technology and social change have made abortion a part of modern health care. At the same time, abortion has become a political issue in American life and a flash point for disagreements about the role of women and individual autonomy in life decisions.

Definition of Abortion

The classic definition of abortion is "expulsion of the fetus before it is viable." This could include spon-

taneous abortion (miscarriage) or induced abortion, in which someone (a doctor, the woman herself, or a layperson) causes the abortion. Before modern methods of abortion, this sometimes meant the introduction of foreign objects such as catheters into the uterus to disrupt the placenta and embryo (or fetus) so that a miscarriage would result. In preindustrial societies, hitting the pregnant woman in the abdomen over the uterus and jumping on her abdomen while she lies on the ground are common techniques used to induce an abortion (Early and Peters 1990). Although these methods can be effective, they may also result in the death of the woman if her uterus is ruptured or if some of the amniotic fluid surrounding the fetus enters her bloodstream. From the Colonial period to the early twentieth century in America, primitive methods such as these were used along with the introduction of foreign objects into the uterus (wooden sticks, knitting needles, catheters, etc.) to cause abortion, frequently with tragic results (Lee 1969).

In modern American society, abortions are performed surgically by physicians or other trained personnel experienced in this technique, making the procedure much safer than when primitive methods were used. The goal of induced abortion still remains the same: Interrupt the pregnancy so that the woman will not continue to term and deliver a baby.

One problem with the classical definition of abortion is the changing definition of viability (the ability to live outside the womb). Premature birth is historically associated with high death and disability rates for babies born alive, but medical advances of the twentieth century have made it possible to save the lives of babies born after only thirty weeks of pregnancy when the usual pregnancy lasts forty weeks. Some infants born at twenty-six to twenty-seven weeks or even younger have survived through massive intervention and support. At the same time, abortions are now sometimes performed at up to twenty-five to twenty-six weeks of pregnancy. Therefore, the old definition of viability is not helpful in determining whether an abortion has been or should be performed (Grobstein 1988).

Reasons for Abortions

There are probably as many reasons for abortions as there are women who have them. Some pregnancies result from rape or incest, and women who are victims of these assaults often seek an abortion. Most women, however, decide to have an abortion because the pregnancy represents a problem in their lives. Some women feel emotionally unprepared to enter parenthood and raise a child; they are too young or do not have a reliable partner with whom to raise a child. Many young women in high school or college find themselves pregnant and must choose between continuing the education they need to survive economically and dropping out to have a baby. Young couples who are just starting their lives together and want children might prefer to develop financial security first to provide better care for their future children. Sometimes people enter into a casual sexual relationship that leads to pregnancy with no prospect of marriage, but even if the sexual relationship is more than casual, abortion is sometimes sought because a woman decides that the social status of the male is inappropriate.

Some of the most difficult and painful choices are faced by women who are happily pregnant for the first time late in the reproductive years (thirty-five to forty-five) but discover in late pregnancy (twenty-six or more weeks) that the fetus is so defective it may not live or have a normal life. Even worse is a diagnosis of abnormalities that may or may not result in problems after birth. Some women and couples in this situation choose to have a late abortion (Hern et al. 1993; Kolata 1992).

In some cases, a woman must have an abortion to survive a pregnancy. An example is the diabetic woman who develops a condition in pregnancy called hyperemesis gravidarum (uncontrollable vomiting associated with pregnancy). She becomes malnourished and dehydrated in spite of intravenous therapy and other treatment, threatening heart failure, among other things. Only an abortion will cure this life-threatening condition.

In other cases, an abortion is sought because the sex of the fetus has been determined through amniocentesis or ultrasound examination and it is not the desired sex. This is more common in some cultures than in others. In the United States, it is exceedingly rare, and the request for abortion in this situation may be precipitated by the risk of a sex-linked hereditary disease.

Incidence of Abortion

If it were not for pregnancy, there would be no abortions. This rather obvious fact must be stated because it is not always noticed. To understand the numbers and rates of abortions, it is necessary to know the denominator: the total number of pregnancies. In the United States, about 6.2 million pregnancies occur each year, of which 1.6 million end in abortion and 4.6 million in live birth (Henshaw and Van Vort 1992; Koonin et al. 1991b). This gives an abortion ratio of 347.8 abortions per 1,000 live births. Since these 1.6 million abortions occur in approximately 67 million women in the reproductive ages (fifteen to forty-five), the abortion rate is 24 abortions per 1,000 women fifteen to forty five. In some areas where contraceptives are not widely available, such as the former Soviet Union and certain countries in Eastern Europe, the abortion rates and ratios are much higher. In some Scandinavian nations, where contraceptives are more freely available and widespread sex education emphasizes prevention of pregnancy and sexually transmitted diseases, the abortion rates and ratios are much lower than in the United States (Hodgson 1981).

The incidence of abortion (total number of cases per unit of time) may fluctuate, but the rates and ratios of abortion tend to remain steady. However, in the early 1970s, when abortion became legal in the United States with the Supreme Court decision in *Roe* v. *Wade* (1973), all three factors were affected. In addition, many illegal abortions performed before the 1970s were simply not reported, so the increase in reported incidence was to some extent an artifact of the changed legal climate. The number of abortions being performed did not change as much as the number of abortions being reported, and the number of deaths due to illegal abortion declined dramatically (Pakter 1977; Tietze 1975, 1977).

When abortion was illegal in the United States, even the many abortions performed properly by skilled physicians were not reported. Women without funds for a safe illegal abortion often committed desperate acts. Restrictions on legal abortion, including prohibition of public funding for the procedure, have produced some of the same results. Women have inserted harmful and even lethal substances such as lye into

2

their vaginas in the mistaken belief that it will cause an abortion. Long knitting needles have been inserted into the uterus and moved around enough to cause an abortion. While this can cause an abortion, penetration of the uterine wall or other organs can occur and be fatal.

Risks of Abortion

Abortion has become not only the most common but also one of the safest operations performed in the United States. This was not always the case. In the nineteenth and early twentieth centuries, abortion was quite dangerous; many women died as a result.

Pregnancy itself is not a harmless condition; women can die during pregnancy. The maternal mortality rate (the proportion of women dying from pregnancy and childbirth) is found by dividing the number of women dying from all causes related to pregnancy, childbirth, and the puerperium (the six-week period following childbirth) by the total number of live births and then multiplying by a constant factor, such as 100,000. The maternal mortality rate in the United States in 1920 was 680 maternal deaths per 100,000 live births (Lerner and Anderson 1963). It had fallen to 38 deaths per 100,000 live births by 1960 and 8 deaths per 100,000 live births by 1994. Illegal abortion accounted for about 50 percent of all maternal deaths in 1920, and that was still true in 1960. By 1980, however, the percentage of deaths due to abortion had dropped to nearly zero (Cates 1982). The difference in maternal mortality rates due to abortion reflected the increasing legalization of abortion from 1967 to 1973 that permitted abortions to be done safely by doctors in clinics and hospitals. The changed legal climate also permitted the prompt treatment of complications that occurred with abortions.

The complication rates and death rates associated with abortion itself can also be examined. In 1970, Christopher Tietze of the Population Council began studying the risks of death and complications due to abortion by collecting data from hospitals and clinics throughout the nation. The statistical analyses at that time showed that the death rate due to abortion was about 2 deaths per 100,000 procedures, compared with the maternal mortality rate exclusive of abortion of 12 deaths per 100,000 live births. In other words, a woman having an abortion was six times less likely to die than a woman who chose to carry a pregnancy to term. Tietze also found that early abortion was many times safer than abortion done after twelve weeks of pregnancy (Tietze and Lewit 1972) and that some abortion techniques were safer than others. The Cen-

ters for Disease Control and Prevention in Atlanta took over the national study of abortion statistics that had been developed by Tietze, and abortion became the most carefully studied surgical procedure in the United States. As doctors gained more experience with abortion and as techniques improved, death and complication rates due to abortion continued to decline. The rates declined because women were seeking abortions earlier during pregnancy, when the procedure was safer. Clinics where safe abortions could be obtained were opened in many cities across the country, improving access to this service.

By the early 1990s, the risk of death in early abortion was fewer than 1 death per 1 million procedures, and for later abortion, about 1 death per 100,000 procedures (Koonin et al. 1992). The overall risk of death in abortion was about 0.4 deaths per 100,000 procedures, compared with a maternal mortality rate (exclusive of abortion) of about 9.1 deaths per 100,000 live births (Koonin et al. 1991a, 1991b).

When and How Abortions Are Performed

In the United States, more than 90 percent of all abortions are performed in the first trimester of pregnancy (up to twelve weeks from the last normal menstrual period). Most take place in outpatient clinics specially designed and equipped for this purpose. Nearly all abortions are performed by physicians, although two states (Montana and Vermont) permit physicians' assistants to do the procedure. A limited number of physicians in specialized clinics perform abortions during the second trimester of pregnancy, but only a few perform abortions after pregnancy has advanced to more than twenty-five weeks. Although hospitals permit abortions to be performed, the number is limited because the costs to perform an abortion in the hospital are greater and hospital operating room schedules do not allow for a large number of patients. In addition, staff members at hospitals are not chosen on the basis of their willingness to help perform abortions, while clinic staff members are hired for that purpose.

Most early abortions are performed with some use of vacuum aspiration equipment. A machine or specially designed syringe is used to create a vacuum, and the suction draws the contents of the uterus into an outside container. The physician then checks the inside of the uterus with a curette, a spoon-shaped device with a loop at the end and sharp edges to scrape the wall of the uterus (Hern 1990).

Before the uterus can be emptied, however, the cervix (opening of the uterus) must be dilated, or stretched, to introduce the instruments. There are two principal ways in which this can be done. Specially designed metal dilators, steel rods with tapered ends that allow the surgeon to force the cervix open a little at a time, are used for most abortions. This process is usually done under local anesthesia, but sometimes general anesthesia is used. The cervix can also be dilated by placing pieces of medically prepared seaweed stalk called laminaria in the cervix and leaving it for a few hours or overnight (Hern 1975, 1990). The laminaria draw water from the woman's tissues and swell up, gently expanding as the woman's cervix softens and opens from the loss of moisture. The laminaria are then removed and a vacuum cannula or tube is placed into the uterus to remove the pregnancy by suction. Following this, the walls of the uterus are gently scraped with the curette.

After twelve weeks of pregnancy, performing an abortion becomes much more complicated and dangerous. The uterus, the embryo or fetus, and the blood vessels within the uterus are all much larger. The volume of amniotic fluid around the fetus has increased substantially, creating a potential hazard. If the amniotic fluid enters the woman's circulatory system, she could die instantly or bleed to death from a disruption of the blood-clotting system. This hazard is an important consideration.

Ultrasound equipment, which uses sound waves to show a picture of the fetus, is used to examine the woman before a late abortion is performed. Parts of the fetus such as the head and long bones are measured to determine the length of pregnancy. The ultrasound image also permits determination of fetal position, location of the placenta, and the presence of any abnormalities that could cause a complication during the procedure.

Between fourteen and twenty weeks of pregnancy, laminaria are placed in the cervix over a period of a day or two, sometimes changing the laminaria and replacing the first batch with a larger number to increase cervical dilation (Hern 1990). At the time of the abortion, the laminaria are removed, the amniotic sac (bag of waters) is ruptured with an instrument, and the amniotic fluid is allowed to drain out. This procedure reduces the risk of an amniotic fluid embolism, escape of the amniotic fluid into the bloodstream, and allows the uterus to contract to make the abortion safer. Using an ultrasound "real time" image, the surgeon then places special instruments such as grasping forceps into the uterus and removes the fetus and placenta (Hern 1990). This has proven to be the safest way to perform late abortions, but it requires great care and skill.

Other methods of late abortion include use of prostaglandin (a naturally occurring hormone), either by suppository or by injection (Hern 1988). Other materials injected into the pregnant uterus to effect late abortion include hypertonic (concentrated) saline (salt) solution, hypertonic urea, and hyperosmolar (concentrated) glucose solution.

Injections are also used with late abortions, especially those performed at twenty-five weeks or more for reasons of fetal disorder. The lethal injection into the fetus is performed several days prior to the abortion along with other treatments that permit a safe abortion (Hern et al. 1993).

Physical and Psychological Effects of Abortion

Studies of the long-term risks of induced abortion, such as difficulties with future pregnancies, show that these risks are minimal. A properly done early abortion may even result in a lower risk of certain obstetrical problems with later pregnancies (Hern 1982; Hogue, Cates, and Tietze 1982). An uncomplicated early abortion should have no effect on future health or childbearing. If the abortion permits postponement of the first-term pregnancy to after adolescence, the usual risks associated with a first-term pregnancy are actually reduced.

Psychological studies consistently show that women who are basically healthy can adjust to any outcome of pregnancy, whether it is term birth, induced abortion, or spontaneous abortion (miscarriage) (Adler et al. 1990). It is highly desirable, however, to have strong emotional support not only from friends and family but also from a sympathetic physician and a lay abortion counselor who will be with the woman during her abortion experience. Most specialty abortion clinics now have abortion counselors who help women talk about their feelings before the abortion and to provide specific information about the procedure and its risks. This counseling is crucial not only in providing proper emotional and social support but also in helping the woman understand what she needs to know about the procedure and prevention of complications. Women who have this kind of support, as well as support from family and friends, generally have few psychological problems following abortion. On the other hand, women who have received hostile, punitive messages about the pregnancy and the decision to have an abortion are likely to experience high levels of stress during the abortion and in later years. These women may have a lingering sense of guilt for having decided to follow through with the abortion procedure.

Denial of abortion can have serious adverse consequences for the children who result from the pregnancies their mothers had wanted to terminate. A long-term study in Czechoslovakia of the offspring of women who were denied abortions has shown a range of adjustment and developmental difficulties in these children (David et al. 1988).

Social Responses to Abortion

The various social responses to abortion range from those of the individual and her immediate circle of family and friends to the organizational, community, and even national levels.

Individual. From an individual's point of view, a decision to have an abortion includes physical concerns (safety, pain, and long-term consequences), emotional aspects, ethical and religious concerns, and the effect on social relationships. These matters are sometimes restricted by laws and other societal regulations. No one has as much information about these issues as the woman who will make the decision, but even then, the decision is complicated and frequently not easy to make. Decisions are influenced by age, socioeconomic status, educational levels, community attitudes, and religious traditions (Ginsburg 1989; Luker 1984).

Family. An abortion affects not just one person but many. A mother thinks about whether another child will make it more difficult to give the necessary love and support to the children she already has. The family may face stressful economic conditions that make it hard to make ends meet. A couple with two jobs may feel that their lives will become impossible with the birth of a child. Whatever the decision, the couple's own parents, siblings, friends, and extended family may play a role by providing emotional support for or opposition to the decision.

The parents of pregnant teenagers who are considering an abortion often have a difficult time. They may wonder where they went wrong as parents, but even in families with a lot of love and good communication, this situation can arise. One recommended approach is to consider all possibilities; abortion is not the best or only solution for everyone or every family. However, for an adolescent, whose risk of serious obstetrical problems is higher than that of a postadolescent, an abortion may have the lowest medical risk.

Teenagers usually have difficulty discussing pregnancy, and especially sexual matters, with their parents, and parents generally have difficulty talking with their children about sex. Sometimes a teacher, cleric, or counselor can serve as an intermediary to facilitate this discussion.

Partner. Other than the woman, her sexual partner may be most directly affected by the abortion decision unless there is no emotional relationship or the woman has elected not to tell him. A woman's decision to have an abortion affects both lives profoundly, and research studies show it is better if the woman's partner is part of the decision and supportive (Shostak and McLouth 1984). Marriages are often made stronger by such a joint decision, regardless of whether the decision is to have an abortion or to continue the pregnancy. The woman cannot be forced to have an abortion, and she has the sole right under law to make the decision. However, unresolved conflict over such a decision can and often does lead to separation or divorce.

A decision to have an abortion is sometimes made in the context of a failing relationship when the woman perceives that her partner will not be there to help her take care of a baby if she continues the pregnancy to term. In this case, the woman not only experiences grief over the loss of the relationship but also loss with the end of the pregnancy that symbolized a bond between her and her partner.

Community. Just as the individual decision-making process concerning abortion contains various components (physical, emotional, social, ethical), there are several levels or aspects to community response, including the general community response (Handwerker 1990). This response can range from public newspaper comment to visible protests and demonstrations in the local community. It can also be the focus of interest by local or national political groups and government attention.

In the United States, the majority of citizens think that abortion should be a matter between the woman and her physician. A small minority (about 12%) think that abortion should never be permitted under any circumstances. Polls show, however, that questions posing special cases (the woman's life is in danger, the pregnancy is the result of rape or incest) produce different responses (McKeegan 1992). Some who support choice would support certain restrictions (e.g., the need for parental consent for adolescents), and some who oppose abortion would grant certain exceptions (e.g., the woman's life is in danger).

There are many conflicting community responses, but among the most visible are the newspaper accounts, editorials, and published letters, some lacerating the writer's adversaries in harsh language. Part of the community response is the formation of organizations with strong belief systems that oppose or support abortion rights, and these groups work hard to mobilize people, sway public opinion, and influence public policy decisions. Some examples include Operation Rescue (opposed to choice) and the National Abortion Rights Action League (supportive of choice).

These community and national responses to abortion have sometimes taken the form of attempts to influence the political process and to codify community attitudes with the passage of local ordinances and federal legislation. Some communities, such as Boulder, Colorado, have displayed this polarization but have become increasingly supportive of choice (Hern 1991), as exemplified by the passage in 1986 of a city ordinance protecting women entering clinics from antiabortion demonstrators. This ordinance became the model for a similar Colorado statute. Nonetheless, antiabortion sentiment has prevailed in other communities.

Regardless of the particular community, however, the national antiabortion movement has become highly mobile, with groups such as Operation Rescue and the Army of God blocking access to clinics, disrupting normal activities around abortion clinics, and pressing antiabortion propaganda on women who seek services at clinics.

More than a thousand violent attacks on abortion clinics and doctors were reported to the National Abortion Federation from 1977 to 1991 (Grimes et al. 1991; Robey 1988), but many incidents went unreported. During this time, more than a hundred clinics and doctors' offices were destroyed by firebombs, arson, or explosives.

Personal attacks have also been made on doctors who perform abortions. These attacks range from public prayers of death (Booth and Briggs 1993; Johnson 1993) to assassinations and attempted assassinations (Bates 1993; Rohter 1993). As a result, many physicians perform abortions behind heavy security protection, even in communities that strongly support abortion rights (Gavin 1993; Hern 1993; Sanko 1993; Stolberg 1993).

National response to antiabortion violence has included passage of federal legislation providing stiff penalties for attacks on clinic workers and patients, signed into law by President Bill Clinton on May 26, 1994.

(*See also:* ABORTION: LEGAL ASPECTS; BIRTH CONTROL: CONTRACEPTIVE METHODS; CONCEPTION: MEDICAL ASPECTS; FAMILY PLANNING; GENETIC COUNSELING; NONMARITAL PREGNANCY; PREGNANCY AND BIRTH)

BIBLIOGRAPHY

Adler, N. E.; David, H. P.; Major, B. N.; Roth, S. H.; Russo, N. F.; and Wyatt, D. E. (1990). "Psychological Responses After Abortion." *Science* 248:41–44.

Bates, M. (1993). "Woman Shoots Abortion Doctor." *The Denver Post*, Aug. 20.

Booth, M., and Briggs, B. (1993). "Abortion Doctor Says His Life Is Threatened." *The Denver Post*, Aug. 13.

Cates, W., Jr. (1982). "Abortion: The Public Health Record." *Science* 215:1586.

David, H. P.; Dytrych, Z.; Matejcek, Z.; and Schuller, V. (1988). *Born Unwanted: Developmental Effects of Denied Abortion.* New York: Springer-Verlag.

Devereux, G. (1955). *A Study of Abortion in Primitive Society.* New York: Julian Press.

Early, J. D., and Peters, J. F. (1990). *The Population Dynamics of the Mucajai Yanomama.* San Diego: Academic Press.

Forrest, J. D., and Henshaw, S. K. (1987). "The Harassment of U.S. Abortion Providers." *Family Planning Perspectives* 19:9–13.

Gavin, J. (1993). "Hern: Rein in Abortion Opponents." *The Denver Post*, Aug. 21.

Ginsburg, F. D. (1989). *Contested Lives: The Abortion Debate in an American Community.* Berkeley: University of California Press.

Grimes, D. A.; Forrest, J. D.; Kirkman, A. L.; and Radford, B. (1991). "An Epidemic of Antiabortion Violence in the United States." *American Journal of Obstetrics and Gynecology* 165:1263–1268.

Grobstein, C. (1988). *Science and the Unborn.* New York: Basic Books.

Handwerker, W. P. (1990). *Births and Power: Social Change and the Politics of Reproduction.* Boulder, CO: Westview Press.

Henshaw, S. K., and Van Vort, J. (1992). *Abortion Factbook, 1992 Edition: Readings, Trends, and State and Local Data to 1988.* New York: Alan Guttmacher Institute.

Hern, W. M. (1975). "Laminaria in Abortion: Use in 1368 Patients in First Trimester." *Rocky Mountain Medical Journal* 72:390–395.

Hern, W. M. (1982). "Long-Term Risks of Induced Abortion." In *Gynecology and Obstetrics,* ed. J. J. Sciarra. New York: Harper & Row.

Hern, W. M. (1988). "The Use of Prostaglandins as Abortifacients." In *Gynecology and Obstetrics,* ed. J. J. Sciarra. New York: Harper & Row.

Hern, W. M. (1990). *Abortion Practice.* Boulder, CO: Alpenglo Graphics.

Hern, W. M. (1991). "Proxemics: The Application of Theory to Conflict Arising from Antiabortion Demonstrations." *Population and Environment* 12:379–388.

Hern, W. M. (1993). "The Pope and My Right to Life." *The New York Times,* Aug. 12.

Hern, W. M.; Zen, C.; Ferguson, K. A.; Hart, V.; and Haseman, M. V. (1993). "Late Abortion for Fetal Anomaly and Fetal

Death: Techniques and Clinical Management." *Obstetrics and Gynecology* 81:301–306.

Hodgson, J. (1981). *Abortion and Sterilization: Medical and Social Aspects.* London: Academic Press.

Hogue, C. J. R.; Cates, W., Jr.; and Tietze, C. (1982). "The Effects of Induced Abortion on Subsequent Reproduction." *Epidemiologic Reviews* 4:66.

Johnson, D. (1993). "Catholics Cool to Antiabortion Demonstrators in Denver." *The New York Times*, Aug. 14.

Kolata, G. (1992). "In Late Abortions, Decisions Are Painful and Options Few." *The New York Times*, Jan. 5.

Koonin, L. M.; Atrash, H. K.; Lawson, H. W.; and Smith, J. C. (1991a). "Maternal Mortality Surveillance, United States, 1979–1986; CDC Surveillance Summaries, July 1991." *Morbidity and Mortality Weekly Report* 40: 1–13.

Koonin, L. M.; Kochanek, K. D.; Smith, J. C.; and Ramick, M. (1991b). "Abortion Surveillance, United States, 1988; CDC Surveillance Summaries, July 1991." *Morbidity and Mortality Weekly Report* 40:15–42.

Koonin, L. M.; Smith, J. C.; Ramick, M.; and Lawson, H. W. (1992). "Abortion Surveillance, United States, 1989; CDC Surveillance Summaries, September 4, 1992." *Morbidity and Mortality Weekly Report* 41:1–33.

Lee, N. H. (1969). *The Search for an Abortionist.* Chicago: University of Chicago Press.

Lerner, M., and Anderson, O. W. (1963). *Health Progress in the United States: 1900–1960.* Chicago: University of Chicago Press.

Luker, K. (1984). *Abortion and the Politics of Motherhood.* Berkeley: University of California Press.

McKeegan, M. (1992). *Abortion Politics: Mutiny in the Ranks of the Right.* New York: Free Press.

Pakter, J. (1977). "National Trends in the Health Impact of Abortion." In *Abortion in the Seventies*, ed. W. M. Hern and B. Andrikopoulos. New York: National Abortion Federation.

Potts, M.; Diggory, P.; and Peel, J. (1977). *Abortion.* Cambridge, Eng.: Cambridge University Press.

Robey, R. (1988). "Shots Fired at Boulder Abortion Clinic." *The Denver Post*, Feb. 6.

Rohter, L. (1993). "Doctor Is Slain During Protest over Abortions." *The New York Times*, Mar. 11.

Sanko, J. (1993). "Doctor: Abortion Foes 'Fascist, Dangerous.'" *The Denver Post*, Aug. 21.

Scheidler, J. M. (1985). *Closed: 99 Ways to Stop Abortion.* Westchester, IL: Crossway Books.

Shostak, A. B., and McLouth, G. (1984). *Men and Abortion: Lessons, Losses, and Love.* New York: Praeger.

Stolberg, S. (1993). "More Like War Than Medicine: Abortion—A Difficult Choice for a Medical Career." *Los Angeles Times*, Mar. 20.

Tietze, C. (1975). "The Effect of Legalization of Abortion on Population Growth and Public Health." *Family Planning Perspectives* 7:123.

Tietze C. (1977). "Comparative Morbidity and Mortality in Abortion and Contraception." In *Abortion in the Seven-ties*, ed. W. M. Hern and B. Andrikopoulos. New York: National Abortion Federation.

Tietze, C., and Lewit, S. (1972). "Joint Program for the Study of Abortion (JPSA): Early Complications of Medical Abortion." *Studies in Family Planning* 3:97.

WARREN M. HERN

Legal Aspects

Abortion in early pregnancy was not a crime during the Colonial period and the first half century of U.S. history. A crime occurred only after "quickening," a point about midway through pregnancy when a woman first perceived fetal movement. Moreover, the crime of abortion was not the subject of legislation, but part of the "common law" received from England, and the crime was a lesser one than homicide.

Early Abortion Legislation

The earliest abortion legislation was passed by the Connecticut legislature in 1821 and banned administration of poisonous substances to a woman after quickening with an intent to produce a miscarriage. This and other early abortion legislation aimed more at the protection of abortion from unscrupulous and dangerous medical practices than at the act of abortion itself. These laws did not punish the woman and were rarely enforced.

By the mid-nineteenth century, however, a newly organized medical profession spearheaded a campaign to outlaw abortion throughout pregnancy. The professional physicians' campaign against abortion was motivated in part by their desire to suppress competition from nonprofessional "irregular" practitioners who primarily performed abortions at that time, as well as by a sincere belief in the immorality of abortion. Promoters of this effort appealed to the public's fear of the medical dangers of abortion, of the changing status of women, and of declining birth rates among native-born white Protestant women who practiced abortion widely at that time as a form of birth control. By the end of the nineteenth century, virtually every state had banned abortion, except in limited circumstances, such as to save the woman's life. These laws remained virtually unchanged until the 1960s.

Improvements in the safety of surgical abortion, a rising civil and women's rights movement, and concern with overpopulation spurred the passage of the first liberalized abortion laws. The plight of women who were exposed to thalidomide, which causes severe birth defects, and yet were denied abortions

7

added poignancy and urgency to the reform movement. Many of the liberalized laws were based on a prototype created by the American Law Institute and allowed abortion to preserve the woman's life or health, including her psychological health; in cases of rape or incest; or when the fetus was threatened with severe defects. Some of the laws also required the woman's decision to be approved by two physicians and a hospital committee. In addition, by the end of 1970, four states—New York, Alaska, Hawaii, and Washington—allowed abortions at the woman's request in early pregnancy.

Simultaneously with this legislative liberalization of abortion laws, an effort was under way to have existing laws against abortion declared unconstitutional by the courts.

Nationwide Legalization

On January 22, 1973, the U.S. Supreme Court declared unconstitutional a Texas law that permitted abortion only to save the woman's life, and a Georgia law based on the American Law Institute model that allowed abortion in a wider range of circumstances. The court held that both laws violated a woman's fundamental constitutional "right to privacy." The effect of the holdings, in *Roe* v. *Wade* (Texas) and *Doe* v. *Bolton* (Georgia), was immediately to legalize abortion nationwide, because any restrictive law was unenforceable as contrary to the U.S. Constitution.

In previous decisions, the Court had held that the Constitution contains an implied right to privacy that protects, among other things, a married couple's right to use contraceptives. In *Roe*, the Court held that the right to privacy, founded on the Fourteenth Amendment's protection against deprivation of liberty without due process of law, was broad enough to encompass a woman's decision to end her pregnancy. The Court further declared the privacy right to be "fundamental" and therefore one that could be limited only to further a compelling state interest.

The Court dealt at length with the question of whether the government's interest in protecting the potential life of the fetus was compelling enough to justify limiting the woman's constitutional right. The Court reviewed the history of the status of the fetus in American legal traditions and concluded that the fetus had never been considered a person in the "whole sense." The Court also examined divergent religious, philosophical, and scientific views on "when life begins" and concluded that when those trained in these respective disciplines could reach no consensus, "the judiciary, at this point in the development of man's

knowledge, is not in a position to speculate as to the answer." The court held, however, that the government has an important and legitimate interest in protecting the potentiality of human life and that that interest grows in importance as pregnancy progresses. At "viability"—the point in pregnancy when the fetus is capable of independent life outside the uterus (approximately the end of the sixth month of pregnancy)—the state's interest in potential life is compelling enough to justify making abortion a crime. Even after that compelling point, the states still must permit abortions necessary to save the woman's life or health, the Court said.

The Court also examined the state's interest in regulating abortion to protect the woman's health. The Court found that since abortion by a competent physician is safer than childbirth in early pregnancy, the state's compelling interest in this type of legislation does not arise until the end of the first trimester of pregnancy. After that point, the state may pass reasonable regulations to protect the woman's health. Prior to that point, however, the abortion decision is primarily a private medical decision to be left to the woman and her doctor, free of state interference.

In *Doe* v. *Bolton*, the companion case challenging the Georgia law, the Court ruled that even a law that allows abortion in somewhat broader circumstances unduly infringes on a woman's constitutional right of choice. The Court further invalidated the requirements of second physician and committee approval, reiterating that early abortion is a decision for the woman alone, to be made in consultation with her treating physician.

Nineteen years later, in the 1992 case of *Planned Parenthood of Southeastern Pennsylvania* v. *Casey*, a newly constituted and more conservative Supreme Court affirmed the basic principles of *Roe* and *Doe*: The Constitution protects a woman's decision to have an abortion, and prior to fetal viability the state may not make abortion a crime. Although the Court still found the legal protection for abortion rooted in the right to privacy, it recognized the key role played by legal abortion in guaranteeing women's equal participation in modern society.

The Court in *Casey*, however, revised the standards against which lesser abortion restrictions would be judged. The Court said that abortion regulations are valid unless they place an "undue burden" on a woman's ability to obtain an abortion—that is, they must have the purpose or effect of placing a substantial obstacle in the path of women seeking abortions. Restrictions that might make abortions a little more difficult to obtain or more expensive are not undue burdens. If a law is not an undue burden, it is valid as long as it furthers permissible interests in maternal health or fetal life.

Roe v. *Wade, Doe* v. *Bolton,* and later *Planned Parenthood of Southeastern Pennsylvania* v. *Casey* definitively invalidated any law that limits the reasons for abortion before viability. States may not pass laws, for example, that provide that abortion is legal only in cases of rape or incest or only when a committee approves the woman's decision. After viability, the state may prohibit abortions not necessary to save the woman's life or health and may require that an abortion method be used that is most likely to result in fetal survival if that method would not endanger the woman's health. Although the Court has ruled that the determination of when viability occurs must be left to the physician, it has also said that the state can require that the physician perform certain tests to determine the status of the fetus when viability "is possible." Nevertheless, abortions at this late stage of pregnancy are extremely rare.

The years since *Roe* and *Doe* have seen a proliferation of abortion legislation and litigation in the areas of minors' rights, married women's rights, the power of the state to regulate abortion facilities, and the government's obligations to fund abortions.

The Rights of Minors

The issue of whether a minor needs parental consent to obtain an abortion was one of the earliest issues to reach the Supreme Court after *Roe*. In 1976, in *Planned Parenthood of Central Missouri* v. *Danforth*, the Court held that laws requiring parental consent to abortion were unconstitutional because they delegated to parents an arbitrary veto power over the minor's decision. The Court hinted, however, that states could require parental consent for minors who were too immature to make the decision.

Later decisions of the Court, including the 1979 case of *Bellotti* v. *Baird*, affirmed that states may generally require parental consent as long as they provide a procedure whereby a minor may apply to a neutral decision maker—usually a judge—for a waiver of the requirement. The judge must waive the requirement if the minor is mature enough to decide about abortion on her own or if an abortion would be in her best interests. The procedure must maintain the minor's confidentiality and be sufficiently expedited so that the minor does not lose the opportunity to have an abortion.

In 1990, in the case of *Hodgson* v. *Minnesota*, the Court extended the rationale of the parental consent

cases to laws that require notice to both of a minor's parents. The Court ruled that states may not require notification to both parents without providing the alternative mechanism whereby a mature minor or one whose best interests are adversely affected may obtain a waiver of the requirement. The Court left open, however, whether laws that require notice to only one parent must provide such an alternative. The lower federal courts have held that they do.

Opponents of notification laws argue that, as a practical matter, they provide an opportunity for parents to prevent their daughters from obtaining an abortion, and that minors afraid to involve their parents will delay seeking abortions, seek them in other states, or seek illegal abortions. More than thirty states have enacted laws requiring parental consent or notification. Approximately twenty-two have laws with a waiver mechanism in effect for mature or "best interests" minors.

The state courts of California and Florida have affirmed greater rights under their state constitutions for minors seeking abortion than are available under the federal constitution. These state courts have held that minors are entitled to an abortion without involving parents or a judge through a waiver procedure.

Husband Involvement

The U.S. Supreme Court has struck down as unconstitutional laws requiring prior consent of or notice to the husband of a woman seeking an abortion. In the 1976 case of *Planned Parenthood of Central Missouri* v. *Danforth*, the Court held that consent laws gave husbands an arbitrary veto power over a woman's constitutionally protected decision.

In 1992, with *Planned Parenthood of Southeastern Pennsylvania* v. *Casey*, the Court held husband notice laws unduly burdensome because of the possibility that women fearful of physical or psychological abuse from their husbands will be deterred from seeking abortions. The lower courts have uniformly rebuffed efforts by sexual partners of women seeking abortions to prevent the procedure.

Regulation of Abortion Facilities

The Supreme Court has held that the state's interest in the woman's health does not justify a requirement that abortions be performed in full-service hospitals throughout pregnancy. The precise point at which hospitalization may be required remains undefined. In *City of Akron* v. *Akron Center for Reproductive Health* (1983), the Court struck down a requirement that all abortions after the first trimester of pregnancy be performed in hospitals, and lower courts have struck down requirements that abortions after sixteen or eighteen weeks of pregnancy be performed in hospitals. These holdings recognize that abortions are widely performed in freestanding clinics with a good record of safety and that a hospitalization requirement raises costs without enhancing safety. Hospitalization requirements also pose significant access problems, as few hospitals are willing to allow the procedure.

The states, however, may require licensing and regulation of abortion facilities as long as those regulations do not amount to an "undue burden," that is, they do not have the purpose or effect of making abortions inaccessible and they further permissible health concerns.

Waiting Periods and Mandatory Information

A number of states have passed laws requiring physicians to provide women seeking abortions with a set list of information, including the risks of abortion and childbirth and a description of the abortion procedure, and to offer a booklet prepared by the state that describes fetal development and agencies for prenatal care and care for the child after birth. After the information is provided, which usually involves an in-person visit by the woman to the abortion facility, she must wait twenty-four hours before returning for the abortion procedure. These requirements pose a considerable burden to women in rural states where abortion providers are few and far between, and the necessity for two trips involves added expense, days off from work, child care, and breaches of confidentiality caused by the need to explain multiple absences from work and school. Opponents of these laws also have argued that some of the mandatory information, such as pictures of fetal development, amount to state propaganda and harassment.

In 1983, the Supreme Court declared these laws unconstitutional as an unnecessary burden on the woman and an intrusion into her relationship with her doctor. In 1992, however, in the *Planned Parenthood of Southeastern Pennsylvania* v. *Casey* decision, the Court overruled its prior decisions and held that such a Pennsylvania law was not unduly burdensome, at least based on projections of how the law would operate in that state. The Court, however, seemed to leave open the door for attacks on the operation of such laws in other, more rural states and, indeed, in Pennsylvania, if the law proved overly burdensome once it was put into effect.

Public Funding

One of the thorniest issues in the ongoing abortion debate has been whether and to what extent the government must pay for a poor woman's abortion if she is eligible for governmental assistance for medical care.

In the 1970s, the Congress and the states passed laws forbidding payment for abortions in the Medicaid program, a joint federal–state program of comprehensive medical assistance for the poorest Americans. In *Maher* v. *Roe* (1977) and again in *Harris* v. *McRae* (1980), the Supreme Court upheld these laws, reasoning that although the government may not directly interfere in a woman's abortion decision, it need not provide financial assistance for her to effectuate her choice.

Since then, courts in eleven states (California, Connecticut, Idaho, Illinois, Massachusetts, Minnesota, New Jersey, New York, Oregon, Vermont, and West Virginia) have ruled that the denial of funding for abortions violates their state constitutions. Among other grounds, these courts reasoned that providing funding for a poor woman's pregnancy and childbirth expenses but denying her funds for abortion inherently coerce her to carry her pregnancy to term. The effect of these decisions is that these states provide funding for poor woman's abortions without the federal financial participation they receive for other care provided under the Medicaid program. A number of other states provide such funding voluntarily (without court orders).

The Supreme Court has also ruled that the rationale of the Medicaid decisions extends to the use of public facilities to provide abortions. States may therefore bar abortions from public hospitals, even when the abortion procedure itself is privately financed.

In *Rust* v. *Sullivan* (1992), the Court upheld the "gag rule," which banned the provision of abortion information in federal family planning programs. Relying on the abortion funding decisions, the Court said the government need not pay for the provision of this information. After *Rust*, Congress attempted to overturn the rule legislatively, but failed to muster the votes needed to override President George Bush's veto. President Bill Clinton revoked the rule on January 22, 1993, his third day in office and the twentieth anniversary of the *Roe* v. *Wade* decision.

The government may not, however, withhold funds from an organization because it provides abortions or abortion information in a separate, privately funded program. The courts have held, nevertheless, that U.S. foreign aid may be withheld from *foreign* organizations that provide abortions or abortion information, even in a separate program, financed with private or foreign government funds. Termed the "Mexico City Policy," this practice of the Reagan and Bush administrations was also annulled by President Clinton on the twentieth anniversary of *Roe* v. *Wade.*

Federal Legislation and Abortion Rights

Legislation has been introduced in Congress that would make the right to abortion a federal statutory right. The legislation was considered particularly urgent before the Supreme Court's 1992 decision in *Planned Parenthood of Southeastern Pennsylvania* v. *Casey*, when it was feared that the Supreme Court would overrule *Roe* v. *Wade.* The Freedom of Choice Act nevertheless remains an important goal of the legal abortion movement because, in addition to guaranteeing a right to abortion, it restores the stricter constitutional standard of *Roe* v. *Wade* and would prevent implementation of laws such as mandatory waiting periods that the *Casey* decision approved. Some prochoice advocates have opposed the proposed legislation because it does not include provisions to guarantee funding of abortion for poor women or to broaden the rights of minors to receive an abortion without parental involvement or court orders.

Various "human life" constitutional amendments have been introduced in Congress. These would overturn the Supreme Court decisions recognizing a right to abortion by amending the U.S. Constitution. Such amendments need the approval of two-thirds of the Congress and three-fourths of the states. None has won congressional approval to date.

Legal Protection of Facilities

Violence and harassment directed at facilities that provide abortions, their staffs, and their personnel have reached epidemic proportions. These acts include massive human blockades of abortion facilities; trespass on those facilities; arsons and bombings; the murder and attempted murder of doctors and clinic personnel; picketing of the homes of physicians and staff; distribution of handbills and posters depicting physicians as "wanted" for murder; and pouring glue into the locks of abortion facilities and injecting the facilities with butyric acid, a substance that leaves a foul odor that is difficult to remove.

While many of these acts are clearly punishable under both state and federal criminal laws, others raise issues of the constitutional rights of those who wish to speak out against abortion.

Picketing and demonstrating are traditional free speech activities protected by the Constitution. The government may nevertheless enact reasonable "time, place, and manner" restrictions on such activities. For example, the number of pickets may be limited, they may be required to remain a certain distance apart, and they may be barred from using sound amplification devices or shouting outside the abortion facility. They may be ordered not to block the doors of the clinics, trespass on clinic property or parking lots, or photograph patients.

With the advent of mass blockades of abortion facilities, courts have ordered "buffer zones" around clinics, banning any demonstration activity from areas adjacent to the facility and requiring demonstrations to take place, for example, across the street. The Supreme Court has upheld the principle of establishing such zones as a means to protect access to clinic facilities.

Some jurisdictions have sought to curb the practice of harassment of individual patients by demonstrators who engage in a practice the antiabortion movement terms "sidewalk counseling." This activity involves the demonstrators' efforts to try to dissuade the woman from having an abortion, but may include accusations of murder, blocking her way, thrusting posters in her face, and generally requiring her to walk a gauntlet of harassing demonstrators. Legislation and court orders on the subject generally state that within a certain number of feet of an abortion or other medical facility, one person may not approach within a close distance of another without express permission. Such legislation generally has been held unconstitutional, and such court orders have been reversed on appeal as violating the demonstrators' free speech rights.

Although peaceful picketing enjoys broad constitutional protection, the Supreme Court has held that governments may ban picketing focused on and taking place in front of a particular residence. The Court recognized that the rights to privacy and to be free of harassment within one's residence outweigh the demonstrators' First Amendment rights.

In addition to asserting their right to freedom of speech, demonstrators occasionally assert the defense of "necessity"—what they view as the moral evil of abortion justifies acts of trespass to stop abortions from taking place. Courts have generally rejected this defense, holding that the right to abortion is constitutionally protected and therefore cannot be considered an evil that justifies criminal conduct.

Although most of the relief against antiabortion harassment has been granted by state courts, abortion facilities have attempted to invoke the power of the federal courts for protection. Such efforts have been particularly important when local law enforcement officials, local elected officials, and local courts are unwilling to afford adequate protection or express antiabortion bias.

The Supreme Court, however, ruled in January 1993 that the federal Civil Rights Act of 1871, the main vehicle upon which the federal courts had relied to protect abortion facilities, was no longer available for that purpose. The Court ruled that the act was meant to protect persons from discrimination against them as a class and that antiabortion demonstrators did not aim their activities against women as a class, but rather against the practice of abortion itself. In response, the Freedom of Access to Clinic Entrances Act was passed by Congress. It creates a new federal crime of interfering with the access to facilities that provide reproductive health care, as well as allowing private parties to collect money damages for its violation. The act has been upheld against constitutional challenge.

In January 1994, the Court ruled that another federal statute, the Racketeer Influenced and Corrupt Organizations Act (RICO), could be used as a remedy against conspiratorial activity aimed at shutting down abortion facilities. The legal issue was whether the RICO law requires conspirators' illegal activity to be motivated by the desire for economic gain. The Court ruled that it does not and that a RICO violation may be found when the conspirators' only motivation is ideological.

(*See also:* ABORTION: MEDICAL AND SOCIAL ASPECTS; BIRTH CONTROL: SOCIOCULTURAL AND HISTORICAL ASPECTS; BIRTH CONTROL: LEGAL ASPECTS; CONCEPTION: LEGAL ASPECTS; PREGNANCY AND BIRTH; PRIVACY AND CONFIDENTIALITY)

BIBLIOGRAPHY

Butler, D. J., and Walbert, D. F. (1992). *Abortion, Medicine, and the Law*, 4th edition. New York: Facts on File.

Callahan, S., and Callahan, D. (1984). *Abortion: Understanding Differences*. New York: Plenum.

Costa, M. (1991). *Abortion: A Reference Handbook*. Santa Barbara, CA: ABC-CLIO.

Garrow, D. J. (1994). *Liberty and Sexuality: The Right to Privacy and the Making of* Roe v. Wade. New York: Macmillan.

Mnookin, R. H. (1985). "*Bellotti* v. *Baird*, a Hard Case." In *In the Interest of Children, Advocacy, Law Reform, and Public Policy*, ed. R. H. Mnookin. New York: W. H. Freeman.

Mohr, J. C. (1978). *Abortion in America: The Origins and Evolution of National Policy, 1800–1900*. New York: Oxford University Press.

Petchesky, R. P. (1990). *Abortion and Woman's Choice*. Boston: Northeastern University Press.

Rubin, E. R. (1987). *Abortion, Politics, and the Courts:* Roe v. Wade *and Its Aftermath*, revised edition. Westport, CT: Greenwood Press.

Tribe, L. H. (1990). *Abortion: The Clash of Absolutes*. New York: W. W. Norton.

Weddington, S. (1992). *A Question of Choice*. New York: Putnam.

CASES

Akron, City of, v. *Akron Center for Reproductive Health* 462 U.S. 416 (1983).

Bellotti v. *Baird* 443 U.S. 622 (1979).

Doe v. *Bolton* 410 U.S. 179 (1973).

Harris v. *McRae* 448 U.S. 297 (1980).

Hodgson v. *Minnesota* 497 U.S. 417 (1990).

Maher v. *Roe* 432 U.S. 464 (1977).

Planned Parenthood of Central Missouri v. *Danforth* 428 U.S. 52 (1976).

Planned Parenthood of Southeastern Pennsylvania v. *Casey* 112 S.Ct. 2791 (1992).

Roe v. *Wade* 410 U.S. 113 (1973).

Rust v. *Sullivan* 111 S.Ct. 1759 (1991).

DARA KLASSEL

ABUSE AND NEGLECT *See* CHILD ABUSE AND NEGLECT: SOCIOLOGICAL ASPECTS; FAMILY VIOLENCE; SPOUSE ABUSE AND NEGLECT

ACQUIRED IMMUNODEFICIENCY SYNDROME *See* AIDS

ADOLESCENCE

A new stage of the life course between childhood and adulthood, called adolescence, began to be recognized at the turn of the twentieth century (Hall 1904). Though biologically mature, the adolescent was relatively free from adult responsibilities; lacking in long-term commitments; oriented to enjoyment, sports, popular music, and peers; receptive to change; and ready to experiment with alternative identities. Adolescence is a time of pubertal change, identity formation, social development, and the acquisition of experiences and credentials promoting entry to adult roles. Moreover, adolescence and early adulthood are critical periods for the development of psychological attributes such as political attitudes and work orientations that tend to persist through adulthood. Psychological attributes such as these may be strongly influenced by contemporaneous historical change, as the concept of generation implies.

Informal socialization in the family and peer group, as well as more formal passage through the institutions of high school and postsecondary schooling, have marked consequences for attitude formation and for adult status placement. It is increasingly recognized that early orientations about efficacy and competence influence later adaptations and goal attainment. Adolescent "planful competence," denoting self-confidence, intellectual investment, and dependability, positively influences men's adult occupational status (Clausen 1993). These attributes imply an ability to delay gratification and a sense of control; successful encounters with problems in adolescence can build confidence and resources that promote effective coping with later life events. Furthermore, early psychological orientations and behavioral tendencies are strengthened over time via the young person's active choice of relationship partners and situations. Individuals select and mold their environments to maintain or reinforce initial traits (Elder and Caspi 1990).

Multiple transitions designating adult status mark the end of adolescence—the completion of formal education, obtaining economic self-sufficiency, independent residence, marriage, parenthood, or entry into full-time work. The variability in their timing makes the duration of adolescence ambiguous and historically variable. The ages at which young people typically acquire adult roles, the character of marking events, and the availability of opportunities to assume adult statuses vary by socioeconomic origin. Given that the majority of young people in modern societies obtain some form of higher education or pursue military service, many experience limited autonomy along with continued economic dependence well into their twenties or even early thirties. In poor urban areas in the United States as well as in some European countries, deteriorating economic conditions prevent substantial proportions of youths from acquiring adult economic roles. In view of such extension of preadult status and consequent ambiguity, it has been proposed that a new stage of "youth" or "postadolescence" be recognized (Klein 1990).

Changing Identities

The establishment of identity is widely viewed as the key developmental task of adolescence, sometimes occurring through gradual exploration but at other times accompanied by intense emotional strain and crisis as adolescents grapple with the question of who they are and what they want to become. Viktor Gecas and Jeylan T. Mortimer (1987) distinguish between identities based on roles, relationships, or status in an organization and those related to character traits (psychological and behavioral attributes). Adolescents are expected to be playful, experimental, carefree, even reckless. Adults, in contrast, are thought to be independent, productive, hardworking, and responsible (Klein 1990). Adolescents' sometimes fierce manifestations of autonomy vis-à-vis their parents belies continued emotional and financial dependency. In school, the student role may acquire increasing autonomy as adolescents mature, but this may be insufficient to satisfy rapidly expanding desires for independence. Youthful role identities, as child (vis-à-vis the parent) and student, imply dependence or subordination. They are increasingly superseded by more adultlike identities as friend or worker.

Given asynchronies in the age-grading systems of different societal institutions, the adolescent (and youth) is subject to recurring status inconsistencies and identity conflicts. Independent, autonomous, and adultlike character identities are confirmed in some contexts but not in others. As a result, it is widely believed that adolescence and youth are stressful life stages; problems diminish with the successful entry into adult roles (Modell, Furstenberg, and Hershberg 1976). Consistently, depressive affect and disorder show marked increases in adolescence, especially among girls (Angold 1988; Rutter, Tizard, and Whitmore 1981); girls' self-esteem also declines as they make the transition into junior high school (Simmons and Blyth 1987). Men's self-perceptions of personal well-being and competence have been found to decline during college and rise during the following decade (Mortimer, Finch, and Kumka 1982).

Because of their capacity to engage in formal operational thought, adolescents can examine their present identities, circumstances, and prospects from multiple vantage points. Adolescents may recognize the multiplicity of choices available to them and the likelihood that their choices may not be optimal. This process of identity exploration is more highly differentiated and sophisticated in areas salient to adult "possible selves." For example, Sally L. Archer (1991) notes that females engage in more sophisticated identity building in the domain of work–family conflict. The resolution of such important identity issues facilitates career choice, the formation of stable intimate relationships, and political-religious ideologies. Optimally, achieved identities will foster a coherent, unified set of self-images and activities that are congruent with available social niches.

There is evidence that cognitive flexibility, high levels of moral reasoning, superior academic performance, achievement motivation, and the ability to adapt and perform effectively under stress result from the successful resolution of identity issues and "crises," especially for adolescent males (Baumeister 1991). "Foreclosed" identities, obtained without benefit of the exploratory "moratorium," involve premature and uncritical commitments to courses of action, following parents or the community. Some fear has been expressed that minority adolescents frequently manifest foreclosed identities, readily accepting the social roles and ideological positions defined by their ethnic/racial communities (Spencer 1991).

Educational Attainment

In view of the clear linkage between adolescent educational achievement and socioeconomic standing in adulthood, considerable attention has been directed to adolescent educational attainment. More than 80 percent of American youths complete high school (American Council on Education 1989). Adolescents of higher social class background have higher educational and occupational aspirations, which, in turn, foster higher attainments (Featherman 1980). Their higher educational strivings are encouraged and facilitated by their parents. Self-directed values in parents, fostered by the more complex and autonomous work tasks of higher-status occupational positions, induce children also to have self-directed values (Kohn, Slomczynski, and Schoenbach 1986). Since these values, in turn, facilitate adaptation to occupational positions of higher socioeconomic status, socioeconomic inequality is perpetuated intergenerationally. The more socioeconomically advantaged parents also engage in more supportive child-rearing behavior, fostering personality traits that are conducive to occupational attainment (Gecas 1979). Close, supportive relationships with fathers foster a sense of competence, work involvement, and positive work values in sons, promoting early adult occupational achievement (Mortimer, Lorence, and Kumka 1986).

Critics of contemporary American high schools argue that the division into academic, vocational, and commercial "tracks" also perpetuates inequality in-

tergenerationally. Enrollment in the college preparatory track seems to increase achievement as well as the likelihood of college attendance. Schools are thus most advantageous for students in the college track, who are given more extensive course work and higher-quality educational experiences (Ekstrom 1991; Games 1991). The cognitive learning, occupational preferences, and career expectations fostered by formal schooling are closely linked to white-collar, professional, and managerial employment (Coleman and Husen 1985).

While students of minority and lower socioeconomic backgrounds are more likely to be placed in nonacademic tracks (Rosenbaum 1976), detachment from actual employment settings limits the effectiveness of many vocational education programs (Grubb 1989). Moreover, if adolescents, particularly "involuntary" minority youths, observe prejudice, career ceilings, inflated job qualifications, housing discrimination, and poor occupational achievement among adult relatives and friends, despite earlier success in school, they may assume an attitude of "What's the use of trying?" (Ogbu 1989). For them, conformity to the norms of the school, including studious behavior, threatens ethnic identity and is construed as "acting white." Accordingly, African-American youths have lower school achievement than whites, higher dropout rates, and are less likely to attend college (Brookins 1991). In fact, while the enrollment of whites in colleges and universities has increased since 1976, the proportion of African-American and Hispanic youths who attend college has declined (American Council on Education 1989).

Work

The secondary school has been criticized because it isolates youths from meaningful contact with adult workers (except teachers) and does not foster effective anticipatory socialization to adulthood. Parents are typically quite favorable about their adolescent children's work, believing that this experience will help them to become responsible and independent, to learn to handle money, and to manage time. However, because jobs for youths are more simple and repetitive than adult work, requiring little training or skills, some commentators question their value. Ellen Greenberger and Lawrence Steinberg (1986) allege that employed adolescents have more cynical attitudes toward work than those who are not employed. However, there is considerable evidence that employment during high school predicts more stable work histories and higher earnings in the years immediately following. David Stern and Yoshi-Fumi Nakata (1989), using data from noncollege youths in the National Longitudinal Survey of Youth, report that more complex work in adolescence predicts lower incidence of unemployment and higher earnings three years after high school.

Furthermore, there is evidence from the Youth Development Study, a longitudinal investigation of a representative panel of urban high school students, that the quality of adolescent work matters for psychological outcomes that could influence adult attainment (Mortimer et al. 1992), such as a sense of competence or personal efficacy, depressive affect, and occupational reward values. For example, boys who reported opportunities for advancement increased in self-competence over a one-year period. Girls who thought they were being paid well also manifested increasing self-efficacy over time (Finch et al. 1991).

Whereas middle-class white youths have the most bountiful work opportunities, minority youths, particularly those who reside in inner cities, are less likely to be employed. Given the benefits from youth employment experience, such as the development of personal responsibility, learning about the world of work, exploring vocational options, and crystallizing occupational values, the lack of job opportunities for minority teenagers is cause for concern.

Upon completion of secondary schooling, those youths who do not go on to college experience a continued "moratorium" (Osterman 1989) for several years. Their jobs are in the secondary sector of the economy, and there is high unemployment and job instability. Such youths lack career orientation and instead emphasize peer relationships, travel, adventure, and short-term jobs to satisfy immediate consumption needs. At the same time, employers express preference for low-wage workers who do not require fringe benefits and who are not likely to unionize. When filling adultlike "primary" jobs, such employers seek evidence of stability or "settling down." The absence of a clear channel of mobility from education to the industrial sector in the United States, unlike Germany and Japan (Hamilton 1990), reduces the level of human capital investment (e.g., job training and continuous work experience) of noncollege youths. In doing so, it depresses the quality of the young adult work force.

Youth Problem Behaviors

Sometimes youth problem behaviors, such as delinquency and substance use, are attributed to the absence of meaningful, valued social roles, despite adolescents' growing capacity to fill them. Some behaviors that are considered problematic or even legally prohibited when engaged in by minors (e.g., smoking, alcohol use, and sexuality) are quite legitimate in adulthood. Richard Jessor and Shirley L. Jessor (1977) see such behaviors as attempts to affirm maturity or to negotiate adult status. More than half of all high school seniors in the United States have experimented with illicit drugs, though the numbers are declining (Kandel 1991). Moreover, the vast majority of high school seniors have used alcohol, and about one of five regularly smokes cigarettes. The potential consequences of substance use and abuse (e.g., addiction, automobile accidents, crime, and health problems) make this quite prevalent behavior problematic. Substance use follows a typical progression: Use of beer or wine and cigarettes generally precedes use of marijuana and other illicit drugs. Movement between "stages" is related to age of onset, peer pressure, lack of stable peer or family relationships, insufficient self-control, stressful life events, and low self-esteem (Rauch and Huba 1991).

Though there is continuity in conduct problems in childhood, adolescent delinquency, and adult criminality, adolescents, particularly males of lower socioeconomic background, have especially high rates of criminal behavior. These are not always reflected in conviction rates because of the tendency to dispose of adolescent arrests informally (Kennedy 1991). However, homicide is the third leading cause of death for midadolescent males and the leading cause of death for African Americans during this life stage (Finkelstein 1991).

Juvenile delinquency has multifaceted causes: macrostructural (e.g., the failure of the society to provide opportunities to obtain widespread success goals legitimately); familial (e.g., indifferent or inconsistent parental monitoring and discipline, or parental criminality); network-related (e.g., involvement in delinquent peer subcultures); and personal (e.g., low levels of moral development, low IQ, and other biological or genetic influences) (see Kennedy 1991). Accordingly, distinctions have been made between "types" of delinquents: "subcultural" delinquents, whose peers encourage delinquent values and activities; "unsocialized psychopathic" delinquents, who have severe deficits in their interpersonal skills and who engage in impulsive, sensation-seeking behavior; and "neurotic-disturbed" delinquents, who use drug and alcohol or fighting as modes of coping with depressed affect (Kennedy 1991).

Given that the family is a major institutional context for socialization and resource acquisition in adolescence, family poverty or disintegration may be expected to have negative consequences. David Quinton (1988) reports that girls from disrupted homes who were reared in institutions were more likely to become pregnant before age nineteen, to marry deviant men, and to experience disturbed family relationships in early adulthood. The economic and emotional turmoil that frequently ensue from divorce and separation can jeopardize healthy development.

African-American adolescents in U.S. inner cities are considered to be especially at risk because of their high rates of poverty and welfare dependency as well as the impoverished and crime-ridden character of the neighborhoods in which they live. African-American adolescents have high rates of school dropout, unemployment, arrest and incarceration, drug use, pregnancy, suicide, HIV infection, and other health problems (Gibbs 1991).

Whereas poverty is not conducive to positive adolescent outcomes, economic resources alone are insufficient for healthy development of youths. Taking a macrostructural, historical perspective, James S. Coleman (1994) argues that societal affluence, in the long term, fosters declining interest of parents in the next generation. In his view, as the multigenerational organization and functions of the family weaken, parental motivation to invest attention, time, and effort in their adolescent offspring also declines. If this is the case, extrafamilial agents and forms of investment in youths may become increasingly necessary.

(See also: ADOLESCENT SEXUALITY; FRIENDSHIP; GANGS; JUVENILE DELINQUENCY; PEER PRESSURE; PERSONALITY DEVELOPMENT; SCHOOL; SELF-ESTEEM; SUBSTANCE ABUSE; TEENAGE PARENTING; TRUANCY; WORK AND FAMILY)

BIBLIOGRAPHY

American Council on Education. (1989). *Minorities in Higher Education: Eighth Annual Status Report*. Washington, DC: Author.

Angold, A. (1988). "Childhood and Adolescent Depression: I. Epidemiological and Aetiological Considerations." *British Journal of Psychiatry* 152:601–617.

Archer, S. L. (1991). "Gender Differences in Identity Development." In *Encyclopedia of Adolescence*, ed. R. M. Lerner, A. C. Petersen, and J. Brooks-Gunn. New York: Garland.

Baumeister, R. F. (1991). "Identity Crisis." In *Encyclopedia of Adolescence*, ed. R. M. Lerner, A. C. Petersen, and J. Brooks-Gunn. New York: Garland.

Brookins, G. K. (1991). "Socialization of African-American Adolescents." In *Encyclopedia of Adolescence*, ed. R. M.

Lerner, A. C. Petersen, and J. Brooks-Gunn. New York: Garland.

Clausen, J. (1993). *American Lives*. New York: Free Press.

Coleman, J. S. (1994). "Social Capital, Human Capital, and Investment in Youth." In *Youth Unemployment and Society*, ed. A. C. Petersen and J. T. Mortimer. Cambridge, Eng.: Cambridge University Press.

Coleman, J. S., and Torsten, H. (1985). *Becoming Adult in a Changing Society*. Paris: Organization for Economic Cooperation and Development.

Ekstrom, R. B. (1991). "Tracking and Educational Achievement." In *Encyclopedia of Adolescence*, ed. R. M. Lerner, A. C. Petersen, and J. Brooks-Gunn. New York: Garland.

Elder, G. H., Jr., and Caspi, A. (1990). "Studying Lives in a Changing Society: Sociological and Personological Explorations." In *Studying Persons and Lives*, ed. A. I. Rabin, R. A. Zucker, and S. Frank. New York: Springer-Verlag.

Featherman, D. L. (1980). "Schooling and Occupational Careers: Constancy and Change in Worldly Success." In *Constancy and Change in Human Development*, ed. O. G. Brim, Jr., and J. Kagan. Cambridge, MA: Harvard University Press.

Finch, M. D.; Shanahan, M. J.; Mortimer, J. T.; and Ryu, S. (1991). "Work Experience and Control Orientation in Adolescence." *American Sociological Review* 56:597–611.

Finkelstein, J. W. (1991). "Aggressive Behavior in Adolescence." In *Encyclopedia of Adolescence*, ed. R. M. Lerner, A. C. Petersen, and J. Brooks-Gunn. New York: Garland.

Games, P. A. (1991). "Educational Achievement and Tracking in High School." In *Encyclopedia of Adolescence*, ed. R. M. Lerner, A. C. Petersen, and J. Brooks-Gunn. New York: Garland.

Gecas, V. (1979). "The Influence of Social Class on Socialization." In *Contemporary Theories About the Family*, Vol. 1, ed. W. R. Burr, R. Hill, F. I. Nye, and I. L. Reiss. New York: Free Press.

Gecas, V., and Mortimer, J. T. (1987). "Stability and Change in the Self-Concept from Adolescence to Adulthood." In *Self and Identity: Individual Change and Development*, ed. T. M. Honess and K. M. Yardley. London: Routledge & Kegan Paul.

Gibbs, J. T. (1991). "Black Adolescents At Risk: Approaches to Prevention." In *Encyclopedia of Adolescence*, ed. R. M. Lerner, A. C. Petersen, and J. Brooks-Gunn. New York: Garland.

Greenberger, E., and Steinberg, L. (1986). *When Teenagers Work*. New York: Basic Books.

Grubb, W. (1989). "Preparing Youth for Work: The Dilemmas of Education and Training Programs." In *Adolescence and Work: Influences of Social Structure, Labor Markets, and Culture*, ed. D. Stern and D. Eichorn. Hillsdale, NJ: Lawrence Erlbaum.

Hall, G. (1904). *Adolescence: Its Psychology and Its Relations to Physiology, Anthropology, Sociology, Sex, Crime, Religion, and Education*. New York: Appleton-Century-Crofts.

Hamilton, S. F. (1990). *Apprenticeship for Adulthood: Preparing Youth for the Future.* New York: Free Press.

Jessor, R., and Jessor, S. L. (1977). *Problem Behavior and Psychosocial Development: A Longitudinal Study of Youth.* New York: Academic Press.

Kandel, D. (1991). "Drug Use, Epidemiology, and Developmental Stages of Involvement." In *Encyclopedia of Adolescence,* ed. R. M. Lerner, A. C. Petersen, and J. Brooks-Gunn. New York: Garland.

Kennedy, R. E. (1991). "Delinquency." In *Encyclopedia of Adolescence,* ed. R. M. Lerner, A. C. Petersen, and J. Brooks-Gunn. New York: Garland.

Klein, H. (1990). "Adolescence, Youth, and Young Adulthood: Rethinking Current Conceptualizations of Life Stage." *Youth and Society* 21:446–471.

Kohn, M. L.; Slomczynski, K. M.; and Schoenbach, C. (1986). "Social Stratification and the Transmission of Values in the Family: A Cross-National Assessment." *Sociological Forum* 1:73–102.

Modell, J.; Furstenberg, F.; and Hershberg, T. (1976). "Social Change and Transitions to Adulthood in Historical Perspective." *Journal of Family History* 1:7–32.

Mortimer, J. T.; Finch, M. D.; and Kumka, D. S. (1982). "Persistence and Change in Development: The Multidimensional Self-Concept." In *Lifespan Development and Behavior,* Vol. 4, ed. P. D. Baltes and O. G. Brim, Jr. New York: Academic Press.

Mortimer, J. T.; Finch, M. D.; Shanahan, M.; and Ryu, S. (1992). "Work Experience, Mental Health, and Behavioral Adjustment in Adolescence." *Journal of Research on Adolescence* 2:25–57.

Mortimer, J. T.; Lorence, J.; and Kumka, D. S. (1986). *Work, Family, and Personality: Transition to Adulthood.* Norwood, NJ: Ablex.

Ogbu, J. U. (1989). "Cultural Boundaries and Minority Youth Orientation Toward Work Preparation." In *Adolescence and Work: Influences of Social Structure, Labor Markets, and Culture,* ed. D. Stern and D. Eichorn. Hillsdale, NJ: Lawrence Erlbaum.

Osterman, P. (1989). "The Job Market for Adolescents." In *Adolescence and Work: Influences of Social Structure, Labor Markets, and Culture,* ed. D. Stern and D. Eichorn. Hillsdale, NJ: Lawrence Erlbaum.

Quinton, D. (1988). "Longitudinal Approaches to Intergenerational Studies: Definition, Design, and Use." In *Studies of Psychosocial Risk: The Power of Longitudinal Data,* ed. M. Rutter. Cambridge, Eng.: Cambridge University Press.

Rauch, J. M., and Huba, G. J. (1991). "Adolescent Drug Use." In *Encyclopedia of Adolescence,* ed. R. M. Lerner, A. C. Petersen, and J. Brooks-Gunn. New York: Garland.

Rosenbaum, J. E. (1976). *Making Inequality: The Hidden Curriculum of High School Tracking.* New York: Wiley.

Rutter, M.; Tizard, J.; and Whitmore, K. (1981). *Education, Health, and Behavior.* Huntington, NY: Krieger.

Shanahan, M. J.; Finch, M. D.; Mortimer, J. T.; and Ryu, S. (1991). "Adolescent Work Experience and Depressive Affect." *Social Psychology Quarterly* 54:299–317.

Simmons, R. G., and Blyth, D. A. (1987). *Moving into Adolescence: The Impact of Pubertal Change and School Context.* New York: Aldine.

Spencer, M. B. (1991). "Minority Development of Identity." In *Encyclopedia of Adolescence,* ed. R. M. Lerner, A. C. Petersen, and J. Brooks-Gunn. New York: Garland.

Stern, D., and Nakata, Y.-F. (1989). "Characteristics of High-School Students' Paid Jobs and Employment Experience After Graduation." In *Adolescence and Work: Influences of Social Structure, Labor Markets, and Culture,* ed. D. Stern and D. Eichorn. Hillsdale, NJ: Lawrence Erlbaum.

JEYLAN T. MORTIMER

ADOLESCENT SEXUALITY

Investigations into adolescent and young-adult sexuality have taken two approaches. The first has focused on variables correlated to sexual behavior. The second approach has been more concerned with the ages at which adolescents first experience sexual intercourse and the rates of teen pregnancies and sexually transmitted diseases.

Correlates of Sexual Behavior

Some correlates of sexual behavior are simple associations between the variable of interest and sexual behavior. Others are more complex, involving several variables in cause–effect paths that include direct and indirect relationships to sexual activity.

Dating relationships and sexuality. Although early adolescents most often engage in sexual intercourse in a dating relationship, surprisingly little is known about how dating experiences are related to sexual activity during this developmental stage. However, early adolescent females are more likely to first engage in coitus in a relationship they characterize as being serious or steady, whereas early adolescent males more often report that their first coitus was in a casual dating relationship. Sexual intimacy is apt to be linked to feelings of emotional intimacy at this stage of development, and the majority of early adolescents report that the reason they engaged in coitus was to give or receive love (Jessor et al. 1983).

Some early female adolescents are pressured into sexual intercourse by their partners. George Cvetkovich and Barbara Grote (1980) report that an inability to say no, wanting to please and satisfy a boyfriend, and feeling as if sex was expected are related to coital activity in white and African-American females. Parallel findings have been reported by other researchers. Richard Jessor and his colleagues (1983) found that a small percentage of the females in their sample engaged in coitus out of a sense of obligation, or because they felt manipulated by their partners. In addition, male, but not female, decision making about intercourse has been found to be related to the couple's coital frequency (Jorgensen, King, and Torrey 1980).

More is known about how sexual expression and dating-relationship dynamics are interrelated for older adolescents and younger adults. Much of the dating and sexual interaction that takes place is shaped by gender-based role expectations. While women rely on nonverbal behaviors to capture men's attention initially and to signal availability for dating, it still falls largely to men to act on these signals by asking women for dates. Further, it is generally perceived to be the male's responsibility to initiate and advance sexual involvement and the woman's responsibility to limit it. Single men and women find sex more pleasurable when these traditional roles are followed (O'Sullivan and Byers 1992). Moreover, the couple is more likely to follow these gender-role prescriptions as commitment increases.

There are at least four ways that commitment and sexual involvement are connected (Christopher and Cate 1985). Some monogamously dating couples restrict their sexual involvement to precoital behaviors. Other couples engage in intercourse very early in their dating history—sometimes on the first date. A third type of couple first experiences coitus as part of their decision about making a steady commitment. A final group engages in limited, precoital sexual involvement until they have made an explicit, monogamous commitment, at which time they fully explore different ways of interacting sexually.

One of the strongest dating-relationship dimensions related to sexual involvement is the degree of love experienced in the relationship. In fact, the level of emotional intimacy in a relationship plays an important role in the coital decision making of most singles, especially women (Christopher and Cate 1984).

Conflict also increases with greater sexual involvement (Christopher and Cate 1985, 1988), although the exact dynamics behind this finding are unclear. It may be that male and female differences in sexual expectations lead to conflict that is resolved, in part, by becoming more sexually involved. Couples may also engage in intercourse without discussing its meaning, and then conflict may follow as a couple attempts to define what their sexual involvement means.

Communication plays an important role in the sexual interaction of older adolescents and young adults.

Communication must be understood in its broader context, as most dating individuals rely on nonverbal cues in their sexual interactions (O'Sullivan and Byers 1992).

Using nonverbal as opposed to verbal cues probably reflects an overt choice by dating partners. Nonverbal cues accomplish two simultaneous communication goals (Cupach and Metts 1991). First, such cues are often ambiguous and indirect. If an individual uses them to initiate sexual involvement and meets rejection, that person can save face by assuming that the cue was misunderstood because of its ambiguous nature. Second, nonverbal cues can be effective ways of bringing about sexual interaction, especially in couples who have been together long enough to understand the meaning behind the cues (O'Sullivan and Byers 1992).

Nonverbal cues are only one way of influencing a partner in a sexual interaction, either to increase or to limit sexual involvement. There are a wide array of sexual-influence tactics that can be used in attempts to influence a partner. Dating individuals, however, usually use a number of tactics together, thereby forming overall influence strategies. Four premarital sexual-influence strategies have been identified (Christopher and Frandsen 1990). The first involves professing how much loving and liking one feels, physically touching a partner, and acting seductively. This strategy is linked to sexual involvement. The second includes making authoritative statements, using logic, offering compromise, and being insistent. It is usually used to limit sexual involvement. The final two strategies involve sexual aggression, with one focusing on threats and use of force and the other focusing on using pressure and manipulation.

Social influences. Family and peers provide two important social influences on adolescent sexual involvement. A consistent finding across studies has been that coming from a single-parent home increases the chances of early coitus in young adolescents (Miller and Moore 1990). Having a mother who was premaritally pregnant and having parents who approve of premarital sexual involvement increase the likelihood of early adolescent coitus (Thornton and Camburn 1987). Alternatively, having parents with a higher level of education decreases the likelihood of early coital activity (Thornton and Camburn 1987).

Family-interaction variables have been shown to play a role in early adolescent sexual activity. Feeling close to one's parents is associated with teens and parents having similar sexual attitudes and with a decreased chance of the teens engaging in coitus (Weinstein and Thornton 1989). In addition, low and high levels of parental-control attempts are associated with increased coital risk, while moderate levels are related to decreased risk (Jessor et al. 1983). Family communication is popularly viewed as an influence, although research has not supported this perception (Weinstein and Thornton 1989). One of the reasons for this lack of a relationship may be that parents rarely talk directly to their children about sexual matters and often rely on plant and animal analogies to explain human sexual interactions, with questionable results (Goldman and Goldman 1982).

Parents influence older adolescents' and young adults' sexual expression only to the extent that parents are chosen as referents (individuals with whom the adolescent identifies and uses as a standard when making decisions about what constitutes correct behavior). When parents are chosen as referents, older adolescents typically refrain from sexual intercourse. Alternatively, if peers are chosen and the peers are perceived as sexually active, the adolescent is also likely to be sexually active (Walsh, Ferrell, and Tolone 1976).

In fact, perceived peer sexual activity has a strong and sizable relationship with the sexual activity of younger and older adolescents (Jessor et al. 1983). Common folk wisdom would hold that the direction of this relationship is from peers to the individual—that falling "into the wrong crowd" will result in a greater likelihood of coital activity in early adolescence. Although it has been found that experiencing general peer pressure to be sexually active results in a greater probability of engaging in intercourse (Furstenberg et al. 1987), there is a need to be careful about the cause–effect direction between adolescents' and friends' sexual activity. A longitudinal investigation showed that only white females were influenced by their same-sex friends' sexual activity to become sexually active themselves (Billy and Udry 1985). In direct contrast to folk wisdom, white males, and to a lesser extent white females, were found to be more likely to become coitally active first, and then to choose friends who were also sexually experienced. Thus, for white males, and some white females, sexual experience may support friend choice rather than friends influencing sexual activity.

Individual factors. Several individual factors are moderately to strongly related to sexual activity in early adolescence. Biology plays an important role—the hormone testosterone contributes to coital activity in males and sexual fantasies and future sexual plans in females (Udry and Billy 1987). Religiosity has an opposite effect. Early adolescents who attend religious services frequently are less likely to engage in

sexual intercourse (Thornton and Camburn 1989). Similarly, future education and occupation aspirations in youth lessen the probability of engaging in sexual intercourse (Jessor et al. 1983).

Adolescents' attitudes about premarital sexuality are usually consistent with their sexual activity. This, however, is not always true; the sexual attitudes of 25 percent of an early teenage sample were inconsistent with their level of sexual experience (Zabin et al. 1984). For example, many nonvirgins felt that intercourse at their age was morally wrong. The fact that teens may change their attitudes as a result of their experiences might explain these inconsistencies. Sexual attitudes can become more positive or negative depending on how rewarding adolescents find their own exploration.

Early adolescents who are coitally active may concurrently engage in other problem behaviors. It has been demonstrated that coital activity is often accompanied by drinking and smoking (Jessor et al. 1983). All three of these behaviors are examples of youths violating age-graded norms. In other words, the same behaviors in older adolescents may not be considered deviant. In a similar vein, illicit drug use has also been found to be strongly related to early coital activity (Rosenbaum and Kandel 1990).

Other individual variables have weaker associations to sexual activity in early adolescence. Contrary to popular beliefs, self-esteem would fall into this category, because self-esteem has not always been found to be related to sexual behavior (cf. Christopher, Johnson, and Roosa 1993). When an association has been found, however, the direction of the effect is dependent on the adolescent's sexual attitudes (Miller and Moore 1990); conservative sexual attitudes and high self-esteem correspond to lower rates of sexual activity, while high self-esteem coupled with liberal attitudes correspond to higher rates of sexual activity. Locus of control, whether success is attributed to one's own ability and effort (internal locus) or to circumstances and fate (external locus), has been shown to be more consistently related to coital activity, but the direction of the relationship appears to be age-related (Day 1992). Younger adolescents with an external locus, and older adolescents with an internal locus, are more likely to engage in coitus. The overall association between coital activity and locus of control, however, is not as strong as with other variables (Jessor et al. 1983).

Some of these variables, such as religiosity and attitudes, are similarly related to sexual behavior for older adolescents and young adults (DeLamater and MacCorquodale 1979). Additional important variables

19

have been identified. Gender is one of the more salient. Single males are more sexually oriented than single females; they see women as providing sexual cues even when women do not perceive themselves as sending such cues (Abbey and Melby 1986), and they wish for greater sexual involvement earlier in dating relationships than do females (Knox and Wilson 1981). These results have led some scholars to conclude that men have a lower threshold for perceiving sexual intent when compared to women (Shotland and Craig 1988).

Other individual variables related to adolescent coital activity include sexual guilt, self-monitoring, and past sexual and dating experience. Sexual guilt has an inhibitory effect on sexual involvement (Mosher and Cross 1971). Self-monitoring is a personality construct that refers to whether individuals make judgments about correct behavior by using cues from others and/or the situation (high self-monitors) or by utilizing their own attitudes and dispositions (low self-monitors). High self-monitors have more one-night stands, a greater number of sexual partners, and are more accepting of casual sex than are low self-monitors (Snyder and Simpson 1984). Finally, early dating and engagement in coitus and a high number of dating partners are often linked to coital activity in later adolescence and young adulthood (Schultz et al. 1977).

Frequency of Coital Activity and Its Outcomes

The second approach to adolescent and young-adult sexuality research has focused on the age at which adolescents first experience sexual intercourse and the rates of teen pregnancy and sexually transmitted diseases (STDs). Samples for this research are usually representative of the U.S. adolescent population as a whole; thus, the results provide a reasonably accurate picture of adolescent sexual activity. These studies have shown that about 50 percent of U.S. adolescents have engaged in coitus by the age of fifteen, with the initial experiences of males preceding females by about a half a year (Sonenstein, Pleck, and Leighton 1991). Rates increase with age; while 25 percent of the females and 35 percent of the males are coitally experienced by age sixteen, by age nineteen these rates climb to 80 percent for females and 86 percent for males (Miller and Moore 1990).

Ethnic and racial differences exist in these estimates. African-American males experience first coitus about two years earlier than white males, whereas African-American females precede white females by

only a half a year (Day 1992; Sonenstein, Pleck, and Leighton 1991). Thirty-five percent of the African-American males aged fourteen or younger report they have engaged in intercourse (Sonenstein, Pleck, and Leighton 1991). Hispanics, the second largest U.S. minority, have not always been identified as a separate ethnic group in these studies. When they have been, results show that Mexican-American males experience their first intercourse an average of one year earlier than white males. Concurrent findings demonstrate, however, that Hispanic males of non-Mexican descent and Hispanic females do not differ from their Anglo counterparts in their average age for first coitus (Day 1992).

The younger ages for sexual involvement of African-American youths is related to the disproportionate number of this minority who live in poverty. An investigation of the sexual activity of inner-city African-American adolescents found that their mean age of first intercourse was 11.8 years and that 23 percent of the males reported they had engaged in coitus by age nine or younger (Clark, Zabin, and Hardy 1984). A similar report stated that lower-class African-American adolescents are more likely to engage in intercourse than middle- and upper-class African-American adolescents (Hogan and Kitagawa 1985).

Although these coital rates are comparable to those of other developed Western countries, U.S. adolescents have the unfortunate distinction of having the highest adolescent pregnancy rates among these nations (Hayes 1987). In 1985, there were 1,031,000 births to teenage women, 31,000 of which were to female adolescents under the age of fifteen (Henshaw and Van Vort 1989). That same year, 42 percent of females between the ages of fifteen and nineteen ended their pregnancies in abortion (Moore 1989). It is estimated that 18 percent of all female adolescents in the United States will become pregnant at least once if these trends continue.

Rates of STDs among adolescents are equally alarming. Although rates vary by disease, teens accounted for 25 percent of the 3 million new cases of STDs in 1985 (Moore 1989). More specifically, teens between the ages of fifteen and nineteen accounted for 29 percent of the reported cases of gonorrhea in 1990. Rates for chlamydia infections, which are often asymptomatic and result in later fertility problems, are estimated to be twice that of gonorrhea (Aral and Holmes 1991). Adolescent cases of acquired immunodeficiency syndrome (AIDS) are of greater concern because infection by the human immunodeficiency virus (HIV) results in eventual death. Contrary to other age cohorts, heterosexual transmission is the most frequent form of transmission among adolescents. The incidence of HIV infections is also rising faster among teens than other groups (DiClemente 1992). Furthermore, the higher incidence of HIV infection among poor and minority youths has led some researchers to conclude that the spread of AIDS among adolescents is following the pattern of other STDs (Aral and Holmes 1991).

(*See also:* ADOLESCENCE; AIDS; LOVE; PEER PRESSURE; PERSONAL RELATIONSHIPS; SEXUALITY; SEXUALITY EDUCATION; SEXUALITY IN THE LIFE CYCLE; SEXUALLY TRANSMITTED DISEASES; TEENAGE PARENTING)

BIBLIOGRAPHY

Abbey, A., and Melby, C. (1986). "The Effects of Nonverbal Cues on Gender Differences in Perceptions of Sexual Intent." *Sex Roles* 15:283–298.

Aral, S. O., and Holmes, K. K. (1991). "Sexually Transmitted Diseases in the AIDS Era." *Scientific American* 264:62–69.

Billy, J. O. G., and Udry, J. R. (1985). "Patterns of Adolescent Friendship and Effects on Sexual Behavior." *Social Psychology Quarterly* 48:381–387.

Christopher, F. S., and Cate, R. M. (1984). "Factors Involved in Premarital Sexual Decision Making." *Journal of Sex Research* 20:363–376.

Christopher, F. S., and Cate, R. M. (1985). "Premarital Sexual Pathways and Relationship Development." *Journal of Social and Personal Relationships* 2:271–288.

Christopher, F. S., and Cate, R. M. (1988). "Premarital Sexual Involvement: A Developmental Investigation of Relational Correlates." *Adolescence* 23:793–803.

Christopher, F. S., and Frandsen, M. M. (1990). "Strategies of Influence in Sex and Dating." *Journal of Social and Personal Relationships* 7:89–105.

Christopher, F. S.; Johnson, D. C.; and Roosa, M. W. (1993). "Family, Individual, and Social Correlates of Early Hispanic Adolescent Sexual Expression." *Journal of Sex Research* 30:45–52.

Clark, S. D., Jr.; Zabin, L. S.; and Hardy, J. B. (1984). "Sex, Contraception, and Parenthood: Experience and Attitudes Among Urban Black Young Men." *Family Planning Perspectives* 16:77–82.

Cupach, W. R., and Metts, S. (1991). "Sexuality and Communication in Close Relationships." In *Sexuality in Close Relationships*, ed. K. McKinney and S. Sprecher. Hillsdale, NJ: Lawrence Erlbaum.

Cvetkovich, G., and Grote, B. (1980). "Psychosocial Development and the Social Problem of Teenage Illegitimacy." In *Adolescent Pregnancy and Childbearing: Findings from Research*, ed. C. Chilman. Washington, DC: U.S. Department of Health and Human Services.

Day, R. D. (1992). "The Transition to First Intercourse Among Racially and Culturally Diverse Youth." *Journal of Marriage and the Family* 54:749–762.

DeLamater, J. D., and MacCorquodale, P. (1979). *Premarital Sexuality: Attitudes, Relationships, Behavior.* Madison: University of Wisconsin Press.

DiClemente, R. J. (1992). "Epidemiology of AIDS, HIV Prevalence, and HIV Incidence Among Adolescents." *Journal of School Health* 62:325–330.

Furstenberg, F. F., Jr.; Morgan, S. P.; Moore, K. A.; and Peterson, J. L. (1987). "Race Differences in the Timing of Adolescent Intercourse." *American Sociological Review* 52:511–518.

Goldman, R., and Goldman, J. (1982). *Children's Sexual Thinking.* London: Routledge & Kegan Paul.

Hayes, C. D., ed. (1987). *Risking the Future: Adolescent Sexuality, Pregnancy, and Childbearing.* Washington, DC: National Research Council.

Henshaw, S. K., and Van Vort, J. (1989). "Teenage Abortion, Birth, Pregnancy Statistics: An Update." *Family Planning Perspectives* 21:85–88.

Hogan, D., and Kitagawa, E. (1985). "The Impact of Social Status, Family Structure, and Neighborhood on the Fertility of Black Adolescents." *American Journal of Sociology* 90:825–836.

Jessor, R.; Costa, F.; Jessor, L.; and Donovan, J. (1983). "Time of First Intercourse: A Prospective Study." *Journal of Personality and Social Psychology* 11:608–626.

Jorgensen, S. R.; King, S. L.; and Torrey, B. A. (1980). "Dyadic and Social Network Influences on Adolescent Exposure to Pregnancy Risk." *Journal of Marriage and the Family* 42:141–155.

Knox, D., and Wilson, K. (1981). "Dating Behaviors of University Students." *Family Relations* 30:255–258.

Miller, B. C., and Moore, K. A. (1990). "Adolescent Sexual Behavior, Pregnancy, and Parenting: Research Through the 1980s." *Journal of Marriage and the Family* 52:1025–1044.

Moore, K. A. (1989). *Facts at a Glance 1989.* Washington, DC: Child Trends.

Mosher, D. L., and Cross, H. J. (1971). "Sex Guilt and Premarital Sexual Experiences of College Students." *Journal of Consulting and Clinical Psychology* 36:27–32.

O'Sullivan, L. F., and Byers, E. S. (1992). "College Students' Incorporations of Initiator and Restrictor Roles in Sexual Dating Interactions." *Journal of Sex Research* 29:435–446.

Rosenbaum, E., and Kandel, D. B. (1990). "Early Onset of Sexual Behavior and Drug Involvement." *Journal of Marriage and the Family* 52:783–798.

Schultz, B.; Bohrnstedt, G. W.; Borgatta, E. F.; and Evans, R. R. (1977). "Explaining Premarital Sexual Intercourse Among College Students." *Social Forces* 56:148–165.

Shotland, R. L., and Craig, J. M. (1988). "Can Men and Women Differentiate Between Friendly and Sexually Interested Behavior?" *Social Psychology Quarterly* 51:66–73.

Snyder, M., and Simpson, J. A. (1984). "Self-Monitoring and Dating Relationships." *Journal of Personality and Social Psychology* 47:1281–1291.

Sonenstein, F. L.; Pleck, J. H.; and Leighton, C. K. (1991). "Levels of Sexual Activity Among Adolescent Males in the United States." *Family Planning Perspectives* 23:162–167.

Thornton, A. D., and Camburn, D. (1987). "The Influences of the Family on Premarital Sexual Attitudes and Behavior." *Demography* 24:323–340.

Thornton, A. D., and Camburn, D. (1989). "Religious Participation and Adolescent Sexual Behavior." *Journal of Marriage and the Family* 51:641–653.

Udry, J. R., and Billy, J. O. G. (1987). "Initiation of Coitus in Early Adolescence." *American Sociological Review* 52:841–855.

Walsh, R. H.; Ferrell, M. Z.; and Tolone, W. L. (1976). "Selection of Reference Group, Perceived Reference Group Permissiveness, and Personal Permissiveness Attitudes and Behavior." *Journal of Marriage and the Family* 38:495–508.

Weinstein, M., and Thornton, A. (1989). "Mother–Child Relations and Adolescent Sexual Attitudes and Behavior." *Demography* 26:563–577.

Zabin, L. S.; Hirsch, M. B.; Smith, E. A.; and Hardy, J. B. (1984). "Adolescent Sexual Attitudes and Behavior: Are They Consistent?" *Family Planning Perspectives* 16(4):181–185.

F. Scott Christopher

ADOPTION

Adoption is a legal process by which a person (the adoptee) acquires the rights and duties of a biological child with respect to an individual who is not that person's biological parent. Usually, as part of the process, the adoptee's legal relationship with his or her biological parents is terminated.

Historically, the purpose of adoption was to benefit the individual doing the adopting (the adopter). Often the adopter's concerns related to the perpetuation of the rites of family religious worship and avoiding the extinction of the family (Goody 1969; Huard 1956; Presser 1971). In modern law, the focus has shifted to advancing the interests of the adoptee (Huard 1956; Zainaldin 1979).

Common events triggering the possibility of adoption are the death of a biological parent; the termination of a biological parent's rights following abuse, abandonment, or neglect of the adoptee; and the divorce of the person's biological parents followed by the remarriage of the custodial parent and a loss of contact with the noncustodial biological parent.

History

Adoption has been known from biblical times and in many cultures (Goody 1969). While Roman adoption practice laid the foundation for legal developments in much of modern Europe, it did not do so for England. Adoption, as such, was only introduced into England in 1926. However, in England, various legal devices sometimes produced essentially the same results as an adoption. For example, the law might recognize a strong presumption that a child born to a married woman was fathered by her husband. Nevertheless, in general, English concerns with the integrity of blood lines and the need to ensure that property was inherited only by "heirs of the blood"—that is, legitimate biological descendants—meant that there was little English adoption law to provide precedent in postrevolutionary America.

Adoption law developed in the United States in response to the needs of dependent children, not infrequently poor, orphaned, or handicapped. Urbanization and immigration led to an increase both in the numbers of such children as well as their concentration in towns and cities. Apprenticeships and other existing social devices for dealing with these children became inadequate (Kawashima 1982; Zainaldin 1979). Philanthropic groups, often with strong religious underpinnings, set out to improve the situation of these children. At the urging of these groups, the first comprehensive statutory schemes dealing with adoption were enacted during the middle of the nineteenth century, the earliest probably being that enacted in Massachusetts in 1851. Today all states have statutes regulating adoption. While these statutes are sometimes similar in concept, they often vary greatly in detail. In addition to the state statutes, Congress enacted the Adoption Assistance and Child Welfare Act of 1980. This law provides financial assistance for the adoption of children with "special needs" (Cole 1983). The "special needs" classification may include children who are physically or emotionally disabled, sibling groups, older children, or children of particular minority or ethnic backgrounds. Further, the federal Indian Child Welfare Act of 1978 governs the adoption of children who are eligible for tribal membership or who are Alaskan Native Americans.

Demographics

The federal government ceased collecting adoption statistics in 1975. Therefore, no reliable current comprehensive official adoption data exist, although individual states usually do have some data. However, some comprehensive data were assembled privately in 1988 using 1986 as a base data year (National Committee for Adoption 1989). This survey indicated that in 1986 there were 104,088 adoptions of adoptees of U.S. origin. In 52,931 instances, the adoptee was already the child of one member of the adoptive couple or was otherwise related to the adoptive parents. In the balance of cases, the children were "unrelated" to the adoptive parents. In this last group, 39 percent of the adoptions were handled by public agencies, 29.4 percent by private agencies, and 31.4 percent by private individuals—often attorneys. Nearly one-fourth of the "unrelated" adoptions involved children with "special needs," and almost half of the "unrelated" adoptions involved children under two years of age. In addition, there were 10,019 adoptions of foreign children in 1986; more than half of these children came from Korea.

Legal Consequences

Generally, the effect of adoption is that the biological parents' rights and duties with respect to the adoptee end, and these rights and duties are acquired by the adoptive parents (Hampton 1988, suppl. 1991). The biological parents cease to owe the adoptee a duty of support, and this duty is imposed on the adoptive parents. Normally the adoptee loses the right to inherit from a biological parent who dies intestate (without making a will), but will acquire the right to inherit from adoptive parents and relatives, although a few states expressly prohibit inheritance from adoptive relatives. One notable exception to this general principle exists where the adoptee is adopted by a stepparent. Here the right to inherit from a biological parent whose rights were otherwise terminated may remain. Also, in some states, an adoptee may still inherit from a biological relative, even though adoption normally gives the adoptee the right to inherit from adoptive relatives. Where the deceased left a will, the will's provisions will be followed. However, the deceased's intentions may not be clear. For example, is a bequest to a "child" intended to include the deceased's biological child who was adopted by a nonrelative before the deceased's death? The outcome may hinge on technical rules used by a given state for interpreting wills, such as whether the deceased used the word "issue" rather than "child," or whether the will was executed before or after the adoption occurred (Rein 1984). Where a testator's intention is not clear, the law tends to rely on presumptions such as that the testator did not intend to include an adoptee as a beneficiary if the testator was a "stranger to the adoption." Complicated legal questions can arise over whether an adoptee is considered a member of an adoptive family for purposes of claims against pension funds; health benefit plans; worker's compensation schemes; and in situations where a suit must be brought against someone who physically injures or kills the child's adoptive parent in, for example, a motor accident.

Because the legal system tends to confer particular benefits on family members, in a number of instances the purposes of the adoption may be to procure particular legal results flowing from the family relationship created by the adoption. Thus, one adult may adopt another where the adopter wishes to make the adoptee a beneficiary of the adopter's estate after the death of the adopter, and the effect of the adoption will be to reduce the taxes on the deceased's estate. Similarly, there is an increasing incidence among homosexual couples of one partner adopting the other partner's biological child. Indeed, in a few states it is possible for one homosexual partner to adopt the other and thereby produce the desired legal consequences. In principle, the legal consequences of adoption are regulated by state statutes. However, not all states have statutes regulating all factual or legal aspects of adoption. Accordingly, the consequences may have to be determined by courts on a case-by-case basis. Thus the legal consequences of adoption may vary significantly from state to state. Indeed, sometimes the law in a given state will treat a person as having been adopted, at least for some purposes, even though no formal adoption occurred, simply because in the circumstances this result is "just."

Process

There are three basic types of adoption process: direct placement by the biological parent or parents, placement through a state agency, and placement through a private agency licensed by the state (Child Welfare League of America 1989). All states permit direct placements where the adopter is a stepparent or close relative. Except in six states, biological parents may also place the adoptee directly with unrelated adoptive parents and in the process may be assisted by unlicensed intermediaries such as lawyers. Increasingly, however, states are insisting that in these "unrelated" private placements the prospective adoptive parents must have been subjected to a screening process before the adoption is finalized. Because agency-based placements are often subject to extensive waiting periods, the majority of healthy young children are adopted through private placement procedures.

Adoption agencies licensed by the state are generally subject to minimum standards set by the state, but they may abide by more rigorous standards developed by outside organizations such as the Child Welfare League of America (Child Welfare League of America 1988). Some adoption agencies are specialized and handle only placements for particular types of children (e.g., those with "special needs"), particular religions, or particular foreign countries of origin (Child Welfare League of America 1989; Gilman 1992).

Agencies and sometimes states often impose extensive conditions on the eligibility of people to adopt and on which children may be placed with particular adoptive parents (Bartholet 1993; Kadushin and Martin 1980; Martin 1988). These conditions may include requirements relating to age, physical and mental health, financial resources, and community reputation. Adoption by unmarried couples, single individuals, and couples whose infertility is not established may also be precluded (Sullivan and Schultz 1990). Traditionally, agencies also paid a great deal of attention to "matching" the physical characteristics of adoptive parents and the adoptee, as well as their socioeconomic backgrounds, religion, and race. Matching was justified as a device to facilitate the adjustment of the adoptee into the new home. Historically, matching also probably was a useful technique for concealing the fact of adoption from both the adoptee and the world at large. Matching and the criteria employed by agencies to restrict eligibility for adoption have been criticized as failures of institutions dominated by a white middle class to acknowledge the diversity of society (Bartholet 1993; Cole 1983; Macaulay and Macaulay 1978). Since the 1980s, there has been increasing acceptance of single-parent adoptions.

Formalized transracial adoption, generally adoption of minority children by white adults, was virtually unknown in the United States until the 1950s. Such adoptions received considerable institutional support during the 1960s, but following severe criticism by the National Association of Black Social Workers in the 1970s, these placements declined. Transracial placements were criticized as failing to provide minority children with the psychological and cultural resources necessary to cope with what was viewed as a racist society and because such placements resulted in the erosion of minority communities (Merritt 1985; National Association of Black Social Workers 1986). Although these placements produce unique problems, the evidence does not suggest that transracial adoptions are inherently disadvantageous (McRoy and Zurcher 1983; Simon and Altstein

1977, 1981, 1987). The National Association of Black Social Workers has suggested that a solution to the relatively high numbers of minority children in foster care is the devotion of increased resources to the reinforcement of minority families and, where necessary, to the expansion of adoption of minority children by minority adults (National Association of Black Social Workers 1986). Similar concerns relating to the erosion of Native American culture and tribal membership led to the enactment by Congress of the federal Indian Child Welfare Act of 1978. This legislation places control of the adoption of children eligible for tribal membership in the hands of the tribe and tribal courts (Dorsay 1984). Adoption placement on the basis of race/ethnicity/tribal membership is subject to criticism because it risks subordinating the adoptee's best interests to extraneous concerns (Bartholet 1993; Rosettenstein 1993, 1994).

The adoption process normally involves three phases: termination of parental rights, placement of the adoptee with an adoptive family, and finalization of the adoption. Sometimes, termination of a biological parent's rights occurs at the instance of the state against the wishes of that parent. Grounds for this termination may include child abuse, abandonment, neglect, failure to support, mental or physical illness of the parent, and in some states the parent's imprisonment or "unfitness" (Schur 1988, suppl. 1991). When the adoption placement occurs through a state agency, it is often because the state has had to assume responsibility for the adoptee following earlier proceedings to terminate parental rights. Where the biological parent is in favor of adoption, parental rights usually are relinquished either by the surrender of the adoptee to an agency, or by the formal consent of the parent to the adoption. To help ensure certainty that the biological parent is willing to give up the adoptee for adoption, consent to the adoption normally cannot be given before the birth of the adoptee. Also, legal procedures are employed that try to reduce the risk that a biological parent will be pressured into consenting. In this regard, generally a parent cannot be paid for consenting to the adoption—that is, the baby cannot be "sold" (Baker 1978). However, adoptive parents routinely pay for expenses associated with the birth, as well as paying agencies and other intermediaries for their services (Cohen 1987; Posner 1987; Zierdt 1991).

Problems sometimes arise with respect to the biological father of the adoptee. His identity or location may or may not be known, or may be known to the adoptee's biological mother but concealed from the adoption authorities. Moreover, the father may be unaware of the mother's pregnancy, or he may know of the birth but have played no active role in either supporting or developing a social relationship with the child. In contexts such as these, states are reluctant to put such fathers in a position where they have the ability to block an adoption or delay it for a period during which the adoptee may be subject to disruption and insecurity (Kadushin and Martin 1980). Nevertheless, the Constitution protects a biological parent's relationship with his or her child, and it provides certain procedural safeguards before this relationship can be terminated. To address these competing concerns, modern law tends to require that a biological father whose identity is known and who has been socially or financially active in the adoptee's life must give his consent to the adoption or, if grounds exist, have his rights terminated on an involuntary basis. Where the father's identity is not known or where he has played a passive role in the adoptee's life, however, the trend is to do no more than attempt to find and notify the father of the proposed adoption and to receive his input on what should happen to the adoptee, without giving him the ability to control the process (Hollinger 1988b, suppl. 1991).

In many instances, a period of time will elapse between the placement of the adoptee with the adoptive parents and the finalization of the adoption (Gilman 1992). Normally, during this delay, an investigator completes a home study and reports to the court on the success of the placement (Sullivan and Schultz 1990). In some states, or in some types of adoptions (e.g, by a stepparent or relative), these studies are not required. However, a state's law may still require a minimum waiting period. At the end of this period, and in all adoptions, a court hearing is held involving a review of all documents and reports. Following a satisfactory review, the court grants a final order of adoption (Kadushin and Martin 1980).

Concealment of Information

Until the 1920s, anonymity in the adoption process was more the exception than the rule. Concealing the identity of the biological parents from the adoptive parents and the adoptee emerged as a device designed to produce greater integration of the adoptee into the adoptive family, protect the biological parents, and shield the adoption from public scrutiny (Bartholet 1993). These goals led to states sealing adoption records and requiring adoption placements to be through intermediaries. Nevertheless, practical considerations such as health concerns have led most states to require that nonidentifying background in-

formation pertaining to the adoptee be made available to adoptive parents (Rosenberg 1992). Indeed, there is increasing litigation arising from the concealment by adoption agencies of information likely to affect the viability of the placement, such as information relating to possible physical or sexual abuse of the adoptee.

To deal with the psychological needs of adoptees and of biological parents, states have become more willing to allow access to background information, even if the effect is to identify the adoptee and the biological and adoptive families (Bartholet 1993; Komar 1991; Lifton 1979; Lindsay and Monserrat 1989; Melina 1989; Rosenberg 1992; Smith and Miroff 1987). Various techniques are employed. In some states, the information is disclosed if a court considers there to be "good cause" for making the disclosure. In other states, a register is maintained of biological and adoptive parents who consent to their identity being revealed should an inquiry be made. In still other states, intermediaries are used to make confidential inquiries as to whether the parties involved are willing to have their identities revealed.

Increasing attention also is being paid to "open" adoptions—that is, adoptions in which contact is maintained between the biological parents and the adoptive family (Amadio and Deutsch 1983; Hardin 1983; Rappaport 1992; Rosenberg 1992; Silber and Dorner 1990). The spectrum of contact may range from limited written communication to formal visitation arrangements. These arrangements may extend to more remote family members, such as biological grandparents. Open adoptions are seen as helping biological parents deal with a sense of grief and as facilitating the adoption process. On the other hand, these adoptions are seen as potentially disruptive to the adoptive family (Askin and Oskam 1982; Gediman and Brown 1989). Open adoptions have been supported particularly in the context of adoptions by stepparents and of older children—that is, in circumstances where the adoptee already had an established relationship with the parents whose rights were being terminated (Hollinger 1988a, suppl. 1991).

(*See also:* CHILD CUSTODY; CHILDREN'S RIGHTS; GUARDIANSHIP; INHERITANCE; REMARRIAGE; REMARRIAGE AND CHILDREN)

BIBLIOGRAPHY

Amadio, C., and Deutsch, S. L. (1983). "Open Adoption: Allowing Adopted Children to 'Stay in Touch' with Blood Relatives." *Journal of Family Law* 22:59–93.
Askin, J., and Oskam, B. (1982). *Search.* New York: Harper & Row.

Baker, N. C. (1978). *Babyselling*. New York: Vanguard Press.

Bartholet, E. (1993). *Family Bonds*. Boston: Houghton Mifflin.

Boskey, J. B. (1988, suppl. 1991). "Placing Children for Adoption." In *Adoption Law and Practice*, ed. J. H. Hollinger. New York: Matthew Bender.

Child Welfare League of America. (1988). *Standards for Adoption Service*, revised edition. Washington, DC: Author.

Child Welfare League of America. (1989). *CWLA's Guide to Adoption Agencies*. Washington, DC: Author.

Cohen, J. M. (1987). "Posnerism, Pluralism, Pessimism." *Boston University Law Review* 67:105–175.

Cole, E. S. (1983). "Advocating for Adoption Services." In *Foster Children in the Courts*, ed. M. Hardin. Boston: Butterworth.

Dorsay, C. J. (1984). *The Indian Child Welfare Act and Laws Affecting Indian Juveniles*. Boulder, CO: Indian Law Support Center.

Gediman, J. S., and Brown, L. P. (1989). *Birth Bond*. Far Hills, NJ: New Horizon.

Gilman, L. (1992). *The Adoption Resource Book*, 3rd edition. New York: HarperCollins.

Goody, J. (1969). "Adoption in Cross-Cultural Perspective." *Comparative Studies in Society and History* 11:55–78.

Hampton, L. P. (1988, suppl. 1991). "The Aftermath of Adoption: The Economic Consequences—Support, Inheritance, and Taxes." In *Adoption Law and Practice*, ed. J. H. Hollinger. New York: Matthew Bender.

Hardin, M. (1983). "Legal Placement Options to Achieve Permanence for Children in Foster Care." In *Foster Children in the Courts*, ed. M. Hardin. Boston: Butterworth.

Hollinger, J. H. (1988a, suppl. 1991). "Aftermath of Adoption." In *Adoption Law and Practice*, ed. J. H. Hollinger. New York: Matthew Bender.

Hollinger, J. H. (1988b, suppl. 1991). "Consent to Adoption." In *Adoption Law and Practice*, ed. J. H. Hollinger. New York: Matthew Bender.

Hollinger, J. H. (1988c, suppl. 1991) "Introduction to Adoption Law and Practice." In *Adoption Law and Practice*, ed. J. H. Hollinger. New York: Matthew Bender.

Huard, L. A. (1956). "The Law of Adoption: Ancient and Modern." *Vanderbilt Law Review* 9:743–763.

Kadushin, A., and Martin, J. A. (1980). *Child Welfare Services*, 3rd edition. New York: Macmillan.

Kawashima, Y. (1982). "Adoption in Early America." *Journal of Family Law* 20:677–696.

Komar, M. (1991). *Communicating with the Adopted Child*. New York: Walker.

Lifton, B. J. (1979). *Lost and Found*. New York: Dial.

Lindsay, J. W., and Monserrat, C. P. (1989). *Adoption Awareness*. Buena Park, CA: Morning Glory.

Macaulay, J., and Macaulay, S. (1978). "Adoption for Black Children: A Case Study of Expert Discretion." *Research in Law and Sociology* 1:265–318.

Martin, C. (1988). *Beating the Adoption Game*, revised edition. New York: Harcourt Brace Jovanovich.

McRoy, R. G., and Zurcher, L. A., Jr. (1983). *Transracial and Inracial Adoptees*. Springfield, IL: Charles C Thomas.

Melina, L. R. (1989). *Making Sense of Adoption*. New York: Harper & Row.

Merritt, W. T. (1985). "Barriers to Adoption." Hearings Before the Senate Committee on Labor and Human Resources, 99th Cong., 1st sess., *Congressional Record* (June 25) 131:214–225.

National Association of Black Social Workers. (1986). *Preserving Black Families: Research and Action Beyond the Rhetoric*. New York: Author.

National Committee for Adoption. (1989). *1989 Adoption Factbook*. Washington, DC: Author.

Posner, R. A. (1987). "The Regulation of the Market in Adoptions." *Boston University Law Review* 67:59–72.

Presser, S. B. (1971). "The Historical Background of the American Law of Adoption." *Journal of Family Law* 11:443–516.

Rappaport, B. M. (1992). *The Open Adoption Book*. New York: Macmillan.

Rein, J. E. (1984). "Relatives by Blood, Adoption, and Association: Who Should Get What and Why." *Vanderbilt Law Review* 37:711–810.

Rosenberg, E. B. (1992). *The Adoption Life Cycle*. New York: Free Press.

Rosettenstein, D. S. (1993). "Custody Disputes Involving Tribal Indians in the United States: A Case Study of the Problems Inherent in Custody Adjudications Involving Non-Isolated Semi-Autonomous Population Subgroups." In *Parenthood in Modern Society: Legal and Social Issues for the Twenty-First Century*, ed. J. M. Eekelaar and P. Sarcevic. Dordrecht, Neth.: Martinus Nijhoff.

Rosettenstein, D. S. (1994). "Transracial Adoption and the Statutory Preference Schemes: Before the 'Best Interests' and After the 'Melting Pot.' " *St. John's Law Review* 68:137–197.

Schur, W. M. (1988, suppl. 1991). "Adoption Procedure." In *Adoption Law and Practice*, ed. J. H. Hollinger. New York: Matthew Bender.

Silber, K., and Dorner, P. M. (1990). *Children of Open Adoption*. San Antonio: Corona.

Simon, R. J., and Altstein, H. (1977). *Transracial Adoption*. New York: Wiley.

Simon, R. J., and Altstein, H. (1981). *Transracial Adoption: A Follow-Up*. Lexington, MA: Lexington Books.

Simon, R. J., and Altstein, H. (1987). *Transracial Adoptees and Their Families*. New York: Praeger.

Smith, D. W., and Sherwen, L. N. (1988). *Mothers and Their Adopted Children: The Bonding Process*, 2nd edition. New York: Tiresias Press.

Smith, J., and Miroff, F. I. (1987). *You're Our Child: The Adoption Experience*. Lanham, MD: Madison.

Sullivan, M. R., and Schultz, S. (1990). *Adopt the Baby You Want*. New York: Simon & Schuster.

Zainaldin, J. S. (1979). "The Emergence of a Modern American Family Law: Child Custody, Adoption, and the Courts, 1796–1851." *Northwestern University Law Review* 73:1038–1089.

Zierdt, C. M. (1991). "Compensation for Birth Mothers: A Challenge to the Adoption Laws." *Loyola University of Chicago Law Journal* 23:25–66.

DAVID S. ROSETTENSTEIN

AGING *See* ELDERS; GRANDPARENTHOOD; LATER-LIFE FAMILIES; MIDDLE AGE; RETIREMENT; WIDOWHOOD

AIDS

Acquired Immunodeficiency Syndrome (AIDS), which impairs the human immune system, is caused by infection with the human immunodeficiency virus (HIV). The definition of AIDS is closely linked to the status of the immunological defenses of the infected person, and an individual may be HIV positive (i.e., infected with the virus) without showing any signs of developing AIDS. One of the earliest signals of HIV infection is swelling of the lymph glands in the neck and armpits, known as persistent generalized lymphadenopathy (PGL). Additional symptoms include fever, fatigue, diarrhea, and loss of weight. A definite diagnosis of AIDS exists when the person's immune system experiences a complete collapse, making the individual susceptible to opportunistic infections (i.e., infections caused by usually harmless microorganisms that become pathogenic when the individual's resistance is impaired).

HIV is transmitted in blood, semen, and vaginal secretions. High-risk behaviors include intravenous drug use and unprotected (i.e., without a condom) anal or vaginal intercourse. The virus can also be transmitted from an HIV-infected mother to her child during pregnancy, although transmission does not occur in every case. Before blood screening began in 1985, the virus was also being contracted from transfusions and blood-clotting agents. HIV cannot be contracted through ordinary social contact with an infected person (e.g., shaking hands or sharing bathroom facilities).

History

AIDS first appeared during the late 1970s as a mysterious illness that was affecting small groups of homosexual men on the East and West coasts of the United States. The interest of the medical establishment was piqued because of the associated diseases (e.g., Kaposi's sarcoma and pneumocystis carinii pneumonia [PCP]), which at that time were extremely rare in the general population. Kaposi's sarcoma, which many of the patients developed, is a malignant tumor affecting the skin and mucous membranes and is usually characterized by the formation of pink to reddish-brown or bluish patches. In general, these tumors are quite rare, slow-growing, vascular in nature, and most commonly affect elderly men of Mediterranean descent; however, in these early AIDS cases, the tumors affected young white males and were found to grow and disseminate rapidly. Overwhelming infection and respiratory failure due to PCP, a form of pneumonia caused by a microorganism that attacks the inner fibrous tissues of the lungs, were the leading causes of death in these early AIDS cases.

Within a brief time, similar AIDS cases were being reported in segments of the population that did not engage in homosexual behaviors. Intravenous drug users, hemophiliacs, and recipients of blood transfusions were being stricken, as were their sexual partners. This led the medical establishment to the conclusion that the passage of a foreign protein or tissue particle from one person to another via previously used syringes, blood transfusions, or body fluids exchanged during sexual activity caused the initiation of AIDS in these populations (Essex 1988).

In 1984, the human T-cell lymphotropic virus (HTLV-III) was isolated as the retrovirus responsible for causing AIDS (Broder and Gallo 1984). A retrovirus does not have DNA, the molecule that holds the genetic code for cell reproduction. Instead, retroviruses have RNA and an enzyme called reverse transcriptase that turns RNA into DNA. After a retrovirus invades a cell, it uses the enzyme to convert its RNA into DNA. This viral DNA then becomes incorporated into the cell DNA. With proper stimulation, the cell's DNA will produce more retroviruses instead of engaging in cellular reproduction. When final cell destruction occurs, the retroviruses are liberated and infect more cells. The first retroviruses studied, prior to the outbreak of AIDS, were confined to the populations of the Caribbean basin, southwestern Japan, central Africa, and northern regions of South America. A subgroup of retroviruses was also isolated in an African species of monkeys and apes (Essex 1988). The early HTLV viruses, which replicated at very slow rates and were low in virulence, were found to be the causative agents in certain forms of T-cell leukemia. It has not been explained how HIV-I and HIV-II, both responsible for AIDS, developed into the rapid replicators they demonstrate themselves to be. HIV may have entered the human species as the final mutation of a precursor virus from a species that has yet to be identified.

One year after the isolation of HIV, tests involving antibodies (proteins produced by the person's immune system to neutralize or help destroy specific foreign substances) and antigens (foreign substances that provoke the body to produce antibodies) were developed. These tests allowed detection of HIV infection well before the onset of any clinical manifestations, opening the door to preventive therapy against the opportunistic infections, especially PCP.

By the end of the 1980s, AIDS had exploded from a medical curiosity that appeared to afflict a segregated segment of the population into a pandemic of global proportions. In 1991, the global prevalence of HIV infection was estimated to be more than 10 million adults. The statistical projections for the year 2000 were 30 million infected adults and 10 million children (Centers for Disease Control and Prevention 1989, 1991).

Groups Affected

Infection by HIV in the majority of pediatric cases reported to the Centers for Disease Control and Prevention occurred via vertical transmission (i.e., transmission of the virus across the placenta from mother to fetus during pregnancy). Most of the mothers of these infected offspring reported a history of intravenous drug use or sexual relations with an HIV-infected man who was also an intravenous drug user. HIV may also be transmitted postnatally to a child through breast-feeding (Peckham et al. 1988). Unfortunately, reliable detection of an HIV infection during an infant's first year of life is uncertain. The antibodies created by an HIV-infected woman's body are passively transmitted to the fetus during pregnancy, whether or not the actual virus is transmitted. Therefore, a test performed to detect antibodies in the child immediately after birth can yield false positive results, meaning that the test results might show HIV positivity when in fact the child is HIV-negative. If no viral infection has occurred, the maternal antibodies will eventually become undetectable after the first fifteen months of the child's life. If the antibody detection test becomes negative and remains so, and if the infant does not develop any opportunistic infections, it may be concluded that the HIV infection has not been transmitted to the infant.

The transmission of HIV in adolescents gained increasing attention as AIDS-related diseases came to

be ranked sixth in the leading causes of death among individuals fifteen to twenty-four years of age. By the end of 1992, more than 1,000 adolescents between thirteen and nineteen years of age had been diagnosed with AIDS, and more than 10,000 young adults between twenty and twenty-four years of age, who were most likely infected with HIV during their teenage years, were diagnosed with AIDS. These data suggest that a substantial number of adolescents are already infected with HIV but are not yet ill and probably do not know they are infected (Lindegren 1994). The increasing proportion of AIDS cases among young adults and adolescents has been attributed to heterosexual contact. In these instances, female adolescents appear to have higher infection rates. Studies have shown that an uninfected woman having regular intercourse with an infected man was twenty times more likely to become infected than was an uninfected man having regular intercourse with an infected woman. This higher infection rate may be related to varying virus concentrations in different body fluids. Because semen contains a higher concentration of viruses than do vaginal secretions, it is possible that HIV is transmitted more efficiently from male to female (Padian, Shiboski, and Jewell 1991).

The incidence of AIDS is also increasing in individuals of more than fifty years in age. According to the Centers for Disease Control and Prevention, 10 percent of all persons reported with AIDS are fifty years of age or older, with a male-to-female ratio of 9 to 1. AIDS tends to progress more rapidly in the elderly and remain undetected until it reaches the later stages (Feldman, Fillit, and McCormick 1994).

Overall, minority groups have been afflicted in disproportionate numbers. For example, African Americans, who comprise 12 percent of the population of the United States, account for 27 percent to 30 percent of all AIDS cases. Hispanics are also disproportionately affected, accounting for 17 percent of all cases while representing only 8 percent of the population (Centers for Disease Control and Prevention 1989, 1991).

Testing and Diagnosis

HIV attacks and destroys CD4 T-lymphocytes, which assist in the regulation of the entire immune system. As the virus continues to replicate and its numbers multiply, more of these cells are lost, and a decrease in the number of CD4 cells increases the risk of opportunistic infections. AIDS can therefore be described as a continuum that begins with infection by the HIV virus leading to decreasing numbers of CD4 cells and eventual progression to opportunistic diseases.

Because variations in CD4 cell counts can be seen in many other diseases, including infectious mononucleosis, a decrease in the number of CD4 cells should not be used to create the initial diagnosis. The correct criteria for diagnosing HIV positivity in persons more than thirteen years of age are the following:

· repeated positive screening tests for HIV antibodies with specific antibodies identified using supplemental tests;
· direct virus isolation and identification in a sample of the individual's tissue;
· HIV antigen detection (i.e., detection of proteins manufactured by the body to combat the virus);
· positive results on any other highly specific licensed test for HIV.

As research into HIV infection progresses, the ease and accuracy of determining whether an individual is HIV-positive have become more refined. The tests, which reflect the high quality control standards in place to guarantee that test results are accurate, allow for adequate pretest counseling and information dissemination with close medical follow-up for those individuals who require it.

With the advent of HIV testing, many states initiated strict guidelines governing the confidentiality of test results and anonymity of the individual during the testing process to protect that person against social stigmatization and economic exploitation. These measures are also intended to encourage widespread testing, so medical care and support services can be instituted early in the process. This widespread testing also allows accurate statistical studies to be done, giving the medical community more information on the spread of HIV infection, the groups affected, and the value of prevention and treatment modalities.

Patient Classification

Once a patient has been diagnosed as HIV-positive, the CD4 cell count becomes crucial for initiation of therapy to fight the infection. The Centers for Disease Control and Prevention revised their classification system for HIV-infected adolescents and adults in January 1993, categorizing individuals on the basis of CD4 T-lymphocyte counts and diseases associated with HIV infection (Centers for Disease Control and Prevention 1992). Patients are placed in one of the following three categories, based on their respective CD4 cell counts:

Category 1: more than 500 cells per microliter
Category 2: 200 to 499 cells per microliter
Category 3: fewer than 200 cells per microliter.

Category 2 patients are often started on azidothymidine (AZT) therapy by their physicians. Category 3 patients are at greater risk for opportunistic infections, so they are usually given antibiotics in addition to the AZT therapy as a preventive measure.

Three clinical categories (asymptomatic, symptomatic not AIDS, and AIDS) are used in addition to these laboratory criteria to classify people with HIV infection (Centers for Disease Control and Prevention 1992). Therefore, diagnosis also involves the CD4/CD8 T-lymphocyte ratios and the development of opportunistic infections (e.g., pulmonary tuberculosis, recurrent pneumonia, and invasive cervical cancer in women).

Symptoms

According to some studies, 40 percent to 60 percent of HIV-infected subjects have experienced acute symptoms similar to mononucleosis or influenza, including sore throat, headache, fever, myalgia (muscular pains), and rash (Ortona and Marasca 1994).

HIV may lead to multiple clinical findings in the infected subject. The most striking skin manifestation is Kaposi's sarcoma, which may be widely disseminated, found on the skin surface, in the mouth, and along the alimentary canal. Seborrheic dermatitis, however, is the most common skin manifestation in HIV-infected subjects. It appears as a dry, scalylike condition affecting areas around the mouth, nose, and eyebrows (LeBoit 1992). In the mouth, a whitish plaque or "thrush" is commonly seen. This results from infection by the fungus candida. There are also a host of viral infections of the skin that are more aggressive and difficult to manage in HIV patients; most notable of these is the herpes simplex virus.

Pneumonia is a frequent occurrence with HIV-infected individuals, and PCP is the most common agent responsible. In the initial years of the AIDS epidemic, many individuals succumbed to the pulmonary complications of HIV infection. However, newer treatment modalities and the administration of preventive antibiotics before the appearance of pneumonia have greatly decreased the number of deaths from PCP. Other infectious agents affecting the lungs are tuberculosis, fungal infections, and cytomegalo virus infection. Biopsy and sample for culture are the principal means of identifying these disorders (Price, Brew, and Sidtis 1988).

Involvement of the central nervous system is also seen in HIV-infected individuals. More than half of HIV-positive subjects demonstrated deterioration of neurological function and ultimately infectious processes of the brain and its supporting structures. Encephalitis and meningitis are frequent infections. Among the agents responsible for these infections are the herpes virus, toxoplasma gondii, and cryptococcal neoformans. The specific infectious agents are identified by analysis of spinal fluid removed during a spinal tap; after the agent is identified, more specific therapy can be instituted (Navia et al. 1986). Brain abscesses resulting from these infections can cause permanent neurologic dysfunction. Involvement of the central nervous system can also lead to AIDS dementia complex. Subjects with AIDS dementia can experience seizures, psychosis (i.e., the inability to distinguish reality from fantasy), weakness, problems walking, and difficulty in recognizing surroundings and loved ones (Price, Brew, and Sidtis 1988).

Treatment

The management and treatment of HIV infections continues to evolve as understanding of the virus, its replication, and its targets becomes more defined. The antiretroviral drugs are the mainstays in AIDS therapy. AZT, the best known of these medications, was one of the first line agents used in the treatment of HIV-infected subjects. The purpose of this drug is to interfere with the actions of the reverse transcriptase, thereby controlling replication of HIV by preventing incorporation of the virus's RNA attributes into the cell's genetic makeup. When administered early in the infection, AZT causes a notable delay in the onset of symptoms that define AIDS. Unfortunately, with continued usage, many of those individuals who initially showed good results were affected with weight loss, neurologic disease, and infectious complications (Katz 1994). A host of side effects, including headaches, weakness, insomnia, and anemia have been displayed by individuals using AZT. The eventual failure of the AZT therapy for these individuals may be due to continued destruction of the immune system or mutation of the virus with resultant development of resistance to the drug. AZT is recommended for individuals with a CD4 cell count of 500 or less. The dose is 100 milligrams given orally five times a day (Cooper 1994).

In addition to AZT, two other antiretroviral agents have been introduced and licensed for use since 1991. The first agent, didanosine (ddI), is licensed as a single agent for HIV patients who have CD4 cell counts of less than 500 and are either intolerant of the side effects of AZT or demonstrate progressing disease despite AZT therapy. The second agent, dideoxycitidine (ddC), which is closely related to ddI, is used in combination with AZT (Schnittman and Fauci 1994).

Besides the antiretroviral therapy, there has developed a strategy of prophylaxis, measures to prevent the occurrence of opportunistic infections in the HIV-positive subject. Of all the possible opportunistic infections, this preventive therapy is directed mainly against PCP. Common agents used against PCP are trimethoprim-sulfamethoxazole (bactrim), dapsone, and aerosolized pentamidine (Katz 1994).

Social Response

Because the majority of those afflicted early in the AIDS epidemic were homosexual, many people fostered an attitude that AIDS was a gay disease, a form of punishment for an unacceptable lifestyle. There were very few support services for those infected. What was available came from organized groups within the gay community. Only after its entry into mainstream America was AIDS recognized as a health problem that could afflict anyone who was unattentive to its presence.

Since that time, however, the social adjustments to AIDS and its effect on American culture have been very dramatic. Contraction of HIV by such famous individuals as Rock Hudson, Ryan White, Arthur Ashe, Magic Johnson, and Greg Louganis has forced the general public to acknowledge the existence of AIDS and rethink social behaviors and sexual activities. New words and phrases have been introduced into daily life, and controversy has arisen about what is appropriate sexual education and at what age these discussions should be initiated.

The psychosocial impact of HIV and AIDS on the family begins with the disclosure of HIV positivity. This single event may shatter the family's image of the HIV-infected member, because of the possible disclosure of involvement in socially unacceptable activities. Anger, fear, and anxiety over the possibility of transmission of the infection arise. These emotional responses to a family's HIV-infected member can lead to refusal to acknowledge and care for the sick individual at a time of greatest need. As the infection progresses, decisions about care and treatment in the terminal stages will need to be made. Strong family support is essential at this time, but the fear of social stigma may lead to secrecy and isolation from support groups that could assist the family unit and the infected individual (Bonuck 1993).

Some AIDS cases have led to a redefining of the family unit. This occurs, for example, when an HIV-positive gay man grants a power of attorney or healthy proxy to his lover as the "next of kin" with full decision-making capabilities, over the objection of the patient's other family members (Sholevar 1990).

Conclusion

Great strides in the treatment of HIV infection, AIDS, and related complicating infections were made during the epidemic's first decade, but a cure was not found. While life expectancy has continued to increase with the development of new treatment modalities, avoiding high-risk behaviors remains the only definitive way to combat HIV infection.

(*See also:* HEALTH AND THE FAMILY; SEXUALITY; SEXUALITY EDUCATION; SEXUALLY TRANSMITTED DISEASES; SEXUAL ORIENTATION)

BIBLIOGRAPHY

Bartlett, J. G., and Finkbeiner, A. K. (1993). *The Guide to Living with HIV Infection.* Baltimore: Johns Hopkins University Press.

Bonuck, K. A. (1993). "AIDS and Families: Cultural, Psychosocial, and Functional Impacts." *Social Work in Health Care* 18:75–86.

Broder, S., and Gallo, R. C. (1984). "A Pathogenic Retrovirus (HTLV-III) Linked to AIDS." *New England Journal of Medicine* 311:1292–1297.

Centers for Disease Control and Prevention. (1989). "Update: Acquired Immune Deficiency Syndrome—United States, 1981–1988." *Morbidity and Mortality Weekly Report* 38:229–248.

Centers for Disease Control and Prevention. (1991). "The HIV/AIDS Epidemic: The First 10 Years." *Morbidity and Mortality Weekly Report* 40:357–369.

Centers for Disease Control and Prevention. (1992). "1993 Revised Classification System for HIV Infection and Expanded Surveillance Case Definition for AIDS Among Adolescents and Adults." *Morbidity and Mortality Weekly Report* 41(RR-17):1–19.

Children's Defense Fund. (1988). *Teens and AIDS: Opportunities for Prevention.* Washington, DC: Author.

Cooper, A. A. (1994). "Early Antiretroviral Therapy." *AIDS* 8(suppl. 3):59–514.

Essex, M. (1988). "Origin of AIDS." In *AIDS*, 2nd edition, ed. V. T. Devila, Jr. Philadelphia: J. B. Lippincott.

Feldman, M. D.; Fillit, H.; and McCormick, W. C. (1994). "The Growing Risk of AIDS in Older Patients." *Patient Care*, Oct. 30, pp. 61–71.

Haffner, D. N. (1987). *AIDS and Adolescents: The Time for Prevention Is Now.* Washington, DC: Washington Center for Population Options.

Holmberg, S. D. (1988). "Prior Herpes Simplex Virus II Risk Factor for Infection." *Journal of the American Medical Association* 259:1048–1050.

Katz, M. H. (1994). *Effect of HIV Treatment on Cognition of Behavior and Emotion.* San Francisco: Department of Public Health, AIDS Office.

LeBoit, P. E. (1992). "Dermatopathologic Findings in Patients Infected with HIV." *Dermatologic Clinics* 1:59–71.

Lindegren, M. L. (1994). "Epidemiology of Human Immunodeficiency Virus Infection in Adolescents, United States." *Pediatric Infectious Disease Journal* 13:525–535.

Navia, B. A.; Cho, E. S.; Petito, C. K.; and Price, R. W. (1986). "The AIDS Dementia Complex." *Annals of Neurology* 19:525–535.

Ortona, L., and Marasca, G. (1994). "The Natural History of HIV Infection Development, Clinical and Humoral Parameters of the Disease." *Rays* 19:4–14.

Padian, N. S.; Shiboski, S. C.; and Jewell, N. P. (1991). "Female to Male Transmission of Human Immunodeficiency Virus." *Journal of the American Medical Association* 266:1664–1667.

Peckham, C. S.; Senturia, Y. D.; Ades, A. E.; and Newell, M. L. (1988). "European Collaborative Study of Mother to Child Transmission of HIV Infection." *Lancet* II:1039–1043.

Price, R. N.; Brew, B.; and Sidtis, J. (1988). "The Brain in AIDS: Central Nervous System HIV-1 Infection and AIDS Dementia Complex." *Science* 239:586–591.

Schnittman, S. M., and Fauci, A. S. (1994). "Human Immunodeficiency Virus and Acquired Immunodeficiency Syndrome: An Update." *Advances in Internal Medicine* 39:305–355.

Shilts, R. (1987). *And the Band Played On.* New York: St. Martin's Press.

Sholevar, G. P. (1990). "Family Systems Intervention and Physical Illness." *General Hospital Psychiatry* 12:313–372.

HENRY P. BELLUTTA

ALIMONY AND SPOUSAL SUPPORT

"Spousal support" and "spousal maintenance" are contemporary terms for historical alimony, an obligation of a person who was married to make payments to the former spouse after the marriage ends. These modern terms indicate changes in concepts about a postdivorce responsibility to contribute financially to an ex-spouse. Since the reform of divorce laws early in the 1970s, differences of opinion about the nature and purpose of spousal support resulted in confusion among both the legal profession and the public. Therefore, one cannot find a single generally accepted theory for modern "alimony" in the United States. This means that different courts may treat people in similar situations differently and that predicting whether spousal support will be awarded by a court is difficult. Tracing the historical development of the law of alimony into maintenance or spousal support is easier than predicting whether any ex-spouse will receive a court order for money payments. However, knowing the development of the law does help one understand that scholars, legislatures, and courts are engaging in a difficult but intellectually exciting process of trying to agree on the nature of contemporary spousal support. Because a high percentage of modern marriages end in divorce, achieving consensus and certainty about spousal support is an important social task.

Historical Origins of Alimony

Nearly one thousand years ago, when the English common law system was beginning to develop, the law of marriage for people in most of Europe was controlled by Catholic Church courts. Marriage was considered a sacred relationship ordained by God and subject to laws of God administered by the ecclesiastical courts (church courts). When people entered marriage they took part in a religious sacrament and were considered in a state of grace or blessing with God (O'Connell 1988). The Church believed that only God, no persons, had the power to end a marriage. The obligations of marriage required the wife to care for the home and the husband to support her at the same standard of living he chose for himself (Krauskopf and Thomas 1974). As long as spouses continued to live together in some degree of harmony and safety, this system operated fairly well.

When a marriage relationship became abusive through the husband treating the wife cruelly, the wife could ask the ecclesiastical courts to grant her permission to live separately from him. Because marriage was a sacred relationship of God, no persons could end the marriage by a complete divorce. Instead, the church courts permitted a wife to leave a husband who was at fault for mistreating her, provided she had been a good wife without fault. They called this a divorce *a mensa et thoro*, a separation from bed and board. The separated spouses were still married, and according to the government's civil law courts, the husband had complete control over any property or earnings of the wife. She had no source of funds or property with which to live. The ecclesiastical courts solved that problem by ruling that the husband's duty to support continued and ordering him to

pay alimony. Thus, alimony originated as an obligation of continuing support from a guilty or at-fault husband to an innocent or without-fault wife after a decree of separation known as a divorce *a mensa et thoro*.

Over the centuries, the civil law courts of England and later of the United States developed property laws and rules for organizing society that protected inherited family estates in land. Land and agricultural pursuits formed the economic basis and most of the wealth of society. The law favored control of family property in one person, who could pass it on undivided to the next generation. That person was nearly always a man.

When the law courts finally took over the functions of the former ecclesiastical courts, the law courts adopted the rules of marriage developed in the ecclesiastical courts. The law courts obligated a married woman to perform household services and to be obedient to her husband. She was not expected to engage in activities outside the home (Brinig and Carbone 1988). Most women had no property or earnings. They married and devoted their lives to household tasks, often including many children. The wife's legal existence merged into that of the husband. He was the legal head of the household and continued to control her property and earnings into the latter part of the nineteenth century, when statutes finally gave married women the right to contract about their property, if they had any. Even in the community property jurisdictions where the spouses were joint owners of property acquired during the marriage, only the husband had power to manage the property. Because wives were economically dependent on their husbands, the obligation for husbands to support wives continued.

During the nineteenth century, the law finally recognized the power of civil courts to order an absolute divorce, which actually ended the marriage. This development recognized the secular (nonreligious) nature of marriage as a civil contract and as a status that law courts regulated for the benefit of society. In the predominantly agrarian society, the family was the basic economic, educational, and social unit. Stability of family life was essential for economically dependent wives and children and also for stable society (Carbone and Brinig 1991). Therefore, even though absolute divorce became possible, social disapproval and strict legal requirements kept divorce a rare event. The rules for granting a divorce *a mensa et thoro*, especially the requirements that the defendant be guilty or at fault and that the plaintiff be innocent or without fault, continued as an effective way to limit divorce. Likewise, even though the marriage ended, the old rules allowed an innocent wife to obtain alimony from a guilty husband. This well-developed law endured in most of the states until the 1970s.

Alimony Prior to the 1970s

The law of alimony prior to the 1970s existed without consensus about a theory or justification for allowing postdivorce support. There were four particular requirements for obtaining an alimony order: wife innocent of marital fault, husband guilty of marital fault, wife in "need" of the support, and husband able to pay. This looked like a continuation of the marital duty of support to meet economic need (Singer 1993). This would be a right to the support because of the married status; however, courts seldom gave reasons why economic need justified the husband's continued duty after the marriage ended. Some courts suggested that the alimony was actually damages for breach of the marriage contract by the husband. The theory was that the husband had breached his marital promise to support the wife for her life and, since she was economically needy, ending the marriage with its support damaged her. Either of these reasons—continuing the marriage duty of support to meet need or damages for breach of the promise to support—is consistent with the usual statement that the amount of alimony should be sufficient to allow the wife to live at the standard of living of the marriage (Singer 1993). In other words, the purpose of the alimony was to allow the wife to continue living at the same standard. However, that purpose could not be achieved in most cases because the husband did not have enough wealth to support two households (his own and hers) at that level. Inability to pay meant that there would be no alimony, or far less than needed. In fact, only about 20 percent of divorces included orders for alimony. Perhaps this situation influenced a few judges to say that the purpose of alimony was only to protect the public purse by providing a minimal amount to keep ex-wives off the welfare rolls.

Fault and innocence requirements for both divorce and alimony had an immensely important practical impact on both the number of divorces and the method of obtaining divorce. Divorces were difficult to obtain because the courts guarded their own power to control the marriage status by refusing a divorce not only to any plaintiff who appeared to be at fault but also to any parties who had agreed to be divorced or who had encouraged misconduct so that they would have a fault ground to use against the other party. An interrelationship between money and free-

dom controlled what happened. As the social stigma of divorce lessened and more pressures to escape an unhappy marriage grew, bargaining for divorce developed. If both parties wanted to be divorced, they perjured themselves in testifying to fault and innocence, denying they had agreed to be divorced, and sometimes manufacturing evidence of fault. (Blumberg 1991). In most states, if a husband wanted a divorce over the objection of his wife who was economically dependent on him, she could threaten to establish the easily proved fault ground of mental cruelty against him and prevent him from being an innocent plaintiff. His only recourse was to talk her into cooperation, usually by promising to give her property or alimony. In other words, the woman who had been promised lifetime support by her husband could insist on property or alimony or refuse to allow him out of the marriage. Thus, the strict fault laws protected economically dependent women and children by preventing divorces and providing bargaining power to obtain financial help as the price of divorce. This all took place by agreement and uncontested divorce hearings. Consequently, courts seldom dealt with the question of whether to grant a contested divorce or with any economic issues. There was little opportunity and no need to consider the theory or purpose of justifying alimony. Granting alimony was, indeed, a practice without a theory (O'Connell 1988).

Divorce Reform

As the pressure for more freedom to divorce grew during the 1960s, the negative side of the fault-based divorce situation surfaced. Nearly everyone criticized the tawdry and shameful illegal collusion and perjury that occurred and continually increased as more persons insisted on their individual right to pursue fulfillment. Divorce by forbidden agreement was a common practice. The pressure to eliminate perjury and hypocrisy from the courthouse brought about the divorce reform movement of the 1970s (Kay 1987; Wadlington 1966). Because the requirements of fault and innocence lay behind the tawdry practices, the reform was aimed at eliminating the fault requirements in order to end a marriage. The initial move allowed a divorce without fault grounds after living separate and apart for an extended time (Blumberg 1991). By 1970, the Commissioners on Uniform Laws recommended that the states pass the Uniform Marriage and Divorce Act (UMDA). Both the UMDA and California adopted irretrievable breakdown of the marriage as a basis for divorce. Within the decade, most states changed or at least added to their divorce laws a no-fault or "breakdown" basis for divorce that did not require fault of the defendant or innocence of the plaintiff. Most states also permitted the parties to agree to be divorced even though courts usually had to determine whether the marriage was broken beyond repair. "No fault" divorce embodied a principle of marriage as a union for personal fulfillment that could be ended at the request of either party, thereby allowing the parties opportunity to remarry (Glendon 1979). Provisions accompanying these reforms in the basis for divorce granted courts the power to, and often required them to, assure a fair settlement of the economic consequences of the marriage and divorce, including equitable property division and alimony or maintenance (Levy 1991).

Judicial responsibility for economic arrangements was supposed to supplant the loss of fault as a bargaining tool to prevent unnecessary divorce and, thereby, obtain economic concessions (Carbone and Brinig 1991). Although fault could remain a relevant consideration on economic issues, most but not all jurisdictions eliminated fault entirely. June Carbone and Margaret Brinig succinctly summarized the effect as changing marriage from a lifelong commitment with enforceable obligations to a contract terminable at will in which the husband's promise of lifetime support became meaningless. "The result . . . was a divorce system that left men financially better off and women worse off than they had been when they married" (Carbone and Brinig 1991, pp. 978–979). Government reports, media accounts, and sociological and legal studies since the mid-1980s echo this conclusion. They consistently show that divorced men have at least 30 percent more economic resources than divorced women (Arendell 1986; Hoffman and Duncan 1988; Parkman 1992; Weitzman 1985). Divorced long-term homemakers and mothers with children are a major source of the "feminization of poverty." Yet spousal support is minimal and awarded in less than 15 percent of divorces (Goldfarb 1989; McLindon 1987; Pennington 1989). Since the courts had the power and authority to enforce fair economic settlement, how did this happen, and is this result appropriate? These questions one must address to evaluate the effects of divorce reform on spousal support.

Several legal changes combined to change the face of divorce and the economic well-being of women and children. First, the reform laws authorized courts to divide between the parties their property. Although most persons had very little property, this was not well known, and the erroneous belief too often was that wives' property share was enough to meet their economic needs (Fineman 1983, 1989; Weitzman 1985). Furthermore, the divorce reform statutes explicitly allowed courts to award property rather than alimony to meet need; thus, property division undermined belief in any role for alimony (Blumberg 1991). Since courts did not determine clearly what amount of money was required to meet economic need, appellate courts could not review whether the trial court's property award was sufficient (Fineman 1989; Krauskopf 1989). In fact, a share of a small amount of property given largely on the basis of the wife's contributions seldom met economic need (Fineman 1989; Weitzman 1985). Secondly, the reform statutes often embodied a concept, new in many states, that ex-wives must use whatever appropriate earning skills they had to provide for their own support and that they would obtain "maintenance" (alimony) only if they could not provide for their reasonable needs with property and their own earnings (Fineman 1989; Levy 1991; UMDA 1987). Many courts interpreted this to mean that the ability to obtain any kind of job was enough to preclude "maintenance" or to limit it to a very short time (Krauskopf 1985, 1988). Coupled with these notions was a philosophy of some scholars and judges that the divorce reform process included a "clean break" principle that the two ex-spouses each should be able to establish new marital ties and go on with life unencumbered by obligations to the first spouse (Levy 1991). A third influential change in law was a shift to sex neutral language in alimony statutes. The U.S. Supreme Court ruled that states could not constitutionally allow alimony only to wives by presuming that only wives, but never husbands, were economically dependent (Orr v. Orr 1979). This change in alimony law was minor because men seldom needed support and women had always had to prove need anyway. But symbolically, the shift to gender-neutral language suggested that men and women were equal in terms of economic self-sufficiency. To the extent that judges replaced the dependency stereotype with an equality stereotype, alimony seemed less needed (Fineman 1989).

Three major social changes may be more significant than the actual change in laws in reducing the economic well-being of women and children. The most important factor is the increase in the number of divorces, which create two households rather than one household to live on a similar amount of money. Obviously, individuals in this situation cannot live as well as previously. The question is whether ex-spouses should lessen their standard of living equally or whether it is fair that men are at least 30 percent, and often far more, better off financially after divorce than women (Hoffman and Duncan 1988; McLindon 1987; Weitzman 1985).

Ironically, the most fundamental influence on both the increase in divorce and the lesser financial condition of women after divorce may be the movement of married women, particularly mothers, into the work force in greater numbers than ever before (Carbone and Brinig 1991). Although employment of women had increased earlier in the century and during World War II, society's desire to provide jobs for returning veterans after the war pushed women back into the home. However, twenty-five years later, many factors combined at the same time that the new divorce reform legislation was being applied to encourage wives' employment: Reproductive control reduced the number of children in families; technology lightened the challenges of homemaking; life spans increased to long after children were out of the nest; inflation increased the cost of living and created incentive for two family incomes; growth of the service economy created jobs; and the desire for individual fulfillment grew, fueled by the civil rights revolution, including the women's movement. In 1970, only 15 percent of married women with children were employed, but more than 66 percent of those with children under eighteen held jobs in 1990 (Oldham 1993). This created an impression that women were economically self-sufficient rather than dependent on the income of husbands. The fact that they had some job or could obtain employment of any kind made it easy for courts to assume that ex-wives could become self-sufficient more quickly (Krauskopf 1985, 1988).

The most amorphous but perhaps the most significant factor on awarding postdivorce support has been the movement toward gender equality. The modern women's movement has many origins and effects, but a major impetus was Betty Friedan's book *The Feminine Mystique* (1963), which argued that women should be permitted, socially and legally, a wider range of experience in life than homemaking. Independent of the divorce reform process, but at the same time, women organized and began to lobby for laws guaranteeing them the same rights and opportunities that were open to men. Although the Equal Rights Amendment to the U.S. Constitution was not ratified, the effort to obtain it raised consciousness and galvanized widespread changes in societal attitudes and in laws that reduced and forbade overt discrimination against women in education, athletic opportunities, employment, political rights, and retirement benefits. Initial efforts concentrated on se-

curing the same legal status and opportunities that men had, rather than recognizing that women would continue to be economically disadvantaged.

There are differences of opinion about the long-range and subtle effects of these efforts for equal opportunities, including effects on divorce economics. Most likely, many effects of the rhetoric of equality operate at one time. For example, many persons, including primarily male judges, honestly believe that women now have equal opportunities to earn and support themselves so that there is little or no justification for postdivorce support (Goode 1982; Kerpelman 1983; Krauskopf 1989; Oldham 1993; Raggio 1988). Male judges, in a form of backlash, may be protecting themselves as well as all men by refusing to recognize a proven need for support (Faludi 1991; Krauskopf 1985; Levy 1991). Divorcing wives, themselves, may want to be treated as though there is no difference between their economic abilities and that of men. Some writers argue that women will never be equal until they become wholly self-supporting (Kay 1987). Lobbying feminists, desiring entitlement to an equal share of the property acquired during a marriage or wishing to eradicate the laws that made husbands the head of the household and wives alone responsible for housekeeping, succeeded in the adoption of a theory of marriage as an economic partnership in which the parties contributed equal value, even though in different ways, to the family (Fineman 1983, 1989; Krauskopf and Thomas 1974). Martha Fineman believes that the emphasis on husband and wife as equal partners continues to obscure the economic need of persons who do homemaking and prevents recognition of different needs and abilities to earn. She describes the equality model and the dependency model as polar ends of the way society views the position of women in marriage and concludes that need has no role to play in a true partnership of equals (Fineman 1983, 1989).

Spousal Support Today

The studies reported in the late 1980s established that awards designated for spousal support exist less often and are more limited in amount than previously, that court awards of property to meet support are few, and that most divorced women and children suffer a significantly more severe reduction in standard of living than do men (McLindon 1987; Pennington 1989; Weitzman 1985). Scholars began to assess whether the lack of child and spousal support was appropriate in view of the adverse economic condition of ex-wives and children. This precipitated analysis and debate about the theory and justification for postdivorce spousal support.

Analysis requires differentiating among many types of marriage relationships. Scholars point out that people in marriages begun in different times and marriages of different lengths and marriages with and without children have different expectations and are in distinctly different situations when the marriage ends (Minow and Rhode 1990). Scholars center their concern and focus primarily on two types: the long-term traditional marriage and a marriage in which one spouse (usually the mother) has had primary responsibility for raising children and maintaining the home (Brinig and Carbone 1988; Carbone and Brinig 1991; Fineman 1989; Glendon 1979; Krauskopf 1985, 1988).

The emerging theory or justification for spousal support that most scholars and many courts are recognizing is compensation for career sacrifices by the homemaker that were made in the interests of the couple's children or the other spouse's career (Beninger and Smith 1982; Carbone and Brinig 1991; Ellman 1989; Parkman 1986). The rationale is that the caretaker of children and home suffers loss in earning capacity so that the other spouse, who is equally benefited by the children and home, may devote nearly all time and energy to income production and increase in earning capacity. In other words, while both enjoy home and children, a transfer in earning capacity occurs: The homemaker's earning capacity decreases, but the employed spouse's earning capacity increases. (Brinig and Carbone 1989; Carbone and Brinig 1991; Krauskopf 1988, 1989).

The long-term traditional marriage involves people married before or near the beginning of the divorce reform movement, the women's movement, and social approval of employment for married women. Most of the women in marriages contracted before 1975 were not employed at all during the marriage or not until children were out of the home. In the older marriages and in those of professional men and businessmen, the husband ordinarily did not want his wife to be employed. Estimates of loss of earning capacity for a person out of the employment market are 1.5 percent per year and as high as 4.3 percent per year for college-educated women (Beninger and Smith 1982; Mincer and Polacheck 1978). These women can never regain the earning capacity sacrificed for the benefit of the family during twenty or thirty years out of the labor market. Many scholars believe that because they are from a different era these women should not be penalized for modern societal changes they did not expect; their husbands should continue

the obligation of support they expected to have for a lifetime. Courts and writers state that unjust enrichment occurs when one alone carries the burden of a reduced earning capacity while the other is advantaged by that sacrifice (*In re Marriage of Franks* 1975; *Jamison* v. *Churchill Truck Lines* 1982; Parkman 1992).

In modern marriages, whether both spouses are employed or not, the wife and mother continues to perform most of the homemaking and the child rearing. Studies show that the wife does 80 percent of the family caretaking tasks (*Columbus Dispatch* 1994; Goldfarb 1989). This includes missing work to care for sick children or to make school visitations. Other studies show that when men do have primary responsibility for children their income and earning capacity decrease (Goldfarb 1989). Forty-five percent of married women with children under three years old are not employed at all, while 33 percent of the employed work only part-time (Oldham 1993). Modern women about to enter the twenty-first century continue to sacrifice their earnings and earning ability for the benefit of their families (Fuchs 1988). There lies the justification for modern postdivorce spousal support. Unless the income producer spouse compensates the homemaker for this loss of earning capacity, the income producer will be unjustly enriched. This probably has been an unarticulated purpose of alimony and maintenance all along; the old continuation of marital support and damages for breach-of-contract language actually covered this purpose (Krauskopf 1985, 1988; Landes 1978). Many scholars center on this phenomenon because they are concerned for the welfare of children. Their theme is that someone must care for and nurture children and that this care of children will be neglected unless the law assures that compensation for the inevitable sacrifices is required when the marriage ends (Brinig and Carbone 1988; Fineman 1989; Oldham 1992). Consistent with these views, others emphasize that support is based on sharing principles much like a business partnership in which partners do different types of work for the good of the partnership (Estin 1993; Starnes 1993).

Courts award spousal support, whether labeled alimony or maintenance or not, primarily in three situations. The first is when one spouse has suffered a long-lasting decrease in earning capacity due to service to the marriage and family. This is almost always the situation in a traditional long-term marriage, where the homemaker spouse had never been employed or had been out of the employment market for many years. After very long marriages, spousal support often is large enough to equalize the postdivorce incomes of the ex-spouses so that they may live at the same standard of living, with each sacrificing if there is not enough money for both to live at the standard of living of the marriage (Burden 1993). Controversy exists about whether the modern primary caretaker of children who is employed also suffers a long-term or permanent loss of earning capacity calling for spousal support. Scholars argue that caretakers of children often hold lower-paying jobs because child care interferes with the devotion to employment required for pay increases, promotion, or more lucrative careers. Whether the recipient is a traditional nonemployed or modern employed homemaker, the spousal support order could be in the form of a periodic payment for an indefinite period of time, such as $500 a month. Because this obligation could last for the parties' lifetimes, it is sometimes called permanent alimony. However, that is a misleading description. "Indefinite spousal support" is more accurate, because certain conditions will allow modification or termination of the obligation to continue payments. The advantage of a periodic order in the situation of long-term earning capacity loss is that an indefinite order adapts to the extreme difficulty of determining exactly when, if at all, the earning capacity decrease will be overcome. If, in the future, the recipient is able to increase earning capacity sufficiently, the order can be modified. Remarriage of the recipient or inability of the obligor to pay also would justify a modification in the order.

The second common situation for spousal support is when one spouse has suffered a temporary reduction in earning capacity because of service to the marriage. There are a variety of situations: The wife gave up going to medical school herself so that the husband could be educated first; the wife took leave from her career for five years while children were born; the wife left her employment when the husband's business or military commitments required them to move. After a relatively short period of time of schooling or reentering the employment market, the sacrificing spouse can be "rehabilitated" enough to be self-sufficient. Spousal support would be ordered by a transfer of property, a cash sum, or, most likely, an amount to be paid periodically for a limited time until the evidence shows that self-sufficiency will be achieved.

Third, all courts grant some compensation to the supporting spouse who supports the other as a student when the marriage ends close to the same time as the student completes the education. The justification is that the student spouse gained a benefit in the form of increased earning capacity due to the educa-

tion they had expected to share during the continuing marriage. This gain may be quite large if the education was professional or graduate, such as medical school. Since the supporting spouse lost both the money contributed to the education and the better standard of living he or she would have enjoyed had the spouse been employed, but will be prevented by the divorce from sharing in the benefit, the courts hold it unfair not to compensate the supporting spouse. Some courts allow only reimbursement for the amount of money contributed plus interest, but others allow broader compensation that takes into account the increase in earning capacity the educated spouse now has (Krauskopf 1988, 1989). The compensation can be ordered to be paid by a transfer of property, a sum of money called an equitable award or reimbursement alimony, or by spousal support payments, usually for a limited time.

Spousal support of the future will be primarily for those persons who cared for home and children or enabled the other spouse to become better educated. Although some economists recommend that divorce laws be changed to require mutual consent of the parties for divorce to give the homemaker more bargaining power, that is not politically likely (Brinig 1993; Parkman 1992). Difficulties in implementing the law of spousal support will remain even if everyone agrees that the justification or theory of spousal support is to compensate the recipient spouse for decreased earning capacity caused by service to the family. Judges granting divorces and support orders have broad discretion to do what they think is fair. Furthermore, the expense of presenting detailed evidence with experts' opinions on the decrease in earning capacity will be too great in most cases. Since evidence of the degree of sacrifice and amount of benefit incurred in any one case always will be uncertain, individual judges' decisions on the amount that should be compensated could vary widely.

For these reasons, guidelines or formulas for determining spousal support will be the method of choice in the twenty-first century. The formulas will be based on the number of years married, the number of years that the recipient was responsible for homemaking, and the combined income of both spouses, which will be multiplied by a figure representing an estimated decrease in earning capacity or value of homemaking (Krauskopf 1989; Oldham 1992).

(*See also:* DIVORCE: LEGAL ASPECTS; DIVORCE: ECONOMIC ASPECTS; MARITAL PROPERTY AND COMMUNITY PROPERTY; PREMARITAL AGREEMENTS; REMARRIAGE)

BIBLIOGRAPHY

Arendell, T. (1986). *Mothers and Divorce: Legal, Economic, and Social Dilemmas.* Berkeley: University of California Press.

Beninger, E., and Smith, J. (1982). "Career Opportunity Cost: A Factor in Spousal Support Determination." *Family Law Quarterly* 16:201–217.

Blumberg, G. (1991). "Reworking the Past, Imagining the Future: On Jacob's Silent Revolution." *Law and Social Inquiry* 16:115–154.

Brinig, M., and Carbone, J. (1988). "The Reliance Interest in Marriage and Divorce." *Tulane Law Review* 62:855–905.

Burden, D. (1993). "Divorce in the Golden Years." *Family Advocate* 16:28–33.

Carbone, J., and Brinig, M. (1991). "Rethinking Marriage: Feminist Ideology, Economic Change, and Divorce Reform." *Tulane Law Review* 65:954–1010.

Columbus Dispatch. (1994). "Women Still Do Bulk of Chores." Jan. 9, p. B6.

Ellman, I. (1989). "The Theory of Alimony." *California Law Review* 77:1–81.

Estin, A. (1993). "Maintenance, Alimony, and the Rehabilitation of Family Care." *North Carolina Law Review* 71:776–803.

Faludi, S. (1991). *Backlash: The Undeclared War Against American Women.* New York: Crown.

Fineman, M. (1983). "Implementing Equality: Ideology, Contradiction, and Social Change." *Wisconsin Law Review,* pp. 789–886.

Fineman, M. (1989). "Societal Factors Affecting the Creation of Legal Rules for Distribution of Property at Divorce." *Family Law Quarterly* 22:279–299.

Friedan, B. (1963). *The Feminine Mystique.* New York: W. W. Norton.

Fuchs, V. (1988). *Women's Quest for Economic Equality.* Cambridge, MA: Harvard University Press.

Glendon, M. A. (1979). "The New Family and the New Property." *Tulane Law Review* 53:697–712.

Goldfarb, S. (1989). "Marital Partnership and the Case for Permanent Alimony." *Journal of Family Law* 27:351–372.

Goode, W. (1982). "Why Men Resist." In *Rethinking the Family: Some Feminist Questions,* ed. B. Thorne and M. Yalum. New York: Longman.

Hoffman, S., and Duncan, G. (1988). "What Are the Economic Consequences of Divorce?" *Demographics* 25:641–644.

Kay, H. H. (1987). "Equality and Difference: A Perspective on No-Fault Divorce and Its Aftermath." *University of Cincinnati Law Review* 56:1–90.

Kerpelman, L. (1983). *Divorce: A Guide for Men.* South Bend, IN: Icarus Press.

Krauskopf, J. (1985). "Maintenance: A Decade of Development." *Missouri Law Review* 50:259–320.

Krauskopf, J. (1988). "Rehabilitative Alimony: Uses and Abuses of Limited Duration Alimony." *Family Law Quarterly* 21:573–589.

Krauskopf, J. (1989). "Theories of Property Division/Spousal Support: Searching for Solutions to the Mystery." *Family Law Quarterly* 22:253–278.

Krauskopf, J., and Thomas, R. (1974). "Partnership Marriage: The Solution to an Ineffective and Inequitable Law of Support." *Ohio State Law Journal* 35:558–600.

Landes, E. (1978). "Economics of Alimony." *Journal of Legal Studies* 7:35–63.

Levy, R. (1991). "A Reminiscence About the Uniform Marriage and Divorce Act." *Brigham Young Law Review,* pp. 43–77.

McLindon, J. (1987). "Separate but Unequal: The Economic Disaster of Divorce for Women and Children." *Family Law Quarterly* 21:351–409.

Mincer, J., and Polacheck, S. (1978). "Women's Earnings Reexamined." *Journal of Human Resources* 13:118–122.

Minow, M., and Rhode, D. (1990). "Reforming the Questions: Feminist Perspectives on Divorce Reform." In *Divorce Reform at the Crossroads,* ed. S. Sugarman and H. H. Kay. New Haven, CT: Yale University Press.

O'Connell, M. (1988). "Alimony After No-Fault: A Practice in Search of a Theory." *New England Law Review* 23:437–513.

Oldham, T. (1992). "Putting Asunder in the 1990s." *California Law Review* 80:1091–1132.

Oldham, T. (1993). "The Economic Consequences of Divorce in the United States." In *Frontiers of Family Law,* ed. A. Bainhaum and D. Pearl. London: Chancery Law Publishing.

Parkman, A. (1992). *No-Fault Divorce: What Went Wrong?* Boulder, CO: Westview Press.

Pennington, J. (1989). "The Economic Implications of Divorce for Older Women." *Clearinghouse Review* (Summer):488–493.

Raggio, L. (1988). "Don't Men Have Rights, Too?—or Lifetime Alimony, an Idea Whose Time Has Come and Gone." In *Alimony, New Strategies for Pursuit and Defense,* ed. L. Raggio and K. Raggio. Chicago: American Bar Association.

Singer, J. (1989). "Divorce Reform and Gender Justice." *North Carolina Law Review* 67:1103–1121.

Singer, J. (1993). "Divorce Obligations and Bankruptcy Discharge: Rethinking the Support/Property Distinction." *Harvard Journal on Legislation* 30:43–114.

Starnes, C. (1993). "Divorce and the Displaced Homemaker: A Discourse on Playing with Dolls, Partnership Buyouts, and Dissociation Under No-Fault." *University of Chicago Law Review* 60:67–122.

Wadlington, W. (1966). "Divorce Without Fault, Without Perjury." *Virginia Law Review* 52:32–87.

Weitzman, L. (1985). *The Divorce Revolution: The Unexpected Social and Economic Consequences for Women and Children in America.* New York: Free Press.

CASES

Franks, In re Marriage of, 189 Colo. 499, 542 P. 2d 845 (1975).

Jamison v. *Churchill Truck Lines*, 632 S.W. 2d 34 (Mo. App. 1982).

Orr v. *Orr*, 440 U.S. 268 (1979).

LEGISLATION

Uniform Marriage and Divorce Act (UMDA). (1987). 307, 308, 9A U.L.A. 338, 347.

JOAN M. KRAUSKOPF

ANNULMENT

Annulment is the judicial pronouncement declaring a marriage invalid. A few ideas must be kept in mind in order to understand the concept of annulment and how it differs from divorce:

1. Every society establishes rules of conduct for its members relating to behavior that impacts the common good. Marriage is an institution designed to enable people to establish stable primary intimate relationships that potentially involve the procreation and rearing of children. While the right to marry is fundamental, each society passes legislation to control and restrict the exercise of this right.

2. The rules governing the valid contracting of legal obligations are not necessarily shared by other social units and vary from society to society. If an individual belongs to multiple social units, the validity of contracts entered into by persons who choose to remain part of that social unit is governed by the laws passed by the legitimate authority of that unit.

3. If the requirements that have been established by the legally binding authority of the social unit and that are in existence at the time of entering the contract are not fulfilled, the contract is considered null and void from its outset.

4. The marriage ceremony takes place in a specific geographic locale. The requirements and regulations established by the state where the exchange of vows takes place may refer to the radical capacity or ability of persons entering marriage to take on the responsibilities and enjoy the rights of marriage (i.e., age and mental competence), the specific form that must be followed (i.e., valid license and official minister who is to witness the exchange of vows), or other regulations that fall into a questionable area between the basic ability or capacity to enter marriage and the format required (i.e., gender of the contracting parties). Whatever the category of requirement or regulation, if *all* norms so determined by the state are not followed, the contract is null and void, invalid; no marriage exists and no rights or obligations are incurred.

Divorce Versus Annulment

Before persons can enter another marriage after they have exchanged vows in a marriage ceremony, the prior marriage must be liquidated. To sever the chains of matrimony or "untie the knot," the case must be adjudicated in a civil court that handles either divorce or annulment.

Divorce presupposes that a valid marriage was entered into by the parties involved and ends a marriage as of the date the divorce decree becomes final. Divorce per se has no effect on the legitimacy of children born of this union or on a claim for alimony.

Annulment implies that a valid marriage never took place because of the inability to perform the responsibilities of marriage. The parties are considered to lack the ability to give valid consent if, at the time and in the place where the marriage ceremony was performed, there was some defect, impediment, or lack of capacity preventing a legal marriage between the parties concerned. When this fact is so judged by legal authority (adjudicated), the legal judgment implies that the marriage is voided *from its inception.* Unless altered by statute, annulment has the legal effect of rendering the children born of this union "illegitimate." A claim for alimony would also be invalid unless the rule is changed by statute or judicial decision.

State legislatures have tended to confuse the distinction between divorce and annulment as they enact divorce statutes. Divorce serves as a substitute for annulment in those jurisdictions that have no statutes allowing courts to grant annulments and becomes a catchall for cases involving such issues as bigamy and impotency.

Grounds for Annulment

The statutes or legislation that determine the impediments to a valid marital contract are not uniform from state to state, and the grounds for annulment vary from one jurisdiction to another. In every case, however, these grounds must be clear, strong, and convincing before an annulment court will issue a decree of nullity following legal proceedings to liquidate a marriage. While the rule of law changes from one jurisdiction to another, some reasons why parties are unable to exchange marital consent include:

1. failure to follow legal format, such as not obtaining a marriage license or neglecting to fulfill other statutory prohibitions

2. being underage—there is a fixed marriageable age that must be respected
3. gender—most societies permit only heterosexuals to marry
4. consanguinity—a marriage would be considered "incestuous and void" if the parties were related by blood, that is, ancestors and descendants such as father and daughter, brothers and sisters, uncles and nieces, aunts and nephews
5. affinity—a relationship established by marriage, such as stepbrother and stepsister
6. impotency—the incapacity to perform the act of sexual intercourse
7. duress (force and fear)—a valid marriage requires free and willing consent of both male and female
8. fraud (deception)—both parties must intend to assume the contractual obligations
9. mental disorder or mental deficiency—persons must possess the ability to understand the nature and consequences of the marriage ceremony.

If any of these impediments were present at the time of the marriage and proven in a court of law, a decree of nullity would be issued indicating that no marriage existed.

Historical Link with Church Law

The concept of annulment draws its heritage from the ecclesiastical courts of England and canon law of the Roman Catholic church. In sharp contrast to Roman law, which considered marriage and its dissolution to be determined by the free will of the parties concerned, the Catholic church believes that a valid marriage entered into by two baptized Christians (classified as "sacramental") cannot be dissolved by any human power. Consequently, if a valid marriage is sacramental and consummated through sexual intercourse, it can be dissolved only by the death of one spouse. Hence the focus on annulment to prove some impediment or defect that would render the contract itself invalid from the outset; this would prove that the marriage never existed.

When an individual falls under the jurisdiction of both state and church law because of an affiliation with a specific religious denomination, the rules of law of both state and church become significant.

For those religious organizations that permit divorce, the usual procedure is to recognize the legal authority of the state to dissolve the marriage in civil court. The denominations would then accept the decree of divorce as valid, thereby freeing both parties to remarry according to the rules of both state and church.

The Roman Catholic church does not allow its members to divorce. If Catholics who previously had exchanged marital vows wish to marry a different partner, a lengthy annulment procedure in the ecclesiastical tribunal is usually required. While the state may allow an individual to remarry within its jurisdiction, the church would forbid a new marriage within the church until an annulment procedure had declared the previous marriage null and void. On the other hand, even though the church has issued a "decree of nullity," the state would require a civil procedure to be completed within the divorce court of the state before allowing either of the parties to enter a new marriage.

(*See also:* DIVORCE: LEGAL ASPECTS; MARRIAGE DEFINITION)

BIBLIOGRAPHY

Anderson, E. A. (1989). "An Exploration of a Divorce Statute: Implications for Future Policy Development." *Journal of Divorce* 12(4):1–18.
Bassett, W. (1968). *The Bond of Marriage.* Notre Dame, IN: University of Notre Dame Press.
Burd, J. (1991). "Splitting the Marriage in More Ways Than One: Bifurcation of Divorce Proceedings." *Journal of Family Law* 30:903–917.
Freed, D. J. (1991). "Family Law in the Fifty States: An Overview." *Family Law Quarterly* 24:309–405.
Kelleher, S. (1973). *Divorce and Remarriage for Catholics.* Garden City, NY: Doubleday.
Nadelson, C., and Polonsky, D. (1984). *Marriage and Divorce.* New York: Guilford.
Parkman, A. M. (1992). *No-Fault Divorce: What Went Wrong?* Boulder, CO: Westview Press.
Phillips, R. (1991). *Untying the Knot: A Short History of Divorce.* New York: Cambridge University Press.
"Same Sex Couples and the Law." (1989). *Harvard Law Review* 102:1603–1628.
Siegle, B. (1986). *Marriage According to the New Code of Canon Law.* New York: Alba House.
Steinbock, B. (1992). "The Relevancy of Illegality." *Hastings Center Report* 22:19–22.
Sugarman, S. D. (1990). *Divorce Reform: At the Crossroads.* New Haven, CT: Yale University Press.
Wisensale, S. K. (1992). "Toward the 21st Century: Family Change and Public Policy." *Family Relations* 41:417–422.
Zimmerman, S. L. (1989). "Comparing the Family Policies of Three States." *Family Relations* 38:190–195.

WARREN F. SCHUMACHER

ATTACHMENT

Attachment is a word commonly used to describe a deep and enduring emotional connection between people, such as romantic partners or parents and their children. Being attached is an integral part of life for people of all cultures and all ages and there is evidence to suggest that humans are biologically prepared to form social attachments. Hundreds of studies have documented the importance of such relationships for happy and healthy functioning from infancy through old age. In addition, researchers have uncovered clues about why some people have difficulty establishing satisfying and lasting attachments.

Attachment Theory

Before the first birthday, virtually every human being develops an emotional attachment to someone. Long before infants are capable of expressing attachment verbally, it is evident in their behavior. They tend to stay in reasonably close proximity to their attachment figure. If they are upset or frightened, they turn to their attachment figure for comfort. The presence of the attachment figure usually makes them feel safe enough to play and explore. The absence of the attachment figure is sufficient cause for distress.

British psychiatrist John Bowlby developed a theory to explain these behaviors. He hypothesized that attachment behavior is regulated by an inborn control system. Because human infants are too immature at birth to care for themselves, their survival depends on developing a relationship with a caregiver. The caregiver's job is to provide such essentials as food, protection, and comfort; the infant's primary task is to stay close to the caregiver. The attachment system helps ensure that the infant will automatically do whatever is necessary to maintain a safe degree of proximity—cry, cling, follow, or signal to be picked up. Whether an infant feels secure or anxious depends, in large part, on the whereabouts of his or her caregiver. This is why attachments are often referred to as emotional bonds.

Although the attachment system is present at birth, attachment relationships take time to develop. For the first couple of months of life, infants will accept care and comfort from almost anyone. By the time they are four or five months old, they become more selective. Between the ages of six and eight months, most infants become capable of crawling. This new ability makes it possible for them to do the kind of exploring that is necessary to learn about the world, but it also opens the possibility of venturing dangerously far from the caregiver. At the very same age, infants first begin to show wariness of unfamiliar people (stranger anxiety) and distress at being separated from their primary caregiver (separation anxiety). An infant who previously smiled at and was happy to be held by nearly everyone suddenly cries when a stranger approaches or the caregiver leaves. At this point, the infant is said to be attached. Most infants are cared for by more than one person and may become attached to all of them. Nevertheless, research has shown that there is typically one person whom the infant prefers over all others, especially when the infant is upset (Ainsworth 1967). Theoretically, this person could be almost anyone; in practice, it tends to be the mother. Bowlby suggested that attachment relationships can be thought of as hierarchically organized. At the top of an individual's attachment hierarchy is the primary attachment figure; on the second level are secondary attachment figures—other familiar but less preferred caregivers. The infant's relationship with the primary attachment figure is special in a variety of ways. For example, it is often characterized by a degree of intimacy that distinguishes it from the infant's relationships with other people, especially physical intimacy in the form of cuddling, nuzzling, sucking, prolonged mutual gazing, and ventral (i.e., belly-to-belly) contact.

Bowlby theorized that attachments are important not only in infancy but throughout life. He argued further that the nature of attachment relationships is essentially the same at any age; there is usually one preferred attachment figure who is turned to for comfort, whose presence provides feelings of security, and from whom separations are distressing. Clearly, there are differences between infant and adult attachments. As individuals mature, they can tolerate separations of greater distance and longer duration. Attachments in early life tend to be complementary; infants and children seek comfort and security from their attachment figures but do not typically provide security and comfort in return. In contrast, adult attachments tend to be reciprocal; two attached adults provide security and comfort to each other. Whereas infants and children are primarily attached to their parents, the primary attachment figure for most adults is their romantic partner (Hazan and Zeifman 1993). This fact suggests that the kind of physical intimacy that characterizes and distinguishes parent–infant and romantic relationships from other types of relationships may be an important factor in attachment formation. Parents kiss, cuddle, and nuzzle their infants and spend hours holding them close and staring into their eyes. Typically, not until the infants grow up and fall in love will they again experience such intimacy. The transition from complementary to reciprocal attachments, when a peer replaces parents as the primary attachment figure, usually occurs sometime during late adolescence or early adulthood (Hazan et al. 1991).

Patterns in Infancy and Childhood

Bowlby theorized that the attachment system, like the other inborn characteristics, could be modified through experience. American psychologist Mary Ainsworth used Bowlby's theory to develop an experimental paradigm for examining the quality of infant–caregiver attachments. The paradigm, known as the Strange Situation, involves eight brief episodes designed to elicit attachment behavior on the part of infants. Experiments begin with the mother and the infant in a laboratory room complete with age-appropriate toys. Twice during the experiment, the mother leaves the room briefly and then returns. Much can be learned about the quality of attachment from observing the way infants behave in the presence and absence of their caregivers, especially during the reunion episodes.

Ainsworth and her colleagues (Ainsworth et al. 1978) identified three distinct types of attachment, which they called secure, ambivalent, and avoidant. Moreover, they discovered that the types of attachment behavior exhibited by infants in the laboratory at twelve months of age could be traced to the way caregivers had treated them in the preceding months. When caregivers responded promptly and warmly to their infants' bids for comfort or contact, the infants tended to form a secure attachment. In the laboratory, they played happily when the mother was present, were upset by her departure, sought contact as soon as she returned, and were sufficiently comforted to resume play and exploratory activity. In Ainsworth's view, these infants had learned that they could count on their caregivers to be responsive, which gave them the confidence they needed for exploration of the unfamiliar environment.

In contrast, infants whose caregivers were not so responsive tended to form insecure attachments. Some caregivers were inconsistent in responding to their infants, being sometimes warmly responsive and at other times intrusive or neglectful. Later, in the laboratory, these infants tended to show ambivalent attachment behavior. They seemed too anxious to enjoy the toys, even with the mother present, were distressed by the separations, sought contact during reunions, but appeared angry and had difficulty settling. Ainsworth saw the behavior of these infants as a way of coping with their unpredictable caregivers. The infants could not be sure that comfort would be forthcoming if they got into trouble, so they opted to stay close rather than venture off to play. Their caregivers' unpredictability left them feeling insecure and made them angry.

The third type of attachment observed was the avoidant pattern, found to be associated with fairly consistent rejection on the part of caregivers. Rather than responding warmly or even inconsistently to their infants' signals for contact, these caregivers regularly rebuffed their infants and even seemed to have an aversion to close contact with them. In the laboratory, the avoidantly attached infants focused their attention on the toys, showed little if any distress when their mothers left the room, and actively avoided contact during the reunions. Ainsworth reasoned that these infants had learned that seeking comfort from their caregivers was futile, perhaps even risky, and adapted by keeping their distance.

According to Bowlby, experiences with the primary caregiver during infancy and childhood form the basis of a mental model of close relationships—a set of beliefs and expectations—that may affect subsequent relationships. For example, an infant may have an avoidant attachment relationship with the caregiver. Key features of the relationship come to be represented in the mind of, and habitually woven into the behavior of, the infant. The representation, which resides in the infant, is then carried forward into new relationships in which it may influence perceptions, feelings, and behaviors. How subsequent relationships unfold—whether they too become avoidant—will be a joint function of the individual's biases (perhaps to expect rejection and avoid contact) and the behavior of new relationship partners.

Patterns in Adolescence and Adulthood

Researchers have identified three patterns of attachment in adolescence and adulthood that are similar to those Ainsworth observed among infants (Hazan and Shaver 1987). Although the behaviors associated with each attachment pattern are different in adulthood and infancy, they seem to be based on the same basic strategies for coping with anxiety. Secure attachment, at any age, is based on the belief that partners can be counted on to provide comfort and support. Securely attached individuals of all ages seek social contact when they are distressed and derive both comfort and confidence from their closest relationships. Adults who are secure in their attachments tend to have relationships characterized by a high degree of intimacy and trust. Their relationships are, on average, more satisfying and more enduring. In addition, the confidence they derive from their close relationships facilitates engagement in other activities, such as work (Hazan and Shaver 1990). Ambivalent attachment, whether in infancy or adulthood, is associated with the belief that attachment figures cannot be counted on to provide comfort. Accordingly, the ambivalent strategy for coping with anxiety is to monitor the whereabouts and reactions of attachment figures continually—a preoccupation that interferes with other activities. Ambivalent adults tend to be obsessive about their relationships, experience extreme jealousy and fears of abandonment, and often feel angry toward their relationship partners (Hazan and Shaver 1987). The lack of security in their relationships can make it more difficult to meet obligations or tend to other activities. For instance, ambivalence has been linked to procrastination and suboptimal performance at work (Hazan and Shaver 1990).

Avoidant attachment, at any point in the lifespan, is based on the belief that attachment figures will be unresponsive and rejecting. Avoidantly attached individuals cope by being overly self-reliant and distracting themselves with nonsocial activities. Avoidant adults tend to have relationships that are typified by emotional distance, a lack of intimacy, less satisfaction, more troubles, and shorter duration (Hazan and Shaver 1987). Avoidant attachment has also been linked to workaholism and a tendency to use work to avoid social activities (Hazan and Shaver 1990).

Stability of Attachment Patterns

One of the most common misconceptions about attachment theory is that mental models of relationships that are formed in infancy remain unchanged throughout life. In other words, the way an individual attaches to his or her caregiver in the first few months of life determines the nature and course of all subsequent relationships. Research has shown that, while attachment patterns are generally stable over time, change is always possible. Investigators have been working to identify the conditions that make stability or change more likely.

Stability of individual differences is thought to result from three different ways in which people interact with their environments (Caspi and Bem 1990). Reactive interaction refers to the fact that individuals pay more attention to information that confirms their mental models than to information that disconfirms it. For example, an avoidant model of relationships can cause an individual to look for and perceive rejection and fail to notice supportiveness, thereby confirming an avoidant view of relationships. Evocative interaction refers to the finding that individuals evoke different responses from their environments. In one experiment, avoidant subjects failed to express their

feelings of anxiety to their partners and, as a result, received less comfort (Simpson, Rholes, and Nelligan 1992). Thus, they evoked the kind of nonsupportiveness that their attachment models would predict. Proactive interaction refers to the fact that individuals have an active role in selecting and creating their environments. Research has shown that adults tend to choose relationship partners that confirm their attachment-related beliefs and expectations, even if those are negative (Swann, Hixon, and De La Ronde 1992).

Data from longitudinal studies have provided support for the claim that mental models of relationships tend to be stable (e.g., Main, Kaplan, and Cassidy 1985; Waters 1978). Individuals who are securely attached during infancy generally grow into children who are socially competent in their relationships with peers; those who are ambivalently or avoidantly attached during infancy tend to have more problematic peer relationships (Arend, Gove, and Sroufe 1979).

Despite the multiple forces promoting the stability of attachment patterns, there is evidence that these patterns can and do sometimes change. Researchers have identified some of the associated processes and circumstances. In infancy, change in attachment patterns can occur as a result of major changes in the infant's environment, especially if the changes affect the behavior of the caregiver. For example, studies have found that changes in the mother's social support network can produce corresponding changes in infant attachment (Crockenberg 1981). Training caregivers to be more responsive has also been found to increase the likelihood of secure attachment on the part of the infant (Van den Boom 1990). In addition, mental models of attachment can be profoundly affected by relationship experiences. One study found that individuals who reported poor childhood relationships with their parents but formed secure attachments to their adult partners were more likely to have had a warm and supportive relationship with another adult (e.g., teacher, family friend) sometime during childhood (Hazan and Hutt 1993). One additional way in which attachment patterns can change is through self-insight coupled with conscious attempts to alter one's relationship behavior. One study reported that parents who were able to overcome insecure childhood attachments and foster security in their own children had a relatively deep understanding of how their attachment experiences had affected them (Main, Kaplan, and Cassidy 1985). In sum, attachment theory as well as attachment research support the view that mental models of attachment are often inadvertently perpetuated by individuals as they interact with their social environments but that changes in either the person or the environment can produce changes in the models.

Conclusion

Understanding human relationships, and especially learning what makes them satisfying and enduring, is a challenging but important task for science. It is difficult to overestimate the importance of close relationships in the lives of individuals of all ages. Such relationships are among the greatest sources of subjective well-being. The disruption of an attachment bond can have serious and long-term negative effects, not only for infants but for adults as well.

Humans have an inborn need for the security and comfort that is best provided by reliable and responsive attachment figures. To be deprived of security and comfort is stressful and, like any prolonged stressor, social deprivation can be both psychologically and physically harmful. Thus, health and happiness depend to a large degree on the quality of closest relationships. Attachment theory offers a framework for understanding how and why humans become emotionally attached to each other, the different ways in which individuals approach and experience their closest relationships, and the importance of such relationships from infancy through old age.

(*See also:* INTIMACY; JEALOUSY; LOVE; PERSONALITY DEVELOPMENT; SHYNESS; TRUST)

BIBLIOGRAPHY

Ainsworth, M. D. S. (1967). *Infancy in Uganda: Infant Care and the Growth of Attachment.* Baltimore: Johns Hopkins Press.

Ainsworth, M. D. S.; Blehar, M. C.; Waters, F.; and Wall, S. (1978). *Patterns of Attachment: Assessed in the Strange Situation and at Home.* Hillsdale, NJ: Erlbaum.

Arend, R.; Gove, F.; and Sroufe, L. A. (1979). "Continuity of Individual Adaptation from Infancy to Kindergarten: A Predictive Study of Ego Resiliency and Curiosity in Preschoolers." *Child Development* 50:950–959.

Bowlby, J. (1969). *Attachment and Loss:* Vol. I, *Attachment.* New York: Basic Books.

Bowlby, J. (1973). *Attachment and Loss:* Vol. II, *Separation: Anxiety and Anger.* New York: Basic Books.

Bowlby, J. (1979). *The Making and Breaking of Affectional Bonds.* London: Tavistock.

Bowlby, J. (1980). *Attachment and Loss:* Vol. III, *Loss: Sadness and Depression.* New York: Basic Books.

Bowlby, J. (1988). *A Secure Base: Parent–Child Attachment and Healthy Human Development.* New York: Basic Books.

Bretherton, I. (1990). "Open Communication and Internal Working Models: Their Role in the Development of Attachment Relationships." In *Nebraska Symposium on Motivation:* Vol. 36, *Socioemotional Development,* ed. R. A. Thompson. Lincoln: University of Nebraska Press.

Caspi, A., and Bem, D. J. (1990). "Personality Continuity and Change Across the Life Course." In *Handbook of Personality: Theory and Research,* ed. L. A. Pervin. New York: Guilford.

Crockenberg, S. B. (1981). "Infant Irritability, Mother Responsiveness, and Social Support Influences on the Security of Infant–Mother Attachment." *Child Development* 52:857–869.

Freedman, J. (1978). *Happy People: What Happiness Is, Who Has It, and Why.* New York: Harcourt Brace Jovanovich.

Hazan, C., and Hutt, M. J. (1993). "Continuity and Change in Internal Working Models of Attachment." Ithaca, NY: Cornell University Department of Human Development and Family Studies.

Hazan, C.; Hutt; M. J.; Sturgeon, J.; and Bricker, T. (1991). "The Process of Relinquishing Parents as Attachment Figures." Presented at the biennial meeting of the Society for Research in Child Development, Seattle, WA.

Hazan, C., and Shaver, P. R. (1978). "Romantic Love Conceptualized as an Attachment Process." *Journal of Personality and Social Psychology* 52:511–524.

Hazan, C., and Shaver, P. R. (1990). "Love and Work: An Attachment-Theoretical Perspective." *Journal of Personality and Social Psychology* 59:270–280.

Hazan, C., and Shaver, P. R. (1994). "Attachment as an Organizational Framework for Research on Close Relationships." *Psychological Inquiry* 5:1–22.

Hazan, C., and Zeifman, D. (1993). "Sex and the Psychological Tether." In *Advances in Personal Relationships*, Vol. 5, ed. D. Perlman and K. Bartholomew. London: Jessica Kingsley.

Main, M.; Kaplan, N.; and Cassidy, J. (1985). "Security in Infancy, Childhood, and Adulthood: A Move to the Level of Representation." *Monographs of the Society for Research in Child Development* 50:66–104.

Shaver, P. R, and Hazan, C. (1993). "Adult Romantic Attachment: Theory and Evidence." In *Advances in Personal Relationships*, Vol. 4, ed. W. H. Jones and D. Perlman. London: Jessica Kingsley.

Simpson, J. A.; Rholes, W. S.; and Nelligan, J. S. (1992). "Support-Seeking and Support-Giving Within Couple Members in an Anxiety-Provoking Situation: The Role of Attachment Styles." *Journal of Personality and Social Psychology* 62:434–446.

Sroufe, L. A., and Fleeson, J. (1986). "Attachment and the Construction of Relationships." In *Relationships and Development*, ed. W. W. Hartup and Z. Rubin. Hillsdale, NJ: Erlbaum.

Swann, W. B., Jr.; Hixon, J. G.; and De La Ronde, C. (1992). "Embracing the Bitter 'Truth': Negative Self-Concepts and Marital Commitment." *Psychological Science* 3:118–121.

Van den Boom, D. (1990). "Preventive Intervention and the Quality of Mother–Infant Interaction and Infant Exploration in Irritable Infants." In *Developmental Psychology Behind the Dikes: An Outline of Developmental Psychology Research in the Netherlands*, ed. W. Koops, H. J. G. Soppe, J. L. van der Linden, P. C. M. Molenaar, and J. J. F. Schroots. Netherlands: Uitgeverij Eburon.

Waters, E. (1978). "The Reliability and Stability of Individual Differences in Infant–Mother Attachment." *Child Development* 49:483–494.

Weiss, R. S. (1988). "Loss and Recovery." *Journal of Social Issues* 44:37–52.

CINDY HAZAN

ATTRACTIVENESS

The subject of physical attraction inevitably appears in a discussion of human courtship and marriage. However, homespun clichés like "beauty is only skin deep," "pretty is as pretty does," and "it is really the inside that counts" deemphasize the importance of good looks. These adages all contain some degree of wisdom, but they deny the power that physical attraction wields over humans in general. Physical appearance can be a very strong force, guiding the types of interactions that people have with others, channeling experiences in both desirable and undesirable ways throughout the lifespan. Sociologists and psychologists have studied topics such as physical features that affect attractiveness, stereotypes of physical appearance, and influence of physical attraction on dating and marriage.

Defining Beauty

While beauty may be in the eye of the beholder, researchers find that a society generally agrees as to who is attractive and who is not. People grouping photographs of strangers just on the basis of physical attractiveness have a consistently high rate of agreement, no matter what age the raters or subjects are. Even small children have been found to agree quite consistently with adult estimates of beauty. Significant differences in rating a person's level of beauty occur only when the person doing the rating is in some relationship with the person they are rating; others are then viewed as less attractive (Simpson, Gangestad, and Lerma 1990).

Some research has examined the parameters of physical features to find out what is considered "attractive." Across all the cultures of the world, however, a single feature of universal beauty has not been found (Ford and Beach 1951). It seems that beauty *is* only skin deep, culturally defined and consensually agreed upon.

Beauty and Attractiveness

Why is beauty so appealing? Elaine Hatfield and Susan Sprecher (1986) propose three reasons: (1) "aesthetic appeal," that is, it pleases the senses; (2) "the glow of beauty," or the assumption that what is beautiful is good; and (3) "beauty rubs off," or the idea that self-esteem and prestige are enhanced by beautiful companions. Whatever the reason, most people want companions who are what they would term "good-looking," whatever that term means to them (Buss and Barnes 1986).

Several psychologists have studied the physical-attractiveness stereotype that says "what is beautiful is good." Confirmation of a physical-attractiveness stereotype surrounding the beauty-is-good hypothesis (Dion, Berscheid, and Walster 1972) can be found with various population samples. Social impressions by individuals judging children (Adams and Crane 1980) and adults (Adams and Huston 1975) have demonstrated that attractive individuals are seen in more favorable ways than their less attractive peers. For example, physically attractive individuals are more likely than their unattractive counterparts to be viewed as possessing better character, more poise, self-confidence, kindness, flexibility, sexual responsiveness, and control of their own destiny. They are seen as socially outgoing and likable, and they are expected to obtain more prestigious occupational success following more advanced education. Physical attractiveness can be a status cue, linked to assumptions of a person's inherited life station (Kalick 1988). Further, attractive individuals are judged less likely than their unattractive peers to possess a "hidden" stigma such as epilepsy. It is known that as early as three or four years of age, and assuredly by the elementary-school-age years, children build social impressions about persons unfamiliar to them based on a beauty-is-good hypothesis. In addition, young adults are not likely to differ appreciably from the elderly in their use of physical appearance in making social-impression evaluations. The beauty-is-good hypothesis is also evident in situations where initial credibility perceptions are made toward persuasive communicators that may increase their effectiveness as a communicator. For example, physically attractive models in advertisements, as compared to unattractive models, are liked more and provide greater source credibility, including both perceived trust and perceived expertise (Patzer 1983). The advertisements themselves are also viewed more positively with an attractive model as opposed to an unattractive model. In oral communication contexts, Judson Mills and Elliot Aronson (1965) found that a stated desire to influence audience opinion was more effective if the speaker was physically attractive. Shelly Chaiken (1979) also found that attractive communicators, as compared to unattractive communicators, induce greater persuasion of agreement during communication.

There is also a negative side to beauty. Highly physically attractive people can have more difficulty maintaining same-sex friendships than others (Krebs and Adinolfi 1975). Some evidence suggests that the beautiful are also subjected to certain prejudices—they are thought to be bourgeois, materialistic, vain, and more likely to have extramarital affairs and get divorced (Dermer and Thiel 1975). Extremely attractive women may have difficulty accepting praise because they cannot distinguish true praise about their admirable qualities from the flattery given so often by men because of physical attraction.

Does anything mitigate this power that beauty has over impressions? Common sense says that age will lessen the importance of appearances, although research does not support that yet as the elderly still support the beauty-is-good hypothesis. One study of women, both single and married, found that more single women felt they had increased in attractiveness with aging, suggesting that marriage may affect impressions of beauty (Giesen 1989). Also, people currently in a dating relationship, as compared to people who are not, will perceive opposite-sex, same-aged persons as less physically and sexually attractive (Simpson, Gangestad, and Lerma 1990). High self-esteem allows individuals the freedom to associate with whomever they want, regardless of looks, and makes it easier for them to approach more beautiful people. Personalities that are less steeped in the traditional gender roles will be less inclined to be swayed by beauty (Anderson and Bem 1981). People with greater concern about their own appearance are more influenced by physical attractiveness than are people with less concern (Glick, DeMorest, and Hotze 1988). Also, people who are willing to engage in sexual relations without commitment place more impoortance on physical attractiveness than personality attributes when choosing a romantic partner (Simpson and Gangestad 1992). Being female may alleviate some of the importance of attractiveness (Margolin and White 1987); however, there may be a discrepancy between what women say they want and what they actually choose in dating partners due to cultural stereotypes that affect what they report (Sprecher 1989). Being aroused can actually increase perceptions of a person's attractiveness, but only if the person being judged is average or above average; homely people will be judged more critically by aroused raters (Istvan, Griffitt, and Weidner 1983).

Research seems to confirm that pretty is not as pretty does, but pretty is, rather, as pretty is assumed to be. There may be some small truth to the beauty-is-good hypothesis. However, because people may treat attractive individuals differently than they treat others, this social process may lead to a self-fulfilling prophecy. If a pretty face is always greeted with admiration and interest, no matter what the pretty person says, the person is likely to internalize those positive self-images.

Dating and Attractiveness

Much of the early research on physical attractiveness in the context of dating has focused on the "matching hypothesis." This hypothesis assumes individuals of comparable social desirability selectively seek each other out for social involvement. However, early research failed to support this hypothesis. Instead, attractive individuals were liked best, regardless of their other characteristics. Given a situation where the possibility of potential rejection is minimized, people will choose the most attractive date available. However, under the right social conditions, when left in a state of ambiguity about acceptance of an offer for a date, males are likely to predict that highly attractive females will be less accepting of their offer than less attractive women (Kalick and Hamilton 1986). It seems that people may match (date someone close to their own level of attractiveness) even while seeking the most attractive companion.

Investigations suggest the saliency of attractiveness is magnified in dating contexts. While the matching hypothesis may be supported when examining same-sex friendships, physically attractive individuals may still be preferred in early dating choices. Furthermore, in the marketplace of dating, a person's attractiveness is increased by showing a high probability of accepting an offer for a date. In a study of interactions in singles bars, the most attractive women were not approached more often than the less attractive women, seeming to show that men were minimizing chances of rejection (Glenwick, Jason, and Elman 1978). So although beauty may be preferred, it may also be unapproachable. On the other hand, extreme unattractiveness may just be unapproached.

The observation that beautiful women have the most dates and a man's attractiveness does not determine his number of dates may indicate the vestige of the "man-asks-the-woman" social norm (Berscheid et al. 1971). Perhaps, however, this is because men tend to state the importance of physical attractiveness more strongly than women. Harold Sigall and David Landy (1973) found that a man accompanied by a beautiful girlfriend was evaluated more favorably than when he was alone, and much more favorably than when he was with an unattractive girlfriend.

Does attractiveness diminish in its influence over the course of a dating period? Eugene W. Mathes (1975) argued that with time and experience certain personality characteristics, as they become known, will diminish or weaken the effects of physical attractiveness. However, his data suggest that physical attractiveness maintains its strong importance, at least over a five-encounter dating period. The preference for other desirable personality characteristics in a dating partner, such as independence, trustworthiness, and modesty, were not as overwhelmingly strong as the preference for an attractive partner. As for popularity, attractiveness is a more important predictor than social skills, intelligence, or personality (Berscheid et al. 1971). Unfortunately for beautiful people, this can lead to problems in keeping relationships on just a friendly basis. It may also lead to the development of cold, aloof strategies that discourage the intimate approaches of strangers or even acquaintances (Hatfield and Sprecher 1986).

Other evidence also suggests that attractive individuals are more likely to engage in and experience fulfilling premarital sexual relations (Stelzer, Desmond, and Price 1987), but it remains unclear whether physical attractiveness plays an important role in promoting social contacts in social settings. However, as time becomes limited, there is reason to believe that the probability of interaction with another may become less influenced by physical attractiveness and more influenced by time constraints (Pennebaker et al. 1979). That is, in social settings such as a bar, as available time to interact with a member of the opposite sex decreases, an individual's perceived (in contrast to real) attractiveness increases.

Marriage and Attractiveness

Roger L. Terry and Elizabeth Macklin (1977) have found that females function on a homogamy principle and expect husbands and wives to be similar in their degree of attractiveness. The male subjects, on the other hand, were more likely to exaggerate the physical attractiveness of a wife. People in this study were able to match a husband to his wife out of four choices with 60 percent accuracy. Intracouple similarity seems to be more important to women (Feingold 1991). Observations on actual married couples are even more likely to support the homogamy principle (e.g., Murstein and Christy 1976). For instance, couples dating for a long term were found to be more similar than casual daters. Regardless of the method used to rate attractiveness (i.e., self, spouse, or objective observer), the more attractive the husband, the more attractive his wife. Highly attractive couples, matched on level of attractiveness, are assumed to have the greatest marital satisfaction (Tucker and O'Grady 1990). Matched couples are also more likely to stay married (White 1980). When observed in natural social settings, couples of similar attractiveness (as rated by observers) engaged in some kind of touching 60 percent of the time, but mismatched couples touched only 22 percent of the time (Silverman 1971). Gregory L. White (1980) found that well-matched couples were the most in love, as rated by Zick Rubin's Love Scale (1970), and were most likely to have grown closer by the nine-month follow-up, whereas mismatched couples were the most likely to have broken up. Engaged and married couples were the best matched, followed by serious daters, and then casual daters. It would seem that "similarity breeds content."

Mismatched couples generally agree that the less attractive partner of the pair has something extra to offer the relationship; they are either unusually loving, unusually self-sacrificing, or unusually wealthy. The more attractive partner may also have more power in the relationship.

In heterosexual couples, if partners find each other attractive, they have a better sexual relationship, but in lesbian couples there seems to be no such convention of beauty (Blumstein and Schwartz 1983). People shown paired photos of matched and mismatched couples judge the matched and attractive pairs to have the best sex lives but also more likely to be split up a year later. In the same study, if a mismatched pair had a good-looking man, then the couple was assumed to be sexually involved, but if the good-looking partner was the woman, then the pair was assumed not to be sexually involved.

Nonetheless, attractiveness may play a particularly unique role in marital selection for women when certain social conditions are considered. Glen H. Elder, Jr., (1969) and Patricia A. Taylor and Norval D. Glenn (1976) have reported that a female's degree of attractiveness is predictive of her husband's occupational status. That is, attractiveness for women, especially from the lower class, is an important variable in determining social mobility through marriage to a high-status male. However, education may be a more influential factor than attractiveness in determining social mobility through marriage. For women who do not go to college, attractiveness is a very important determinant of whether or not they will marry a high-status husband. J. Richard Udry and Bruce K. Eckland (1984) rated the attractiveness of 1,300 men and women in high school yearbooks and then followed up on who married whom and what jobs they had fifteen years later. The more attractive a woman, the more educated and rich her husband was (although this was not replicated by Stevens, Owens, and Schaefer 1990). The women rated as beautiful were also ten times more likely to be married than the women rated as unattractive. The men rated as most attractive had less-educated wives, were less-educated themselves, and had lower-status jobs than the men rated as less attractive. Men were equally likely to be married, however, regardless of their physical attractiveness.

Physical attractiveness, at least for women, is seen, therefore, as something that can be traded for other socially desirable traits. Interracial dating has been studied to evaluate this exchange theory, hypothesizing that an attractive person of a minority group may maintain "equity" in a relationship with a less attractive member of the majority. Objective judges of interracial couples tend to find a significant difference in attractiveness of the couples, but the self and partner ratings of attractiveness show that the couples see themselves as matched (Murstein, Merighi, and Malloy 1988).

Attractiveness can also affect relationships by threatening them (McIntosh and Tate 1992). Jealousy-arousing situations are the most angering for women and men if the interloper is unattractive. However, while men are most likely to "start going out with other people" if the interloper is attractive, women are most likely to do the same if the interloper is unattractive (Shettel-Neuber, Bryson, and Young 1978).

Although it is a good idea not to judge a book by its cover, people still want to be with the most attractive person available in actual interactions. Appearance can produce strong feelings and behaviors, showing that even though the outside may not count for everything, it does count for something.

(*See also:* ATTACHMENT; COMMITMENT; EXCHANGE THEORY; MARITAL QUALITY; MATE SELECTION; PERSONAL RELATIONSHIPS; SELF-ESTEEM; SHYNESS)

BIBLIOGRAPHY

Adams, G. R., and Crane, P. (1980). "An Assessment of Parents' and Teachers' Expectations of Preschool Children's Social Preference for Attractive or Unattractive Children and Adults." *Child Development* 51:224–231.

Adams, G. R., and Huston, T. L. (1975). "Social Perception of Middle-Aged Persons Varying in Physical Attractiveness." *Developmental Psychology* 11:657–658.

Anderson, S. M., and Bem, S. L. (1981). "Sex Typing and Androgyny in Dyadic Interaction: Individual Differences in Responsiveness to Physical Attractiveness." *Journal of Personality and Social Psychology* 41:74–86.

Berscheid, E.; Dion, K.; Walster, E.; and Walster, G. W. (1971). "Physical Attractiveness and Dating Choice: A Test of the Matching Hypothesis." *Journal of Experimental Social Psychology* 7:173–180.

Blumstein, P., and Schwartz, P. (1983). *American Couples.* New York: William Morrow.

Buss, D. M., and Barnes, M. (1986). "Preferences in Human Mate Selection." *Journal of Personality and Social Psychology* 50:559–570.

Chaiken, S. (1979). "Communicator Physical Attractiveness and Persuasion." *Journal of Personality and Social Psychology* 37:1387–1397.

Dermer, M., and Thiel, D. L. (1975). "When Beauty May Fail." *Journal of Personality and Social Psychology* 31:1168–1176.

Dion, K. K.; Berscheid, E.; and Walster, E. (1972). "What Is Beautiful Is Good." *Journal of Personality and Social Psychology* 24:285–290.

Elder, G. H., Jr. (1969). "Appearance and Education in Marriage Mobility." *American Sociological Review* 34:519–533.

Feingold, A. (1991). "Sex Differences in the Effects of Similarity and Physical Attractiveness on Opposite-Sex Attraction." *Basic and Applied Social Psychology* 12:357–367.

Ford, C. S., and Beach, F. A. (1951). *Patterns of Sexual Behavior.* New York: Harper & Row.

Gieson, C. B. (1989). "Aging and Attractiveness: Marriage Makes a Difference." *International Journal of Aging and Human Development* 29:83–94.

Glenwick, D. S.; Jason, L. A.; and Elman, D. (1978). "Physical Attractiveness and Social Contact in the Singles Bar." *Journal of Social Psychology* 105:311–312.

Glick, P.; DeMorest, J. A.; and Hotze, C. A. (1988). "Self-Monitoring and Beliefs About Partner Compatibility in Romantic Relationships." *Personality and Social Psychology Bulletin* 14:485–494.

Hatfield, E., and Sprecher, S. (1986). *Mirror, Mirror: The Importance of Looks in Everyday Life.* New York: State University of New York Press.

Istvan, S.; Griffitt, W.; and Weidner, G. (1983). "Sexual Arousal and the Polarization of Perceived Sexual Attractiveness." *Basic and Applied Social Psychology* 4:307–318.

48

Kalick, S. M. (1988). "Physical Attractiveness as a Status Cue." *Journal of Experimental Social Psychology* 24:469–498.

Kalick, S. M., and Hamilton, T. E., III. (1986). "The Matching Hypothesis Reexamined." *Journal of Personality and Social Psychology* 51:673–682.

Krebs, E., and Adinolfi, A. A. (1975). "Physical Attractiveness, Social Relations, and Personality Style." *Journal of Personality and Social Psychology* 31:254–253.

McIntosh, E. G., and Tate, D. T. (1992). "Characteristics of the Rival and the Experience of Jealousy." *Perceptual and Motor Skills* 74:369–370.

Margolin, L., and White, L. (1987). "The Continuing Role of Physical Attractiveness in Marriage." *Journal of Marriage and the Family* 49:21–27.

Mathes, E. W. (1975). "The Effects of Physical Attractiveness and Anxiety on Heterosexual Attraction over a Series of Five Encounters." *Journal of Marriage and the Family* 37:769–774.

Mills, J., and Aronson, E. (1965). "Opinion Change as a Function of Communicator's Attractiveness and Desire to Influence." *Journal of Personality and Social Psychology* 1:173–177.

Murstein, B. I., and Christy, P. (1976). "Physical Attractiveness and Marriage Adjustment in Middle-Aged Couples." *Journal of Personality and Social Psychology* 34:537–542.

Murstein, B. I.; Merighi, J. R.; and Malloy, T. E. (1988). "Physical Attractiveness and Exchange Theory in Interracial Dating." *Journal of Social Psychology* 129:325–334.

Patzer, G. L. (1983). "Source Credibility as a Function of Communicator Physical Attractiveness." *Journal of Business Research* 11:229–241.

Pennebaker, J. W.; Dyer, M. A.; Caulkins, R. S.; Litowitz, D. L.; Ackerman, P. O.; Anderson, D. B.; and McGraw, K. M. (1979). "Don't the Girls Get Prettier at Closing Time: A Country and Western Application to Psychology." *Personality and Social Psychology Bulletin* 5:122–125.

Rubin, Z. (1970). "Measurement of Romantic Love." *Journal of Personality and Social Psychology* 16:265–273.

Shettel-Neuber, J.; Bryson, J. B.; and Young, L. E. (1978). "Physical Attractiveness of the 'Other Person' and Jealousy." *Personality and Social Psychology Bulletin* 4:612–615.

Sigall, H., and Landy, D. (1973). "Radiating Beauty: The Effects of Having a Physically Attractive Partner on Person Perception." *Journal of Personality and Social Psychology* 28:218–224.

Silverman, I. (1971). "Physical Attractiveness." *Sexual Behavior* (September):22–25.

Simpson, J. A., and Gangestad, S. W. (1992). "Sociosexuality and Romantic Partner Choice." *Journal of Personality* 60:31–51.

Simpson, J. A.; Gangestad, S. W.; and Lerma, M. (1990). "Perception of Physical Attractiveness: Mechanisms Involved in the Maintenance of Romantic Relationships." *Journal of Personality and Social Psychology* 59:1192–1201.

Sprecher, S. (1989). "The Importance to Males and Females of Physical Attractiveness, Earning Potential, and Expressiveness in Initial Attraction." *Sex Roles* 21:591–607.

Stelzer, C.; Desmond, S. M.; and Price, J. H. (1987). "Physical Attractiveness and Sexual Activity of College Students." *Psychological Reports* 60:567–573.

Stevens, G.; Owens, D.; and Schaefer, E. C. (1990). "Education and Attractiveness in Marriage Choices." *Social Psychology Quarterly* 53:62–70.

Taylor, P. A., and Glenn, N. D. (1976). "The Utility of Education and Attractiveness for Females' Status Attainment Through Marriage." *American Sociological Review* 41:484–498.

Terry, R. L., and Macklin, E. (1977). "Accuracy of Identifying Married Couples on the Basis of Similarity of Attractiveness." *Journal of Psychology* 97:15–20.

Tucker, M. W., and O'Grady, K. E. (1990). "Effects of Physical Attractiveness, Intelligence, Age at Marriage, and Cohabitation on the Perception of Marital Satisfaction." *Journal of Social Psychology* 13:253–269.

Udry, J. R., and Eckland, B. K. (1984). "The Benefits of Being Attractive." *Psychological Reports* 54:47–56.

White, G. L. (1980). "Physical Attractiveness and Courtship Progress." *Journal of Personality and Social Psychology* 39:660–668.

JONATHAN D. MIDGETT
GERALD R. ADAMS

ATTRIBUTION IN RELATIONSHIPS

The term "attribution" refers to the interpretation of an event by inferring what caused the event to occur. This interpretation also may extend to inference of responsibility for an event and judgment about the trait qualities of another person or of oneself. As an illustration of a common situation involving attributional activity, a husband may ask why his wife left the room with a sudden burst of tears in the middle of what he perceived to be an innocent conversation about their respective days at the office (i.e., what was the causal factor?). He also may wonder whether what he said was responsible for her emotional display (i.e., where does the responsibility lie?) or whether her emotional display pertains to something about her personality (e.g., a trait of having sudden emotional outbursts).

The concept of attribution was developed by Fritz Heider (1958) and articulated into testable theories by Edward E. Jones and Keith E. Davis (1965) and Harold H. Kelley (1967). In his self-perception theory, Daryl J. Bem (1972) extended attributional theorizing to encompass self-attributions. Bem posited that people take some meaningful form of action and then, in forming a perception about that action, use their own behavior and the context in which it occurs to judge their attitudes, beliefs, and other internal states. For example, a wife whose husband has suddenly, and with visible upset, ended their conversation may look back at her behavior and conclude, "I was being insensitive in those remarks I made about our friends. No wonder he was upset."

For the situation involving a person's sudden emotional outburst, these theories suggest that observers infer the bases for the behavior by logical analysis of such information as (1) the person's behavior in previous similar situations (i.e., consistency information—is it common to show emotions in this way?); (2) the partner's insensitive behavior toward the person (i.e., consensus information—does the person often become upset during their conversations?); (3) any specific events that distinguish this circumstance (i.e., distinctiveness information—did something unusual and highly embarrassing happening at the office that day?); and (4) the person's intention to show hurt about some past concern or the partner's intent to cause upset and whether either type of intention reveals something about the personalities involved.

Attribution theory in social psychology became a prominent topic for examination in the 1970s. As early as the mid-1970s, an extension of attributional theorizing focused on close heterosexual relationships (i.e., relations in which two people's lives reflect strong and regular interconnections of their thoughts, feelings, and behavior). A major theoretical analysis that contributed to this extension was the divergent perceptions hypothesis created by Jones and Richard E. Nisbett (1972). This hypothesis pertains to a situation in which an actor and an observer arrive at different explanations for the same action. It states that the actor would attribute personal behavior to the forces in the situation, while the observer would attribute the same behavior to personality characteristics of the actor.

Jones and Nisbett's explanation for why the divergent perspectives tendency occurs emphasized cognitive–perceptual dynamics, namely, that (1) the actor perceptually views the situation as central in his or her field of thought and perception, whereas the observer views the actor as central; and (2) the actor will have evidence that he or she has shown variation in behavior across different situations, whereas the observer often will not have access to that evidence. Another type of explanation that is quite germane to the situation couples often encounter is that actors are motivated to protect their self-esteem in situations in which their behavior leads to questionable outcomes. Actors may be inclined to attribute their behavior to the situation in order to better protect their self-esteem, while observers may be motivated to attribute bad outcomes to the actor's personality as a means of punishing or controlling the actor (Harvey, Harris, and Barnes 1975). Heider's (1958) conception of attributional phenomena emphasized this type of integration of cognition and self-esteem or motivational elements.

Close Relationships

The first investigation to study connections between attributions and close relationships was conducted by Bruce R. Orvis, Kelley, and Deborah Butler (1976). College-age couples were asked to list examples of behavior, for themselves and their partner, for which each had a different explanation. Several categories of behavior yielded divergent attributions (e.g., "actor criticizes or places demands upon the partner"). More generally, for behavior resulting in negative outcomes, respondents exonerated themselves and blamed their partners. Later work suggests that this egocentric bias in attribution by close relationship partners holds mainly for couples experiencing distress. Those respondents who are less distressed attribute bad outcomes to the situation and good outcomes to their partner or to their collaboration with their partner.

An important implication of the results of Orvis, Kelley, and Butler's investigation is that attributions made directly to one's partner, or indirectly in public and available to one's partner, may represent an attempt to influence the partner about why problematic events are occurring. For example, a wife may say, "Our problems have been caused mainly by my husband's inability to break the controlling influence his parents have over what he does." Whether or not the wife believes that this control factor is critical, she may be making the attribution in an attempt to influence her spouse to sever the control his parents have in his life. Helen Newman (1981) elaborated on attribution as a form of persuasion and ongoing communication in close relationships.

This early work by Orvis, Kelley, and Butler confirmed the value of the divergent perspectives hypothesis, with the important qualification that attributions often reflect self-esteem motivation when couples are making attributions about their relationships. Another amplification of this hypothesis was revealed in a study by John H. Harvey, Gary L. Wells, and Marlene D. Alvarez (1978). They showed that relationship partners who are distressed not only diverge in their attributions about relationship problems, but also cannot readily predict one another's attributions about the sources of the problems.

Attributional Biases

Since 1970, the predominant research on attributions in close relationships has focused on attributional biases. The aforementioned egocentric bias has been repeatedly found in different relationship situations (e.g., Fincham 1985; Jacobson et al. 1985). Theorists have suggested that this bias may have causal impact on satisfaction in relationships or it could serve as a secondary indicator that the relationship has already achieved a distressed status. Frank D. Fincham, Thomas N. Bradbury, and their colleagues (e.g., Bradbury and Fincham 1992) have presented evidence that attributions play a causal role in close relationship development and breakdown. Their theoretical analysis, referred to as a contextual mode, emphasizes that context always must be taken into account in understanding relationship phenomena. They argue that behaviors exchanged in an interaction can have different meanings, depending on other events occurring in the interaction.

Another area of study on attributions in relationships concerns gender differences. Amy Holtzworth-Munroe and Neil J. Jacobson (1985) found that, in general, during the course of relationships, women tend to do more processing and analyzing of the causes of issues and events than do men. On the other hand, men appear to become quite active in their analysis when the relationship begins to encounter serious turmoil. This finding, therefore, suggests that a man's involvement in extensive attributional work in a relationship may be a good barometer of the seriousness of distress being jointly experienced in the relationship. It also is consistent with earlier work on possible gender differences in how women and men experience the breakdown of relationships (e.g., Weiss 1975).

Other Directions

Researchers have extended attributional perspectives to a variety of relationship phenomena, including linking attributions, communications, and effect in ongoing relationships (Vangelisti 1992); the types of attributions made by violent men regarding their marriages (Holtzworth-Munroe 1988); and attributions made by female victims of marital violence (Andrews 1992). The primary conclusion of these extrapolations is that attributions play a key role in relationship events, often being implicated in causal sequences.

Attribution is also being viewed as part of people's natural stories, narratives, or accounts relating to their relationships. According to this approach, people often form understandings and make attributions about their daily relationships in the form of storylike constructions that usually are developed initially in private and then communicated to other people. Such diverse writings as those of Robert S. Weiss (1975), Roy F. Baumeister (1991), Jerome Bruner (1990), and Daniel P. McAdams (1985) may be interpreted as embracing this approach. Illustrative research stresses the collection of people's naturalistic attributional accounts and the linking of those accounts to relationship behavior (e.g., Vaughan 1986).

(*See also:* COMMUNICATION; CONFLICT; FAMILY STORIES AND MYTHS; PERSONAL RELATIONSHIPS; SELF-ESTEEM)

BIBLIOGRAPHY

Andrews, B. (1992). "Attribution Processes in Victims of Marital Violence." In *Attributions, Accounts, and Close Relationships*, ed. J. H. Harvey, T. L. Orbuch, and A. L. Weber. New York: Springer-Verlag.

Baumeister, R. F. (1991). *Meanings of Life*. New York: Guilford.

Bem, D. J. (1972). "Self-Perception Theory." In *Advances in Experimental Social Psychology*, Vol. 6, ed. L. Berkowitz. New York: Academic Press.

Bradbury, T. N., and Fincham, F. D. (1992). "Attributions and Behavior in Marital Interaction." *Journal of Personality and Social Psychology* 63:713–628.

Bruner, J. (1990). *Acts of Meaning*. Cambridge, MA: Harvard University Press.

Fincham, F. D. (1985). "Attributional Processes in Distressed and Nondistressed Couples." *Journal of Abnormal Psychology* 94:183–190.

Harvey, J. H.; Harris, B.; and Barnes, R. D. (1975). "Actor-Observer Differences in the Perceptions of Responsibility and Freedom." *Journal of Personality and Social Psychology* 32:22–28.

Harvey, J. H.; Weber, A. L.; and Orbuch, T. L. (1990). *Interpersonal Accounts*. Oxford: Basil Blackwell.

Harvey, J. H.; Wells, G. L.; and Alvarez, M. D. (1978). "Attribution in the Context of Conflict and Separation in Close Relationships." In *New Directions in Attribution Research*, Vol. 2, ed. J. H. Harvey, W. J. Ickes, and R. F. Kidd. Hillsdale, NJ: Lawrence Erlbaum.

Heider, F. (1958). *The Psychology of Interpersonal Relations.* New York: Wiley.

Holtzworth-Munroe, A. (1988). "Causal Attributions in Marital Violence." *Clinical Psychology Review* 89:331–344.

Holtzworth-Munroe, A., and Jacobson, N. J. (1985). "Causal Attributions of Married Couples." *Journal of Personality and Social Psychology* 48:1398–1412.

Jacobson, N. S.; McDonald, D. W.; Follette, W. C.; and Berley, R. A. (1985). "Attributional Processes in Distressed and Nondistressed Married Couples." *Cognitive Therapy and Research* 9:35–50.

Jones, E. E., and Davis, K. E. (1965). "From Acts to Dispositions: The Attribution Process in Person Perception." In *Advances in Experimental Social Psychology*, Vol. 2, ed. L. Berkowitz. New York: Academic Press.

Jones, E. E., and Nisbett, R. E. (1972). "The Actor and the Observer: Divergent Perceptions of the Causes of Behavior." In *Attribution: Perceiving the Causes of Behavior*, ed. E. E. Jones, D. Kanouse, H. Kelley, R. Nisbett, S. Valins, and B. Weiner. Morristown, NJ: General Learning Press.

Kelley, H. H. (1967). "Attribution Theory in Social Psychology." In *Nebraska Symposium on Motivation*, Vol. 15, ed. D. Levine. Lincoln: University of Nebraska Press.

McAdams, D. P. (1985). *Power, Intimacy, and the Life Story.* Homewood, IL: Dorsey Press.

Newman, H. (1981). "Communication Within Ongoing Intimate Relationships: An Attributional Perceptive." *Personality and Social Psychology Bulletin* 7:59–70.

Orvis, B. R.; Kelley, H. H.; and Butler, D. (1976). "Attributional Conflict in Young Couples." In *New Directions in Attribution Research*, Vol. 1, ed. J. Harvey, W. Ickes, and R. Kidd. Hillsdale, NJ: Lawrence Erlbaum.

Vangelisti, A. L. (1992). "Communication Problems in Committed Relationships." In *Attributions, Accounts, and Close Relationships*, ed. J. H. Harvey, T. L. Orbuch, and A. L. Weber. New York: Springer-Verlag.

Vaughan, D. (1986). *Uncoupling.* New York: Oxford University Press.

Weiss, R. S. (1975). *Marital Separation.* New York: Basic Books.

JOHN H. HARVEY
NILS OLSEN

B

BANKRUPTCY

In everyday conversation, the word "bankrupt" is used synonymously with the term "insolvent" or "broke," but in fact the term "bankrupt" is no longer used in bankruptcy law. One who is the subject of a bankruptcy proceeding filed since October 1979 is referred to as a "debtor." All bankruptcy proceedings are administered in the federal, as opposed to the state, courts pursuant to Article I, Section 8, Clause 4 of the Constitution of the United States. The bankruptcy power was placed in federal control by the drafters of the Constitution for the sake of uniformity because the individual states had treated debtors very differently prior to the Constitutional Convention.

The Bankruptcy Code offers four chapters among which debtors may choose: Chapters 7, 11, 12, and 13. Each chapter is a chapter of Title 11, U.S. Code (the "Bankruptcy Code"). The vast majority of cases filed in bankruptcy courts are Chapter 7 cases. The filing of a bankruptcy petition creates an estate. Both individuals and businesses must give over to a trustee all estate assets that cannot be excluded by virtue of exemption law as of the date of the filing of the petition in bankruptcy. The trustee then liquidates the assets and distributes available funds to creditors according to the priorities established in the Bankruptcy Code. Debts given priority include fees incurred in the administration of the bankruptcy, wages owed by the debtor, alimony, child support, and certain taxes. Businesses filing for Chapter 7 do not operate again (although sometimes the name is sold along with other assets and a new company uses the name). Businesses filing for Chapter 11 do continue to operate. Chapter 11 allows for reorganization of troubled businesses and is sometimes used by large corporations. Chapter 11 cases receive most of the press coverage,

but they represent a small percentage of bankruptcy cases filed.

Chapters 13 and 12 are extremely similar, and both are reorganization chapters for individuals. Chapter 12, enacted after Chapter 13, was designed to assist small farmers and follows Chapter 13 in most respects. Chapter 13 is preferred over Chapter 7 by most individuals who are able to take advantage of it. A person filing for Chapter 13 must have a source of regular income and must file a plan with the court showing how the debts will be repaid over a three- to five-year period. There are some definite advantages over Chapter 7. In Chapter 13, anyone who cosigned or guaranteed the debt of a person who files for Chapter 13 will also be protected by an automatic stay of collection actions. Also, Chapter 13 debtors' assets are not rounded up and liquidated, as is the case under Chapter 7. If the debtor has few assets to protect, however, Chapter 7 is preferable.

For individuals, bankruptcy provides two important benefits: the automatic stay and the discharge. The automatic stay provides that once a petition in bankruptcy is filed, no one may start or continue any action to collect a debt without specific permission of the bankruptcy court. There are some exceptions to this rule, such as actions to establish or modify an order for alimony and actions to enforce criminal law, but generally the automatic stay is an extremely powerful and useful tool. A person with severe credit problems is usually being harassed by a number of creditors. The automatic stay provides relief from such harassment. A creditor who chooses to ignore the automatic stay and who continues to harass an individual debtor will be ordered to pay damages to the debtor.

The discharge is the permanent benefit of bankruptcy. Assuming that the debtor has not illegally or fraudulently reported assets or liabilities, the bankruptcy court will grant a discharge of debts, relieving the debtor's legal duty to pay all debts outstanding at the time of the filing of the petition. No one may call upon a person to pay a discharged debt, and no one may discriminate against a person who has received a discharge in a bankruptcy proceeding.

The bankruptcy courts' determination of whether a debt is dischargeable begins with the general policy decisions articulated by Congress in the Bankruptcy Code. Generally, debts not dischargeable include obligations to support a child or former spouse, student loan obligations, fines, judgments against the debtor for intentional harm to another or harm caused while intoxicated, and debts that were fraudulently obtained. Parties may then ask the court to determine whether a particular debt falls into one of the general categories—for example, whether an obligation to a former spouse is in the nature of a property settlement (dischargeable) or is alimony or support (not dischargeable). A state court's determination as to the nature of a debt for dischargeability is not binding on a federal bankruptcy court—for example, even though a state court calls a debt alimony, a bankruptcy court may determine that the funds are not necessary for support and allow the debtor to discharge the debt.

Once a discharge is granted, no further discharge may be granted in any bankruptcy case commenced within six years of the filing of the first case. One need be mindful of this fact when a creditor requests reaffirmation of a debt. A reaffirmation of a debt voids the effect of the discharge as to that debt. While reaffirmation agreements are legal if the correct procedure is followed and the court approves the agreement, they are dangerous for debtors who will have neither a discharge of the reaffirmed debts nor bankruptcy as a safety net for the next six years should illness or unemployment arise.

Under Chapter 7, individuals must turn over most existing assets to a trustee to be liquidated, with the exception of certain items. The assets that such debtors need not turn over are either nonestate assets or exempt assets. The Bankruptcy Code provides that estate property includes physical property whether in the possession of the debtor or not, rights to lawsuits, certain types of property acquired within six months after the filing of the petition, and certain types of community property. Property that does not become property of the estate includes property held but not owned or leased by the debtor and the property rights of a debtor in a trust or pension plan complying with stated requirements of specific state and federal law, such as ERISA qualified pension plans.

The law allowing exemption of certain assets from inclusion in the bankruptcy estate is intended to provide debtors with a "fresh start," advancing the public policy that individuals are more likely to be productive members of society if not left penniless and unable to support themselves or their dependents. The types of assets debtors may exempt by virtue of bankruptcy law include up to $15,000 of value in a house (or cash equivalent if no house is owned), up to $2,400 in value of an automobile, and furnishings and clothing up to an aggregate of $8,000, with no one item having a value of more than $400. Other federal bankruptcy exemptions include unmatured life insurance, unemployment benefits, certain kinds of pension or annuity benefits, and certain kinds of recoveries from personal injury lawsuits.

The exception to the rule in the Constitution that bankruptcies must be administered in a uniform fashion is that federal law allows the states to decide whether a debtor may choose, or be compelled, to use state or federal nonbankruptcy exemptions in lieu of those provided in the Bankruptcy Code. Some states' exemptions are very generous to debtors. Florida allows debtors to exempt the entire unmortgaged value of 160 acres of homestead property in the country and one-half acre in cities, regardless of value. Texas has a similar limitation on the acreage, but not the value, of the homestead and allows a homestead exemption for business property as well.

The states also vary as to exemptions of assets other than real property. In New York, personal property exemptions cannot be applied against creditors who enabled the purchase of an item, and specific exemptions include a seat or pew occupied by the judgment debtor or the family in a place of public worship and 90 percent of any money due for the sale of milk produced on a farm operated by the debtor. California offers two sets of personal property exemptions. One is very similar to the federal bankruptcy exemptions. The other allows a variety of specific exemptions, including that for educational financial aid and funds held on deposit for inmates in correctional facilities. In practice, most Chapter 7 cases are considered to be "no asset" cases because after accounting for home mortgages, liens on automobiles, and exempt assets there are no assets remaining to turn over to a trustee.

Notwithstanding the antidiscrimination injunction that applies once discharge has been ordered, a bankruptcy case will almost certainly have a negative effect on an individual's credit rating. The ability to obtain credit cards or loans for cars or homes could be hampered by bankruptcy because large databases of credit histories are kept by reporting services such as Dun & Bradstreet and are used by banks and credit unions. Bankruptcy most often results from mismanagement of credit. Although credit-issuing entities seem to encourage unwise use of credit, such as to purchase small consumer items, they are understandably reticent about extending new credit to an individual who is a known risk.

(*See also:* ALIMONY AND SPOUSAL SUPPORT; CHILD SUPPORT; DIVORCE: ECONOMIC ASPECTS; MARITAL PROPERTY AND COMMUNITY PROPERTY; POVERTY; UNEMPLOYMENT)

BIBLIOGRAPHY

Arena, R. M., and Fitzgerald, J. K. (1994). *Bankruptcy and Divorce: Support and Property Division.* New York: Wiley.

Baird, D. G. (1993). *The Elements of Bankruptcy,* revised edition. Westbury, NY: Foundation Press.

Epstein, D. G. (1991). *Debtor–Creditor Law in a Nutshell.* St. Paul, MN: West Publishing.

Hammond, B. (1993). *Life After Debt: How to Repair Your Credit and Get Out of Debt Once and For All.* Hawthorne, NJ: Career Press.

HONOR S. HEATH

BEHAVIOR PROBLEMS *See* ADOLESCENCE; DISCIPLINE; GANGS; JUVENILE DELINQUENCY; PERSONALITY DEVELOPMENT; RUNAWAY CHILDREN; SUBSTANCE ABUSE; SUICIDE; TRUANCY

BIRTH CONTROL

This entry consists of the following three articles:

Sociocultural and Historical Aspects
   Vern L. Bullough
   Bonnie Bullough
Contraceptive Methods
   Maxine J. Klein
Legal Aspects
   Eve W. Paul

Sociocultural and Historical Aspects

Birth control refers to control over and decisions about the timing and number of births that a woman or couple has; it is a part of family planning but includes more than contraception.

People have used various forms of birth control throughout history, including abstinence (both short-term and, for some individuals, lifetime continence); abortion (abortifacients are common in both historical and oral sources); infanticide (disposing of unwanted infants); and surgical intervention (ranging from castration to creating a hypospadias condition in the male by making an exit for sperm and urine at the base of the penis). Forms of contraception have ranged from "natural" means, such as withdrawal or use of other orifices, to a variety of mechanical means, including IUDs (intrauterine devices) and various barriers such as the condom.

Historically, however, birth control was not a general matter for public discourse. Although various medical writers described methods, some more effective than others, and theologians took conflicting stands about nonprocreative sexual activities, full-scale debate on the issue did not occur until almost the beginning of the nineteenth century.

Widespread Public Discussion

Key to the beginning of widespread public discussion was concern with overpopulation. This issue was first put before the public by the Reverend Thomas Robert Malthus (1766–1834) in his *Essay on the Principle of Population* (1798). The essay was first published anonymously, but Malthus signed his name to a second, expanded edition published in 1803. Malthus argued that human beings were possessed by a sexual urge that led them to multiply faster than their food supply, and unless some checks could somehow be applied, the inevitable results of such unlimited procreation were misery, war, and vice. Population, he argued, increased geometrically (1, 2, 4, 8, 16, 32 . . .), while food supply only increased at an arithmetic rate (1, 2, 3, 4, 5, 6, . . .). Malthus's only solution to the problem was to urge humans to exercise control over their sexual instincts (i.e., abstinence) and to marry as late as possible. Sexually, Malthus was an extreme conservative who went so far as to classify as vice all promiscuous intercourse, "unnatural" passions, violations of the marriage bed, use of mechanical contraceptives, and irregular sexual liaisons.

Many of those who agreed with Malthus about the threat of overpopulation disagreed with him on the solutions and instead advocated the use of contraceptives. Such followers came to be known as neo-Malthusians. In essence, however, the terms of the debate over birth control came to be centered on attitudes toward sexuality. Malthus recognized the need of sexual activity for procreation but not for pleasure.

The neo-Malthusians held that continence was no solution because sex urges were too powerful and nonprocreative sex was as pleasurable as procreative sex.

Much of the available information about contraception had been passed from mother to daughter, and although some methods might have been more effective than others, little research had been done. To overcome an apparent lack of real knowledge, the neo-Malthusians felt it was essential to spread information about methods of contraception. The person in the English-speaking world generally given credit for first doing so was the English tailor Francis Place (1771–1854). Place was concerned with the widespread poverty of his time, which was accentuated by the growth of industrialization and urbanization as well as the breakdown of the traditional village economy. Large families, he felt, were more likely to live in poverty than smaller ones, and to help overcome this state of affairs, Place published in 1822 his *Illustrations and Proofs of the Principle of Population*. He urged married couples to use "precautionary" means to plan their families better, but he did not go into detail. To remedy this lack of instruction, he printed handbills in 1823, addressed simply *To the Married of Both Sexes*. The publication described a way to avoid pregnancy by inserting a dampened sponge, with a string attached, into the vagina prior to "coition." Later pamphlets by Place and some of his followers added other methods, all involving the female. Pamphlets of the time, by Place and others, were never subject to any legal interference, although they were brought to the attention of the attorney general. Place ultimately turned to other issues, but his disciples, notably Richard Carlile (1790–1843), took up the cause. It became an increasingly controversial subject, in part because Place and Carlile were social reformers as well as advocates of birth control. Carlile was the first man in England to put his name to a book devoted to the subject of birth control, *Every Woman's Book* (1826).

Early U.S. Birth Control Movement

In the United States, the movement for birth control may be said to have begun in 1831 with publication by Robert Dale Owen (1801–1877) of the booklet *Moral Physiology*. Owen, following the lead of Carlile, advocated three methods of birth control. He felt coitus interruptus was the best choice because a vaginal sponge, his second alternative, was not always successful and because a condom, his third alternative, was very expensive and could be used only once. Far more influential, however, was a Massachusetts physician, Charles Knowlton (1800–1850), who published his *Fruits of Philosophy* in 1832. In his first edition, Knowlton advocated douching, a not particularly effective contraceptive. However, the book is best remembered for the controversy it caused. As he lectured on the topic throughout Massachusetts, he was jailed in Cambridge, fined in Taunton, and twice acquitted in trials in Greenfield. These actions increased public interest in contraception, and Knowlton had sold some 10,000 copies of his book by 1839. In subsequent editions of his book, Knowlton added other more reliable methods of contraception.

Once the barriers to publications describing methods of contraception had fallen, a number of other books appeared throughout the English-speaking world. The most widely read material was probably the brief descriptions included in *Elements of Social Science* (1854), a sex education book. Originally issued anonymously, some of the later editions were signed by the author, George Drysdale (1825–1904). Drysdale was what might be called a social conservative in the contraceptive movement—that is, he felt the only cause of poverty was overpopulation, something that his more radical freethinking rivals could not accept. For the "radicals," conception was just one cause of poverty, and they regarded contraception as just part of an effort toward a basic reform of society aimed at eliminating the grosser inequities among the classes.

Influence of Eugenics

Giving a further impetus to the more conservative aspects of birth control was the growth of the eugenics movement. The eugenicists, while concerned with the high birthrates among the poor and the illiterate, emphasized the problem of low birthrates among the more "intellectual" upper classes. Eugenics came to be defined as an applied biological science concerned with increasing the proportion of persons of better-than-average endowment in succeeding generations. The eugenicists threw themselves into the campaign for birth control among the poor and illiterate, while urging the "gifted" to produce more.

The word "eugenics" was coined by Francis Galton (1822–1911), a great believer in heredity, who also had many of the prejudices of an upper-class Englishman in regard to social class and race. Galton's hypotheses were given further "academic" respectability by Karl Pearson (1857–1936), the first holder of the Galton endowed chair of eugenics at the University of London. Pearson believed that the high birthrate of the poor was a threat to civilization, and if members of the "higher" races did not make it their duty to reproduce, they would be supplanted in time by the members of the "lower" races.

When put in this harsh light, eugenics gave "scientific" support to those who believed in racial and class superiority. It was just such ideas that Adolph Hitler attempted to implement in his "solution" to the "racial problem." Although Pearson's views were eventually opposed by the English Eugenics Society, the American eugenics movement, founded in 1905, adopted his view. Inevitably, a large component of the organized family planning movement in the United States was made up of eugenicists. The fact that Pearson-oriented eugenicists also advocated such beliefs as enforced sterilization of the "undesirables" inevitably tainted the groups in which they were active even when they were not the dominant voices.

Dissemination of Information Regulation

Even without the burden of the early eugenicists' belief in racial and class superiority, the birth control movement often found it difficult to contact the people it most wanted to reach, namely poor, overburdened mothers who did not want more children.

Following the passage of the first laws against pornography, in England in 1853, information about contraception was interpreted to be pornographic since, of necessity, it included discussion of sex. Books on contraception that earlier had been widely sold and distributed were seized and condemned. Such seizures were challenged in England in 1877 by Charles Bradlaugh (1833–1891) and Annie Besant (1847–1933). They were convicted by a jury that really wanted to acquit them, and the judgment was overturned on a technicality. In the aftermath, information on contraception circulated widely in Great Britain and its colonies.

In the United States, however, where similar legislation was enacted by various states and by the federal government, materials that contained information about birth control and were distributed through the postal system quickly ran into the censoring activities of Anthony Comstock (1844–1915), who had been appointed as a special postal agent in 1873. One of his first successful prosecutions was against a pamphlet on contraception by Edward Bliss Foote (1829–1906). As a result, information about contraceptives was driven underground. Only those Americans who went to Europe regularly kept up with contemporary developments such as the diaphragm, which began to be prescribed in Dutch clinics at the

end of the nineteenth century. The few physicians who did keep current in the field tended to restrict their services to upper-class groups. The change in this situation is generally credited to a nurse, Margaret Sanger (1879–1966).

In 1914, Sanger began to publish *The Woman Rebel*, a magazine to stimulate working women to think for themselves and to free them from bearing unwanted children. To encourage women to think about possible alternatives, Sanger decided to defy the laws pertaining to the dissemination of contraceptive information by publishing a small pamphlet, *Family Limitation* (1914). After her arrest and preliminary hearing, but before her formal trial, Sanger fled to Europe. During her absence (much of which was spent learning about European contraceptive methods), her husband, William Sanger (1873–1961), who had little to do with his wife's publishing activities, was tricked into giving a copy of the pamphlet to a Comstock agent. For this he was arrested and convicted, an act that led to the almost immediate return of his wife.

By 1917, a third element had been added to the forces behind the movement for more effective birth control information, namely the woman's movement (or at least certain segments of it). They joined with the radical reformers and the eugenicists in an uneasy coalition for dissemination of contraceptives. The change in public opinion about contraception was effectively demonstrated by the government's decision not to prosecute Sanger after her return, an action made easier by the death of Comstock.

Sanger, though relieved at being freed from prosecution, was still anxious to spread the message of birth control to the working women of New York. To reach them, Sanger opened the first U.S. birth control clinic. The clinic was patterned after the Dutch model. The well-publicized opening attracted long lines of interested women as well as several vice officers. After some ten days of disseminating information and devices, Sanger and two other women—Ethel Byrne (Sanger's sister) and Fania Mindell (a social worker)—were arrested. Byrne, who was tried first and sentenced to thirty days in jail, promptly went on a hunger strike, attracting so much national attention that after eleven days she was pardoned by the governor of New York. Mindell, who was also convicted, was fined only $50. By the time of Sanger's trial, the prosecution was willing to drop charges provided she would agree not to open another clinic. She refused, was sentenced to thirty days in jail, and immediately appealed her conviction. The New York Court of Appeals rendered a rather ambiguous decision in acquitting her, holding that it was legal to disseminate contraceptive information for the "cure and prevention of disease." They failed to specify the disease. Sanger, interpreting unwanted pregnancy as a disease, continued her campaign unchallenged using this legal loophole.

New York, however, was just one state; there were a variety of state laws to be overcome before information about contraceptives could be widely disseminated. Even after the legal barriers began to fall, public policies of many agencies made it difficult to distribute information. Volunteer birth control clinics were often prevented from publicly advertising their existence. It was not until 1965 that the U.S. Supreme Court, in the case of *Griswold* v. *Connecticut*, removed the obstacle to dissemination of contraceptive information to married women. It took several more years before dissemination of information to unmarried women was legal in every state.

Teenagers and Birth Control

With legal obstacles for adults removed, and a variety of new contraceptives available, the problem remained one of dissemination of information and encouraging people to utilize contraceptives. This remains a difficult problem, particularly in the case of teenagers. Many so-called family life or sex education programs refuse to deal with the issue of contraceptives and instead emphasize continence as the only alternative. However, attempted continence has the highest failure rate of any of the possible methods of birth control. This failure has resulted in an increase in unmarried teenage mothers. The unmarried emphasis is important because in the past, even up to 1960, most of these pregnant teenagers would have married. In fact it is the change in marriage patterns and in adoption patterns, more than the sexual activity of teenagers, that has led to public concern over unmarried teenage mothers. Societal belief patterns have increasingly frowned upon what might be called forced marriages of pregnant teens, and the welfare system itself was modified to offer support to the single mother, making adoption no longer the only alternative.

Vast numbers of programs have been introduced, most of them funded by government grants, to teach the teenagers most at risk to be more responsible sexually. Few of the programs have included a component about contraceptives. Most of them talk about self-esteem, the need for adult responsibility, and the importance of continence. However, it seems they all have failed to change the statistics. The programs

dealing with contraceptive alternatives for those who cannot maintain continence are most effective.

As contraception and family planning have come to be part of the belief structure of the American family, large segments of the population remain either frightened by, unaware of, or unconvinced by discussions about birth control. The history of much of the contraceptive movement being aimed at the poor and minorities raises fear of not only discrimination but also racial suicide. Lack of awareness can certainly be overcome by education, but the biggest failure here is in dealing with young people. They are the most in need of the information and possess the greatest amount of misinformation.

Birth Control Misinformation

The greatest misinformation about birth control is among teenagers, in part because many segments of the general population remain fearful of frank discussions of sexuality among young people. This is a remnant of hostility to sexual pleasure, which has a long tradition in the Western world, and although most adults have come to terms with their own sexuality, they are still not willing to accept it in children. This is despite the fact that 53 percent of American adolescents have become sexually active before age eighteen, with 5 percent doing so before their fourteenth birthday (Dawson 1986).

More than one million teenagers become pregnant each year, and the majority of these pregnancies are unplanned. About one half of these teenage girls obtain abortions, and the other half give birth (Henshaw and Van Vort 1989). In trying to explain why this is the case, researchers have come up with four necessary conditions that should be met for teenagers to use contraceptives: existence of reliable contraceptives, birth-control education, easy access to contraceptives, and motivation to employ contraception. In the case of most U.S. teenagers, only the first—the existence of reliable contraceptives—is met. Eighty percent of school districts in major U.S. cities provide information on sex-related topics (Muraskin 1986). However, only about half of American teenagers are exposed to contraceptive education, and only a third of them know such a rudimentary fact as when in her cycle a woman is most fertile. Most programs aimed at lessening teenage pregnancy refuse to deal with contraceptives and their availability. On the other hand, during the three years that a high school in St. Paul, Minnesota, taught sex education and ran a contraceptive clinic, the pregnancy rate dropped from seventy-nine to thirty-five per thousand (*Population*

Today 1986). A Baltimore controlled experiment using four high schools—two where contraceptive information was made available and two where it was not—showed that availabiltiy of contraceptive information not only reduced pregnancy but also delayed the age of first intercourse. After thirty-eight months the pregnancy rate had declined by 30 percent in the program schools, whereas it had increased by 58 percent in the two control groups (Zabin 1986).

(*See also:* ABORTION: MEDICAL AND SOCIAL ASPECTS; ADOLESCENT SEXUALITY; BIRTH CONTROL: LEGAL ASPECTS; FAMILY PLANNING; INFANTICIDE; SEXUALITY EDUCATION)

BIBLIOGRAPHY

Bullough, V. L., and Bullough, B. (1990). *Contraception.* Buffalo, NY: Prometheus.

Chandrasekhar, S. (1981). *A Dirty, Filthy Book: The Writings of Charles Knowlton and Annie Besant on Reproductive Physiology and Birth Control and an Account of the Bradlaugh-Besant Trial.* Berkeley: University of California Press.

Dawson, D. A. (1986). "The Effects of Sex Education on Adolescent Behavior." *Family Planning Perspectives* 18: 162–170.

Fryer, P. (1965). *The Birth Controllers.* London: Secker & Warburg.

Henshaw, S. K., and Van Vort, J. (1989). "Patterns and Trends in Teenage Abortion and Pregnancy." In *Teenage Pregnancy in the United States,* ed. S. K. Henshaw, A. M. Kenney, D. Somberg, and J. Van Vort. New York: Alan Guttmacher Institute.

Population Today. (1986). "Contraceptive Push Urged." 18: 4, 8.

Reed, J. (1978). *From Private Vice to Public Virtue: The Birth Control Movement and American Society Since 1830.* New York: Basic Books.

Soloway, R. A. (1982). *Birth Control and the Population Question in England, 1877–1930.* Chapel Hill: University of North Carolina Press.

Wood, C., and Suitters, B. (1970). *The Flight for Acceptance: A History of Contraception.* Aylebury, Eng.: MTP.

Zabin, L. S. (1986). "Evaluation of a Pregnancy Prevention Program for Urban Teenagers." *Family Planning Perspectives* 18:119–126.

VERN L. BULLOUGH
BONNIE BULLOUGH

Contraceptive Methods

There are many forms of contraception, the prevention of pregnancy. How they work, their effectiveness, and the pros and cons of each should all be taken into account when choosing the contraceptive method best suited for an individual or couple.

Oral Contraception

The combination pill—the most widely used birth control pill (BCP)—consists of an estrogen component and a progestin (synthetic progesterone) component. Women opting for this method take active (hormone-containing) pills for three out of four weeks. There are multiple effects of the BCP components that facilitate contraception. The estrogen component can prevent possible ovulation. Estrogen also works to stabilize the lining of the uterus to maintain cyclic bleeding. The progestin provides the majority of the contraceptive benefits, including prevention of ovulation, alteration of the lining of the uterus to make it unreceptive to a fertilized egg, if conception occurs, and significant thickening of the cervical mucus, thereby not allowing sperm to penetrate and reach the egg.

The reported failure rate of BCP is 0.1 to 3 percent. The majority of failures comes from not starting the pill at the appropriate time in the cycle. Common side effects associated with oral contraceptives are nausea, headache, and breakthrough bleeding (midcycle bleeding). These usually can be controlled by altering the formulation used. Common concerns associated with BCP use include the risk of heart attacks, strokes, and blood clots. Such risks were most often seen with the high-dose birth control pills that were first on the market and are not frequently used today. There appears to be no increase in these serious risks in pill users who do not smoke. Another common concern about BCPs is whether there is an increased risk of breast cancer in women who take them, although this has not been proven to be true. Research has shown, however, that the pill may protect against uterine and ovarian cancer. There are some women who develop high blood pressure while on the pill. This may make it necessary for them to stop taking the pill; in this case, they can use a progestin-only formulation (such as Norplant or Depoprovera). The only absolute contraindications to taking BCPs is a personal history of blood clots, breast cancer, or liver disease.

Long-Acting Steroid Methods

The Norplant system consists of six silastic rods, containing progestin only, placed under the skin of the woman's upper arm by the clinician during a minor surgical procedure. Each rod is approximately two inches long, one-eighth inch wide, and contains the progestin called levonorgestrel. The capsules release 80 µg (micrograms) of levonorgestrel in twenty-four hours, an amount that declines after the first year of use. The contraceptive effect lasts five years, at which time the woman may have the rods removed and replaced, although they can be removed at any time. Fertility is restored immediately after their removal. Because body weight affects the actual level of levonorgestrel in the blood, overweight individuals may not have enough hormone circulating to provide contraception for the entire five years. When the device was first introduced, women over 150 pounds were to be counseled adequately that the Norplant system may not work for the entire five years.

Norplant prevents conception by inhibiting ovulation, decreasing sperm penetration by thickening cervical mucus, or thinning the lining of the uterus to prevent implantation of a fertilized egg (all of the progestin effects of BCPs). The most common side effect is bleeding irregularity, especially during the first year. The same contraindications as for BCPs apply to Norplant. Of the reversible hormone methods, Norplant is the most effective form of contraception, comparable to sterilization.

Depoprovera is a long-acting progestin-only contraceptive, administered to the woman as an injection of 150 mg (milligrams) every three months.

The injection works in the same way as Norplant and is as effective as sterilization. The major side effects of Depoprovera are weight gain and irregular bleeding. A period of six to eight months may be necessary to clear the effects of the drug from the body following the last injection. Therefore, reproductive function may not return immediately.

Intrauterine Contraceptive Device (IUD)

The intrauterine device is just that, a device placed in the lining of a woman's uterus (endometrial canal) by a clinician to prevent unwanted pregnancies. However, the pregnancy rate with an IUD is approximately 1.5 percent. There are two IUDs now used in the United States: the ParaGard (a copper IUD) and the Progestasert (a progesterone-releasing IUD).

The mechanism of action involves creating an environment in the uterus that causes sperm to die, thereby not allowing them to reach the egg. The IUD may affect tubal function and set up a mild irritation in the uterus to prevent implantation, if fertilization occurs. The IUD is usually inserted during the menses, since it is easier to pass through the cervix at this time, unscheduled bleeding is not started, and the risk of pregnancy is eliminated. Although the ParaGard is approved for eight years, the Progestasert must be changed yearly. The IUD can be removed at any time, and fertility is usually restored immediately.

The major determinant in deciding if the IUD is the best contraceptive for a woman is her risk of getting a pelvic infection. This risk is related to previous infections and monogamy. The risk of infection is only increased at the time of insertion. An IUD is also easier to place in a woman who has had children. A woman with irregular cycles may not be the best candidate for the IUD, as she may have difficulty determining if she is pregnant. Previously held ideas that IUDs cause abortions or tubal pregnancies are not true. In fact, copper IUDs may reduce the risk of tubal pregnancies.

Barrier Methods

Barrier methods of contraception do just as their name implies, they provide a "barrier" between sperm and egg to prevent conception.

Condoms are contraceptives used by males. A condom is placed on the erect penis prior to intercourse to prevent semen from being deposited in the vagina. The semen is instead deposited in a small reservoir receptacle at the end of the condom. An added benefit of condoms is that, used properly, they can prevent sexually transmitted diseases. The reported failure rate of condoms is 12 percent. This can be improved by the use of spermicide as well.

The diaphragm is a dome-shaped piece of latex with a metal ring that bends to allow insertion into the vagina and then returns to its original shape. Usually, a woman needs to be fitted for the right diaphragm by a clinician. Practice is often necessary to learn proper insertion and removal. The diaphragm's main purpose is to provide a means of keeping the spermicide over the cervix. The reported failure rate of the diaphragm can be as high as 18 percent.

The cervical cap, like the diaphragm, covers the cervix. However, the cervical cap has a somewhat tighter fit, and the actual fitting process is more difficult. The cervical cap, although more difficult to use, can be left in place for 48 hours, the main advantage over a diaphragm. Also, less spermicide is necessary. The failure rate is the same as the diaphragm's.

The contraceptive sponge is placed in the vagina near the cervix up to twenty-four hours prior to intercourse. Its effectiveness is similar to that of the diaphragm, although the effectiveness in women who have already had children is debatable.

Vaginal spermicides are available in many formulations, such as inserts or foam. Their effectiveness is similar to that of the sponge, but when used in combination with condoms, the sponge, or the diaphragm, effectiveness can be improved.

Sterilization

A brief note should be made about sterilization as a means of contraception. More than one-third of American couples use sterilization for contraception. The failure rates range from 0.15 percent to 0.4 percent. This option, which should be considered permanent, requires an operative procedure to interrupt either the fallopian tubes (for the female) or the vas deferens (for the male), thereby preventing the egg or the sperm from completing their journey. Sexual function is not affected.

Periodic Abstinence—Natural Family Planning

Some couples prefer to use no artificial means of contraception. This idea is also preferred by some religious groups. Periodic abstinence, or the rhythm method, involves monitoring the menstrual cycle and determining the approximate time of ovulation and then avoiding intercourse around this time. Ovulation may be determined by a combination of monitoring the woman's temperature, recording the menstrual cycle on the calendar, and checking the quantity and quality of cervical mucus. The failure rate is relatively high, approximately 20 percent, as exact ovulation time may be difficult to determine, even if all of the above steps are followed.

(*See also:* CONCEPTION: MEDICAL ASPECTS; FAMILY PLANNING; GENETIC COUNSELING; PREGNANCY AND BIRTH)

BIBLIOGRAPHY

Grimes, D. (1993). *The Contraceptive Report*. Liberty Corner, NJ: Emron.
Nelson, A. C. (1993). "Contraceptive Choices for the 1990s." *Clinical Practice in Sexuality* 9:15–20.
Physicians' Desk Reference, 47th edition. (1993). Oradell, NJ: Medical Economics Data.
Speroff, L., and Darney, P. (1992). *A Clinical Guide for Contraception*. Baltimore: Williams & Wilkins.
Trussell, J.; Hatcher, R. A.; Cates, W., Jr.; Stewart, F. H.; and Kost, K. (1990). "Contraceptive Failure in the United States." *Studies in Family Planning* 21:51–54.
Walker, D. M. (1993). "Contraception, Sterilization, and Abortion." In *Handbook of Gynecology and Obstetrics*, ed. J. Brown and W. R. Crombieholm. Norwalk, CT: Appleton and Lange.

MAXINE J. KLEIN

Legal Aspects

Effective means of contraception were first mass-produced during the nineteenth century, enabling the majority of people to benefit from them. The suppression of contraceptive information in the United States began in the 1870s, led by Anthony Comstock, a fanatical Puritan reformer and secretary of the Society for the Suppression of Vice. The "Comstock laws" were originally passed by Congress in 1873. These laws prohibited the mailing, shipping, or importation of "obscene" or "immoral" matter, which until 1971 was defined to include articles, drugs, or medicines for the prevention of conception and, in part, the dissemination of printed materials about contraceptives. Many states enacted "little Comstock laws," prohibiting the sale, advertising, or display of "articles for the prevention of conception."

Margaret Sanger, a nurse born in Corning, New York, in 1879, led a national crusade to legalize birth control. She went to jail in 1917 for distributing contraceptives to immigrant women in a Brooklyn clinic. She founded the American Birth Control League, today known as the Planned Parenthood Federation of America. As a result of challenges to the federal Comstock laws brought by birth control advocates, those statutes were interpreted by courts and administrative agencies over the years to provide for numerous exceptions. In 1971, Congress passed amendments introduced by Representative James H. Scheuer (D-NY), which deleted from these laws all reference to articles for the prevention of conception. At the same time, however, Congress added a new section, designating as "nonmailable matter" contraceptives and printed materials concerning contraceptives that were not solicited by the addressee. This last vestige of the federal Comstock laws was declared unconstitutional by the U.S. Supreme Court in 1983 in *Bolger* v. *Youngs Drug Products Corp.*, on First Amendment grounds.

The most stringent of the state "little Comstock laws" was enacted in Connecticut, where a statute actually made it a crime to *use* contraceptives. In 1965, in the case of *Griswold* v. *Connecticut*, the U.S. Supreme Court struck down the Connecticut statute and recognized the right of married persons to practice birth control free from government interference. The Court found in the Constitution a right of privacy that protects decision making in such personal matters as having a child. Subsequently, in *Eisenstadt* v. *Baird* (1972), the Court held that unmarried people have the same right of privacy. In *Population Services International* v. *Carey* (1977), the Supreme Court struck down a New York statute that barred the advertisement or display of contraceptives. Since that time, virtually all state laws restricting the dissemination of information about, the advertising of, or the sale or distribution of contraceptives have either been repealed or are invalid and unenforced.

The *Population Services International* case also struck down a New York State ban on the sale of over-the-counter contraceptives to minors. Since then, a number of U.S. Supreme Court decisions have upheld the right of mature minors to a degree of privacy in their reproductive decisions. Advances in statutory and judge-made law have made contraception widely available to young people on a confidential basis.

The trend since the 1960s has been to affirm federal and state support of improved access to voluntary family planning information and services. In 1970, the federal Family Planning Services and Population Research Act was signed into law. Commonly known as Title X of the Public Health Service Act, this legislation has been repeatedly reauthorized and extended and still provides funding to public agencies and nonprofit private organizations to "assist in establishment of . . . voluntary family planning projects which shall offer a broad range of acceptable and effective family planning methods. . . ." Other federal legislation provides funding for family planning services for recipients of Aid to Families with Dependent Children (AFDC), Medicaid recipients, active duty members of the uniformed services, and others.

Most states now have statutes or case law authorizing state agencies to administer family planning programs. The only state regulation now permissible relates to the manner of distribution or advertising of contraceptives. For example, some states still restrict vending machine sales of condoms, and even these restrictions are rapidly disappearing with the advent of AIDS and the importance of condoms for disease prevention.

A wave of social reaction during the presidencies of Ronald Reagan and George Bush, although mainly directed against abortion, also threatened family planning. New regulations under Title X of the Public Health Service Act proposed by the Reagan administration in 1987 would have blocked funding to any family planning agency offering abortion counseling, referral, or services. These regulations were tied up in litigation until 1993, when they were revoked by President Bill Clinton as one of the first acts of his administration. The Reagan administration also promulgated the "squeal rule," which would have required providers of federally funded contraceptive services to notify the parents of minors. This was declared invalid by the courts as inconsistent with the Title X legislation, one of the primary purposes of which was to prevent unintended adolescent preg-

nancy. U.S. efforts to fund international family planning were severely hampered during the Reagan and Bush administrations by the "Mexico City policy," which barred funding to American agencies providing services abroad if those agencies, using private funds, provided abortion counseling, referral, or services. This policy was also revoked by President Clinton.

New methods of contraception (which, since a change in the statute in 1976, include devices as well as drugs) must still be approved by the Food and Drug Administration (FDA). While the agency was faulted by some people for delaying approvals in the 1970s and 1980s, the FDA has approved two major new methods since 1990: Depoprovera, an injectable contraceptive, and Norplant, a silastic hormone-releasing implant.

Advocates of birth control believe that the key to its universal acceptance is accurate and age-appropriate sexuality education in the schools, from kindergarten through grade twelve. Although most states have adopted sex education programs, the battles over the content of these programs continue in local school board elections nationwide.

(*See also:* ABORTION: LEGAL ASPECTS; BIRTH CONTROL: SOCIOCULTURAL AND HISTORICAL ASPECTS; CONCEPTION: LEGAL ASPECTS; FAMILY PLANNING; SEXUALITY EDUCATION)

BIBLIOGRAPHY

Chesler, E. (1992). *Woman of Valor: Margaret Sanger and the Birth Control Movement in America*. New York: Simon & Schuster.
Gordon, L. (1990). *Woman's Body, Woman's Right: Birth Control in America*, revised and updated edition. New York: Viking Penguin.
Reed, J. (1983). *The Birth Control Movement and American Society: From Private Vice to Public Virtue*. Princeton, NJ: Princeton University Press.
U.S. Department of Health, Education, and Welfare. (1978). *Family Planning, Contraception, Voluntary Sterilization, and Abortion: An Analysis of Laws and Policies in the United States, Each State and Jurisdiction (as of October 1, 1976, with 1978 Addenda)*. Washington, DC: U.S. Government Printing Office.
Wood, C., and Suitters, B. (1970). *The Fight for Acceptance: A History of Contraception*. Aylesbury, Eng.: Medical and Technical Publishing.

CASES

Bolger v. *Youngs Drug Products Corp.*, 463 U.S. 60 (1983).
Griswold v. *Connecticut*, 381 U.S. 479 (1965).
Eisenstadt v. *Baird*, 405 U.S. 438 (1972).
Carey v. *Population Services International*, 431 U.S. 678 (1977).

EVE W. PAUL

C

CAREGIVING *See* Child Care; Parent Education; Substitute Caregivers

CELIBACY

Historically, celibacy has been defined as the state of not being married and has applied particularly to those who have taken religious vows to remain single. In the life of the religious, celibacy has long been an essential part of a spiritual discipline, a practice for the devotee to advance in spiritual growth. Celibacy offers a way for the religious individual to have his or her attention most fully absorbed in the commitment to seeking and experiencing God. Often, these individuals set themselves apart from the larger society, and this has led to the growth of male and female monasticism. Celibacy is traditional in many of the world's religions, including Hinduism, Buddhism, Taoism, Jainism, and Christianity (within Roman Catholicism and the Eastern Orthodox church) but not Judaism, Islam, or Confucianism. In North and Central America, there are more than 250,000 priests, nuns, and monks leading celibate lives, although these numbers are said to be on the decline (Wade 1971).

There has also been a tradition of secular celibacy, especially in Eastern cultures; in the West, it has had a confused and fragmentary history. There have been no large movements advocating secular celibate life. At its worst, proponents of celibacy have used it to uphold a repressive, antisexual ideology. At its best, celibacy has been an important commitment for certain social groups—such as the Shakers—who were seeking ways to achieve self-fulfillment and societal change.

Since the 1970s, the term "celibacy" has taken on a larger meaning and is often used synonymously with chastity. In this sense, celibacy refers to a behavior, to the absence of sexual activity, whether for long or short periods of time, without regard to marital status or any other sociological factors. It is simply understood as a psychophysical state, wherein one's physical behavior is usually accompanied by a congruent mental and emotional outlook. Celibacy has a strong mental and emotional component just as sexual expression does. Celibacy does not mean having no sexual feelings; rather, it can be thought of as the "rest" stage of sexuality, in which a less active response predominates. As with sexual activity, celibacy is generally a voluntary choice for human beings, apparently the only creatures who can freely choose to be sexually active or celibate (Brown 1989).

After the sexual revolution of the 1960s began to lose its allure, more and more individuals began to experiment with celibate lifestyles, sometimes even within a committed relationship. From the mid-1980s on, as sexual behavior changed in response to the AIDS epidemic, celibacy gained far more acceptance as a positive social behavior. In addition to its obvious practical benefits as a preventive health measure for any sexually transmitted disease, including AIDS, celibacy can serve as a behavioral approach to the treatment of a range of sexual problems; a person can step back and deal directly with underlying causes. In cases of sexual addiction, for example, in which the yearning for intimacy is almost never satisfied through sex, celibacy can open the door to other ways of creating and sustaining intimacy.

No major scientific study of the effects of celibacy has been undertaken. Observations that celibacy is beneficial for physical, mental, and emotional health have proven difficult for researchers to measure, partly because those who are celibate are generally also involved in a number of other health-enhancing practices. However, anecdotal reports from those who have chosen a celibate lifestyle suggest that celibacy can lead to the exploration of new modes of personal communication and intimate relating for men and women alike. Men report that celibacy often enables them to pursue a variety of personal goals, such as deepening their commitment to achievement in creative work or focusing on the process of spiritual development. Celibacy can provide a way for a man to open his heart to lovers, friends, and family. Boundaries in his emotional life can be broken by deemphasizing sexual goals. He can more deeply appreciate his masculinity by allowing the separation of his virility from his sexuality (Brown 1989).

Women who practice celibacy report that it allows them to break old patterns of behavior, dependencies, and limits. Becoming celibate enables them to experience a greater degree of self-sufficiency and freedom while exploring new dimensions in relationships. Women who are celibate often report increased creativity and energy in all aspects of their lives, along with feelings of peacefulness, "centeredness," and the enlivened capacity to pursue a more spiritual life. A period of celibacy can free a woman from the narrow focus of sexual activity and provide a time in which feelings in a particular relationship can deepen without the added complications of sex; it can allow a love relationship to develop and unfold in a more unbounded field.

Whether it is undertaken as a lifetime commitment in a spiritual community or practiced for a certain period of time outside or within a marriage, celibacy in American society is a positive vehicle to further personal growth, although accurate estimates of how many people are voluntarily celibate are difficult to assess. Celibacy is a private behavior for most, and there is no celibacy "movement" as such. However, the combination of health concerns, the desire to counter an undue societal emphasis on sexuality, and an interest in spiritual development means that celibacy will continue as a viable option for those searching for a deeper, more intimate experience of love and a more balanced approach to living fulfilled lives.

(*See also:* COMMITMENT; COMMUNICATION; INTIMACY; LOVE; SEXUALITY; UTOPIAN COMMUNITIES)

BIBLIOGRAPHY

Brown, M. G. (1989). *The New Celibacy: A Journey to Love, Intimacy, and Good Health in a New Age.* New York: McGraw-Hill.

Gagnon, J. H., and Simon, W. (1973). *Sexual Conduct: The Social Sources of Human Sexuality.* Chicago: Aldine.

Gallagher, C. A., and Vandenberg, T. (1989). *Celibacy Myth: Loving for Life.* New York: Crossroad.

Goergen, D. (1974). *The Sexual Celibate.* New York: Seabury.

Menninger, W. (1976). *Happiness Without Sex.* New York: Sheed, Andrews, and McMeel.

Sipe, A. W. (1990). *A Secret World: Sexuality and the Search for Celibacy.* New York: Brunner/Mazel.

Sovatsky, S. (1994). *Passions of Innocence: Tantric Celibacy and the Mysticism of Eros.* Rochester, VT: Destiny Books.

Wade, J. D. (1971). *Chastity, Sexuality, and Personal Hang-Ups.* New York: Alba House.

M. GABRIELLE BROWN

CHILD ABUSE AND NEGLECT

This entry consists of the following three articles:

Sociological Aspects
   Richard J. Gelles
Emotional and Psychological Aspects
   Stanley Parker
Legal Aspects
   Gregory Loken

Sociological Aspects

The rapid increase in public awareness of child abuse and neglect has led professionals and lay people alike to conclude that child abuse and neglect is a new phenomenon that has increased to epidemic proportions. Although abuse and neglect of children receive considerably more attention today, it has been part of the lives of children throughout history. The history of Western society is one in which many children have been subjected to unspeakable cruelties. In ancient times infants had no rights until the right to live was bestowed on them by their fathers, typically as part of some formal cultural ritual (Radbill 1980). When the right to live was withheld, infants were abandoned or left to die. Although it is not known how often children were killed or abandoned, it is known that infanticide was widely accepted among ancient and prehistoric cultures. Infanticide continued through the eighteenth and nineteenth centuries.

Killing children was not the only form of harm inflicted by generations of parents. Since prehistoric times, children have been mutilated, beaten, and maltreated. Such treatment was not only condoned, it also was often mandated as the most appropriate method of child rearing. Children were hit with rods, canes, and switches. Fathers in Colonial America were implored to "beat the devil" out of their children (Greven 1991).

Terms and Definition

An enduring problem in the study of child abuse and neglect has been the development of a useful, clear, acceptable (and accepted) definition of "abuse and neglect." C. Henry Kempe and his colleagues (1962) first defined the "battered child syndrome" as a clinical condition (meaning that diagnosable medical and physical symptoms existed) involving those who have been deliberately injured by a physical assault. Kempe's definition of abuse, however, was restricted only to acts of physical violence that produce diagnosable injuries.

The National Center on Child Abuse and Neglect (NCCAN) uses a broader definition of child abuse and neglect, one now included in federal law. This definition served as a model for the definitions used in all fifty states in laws requiring the reporting of suspected instances of abuse or neglect. According to this definition, child abuse and neglect is the physical or mental injury, sexual abuse, negligent treatment, or maltreatment of a child under the age of eighteen by a person who is responsible for the child's welfare under circumstances which indicate that the child's health or welfare is harmed or threatened thereby.

Others prefer an even broader definition. David G. Gil (1975) defines abuse and neglect as any act of commission or omission by a parent, an individual, an institution, or by society as a whole that deprives a child of equal rights and liberty and/or interferes with or constrains the child's ability to achieve his or her optimal developmental potential.

The years of debate and discussion have not resulted in a definitive definition of child abuse, and debate still continues over the issues of consequence and intent. One problem is that the terms "abuse" and "neglect" are political concepts and not scientific or legal concepts. Abuse and neglect are essentially any acts that are considered deviant or harmful by a group large enough or with sufficient political power to enforce the definition. However, no one set of objective acts can be uniformly and consistently characterized as abusive. What is defined as abuse or neglect depends on a process of negotiation. What is now considered child abuse is the product of a long-term effort to educate clinicians, policymakers, and the public about what acts and actions are considered harmful to children.

Definitions of abuse and neglect that can be applied cross-culturally are even more difficult to specify or agree on (Finkelhor and Korbin 1988; Gelles and Cornell 1983; Korbin 1981). Jill Korbin (1981) points out that since there is no universal standard for optimal child rearing, there can be no universal standard for what constitutes child abuse and neglect. David Finkelhor and Korbin (1988) explain that a definition of child abuse that could be used internationally should accomplish at least two objectives: It should distinguish child abuse clearly from other social, economic, and health problems of international concern; and it should be sufficiently flexible to apply to a range of situations in a variety of social and cultural contexts. They note that some of what is talked about as child abuse in Western societies has very little meaning in other societies. Finkelhor and Korbin (1988) propose the following definition of child abuse for cross-cultural research: Child abuse is the portion of harm to children that results from human action that is proscribed (negatively valued), proximate (the action is close to the actual harm—thus, deforesting land that results in child malnutrition does not fit this definition), and preventable (the action could have been avoided).

Types of Abuse and Neglect

Child abuse and neglect is a general term that covers a wide range of acts of commission and omission, either carried out by a perpetrator or allowed to happen, that result in injuries ranging from death, to serious disabling injury, to emotional distress, to malnutrition and illness. The following are the six major types of abuse and neglect (NCCAN 1988):

1. Physical abuse: Acts of commission that result in physical harm, including death, to a child.
2. Sexual abuse: Acts of commission, including intrusion or penetration, molestation with genital contact, or other forms of sexual acts in which children are used to provide sexual gratification for a perpetrator.
3. Emotional abuse: Acts of commission that include confinement, verbal or emotional abuse, or other types of abuse such as withholding sleep, food, or shelter.
4. Physical neglect: Acts of omission that involve refusal to provide health care, delay in providing health care, abandonment, expulsion of a child from a home, inadequate supervision, failure to meet food and clothing needs, and conspicuous failure to protect a child from hazards or danger.

5. Educational neglect: Acts of omission and commission that include permitting chronic truancy, failure to enroll a child in school, and inattention to specific educational needs.

6. Emotional neglect: Acts of omission that involve failing to meet the nurturing and affection needs of a child, exposing a child to chronic or severe spouse abuse, allowing or permitting a child to use alcohol or controlled substances, encouraging the child to engage in maladaptive behavior, refusal to provide psychological care, delays in providing psychological care, and other inattention to the child's developmental needs.

Incidence and Prevalence

Various methods have been used in attempts to achieve an accurate estimate of child abuse and neglect in the United States. In 1967, Gil (1970) conducted a nationwide inventory of reported cases of child abuse (before, however, all fifty states had enacted mandatory reporting laws). He found 6,000 confirmed cases of child abuse. Gil also used a self-report survey to estimate that 2.53 million to 4.07 million children were abused each year.

The NCCAN has conducted two surveys designed to measure the national incidence of reported and recognized child maltreatment (Burgdorf 1980; NCCAN

Table 1 National Maltreatment Incidence Estimates

Form and Severity of Maltreatment	Number of In-Scope Children	Incidence Rate[a]
All Maltreated Children	1,025,900	16.30
All Abused Children[b]	580,400	9.20
Physical abuse	311,200	4.90
Sexual abuse	138,000	2.20
Emotional abuse	174,400	2.80
All Neglected Children[b]	498,000	7.90
Physical neglect	182,100	2.90
Emotional neglect	52,200	0.80
Educational neglect	291,100	4.60
Severity of Child's Injury		
Fatal	1,100	0.02
Serious	157,100	2.50
Moderate	740,000	11.70
Probable	127,800	2.00

[a] Per 1,000 per year.
[b] Totals may be lower than sum of categories because a child may have experienced more than one category of maltreatment.
SOURCE National Center on Child Abuse and Neglect (1988).

1988). Both surveys assessed how many cases were known to investigatory agencies, professionals in schools, hospitals, and other social service agencies. A total of 1,025,900 maltreated children were known by the agencies surveyed in 1988 (see Table 1).

A second source of data on the extent of child abuse comes from the National Study of Child Neglect and Abuse Reporting conducted each year by the American Association for Protecting Children, a division of the American Humane Association. This study measures the number of families, alleged perpetrators, and children involved in official reports of child maltreatment (American Association for Protecting Children 1989). During 1987, the last year the survey was conducted, 2,178,384 children were reported to state agencies for suspected child abuse and neglect. Of these, it is estimated that 686,000 reports were substantiated, or considered valid reports, by the state Child Protective Service agencies. The National Committee for Prevention of Child Abuse estimates that nearly 3 million reports of child abuse and neglect were made in 1992 (McCurdy and Daro 1993).

A source of data not based only on official reports or official awareness are the National Family Violence Surveys carried out in 1976 and again in 1985 by Richard Gelles and Murray Straus (Gelles and Straus 1987, 1988; Straus and Gelles 1986; Straus, Gelles, and Steinmetz 1980). The National Family Violence Surveys interviewed two nationally representative samples of families—2,146 family members in 1976 and 6,002 family members in 1985.

Milder forms of violence—violence that most people think of as physical punishment—as represented by the first three items in Table 2 were, of course, the most common. However, even with the severe forms of violence, the rates were surprisingly high. Abusive violence was defined as acts that had a high probability of injuring the child. These included kicking, biting, punching, hitting or trying to hit a child with an object, beating up a child, burning or scalding, and threatening to or using a gun or a knife. Slightly more than 2 parents in 100 (2.3%) engaged in one act of abusive violence during the year prior to the survey. Seven children in 1,000 were hurt as a result of an act of violence directed at them by a parent in the year prior to the survey.

Projecting the rate of abusive violence to all children under the age of eighteen years who lived in the home suggests that 1.5 million children experience acts of abusive physical violence each year. Likewise, projecting the rate of injury suggests that about 450,000 children are injured each year as a result of parental violence.

Table 2 Frequency of Parental Violence Toward Children Under Eighteen Years of Age

Violent Behavior	Percentage of Occurrences in Past Year				Percentage of Occurrences Ever Reported
	Once	Twice	More Than Twice	Total	
Threw object at child	1.5	0.7	0.9	3.1	4.5
Pushed, grabbed, or shoved child	5.8	7.5	14.9	28.2	33.6
Slapped or spanked child	8.1	8.5	39.1	55.7	74.6
Kicked, bit, or punched	0.7	0.5	0.3	1.5	2.1
Hit or tried to hit child with something	2.4	2.0	5.3	9.7	14.4
Beat up child	0.3	0.1	0.2	0.6	1.0
Burned or scalded child	0.2	0.1	0.1	0.4	0.6
Threatened child with knife or gun	0.1	0.1	0.0	0.2	0.3
Used a knife or gun	0.1	0.1	0.0	0.2	0.2

SOURCE Second National Family Violence Survey (Gelles and Straus 1988).

Sexual abuse. A comprehensive review of studies on the incidence and prevalence of child sexual abuse reports that estimates of the prevalence range from 6 percent to 62 percent for females and from 3 percent to 31 percent for males (Peters, Wyatt, and Finkelhor 1986). This variation may be accounted for by a number of methodological factors, such as differences in definitions of abuse, sample characteristics, interview format (e.g., in-person versus telephone interview), and a number of questions used to elicit information about abuse experiences.

Child homicide. Homicide is one of the five leading causes of death for children between one and eighteen years of age. More than 1,300 children are killed by their parents or caretakers each year (McCurdy and Daro 1993). Even with an estimate this high, researchers believe that homicide of infants is probably underreported in health statistics (Jason, Gilliland, and Tyler 1983). Infants from one week to one year of age are most likely to be killed by a parent. Parents and caretakers including stepparents are the most likely perpetrators of child homicide of children under five years of age. The cause of death is usually a beating, burns, or neglect, and the circumstances of the death are either discipline or neglect of the victim (Christoffel 1990).

Patterns and Causes of Child Abuse

The first research articles on child abuse and neglect characterized offenders as suffering from vari-

ous forms of psychopathology (Bennie and Sclare 1969; Galdston 1965; Steele and Pollock 1974). More recent approaches to child maltreatment tend to recognize the multidimensional nature of abuse and locate the roots of physical abuse and neglect in the structure of the family and/or society.

Five factors have been consistently found to be related to the physical abuse of children. These factors are intergenerational transmission of abuse; low socioeconomic status; social and structural stress; social isolation and low community embeddedness; and family structure.

The single most consistent finding reported in the child-abuse literature is that experiencing abuse as a child increases the likelihood of becoming an abusive caretaker (Gelles 1973; Gil 1970; Kempe et al. 1962; Straus, Gelles, and Steinmetz 1980). However, as Deborah A. Potts, Sharon D. Herzberger, and A. Elizabeth Holland (1979) point out, the relationship between being abused and becoming an abuser is probabalistic, not deterministic. According to Joan Kaufman and Edward Zigler (1987), who reviewed the major research studies on the cycle of physical abuse, 30 percent of abused children grow up to be abusive.

A disproportionate number of cases of abuse come from low-income families (Elmer 1967; Gelles 1973; Gil 1970; Maden and Wrench 1977; Parke and Collmer 1975; Pelton 1978; Straus, Gelles, and Steinmetz 1980). There is a need for caution in interpreting data on the relationship between child abuse and social class, because lower-class families are much more vulnerable to being officially recorded for abusive behavior. Survey data that are less subject to the biases of official report data confirm the higher rates of abuse among the lower class.

The mechanism through which low socioeconomic status works to bring about child abuse is social stress. Abusive and neglectful families are reported as experiencing more stressful life events than nonmaltreating families (Elmer 1967; Gelles 1973; Gil 1970; Parke and Collmer 1975; Straus, Gelles, and Steinmetz 1980). One of the more significant social stressors related to abuse and neglect is unemployment. Among families in which the father is unemployed or employed part-time, the risk of abuse is higher than in households where the father has full-time work (Galdston 1965; Gil 1970; Straus, Gelles, and Steinmetz 1980). Poor housing conditions and larger-than-average family size are also risk factors for maltreatment (Gil 1970; Johnson and Morse 1968; Straus, Gelles, and Steinmetz 1980). Other stressful life conditions found related to abuse include a new baby present in the home, the presence of a handicapped person in the home, illness or death of a family member, and child care problems. Stress produced by child-related factors can also lead to abuse. Babies with low birthweights; children born prematurely; and children with physical, mental, or developmental disabilities are at higher risk for abuse than are children without these conditions (Elmer 1967; Freidrich and Boriskin 1976; Gil 1970; Newberger et al. 1977).

Parents who abuse their children tend to be socially isolated from both formal and informal social networks (Elmer 1967; Garbarino and Gilliam 1980; Milner and Chilamkurti 1991). Lack of formal or informal social networks deprives abusive parents of support systems that would aid them in dealing with social or family stress. Moreover, lack of community contacts makes these families less likely to change their behavior to conform with community values and standards (Steinmetz 1978). Thus, they are particularly vulnerable to violent responses to stress while not perceiving their behavior as deviant.

Certain family structures are common among abusive and neglectful families. Single parents are at higher risk to abuse their children; however, this is a function of the fact that single-parent families have lower income than do dual-caretaker homes (Gelles 1989). Within intact homes, a major structural feature found related to the use of abusive violence toward children is inequality. Straus and his colleagues (1980) found that the rate of severe violence toward children was highest in homes where there was little shared decision making. Those homes in which decision making was dominated by either the husband or the wife and where little family equality existed were among the most violent.

Models to Explain Abuse

The earliest research on child abuse and neglect advanced a psychopathological model: Mental illness caused people to abuse their children. Other intra-individual models proposed that abuse was caused by alcohol and/or drugs. Four theoretical models of child abuse and neglect are the economic model, the sociocultural explanation, the ecological model, and the exchange theory approach.

The economic or social-structural model explains that violence and abuse arise out of socially structured stress. Stresses such as low income, unemployment, and illness are unevenly distributed in the social structure. When violence is the accepted response or adaptation to stress, stress leads to violence and abuse (Coser 1967).

Some students of violence have explained the occurrence of family violence, including child abuse, by drawing on sociocultural attitudes and norms concerning violent behavior. Societies, cultures, and subcultures that approve of the use of violence are thought to have the highest rates of domestic violence and child abuse (Straus, Gelles, and Steinmetz 1980).

James Garbarino (1977) has proposed an ecological model of child maltreatment. The model rests on three levels of analysis: (1) the relationship between organism and environment; (2) the interacting and overlapping system in which human development occurs; and (3) environmental quality. Garbarino proposes that maltreatment arises out of a mismatch between parent, child, and family to neighborhood and community.

Exchange theory (Gelles 1983) proposes that family violence and child abuse are governed by the principle of costs and rewards. Abuse is used when the rewards are higher than the costs. The private nature of the family, the reluctance of social institutions and agencies to intervene—in spite of mandatory child abuse reporting laws—and the low risk of other interventions reduce the costs of abuse and violence. The cultural approval of violence as both an expressive behavior and an instrumental behavior raises the potential rewards for violence.

Consequences of Abuse and Neglect

A number of people believe that untreated abused children frequently grow up to be delinquents, murderers, and batterers of the next generation of children (Schmitt and Kempe 1975). Criminologist Cathy S. Widom (1989) identified a large sample of validated cases of child abuse and neglect from approximately the mid-1970s, established a control group of non-abused children, and assessed official arrest records to establish occurrences of delinquency, criminal behavior, and violent criminal behavior. She reports that abused and neglected children have a higher likelihood of arrest for delinquency, adult criminality, and violent criminal behavior than the matched controls.

Abused children have been frequently described as having a number of cognitive, emotional, and social difficulties (Starr 1988). Studies find various social and emotional deficits, including communication problems, poor performance in school, and learning disabilities (Starr 1988). Adults who were abused as children are also thought to have higher rates of drug and alcohol abuse, criminal behavior, and psychiatric disturbances (Smith, Hansen, and Nobel 1973).

Prevention of Abuse and Neglect

All fifty states enacted mandatory reporting laws for child abuse and neglect by the late 1960s. These laws require certain professionals (or in some states, all adults) to report cases of suspected abuse or neglect. When the report comes in, state protective service workers typically investigate the report to determine if it is accurate and if the family needs help. Although a wide array of options are available to public social workers, they typically have two basic options: (1) removal of the child from the parents and placement in a foster home or institution or (2) providing the family with social support such as counseling, food stamps, day-care services, or a homemaker.

Neither solution is ideal, and there are risks in both. Removing a child from a home involves two risks. First, the child may not understand why he or she is being removed. Children have little basis of comparison, and they might not realize that they are being treated differently from other children. To them, the removal might be just another instance of them doing something wrong and being punished. Children who are removed from abusive homes may well be protected from physical damage but still suffer emotional harm. A second problem is finding suitable placement for an abused child. Given that abused children may suffer physical and emotional damage, they frequently require special care. They could well become a burden for any foster home or institution that has to care for them. The risk of abuse might actually be greater in a foster home or institution than in the home of the

biological or adoptive parents from which the child was taken.

The risk of leaving children in abusive homes and providing support services is that the support services may not resolve the problems that led to the abuse and the child may be abused again or killed. Thirty to 50 percent of the children killed by parents or caretakers are killed *after* they have been identified by child welfare agencies and have been involved in interventions; they are either left in their homes or returned home after a short-term removal (Anderson et al. 1983; Besharov 1991; Daro 1987; Mayor's Task Force on Child Abuse and Neglect 1983; Mitchel 1989; Texas Department of Human Resources 1981).

There are only a handful of evaluations of prevention and treatment programs for child maltreatment. Pediatrician David Olds and his colleagues (1986) evaluated the effectiveness of a family support program during pregnancy and the first two years after birth for low-income, unmarried, teenage, first-time mothers. Of those children of unmarried teenage mothers who were provided with the full complement of home visits during the mother's pregnancy and for the first two years after birth, 4 percent had confirmed cases of child abuse and neglect reported to the state child protection agency. This figure is in contrast with 19 percent of the comparison groups that had cases of maltreatment reported.

A new prevention program is the Healthy Start or the "Hawaii Model." This prevention effort targets high-risk families at the time of the birth of their children. Healthy Start provides home visits designed to expand the caretaker's knowledge about available services and enhance the ability to obtain these services. The visits are weekly for about a year, diminishing then to monthly, and finally to quarterly until the child is five years old. Evaluations of Healthy Start home visiting programs are limited to comparing child maltreatment reports for families enrolled in the program to those not enrolled. Initial results suggest lower rates of child abuse among enrolled high-risk families compared to nonenrolled high-risk families (Fuddy 1992).

Deborah Daro and Ann H. Cohn (1988) reviewed a number of evaluations of child maltreatment programs. They found that there was no noticeable correlation between a given set of services and positive client outcomes. In fact, the more services a family received, the worse the family got. Lay counseling, group counseling, and parent education classes resulted in more positive treatment outcomes. The optimal treatment period appeared to be seven to eighteen months. Projects successful in reducing abuse separated children from abusive parents, either by placing the children in foster homes or by requiring the maltreating adult to move out of the house.

(*See also:* CHILD ABUSE AND NEGLECT: EMOTIONAL AND PSYCHOLOGICAL ASPECTS; CHILD ABUSE AND NEGLECT: LEGAL ASPECTS; CHILDHOOD; CONFLICT; DISCIPLINE; DYSFUNCTIONAL FAMILY; FAMILY VIOLENCE; INCEST; INFANTICIDE; PARENT EDUCATION; STRESS)

BIBLIOGRAPHY

American Association for Protecting Children. (1989). *Highlights of Official Child Neglect and Abuse Reporting, 1987*. Denver: American Humane Association.

Anderson, R.; Ambrosino, R.; Valentine, D.; and Lauderdale, M. (1983). "Child Deaths Attributable to Abuse and Neglect: An Empirical Study." *Children and Youth Services Review* 5:75–89.

Bennie, E., and Sclare, A. (1969). "The Battered Child Syndrome." *American Journal of Psychiatry* 125:975–979.

Besharov, D. J. (1991). "Reducing Unfounded Reports." *Journal of Interpersonal Violence* 6:112–115.

Burgdorf, K. (1980). *Recognition and Reporting of Child Maltreatment*. Rockville, MD: Westat.

Christoffel, K. K. (1990). "Violent Death and Injury in U.S. Children and Adolescents." *American Journal of Diseases of Children* 144:697–705.

Coser, L. A. (1967). *Continuities in the Study of Social Conflict*. New York: Free Press.

Daro, D. (1987). *Deaths Due to Maltreatment Soar: Results of the Eighth Semiannual Fifty-State Survey*. Chicago: National Committee for Prevention of Child Abuse.

Daro, D., and Cohn, A. H. (1988). "Child Maltreatment Evaluation Efforts: What Have We Learned?" In *Coping with Family Violence: Research and Policy Perspectives*, ed. G. T. Hotaling, D. Finkelhor, J. T. Kirkpatrick, and M. A. Straus. Newbury Park, CA: Sage Publications.

Elmer, E. (1967). *Children in Jeopardy: A Study of Abused Minors and Their Families*. Pittsburgh: University of Pittsburgh Press.

Finkelhor, D. (1984). *Child Sexual Abuse: New Theory and Research*. New York: Free Press.

Finkelhor, D., and Baron, L. (1986). "High-Risk Children." In *A Sourcebook on Child Sexual Abuse*, ed. D. Finkelhor. Newbury Park, CA: Sage Publications.

Finkelhor, D., and Korbin, J. (1988). "Child Abuse as an International Issue." *Child Abuse and Neglect: The International Journal* 12:3–23.

Freidrich, W., and Boriskin, J. (1976). "The Role of the Child in Abuse: A Review of Literature." *American Journal of Orthopsychiatry* 46:580–590.

Fuddy, L. (1992). "Hawaii's Healthy Start's Success." Paper presented at the Ninth International Conference on Child Abuse and Neglect, Chicago.

Galdston, R. (1965). "Observations of Children Who Have Been Physically Abused by Their Parents." *American Journal of Psychiatry* 122:440–443.

Garbarino, J. (1977). "The Human Ecology of Child Maltreatment." *Journal of Marriage and the Family* 39:721–735.

Garbarino, J., and Gilliam, G. (1980). *Understanding Abusive Families*. Lexington, MA: D. C. Heath.

Gelles, R. J. (1973). "Child Abuse as Psychopathology: A Sociological Critique and Reformulation." *American Journal of Orthopsychiatry* 43:611–621.

Gelles, R. J. (1983). "An Exchange/Social Control Theory." In *The Dark Side of Families: Current Family Violence Research*, ed. D. Finkelhor, R. Gelles, M. Straus, and G. Hotaling. Newbury Park, CA: Sage Publications.

Gelles, R. J. (1989). "Child Abuse and Violence in Single-Parent Families: Parent Absence and Economic Deprivation." *American Journal of Orthopsychiatry* 59:492–501.

Gelles, R. J. (1992). "Poverty and Violence Toward Children." *American Behavioral Scientist* 35:258–274.

Gelles, R. J., and Cornell, C., eds. (1983). *International Perspectives on Family Violence*. Lexington, MA: Lexington Books.

Gelles, R. J., and Straus, M. A. (1987). "Is Violence Toward Children Increasing? A Comparison of 1975 and 1985 National Survey Rates." *Journal of Interpersonal Violence* 2:212–222.

Gelles, R. J., and Straus, M. A. (1988). *Intimate Violence*. New York: Simon & Schuster.

Gil, D. G. (1970). *Violence Against Children: Physical Child Abuse in the United States*. Cambridge, MA: Harvard University Press.

Gil, D. G. (1975). "Unraveling Child Abuse." *American Journal of Orthopsychiatry* 45:346–356.

Greven, P. (1991). *Spare the Child: The Religious Roots of Punishment and the Psychological Impact of Physical Abuse*. New York: Alfred A. Knopf.

Jason, J.; Gilliland, J.; and Tyler, C., Jr. (1983). "Homicide as a Cause of Pediatric Mortality in the United States." *Pediatrics* 72:191–197.

Johnson, B., and Morse, H. (1968). "Injured Children and Their Parents." *Children* 15:47–152.

Kaufman, J., and Zigler E. (1987). "Do Abused Children Become Abusive Parents?" *American Journal of Orthopsychiatry* 57:186–192.

Kempe, C. H.; Silverman, F.; Steele, B.; Droegemueller, W.; and Silver, H. (1962). "The Battered Child Syndrome." *Journal of the American Medical Association* 181:17–24.

Korbin, J. (1981). *Child Abuse and Neglect: Cross-Cultural Perspectives*. Berkeley: University of California Press.

Maden, M. F., and Wrench, D. F. (1977). "Significant Findings in Child Abuse Research." *Victimology* 2:196–224.

Mayor's Task Force on Child Abuse and Neglect. (1983). *Report on the Preliminary Study of Child Fatalities in New York City*. New York: Author.

McCurdy, K., and Daro, D. (1993). "Current Trends in Child Abuse Reporting and Fatalities: NCPCA's 1992 Annual

Fifty-State Survey." Chicago: National Committee for Prevention of Child Abuse.

Milner, J. S., and Chilamkurti, C. (1991). "Physical Child Abuse Perpetrator Characteristics: A Review of the Literature." *Journal of Interpersonal Violence* 6:345–366.

Mitchel, L. (1989). "Report on Fatalities from NCPCA." *Protecting Children* 6:3–5.

National Center on Child Abuse and Neglect (NCCAN). (1988). *Study Findings: Study of National Incidence and Prevalence of Child Abuse and Neglect, 1988.* Washington, DC: U.S. Department of Health and Human Services.

Newberger, E.; Reed, J.; Daniel, J.; Hyde, J.; and Kotelchuck, M. (1977). "Pediatric Social Illness: Toward an Etiologic Classification." *Pediatrics* 60:178–185.

Olds, D. L.; Henderson, C. R., Jr.; Tatelbaum, R.; and Chamberlin, R. (1986). "Preventing Child Abuse and Neglect: A Randomized Trial of Nurse Home Visitation." *Pediatrics* 77:65–78.

Parke, R. D., and Collmer, C. W. (1975). "Child Abuse: An Interdisciplinary Analysis." In *Review of Child Development Research*, Vol. 5, ed. M. Hetherington. Chicago: University of Chicago Press.

Pelton, L. (1978). "Child Abuse and Neglect: The Myth of Classlessness." *American Journal of Orthopsychiatry* 48:608–617.

Peters, S. D.; Wyatt, G. E.; and Finkelhor, D. (1986). "Prevalence." In *A Sourcebook on Child Sexual Abuse*, ed. D. Finkelhor. Newbury Park, CA: Sage Publications.

Potts, D. A.; Herzberger, S. D.; and Holland, A. E. (1979). "Child Abuse: A Cross-Generational Pattern of Child Rearing?" Paper presented at annual meeting of Midwest Psychological Association, Chicago.

Radbill, S. A. (1980). "A History of Child Abuse and Infanticide." In *The Battered Child*, 3rd edition, ed. R. Helfer and C. H. Kempe. Chicago: University of Chicago Press.

Schmitt, B., and Kempe, C. H. (1975). "Neglect and Abuse of Children." In *Nelson Textbook of Pediatrics*, ed. V. Vaughan and R. McKay. Philadelphia: Saunders.

Smith, S.; Hansen, R.; and Nobel, S. (1973). "Parents of Battered Babies: A Controlled Study." *British Medical Journal* 5:388–391.

Spinetta, J., and Rigler, D. (1972). "The Child-Abusing Parent: A Psychological Review." *Psychological Bulletin* 77:296–304.

Starr, R. H., Jr. (1988). "Physical Abuse of Children." In *Handbook of Family Violence*, ed. V. B. Van Hasselt, R. L. Morrison, A. S. Bellack, and M. Hersen. New York: Plenum.

Steele, B. F., and Pollock, C. (1974). "A Psychiatric Study of Parents Who Abuse Infants and Small Children." In *The Battered Child*, ed. R. Helfer and C. H. Kempe. Chicago: University of Chicago Press.

Steinmetz, S. K. (1978). "Violence Between Family Members." *Marriage Family Review* 1:1–16.

Straus, M. A., and Gelles, R. J. (1986). "Societal Change and Change in Family Violence from 1975 to 1985 as Revealed in Two National Surveys." *Journal of Marriage and the Family* 48:465–479.

Straus, M. A.; Gelles, R. J.; and Steinmetz, S. K. (1980). *Behind Closed Doors: Violence in the American Family.* Garden City, NY: Doubleday/Anchor.

Texas Department of Human Resources. (1981). *A Study of Child Deaths Attributed to Abuse and Neglect.* Austin: Child Abuse and Neglect Resource Center.

Widom, C. S. (1989). "The Cycle of Violence." *Science* 244:160–166.

Wolfner, G., and Gelles, R. J. (1993). "A Profile of Violence Toward Children." *Child Abuse and Neglect: The International Journal* 17:197–212.

RICHARD J. GELLES

Emotional and Psychological Aspects

The effects of child abuse on a child's development and later adult behavior can be severely destructive, and recovery can be extremely difficult. The effects of child abuse can also be difficult to differentiate from other childhood trauma, such as poverty, disease, and accidents. In this entry, neglect, physical abuse, sexual abuse, and emotional abuse are all considered to be aspects of child abuse.

The abuse of children is widespread and has deep historical roots in American culture. Traditionally children have been viewed as "property" to be used by parents, especially fathers, as the adults saw fit. Societal intrusions into domestic relations were devalued and minimized. This traditional view of the family is in conflict with an emerging view that sees children not as the property of parents, but rather as a resource of society at large that parents "hold" in a sacred trust. These two belief systems are in conflict. This is illustrated by the emergence of large state-supported human service systems to investigate, prosecute, and treat child abuse. The beliefs that children are not the property of parents and that a child's healthy development is the business and responsibility of all individuals are based on a philosophy that views children as part of a larger social system. Essentially, how a child is parented is important to society because that child will eventually become an adult and function as part of the social environment. Therefore, society is a stakeholder in the future parents are creating. Society's "trust" is in their ability to produce a child who will be an effective, appropriate, and productive adult. Child abuse reduces the quality of the social environment by seriously diminishing the ability of future adults to be productive and contributing members of society.

Child abuse takes place in the context of a relationship between the child and another person who has the power to accomplish the abuse. This power may derive from the abuser's status as a parent or adult, or may derive from the abuser's superior physical and/or psychological strength. The victim's experience of the abuse can be evaluated across a number of variables.

Variables Related to Degree of Harm

Six variables that appear to influence the degree of harm done by the abuser are the duration of the abusive relationship, the severity of the abuse, the ability of the victim to predict the abuse, the degree of secrecy, the role of the abuser in the victim's life, and the ability of the victim to externalize the abuse.

Duration. The longer the abuse continues, the more harm will be done to the child. The child who suffers from one angry outburst by a parent who physically loses control will not be as likely to integrate the abuse into his or her identity. More than likely, the child will interpret this as a nonnormal event, and while the event may be traumatic and frightening, the victim will probably not develop a self-concept as a victim. This is especially true if the offending parent is responsible enough to admit to the overreaction. This kind of event occurs in a normally loving interactive and supportive parent–child relationship. In a parent–child relationship where physical harm is rare, but the parent communicates blame to the child for the parent's excessive behavior, then the victim will integrate the self-blame and tend to develop a self-image consistent with the parent's teaching. This kind of emotional abuse will tend to affect the victim more acutely the longer it continues. The combining of emotional abuse and neglect over long periods of time can severely affect the developmental process of the child. The general rule is that the longer the abusive relationship continues, the stronger the destructive effect on the child.

Severity. Extremely severe physical and/or sexual abuse, even for relatively short durations, can have strong effects on the victim. Especially devastating can be the coupling of physical abuse with the constant emotional abuse presented by the abuser's use of threats to ensure compliance.

Predictability. If the abuser's behavior is predictable, the child can gain some sense of control. If the abuser's threats are tied to specific behaviors that the child can understand, the child can act to limit the abuse. If the child's ability to predict the abuse accurately empowers the victim to act to avoid the worst of the abuse, the assumption is that the harm to the child will be modified. Families with a physically abusive father who abuses only when drinking learn to alter their behavior based on the father's alcohol intake. The alcohol abuse may serve as an early warning system to the coming of physical abuse.

Degree of secrecy. A child has access to other people who are able to label the abuse as inappropriate, and if they can provide an environment that counters the victim's sense of responsibility for the abuse, then the victim will be harmed less. If victims suffer alone, and exist in an environment of denial, they will internalize the abuse and blame themselves. Children who have little contact with anyone other than the abuser will be more likely to see themselves as the cause and deserving of the abuse. They will more likely "normalize" their victim experience.

Role of the abuser. It is assumed that a parent violation of the parent–child relationship is more devastating than an assault by a stranger. The greater the degree of trust normally associated by the child in the relationship, the greater the sense of betrayal and violation. Additionally, the greater the confusion of the child, the greater the development of distrust in his or her own perceptions.

Externalizing abuse. The more a child has accomplished in age-appropriate developmental tasks, the less likely he or she will be harmed by abuse. The important variable related to chronological age is the children's ability to externalize the abuse and not blame themselves. As children mature, they develop the skill to "objectify" themselves as part of the abusive environment. The greater the ability to see themselves as a recipient of abusive behaviors, rather than the cause, the greater will be their ability to reduce the effects of the abuse.

Guidelines for Ending Abuse

There is no one best intervention to prevent or to treat abusive relationships, because the effects of abuse vary. Each individual brings to the abusive relationship a unique history and the ability to use power; therefore, there are different means to end violence. No intervention can guarantee that there will be no future abuse, but the intervention that comes closest to being risk-free is the effective separation of the perpetrator and the victim. The best predictor of future abuse is past abuser behavior, which makes the separation of the abuser and abused appear to be an attractive option and often—especially in more severe cases—the safest and "cleanest" option. For practitioners in the field, however, the reality is often that separation by itself is not an effective option. For example, a mother who beats her child may lose that child to the social agency in charge of abuse, only to bear a new victim, who also may be removed after abuse is documented. The cycle can continue and may result in high economic and psychological costs. Another example would be a father removed by the criminal justice system, only to return secretly with the nonoffending parent's support. The answers to reducing child abuse are complex, but some guidelines exist to help provide support for ending abusive relationships.

Abuse thrives in a closed system. Physical abuse within the family is more likely to continue and increase in severity if the abuse is kept secret. The first expectation in the treatment of abusive relationships is the complete and open acknowledgment that abuse has occurred. Denial of the event by the perpetrator, nonoffending parent, siblings, or the victim will increase the danger of repetition. The more openly information about the abuse is shared, the greater the potential for reducing the destructive effects on the victim. Often, the denial by loved ones, such as the nonoffending parent or trusted school officials, can magnify the effects of the abuse on the victims. Intervention is in the best interest of the child. Families that solve this problem alone, within their own boundaries, are few. Families may not deny the abuse but will often attempt to minimize the effects. Victims are often quick to forgive in the hope that they can "put it all behind them."

Taking complete responsibility for one's own violent behavior is the second guideline. For abusers to take responsibility means that they must come to believe that violent behavior is a choice and that they can take control of their behavior. This means an understanding of a particular abuser's cycle of violence. They must believe and act upon the concept that their violence takes place within a context of beliefs and behaviors that lead to violence. They learn to predict violent behavior by identifying early warning behaviors and thoughts and then *choose* to alter their behavior. This type of intervention usually takes a great deal of time and work by the abuser. However, significant and real behavioral change by an abusing loved one can lead to important positive results for the victim.

Effects of Abuse

The effects of emotional, physical, and/or sexual violence on a child can take a variety of forms. Additionally, society is becoming more sensitized to the effects on children who are "secondary" victims of violence—children who are exposed to violence perpetrated not directly on themselves but rather on oth-

ers within their environment. A child who directly or indirectly observes a father physically abusing the child's sibling may suffer some of the same dysfunction as the victim.

The concept of "identification with the aggressor" may help to explain how many children are taught to normalize violence within the family whether or not they are direct victims. The child for whom violence becomes normal and familiar during childhood will be more likely to legitimize violence as an adult. One effect of abuse on children is that they will have a greater tendency to become either perpetrators or victims or both.

Research does not generally support the idea that abused children will become abusers; being an abused child does not lead automatically to becoming an abuser. Clearly, though, the child-abuse history of a perpetrator may be part of how the perpetrator learns, as a victim or secondary victim, to legitimize the use of violence. Becoming violent as a child and/or as an adult is one effect of child abuse.

Abuse often makes children more difficult to manage and nurture. This concept violates the cultural ideal that children are innocent, defenseless, and powerless. The very ability of children to learn and adapt often results in abused children learning coping mechanisms that inhibit normal development.

Children who are abused often develop effective denial systems to cope with the abuse. The child learns to "separate" or dissociate himself or herself from the abusive experience. This is a normal defense mechanism used to compartmentalize feelings or experiences too difficult to accept. For the abused child, the need to dissociate can be so strong that it has lasting destructive effects. Victims of child abuse demonstrate problems as adults that can interfere with their ability to parent effectively. The cycle of abuse then passes to the next generation. One key to breaking this cycle is to end the secrecy surrounding child abuse.

(*See also:* CHILD ABUSE AND NEGLECT: SOCIOLOGICAL ASPECTS; CHILD ABUSE AND NEGLECT: LEGAL ASPECTS; CHILD CARE; CHILDREN'S RIGHTS; DYSFUNCTIONAL FAMILIES; FAMILY VIOLENCE; INCEST; PERSONALITY DEVELOPMENT; SELF-ESTEEM)

BIBLIOGRAPHY

Azar, S. T., and Siegel, B. R. (1990). "Behavioral Treatment of Child Abuse: A Developmental Perspective." *Behavior Modification* 14:279–300.

Azar, S. T., and Wolfe, D. A. (1989). "Child Abuse and Neglect." In *Behavioral Treatment of Childhood Disorders*, ed. E. J. Marsh and R. A. Barkley. New York: Guilford.

Cicchetti, D. (1989). "How Research on Child Maltreatment Has Informed the Study of Child Development: Perspectives from Developmental Psychopathology." In *Child Maltreatment: Research and Theory on the Causes and Consequences of Child Abuse and Neglect*, ed. D. Cicchetti and V. Carlson. New York: Cambridge University Press.

Daro, D. (1990). *Confronting Child Abuse: Research for Effective Program Design*. New York: Free Press.

Fantuzzo, J. W. (1990). "Behavioral Treatment of the Victims of Child Abuse and Neglect." *Behavior Modification* 14:316–339.

Finkelhor, D.; Gelles, R. J.; Hotaling, G. T.; and Straus, M. A. (1983). *The Dark Side of Families*. Newbury Park, CA: Sage Publications.

Gelles, R. J. (1973). "Child Abuse as Psychopathology: A Sociological Critique and Reformulation." *American Journal of Orthopsychiatry* 43:611–621.

Gelles, R. J., and Straus, M. (1988). *Intimate Violence*. New York: Simon & Schuster.

Hansen, D. J., and MacMillan, V. M. (1990). "Behavioral Assessment of Child-Abusive and Neglectful Families." *Behavior Modification* 14:255–278.

Isaacs, C. D. (1982). "Treatment of Child Abuse: A Review of the Behavioral Interventions." *Journal of Applied Behavior Analysis* 15:273–294.

Kaufman, J., and Zigler, E. (1989). "The Intergenerational Transmission of Child Abuse and the Prospect of Predicting Future Abusers." In *Child Maltreatment: Research and Theory on the Causes and Consequences of Child Abuse and Neglect*, ed. D. Cicchetti and V. Carlson. New York: Cambridge University Press.

Kaufman, K. L., and Rudy, L. (1991). "Future Directions in the Treatment of Physical Child Abuse." *Criminal Justice and Behavior* 18:82–97.

Melton, G. B. (1990). "Child Protection: Making a Bad Situation Worse?" *Contemporary Psychology* 35:213–214.

Renvoize, J. (1993). *Innocence Destroyed*. New York: Routledge.

Straus, M. A.; Gelles, R. J.; and Steinmetz, S. (1980). *Behind Closed Doors: Violence in the American Family*. Garden City, NY: Doubleday/Anchor.

Wolfe, D. A. (1988). "Child Abuse and Neglect." In *Behavioral Assessment of Childhood Disorders*, 2nd edition, ed. E. J. Marsh and L. G. Terdal. New York: Guilford.

Wolfe, D. A. (1991). *Preventing Physical and Emotional Abuse of Children*. New York: Guilford.

STANLEY PARKER

Legal Aspects

Although children have always been vulnerable to abuse, exploitation, and neglect, the law has only recently provided them with any substantial refuge. Roman law, indeed, specifically permitted parents to expose infants immediately after birth and gave fathers the power of life and death over their offspring, as well as the right to sell them. Medieval civilization brought with it formal efforts by church and state to discourage infanticide and abandonment of children, but in practice the well-being of children still depended almost entirely on the disposition and resources of their parents (Duby 1988; Herlihy 1985). Before the modern era, orphans and abandoned children often depended on the kindness of strangers, yet the informal efforts of private individuals and communities may well have been remarkably effective both in saving the lives of those children and in providing them with a healthy context in which to grow.

Whether the Reformation and early modern times ushered in greater concern for, or repression of, children (or both at the same time) has divided historians (Ozment 1983; Stone 1979). In the 1700s, Sir William Blackstone ([1783] 1978, p. 452) summed up the English common law tradition, which was to become the basis for American law, in deceptively simple terms: "The power of a parent by our English laws is . . . moderate; but still sufficient to keep the child in order and obedience. He may lawfully correct his child, being under age, in a reasonable manner; for this is for the benefit of his education." Yet what was "moderate" power, and what was "reasonable" correction? Because children enjoyed no access to common law courts to complain of parental mistreatment, these questions were of little practical import. In Blackstone's view, moreover, parents were permitted to abandon, or refuse to support, their offspring, with only a small fine to fear as penalty.

Despite enormous efforts to improve the lot of children in the nineteenth and early twentieth centuries, no significant legal protections against child abuse and neglect existed until the mid-1960s. In the wake of a dramatic article by C. Henry Kempe and his colleagues (1962) documenting the "battered child syndrome"—which no doubt had all the more impact because of the enormous optimism of the period regarding government intervention as a means of solving social problems—a quiet revolution occurred in American law. By 1967, every state in the country had adopted a "child abuse" reporting statute. Soon after, Congress enacted the Child Abuse Prevention and Treatment Act of 1974 to establish the National Center on Child Abuse and Neglect and to encourage further development of state laws to protect children from maltreatment and neglect (Schwartz and Hirsh 1982). The result has been the creation of an extraordinarily complex body of law and an elaborate system of services, with each state—and often each city or county—presenting special problems of legal interpretation and administrative structure.

At the same time, however, the states have achieved a remarkable degree of consensus in their latter-day assault on child abuse and neglect. The 1974 federal act and its amendments established a variety of general guidelines for state legislation tied to significant financial incentives for states to conform. State legislatures eagerly swallowed the bait, and as a result it is possible to trace a variety of principles—as well as problems—common to laws addressing child abuse and neglect throughout the country and to identify the social services that those laws have produced.

Legal Definitions

While the initial attention of policymakers in the 1960s was focused on "battered" children, child protection law quickly developed a far broader reach. Now, all state laws cover not only affirmative misconduct of parents and caretakers toward children under eighteen years of age ("abuse"), but also the failure of those persons to provide for the needs of children in their care ("neglect"). Indeed, state laws typically include within their scope conduct of parents that threatens future harm to a child and circumstances (e.g., retardation or mental illness) that might in the future impair an adult's ability to provide adequate care for a child. Finally, better understanding of the wide variety of children's health and development needs has caused legislators to look beyond physical injuries to children and to include the sexual integrity and emotional health of children as objects of legal protection as well.

On the other hand, states have uniformly limited the reach of child abuse and neglect statutes to conduct by those responsible for the child's welfare. (Thus, an assault on a child by a stranger, or even a friend or neighbor would not, unless the adult was acting as a caretaker, constitute "abuse" or "neglect" under the law.) Likewise, state laws typically limit their scope to cases where, in the words of the Child Abuse Prevention and Treatment Act of 1974, the child's "health or welfare is harmed or threatened." This may exclude long-ago abuse or neglect that is not likely to be repeated, or more recent parental misconduct of a minor nature.

Apart from these general principles, however, the task of providing reasonably precise legal definitions of what conduct constitutes "child abuse" or "child neglect" has proved extremely difficult—so difficult, in fact, that the American Bar Association struggled for more than a decade to formulate "model" definitions before abandoning the task (Besharov 1985). Richard Gelles (1976) has maintained that, with mi-

nor exceptions such as filicide, there is no objective behavior that can automatically be recognized as child abuse; child abuse is the product of social labeling. Ultimately, state statutes have settled on a number of widely accepted labels to describe the scope of laws in the area, but they have left it to courts and child protection workers to provide working definitions of the terms.

"Physical abuse" typically refers to any bodily injury suffered by a child that has been willfully or negligently inflicted, or any injury for which a parent or custodian has not given an explanation or, most commonly, has given an explanation at odds with the medical evidence. While generally provoking the least controversy over its legal definition, physical abuse cases can present thorny problems in court. First, it is not always possible to distinguish cleanly between physical discipline of a child by a parent, which is sanctioned if "reasonable" by common law, and physical abuse. Second, the "reasonable" use of physical force on children is in part governed by cultural context. Vague statutory language gives no guidance as to whether Anglo-American standards of "reasonable" discipline will be enforced against parents of differing ethnic backgrounds, nor as to whether child-rearing practices (e.g., female circumcision) that other societies freely sanction constitute "abuse" in the United States. Third, even where the existence of physical abuse is undoubted, it is frequently difficult to determine which parent or caretaker is responsible, especially in cases involving infants or toddlers.

"Sexual abuse" is generally assumed to include any overt sexual contact with, or conduct toward, a child—specifically, sexual intercourse with a child, any other intentionally sexual touching of a child's genitals or intimate body parts, or the use of a child in pornography or prostitution. Other conduct may also, depending on context and local law, fall under the legal definition of "sexual abuse"—for example, exhibitionism and the intentional (but not sexually motivated) touching of a child's private parts. Because this sexual abuse is defined in significant part by the adult's intention, and because obtaining physical evidence to corroborate an allegation is frequently impossible, cases in this area present the knottiest problems of proof and the greatest risk of false accusations (Besharov 1990). Further, defining the limits of touching (or nudity) within a family or child-care context is often very difficult. In part because of the risks of erroneous outcomes and the mere "harm done by inquiry" in this volatile area, Joseph Goldstein, Anna Freud, and Albert J. Solnit (1979) have even urged that "sexual abuse" findings be confined to cases in which a parent has been convicted of a criminal sex offense against a child—a radical position not adopted by any state.

"Emotional abuse" or "psychological maltreatment" of children is covered by statute in many states, but its precise boundaries are extremely difficult to define. Douglas J. Besharov (1990) describes it as "an assault on the child's psyche, just as physical abuse is an assault on the child's body." Tying a child up, confining him or her to a closet, engaging in habitual patterns of belittling or scapegoating, or threatening a child with other forms of abuse are encompassed by this category (Sedlak 1991). Yet of all forms of abuse, this is the most difficult to separate from legitimate, if immature or overly angry, parenting, and states have approached it with far more caution when defining "child abuse" (Schwartz and Hirsh 1982). Further, it is this form of abuse that is most likely at trial to provoke disagreement among experts about its existence and, if it exists, the harm inflicted on the child.

"Neglect" is the legal category prompting more state intervention than any other and is covered by statute in all states. Its scope is the broadest, and some would say the vaguest, of all types of abuse and neglect. At its core, "neglect" refers to outright abandonment of a child or gross failure by a caretaker to provide basic physical necessities or critically needed medical treatment, but the language of state statutes typically extends far wider. Such statutes permit state intervention regarding any parental conduct or negligence that is "detrimental" to a child's "physical or mental health" or "morals." Some courts have ruled such language to be so vague or overbroad as to violate the constitutional right of parents to "family integrity" (*Alsager* v. *District Court* 1975). Many see in wide-ranging "neglect" jurisdiction grave risks of discrimination by child protective professionals against ethnic minorities and the poor through imposition of ill-defined middle-class parenting standards (Goldstein, Freud, and Solnit 1979). Others point to the overwhelming burden such broad authority places on the limited personnel and resources of state social service systems, which consequently limits the state's effectiveness in addressing the most serious cases of child endangerment (Besharov 1985).

Yet for all their definitional inadequacies, state statutes governing child abuse and neglect have survived virtually all attempts in court to strike them down and, if anything, enjoy broader public support than ever before. Indeed, public pressure has led since the 1970s to continual expansion of their scope—without substantial real increases in the commitment of re-

sources to the courts and government agencies designated with the task of protecting children.

The Child Protection "System"

The complexity of defining child abuse and neglect is mirrored in the systems established by state and federal law to address it. With regard to reporting requirements, investigative methods, adjudication standards, and placement/service options, states and communities differ widely on details, but again, a substantial range of consensus exists.

All states allow anyone, to begin with, to report, whether anonymously or not, the suspected abuse or neglect of a child and provide broad protections against liability for false reports as long as they are made in good faith. More crucially, however, every state mandates the reporting of cases raising reasonable grounds to suspect the existence of child "abuse" or "neglect" by a wide array of professionals, including physicians, nurses, coroners, dentists, mental health therapists, social workers, teachers, child-care workers, and law enforcement personnel. Many states add to mandated reporters others who have regular contact with children, such as pharmacists, foster parents, clergy, attorneys, substance abuse counselors, camp counselors, and family mediators. (A few states require reporting by virtually anyone coming in contact with a child, a mandate so broad as arguably to become meaningless.) Usually, the reporting requirement applies only to cases that come before these individuals in a "professional" or employment-related capacity. Failure to report a case falling under these requirements is typically ground for civil liability and criminal penalties, as well as professional sanctions.

States differ as to the agencies designated to receive reports of abuse or neglect, with city or county social service agencies, local police, or statewide "hot lines" as typical destinations. Once made, a report will both prompt an investigation of the child's circumstances and become part of state records permanently maintained in an office usually called the child abuse "registry." Those records are accessible not only to child protective personnel but also to private agencies and businesses providing care or services to children for the purpose of investigating the background of employees. Many states require such background checks on potential employees who will have regular contact with children.

The reporting system is vital to state intervention on behalf of children whose mistreatment would otherwise continue to be invisible, but the system has created its own share of special problems. The wide range of conduct included within legal definitions of abuse and neglect is compounded, with regard to reporting, by mandates covering even suspected maltreatment. Further, those mandates can often collide dramatically with expectations of confidentiality by parents seeking professional help, especially from attorneys, therapists, and clergy (Mosteller 1992). Those who are the subjects of unfounded reports may find that the continued presence of the reports in the state's registry damages their reputations and employment prospects, yet they may have only very limited opportunities to have the reports expunged (Phillips 1993). Finally, the very success of the reporting system is in some respects a danger to the rest of the system, for the careful investigation and disposition of more than 1.5 million reports nationally every year is a task arguably beyond even the best efforts of government agencies.

Once a report has been made, state laws or regulations usually provide that an investigation must commence within a few days. There typically is not, however, a time limit on when the investigation must end, and many children who are the subjects of reports face significant danger in the meantime. All states have procedures for summary removal of children from the home where reasonable cause exists to believe that they would face serious and imminent harm if left at home. State law may permit certain persons such as doctors or police officers to remove a child without a prior hearing. All states provide, however, for expedited court hearings at which the local child protective agency may request an order for summary removal, without any need to provide parents with prior notice or the opportunity to be present. If a child is summarily removed, however, state laws normally require that a full hearing must soon follow at which a parent can contest the action.

Ultimately, the factual determination as to whether a child has been abused or neglected occurs in court before a judge, but hearings in this area have several characteristics distinguishing them from most other court proceedings. First, they are not open to either the public or the press; names and records are kept confidential. Second, the judge before whom they are heard is usually designated specially to hear family and juvenile matters. While this can mean that these judges develop expertise in the area, it can also create a "ghetto" effect, with family courts receiving less attention and resources than other courts. Finally, rules of evidence in abuse and neglect hearings are in practice somewhat looser than in other proceedings; in particular, reports and records compiled by child protective personnel, social workers, and court-

appointed psychologists typically have enormous weight but are not easily challenged on grounds of hearsay nor subject to rigorous scrutiny for accuracy before being admitted.

The U.S. Supreme Court has ruled that parents do not have a constitutional right to court-appointed counsel at abuse and neglect hearings (*Lassiter* v. *Department of Social Services* 1981), but many states provide for it anyway. In practice, many parents choose not to contest their child's removal; rather than face allegations of abuse or neglect in court, they place their child in state care on a "voluntary" basis. The child on whose behalf the state has brought the petition may also, depending on state law, be entitled to separate, state-funded counsel. For immature or disabled minors it may also be necessary to appoint a "guardian ad litem," charged with representing the child's "best interests" to the court.

If the state demonstrates the presence of statutorily defined abuse or neglect by a preponderance of the evidence, the court will enter a finding against the parents and then choose among several options based on the court's assessment of the "best interests" of the child. The child may be sent back home, with or without court-ordered supervision and services. Occasionally a responsible relative or even a family friend may be given custody of the child. Most commonly after a finding of abuse or neglect, however, the child will be placed for an indefinite period in state-funded foster care.

State foster care originally took the form of orphanages or "houses of refuge" but now generally falls into one of two categories. Infants and younger children usually are placed in "foster families"—that is, with private individuals or couples who receive a stipend to care for the child and who are supervised by caseworkers of a state or private child-care agency. Adolescents and severely disabled children are frequently cared for in "group homes" with a small number of similar children by a rotating staff of child-care workers. Whatever its setting, foster care is in theory supposed to be strictly temporary, and federal law encourages vigorous efforts toward reunification of children with their biological or adoptive parents and a fresh court review every eighteen months after a placement in foster care (Child Welfare Act of 1980; Mnookin 1975).

Temporary displacement of parental custody is not by any means the state's most drastic option in cases of child maltreatment. Where "serious" or "permanent" neglect or abuse can be shown, the state may petition for termination of all of a parent's rights in a child, thus freeing the child for adoption by others. In

Santosky v. *Kramer* (1982), though, the U.S. Supreme Court held that the state must demonstrate parental misconduct or abandonment in termination proceedings by "clear and convincing evidence." In practice, this higher standard of proof makes such petitions far harder to sustain than those requesting mere removal from parental custody.

Even more punitive than the power of termination is the state's ability to prosecute parents and caretakers under criminal statutes forbidding the endangerment, abandonment, sexual exploitation, or abuse of a child. It is difficult to imagine that such statutes serve as much of a deterrent to parents not otherwise disposed to give decent care to their offspring; moreover, such prosecutions are relatively rare. The threat of criminal penalties can nevertheless be a potent asset to the state in persuading parents to agree to voluntary placement of their child or to provide no contest to placement proceedings. Yet this asset does not come without a price: The potential for prosecution can create tensions within the system between police and prosecutors on one side and child protective workers and family reunification specialists on the other, each side believing its jurisdiction should be primary. To reduce the potential for conflict, some communities have formed special teams or task forces bringing together representatives of all government agencies with potential interest in child maltreatment cases.

Special Issues

No amount of cooperation or tinkering, unfortunately, can fully resolve some of the fundamental dilemmas at the heart of society's effort to combat child abuse and neglect. Brief summaries of three such long-term challenges to the system follow.

Constitutional limits. Beginning in the 1920s, the U.S. Supreme Court began a long process of defining the right of parents to be free from state interference with decisions involving childbearing or child rearing. In the same period, the Court recognized the authority of government to protect children from "harm" at the hands even of their parents. With society's understanding of child development still at a relatively primitive level, however, the meaning of "harm," and so the boundary between state and parental power, are almost hopelessly muddled. The continuing expansion of parental conduct defined by medical science as "harmful" to children threatens the system with fundamental conceptual chaos. Thus, the use of drugs or alcohol by a pregnant woman, now known to endanger the unborn child, is viewed by some as clearly within the state's child-abuse jurisdiction, while others see such intervention as at best counterproductive and at worst a direct attack on the right to abortion granted women by the U.S. Supreme Court in 1973.

Evidentiary dilemmas. Once the concept of child abuse expanded beyond clearly visible physical injury to a child, the law has faced excruciating difficulties in obtaining useful and accurate evidence to support state intervention. The most telling examples have concerned sexual abuse cases wherein the state has often sought to use out-of-court statements of children as evidence as well as expert testimony based on such statements. Such testimony has been strongly indicted both for its high potential for error (Askowitz 1992; Coleman and Clancy 1990) and for its conflict with a defendant's right to effective cross-examination of witnesses against him or her (*Coy* v. *Iowa* 1988). Because many allegedly abused and neglected children are far too young to be able to testify credibly in court and because the conduct in question occurs in private, the risk of erroneous decision making will likely remain very high.

Foster care inadequacies. If the primary object of the child protective system is to help children and not simply to punish inadequate parents, then it may be considered successful only to the extent that its alternatives to parental care provide nurturing and long-term opportunities for successful growth into adulthood. However, the foster care system is frequently wanting in almost every respect. Many children are shuffled from one placement to another with numbing frequency (Mnookin 1975), and on leaving foster care in their late teens, many are grossly unprepared to live independently. Foster families often receive little training, supervision, or support (Mushlin 1988) and are even actively discouraged from becoming "too attached" to a child in their care (*In re Jewish Child Care Association* 1959). Yet because of the difficulty of meeting the high burden required to terminate parental rights, many children whose parents remain incapable of caring for them must languish in foster care with no hope of adoption or a comparably stable environment. Unless society is willing to direct far more energy and resources toward improving state-provided care for abused and neglected children, the noble government experiment with child protection may yet prove to be a dismal failure.

(*See also:* CHILD ABUSE AND NEGLECT: SOCIOLOGICAL ASPECTS; CHILD ABUSE AND NEGLECT: EMOTIONAL AND PSYCHOLOGICAL ASPECTS; CHILD CUSTODY; CHILDREN'S RIGHTS; FOSTER PARENTING; GUARDIANSHIP)

BIBLIOGRAPHY

Askowitz, L. R. (1992). "Comment: Restricting the Admissibility of Expert Testimony in Child Sexual Abuse Prosecution." *University of Miami Law Review* 47:201–240.

Besharov, D. J. (1985). "'Doing Something' About Child Abuse: The Need to Narrow the Grounds for State Intervention." *Harvard Journal of Law and Public Policy* 8:539–589.

Besharov, D. J. (1986). "Child Abuse: Arrest and Prosecution Decision Making." *American Criminal Law Review* 24:315–374.

Besharov, D. J. (1990). *Recognizing Child Abuse.* New York: Free Press.

Blackstone, W. ([1783] 1978). *Commentaries on the Laws of England.* New York: Garland.

Coleman, L., and Clancy, P. E. (1990). "False Allegations of Child Sexual Abuse." *Criminal Justice* 5:14–47.

Duby, G., ed. (1988). *A History of Private Life: Revelations of the Medieval World.* Cambridge, MA: Harvard University Press.

Fahn, M. S. (1991). "Allegations of Child Sexual Abuse in Custody Disputes." *Family Law Quarterly* 25:193–216.

Fossey, R. (1991). "Child Abuse Investigations in the Public Schools." *Education Law Reporter* 69:991–1008.

Gelles, R. (1976). "Demythologizing Child Abuse." *Family Coordinator* 25:135–141.

Gies, F., and Gies, J. (1987). *Marriage and the Family in the Middle Ages.* New York: Harper & Row.

Goldstein, J.; Freud, A.; and Solnit, A. J. (1973). *Beyond the Best Interests of the Child.* New York: Free Press.

Goldstein, J.; Freud, A.; and Solnit, A. J. (1979). *Before the Best Interests of the Child.* New York: Free Press.

Herlihy, D. (1985). *Medieval Households.* Cambridge, MA: Harvard University Press.

Kempe, C. H.; Silverman, F.; Steele, B.; Droegemueller, W.; and Silver, H. (1962). "The Battered Child Syndrome." *Journal of the American Medical Association* 181:17–24.

Light, R. J. (1973). "Abused and Neglected Children in America: A Study of Alternative Policies." *Harvard Educational Review* 43:556–598.

Martin, L. H. (1991). "Caseworker Liability for the Negligent Handling of Child Abuse Reports." *University of Cincinnati Law Review* 60:191–219.

Mnookin, R. (1975). "Child Custody Adjudication: Judicial Functions in the Face of Indeterminacy." *Law and Contemporary Problems* 39:226–293.

Mosteller, R. P. (1992). "Child Abuse Reporting Laws and Attorney–Client Confidences: The Reality and the Specter of Lawyer as Informant." *Duke Law Journal* 42:203–278.

Mushlin, M. B. (1988). "Unsafe Havens: The Case for Constitutional Protection of Foster Children from Abuse and Neglect." *Harvard Civil Rights–Civil Liberties Law Review* 23:199–280.

Ozment, S. (1983). *When Fathers Ruled: Family Life in Reformation Europe.* Cambridge, MA: Harvard University Press.

Phillips, M. R. (1993). "Note: The Constitutionality of Employer-Accessible Child Abuse Registries." *Michigan Law Review* 92:139–194.

Roncière, C. de la. (1988). "Tuscan Notables on the Eve of the Renaissance." In *A History of Private Life: Revelations of the Medieval World,* ed. G. Duby. Cambridge, MA: Harvard University Press.

Sedlak, A. J. (1991). "National Incidence and Prevalence of Child Abuse and Neglect: 1988." Report to National Center on Child Abuse and Neglect, Washington, DC.

Stone, L. (1979). *The Family, Sex, and Marriage in England, 1500–1800,* abridged edition. New York: Harper & Row.

Schwartz, A., and Hirsh, H. (1982). "Child Abuse and Neglect: A Survey of the Law." *Medical Trial Techniques Quarterly* 28:293–334.

CASES

Alsager v. *District Court of Polk County, Iowa* (Juvenile Division), 406 F.Supp. 10 (S.D. Iowa 1975), *aff'd* 545 F.2d 1137 (8th Cir. 1976).

Coy v. *Iowa,* 487 U.S. 1012 (1988).

Jewish Child Care Association, In re, 5 N.Y.2d 222, 156 N.E.2d 700 (1959).

Lassiter v. *Department of Social Services,* 452 U.S. 18 (1981).

Santosky v. *Kramer,* 455 U.S. 745 (1982).

PUBLIC LAWS

Child Abuse Prevention and Treatment Act of 1974, P.L. 93-247 (renamed Child Abuse Prevention and Treatment and Adoption Reform Act, codified at 42 U.S.C. § 5101, *et seq.*).

Child Welfare Act of 1980, P.L. 96-272 (codified at 42 U.S.C. § 670, *et seq.*).

GREGORY LOKEN

CHILD CARE

Broadly interpreted, the term "child care" includes all care provided for young children by persons other than the primary caregiver. In most families, mothers are the primary caregiver, but fathers, grandparents, and other individuals may also take this role. Individuals who provide child care include other family members, baby-sitters, and caregivers in center-based care. Lessons, clubs, and activities may function as child care if children attend regularly. Older children can sometimes care for themselves (Hofferth et al. 1991).

Child care also refers to the care used by employed parents. Most researchers have used this definition because it is assumed that care used for employment may differ from the care that a child would typically experience in a family. However, parents also use child care for shorter periods when they are engaged in activities such as shopping, errands, appointments, and leisure. Child care is also used to supplement a child's educational and social experiences.

Importance of Child Care

The economic structure of society has significantly influenced how families care for children (Lamb et al. 1992). Since women are usually the primary caregivers, the nature of their work roles has an important effect on child care. In the past, mothers, as well as fathers, could provide food, clothing, and shelter for their families through work located in or near the family home. As work became more mechanized with the Industrial Revolution, many men started working away from the home and child care became the primary responsibility of women.

Important changes have occurred in the composition of the labor force since 1960. For a variety of personal and economic reasons, most mothers with young children are now in the labor force. The percentage of American mothers, with children under the age of eighteen, in the labor force has risen from 18 percent in 1950 to 67 percent in 1991 (Lerner 1994). The responsibilities of employment outside the home have been combined with the traditional care of home and children.

The time when mothers work outside the home has also changed (U.S. Bureau of the Census 1990). Initially, women worked only before marriage, before children were born, or after children were mature enough to care for themselves (Ahlburg and De Vita 1992). Now, more than half (56%) of all mothers with children under one year of age are employed. The percentage of employed mothers with older children is even higher. Sixty-five percent of mothers with children age three to five, 73 percent of mothers with children age six to thirteen, and 76 percent of mothers with children age fourteen to seventeen are employed (Lerner 1994). When mothers simultaneously engage in employment and child rearing, supplemental caregivers are needed to care for young children (Moen 1992).

Available Child Care

Child care can be divided into three major categories: care in the child's home by relatives or nonrelatives, care outside the child's home by relatives or nonrelatives, and center-based care. There often is a great deal of variation within each of these categories,

including the time that care is available, the cost and quality of care, the professional status of the caregiver, and the relationship between the caregiver and the family. The age of the child and whether the mother is employed or a homemaker are major influences on the care arrangements used. Many families report that no one type of care is sufficient to meet all their child-care needs; they must use a variety of caregivers (Hofferth et al. 1992).

In many families, parents and relatives provide most of the child care. Some parents can work at different times, which means that there is always a parent at home to care for the children (Presser 1988). In other cases, older children (usually over the age of ten) care for younger siblings, especially when children need care for only a short period of time. However, mothers generally retain the major responsibility for children.

Grandparents and other relatives provide a great deal of care for families, ranging from occasional care for recreational purposes to full-time, regular care while the parents are employed. About 5 percent of children and their parents live in the grandparents' home, a pattern more common in African-American and Hispanic families. Relatives are especially important caregivers while the children are infants and toddlers, a time when other caregivers are difficult to find (Jendrek 1993). This care is unique because relatives have a past and anticipated future relationship and commitment to the children and may also care for them without charge.

Some individuals unrelated to the family also provide care in the child's home. Caregivers such as nannies may live in the family home and perform other household duties as well, while baby-sitters (often teenagers) provide occasional care for only a few hours. Some families jointly hire and share the services of an in-home caregiver. Other families form play groups for their children and trade child care on a regular basis.

Children also receive care outside their home. In 37 percent of the cases in 1988, care of children age five and under was provided in another home, either by a relative or a nonrelative (Lerner 1994). This care takes place in the form of family day care (home day care), the care of a small number of children, usually six or fewer, in a private home (Peters and Pence 1992). Many home day-care providers have young children of their own, but individuals without children or with grown children also become providers. Care on a regular basis is usually provided for a fee unless the caregiver is a relative. Some caregivers enroll a larger number of children and use additional adults to provide group day care (Kontos 1992). In most states, family day care is regulated through licensing or registration, although a majority of such homes are unregulated.

The small number of children in day-care homes produces a desirable adult–child ratio, although the quality and the stability of the care depend on the characteristics of the caregiver. While most providers have experience with young children, few may have formal training in child development. Providers may find home day care a positive way to combine care of their own children with the ability to earn income, but the presence of young nonfamily children in the home is stressful and the turnover rate of providers is high (Atkinson 1992; Nelson 1991).

Center-based child care is the most common arrangement for preschool children with employed mothers, but many mothers who are not employed also use center-based care for preschool children. This form of care has shown the largest increase in use since the early 1970s (Hofferth et al. 1991).

The programs are often staffed with professionally trained directors and teachers, and enrollment ranges from 15 to more than 100 children. Nursery schools generally provide a half-day program of cognitive enrichment and socialization for children three to five years of age. Although many educational philosophies exist, most programs provide hands-on learning experiences that help children learn about the world by experimenting with materials and ideas. A second goal for many nursery school programs is to help children learn how to function within a group and cooperate with peers and adults successfully. Cooperative programs have a paid professional head teacher but use parent volunteers for the rest of the teaching staff. Parents' day-out programs provide informal care for a few hours a week.

Most day-care centers include both all-day care and an educational program. Employed parents typically need child care from early in the morning to late afternoon, so teachers care for the children much of the day. The curriculum generally includes periods of active play, planned activities, rest periods, and meals and snacks. Most states set basic standards for centers in terms of programs, buildings and equipment, and staff certification. Some centers and caregivers meet even higher standards through accreditation by professional organizations. Although children often attend day-care centers when they are between two and five years of age, there is a growing demand for center-based programs for infants and toddlers. Religious organizations, employers, and community agencies sponsor

nonprofit centers to meet this need. Other centers operate as for-profit businesses (Klein 1992).

Older children also need care when school hours do not mesh with parental hours of employment. The term "latchkey child" reflects concern for children who spend significant amounts of time without adult supervision. In response, many programs have been developed to provide care before and after school, usually at the school itself, offering breakfast and snacks as well as supervision and games until parents can pick up their children. Approximately two million children are regularly unsupervised after school (Lerner and Galambos 1991). If children are sufficiently mature, parents can supervise from a distance (i.e., checking periodically in person or by telephone), and if the unsupervised time does not last too long, this experience may help children learn how to take responsibility for themselves.

Other programs provide services for children with special needs. Head Start, begun during the 1960s as part of the War on Poverty, is the best known. The goal of this program is to give young children a boost that will help them succeed in school and life. Activities are designed for cognitive stimulation, socialization, and emotional support. The programs also provide comprehensive services for parents and health and nutrition programs for children. "At-risk" programs provide comprehensive services for children considered to have a high risk of failure in school. An increasing number of programs are being developed in cooperation with public schools, and in some states, extensive programs are available to provide parents with support services and information about children from birth to eight years of age. In addition, a small but growing number of employers support child care by providing on-site care, information and referral services, flexible financial benefits, and flexible work schedules for parents (Kahn and Kammerman 1987).

Effects of Child Care

Much of the research since 1960 has investigated the positive and negative effects that child care may have on children. When mothers began entering the labor force in large numbers, experts in child development expressed concern about the effect of mothers' absences on the emotional relationship between children and parents. The emotional bond that begins early in life has a critical influence on a child's social, emotional, and cognitive development. Most experts agree that children need a stable and continuous relationship with a sensitive and responsive caregiver to develop a secure emotional attachment. Concern that this bond would be weakened when the child attended day care grew from studies of short-term and long-term parent–child separations. In these situations, children who were separated from their parents were later found to show permanent negative effects (Hayes et al. 1990).

Initial research with child care in high-quality university day-care centers found little evidence that day care produced damage to children. For children with restricted home environments, the high-quality child care often provided important benefits. Subsequent research in child care that more accurately represents typical arrangements has resulted in some concerns, especially for infants spending long hours away from parents.

More current research suggests that the *quality* of child care is a critical factor determining how children are influenced by child care. Researchers have shown that children with extensive nonparental care in their first year of life may be more highly influenced by the quality of the care than children who enter day care when older (Belsky 1990). In addition, the cultural context of the care may be a significant influence. For example, research has shown significant differences in effects of child care for children living in the United States and children living in Sweden (Lamb et al. 1992).

Other research has examined the effect of day care on children's social development. Children enrolled in child care typically have more experience interacting with peers than children raised at home, creating both positive and negative results. Children with child-care experience typically show greater independence, self-confidence, and social adeptness, but they may also show evidence of greater aggression and noncompliance to adult requests (Booth 1992). Research in programs such as Head Start found that children made initial gains in cognitive development as measured by IQ tests, but these differences in IQ levels later diminished after children attended elementary school (Booth 1992).

Characteristics of the children themselves have been found to be an important influence on their adaptation to day care. The age and consequent abilities of children are an important factor in how easily they adapt to changes in caregivers. Children between the ages of six and eighteen months, who are developing an understanding of permanence and change in their world, may find it difficult to adjust to a new caregiver. Older children with better language skills and a more sophisticated understanding of their environment can handle these changes more easily. Individ-

ual children also differ in the ease with which they handle adjustments. Children with an "easy" temperament can handle disruptions calmly, but children who are more sensitive to change require additional time and adult support. The child's gender may also influence adjustment. In some but not all studies, mothers' employment was found to have a negative effect upon boys and to have a positive or neutral effect upon girls (Lerner and Galambos 1991).

Research has also shown that parental selection of child care is an important variable that influences the effect of child care. Parents do not select child care randomly; they tend to choose care similar to their own family care. Families using poor-quality child care have often been found to have higher stress levels, and this poor-quality care may be especially damaging to children already living in less than supportive home environments. However, good-quality child care may be beneficial for these children, in compensation for stressful home environments (Belsky 1990).

The relationship between maternal employment and children's development is complex; there are many indirect linkages. Research studies have been limited in the scope of questions asked, and caution must be taken in generalizing. However, mothers' employment status by itself does not create a negative experience for children. To predict the effect of child care accurately, the characteristics of the child, his family, the child care, parental employment, and the context of the society must all be considered.

Availability, Cost, and Quality of Child Care

Experts disagree about the adequacy of the supply of child care. The cost of care has not gone up significantly since the mid-1970s, but the demand for care has greatly increased. Although this indicates that the supply of care must be meeting the demand for care, researchers point to the difficulties many families have in finding child care for employment. Part of the problem may be a shortage of the quality care wanted by parents, even though the overall supply of child care may be adequate. In addition, specific types of care are often hard to find, including care for infants, school-age children, children with special needs, and part-time care. There are also significant differences in the supply of child care in various regions of the country (Booth 1992).

Child care is a major expenditure for many families. For low-income families, the cost of child care may be similar to that for food and housing and take up to one-fourth or more of the family income. Some low-income families can find care subsidized by government programs, although this care is limited. Families with higher incomes may spend as little as 6 percent of their total income on child care, and families with sufficiently high income can take advantage of child-care tax credits. The cost of child care also differs by the type of care used. In-home care such as that provided by a nanny is generally the most expensive per hour; center-based care and family day care are usually in between; and care provided by relatives is the least expensive. Families who use child care for purposes of the child's enrichment pay more per hour than child care for purposes of parental employment, but the latter is used for more hours, resulting in a greater total cost of care (Blau 1991).

The quality of the child care is especially important when children spend many hours away from home. Experts define quality in different ways but generally agree on several important factors. The easiest aspects of quality to identify are those associated with the structure of the child care. These include the ratio of the number of adults to the number of children, the total number of children in a group, the education and training of the caregiver, and the continuity of caregivers. Interactive dimensions of quality may be even more important but are more difficult to measure. These include the relationship between the child and the caregiver; the program, including learning activities and unstructured time; the physical environment, including the organization of equipment and space; and the child's relationship with peers. To be effective, programs and activities should be sensitive to and fit the development level of the children (Hayes, Palmer, and Zaslow 1990).

Evaluation of care may vary depending on the experience of the person doing the evaluation. One may view care from a top-down perspective (characteristics of the setting, equipment, and the programs as seen by adults) or from the bottom up, as children experience care. Quality may also be viewed from the inside (staff) or from the outside (parents). A societal perspective may also be used to view child care, assessing how programs serve the community and the larger society. In a comparison of child care in different countries, Michael E. Lamb and his associates (1992) have documented how interpretations of quality differ according to the context and values of the community and family.

Parents generally say that they are satisfied with the child care they use, although some would prefer other care and many become more critical when they are no longer using the care. Parents say that the quality of the care is the characteristic most valued when selecting child care, and the most important

aspect of quality for parents is the nature of the provider–child relationship (Hofferth et al. 1992).

Selection of Child Care

Parents' actions and decisions are critical in the selection of child care. The search for good-quality child care requires an investment of parental time and energy and often begins with an assessment of family needs and values. How many hours a day is care needed and during what days in the week? Most child care used to meet employment needs is available during weekdays, but it may be difficult to find on weekends, during the night, or at other irregular time periods. The age of the children is also important; care is usually easier to find for children ages three to five than for infants and toddlers.

With this knowledge, parents can explore available child-care arrangements. Most parents say that they learn about their child care from friends, coworkers, and relatives. However, regulated family day care and day-care centers are listed with state agencies, and information and referral centers can provide personalized information and listings of caregivers with openings in a specific area.

Most parents need backup arrangements for times when the main caregiver is unavailable or the child is sick. Although the turnover rate of individual caregivers in center-based care is high, the service is usually continuous. However, if an individual caregiver is unable to work, the parent has to find a replacement. This problem is most severe for mothers with low income, and many jobs have insufficient leave time for child-care emergencies.

Finding suitable child care involves consideration of parental and child needs as well as the supply of child care and the demands of a job. It may be impossible to find one type of child care that will meet all these needs. Many families find it necessary to use several types of child care and caregivers to create an adequate system of care-giving arrangements.

Child-Care Policy Issues

Parents in the United States have primary responsibility for the quality of the care and the education of their young children. However, when children receive care through public funding, other issues emerge. Child care has also become an important business, with more than $40 billion spent yearly for child care. What rights and responsibilities should parents, employers, schools, religious groups, and the community have for child care? If governments certify that child care meets basic standards, what should these standards be? Should parents who do not work outside the home receive support for the care they provide for children?

There are no federal regulations regarding child-care facilities, and the standards set by states vary greatly. Some states require a degree in early childhood education or course work in child development, but little or no professional preparation is required in other states. Standards are usually the strongest in day-care centers. Family day-care providers are often required to have little formal preparation beyond first-aid or child-abuse training. Almost no regulations are placed on relatives or baby-sitters who provide care in the home, and the requirements for teaching pre-school children are generally lower than for teaching young children in public schools.

Although the care of young children is a private responsibility of parents, the well-being of children is also a societal concern. In some countries, this concern is expressed through government programs for all young children and their families through direct and indirect services. Child care in the United States is a normal part of life for most families and is used for a variety of purposes. However, there is no clear child-care policy and little coordination of information or services from groups providing and monitoring care. The challenge for child care is to ensure that children receive high-quality care the simultaneously addresses the needs of family members and the concerns of employers, caregivers, religious institutions, schools, and society.

(*See also:* DUAL-EARNER FAMILIES; FAMILY POLICY; FAMILY VALUES; GRANDPARENTHOOD; PERSONALITY DEVELOPMENT; SUBSTITUTE CAREGIVERS; WORK AND FAMILY)

BIBLIOGRAPHY

Ahlburg, D., and De Vita, C. J. (1992). "New Realities of the American Family." *Population Bulletin* 47(2). Washington, DC: Population Reference Bureau.

Atkinson, A. M. (1992). "Stress Levels of Family Day Care Providers, Mothers Employed Outside the Home, and Mothers at Home." *Journal of Marriage and the Family* 54:379–386.

Beardsley, L. (1990). *Good Day, Bad Day: The Child's Experience of Child Care.* New York: Teachers College Press.

Belsky, J. (1990). "Child Care and Children's Socioemotional Development." *Journal of Marriage and the Family* 52:885–903.

Blau, D. M. (1991). *The Economics of Child Care.* New York: Russell Sage Foundation.

Booth, A., ed. (1992). *Child Care in the 1990s: Trends and Consequences.* Hillsdale, NJ: Lawrence Erlbaum.

Bronfenbrenner, U. (1992). "What Do Parents Do?" In *Rebuilding the Nest: A New Commitment to the American Family,* ed. D. Blankenhorn, S. Bayme, and J. Bethke Elshtain. Milwaukee: Family Service America.

Clarke-Stewart, A. K. (1991). "A Home is Not a School: The Effects of Child Care on Children's Development." *Journal of Social Issues* 47:105–124.

Hayes, C.; Palmer, J. L.; and Zaslow, M. J., eds. (1990). *Who Cares for America's Children?* Washington, DC: National Academy Press.

Hofferth, S. L.; Brayfield, A.; Deich, S.; and Holcomb, P. (1991). *National Child-Care Survey, 1990.* Urban Institute Report 91-5. Washington, DC: Urban Institute Press.

Jendrek, M. P. (1993). "Grandparents Who Parent Their Grandchildren: Effects on Lifestyle." *Journal of Marriage and the Family* 55:609–621.

Kahn, A., and Kamerman, S. (1987). *Child Care: Facing the Hard Choices.* Westport, CT: Auburn House.

Klein, A. G. (1992). *The Debate over Child Care, 1969–1990,* Albany: State University of New York Press.

Kontos, S. (1992). *Family Day Care: Out of the Shadows and Into the Limelight.* Washington, DC: National Association for the Education of Young Children.

Lamb, M. E.; Sternberg, K. J.; Hwang, C. P; and Broberg, A. G., eds. (1992). *Child Care in Context.* Hillsdale, NJ: Lawrence Erlbaum.

Lerner, J. V. (1994). *Working Women and Their Families.* Newbury Park, CA: Sage Publications.

Lerner, J. V., and Galambos, N. (1991). *Employed Mothers and Their Children.* New York: Garland.

Moen, P. (1992). *Women's Two Roles: A Contemporary Dilemma.* Westport, CT: Auburn House.

Nelson, M. K. (1991). *Negotiated Care: The Experience of Family Day Care Providers.* Philadelphia: Temple University Press.

Peters, D. L., and Pence, A. R. (1992). *Family Day Care: Current Research for Informed Public Policy.* New York: Teachers College Press.

Phillips, D., ed. (1987). *Quality in Child Care: What Does Research Tell Us?* Washington, DC: National Association for the Education of Young Children.

Powell, D. R. (1989). *Families and Early Childhood Programs.* Washington, DC: National Assocation for the Education of Young Children.

Presser, H. B. (1988). "Shift Work and Child Care Among Dual-Earner American Parents." *Journal of Marriage and the Family* 50:133–148.

Reeves, D. L. (1992). *Child-Care Crisis: A Reference Handbook.* Santa Barbara, CA: ABC-CLIO.

Spodek, B., ed. (1993). *Handbook of Research on the Education of Young Children.* New York: Macmillan.

Steglin, D. A. (1992). *Early Childhood Education: Policy Issues for the 1990s.* Norwood, NJ: Ablex.

U.S. Bureau of the Census. (1990). "Who's Minding the Kids? Child-Care Arrangements, 1986–87." *Current Pop-*

ulation Reports. Series P-70, no. 20. Washington, DC: U.S. Government Printing Office.

Whitebook, M.; Howes, C.; and Phillips, D. (1989). *Who Cares? Child-Care Teachers and the Quality of Care in America*. Final Report: The National Child-Care Staffing Study. Oakland, CA: Child-Care Employee Project.

Zigler, E., and Lang, M. E. (1991). *Child-Care Choices: Balancing the Needs of Children, Families, and Society.* New York: Macmillan.

ALICE M. ATKINSON

CHILD CUSTODY

"Child custody" is the term used in the law to describe the bundle of rights and responsibilities that parents have regarding their biological or adopted children. Custody includes the right to have the child live with the parents and to make decisions about the health, welfare, and lifestyle of the child. In this entry, "child" refers to a minor under age eighteen years.

Issues about custody arise in three distinct contexts: when government proposes to interfere with parental custody in an intact family, when parents separate and a decision about custody must be made between them, and when third parties seek custody in preference to parents.

Intact Families

Parents who live together in an intact family make decisions for the children in their custody with relatively little interference from government. American law accords great deference to family autonomy and privacy. When governmental interference does occur, it is focused on and initiated by concern about harm to children.

The most important area in which government interferes with parental custody is in abuse and neglect situations. All states have statutes that give the juvenile court authority to remove children from the custody of their parents for failure to meet minimal societal norms of parenting. Although the statutes differ considerably from state to state, they typically authorize intervention because the child is physically or sexually abused or because the parent fails to provide necessary care, food, clothing, medical care, or shelter so that the health of the child is endangered (Clark 1988).

Allegations of parental misconduct are processed by the juvenile court, which, unlike other courts, is charged with investigating and evaluating the charges

for the purpose of initially providing services to the family so the child remains in the home if possible. These treatment and preventive services may interfere with parental custodial decision making by requiring certain conduct or providing supervision, but they do not remove the child from the residential custody of the parents.

If parental failure continues in spite of limited state intervention, the court, after a hearing, may order the child removed from the home and custody transferred to a public or licensed private social agency to provide care and treatment of the child. Although the legal process is a transfer of custody to an agency, the actual physical care of the child is then placed with foster parents (Wald 1976).

A transfer of custody by a juvenile court is a limited type of custody. It means that the physical care of the child is removed from the parental residence and decisions about the daily care of the child are made by the agency or by the foster parents; the right to make major decisions, such as decisions about religious training, surgery or other significant medical treatment, or consent to adoption by a new set of parents, remains with the child's parents. The term used to describe the right to make these major decisions is that of "parental rights."

The purpose of removing a child from the custody of parents in a juvenile court proceeding is to protect and provide for the child, with the ultimate objective of returning the child to a parental home that is adequate to meet at least minimal parenting requirements. Therefore, in addition to providing care for the child, the state is required by juvenile court statutes to attempt to rehabilitate the parents so they can adequately care for the child.

The ultimate state intervention in parental custody comes when the state alleges that the parents have not been rehabilitated and are not capable of caring for the child. At this point the proceeding is one to terminate the parental rights of the parents—that is, to end all rights to have the child live with them and to make decisions about the child. Termination of parental rights makes a child legally available for adoption, although adoption does not necessarily follow termination in all cases.

Obviously, a termination of parental rights is one of the most serious proceedings relating to parents and children. The U.S. Supreme Court has held that the burden of proof on the state is the heaviest one available: beyond a reasonable doubt. Most states require that counsel be appointed for parents who cannot afford their own, but the U.S. Supreme Court has held that due process does not require the appointment of counsel for an indigent person in a case where the weight of evidence favoring termination was sufficiently great that the presence of counsel would not have affected the outcome.

Separated Parents

The concept of child custody receives its major attention in the law when parents separate. At that point it is necessary to determine what living arrangements will be made for the children and how parents will exercise their custodial rights and responsibilities separately. The most common situation in which this occurs is when parents divorce and the family dissolves as an entity. Divorce severs the husband–wife relationship, but it does not end the parental relationships; it only alters those ties.

Types of custody. When parents separate, there are four different types of custodial arrangements available. These are sole custody, split custody, joint legal custody, and joint legal and physical custody.

Historically, sole custody was the only kind of custodial arrangement provided by the law when parents separated. It continues to be the most common custodial form. Sole custody means that the child resides with the parent awarded sole custody, and that parent has authority to make decisions for the child on lifestyle issues, such as education, religion, medical treatment, and general welfare. The other parent has the right of visitation but limited authority.

Split custody is really a form of sole custody, with the sole custody of the children divided between the parents; each parent has sole custody of one or more of the children. A very small number of custody arrangements involve split custody.

Joint custody is a relatively new custody form and was unknown in the law until the 1970s. Since then, however, almost all states have authorized courts to award joint custody. There are two types of joint custody. One form that has become popular is known as joint legal custody. In joint legal custody, the decision-making aspect of custody is separated from the physical care aspect. Both parents exercise decision-making authority for the child, but the child resides with one parent, usually the mother. In some states, joint legal custody with physical custody to one parent, usually the mother, is the most common postdivorce custody form.

The other type of joint custody is joint legal and physical custody, where the parents share decision-making authority and the child resides in both households. The amount of time may be equally divided between parental homes, or the child may spend a majority of time with one parent and a lesser amount with the other parent. The issue of how much time a parent must have a child for the arrangement to be considered joint physical custody is not addressed in the custody statutes. Eleanor E. Maccoby and Robert H. Mnookin (1993), who have conducted a large-scale study in California of divorce and child custody, asked parents for their perceptions of joint physical custody, or as they termed it, "dual residence." They found that if the child spent four or more overnights in a two-week period with each parent (about 28 percent of the time), the parents said the child lived with both of them.

Shared time or dual residence as a custody form has been controversial (Schulman and Pitt 1982). It is estimated that this form is used in less than 10 percent of all cases, but it seems to be gradually growing in popularity, probably reflecting changing parenting roles in intact families.

Standards for awarding custody. The universal rule that guides the courts in deciding which parent should have custody is "the best interests of the child." Although common law originally gave the father the right to custody of his children (Klaff 1982), American courts had adopted the best interests of the child as the polestar in custody decisions by the end of the nineteenth century (Grossberg 1985; Zainaldin 1979). For most of the twentieth century the best interests of the child was equated with mother custody, particularly for young children. Then, beginning in the 1970s, the preference for mothers began to disappear formally from the law, abolished by statute or case law in the wake of concerns about gender equity. Since then, the assessment of what is in the best interests of the child has been greatly influenced by *Beyond the Best Interests of the Child* (Goldstein, Freud, and Solnit 1979), a book that stressed the importance of the relationships, particularly the psychological ties that children have with their parents.

Parental sexual behavior is often brought to the attention of the court, to be considered in awarding custody. The general rule is that parental conduct that does not affect the child is not to be considered. Courts have differing reactions as to whether sexual behavior affects the care of the child. A parent who has a sexual partner move in with the family may find that some courts feel this affects parenting ability. Where the sexual partner is of the same gender as the parent, judicial reaction is even more problematic (Polikoff 1990).

Another issue that arises in custody decisions relates to whether the religious practices of a parent may be considered in awarding custody. The matter is complicated by the fact that the First Amendment protects the parent's religious views (Mangrum 1981). Courts, however, tend to consider whether the religious views of the parent will affect the child.

One thing that cannot be the controlling consideration in awarding custody is the racial identity of the child and the parents. The U.S. Supreme Court held in *Palmer* v. *Sidoti* (1984) that a custody decision cannot be based solely on racial considerations. In that case a divorced white mother who had been awarded custody of her daughter married a black man. The trial court had transferred custody of the child to her father, reasoning that living with her mother in a racially mixed home in the state of Florida would not be in the child's best interests. The U.S. Supreme Court reversed the decision. It said: "The effect of racial prejudice, however real, cannot justify a racial classification removing an infant child from the custody of its natural mother found to be an appropriate person to have such custody."

Application of "the best interests of the child" criterion implies that the court's decision will provide the very best possible solution for the child. Unfortunately, as numerous critics have pointed out, obtaining the best possible solution is more illusory than real. Human knowledge is too limited and problematic to give clear guidance when making decisions that will be affected by unpredictable future events. In addition, the courts often lack the time and staff to gather sufficient information with which to determine the best possible solution (Charlow 1987; Erlanger, Chambliss, and Melli 1987; Melli 1993; Mnookin 1975). Scholars have also expressed concern that the lack of predictability on what constitutes the best interests of the child encourages litigation—a result that is universally regarded as undesirable (Mnookin and Kornhauser 1979). Considerable attention has been devoted to searching for some limiting preference that would reflect the best interests of most children. The preference on which there has been the most agreement is that of the "primary caretaker" (Chambers 1984).

Regardless of the standard applied, the overwhelming number of children in single-parent families live with their mothers. Most studies show mother custody at about 70 percent to 80 percent, with father custody, split custody, and shared custody accounting for the rest (Maccoby and Mnookin 1993).

The role of the court. A custody arrangement is made by an order of the court as part of the divorce proceeding. However, in the great majority of cases the actual decision is made not by the court but by agreement of the parents. Most estimates are that 95 percent of the custody orders are based on parental agreement. In their California study, Maccoby and Mnookin (1993) found that only 3.5 percent of the cases required a decision by the court; the rest were arranged by the parents themselves or, if the parents were in disagreement, were negotiated and settled with the aid of their lawyers.

The role of the child. Given the importance of a custody determination to a child, several issues arise as to the role of the child in such a proceeding. Most states view the child's preference as relevant to a custody decision. The weight to be given to the child's wishes usually depends on the child's age and maturity of judgment. Some state statutes require that the child's preference be honored if the child is older than a certain age, such as fourteen years (Clark 1988).

A related issue is whether a child has a right to be represented in the custody proceedings. This issue recognizes the concern that custody litigation may lose sight of the best interests of the child. Hostile parents and their lawyers may fail to inform courts about issues important to the well-being of the child. Some statutes and courts have responded by requiring the appointment of a representative, sometimes called a guardian ad litem, for the child ("Lawyering for the Child" 1978; Mnookin 1975). The U.N. Convention on the Rights of the Child (1989) provides in Article 12 that states should assure a child the right to be heard in custody proceedings either directly or through a representative.

The role of mediation. When parents are in conflict about the custodial arrangements, there is substantial agreement that the traditional dispute resolution process of the law, litigation, is not suited for the problem. The most frequently suggested alternative is mediation (Milne and Folberg 1988). A few states, such as California and Wisconsin, have mandatory mediation of custody disputes; other states make mediation available to disputing parties. The research on mediation is very limited, but it appears to result in more user satisfaction than do litigation experiences (Pearson and Thoennes 1988). However, its use is controversial. Critics claim that mediation results in undesirable shared custody arrangements (Bruch 1988), and feminists express concern about unfair pressures on mothers in the process (Grillo 1991).

Modification of custody. Custody arrangements are not final; they may be changed by the parties or modified by the court. Maccoby and Mnookin (1993) found that over the three and a half years of their study, there was a fair amount of change in the residential arrangements of the children. Mother sole custody was the most stable arrangement, with 81 percent of the children who lived with their mother at the time of the first interview still living there at the time of the third interview. The other two types of physical custody arrangements, father custody and dual residence, were much less stable, with 51 percent of the children in those arrangements making at least one change.

In addition to informal changes made by the parties themselves (these are often not ratified by a change in the formal court order), the court may modify the custody award because it is never considered a final order and is, therefore, subject to modification. This nonfinality for custody orders reflects concern about the need to protect children from harmful circumstances, but it conflicts with an equally important policy favoring stability for children. For this reason there has been a clear trend in the law toward making changes difficult, discouraging parents from relitigating custody decisions. Most states, for example, limit the consideration of a custodial change to situations where it can be shown that there has been a change in circumstances since the date of the custody decree, or where evidence not considered by the court in granting the decree is now presented for the first time. Some jurisdictions are even more restrictive, prohibiting the consideration of requests for changes for a set period of time, such as two years after the entry of the original order, unless the existing physical custody arrangement seriously endangers the child.

Once the set of conditions for considering a custody change has been established, the issue is whether a change in custody is in the best interests of the child. Again, concern that custodial change is not good for the child is an important consideration. Usually, there is a presumption that staying in the present placement is in the child's best interest. Apart from concerns about changing children's living situations, courts consider the same kinds of issues on modification as they do in making the original order.

Concerns about the ability of parents to relitigate the issue of custody has also resulted in federal legislation, known as the Parental Kidnapping Prevention Act (1980), that requires states to give full faith and credit to custody decrees of the child's home state. Historically, a parent dissatisfied with a custody decision could take the child and file a petition for custody in the state of that parent's current residence. Because jurisdiction over custody was based on the presence of the child in the state, that court had jurisdiction to modify the earlier order.

Joint physical custody poses particular problems of modification because any change in parental circum-stances can easily upset a complicated dual residence arrangement. Therefore, courts are more willing to consider requests to change dual residence arrangements. Usually, for example, a prohibition against change in custody for the first two years after the original order is not applied to joint physical custody situations.

Relocation by the custodial parent. One of the most problematic custody issues is not a change in custody but a proposed move by the custodial parent. In America's mobile society, the custodial parent may decide to move for a better job or job prospects, to be near helpful family members, or because of remarriage. Unfortunately, if the new place of residence is at a considerable distance, the visitation rights of the noncustodial parent may be severely limited by the move. Consequently, some states by statute require the custodial parent to seek court permission to move, or the divorce decree may contain a prohibition against moving by the custodial parent. Usually, the move that is prohibited is outside the state, but the issue is really one of distance, and some statutes recognize this.

Most cases condition relocation on the best interests of the children but are inconsistent in how they assess the best interests issue. Some require the custodial parent to show that the move is for a good reason, but judicial reactions to whether the reason is good vary. Other courts allow the custodial parent to move unless the noncustodial parent shows that the move is not in the child's best interests. Some scholars see a prohibition on the move by the custodial parent as an unconstitutional infringement on the parent's right to travel (Spitzer 1985).

Searching for a proper balance in relocation cases is difficult. For one thing, there have been no legislation or judicial decisions restricting a noncustodial parent who wishes to move a long distance even though that will limit visitation just as much as a move by the custodial parent. Critics also point out that most custodial parents are mothers, and the willingness of courts to discount their reasons for moving may amount to gender bias (Patis 1986).

Visitation. When one parent has sole physical custody, which is the situation in about 90 percent of the cases, the other parent is entitled to spend time with the child during what is usually called "visitation." The term is very inadequate to describe what society hopes will continue to be a meaningful relationship between the child and the noncustodial parent. Therefore, some states have tried other terms to describe the arrangement, such as "parent–child contact time" or "physical placement."

Visitation is usually regarded as a right of the noncustodial parent to which that parent is entitled unless visitation would seriously harm the child. Therefore, a custodial parent who objects to visitation by the noncustodial parent has the burden of showing that contact with the child's other parent would be harmful to the child.

Difficult situations are presented to decision makers when the conflict between the parents is so great that the children are drawn into it and object to seeing a parent because they have, in effect, taken the view of the parent with whom they live. However, even when children object to seeing their noncustodial parent, most courts will order visitation.

The prevailing rule that the noncustodial parent has a right to see and spend time with the child, absent a showing of some type of harm to the child, reflects a public policy recognizing that continued contact with both parents is desirable. Although it has been argued that stability and a positive relationship with one parent are the most important factors in the development of a child and that parental conflict over the noncustodial parent's time with the child is so divisive that it ought to be controlled by the custodial parent (Goldstein, Freud, and Solnit 1979), the value of continued association with both parents is supported by the weight of social science research (Maccoby et al. 1993). Continued contact with a noncustodial parent is important to a child in terms of both social and financial support. There is evidence, for example, that noncustodial parents who visit their children more frequently also pay more child support (Anditti 1991; Dudley 1991; Seltzer, Schaeffer, and Charng 1989).

The most common visitation arrangement is overnight every other weekend (Maccoby and Mnookin 1993; Wallerstein and Kelly 1980). Maccoby and Mnookin found that for the families they studied overnight visitation was also the most stable arrangement, remaining fairly constant over the three and a half years of the study. Daytime visitation in mother residence families (more than two-thirds of the cases in the study) was much more unstable; children with no regular visitation with fathers had increased from 25 percent at the first interview to 39 percent at the end of the study. For children in father residence the picture was quite different; the proportion of children with daytime visits with their noncustodial mothers increased from 16 percent to 36 percent, while no visits dropped from 39 percent to 18 percent.

Enforcement of visitation. When the custodial parent interferes with or prevents visitation by the noncustodial parent, the principal remedy of the law is contempt of court with a fine or imprisonment.

Such a severe remedy against a custodial parent is, of course, rarely used. Some courts and legislatures have provided for the reduction or withholding of child support in response to visitation infractions (Czapanskiy 1989). Unfortunately, such a remedy primarily affects the child.

Custody between unmarried parents. Increasing numbers of children are born to parents who are not married to each other and who may not even live together. In those cases, the custodial rights of the father are dependent, first of all, on the establishment of paternity. Historically, even after paternity was established, the mother had a superior right to custody of the child. Since about 1970, however, developments in the law regarding the constitutional rights of unmarried fathers have raised questions about this maternal preference. There is a definite trend in the law toward applying the same rules to custody disputes between unmarried parents as between married parents, particularly in cases where the unmarried father has lived with and cared for the child. The unmarried father who has never lived with the child or established a parent–child relationship in some other way may find his custody rights to be more limited than those of the mother.

Third-Party Disputes

A child custody dispute may arise between a parent and a nonparent in a variety of contexts. Perhaps the most common situation involves a stepparent. Stepfamilies are a fast-growing family type; estimates of divorced custodial parents who remarry range as high as 70 percent (Buser 1991; Chambers 1990). Other cases in which a nonparent may seek custody involve the same-gender partner of the child's parent; another relative; or a third party with whom a parent has placed the child during an extended period. In all of these cases, the child may have lived with the nonparent for most of the child's life, and the nonparent may have been the primary caretaker of the child, forming a very close psychological parent–child bond.

In these types of custodial disputes, the nonparent faces two hurdles. The first is that the court may find that it has no authority even to hear the petition of the nonparent for custody. Only about 50 percent of the states have enacted legislation that gives courts jurisdiction to hear these petitions (Victor, Robbins, and Bassett 1991). The second problem faced by a nonparent seeking custody is that the rule of the best interests of the child, which guides decisions between parents, is not controlling. On the contrary, the traditional rule is that in a custody dispute between a parent and nonparent, the parent is entitled to custody unless that parent is found to be unfit (Buser 1991; Clark 1988). The effect of giving primacy to the interests of the biological parent when the other choice is a nonparent means that the best interests of the child may be disregarded. Therefore, some state statutes explicitly provide for the use of a best interests of the child rule in these cases. Courts sometimes adopt that rule even in the absence of legislation (Clark 1988; Victor, Robbins, and Bassett 1991).

Legal scholars have puzzled over the persistence of a rule that seems to place the child's best interests after those of the parent. Probably the most important factor in these cases is concern about the importance of "blood" ties and the belief that the child's biological parent will in the long run be the most successful caretaker for the child. In addition, there is often a sympathy for a biological parent who has, perhaps after a period of years, now realized how important the child is (Chambers 1990). Finally, in the case of the same-gender partner, the court may express some of the societal ambivalence toward that family form.

Custody for nonparents is an area in which the law is developing and in which changing values and attitudes may result in changes in the law. This is particularly true as the importance of the concept of the psychological parent is more widely accepted (Clark 1988).

Nonparents often seek another custodially related right, that of visitation. Here they have been more successful, perhaps because one of the major nonparent groups interested in securing visitation rights has been grandparents, who have shown themselves to be very effective lobbyists (Clark 1988). All fifty states have statutes authorizing courts to grant visitation rights—if in the best interests of the child—to grandparents and also in some cases to other nonparents. Usually, these other nonparents are limited to close relatives or to nonparents who have lived with the child in a parent–child relationship (Victor, Robbins, and Bassett 1991).

(*See also:* CHILD ABUSE AND NEGLECT: LEGAL ASPECTS; CHILDREN'S RIGHTS; CHILD SUPPORT; DIVORCE: LEGAL ASPECTS; DIVORCE: EFFECTS ON CHILDREN; FOSTER PARENTING; GAY AND LESBIAN PARENTS; GRANDPARENTHOOD; GUARDIANSHIP; REMARRIAGE AND CHILDREN; SUBSTITUTE CAREGIVERS)

BIBLIOGRAPHY

Arditti, J. A. (1991). "Child Support Noncompliance and Divorced Fathers: Rethinking the Role of Parental Involvement." *Journal of Divorce and Remarriage* 14:107–120.

Bruch, C. S. (1988). "And How Are the Children? The Effects of Ideology and Mediation in Child Custody Law and the Children's Well-Being in the United States." *International Journal of Law and the Family* 2:106–126.

Buser, P. J. (1991). "The First Generation of Stepchildren." *Family Law Quarterly* 25:1–18.

Chambers, D. L. (1984). "Rethinking the Substantive Rules for Custody Disputes in Divorce." *Michigan Law Review* 83:477–569.

Chambers, D. L. (1990). "Stepparents, Biologic Parents, and the Law's Perception of 'Family' After Divorce." In *Divorce Reform at the Crossroads*, ed. S. D. Sugarman and H. H. Kay. New Haven, CT: Yale University Press.

Charlow, A. (1987). "Whose Child Is It Anyway? The Best Interests of the Child and Other Fictions." *Yale Law and Policy Review* 5:267–290.

Clark, H. H., Jr. (1988). *The Law of Domestic Relations in the United States*, 2nd edition. St. Paul, MN: West Publishing.

Czapanskiy, K. (1989). "Child Support and Visitation: Rethinking the Connections." *Rutgers Law Journal* 20:619–665.

Dudley, J. R. (1991). "Exploring Ways to Get Divorced Fathers to Comply Willingly with Child Support Agreements." *Journal of Divorce and Remarriage* 14:121–135.

Erlanger, H. S.; Chambliss, E.; and Melli, M. S. (1987). "Participation and Flexibility in Informal Processes: Cautions from the Divorce Context." *Law and Society Review* 21:585–604.

Furstenberg, F. F., Jr., and Cherlin, A. J. (1991). *Divided Families.* Cambridge, MA: Harvard University Press.

Goldstein, J.; Freud, A.; and Solnit, A. J. (1979). *Beyond the Best Interests of the Child*, 2nd edition. New York: Free Press.

Grillo, T. (1991). "The Mediation Alternative: Process Dangers for Women." *Yale Law Journal* 100:1545–1610.

Grossberg, M. (1985). *Governing the Hearth.* Chapel Hill: University of North Carolina Press.

Jacob, H. (1988). *Silent Revolution.* Chicago: University of Chicago Press.

Klaff, R. (1982). "The Tender Years Doctrine: A Defense? *California Law Review* 70:335–372.

"Lawyering for the Child: Principles of Representation in Custody and Visitation Disputes Arising from Divorce." *Yale Law Journal* 87:1126–1190.

Maccoby, E. E.; Buchanan, C. M.; Mnookin, R. H.; and Dornbusch, S. M. (1993). "Postdivorce Roles of Mothers and Fathers in the Lives of Their Children." *Journal of Family Psychology* 7:24–38.

Maccoby, E. E., and Mnookin, R. H. (1993). *Dividing the Child.* Cambridge, MA: Harvard University Press.

Mangrum, R. C. (1981). "Exclusive Reliance on Best Interest May Be Unconstitutional: Religion as a Factor in Child Custody Cases." *Creighton Law Review* 15:25–82.

Melli, M. S. (1993). "Toward a Restructuring of Custody Decision Making at Divorce: An Alternative Approach to the Best Interests of the Child." In *Parenthood in Modern*

Society, ed. J. M. Eekelaar and P. Sarcevic. Dordrecht, Neth.: Martinus Nijhoff.

Milne, A., and Folberg, J. (1988). "The Theory and Practice of Divorce Mediation: An Overview." In *Divorce Mediation*, ed. J. Folberg and A. Milne. New York: Guilford.

Mnookin, R. H. (1975). "Child Custody Adjudication: Judicial Functions in the Face of Indeterminacy." *Law and Contemporary Problems* 39:226–293.

Mnookin, R. H., and Kornhauser, L. (1979). "Bargaining in the Shadow of the Law: The Case of Divorce." *Yale Law Journal* 88:950–997.

Patis, A. G. (1986). "Residence Restrictions on Custodial Parents: Sex-Based Discrimination?" *Golden Gate University Law Journal* 16:419–484.

Paul, J. C. (1989). "You Got the House. I Get the Car. You Get the Kids. I Got Their Souls. The Impact of Spiritual Custody Awards on the Free Exercise Rights of Custodial Parents." *University of Pennsylvania Law Review* 138:583–613.

Pearson, J., and Thoennes, N. (1988). "Divorce Mediation Results." In *Divorce Mediation*, ed. J. Folberg and A. Milne. New York: Guilford.

Polikoff, N. (1990). "This Child Does Have Two Mothers: Redefining Parenthood to Meet the Needs of Children in Lesbian-Mothers and Other Nontraditional Families." *Georgetown Law Journal* 78:459–575.

Schepard, A. (1985). "Taking Children Seriously: Promoting Cooperative Custody After Divorce." *Texas Law Review* 64:687–788.

Schulman, J., and Pitt, V. (1982). "Second Thoughts on Joint Custody: Analysis of Legislation and Its Implications for Women and Children." *Golden Gate University Law Review* 12:539–571.

Scott, E. (1992). "Pluralism, Parental Preference, and Child Custody." *California Law Review* 80:615–672.

Seltzer, J. A.; Schaeffer, N. C.; and Charng, H. (1989). "Family Ties After Divorce: The Relationship Between Visiting and Paying Child Support." *Journal of Marriage and the Family* 51:1013–1031.

Spitzer, A. L. (1985). "Moving and Storage of Postdivorce Children: Relocation, the Constitution, and the Courts." *Arizona State Law Journal* 1985:1–78.

United Nations Convention on the Rights of the Child. (1989). *International Legal Materials*, Vol. 48. New York: United Nations.

Victor, R. S.; Robbins, M. A.; and Bassett, S. (1991). "Statutory Review of Third-Party Rights Regarding Custody, Visitation, and Support." *Family Law Quarterly* 25:19–57.

Wald, M. (1976). "State Intervention on Behalf of Neglected Children." *Stanford Law Review* 28:623–706.

Wallerstein, J. S., and Kelly, J. B. (1980). *Surviving the Breakup*. New York: Basic Books.

Weitzman, L. J. (1985). *The Divorce Revolution*. New York: Free Press.

Zainaldin, J. S. (1979). "The Emergence of Modern American Family Law." *Northwestern University Law Review* 73:1038–1089.

CASE

Palmer v. *Sidoti*, 104 S.Ct. 1879 (1984).

STATUTE

Parental Kidnapping Prevention Act, 28 U.S.C. §1738A (1980).

MARYGOLD S. MELLI

CHILDHOOD

Childhood is usually defined in relation to adulthood: the condition of being an immature person, of having not yet become an adult. In some societies, physical or reproductive maturity marks the transition to adulthood, but in modern Western societies full adult status is not usually achieved until several years after puberty. Childhood is legally defined here as a state of dependency on adults or as the status of those excluded from citizenship on the grounds of their youth. Dependence and exclusion from citizenship are in turn justified in terms of young people's incapacity to look after themselves or their emotional and cognitive unfitness for adult rights and responsibilities. Hence, psychological immaturity becomes a further criterion for deciding who counts as a child. The definition of childhood, then, involves complex cultural judgments about maturity and immaturity, children's assumed capabilities, and their difference from adults. Therefore, childhood is a social category, not merely a natural one.

Modern legal systems institutionalize childhood by setting an age of majority at which a person becomes a legal subject responsible for their own affairs and able to exercise citizenship rights. The United Nations Convention on the Rights of the Child defines a child as anyone under the age of eighteen unless, under the laws of his or her country, the age of majority comes sooner. Even with such legalistic dividing lines, there are still areas of ambiguity. Within any one country there may be various markers of adult status, so that one ceases to be a child for some purposes while remaining one for others. For example, the right to vote and the right to marry without parental consent may be acquired at different times.

Modern Western Conception of Childhood

Childhood has not been defined and experienced in the same ways in all societies at all times. The modern

Western conception of childhood is historically and culturally specific. Philippe Ariès (1962) was one of the first to suggest that childhood is a modern discovery. He argued that in medieval times children, once past infancy, were regarded as miniature adults; they dressed like adults and shared adult's work and leisure. Children were not assumed to have needs distinct from those of adults, nor were they shielded from any aspects of adult life. Knowledge of sexual relations was not considered harmful to them and public executions were a spectacle attended by people of all ages. In claiming that there was no concept of childhood prior to modern times, however, Ariès overstated his case (see Pollock 1983; Archard 1993). Shulamith Shahar (1990) suggests that medieval thinkers did see young children as being less developed in their mental and moral capacities than adults. It is clear from Ariès's own evidence that children did not always do the same work as adults and that they occupied a distinct place within society.

David Archard (1993) makes a useful distinction here between a concept of childhood and a conception of childhood. A concept of childhood requires only that children are in some way distinguished from adults; a conception entails more specific ideas about children's distinctiveness. The existence of a concept of childhood in the past does not mean that those people shared the modern conception of childhood. Medieval writers thought of childhood rather differently from how it is viewed today. They dwelt on the status and duties of children and on the rights accorded them at various stages of maturity (Shahar 1990). Childhood was defined primarily as a social status rather than as a psychological, developmental stage. Attitudes to children began to change, very slowly, in the sixteenth and seventeenth centuries, affecting upper-class boys first, then their sisters (Ariès 1962; Pinchbeck and Hewitt 1969). By the nineteenth century, middle-class children were confined to home and school, but many working-class children continued to work and contribute to the support of their families (see Davin 1990; Pinchbeck and Hewitt 1973). Gradually, however, children as a whole were excluded from the adult world of work and the period of dependent childhood lengthened.

Both historians and anthropologists have argued that modern Western societies make an unusually sharp distinction between childhood and adulthood. (Ariès 1962; Benedict 1938; Mead and Wolfenstein 1955). Western children are excluded by law and convention from many aspects of adult social life. They spend most of their time either within their families or within institutions designed to care for, educate, or entertain them separately from adults. They therefore have little contact with adults outside the circle of family and friends apart from child-care professionals. Many of the special arrangements made for children serve to emphasize their difference from adults: their clothes, toys, games, songs and books, even the colors of their bedrooms. Children are treated not simply as inexperienced members of society, but as qualitatively different from adults.

Childhood is also conceptualized as a process of development toward adulthood. In the nineteenth century, childhood began to be mapped out as a series of developmental stages that determined the character of the adult individual. Both Archard (1993) and Nikolas Rose (1989) accord a decisive role at this time to the emerging discipline of psychology. Rose argues that in making it the object of scientific inquiry, psychology constructed or invented childhood and claimed a particular expertise in categorizing children, measuring their aptitudes, managing and disciplining them—and has done so ever since (Rose 1989).

Living in a society where childhood is thought of as a series of developmental stages has specific effects on children. For example, schooling is organized as a series of age-graded progressions, which means that children are not only relatively segregated from adults but also from children of different ages. Children themselves acquire ideas about what is appropriate for people of their own age and may try to negotiate specific freedoms or privileges on this basis. Ordering children's lives in this way also influences what they are capable of achieving. It has been argued that the restriction of children to age-graded institutions may help to construct the very developmental stages that are seen as universal features of childhood (Skolnick 1980; Archard 1993). For a child to behave in the manner of someone older is often thought inappropriate, so the term "precocious" has become an insult. Age-grading may help to keep children childish. Historical and anthropological evidence suggests that children in other societies and in the past were far more independent and capable of taking care of themselves than Western children are today (Jackson 1982).

The idea of childhood as a developmental phase means that childhood is usually seen as important largely in terms of its consequences for adulthood. This is, as a number of researchers have pointed out, a very adult-centered view (Leonard 1990; Thorne 1987; Waksler 1986). Children are thought of as incomplete adults whose experiences are not worth investigating in their own right, but only insofar as they constitute learning for adulthood. Developmental theories presuppose that children have different capacities at different ages, yet children are frequently characterized as the polar opposites of adults: children are dependent, adults are independent; children play, adults work; children are emotional, adults are rational. The definitions of both childhood and adulthood are, moreover, gendered. Models of ideal adulthood are frequently in effect models of manhood, so that there is often a correspondence between attributes deemed childish and those deemed feminine—such as emotionality—and conversely those deemed adult and masculine—such as rationality (Jackson 1982; Thorne 1987).

The definition of childhood as a developmental stage and psychological state masks the fact that it is still a social status. Because childhood is defined as a stage or state of incapacity, children are thought to be incapable of exercising adult rights. There is considerable debate about whether this assumption is justified or not and about what rights are appropriate to children (see Thorne 1987; Archard 1993). Childhood is an exclusionary status (Hood-Williams 1990) in that children are neither citizens nor legal subjects and are under the jurisdiction of their parents. Their subordinate position is also evident in their interaction with adults. A child is expected to be deferential and obedient; a "naughty" child is one who defies adult authority.

Children Within Families

Within families, children are defined as dependents, subject to parental authority. Economic dependence is a crucial, and often neglected, aspect of children's status within families (see Leonard 1990; Hood-Williams 1990; Delphy and Leonard 1992). Children's lifestyles are dependent on their parents' income and their parents' decisions about how that income should be spent. The goods children receive come in the form of gifts or maintenance; they have things bought for them rather than buying them for themselves. Children can exercise choice over these purchases only if their parents allow them to choose. A child may well receive pocket money, or money as gifts, but this too is given at adults' discretion and adults may seek to influence how it is spent. Dependent, adult-mediated consumption is one facet of the power that parents have over children.

It has been argued that parents today have less power and autonomy than in the past because child rearing is now policed and regulated by experts and state agencies (Donzalot 1980; Ehrenreich and English 1978). Nonetheless, parents have a great deal of latitude in rearing their children as they wish, in setting acceptable standards of behavior, and in deciding what their children should eat and wear and how they should be educated and disciplined. Others' interference in these matters is regarded as violation of family privacy and an assault on parents' rights. Because modern families are seen as private institutions, state or public regulation generally only intrudes where parents are deemed to have abused their power or not exercised it effectively enough—where children are abused, neglected, or delinquent. As Barrie Thorne (1987) points out, the situation of children enters the public domain only when they are seen as victims of adults or a threat to adult society. Children also come into public view if their parents separate and contest custody, asserting the primacy of his or her rights over those of the other. Only during the late twentieth century have children been accorded any rights in deciding with which parent they prefer to live.

John Hood-Williams (1990) argues that children's lives within families are regulated in unique ways. Confinement to highly localized, restricted social spaces is part of the everyday parameters of childhood, as is the ordering of children's time by others. Childhood is also remarkable, says Hood-Williams, for the degree of control exercised over the body by others. Children's deportment, posture, movement, and appearance are regulated; they are touched, kissed, and fussed over to a degree unparalleled in any other social relationship. Children are also the people most likely to be subject to corporal punishment; many American and British parents hit their children on occasion (Gelles 1979; Newsom and Newsom 1965, 1968).

Styles of child rearing, however, have become undoubtedly less authoritarian than they were in the late nineteenth century. Increased concern about children's special needs has resulted in more emphasis on the quality of child care, and each new model of child development has involved changes in standards of ideal parenting, especially mothering (see Hardyment 1983). Families are often described as child-centered. Certainly children's needs are given a high priority, but these are defined for them by adults, tied in part to the responsibility placed on parents to raise children who will conform to wider social norms. It is widely recognized that socialization, or the social construction of subjectivity, of identities, desires, and aptitudes begins with early experience of family life.

An important aspect of this process is the reproduction of family members, of each new generation of adults who will marry and have children. Although family structures are changing, the majority of the Western population still fulfills these expectations. To take up positions as husbands and wives, fathers and mothers, individuals are required to be identifiably masculine or feminine and to be predominantly heterosexual. Despite opposition from feminist, lesbian, and gay activists, the family remains a heterosexual institution founded on hierarchies of age and gender (see Delphy and Leonard 1992).

This raises questions about how childhood experiences influence sexual and romantic desires and expectations of marriage and family life. Much of what children learn derives from their experience of family life and the sense they make of it. This is evident, for example, in the way young children play house, recreating the patterns of relationships they see around them. The single most important factor in the shaping of future sexual and familial identities and experiences is gender. To enter into any social relationships whatsoever, children must be defined, and must position themselves, as girls or boys; there is no gender-neutral option. Gender then becomes an organizing principle around which sexual, emotional, and romantic desires are ordered (Jackson 1982; Davies 1989; Crawford et al. 1992).

Sexual learning in early childhood, for both sexes, is limited by adults' concealment of sexual knowledge from children. Children usually first learn about sexual relations as a reproductive, heterosexual act, but this does not mean that children learn nothing else of sexual significance. They learn, for instance, about bodily attractiveness, deportment, and modesty in a way that is shaped by adult sexual assumptions and impinges particularly on girls (Jackson 1982; Haug 1987). They become acquainted with codes of romance from such sources as fairly tales (Davies 1989). This is true of both sexes, but again it is girls who are encouraged to take part in feminine romantic rituals and to become more fluent in discourses of love and emotion (Jackson 1993). Numerous researchers suggest that romantic ideals profoundly affect the way in which young women later come to terms with their sexuality (Lees 1993; Thompson 1989; Thomson and Scott 1991). Boys, on the whole, become less emotionally fluent, find intimacy problematic, and make sense of sexuality through a language of masculine bravado (Seidler 1989; Wood 1984). This may help set the pattern, so often observed in studies of marriage, where women seek forms of emotional closeness that men are unable to provide (Cancian 1989).

Nancy Chodorow (1978) argues, from a psychoanalytic perspective, that this pattern of heterosex-

ual incompatibility is reproduced because women care for children. Girls grow up in a close identificatory relationship with their mothers and so develop the desire to nurture and be nurtured. Boys can establish their masculinity only by distancing themselves from the feminine, becoming more autonomous and less able to establish emotional closeness with others. This process is envisaged as occurring largely at an unconscious level. Other perspectives suggest that children's emotional and sexual desires develop through their active negotiation of gendered positions within the social world (Davies 1989; Haug 1987; Jackson 1993; Crawford et al. 1992). In either case, the experiences of children have an effect on their later lives and on the expectations they bring to adult sexual, marital, and family relationships.

(*See also:* CHILD ABUSE AND NEGLECT: SOCIOLOGICAL ASPECTS; CHILD CUSTODY; CHILDREN'S RIGHTS; FAMILY GENDER ROLES; FAMILY POLICY; GENDER; GENDER IDENTITY; HISTORY OF THE FAMILY; PERSONALITY DEVELOPMENT)

BIBLIOGRAPHY

Archard, D. (1993). *Children: Rights and Childhood.* London: Routledge & Kegan Paul.

Ariès, P. (1962). *Centuries of Childhood.* London: Jonathan Cape.

Benedict, R. (1938). "Continuities and Discontinuities in Cultural Conditioning." *Psychiatry* 1:161–167.

Cancian, F. (1989). *Love in America.* Cambridge, Eng.: Cambridge University Press.

Chodorow, N. (1978). *The Reproduction of Mothering.* Berkeley: University of California Press.

Crawford, J.; Kippax, S.; Onyx, J.; Gault, U.; and Benton, P. (1982). *Emotion and Gender: Constructing Meaning from Memory.* Newbury Park, CA: Sage Publications.

Davies, B. (1989). *Frogs and Snails and Feminist Tales.* Sydney: Allen and Unwin.

Davin, A. (1990). "When Is a Child Not a Child?" In *The Politics of Everyday Life*, ed. H. Corr and L. Jamieson. London: Macmillan.

Delphy, C., and Leonard, D. (1992). *Familiar Exploitation.* Oxford: Polity.

Donzalot, J. (1980). *The Policing of Families: Welfare Versus the State.* London: Hutchinson.

Ehrenreich, B., and English, D. (1978). *For Her Own Good: 150 Years of Experts' Advice to Women.* New York: Doubleday.

Gelles, R. (1979). *Family Violence.* Newbury Park, CA: Sage Publications.

Hardyment, C. (1983). *Dream Babies: Child Care from Locke to Spock.* London: Jonathan Cape.

Haug, F., ed. (1987). *Female Sexualization.* London: Verso.

Hood-Williams, J. (1990). "Patriarchy for Children: On the Stability of Power Relations in Children's Lives." In *Childhood, Youth, and Social Change: A Comparative Perspective,* ed. L. Chisholm, P. Buchner, H.-H. Kruger, and P. Brown. London: Falmer.

Jackson, S. (1982). *Childhood and Sexuality.* Oxford: Basil Blackwell.

Jackson, S. (1993). "Even Sociologists Fall in Love: An Exploration in the Sociology of Emotions." *Sociology* 27:201–220.

Lees, S. (1993). *Sugar and Spice: Sexuality and Adolescent Girls.* London: Penguin Books.

Leonard, D. (1990). "Persons in Their Own Right: Children and Sociology in the UK." In *Childhood, Youth, and Social Change: A Comparative Perspective,* ed. L. Chisholm, P. Buchner, H.-H. Kruger, and P. Brown. London: Falmer.

Mansfield, P., and Collard, J. (1988). *The Beginning of the Rest of Your Life.* London: Macmillan.

Mead, M., and Wolfenstein, M. (1955). *Childhood in Contemporary Cultures.* Chicago: University of Chicago Press.

Newsom, J., and Newsom, E. (1965). *Patterns of Infant Care in an Urban Community.* London: Penguin Books.

Newsom, J., and Newson, E. (1968). *Four Years Old in an Urban Community.* London: Penguin Books.

Pinchbeck, I., and Hewitt, M. (1969). *Children in English Society,* Vol. 1. London: Routledge & Kegan Paul.

Pinchbeck, I., and Hewitt, M. (1973). *Children in English Society,* Vol. 2. London: Routledge & Kegan Paul.

Pollock, L. A. (1983). *Forgotten Children: Parent–Child Relations from 1500–1900.* Cambridge, Eng.: Cambridge University Press.

Rose, N. (1989). *Governing the Soul: The Shaping of the Private Self.* London: Routledge & Kegan Paul.

Seidler, V. (1989). *Rediscovering Masculinity.* London: Routledge & Kegan Paul.

Shahar, S. (1990). *Childhood in the Middle Ages.* London: Routledge & Kegan Paul.

Skolnick, A. (1980). "Children's Rights, Children's Development." In *Children's Rights and Juvenile Justice,* ed. L. T. Empey. Charlottesville: University of Virginia Press.

Thompson, S. (1989). "Search for Tomorrow: On Feminism and the Reconstruction of Teen Romance." In *Pleasure and Danger,* ed. C. Vance. London: Pandora.

Thomson, R., and Scott, S. (1991). *Learning About Sex: Young Women and the Social Construction of Sexual Identity.* London: Tufnell Press.

Thorne, B. (1985). "Revisioning Women and Social Change: Where Are the Children?" *Gender and Society* 1:85–109.

Waksler, F. C. (1986). "Studying Children: Phenomenological Insights." *Human Studies* 91:71–82.

Wood, J. (1984). "Groping Towards Sexism: Boys' Sex Talk." In *Gender and Generation,* ed. A. McRobbie and M. Nava. London: Macmillan.

STEVI JACKSON

CHILDREN'S RIGHTS

A country can be judged by countless measures, but for many the most significant are its treatment of children under eighteen years of age and the legal protection that society affords them. Although most people profess to love children, is this merely an abstraction, or are political and social environments truly child-centered? Are children accorded the rights, dignity, and benefits worthy of their status as citizens and human beings, or does their legal incapacity result in their needless subjection to abuse, exploitation, and other dangers? Does society permit, to the detriment of children, the unrestricted exercise of parental prerogative and the neglect of elected officials who realize that "children don't vote"?

Since the late 1960s, the American legal system has been responding more favorably to these questions, but many advocates for children believe it still has far to go. The "children's rights movement" began in the late 1960s and has been an effort by organized advocacy groups, academics, lawyers, lawmakers, judges, and others to help the law evolve into a more humane instrument on behalf of the country's most vulnerable population. The pace of legal developments in the field of children's rights has been steadily accelerating, and the issues dealt with today differ considerably from those in the 1960s and 1970s. During those decades, children's rights, especially to the public, meant that children should receive (except where clearly inappropriate) the same freedoms and treatment accorded to adults. This included the right to liberty, free speech, and due process of law—all areas where major legal battles were fought.

Because of that brief focus of the movement on giving children many of the same rights as adults, the cause of children's rights has often wrongfully been viewed by many as simply a war of youth liberation or overcoming adult oppression of young people. However, freedom from parental authority, control, and discipline has never been a major theme of serious children's rights advocates. Most groups have focused on child victims of abuse and neglect and how government agencies can better protect them. The most active advocates for children in America are not engaged in a drive to secure children's independence from adult supervision, but rather are addressing such issues as improving the country's system of enforcing child support obligations, preventing child sexual exploitation, and helping assure that children receive adequate education and health care.

Early Children's Rights Activity

Early American history largely consigned children to the status of parental property or chattel (primarily the father's chattel). This was an import from the laws of England. Absolute parental control of the child, unfettered by the state, was largely a reflection of the agrarian society and the family itself as a work unit. Even where a child became orphaned or was so severely mistreated by parents or guardians that courts sentenced the abusers to prison, the child would often be indentured into the service of a new parent-master. This concept of children having an economic value was matched with even sterner religious views of the time, in which children were seen as inherently evil and needing a strict, punitive upbringing.

In the nineteenth century, there was a level of children's rights activity unmatched before or since. "Child saving" became a central theme of social reformers who wanted a public policy shift from punishment to education and rehabilitation. Many private, public, and especially progressive religious organizations became involved in efforts to create institutions—orphanages, houses of refuge, and reform schools—for abandoned, destitute, delinquent, wayward, and vagrant youths. Societies for the prevention of cruelty to children were established. The first child labor and compulsory schooling laws were enacted. Just before the turn of the twentieth century, these new concepts of child protection were institutionalized in the country's first juvenile courts, the earliest being in Chicago in 1899. By 1917, all but three states had such special courts.

Until the mid-1960s, the focus of most U.S. Supreme Court attention to children's rights centered on conflicts between parents and the state. For example, the 1923 decision in *Meyer* v. *Nebraska* enunciated the fundamental legal right of parents to establish a home and bring up children, including dictating their education. In that case, the Court struck down a state law prohibiting foreign-language education in all primary schools. The Court held that the community's interest in children—resulting in the dictating of educational policy—could not prevail over parents' rights to control their child (and thus the child's education). Essentially, this opinion of the Court strongly asserted the doctrine of parental ownership of children, and it has been relied on in other children's rights cases before the Court. An example was *Parham* v. *J.R.*, a 1979 decision permitting parents to commit their children to mental institutions, as long as a neutral fact-finder

had reviewed the situation and found the commitment to be medically justified.

There was, however, one important pre-1960 U.S. Supreme Court decision that remains a hallmark of legal articulation of the rights of children. In 1944, the Court recognized, in the case of *Prince* v. *Massachusetts*, a broad *parens patriae* (also known as in loco parentis) responsibility of government to intervene to protect children from parentally inflicted harm. In upholding a state's child labor laws, the Court stated that the family itself was not beyond regulation in the public interest and that the state had a wide range of power for limiting parental freedom and authority in matters affecting the child's welfare. This decision is frequently cited in lower-court opinions approving medical care and other needed services for children over parental objections. No statement of the Court on children's rights is as powerful as its pronouncement in *Prince* that, although parents may be free to become martyrs themselves, they are not free to make martyrs of their children.

Contemporary Children's Rights Movement

At about the middle of the twentieth century, the term "best interests of the child" began to be used regularly by judges in court opinions related to child custody. By the early 1960s, concern about child abuse had finally emerged as a public policy issue. The concepts of "best interests" and "child protection" are difficult to define narrowly, but they remain the cornerstone of children's rights policy.

In 1967, the U.S. Supreme Court issued a decision that marked a new era in the relationship between children and the legal system. For close to seventy years, the country's juvenile courts had largely acted as informal community tribunals where rules of evidence, due process, legal representation, and other elements of the justice system that adults had come to take for granted were often largely ignored. In the case of *In re Gault*, nullifying a juvenile delinquency adjudication and sentence that had been given by a juvenile court without the affected child being afforded the right to counsel, the Supreme Court clearly rejected the unrestricted authority of the "benevolent" juvenile court system that permitted children to be incarcerated without the legal protections afforded adults. *Gault* breathed new life into the phrase "children's rights."

It is important to note that the *Gault* case only addressed such due process issues as the right to legal representation in the context of cases where children's liberty could be restricted for commission of an offense. There is yet to be an analogous Supreme Court ruling on the constitutional right of abused, neglected, and abandoned children to be represented by counsel in judicial matters affecting them. Likewise, the Supreme Court has never entertained any case suggesting the constitutional need for children affected by custody, visitation, or adoption actions to receive independent legal representation (and few states have laws mandating such representation for children).

In another pivotal decision, *Tinker* v. *Des Moines Independent Community School District*, the Court in 1969 struck down a school policy prohibiting the wearing of black armbands (worn to protest the war in Vietnam) by students. Rights under the First Amendment of the Constitution, said the Court, are available to students unless their exercise would materially and substantially disrupt the work and discipline of the school. School students do not shed their constitutional rights to freedom of speech or expression at the schoolhouse gate, stated the Supreme Court in a most important pronouncement.

Within a few years of the Supreme Court issuing such pivotal decisions as *Gault* and *Tinker*, writing on children's rights began to multiply. One of the most important of these articles was "Children Under the Law" (Rodham 1973), which thoroughly explored the implications of legal issues that were then quite new to American jurisprudence.

The article discussed such matters as the direction in which laws related to the protection and procedural rights of children were likely to evolve; the areas in which the rights of children might responsibly be extended; and how attorneys could use the law creatively to do something meaningful for delinquents and severely abused children and their families. It never advocated more widespread litigation by children against their parents, but rather called for children to be provided with independent legal counsel in all existing court actions where their interests were being adjudicated. It further supported legal protection against the harm that government may itself cause to children and asserted that it was important to recognize the limited ability of the legal system to prescribe and enforce the quality of social arrangements.

This article was one of the first by a legal scholar to express concern about the potential evils of government intrusion into family autonomy and privacy under the guise of child protection. It asserted that intervention by instruments of the state is fraught with peril and that children and their families, once caught in the web of the system, may have virtually no power, or even a voice, to make that system meet their needs.

Standards on the Rights of Children

Proclamations on the rights of children are not new. President Herbert Hoover's White House Conference on Child Health and Protection in 1930 issued a Children's Charter, and subsequent White House Conferences on Children have produced similar documents. Many of these look remarkably like more contemporary articulations of rights for children. In 1959, the United Nations approved a modest but much-cited ten-point Declaration of the Rights of the Child. In the early 1970s, writers John Holt and Richard Farson both promulgated bills of rights for children, as did New York attorneys Henry Foster and Doris Jonas Freed.

To mark the twentieth anniversary of the U.N. Declaration of the Rights of the Child, the United Nations proclaimed 1979 the International Year of the Child and embarked on a decade-long project to place into international treaty form the values contained in the declaration. What emerged in 1989, the Convention on the Rights of the Child, is a comprehensive compilation of rights of children—including civil-political, economic-social-cultural, and humanitarian—for all nations of the world to use as a common agreement on the minimum rights that governments should guarantee to children. The convention is drafted in language that strongly emphasizes the rights of the individual child, rather than collective children as members of families or groups. It has been called a "Magna Carta for children."

The convention had been signed or ratified by most of the nations of the world by 1995, including almost all the world's democracies. The United States, which was not among them, has been very slow to take presidential or senatorial action on international human rights treaties, and for many years this convention has been under study by the federal executive branch. The comprehensiveness of the convention's text, coupled with the fact that many of the rights articulated within it fall within the jurisdiction of state rather than federal law, have contributed to the convention getting bogged down in the bureaucracy.

Prior to this convention, there had been more than eighty international legal instruments developed over a sixty-year period that in some way addressed the special status of children. However, the new convention is the penultimate articulation of children's rights in the sense that when nations ratify it they become bound by its provisions. The many articles of the convention stress the importance of actions being in the best interests of the child; recognize the child's evolving capacities; provide protection to the child from abuse, neglect, and exploitation; address the child's civil rights and rights in the juvenile justice system; affect the child's ability to be heard and represented meaningfully in official actions; focus on the child's right to an adequate education, standard of living, health and rehabilitative care, mental health, adoption, and foster care services; place importance on the child's access to diverse intellectual, artistic, and recreational resources; and protect children from involvement in armed conflict.

Some state legislatures have enacted their own state bills of rights for children and, in particular, addressed the needs of child victims of crime. There also have been proponents of federal and state constitutional amendments that address the rights of children. However, the amount of legislative activity related to children's rights statements specifically has been very limited.

Questions for the Future

In 1992, a twelve-year-old Florida boy brought the issue of children's rights to the forefront of America's consciousness. He was known only as Gregory K., and he simply wanted a "place to be," a permanent home (i.e., adoption) rather than a string of foster care placements.

While he was in state-sponsored foster care, Gregory sought to commence termination of his biological mother's parental rights, citing the fact that he had spent only a few months in her care during the previous eight years. Because Gregory did not proceed in the usual way (i.e., through an adult guardian, guardian *ad litem*, or "next friend"), he raised a still unsettled question that is at the heart of the children's rights struggle: Should children have standing to commence, be parties to, and be able to secure their own lawyers for litigation in matters pivotal to their own care and custody?

In addition, recognizing that too many children are subjected to severe physical and sexual abuse—and chronic neglect—within their homes, proponents of children's rights have posed a second, as yet unanswered, question: Should not children be given the right to take action, if the state fails to do so, to protect themselves and find security and stability with a loving and properly nurturing family?

The answers to these questions may well stay unresolved until the courts and legislatures take further action on the rights of the children.

(*See also:* CHILD ABUSE AND NEGLECT: LEGAL ASPECTS; CHILD CUSTODY; CHILD SUPPORT; DIVORCE: LEGAL ASPECTS; FAMILY LAW; FOSTER PARENTING; GUARDIANSHIP)

BIBLIOGRAPHY

"Children's Legal Rights." (1993). *CQ Researcher*, April 23, pp. 337–360.

Cohen, C. P., and Davidson, H. A. (1990). *Children's Rights in America: U.N. Convention on the Rights of the Child Compared with United States Law*. Washington, DC: American Bar Association Center on Children and the Law.

Kramer, D. T. (1994). *Legal Rights of Children*, 2nd edition. Colorado Springs, CO: Shepard's/McGraw-Hill.

Rodham, H. (1973). "Children Under the Law." *Harvard Educational Review* 43:487–514.

Rodham, H. (1977). "Children's Policies: Abandonment and Neglect." *Yale Law Journal* 86:1522–1531.

Special Symposium Issue on the Rights of Children. (1993). *Family Law Quarterly* 27.

Woodhouse, B. B. (1993a). "Children's Rights: The Destruction and Promise of Family." *Brigham Young Law Review*, pp. 497–515.

Woodhouse, B. B. (1993b). "Hatching the Egg: A Child-Centered Perspective on Parents' Rights." *Cardozo Law Review* 14:1747–1865.

CASES

Gault, In re, 387 U.S. 1 (1967).
Meyer v. *Nebraska*, 262 U.S. 390 (1923).
Parham v. *J.R.*, 442 U.S. 584 (1979).
Prince v. *Massachusetts*, 321 U.S. 159 (1944).
Tinker v. *Des Moines Independent Community School District*, 393 U.S. 503 (1969).

HOWARD A. DAVIDSON

CHILD SUPPORT

The term "child support" has come to be defined narrowly in the United States to mean a payment by a noncustodial parent to a custodial parent (or other caregiver, such as another relative of the child) to assist the custodial parent to meet the monetary costs of raising the child.

Child support could also be defined much more broadly to cover all monetary and nonmonetary contributions by the custodial parent or parents and others toward raising a child. When two parents raise a child together, many of their contributions to child rearing are nonmonetary: physical care of the child, such as feeding, bathing, dressing, and nursing when sick; emotional and intellectual care of the child, such as comforting, counseling, and assisting with homework; and chores related to the child, such as meal preparation, housecleaning, foodshopping, and laundering of clothing. In addition, there are the planning and management functions of parenthood, such as arranging to take the child to regular doctor and dental appointments, attending PTA meetings, making sure the child has clothes that fit and are appropriate, and arranging for the child to be involved in sports activities, music lessons, and other extracurricular activities. In many families, the parents receive assistance with some of these functions from their parents or other relatives, and sometimes they receive monetary or in-kind assistance as well, such as housing, meals, or the like.

When parents are not raising their child together—whether because of nonmarriage, divorce, separation, or institutionalization of a spouse—the custodial parent takes on all of the nonmonetary support responsibilities except those that the noncustodial parent is capable of providing and willing to give. For those noncustodial parents who remain involved in their children's lives, a few days or weeks of "visitation" per year is the usual extent of the nonmonetary contribution. The noncustodial parent's monetary contribution to the children's upbringing is called "child support." Whatever additional monetary needs the children have that cannot be met by the custodial parent are sometimes met by the state, in the form of public benefits, or are left unmet.

All families receive monetary and in-kind assistance from the government to help them raise their children. Some kinds of assistance (e.g., public schools, libraries, and recreational facilities) are freely available to all parents. Others (e.g., subsidized preschool or child-care services, public assistance, food stamps, Medicaid, and subsidized housing) are available on a means-tested basis to low-income parents. Still others (e.g., the tax exemption for each child, the tax deduction for home mortgage interest, and partially subsidized cultural institutions such as museums and performing arts institutions) benefit only or primarily parents who are monetarily more well off than the average.

All of these are forms of child support, but the connections between child support and public benefits, especially Aid to Families with Dependent Children (AFDC) and Medicaid, have been getting closer and more complex.

AFDC (commonly called "welfare") is provided by the government to extremely low-income (below the poverty level in all states—far below in most) families with children where the children are deprived of the care of one parent because of death, absence, or disability. Each state sets its own AFDC level of payment, which, in the continental United States, varies from $120 per month for a family of three in Mississippi to $633 per month for a family of three in California (Blong and Leyser 1993). Family members who are receiving AFDC also receive Medicaid, which is also available to limited categories of other low-income individuals and families.

Intrinsically, there is no necessary connection between child support and welfare. In the United States, however, the federal government has required states to assess and collect child support on behalf of children who receive AFDC, to reimburse the government for the welfare payments made on behalf of those children. State-funded welfare programs for families that do not qualify for AFDC have tended to have similar requirements concerning child support. This has created a link between child support and public assistance that has proved to be both beneficial and problematic.

Traditional State Regulation

The states traditionally have had exclusive control over the creation and breakup of family relationships, including custody and support of children. Each state's laws on child support differed in many ways, but they were similar in two respects. First, the burden of obtaining and enforcing a child support order was placed totally on the custodial parent, who often could not afford an attorney and thus ended up with little or no child support. Second, the amounts of child support ordered were generally woefully inadequate (Clark 1987; Erickson 1992). The only children who were not deprived by this system were those whose noncustodial parents—usually fathers, but sometimes mothers—voluntarily supported them at a reasonable level. By the early 1970s, despite passage of the Uniform Marriage and Divorce Act (UMDA 1968) in more than a dozen states, and passage of an interstate compact on child support enforcement (URESA 1968) in all states, levels of child support were far from uniform as applied to similarly situated families in different states. Nonmarital children routinely received far less child support than marital children, and it was relatively easy for a noncustodial parent to escape paying child support by moving to another state.

Federal Regulation of Child Support

In *Levy* v. *Louisiana* (1968), the U.S. Supreme Court handed down the first in a series of cases establishing the rights of nonmarital (then called "illegitimate") children to equal treatment under the law, including in the area of child support (*Gomez* v. *Perez* 1973). In *Stanton* v. *Stanton* (1975), the court held that female children had a right to be supported to the same age as male children.

The year 1975 was also the effective date of the Social Services Amendments of 1974, which created Title IV-D of the Social Security Act. Title IV-D established the federal child support enforcement program (sometimes called the "IV-D" program). The passage of Title IV-D marked the inception of a connection between child support and AFDC. The federal government required all states to condition receipt of AFDC by a custodial parent on that parent's cooperation in efforts to locate the absent parent and obtain child support from that parent. The child support is then used to repay the government for the AFDC paid to the family.

When Congress realized what a poor job the states were doing of locating absent parents and obtaining child support—and what this meant in terms of AFDC costs—Congress began to take a greater role in child support assessment and enforcement. Congress made substantial amendments to Title IV-D in 1984 (Child Support Enforcement Amendments of 1984). Finally, with the passage of the Family Support Act of 1988, it could be said that the child support arena was no longer occupied almost exclusively by the states but was controlled to a great extent by federal laws and regulations. Subsequent federal laws, including the Omnibus Budget Reconciliation Act of 1993 (OBRA '93), have further federalized child support.

Each state must have a IV-D agency, and the state agency must provide services to custodial parents to locate absent parents, establish paternity, obtain support orders, and enforce those orders. Any custodial parent—rich or poor—is entitled to services from the IV-D agency, although custodial parents who are not receiving AFDC may be charged small fees.

The Child Support Obligation

Parents in all states are legally liable for the support of their biological children, whether born in or out of wedlock, and for the support of any children they adopt. The obligation to support a child normally lasts until the child is adopted by someone else, dies, becomes emancipated, or reaches the age of majority for child support purposes, which is eighteen in most states and twenty-one in a few. In some states, however, a parent may be required to support a child beyond the age of majority if the child is disabled or in school (Clark 1987).

Paternity establishment. A father is liable for the support of a nonmarital child when paternity has been established (Clark 1987). A 1993 federal law (OBRA '93) requires all birthing hospitals to attempt to obtain acknowledgments of paternity in the hospital, because an unwed father is more likely to be present and to admit paternity during the time surrounding birth than later on.

Federal laws also mandate that states require genetic testing (blood tests) in disputed paternity cases and that a high probability of paternity established by genetic tests must create a presumption of paternity (OBRA '93). State statutes of limitations must permit paternity claims to be brought at least until the child's eighteenth birthday. Some states permit paternity to be established for child support purposes up to age twenty-one or even above under certain circumstances (U.S. Department of Health and Human Services 1992a).

A man is legally liable for the support of any children born to his wife or conceived by her during their marriage, even if the child is not his biological child, unless and until there is a court order declaring that he is not the legal father (Clark 1987).

Locating absent parents. A parent who does not want to pay child support often moves and hides his or her whereabouts. If the custodial parent is unable to locate the absent parent or his or her assets, a child support order will not be of any use.

Often, a resourceful and persistent custodial parent can track down the absent parent by checking with relatives, friends, former employers, and utility companies (Takas 1985). If self-help proves unsuccessful, the custodial parent can seek the assistance of government parent locator services. There is a Federal Parent Locator Service (FPLS), and each state must have a State Parent Locator Service (SPLS). Any custodial parent may request "locate only" services from the state IV-D office. The most important locate information is the parent's Social Security number, although an absent parent can often be found by means of name and date of birth. The SPLS will conduct computer searches of certain state agencies and criminal justice files. If this search is unsuccessful, the SPLS may forward the request to the FPLS, which will search federal files such as those of the IRS, Social Security Administration, Veterans Administration, Department of Defense, and the National Personnel Records Center. If the absent parent is believed to be in another state, the SPLS may also forward the request to that other state's SPLS.

Deciding whether to seek child support. If the custodial parent is not receiving welfare, she or he may decide whether to seek child support from the noncustodial parent. Most people assume that all custodial parents want to seek child support, but that is not the case. For some custodial parents—even those of small means—the benefits of obtaining funds from the other parent are far outweighed by the detriments. An absent parent may have abused the custodial parent or the child; may be drug- or alcohol-dependent; or may be a person who, for other reasons, will be dangerous or will not be able to be a good parent. A custodial parent also may fear that seeking child support may lead to a custody battle. Even if the absent parent gains only visitation, not custody, that parent will have the power to interfere with the lives of those in the custodial parent's family—the custodial parent and his or her family of origin, the child, and any new spouse or child—in many significant ways. For example, the absent parent may be able to prevent the custodial parent from moving, even if a move would be in the best interests of the family unit, by alleging that a move would interfere with visitation. Thus, many custodial parents—the majority of whom are mothers—consider the ability to choose whether to seek child support to be a very valuable one.

If a custodial mother needs welfare to support her child, however, she must cooperate with the government's efforts to seek child support (and establish paternity, if necessary). She must cooperate even if she believes that establishment of paternity will not be in the best interests of the child and, in fact, will be dangerous to the child. The only alternative is to prove that the case fits within a very narrow category of cases in which the government decides that the custodial parent has "good cause" not to cooperate in establishing paternity or seeking child support. The cooperation requirement is especially problematic for battered women, because "good cause" is so difficult to prove.

Child Support Guidelines

The traditional method of setting the amount of child support was for a judge to determine the amount deemed appropriate, often based on "factors" set forth in the state statute, such as the "needs" of the child, the "means" of the parents, and the standard of living the child would have enjoyed if the marriage or relationship continued (UMDA 1968). Because these factors are vague, the amounts ordered by two judges looking at identical cases could be very different. To encourage both uniformity and adequacy, Congress mandated the use of numerical formulas, known as "guidelines."

Federal requirements. Pursuant to federal law, each state must have in place one set of guidelines for establishing and modifying all child support orders within the state. At a minimum, the guidelines must take into consideration all income and earnings of the absent parent, be based on specific descriptive and numerical criteria, result in computation of the dollar amount of the child support obligation, and provide for the children's health-care needs.

There must be a rebuttable presumption, in any proceeding for child support, that the amount of the order that would result from the application of the guidelines is the correct amount to be awarded. Only a written or specific finding on the record that the use of the guidelines would be unjust or inappropriate in a particular case is sufficient to rebut the presumption in that case. Such a finding must be predicated on criteria established by the state. While development of the specific criteria for rebuttal is left to each state's discretion, the state's criteria must take into consideration the best interests of the child. Findings that rebut the guidelines must state the amount of support that would have been required under the guidelines and include a justification of why the order varies from the guidelines, even if the parents have agreed to an amount different from the presumptive guidelines amount (Erickson 1992).

State guidelines. The guidelines that have been adopted by the state pursuant to federal law fall into three categories: the Melson formula, the percentage-of-income approach, and the income-shares model.

All three models allegedly attempt to attain a level of support that approximates the support level in a two-parent family. However, the economic data on which they are based are subject to serious criticism in this regard (Erickson 1992), and if the custodial parent (usually the mother) is the lower-income parent (which she usually is), that goal will not be attained, and the children will end up living at a much lower standard of living than the noncustodial parent.

The Melson formula, which is followed in four states (Delaware, Hawaii, Montana, and West Virginia), seems to be the most equitable when applied to low-income parents, whether the parent is the custodial or the noncustodial parent (Erickson 1992). First, a poverty level self-support reserve is allotted to each parent. Then the formula allocates between the parents—according to their remaining income—poverty-level support to the children. Finally, the court allocates for additional child support a certain percentage of any amount the noncustodial parent has left. For example, in Delaware the percentages are 18 percent for one child, 27 percent for two children, and

35 percent for three children (National Center for State Courts 1991).

The percentage-of-income approach is the least complicated guidelines model. It simply assesses the noncustodial parent a certain percentage of his or her income for child support, depending on the number of children. The Wisconsin percentages, for example, are 17 percent of gross income for one child, 25 percent for two, 29 percent for three, 31 percent for four, and 34 percent for five or more (National Center for State Courts 1991).

The income-shares model, which has been adopted in more than thirty states (Erickson 1992), is based on combined parental income. For example, New York, in accordance with the New York Family Court Act, assesses 17 percent of a combined parental adjusted gross income as child support for one child and allocates it between the parents according to their percentage share of the combined income. Thus, a parent whose income was 40 percent of the combined parental income would be allocated 40 percent of the child support. There are many variations on the income-shares model, and some of them require the court to add on to the basic child support obligation an additional amount for certain extraordinary expenses, such as child care that the custodial parent needs in order to be employed or attend school, and extraordinary medical expenses of the child.

Federal and State Enforcement Mechanisms

Because child support enforcement was traditionally controlled by the individual states, some remedies for intrastate enforcement were available, although cumbersome and often unsuccessful. Enforcement of an order was almost impossible, however, if the noncustodial parent moved out of state. The states attempted to deal with this problem in various ways, but even the Uniform Reciprocal Enforcement of Support Act (URESA)—an interstate compact—did not come close to an adequate solution (Haynes and Dodson 1989). Congress mandated improvements in both intra- and interstate enforcement remedies.

Intrastate. Congress has required the states to enact certain laws and to put into effect certain procedures for child support enforcement. There are federal requirements as to the following enforcement mechanisms: income withholding, reducing arrears to judgment, bonds and other security, liens, income tax refund intercept, and credit reporting. Most states also have provisions for enforcing child support by means of civil contempt proceedings (which may lead

to civil incarceration) and criminal nonsupport prosecutions (Haynes et al. 1990).

Federal laws make income withholding standard operating procedure to enforce child support. In 1981, Congress mandated that states subject unemployment insurance benefits to withholding to collect unpaid child support debts. In 1984, Congress mandated that states have procedures requiring wage withholding in all cases handled by the IV-D agencies, without the need for any further action by the court, upon the occurrence of the earliest of certain triggering events: (1) when arrears are equal to one month's amount of support; (2) when the obligor requests withholding; or (3) when the obligee requests withholding and the state determines under rules it has established that the request should be approved (e.g., when the obligor is habitually late). In cases not being handled by the IV-D agencies, wage withholding must occur upon the accrual of arrears as specified by the state (which could be more or less than one month's support) (Child Support Enforcement Amendments of 1984).

With the Family Support Act of 1988, Congress strengthened the income withholding requirements. In all new IV-D orders and in orders where the IV-D agency is seeking a modification, there must be a provision for immediate wage withholding unless the court finds there is "good cause" not to require immediate withholding, or if the parties reach a written agreement that provides for an alternative arrangement. If, for one of these two reasons, immediate withholding is not ordered, withholding must be available if arrears accrue in an amount equal to one month's support. In cases not being enforced by the IV-D agency, state law must provide for immediate wage withholding for all support orders issued after January 1, 1994, unless there is good cause or a written agreement providing for an alternative support arrangement.

The federal Consumer Credit Protection Act (CCPA) restricts the percentage of earnings that can be withheld from the income of an obligor. The usual limit is 25 percent, but for support orders the limit is higher: 50 percent of disposable earnings where the obligor is obligated to support a second family and 60 percent where there is no second family. These limits increase to 55 percent and 65 percent, respectively, when the collection is for arrears that are more than twelve weeks old.

The CCPA applies only to earnings, not to income from other sources, so that a state could withhold a higher percentage of an obligor's workers' compensation or Social Security disability or retirement benefits, unless the state law either defined such income as earnings or had a state limit on withholding from such benefits (Erickson 1995).

One of the most effective enforcement mechanisms for noncustodial parents whose income is from a source that makes income withholding difficult—such as self-employed individuals—is income tax refund intercept. If the government owes an income tax refund to a taxpayer, and the taxpayer is a noncustodial parent who owes child support arrears, the refund can be sent to the custodial parent instead of the noncustodial parent. Federal law requires states that have an income tax to have laws providing for state income tax refund intercept for child support arrears in both intrastate and interstate cases. A custodial parent who is receiving child support enforcement services from the IV-D agency may also benefit from the federal income tax refund intercept program (Erickson 1992).

Interstate. If a state has jurisdiction over the noncustodial parent, the state can continue to enforce its child support order against that person even if he or she moves out of the state. However, in most cases, actual collection of support will be impossible, because the court often will not have jurisdiction over his or her income or property.

URESA was intended to solve this problem, but its procedures are slow and cumbersome. Successful use of URESA requires close cooperation of the states where the two parents reside. There are so many problems with URESA that the National Conference of Commissioners on Uniform State Laws has drafted the Uniform Interstate Family Support Act (UIFSA), which would replace URESA. The U.S. Commission on Interstate Child Support has recommended that each state adopt UIFSA, and several states have already done so (Erickson 1993).

The Uniform Enforcement of Foreign Judgments Act provides another method of enforcement if arrears have accrued. The custodial parent files the judgment in the noncustodial parent's state; then, any enforcement provisions of his or her state (such as income withholding) can be used (Erickson 1992).

In 1984, an interstate income withholding procedure was mandated by federal law (Child Support Enforcement Amendments of 1984). Although, like URESA, it requires interstate cooperation, it is a more direct and less time-consuming method (Erickson 1992).

International Comparisons

Other industrialized nations generally provide more support for families with children than does the United States. The biggest differences between the

United States and other modern, industrialized countries relate to the provision of maternity/paternity benefits and children's allowances. In addition, many countries have had procedures in place for many years whereby the government—not the support parent—is responsible for collection of child support.

With regard to maternity/paternity benefits, there is a requirement in the United States that parents employed by medium- or large-size companies be permitted up to three months of time off when a baby is born, when a child is adopted, or when the employee or a family member is ill (Family and Medical Leave Act of 1993). If the employee's job cannot be held open for him or her, the employee must be offered another job upon returning from the leave of absence. There is no requirement, however, that the leave be partially or fully paid; thus, many parents cannot afford to take the time off. Some employees have accumulated "sick days" that may be used when the employee is unable to work due to illness or disability (including disability resulting from pregnancy and childbirth), but federal law does not mandate that employers provide sick days as part of their fringe benefits package. Many other countries provide payment to employees for maternity/paternity leave, for varying periods of time (U.S. Department of Health and Human Services 1992b).

Many countries also provide children's allowances. A children's allowance is a monetary grant to a family for a child, usually regardless of family income and circumstances. Sometimes it is categorized as a "family allowance." Virtually every industrialized country—except the United States—has some kind of family allowance program (U.S. Department of Health and Human Services 1992b). Because a children's allowance—unlike AFDC—usually is not means-tested, it does not carry a stigma such as has attached to "welfare" in the United States. The government can recoup much of the child's allowance via taxes if the child's family is not poor.

Parents in some other countries are also given more assistance with child support enforcement. In fact, in many countries the government provides the child support to the custodial parent and then attempts to reimburse itself by pursuing the noncustodial parent. For example, such a system has been in operation in Sweden since 1964 (Maclean 1992). Proposals in the United States for similar programs have been termed child support assurance (CSA) proposals.

Finally, as in the United States, some form of means-tested public benefit, such as "welfare," is the final safety net in many other countries as well (U.S. Department of Health and Human Services 1992b).

Proposals for Changes

In addition to UIFSA, which has been discussed, the U.S. Commission on Interstate Child Support made other recommendations for improvements in the child support enforcement arena, and many of these would result in more rigorous intrastate as well as interstate enforcement. Some recommendations, such as removing drivers' licenses and professional licenses from persons who owe child support arrears if they are able but refuse to pay the support, are already being used in several states. Others, such as the recommendation that child support be payable up to age twenty-two if a child is in school, probably have little chance of passage in most state legislatures; thus, a federal mandate would be necessary.

The commission also recommended that the federal government fund demonstration projects to determine the feasibility and utility of a CSA program. CSA proposals predated the commission's report. The first major CSA proposal was the Downey-Hyde proposal, in 1991. The welfare "reform" bill that was proposed by President Bill Clinton's administration contained authorization for CSA demonstration projects, but not for CSA on a national basis.

The basic concept of CSA is that the government would provide a monetary benefit to the custodial parent of any child for whom there is a child support order. In the Downey-Hyde proposal, the proposed benefit ranged from $2,000 per year for one child to $4,000 per year for four or more. The government would then attempt to recoup the amount of the assured benefit by enforcing the child support order against the noncustodial parent. As indicated, some countries implemented this type of program many years ago. Many CSA proposals are limited in that they would exclude children whose custodial parents have not "cooperated" in paternity establishment or child support proceedings, or whose noncustodial parents have died, disappeared, or are unknown. Most proposals also do not benefit children who are receiving public assistance because every dollar of CSA received would decrease the amount of public assistance by the same amount. CSA could be a major step toward lifting children out of poverty if the levels of the "assured" benefit were high enough, if it were "assured" to all children, if "good cause" exemptions were expanded, and if it benefited the poorest children—those already receiving AFDC.

(*See also:* CHILD CUSTODY; DIVORCE: LEGAL ASPECTS; DIVORCE: ECONOMIC ASPECTS; DIVORCE: EFFECTS ON CHILDREN; ENTITLEMENTS; POVERTY)

BIBLIOGRAPHY

Blong, A., and Leyser, B. (1993). *Living at the Bottom: An Analysis of AFDC Benefit Levels.* Washington, DC: Center on Social Welfare Policy and Law.

Clark, H. H. (1987). *The Law of Domestic Relations.* St. Paul, MN: West Publishing.

Erickson, N. (1992). *Child Support Manual for Attorneys and Advocates.* New York: National Center on Women and Family Law.

Erickson, N. (1993). *1993 Update to Child Support Manual for Legal Services Attorneys and Advocates.* New York: National Center on Women and Family Law.

Erickson, N. (1995). *Child Support Orders Against Recipients of Means-Tested Public Benefits.* New York: National Center on Women and Family Law.

Haynes, M.; Ball, J.; Landstreet, E.; and Sablan, V. A. (1990). *Child Support Reference Manual.* Washington, DC: American Bar Association.

Haynes, M., and Dodson, D. (1989). *Interstate Child Support Remedies.* Washington, DC: American Bar Association.

Maclean, M. (1992). "Background Facts from Country Reports." In *Economic Consequences of Divorce: The International Perspective*, ed. L. Weitzman and M. Maclean. New York: Oxford University Press.

National Center for State Courts. (1991). *Child Support Guidelines: A Compendium.* Arlington, VA: National Center for State Courts.

Subcommittee on Human Resources, Committee on Ways and Means, U.S. House of Representatives. (1992). Written Comments on the Downey-Hyde Child Support Enforcement and Assurance Proposal. Washington, DC: U.S. Government Printing Office.

Takas, M. (1985). *Child Support.* New York: Harper & Row.

U.S. Department of Health and Human Services (1992a). *Essentials for Attorneys in Child Support Enforcement.* Washington, DC: Author.

U.S. Department of Health and Human Services (1992b). *Social Security Programs Throughout the World, 1991.* Washington, DC: Author.

CASES

Gomez v. *Perez*, 409 U.S. 535 (1973).
Levy v. *Louisiana*, 391 U.S. 68 (1968).
Mills v. *Habluetzel*, 456 U.S. 91 (1982).
Pickett v. *Brown*, 462 U.S. 1 (1983).
Stanton v. *Stanton*, 421 U.S. 7 (1975).

STATUTES, BILLS, AND REGULATIONS

Child Support Enforcement Amendments of 1984, P.L. 98–378, 98 Stat. 1305.

Consumer Credit Protection Act, 15 U.S.C. §1673.

Family and Medical Leave Act of 1993, 29 U.S.C. §2601–2654.

Family Support Act of 1988, P.L. 100–485, 102 Stat. 2343.

New York Family Court Act §413 1(b)(3)(f).

Omnibus Budget Reconciliation Act of 1993 (OBRA '93), P.L. 103–66.

Social Services Amendments of 1974, P.L. 93–647, 88 Stat. 2337.

Uniform Enforcement of Money Judgments Act. National Conference of Commissioners on Uniform State Laws 1968, *Uniform Laws Annotated.* St. Paul, MN: West Publishing.

Uniform Interstate Family Support Act, *Family Law Reporter* (1993), 19:2001.

Uniform Marriage and Divorce Act (UMDA). National Conference of Commissioners on Uniform State Laws 1968, *Uniform Laws Annotated.* St. Paul, MN: West Publishing.

Uniform Reciprocal Enforcement of Support Act (URESA). National Conference of Commissioners on Uniform State Laws 1968, *Uniform Laws Annotated.* St. Paul, MN: West Publishing.

NANCY S. ERICKSON

CHRONIC ILLNESS

The twentieth century witnessed a dramatic transformation in patterns of health, sickness, and death among persons living in industrialized countries. One important change was a decline in the rate of death from infectious diseases and a substantial increase in the average lifespan. The second major change, which became apparent in the 1950s, was an increase in the prevalence of chronic or long-term illness. Chronic illnesses and disabilities afflict more than 50 percent of all Americans, causing various levels of physical and mental impairment. Some chronic health conditions are relatively mild and can be controlled by medical therapies and/or changes in activities and diets. On the other hand, chronic illnesses can be severe, deteriorative, and terminal, causing disability and creating the need for extensive medical treatment and long-term care. Asthma, diabetes, heart disease, hypertension, stroke, cancer, arthritis, cystic fibrosis, sickle-cell disease, cirrhosis of the liver, renal disease, and mental illness are examples of chronic illnesses. The growth of chronic illnesses represents an important change in the nature of the health-care burden in modern societies. It has increased the role of families in providing medical care for their members who are chronically ill or disabled, and it has led medical and social theorists to rethink their assumptions about the impact and management of sickness.

Social and Historical Context

Sickness and death in preindustrial America were caused mostly by exposure to bacteria and parasites, which gave rise to acute illnesses such as influenza, scarlet fever, whooping cough, polio, pneumonia, and tuberculosis. Acute illnesses often occur suddenly and are characterized by a sharp increase in discomfort or pain due to an inflammation, and they usually have a short course. Prior to the 1900s, acute health conditions rarely could be treated successfully by medical therapies, so they were self-limiting in that they led to spontaneous recovery or to death within a fairly short period of time. Acute infectious illnesses, whether endemic or epidemic, contributed heavily to the high mortality rates and short lifespans among persons living in agricultural and early industrial societies. They also created the need for medical care, which was primarily provided by the family. In Colonial America, the family was not only the central economic unit but also a multifunctional unit that was expected to perform a broad array of social and economic tasks, including care for the sick. While a variety of competing medical practitioners were available for consultation and medical assistance during this period, the rural and small-town atmosphere created both ideological and structural barriers to relying on these medical practitioners (Starr 1982). To survive, family members typically developed a wide range of skills and abilities and, both religiously and politically, were invested with a strong orientation toward self-reliance.

In the 1700s, industrialization sparked a major transformation in the social, political, and economic life of people living in Western countries. Industrialization and technology completely restructured the workplace, leading to a system of monopoly capitalism based on class and wealth and a global economy dominated by a handful of Western nations. In its early stages, industrialization produced a rapid deterioration in the living and working conditions of people in developing countries. Traditional family and economic systems were disrupted as populations migrated into urban areas in pursuit of employment, and the lack of clean water and sanitation, the spread of environmental toxins, population concentration, malnutrition, and the nature of industrial work increased sickness and death from contagious diseases. Gradually, public health measures and improvements in diet, housing, water supplies, and sanitation reduced the spread of deadly contagious diseases in developing countries. As these core Western nations industrialized and gained economic and military domination, their control rapidly spread to underdeveloped countries. Through colonialism and the exploitation of material and human resources, many underdeveloped countries saw their economic systems disrupted and experienced dramatic increases in infectious diseases. By the end of the nineteenth century, there were significant differences between developed and underdeveloped countries in terms of sickness and death from infectious diseases, malnutrition, and living conditions.

Improvements in hygiene, sanitation, living conditions, and nutrition curtailed the rate of sickness and death from acute illnesses in developed countries. The second phase in the control of contagious diseases was the development of the medical sciences, which reached maturity between 1890 and 1920. Medical inventions and discoveries during this era led scientists and physicians to reformulate the problem of disease and focus on direct medical intervention to heal diseases. For many years, American physicians were divided in their approach to healing disease. Some, especially those trained in Europe, had an aversion to reducing their work to manual labor by touching the human body, while others practiced heroic medicine, where patients were often bled and purged to heal disease. By 1850, they began to accept the notion that diseases leave "telltale footprints" on the tissues of the body, and the physical examination was established as the best way to diagnose illness (Reiser 1978). A major breakthrough in medicine came in the late 1800s when scientists, most notably Robert Koch and Louis Pasteur, confirmed the link between bacteria and acute illnesses. Tuberculosis, known as the "white plague," was still the leading cause of sickness and death in Europe and the United States. Koch isolated the tubercle bacillus, the germ that caused tuberculosis, and established the science of bacteriology. Pasteur proved that many diseases were caused by the spread of bacteria and advanced the use of vaccinations to prevent disease.

These advances in medical science, along with the development of more accurate diagnostic technologies and antiseptic surgery, gave birth to modern, scientific medicine. The germ theory of sickness became the basis of medical practice and the medical approach to dealing with disease. It was a key factor in the medical physician's ability to achieve cultural authority (Starr 1982) and become preeminent among health-care providers. Medical interventions were eventually credited with playing a central role in reducing infectious disease, and this generated great enthusiasm that medical science would eventually find a cure for all diseases. Pursuit of the "magic bullets" of medicine, or drugs that would "miraculously" heal diseases, became the focus of medical science and education. Control over contagious diseases and the germ theory of sickness gave rise to a specific conceptualization of health and illness that Eliot G. Mishler (1981) has described as the medical model of disease. The medical model of disease assumes that there is a sharp and clear distinction between sickness and health, based on the belief that sickness can be readily detected by diagnostic tests and confirmed by physicians. Because it is based on acute, infectious diseases, this model also assumes that diseases have specific causes, clearly distinguishing characteristics, and that they can be healed by medical therapies. Thus, disease was stripped of social context and seen essentially as a biophysical event.

The development of modern medicine was part of a larger trend toward professionalization and specialization that led to a reconceptualization of the family as a specialized institution. The most important change in the family wrought by industrialization was a loss of family function. The modern nuclear family was seen as ideally suited to meet the demands of the industrial workplace and to carry out two functions: child rearing and meeting the emotional needs of its members. At the same time, this family was viewed as extremely vulnerable to certain types of strain and as constituting an "intrinsically puny work group" (Hill 1954) when it came to meeting the demands of caring for sick people. Talcott Parsons, a leading family sociologist of the 1950s, argued that the use of physicians and hospital care was functional for families in that it protected them against the disruptive aspects of illness and helped motivate the sick person to get well (Parsons and Fox 1952). Parsons also developed the concept of the sick role, which described the social expectations governing the behavior of sick persons. Essentially, sick people were seen as exempt from their usual social responsibilities but were obliged to try to get well. An integral part of getting well was seeking competent medical help and complying with the advice and medical regimens of physicians. The sick-role concept reinforced the medical model by assuming that illness was a temporary departure from health. By the 1950s, however, acute illnesses were being replaced by long-term chronic health conditions.

Transformation in Burden

In 1900, the majority of deaths were still caused by infectious diseases; these illnesses accounted for less than 6 percent of all deaths in developed countries by 1987 (McKinlay and McKinlay 1987). The decline in death from infectious disease has led to substantial increases in the average life expectancy, from fewer than fifty years prior to 1900 to an average life expectancy of seventy years for men and seventy-eight years for women by the end of the twentieth century. These improvements in health and longevity, however, have been accompanied by a shift in the illness burden from acute to chronic illnesses. A chronic illness is defined as having one or more of the following characteristics: It is long-term or permanent; it leaves a residual disability; its cause, natural course, and treatment are ambiguous; it is degenerative; it requires special training of the patient for rehabilitation; and/or it requires a long period of supervision (Maddox and Glass 1989; National Commission on Chronic Illness 1956). Chronic illnesses are now responsible for most sickness and disease; two chronic diseases, heart disease and cancer, account for slightly more than 50 percent of all deaths. Rates of chronic illness vary by age, gender, race, and social class. Older people are more likely to have a chronic health condition than are younger people: Four of every five persons over age sixty-five have at least one chronic illness (Freund and McGuire 1991). Women have higher rates of chronic illness than men, although women are less likely than men to have life-threatening chronic illnesses. African Americans and low-income groups have higher rates of chronic illness than do whites and people who are affluent.

Most chronic illnesses are long-term and incurable; they are not caused by germs, nor can they be prevented by direct medical interventions such as immunization. The causes of chronic illnesses are often complex; many, such as sickle-cell anemia (found mostly among African Americans) and Tay-Sachs disease (found among Jews of East European descent) have a genetic or hereditary component. In other cases, genetic, sociocultural, and economic factors combine to influence patterns of chronic illness. Inadequate diets, poor housing and living conditions, sedentary lifestyles, tobacco and drug use, stress, poverty, and exposure to environmental toxins all affect the likelihood of acquiring a chronic illness. These social factors do not have the same effect on all people. For example, poor people experience more sickness than affluent people, partially due to poor people's higher rates of inadequate housing, malnutrition, and stressful living conditions. The nature of chronic illness places it at odds with the organization and focus of the medical system. Medical research has long focused on finding explicit biological factors that cause disease and medical therapies that effect healing. Chronic illnesses, however, are caused by a multiplicity of factors, and their most salient feature is their permanency. Because neither the patient nor the physician experi-

ences the gratification of a full and complete recovery, chronic illnesses have been described as medical failures. A twenty-five-year-old hemophiliac is quoted as saying: "The most important thing to remember about a chronic illness is that it is exactly that: chronic. It never goes away. It pervades every moment and aspect of life, often from birth until death" (Patterson 1988, p. 69).

In addition to being long-term or permanent, the diagnosis and treatment of chronic illness can be very challenging. Symptoms of chronic illnesses often appear gradually and are vague, making it difficult to obtain an early and accurate diagnosis from doctors or laypersons. A study of children with cystic fibrosis, for example, found that despite the presence of severe symptoms of illness, the majority of children (62%) were not accurately diagnosed during the first medical contact (Venters 1981). David C. Stewart and Thomas J. Sullivan (1982) studied sixty individuals with multiple sclerosis and found that it took an average of five and a half years for these patients to be diagnosed correctly. Once an accurate diagnosis is obtained, there is often no clearly effective medical therapy or, in other cases, the patient finds that he or she must cope with a long-term, burdensome medical regimen. Patient compliance becomes a major issue because many medical therapies are expensive, inconvenient, and may have undesirable side effects. Partly in response to the medical ambiguities that accompany chronic illnesses, patients have become much more active in managing their own medical care. Research has documented a growing tendency among patients to challenge and negotiate with physicians in obtaining a diagnosis (Hill 1994; Stewart and Sullivan 1982) and to alter or reject physician-prescribed medical treatments.

Patients and their families are very likely to be engaged actively in managing their own health and health care (Kronenfeld 1979). While this activist stance of laypersons appears to be a relatively new phenomenon, medical sociologists have pointed out that patients and their families have always played a central role in defining and treating illness symptoms. Using the social constructionist perspective, Mishler (1981) viewed health and illness as socially constructed categories, since their definitions vary substantially based on cultural values and social norms. Even within the same culture, there are often differences between laypersons and physicians in their responses to symptoms of illness. This discrepancy between physician and patient views of illness is best described in David Mechanic's (1982, p. 1) distinction between illness and illness behavior:

Illness usually refers to a limited scientific concept denoting a constellation of symptoms or a condition underlying them. Illness behavior, on the other hand, describes the manner in which persons monitor their bodies, define and interpret their symptoms, take remedial action, and utilize the health care system. People differentially perceive, evaluate, and respond to illness, and such behaviors have enormous influence on the extent to which illness interferes with usual life routines, the chronicity of the condition, the attainment of appropriate care, and the cooperation of the patient in the treatment situation.

Mechanic noted that physicians often diagnose illness even when symptoms are absent or assume health when symptoms cannot be verified medically. Patients, on the other hand, view health in terms of their overall sense of well-being and the extent to which symptoms they experience interfere with their ability to function in important life activities. Patients with chronic illness are especially likely to use their own interpretations in coping with the illness.

Living with Chronic Illness

There is considerable variability among chronic illnesses in their characteristics and the extent to which they impose limitations on their victims. However, when the chronic illness is a severe, life-threatening, and/or deteriorative one, the first step in living with the illness is emotional acceptance of the diagnosis and its implications. The diagnosis of a severe chronic illness is usually a stressful event that generates intense emotional distress in patients and their families. A great deal of research has focused on how parents react to the birth of a child with chronic illness or disability. These studies have described such a child as a "complete distortion of the dreamed-of and planned-for infant" (Bristor 1984) and noted that parents respond with shame, guilt, and mourning. These feelings are exacerbated when parents feel responsible for the condition or that it could have been avoided. Their emotional distress is often manifested as feelings of extreme vulnerability, helplessness, and uncertainty over the future (Cohen 1993). With time, however, these feelings wane as individuals accept the diagnosis and begin to cope with its implications. Summarizing research on family responses to serious medical diagnoses, Laurie Fortier and Richard Wanlass (1984) suggest five stages of adjustment: (1) the initial impact, marked by extreme stress; (2) a period of denial; (3) feelings of grief, self-doubt, blame; (4) focusing outward by objectively evaluating the situation; and (5) closure, or achieving a sense of hope.

Models of adjustment to chronic illness or disability usually assume that individuals and their families eventually accept the medical diagnosis and the prescribed treatments. Researchers, however, have found this is often not the case; persistent elements of denial may continue throughout the course of the illness. A study of African-American families with children who have sickle-cell anemia found that mothers denied their children's diagnosis for a number of reasons, including race- and class-based discrepancies between patient and doctor perceptions of illness, the belief that their children were not like others who had the disease, and because they did not want to face the reproductive implications of passing on the disease to future children (Hill 1994). While denial has typically been viewed as maladaptive, some research has indicated that denial can have both beneficial and harmful effects (Handron 1993; Kasl 1983). People often deny the disease or its implications so they can continue to participate in important roles and activities. Denial has been found to reduce psychological distress and the rate of mortality from some diseases, and to enhance work and family role performance. On the other hand, denial may also lead to noncompliance and can be especially risky when a disease, such as hypertension, has few symptoms but potentially severe health consequences.

Living with a chronic illness often leads to changes in one's lifestyle, activities, and relationships. Sometimes these changes are relatively minor and can stabilize the chronic illness and enhance the person's overall sense of health and well-being. More severe chronic illnesses, however, may require substantial changes in the life of the ill person, and these are often experienced as a series of losses—the loss of freedom, of hobbies, of employment, of physical appearance, and even of friendships. It may also cause the loss of physiological or anatomical functions, or impairments that can lead to disabilities, such as the inability to walk, climb stairs, work, or live independently. As control over one's life, body, and activities is highly valued, chronic illness can lead to stigma and devaluation. Chronic pain or ongoing, recurrent, unpredictable pain is another characteristic of chronic illness that causes feelings of loss of control. This pain can be constant and all-consuming, making symptom management and participation in everyday activities difficult. Peter E. S. Freund and Meredith B. McGuire (1991) have noted that chronic pain can jeopardize social relationships and lead to isolation, as it often invokes invalidating responses from others.

The pain experienced by persons who are chronically ill often has no organic basis and cannot be verified medically, so others may doubt its existence. This can lead to the loss of social relationships with others as the empathy and support of friends and relatives begin to wear thin.

Chronic illness is accompanied by a great deal of uncertainty, since even with the best medical care, its course and severity can vary from patient to patient. Mothers of children with sickle-cell anemia experienced considerable uncertainty over how the disease would affect their children, especially when the diagnosis was made prior to the manifestation of symptoms (Hill 1994). Patients may be uncertain about how to use prescribed medical treatments and concerned about their side effects. In pursuing everyday activities, many persons with chronic illness are plagued by moment-to-moment worries about whether or when the body might fail them and what the consequences will be. Rose Weitz (1990) interviewed persons who have acquired immunodeficiency syndrome (AIDS), which, like many other chronic illnesses, is characterized by "unpredictable flare-ups and remissions." She reported that people living with AIDS experienced much uncertainty about the meaning of illness symptoms, why they had become ill, their ability to function the next day, whether they would be able to live or die with dignity, and whether their health regimens would prolong their lives or heal the disease. Because self-image is integrally tied to the body and a sense of having control over it, the self-image can be dramatically altered by chronic illness. Juliet M. Corbin and Anselm Strauss (1988, p. 49) have noted, "When a severe chronic illness comes crashing into someone's life, it cannot help but separate the person of the present from the person of the past and affect or even shatter any images of self held for the future."

Community resources, both formal and informal, are available to help persons with chronic illness adjust to the limitations imposed by the illness and participate as fully as possible in social and economic activities. Hospitals, schools, and state and private institutions offer support groups for people with various chronic conditions. Support groups provide education about the illness or disability, information about resources available in meeting daily needs, and assistance in adjusting emotionally to the disease. A central theme in many organizations is empowerment, or providing the individual with the maximum amount of control over his or her life. Sarah Rosenfield (1992) reported that community resources can enhance the subjective quality of life for persons with chronic illnesses. In examining some organizations that provide services to persons with chronic mental illness, she found that programs that increase economic resources through vocational training and financial support are salient for life satisfaction. These interventions often increased the individual's subjective assessment of status and sense of mastery. Rosenfield's work suggests that the deinstitutionalization of individuals with mental illness can be successful with the development of supportive community resources.

The most important institution in coping with the illness, however, is the family. The family is the primary unit in health and medical care, and the most important social context in which illness occurs and is managed.

Family Caregiving

The rise of chronic illness has led researchers to reassert the role of the family in caring for the sick. While most chronic illnesses are incurable, medical science has developed technologies and interventions that have extended the lifespans of many persons who are chronically ill. Thus, many diseases that once signaled early death now result in the need for long-term caregiving. These higher survival rates and the growing emphasis on reducing medical costs have increased family responsibility for caring for their sick members. Family caregiving, however, means that chronic illness produces not only temporary emotional distress and disorganization but also can create long-term strains and hardships in the family system. Examining caregiving within the context of stress theory, Carol S. Aneshensel, Leonard I. Pearlin, and Roberleigh H. Schuler (1993) make a distinction between primary stressors, caused by performing the work required to care for the sick family members, and secondary stressors, problems that emerge in social roles and relationships as a result of caregiving. This distinction highlights the fact that caregiving involves more than the performance of medical tasks; it also may disrupt the normal life cycle, alter family roles and relationships, lead to economic hardships, exacerbate family conflicts, constrict work and social activities, and challenge the basic equilibrium in the family system.

The majority of persons in need of family caregivers are the elderly, as chronic conditions and deterioration increase with age. Eighty percent of the noninstitutionalized elderly have one or more chronic health problems, and family members provide care for more than five million elderly individuals with chronic illness (Freund and McGuire 1991). Heart disease, cancer, stroke, arthritis, and dementia are the major chronic illnesses leading to disability among the elderly. Caregiving for the elderly may begin with minimal assistance in meeting daily living tasks and become more exhausting and taxing as aging and physical deterioration continue. When the health status of an elderly person dramatically declines, family members usually rally in support by providing care for their loved one. However, there is a tendency for that support to wane over time and for the primary caregiver to be selected by default: because she is a woman, is not employed outside the home, or lives nearby (Aneshensel, Pearlin, and Schuler 1993). As few elderly people have young children, caregiving often falls to children who are middle-aged or even elderly. Caregiving may cause long-standing family disagreements to reemerge, and both caregivers and care receivers may experience conflicting emotions of compassion, love, and anger as frustration toward each other.

Family caregiving for the more than three million Americans who have Alzheimer's disease can be highly stressful and lead to family dysfunction. Alzheimer's is a form of dementia that results in progressive memory loss, diminished mental and intellectual capabilities, and a deterioration in the ability to perform many everyday activities. In the early stages, family caregivers may recognize that there is a health problem and respond by providing minimal types of assistance. Aneshensel, Pearlin, and Schuler (1993) found that the average caregiver for patients with Alzheimer's disease had been providing care for more than three years before a doctor was consulted. As in the case with other chronic conditions, the tasks required of caregivers may vary considerably. Yet the tendency of individuals with Alzheimer's disease to deteriorate cognitively and physically causes unique caregiving problems. Studies have suggested that cognitive impairment increases strain because it creates an ambiguity in the family boundary: The patient's failure to recognize or emotionally respond to the caregiver creates confusion over whether the patient is in or out of the family system (Boss, Caron, and Horbal 1988). Caregiving for elderly people is often time-bounded, however, as serious, degenerative disease among elderly people often leads to death or institutional care.

Family caregiving for children, on the other hand, can start from birth and last indefinitely, especially if the illness or disability prolongs their dependency. Research indicates that about 20 percent of all children have a chronic illness or disability, and 10 per-

cent have problems that create caregiving requirements, including the three million children under age eighteen who are disabled (Butler, Rosenbaum, and Palfrey 1987; Sexson and Madan-Swain 1993). Childhood chronic illness can result in severe financial strains, marital discord, and family isolation and disorganization. It may also undermine essential family tasks such as reproduction and child rearing and disrupt the normal family life cycle, especially when it prolongs the child's normal period of dependency. Studies have focused on the demand for family caregiving created by chronic illness or disability. The amount of work that families perform depends primarily on the type of illness and the extent of impairment. Caregiving for illnesses such as epilepsy, arthritis, and diabetes may require managing the illness daily with special diets and/or drug therapies, and coping with occasional acute medical crises. Other illnesses, however, such as kidney disease, cystic fibrosis, and spina bifida, often require extensive home care labor and frequent contact with medical professionals.

Cystic fibrosis is the most common genetic disorder among whites, affecting 1 in 2,000 live births. It occurs in other racial groups much less frequently. A study of caregiving for children with cystic fibrosis pointed to the demanding medical treatments parents must administer, which include oral medications and special diets, aerosol therapy and bronchial drainage (prescribed two to four times a day, requiring about an hour each time), exercise, and mist tent therapy at night (Patterson 1985). Medical therapies such as these are complex, difficult to learn, and can occupy so much time that they become the center of family life. They may also be risky and interfere with normal parental behavior that ordinarily centers on being nurturing and supportive. One study on pediatric ambulatory dialysis found that parents have difficulty reconciling parenting with the administration of medical regimens:

Parents are asked to monitor the child's physical state intensely. They are also told not to allow the child's medical problems to become the main family focus. Parents are instructed that an error in the sterile technique could result in their child's serious illness, yet staff is also concerned that parents should not experience excessive anxiety. Parents are asked to function as both medic and parent, and yet it is also expected that the child will be able to progress through the normal stages of separation and individuation [LePontis, Moel, and Cohn 1987, p. 83].

In addition to the work and anxiety entailed in carrying out medical tasks, parents must also address the psychological and emotional needs of the child with chronic illness or disability. While most children with physical disabilities do not develop mental health problems, they are much more likely to do so than healthy children because of greater social isolation, alienation, and poor school performance (Patterson and Geber 1991). Both parents and medical care experts endeavor to prevent these problems by encouraging normal life experiences and bolstering coping skills, self-esteem, and confidence of children who are chronically ill. Parents must also try to maintain a sense of balance in meeting the needs of their ill and healthy children. Siblings of children with chronic illness often receive less attention from parents while performing more household tasks, which can lead to sibling resentment and rivalry.

The notion of family caregiving often obscures the fact that gender is a crucial determinant of the impact of a chronic illness or disability on the family; it affects responses to medical diagnoses, definitions of social support, and the distribution and style of caregiving work. Fathers respond more negatively to the birth of a child with disability than do mothers; in one study fathers listed more symptoms of stress and were more negative about the impact of the child on their marriage (Waisbren 1980). Oscar Barbarin, Diane Hughes, and Mark Chesler (1985) found that parents of children with cancer, both fathers and mothers, cited spousal support as essential to their ability to cope; mothers, however, saw support as help from fathers in caring for the child, while fathers saw the mother's availability in the home as support. The most important impact of gender on caregiving is that social norms still define women as primarily responsible for caregiving. Studies have consistently found that 75 percent to 80 percent of those who have primary or sole responsibility for caregiving are women. Caregiving substantially increases the amount of work performed by women. For example, Naomi Breslau (1983) reported that families of children with disabilities spent a great deal more time on home therapies, doctor visits, and domestic work than did families of healthy children. Mothers who are caregivers for chronically ill family members often have difficulty meeting their role obligations, especially if they are employed outside the home or are single parents.

There is also a gender division in the type of work men and women perform, as well as in their styles of caregiving. Men perform more instrumental tasks for relatives with disability or illness, such as lawn maintenance, lifting, and assisting with financial matters. Men have an activity-oriented, managerial, and emotionally detached style of caregiving, and when they are the primary caregiver, they receive more help from others in carrying out their tasks (Boss, Caron, and Horbal 1988; Ungerson 1987). Women view caregiving as a duty and obligation and have styles that are more expressive and supportive. They provide more personal service than do men, receive less assistance from others in performing their work, but do have more sources of emotional support. These gender differences in the type and style of caregiving may explain why women who are caregivers experience more stress than do men. A study by Anne E. Kazak and Robert S. Marvin (1984) focused on mothers of children with handicaps and those of healthy children and found that mothers of children with handicaps were more isolated, saw their children as more demanding and dependent, and felt their children were less able to deal with their social and physical environments. In this study, 50 percent of the mothers were at a high risk for developing other problems. Mother-caregivers have also been found to have high levels of anxiety and depression, especially when caregiving requires demanding tasks; these mothers viewed motherhood as "frustrating, unhappy, and wearing" (Breslau, Salkever, and Staruch 1982). Mothers often experience significant declines in their own health status (Patterson, Leonard, and Titus 1992).

The impact of caregiving on families is also mediated by economic and sociocultural influences. People who are poor have higher rates of sickness, chronic illness, and mortality than do affluent people, but less access to adequate medical care. John A. Butler, Sara Rosenbaum, and Judith S. Palfrey (1987) found that 12 percent of low-income children with the most severe disabilities in the United States had no regular physician, and 7 percent to 32 percent had no insurance coverage. Medicaid, a federal-state program designed to provide medical care to the poor, now covers fewer than 50 percent of low-income persons because eligibility guidelines often require having an income well below the poverty line. The elderly are more likely to be covered by Medicare, a federal insurance program, and the nonpoor elderly may have additional forms of insurance. Insurance programs, however, have made little progress in defraying expenses incurred by families who provide home care. Due to cultural and economic influences, African Americans are especially likely to care for the elderly at home, and the availability of a broad range of informal caregivers helps mediate the strain of caregiving. A study of women caring for elderly parents provided further data on how economics influence caregiver roles. In this study, Patricia G. Archbold (1983) found that affluent caregivers were care managers who used a variety of institutional resources to coordinate their parents' care, while low-income women were care providers who performed the heavy physical work of nursing care and personal service.

Coping Resources and Strategies

Coping has been defined as the things people do to avoid or minimize the stress that would otherwise result from problematic conditions of life (Pearlin and Aneshensel 1986). Researchers have focused on two interrelated dimensions of coping: coping resources and coping strategies. Coping resources are the psychological and material assets available to individuals and their families in responding to stressful situations. Coping strategies, on the other hand, are the actual behaviors or responses people use in dealing with stressful events. At the individual level, coping resources include one's education, income, self-esteem, a sense of mastery, and psychological hardiness, all of which enhance one's ability to deal effectively with life strains.

Family systems theorists have noted that there is a powerful interactive effect between the family and illness, in that illness not only affects the family but also the family actively structures and mediates the impact of the illness (Shapiro 1983). In early studies on family adaptation to crises, Reuben Hill (1954) identified integration and adaptability as key family resources. Integration refers to having strong ties of affection, pride in family tradition, and a history of sharing in activities; adaptability means having flexible social roles, sharing responsibility for performing tasks, and communicating openly. Other studies have shown that coping is enhanced when the family does not blame itself for the illness but feels confident in its ability to manage the situation. This often requires that the family not organize itself completely around the illness or the needs of the sick person, but continue to be sensitive and responsive to the needs of all family members. The family's health-care attitudes and behaviors, patterns of communication and emotional expressiveness, role relationships, available caregivers, and financial stability are all important resources in managing illnesses.

Social support has become a key element in stress theory, as it has been shown to be an essential mediator of the stress produced by undesirable life events. Also, because the course of chronic illnesses is often affected by stress, social support may actually ameliorate the physical symptoms of illness and enhance survival. Many types of social support have been examined, but the three most basic types are emotional support, which fosters feelings of comfort; cognitive support, which entails providing information, knowledge, and advice; and material support, the offer of goods and materials (Jacobsen 1986). Most people expect informal support from their friends and family members, often finding such support available and adequate. However, there is a tendency for informal sources of support to be available during acute stages of the illness, such as the diagnosis or terminal stage, but to wane when the illness continues over an extended time. Formal sources of social support may be available on a more consistent basis and provide the advantage of talking with experts or people experiencing similar problems. Participation in formal support groups by caregivers for children with developmental disabilities has been found to lower levels of stress and depression. Findings such as these have led to a growth in the organization of support groups that focus on building family strengths and providing counseling and referral services.

A variety of coping strategies have been identified among persons who experience life strains, including prayer, stoicism, physical activity, denial, withdrawal, and ignoring the problem. The two most common strategies for coping with long-term chronic illness and its debilitating effects, however, are normalization and the attribution of meaning. After the initial impact of the diagnosis of chronic illness wanes, family members are eager to resume their normal lives. Whatever the level of physical or mental impairment caused by the illness, most people do not want the illness to threaten the self-identities, social roles, or activities they value or to become the dominant factor in their interactions with others. To avoid this, they attempt to normalize the situation by minimizing the illness and conveying the impression of normalcy to others. One normalizing strategy is to describe behaviors associated with the illness, such as pain, crying, fatigue, forgetfulness, diet changes, and drug therapies, as things that all people experience or engage in from time to time. Parents often make sure that their children with illness or disability participate in as many normal school and household activities as necessary. In some cases, people with chronic illness invest a great deal of energy in their efforts to manage impressions and responses of others; they may disguise symptoms, avoid embarrassing situations, or control the information available to others. Normalization may, however, conflict with the demands of the illness or be hampered by visible and intrusive illness symptoms and medical regimens.

The attribution of meaning, a coping strategy that refers to defining the illness in a positive manner, is also an effort to maintain a certain balance in family life. Parents and other family members often view the illness as increasing family cohesion, their patience, and their faith in God or as leading them to develop more meaningful goals and values. Parents may also redefine the expectations they have for their child with chronic illness or disability in a way conducive to maintaining a positive self-image. In a study focusing on preventing mental health problems among children with chronic illness, Joan M. Patterson and Gayle Geber (1991) point out that meanings are at the core of determining whether a disability leads to a handicap, which is a discrepancy between role expectations and actual role performance. The process of definition allows people with chronic illness and their families to endow the illness with meaning, as noted by Maurice Venters (1981) in her study of families with children who have cystic fibrosis. For example, one parent defined caring for the child this way:

> God has chosen our family to care for this special child. He knew we were a giving, loving family and were strong enough to take the difficult times as well as the good times. Children are meant to be loved, and so we have a special mission in life to carry out God's will [Venter 1981, p. 294].

Medical progress has been made in treating and controlling chronic illnesses; however, few people believe those illnesses will be completely eliminated by biomedical interventions, as they are intricately related to aging and ever-changing environmental and social factors. Some people respond to the threat of chronic illnesses, many of which are associated with lifestyle choices, by advocating individual responsibility for health care. This suggests that people should rely on the medical system less and focus on adopting healthy lifestyles. Others have begun to emphasize that the traditional emphasis on finding biophysical cures for diseases should be redirected toward continuing improvements in preventive care and a focus on caring rather than curing. This caring has been defined as "a positive emotional and supportive response . . . to affirm our commitment to their well-being, our willingness to identify with them in their pain and suffering, and our desire to do what we can to relieve their situation" (Callahan 1990, p.111).

Studies of family caregiving have often focused on caring as burdensome and disruptive to families, es-

pecially women, and as a threat to family stability. However, researchers have begun to emphasize the subjective and experiential aspects of caregiving that arise from the meanings assigned to the work (Fisher and Tronto 1990; Traustadottir 1991). While the work performed by caregivers needs to be recognized, it need not be viewed as burdensome or unworthy. Rather, caregiving work has been redefined as potentially empowering, as it involves caring about the quality of life for persons with chronic illness and disability and working to make the community and society more responsive to their needs.

(*See also:* DISABILITIES; ELDERS; HEALTH AND THE FAMILY; PSYCHIATRIC DISORDERS; STRESS)

BIBLIOGRAPHY

Aneshensel, C. S.; Pearlin, L. I.; and Schuler, R. H. (1993). "Stress, Role Captivity, and the Cessation of Caregiving." *Journal of Health and Social Behavior* 34:54–70.

Archbold, P. G. (1983). "Impact of Parent-Caring on Women." *Family Relations* 32:39–45.

Barbarin, O.; Huges, D.; and Chesler, M. (1985). "Stress, Coping, and Marital Functioning Among Parents of Children with Cancer." *Journal of Marriage and the Family* 47:473–480.

Battle, C. U. (1984). "Disruptions in the Socialization of a Young, Severely Handicapped Child." In *The Psychological and Social Impact of Physical Disability*, ed. R. P. Marinelli and A. E. Dell Orto. New York: Springer-Verlag.

Beckman, P. J. (1983). "Influence of Selected Child Characteristics on Stress in Families of Handicapped Infants." *American Journal of Mental Deficiency* 88:150–156.

Billings, A. G., and Moos, R. H. (1981). "The Role of Coping Responses and Social Resources in Attenuating the Stress of Life Events." *Journal of Behavioral Medicine* 4:139–157.

Boss, P.; Caron, W.; and Horbal, J. (1988). "Alzheimer's Disease and Ambiguous Loss." In *Chronic Illness and Disability*, ed. C. S. Chilman, E. W. Nunnally, and F. M. Cox. Newbury Park, CA: Sage Publications.

Breslau, N. (1983). "Care of Disabled Children and Women's Time Use." *Medical Care* 21:620–629.

Breslau, N.; Salkever, D.; and Staruch, K. S. (1982). "Women's Labor Force Activity and Responsibilities for Disabled Dependents: A Study of Families with Disabled Children." *Journal of Health and Social Behavior* 23:169–183.

Bristor, M. W. (1984). "The Birth of a Handicapped Child: A Wholistic Model for Grieving." *Family Relations* 33:25–32.

Brown, E. R. (1979). *Rockefeller Medicine Man: Medicine and Capitalism in America*. Berkeley: University of California Press.

Butler, J. A.; Rosenbaum, S.; and Palfrey, J. S. (1987). "Ensuring Access to Health Care for Children with Disabilities." *New England Journal of Medicine* 317:162–165.

Callahan, D. (1990). "The Primary of Caring: Choosing Health-Care Priorities." *Commonweal*, February 23, pp. 107–112.

Carter, B. D.; Urey, J. R.; and Eid, N. S. (1992). "The Chronically Ill Child and Family Stress: Family Developmental Perspectives on Cystic Fibrosis." *Psychosomatics* 33: 397–403.

Cohen, M. H. (1993). "The Unknown and the Unknowable: Managing Sustained Uncertainty." *Western Journal of Nursing Research* 15:77–96.

Corbin, J. M., and Strauss, A. (1988). *Unending Work and Care: Managing Chronic Illness at Home.* San Francisco: Jossey-Bass.

Crawford, R. (1986). "Individual Responsibility and Health Politics." In *The Sociology of Health and Illness*, 2nd edition, ed. P. Conrad and R. Kern. New York: St. Martin's Press.

Dubos, R. (1959). *Mirage of Health: Utopias, Progress, and Biological Change.* New York: Harper & Row.

Fisher, B., and Tronto, J. (1990). "Toward a Feminist Theory of Caring." In *Circles of Care: Work and Identity in Women's Lives*, ed. E. K. Abel and M. K. Nelson. New York: State University of New York Press.

Fortier, L., and Wanlass, R. (1984). "Family Crisis Following the Diagnosis of a Handicapped Child." *Family Relations* 33:13–24.

Freund, P. E. S., and McGuire, M. B. (1991). *Health, Illness, and the Social Body: A Critical Sociology.* Englewood Cliffs, NJ: Prentice Hall.

Hamlett, K. W.; Pellegrini, D. S.; and Katz, K. S. (1992). "Childhood Chronic Illness as a Family Stressor." *Journal of Pediatric Psychology* 17:33–47.

Handron, D. S. (1993). "Denial and Serious Chronic Illness: A Personal Perspective." *Perspectives in Psychiatric Care* 29:29–33.

Hill, R. (1954). "Social Stresses on the Family." *Social Casework* 39:139–156.

Hill, S. A. (1994). *Managing Sickle-Cell Disease in Low-Income Families.* Philadelphia: Temple University Press.

Hines-Martin, V. P. (1992). "A Research Review: Family Caregivers of Chronically Ill African-American Elderly." *Journal of Gerontological Nursing* 18:25–29.

Hymovich, D. P., and Hagopian, G. A. (1992). *Chronic Illness in Children and Adults: A Psychosocial Approach.* Philadelphia: Saunders.

Jacobsen, D. E. (1986). "Types and Timing of Social Support." *Journal of Health and Social Behavior* 27:250–264.

Kasl, S. V. (1983). "Social and Psychological Factors Affecting the Course of Disease: An Epidemiological Perspective." In *Handbook of Health, Health Care, and the Health Professions*, ed. D. Mechanic. New York: Free Press.

Kazak, A. E., and Marvin, R. S. (1984). "Differences, Difficulties, and Adaptation: Stress and Social Networks in Families with a Handicapped Child." *Family Relations* 33:67–77.

Koch, A. (1985). "If Only It Could Be Me: The Families of Pediatric Cancer Patients." *Family Relations* 34:63–70.

Kronenfeld, J. J. (1979). "Self-Care as a Panacea for the Ills of the Health-Care System: An Assessment." *Social Science and Medicine* 13A:263–267.

Krulik, T. (1980). "Successful 'Normalizing' Tactics of Parents of Chronically Ill Children." *Journal of Advanced Nursing* 5:573–578.

LePontis, J.; Moel, D. I.; and Cohn, R. A. (1987). "Family Adjustment to Pediatric Ambulatory Dialysis." *American Journal of Orthopsychiatry* 51:78–83.

Lerner, M. J.; Somers, D. G.; Reid, D.; and Tierney, M. C. (1989). "A Social Dilemma: Egocentrically Biased Cognitions Among Filial Caregivers." In *Social Psychology of Aging*, ed. S. Spacapan and S. Oskamp. Newbury Park, CA: Sage Publications.

Litman, T. J. (1974). "The Family as a Basic Unit in Health and Medical Care: A Social-Behavioral Overview." *Social Science and Medicine* 8:495–519.

Maddox, G. L., and Glass, T. A. (1989). "Health Care of the Chronically Ill." In *Handbook of Medical Sociology*, 4th edition, ed. H. E. Freeman and S. Levine. Englewood Cliffs, NJ: Prentice Hall.

McKinlay, J. B., and McKinlay, S. M. (1987). "Medical Measures and the Decline of Mortality." In *Dominant Issues in Medical Sociology*, 2nd edition, ed. H. D. Schwartz. New York: McGraw–Hill.

Mechanic, D. (1982). "The Epidemiology of Illness Behavior and Its Relationship to Physical and Psychological Distress." In *Symptoms, Illness Behavior, and Help-Seeking*, ed. D. Mechanic. New York: Prodist.

Mechanic, D. (1992). "Health and Illness Behavior and Patient–Practitioner Relationships." *Social Science and Medicine* 34:1345–50.

Mishler, E. G. (1981). "Critical Perspectives on the Biomedical Model." In *Social Contexts of Health, Illness, and Patient Care*, ed. E. G. Mishler, L. A. Singham, S. T. Hauser, R. Liem, S. D. Osherson, and N. E. Waxler. Cambridge, Eng.: Cambridge University Press.

National Commission on Chronic Illness. (1956). *Chronic Illness in the United States: Care of the Long-Term Patient*, Vol. II. Cambridge, MA: Harvard University Press.

Parsons, T., and Fox, R. (1952). "Illness, Therapy, and the Modern Urban American Family." *Journal of Social Issues* 13:31–44.

Patterson, J. M. (1985). "Critical Factors Affecting Family Compliance with Home Treatment for Children with Cystic Fibrosis." *Family Relations* 34:79–88.

Patterson, J. M. (1988). "Chronic Illness in Children and the Impact on Families." In *Chronic Illness and Disability*, ed. C. S. Chilman, E. W. Nunnally, and F. M. Cox. Newbury Park, CA: Sage Publications.

Patterson, J. M., and Geber, G. (1991). "Preventing Mental Health Problems in Children with Chronic Illness or Disability: Parent to Parent Conference." *Children's Health Care* 20·150–161

Patterson, J. M.; Leonard, B. J.; and Titus, J. C. (1992). "Home Care for Medically Fragile Children: Impact on Family Health and Well-Being." *Journal of Developmental Behavior and Pediatrics* 13:248–255.

Pearlin, L. I., and Aneshensel, C. S. (1986). "Coping and Social Supports: Their Functions and Applications." In *Applications of Social Science to Clinical Medicine and Health Policy*, ed. L. Aiken and D. Mechanic. New Brunswick, NJ: Rutgers University Press.

Reiser, S. J. (1978). *Medicine and the Reign of Technology.* New York: Cambridge University Press.

Rosenfield, S. (1992). "Factors Contributing to the Subjective Quality of Life of the Chronic Mentally Ill." *Journal of Health and Social Behavior* 33:299–315.

Seaburn, D. B.; Lorenz, A.; and Kaplan, D. (1992). "The Transgenerational Development of Chronic Illness Meanings." *Family Systems Medicine* 10:385–394.

Sexson, S. B., and Madan-Swain, A. (1993). "School Reentry for the Child with Chronic Illness." *Journal of Learning Disabilities* 26:115–125.

Shapiro, J. (1983). "Family Reactions and Coping Strategies in Response to the Physically Ill or Handicapped Child: A Review." *Social Science and Medicine* 17:913–931.

Shapiro, J., and Tittle, K. (1986). "Psychosocial Adjustment of Poor Mexican Mothers of Disabled and Nondisabled Children." *American Journal of Orthopsychiatry* 56:289–302.

Starr, P. (1982). *The Social Transformation of American Medicine.* New York: Basic Books.

Stewart, D. C., and Sullivan, T. J. (1982). "Illness Behavior and the Sick Role in Chronic Disease." *Social Science and Medicine* 16:1397–1404.

Traustadottir, R. (1991). "Mothers Who Care: Gender, Disability, and Family Life." *Journal of Family Issues* 12:211–228.

Turner-Henson, A.; Holaday, B.; and Swan, J. H. (1992). "When Parenting Becomes Caregiving: Caring for the Chronically Ill Child." *Family and Community Health* 15:19–30.

Ungerson, C. (1987). *Policy Is Personal: Sex, Gender, and Informal Care.* New York: Tavistock.

Venters, M. (1981). "Familial Coping with Chronic and Severe Childhood Disease: The Case of Cystic Fibrosis." *Social Science and Medicine* 15A:289–297.

Waisbren, S. E. (1980). "Parents' Reaction After the Birth of a Developmentally Disabled Child." *American Journal of Mental Deficiency* 84:345–351.

Weitz, R. (1990). "Uncertainty and the Lives of Persons with AIDS." In *The Sociology of Health and Sickness*, 3rd edition, ed. P. Conrad and R. Kern. New York: St. Martin's Press.

SHIRLEY A. HILL

CODEPENDENCY

"Codependency" is a word most often used to describe the behavior of a spouse of a chemically dependent person. However, the phenomenon of the tendency of one human being to become focused on another to the point of obsession can be observed in many situations of illness and stress and in different relationships, including parents and children, siblings, lovers, and friends.

During the 1980s and early 1990s, codependency was widely discussed on television talk shows, and it was the subject of many best-selling books. Interest in recovery developed into a sort of grassroots movement, primarily among white middle-class social groups in the United States. A network of nationally known specialists in the field, popular lecturers, writers, and therapists emerged to theorize on its nature and cause.

Codependency has been called a manifestation of a dysfunctional family system. Some experts contend that it is the root cause of all addiction, while others say that codependency is a disease in itself. Still others argue that it is a result of cultural conditioning, especially of women. Whichever definition is ascribed to, there seems to be general agreement that codependency is a common and widespread condition in society. There is also agreement that it is treatable, that the behaviors can be confronted and changed, and that codependent people can and do recover.

However, the concept of codependency has also been criticized for being over generalized and under researched. Social commentators have accused proponents of mercenary motives: "Inventing a ubiquitous disease—codependency—creates a huge market for a cure" (Kaminer 1993, p. xvi). Evidence of its prevalence has been largely anecdotal, coming from the observations of therapists and the personal testimony of people in self-help groups, rather than from scientific research.

Roots and Traits of Codependency

There are as many definitions of codependence as there are experts in the field. In 1989, a group of therapists and other professionals gathered at a forum session before the first national conference on the subject and proposed the following definition: "Codependency is a pattern of painful dependence on compulsive behaviors and on approval from others in an attempt to find safety, self-worth, and a sense of identity. Recovery is possible" (Whitfield 1991, p. 10).

An important point to understand is that codependency is a condition that occurs in terms of an individual's relationship with someone else with an addiction (e.g., an alcoholic, a drug addict, a compulsive gambler). Just as it has been observed that chemical dependency runs in families, it follows that codependency does as well. Sharon Wegscheider-Cruse, a leading proponent of codependency, states it is her belief that 96 percent of the population of the United States could be described as codependent, which she defines as "all persons (1) who are in a love or marriage relationship with an alcoholic; (2) have one or more alcoholic parents or grandparents; (3) grew up in an emotionally repressive family" (Schaef 1986, p. 18). Elaborating on the personal attributes of these codependent individuals, Pia Mellody (1989) describes five core symptoms of codependence: low self-esteem, poor boundaries, limited self-expression, poor self-care, and extreme actions.

A "primary" codependent's condition usually begins in childhood as a reaction to and as a compensation for parental dysfunction (Whitfield 1991). These individuals often make promises to themselves that they will never marry a chemically dependent person because they do not want to put their children through the pain of growing up in the same type of dysfunctional family. There is always the possibility, however, that the primary codependent will unconsciously choose a mate with another compulsive disorder, such as gambling, which can trigger enabling behavior just as easily as chemical dependency.

Individuals who find themselves married to a person with an addiction usually attempt to control their spouse with behaviors such as emptying the spouse's bottles of alcohol, spying on their whereabouts, and covering for their irresponsible actions. This is consistent with Melody Beattie's opinion that "a codependent person is one who has let another person's behavior affect him or her, and who is obsessed with controlling that person's behavior" (Beattie 1987, p. 31). Codependent spouses tend to internalize the shame and embarrassment caused by the addicted person's conduct. This reinforces the shame of a primary codependent's childhood, further convincing the person that there must be something wrong with him or her. "Shame is the essence of codependency" (Bradshaw 1988b, p. 14).

Codependence has long been thought to be associated with mental and emotional illness (Whitfield 1991), but it is also claimed by some to be related to physical illness, such as "headaches; backaches; respiratory, heart, and gastrointestinal problems . . . hypertension . . . [and] even cancer" (Schaef 1986, pp.

58–59). Therefore, it is not surprising that codependency has also come to be known as a "disease of lost selfhood" (Whitfield 1991, p. 3). One of the mysterious characteristics of codependence is that it is not just a reaction to the partner's chemical dependency or compulsion, as the symptoms of codependency often escalate when the family member who is ill recovers or dies (Mellody 1989).

Most examples of codependent behavior involve women—wives, mothers, and daughters—who nurture their husbands, parents, and children, as they are encouraged to do by the society in which they live. However, some feminists argue that codependency is a concept that is demeaning to women, because it blames them for the roles and tasks they are assigned in the patriarchal system. Charlotte Davis Kasl calls it "a disease of inequality—a predictable set of behavior patterns that people in a subordinate role typically adopt to survive in the dominant culture. Codependency is a euphemism for internalized oppression" (Kasl 1992, p. 279). Anne Wilson Schaef, who wrote one of the first books on the subject, believes that codependency is the manifestation of a society whose institutions, such as marriage, foster addiction; therefore, it has "no respect for age, color, social standing, or sex" (Schaef 1986, p. 45).

The major trap in codependence is the danger of becoming a "relationship addict" (Schaef 1986, p. 48). In this case, the codependent individual has become as dependent on the partner as the partner is dependent on the addiction. This makes recovery for either member of the relationship very difficult.

Healing from Codependence

As the fellowship of Alcoholics Anonymous (AA) grew in the late 1930s, the wives of the early members met and talked about their own issues while their husbands were at the meetings. In 1948, Lois Wilson, the wife of AA cofounder William Wilson ("Bill W."), helped to create Al-Anon, "a fellowship of relatives and friends of alcoholics who share their experience, strength, and hope in order to solve their common problems" (Al-Anon Family Groups 1991, p. 2). Matching the growth of AA, Al-Anon has grown into a worldwide organization with thousands of members. Their philosophy is that "alcoholism is a family illness, and that changed attitudes can aid recovery" (Al-Anon Family Groups 1991, p. 2).

With the support of their friends in Al-Anon, members make concerted efforts to change their enabling, codependent behaviors. No longer do they clean up after and make excuses for their partners. Al-Anon members go through their own healing process, and healing from codependency can sometimes influence the chemically dependent partner to get well. However, Al-Anon primarily encourages members to "take your eyes off the alcoholic and put them on yourself." This makes the individuals reexamine their own habits, such as controlling, nagging, and manipulating.

Janet Geringer Woititz, who studied children of alcoholics, revealed that they have lower self-esteem than children from nonalcoholic homes. This led her to question what would happen to these children as they grew up. As "self-perceptions do not change over time without some form of intervention," she suggested that "an important population to pay attention to are the Adult Children of Alcoholics" (Woititz 1983, p. xvii). The Adult Children of Alcoholics (ACOA) self-help meetings, which first began in the United States in 1977, focus on family-of-origin issues and encourage members to express the full range of their emotions (Whitfield 1991).

Healing involves examination of the true origins of the codependent's problems and a realization that these problems started long before the family member developed his or her own dependency. Often, the codependent's pain goes back to childhood feelings of shame and insecurity, because it is the "inner child" who is the "repository of self-worth" (Wegscheider-Cruse 1987, p. 23). Charles L. Whitfield, who has said that the "adult child syndrome" is the same as codependence, points out that healing from codependency always involves finding a lost part, called the "inner child" or the "true self," the special, unique gift within each human being (Whitfield 1991, pp. 20, 22).

Conclusion

In 1986, the CoDependents Anonymous (CoDA) organization was founded, expressly to focus on freeing members from unnecessary suffering in their relationships in general (Whitfield 1991). However, there are many self-help groups in addition to AA, Al-Anon, ACOA, and CoDA, as well as many professional therapeutic approaches to codependency. It is up to the individual to decide which organization or therapy will provide the best support for his or her particular situation. The claimed success of self-help groups (which remains largely unmeasured) is based on the simple formula of admission of the truth and sharing in a confidential environment. "We simply cannot underestimate the healing effects of being with other persons who are struggling with the same problems" (Schaef 1986, p. 97).

(*See also:* Attachment; Dysfunctional Family; Family Therapy; Marriage Counseling; Personality Development; Self-Help Groups; Substance Abuse)

BIBLIOGRAPHY

Al-Anon Family Group. (1991). *Al-Anon's Twelve Steps and Twelve Traditions*. New York: Author.

Beattie, M. (1987). *Codependent No More*. New York: Harper & Row.

Bradshaw, J. (1988a). *The Family*. Deerfield Beach, FL: Health Communications.

Bradshaw, J. (1988b). *Healing the Shame that Binds You*. Deerfield Beach, FL: Health Communications.

Kaminer, W. (1993). *I'm Dysfunctional, You're Dysfunctional*. New York: Vintage Books.

Kasl, C. D. (1992). *Many Roads, One Journey*. New York: HarperCollins.

Mellody, P. (1989). *Facing Codependence*. New York: HarperCollins.

Schaef, A. W. (1986). *Co-Dependence: Misunderstood—Mistreated*. New York: HarperCollins.

Wegscheider-Cruse, S. (1987). *Learning to Love Yourself*. Deerfield Beach, FL: Health Communications.

Whitfield, C. L. (1991). *Co-Dependence: Healing the Human Condition*. Deerfield Beach, FL: Health Communications.

Woititz, J. G. (1983). *Adult Children of Alcoholics*. Deerfield Beach, FL: Health Communications.

LYNN JOHNSON-MARTIN

COHABITATION

Among the changes in living arrangements experienced by Americans since 1960, the rise in the number of nonmarital couples cohabitating is especially noticeable. Sharing living quarters with a sexual partner without a formal marriage—a pattern variously known as consensual unions, living together, nonmarital cohabitation, unmarried-couple households, and domestic partners—has become widely practiced. The U.S. Bureau of the Census even coined the acronym POSSLQ'S (People of the Opposite Sex Sharing Living Quarters) to depict heterosexual participants in such relationships. This alternative lifestyle is not a recent phenomenon, however, nor is it a uniquely Western one; coresiding couples are found in many past as well as present societies. For example, in the United States, a historically familiar form of living together is the common-law relationship—a couple living together, having and rearing children, and so on, outside the framework of legal matrimony. Although the concept of common-law marriages was eventually abandoned by a majority of jurisdictions, it is still recognized by many states.

Unmarried cohabitation is also increasing in most other Western nations, such as Australia, Canada, France, Great Britain, and Sweden. In Sweden, for instance, it is estimated that about one-fourth of couples live in this type of arrangement, and it is generally recognized that the majority of Swedes now cohabit before marriage. In 1992, there were 3.3 million unmarried-couple households in the United States. This represented a 650 percent increase from 1960. More important, the proportion of first marriages preceded by cohabitation increased from only 8 percent for marriages in the late 1960s to about 50 percent for marriages in the 1990s (Bumpass and Sweet 1989; Popenoe 1993). Moreover, this changing behavior has been accompanied by a shift in attitudes, in which the participants "express little concern with cohabitation being a moral issue or with the disapproval of parents or friends" (Bumpas, Sweet, and Cherlin 1991, p. 921).

These figures no doubt underrepresent the number of unmarried consensual partners because it is difficult to know precisely how many of these relationships there are. Couples sometimes maintain separate addresses even though they actually coreside in one or the other's quarters most of the time. Others do not report their living arrangements in the first place (Bedard 1992). In any event, there is little question that a growing proportion of people is coming to view this nonmarital arrangement as an acceptable one; for many, it is viewed as a normal step in the courtship process. This is even apparent among the remarried population. During the 1960s, 25 percent of remarriages were preceded by cohabitation; by the end of the 1980s, 70 percent were (U.S. Bureau of the Census 1992).

Why Cohabit?

People selecting cohabitation do so because they view it as meeting a variety of their needs, because it supports some of their major beliefs or values, or for many other reasons. They may form consensual unions out of loneliness, disappointment with traditional dating and courtship, fear of marital commitment, or simply because they wish to experiment with a new living arrangement—one that gives them greater freedom and privacy. For many couples, cohabiting offers the financial advantage of reducing the costs of daily living. Many others are attracted to this lifestyle because it provides regular access to a sexual

partner under minimal conditions for contracting a sexually transmitted disease, such as AIDS. For still others, cohabitation meets their desire to test compatibility for eventual marriage. Clearly, there are many different motivations underlying the decision to establish an unmarried-couple household.

Many couples drift into cohabiting as a matter of convenience, with little or no prior discussions of the motivations, responsibilities, expectations, goals, or long-term implications of this action. In this connection, Carl Ridley and his associates (1978) identified four commonly observed types of cohabiting relationships (Linus-blanket, emancipation, convenience, and testing), each of which varies as a marriage preparation experience. Linus-blanket type relationships result from the dependence or insecurity of one of the partners, who prefers a relationship with *anyone* to being alone. Not surprisingly, such relationships generally tend to be short-lived. Emancipation relationships involve using cohabitation primarily to gain independence from parental values and influence. Convenience relationships involve partners who live together sexually more for practical reasons than for intimacy. Sustaining some level of mutual convenience is difficult but essential in order to prevent the possibility of exploitation. The testing mode of cohabitation essentially views the relationship as a trial marriage.

Ridley and his colleagues stressed the importance of clarifying motivations and goals for cohabiting before the step is taken. The experience could be of some value as preparation to marriage, either to test a particular relationship or to help the individual mature and become better able to sustain intimate relationships. On the other hand, cohabiting for the wrong reasons, or for persons who are not prepared emotionally or otherwise, can lead to considerable frustration and disappointment.

Even though the average length of cohabitation is about a year and a half, people terminating such relationships (especially if they have been of longer duration) often suffer an emotional trauma similar to those undergoing the divorce process (Newcomb 1979).

The Demography of Cohabitation

Although only about 5 percent of all couples in America are cohabitating at any given time, many more have done so at some time. Toward the end of the 1980s, for example, more than a third of women of childbearing age had lived with a boyfriend or partner at some point without being married to them. Among

COHABITATION

all first cohabiting unions (either before first marriage or sometime later), slightly more than half resulted in marriages (some of which ended in divorce), slightly more than 37 percent dissolved without marriage, and 10 percent were still ongoing (London 1991).

Cohabitors, as one might suspect, tend to be concentrated among younger age groups; more than three-fifths are thirty-four years old or younger; approximately 85 percent are under age forty-five. Only a small percentage are age sixty-five or older. This latter group, though comparatively small, is of some interest, since they represent a generation that did not particularly condone this lifestyle. The proportion and number of unmarried couples involving persons age sixty-five or older have declined significantly since 1970. Such couples numbered 115,000 in 1970, representing 22 percent of all unmarried-couple households. By 1992, they numbered about 73,000 couples and represented less than 5 percent of all unmarried-couple households. Such changes are noteworthy, given the significant increase in the elderly population in the United States. They may be explained by revised Social Security regulations, which make remarriage more practical for elderly people, and also by the large increase in younger unmarried couples who choose to live together. The advantages of nonmarital cohabitation for older persons are likely to be similar to those for younger persons. However, older couples may face greater disapproval from their age cohorts, friends, and associates. They are also more likely to encounter resistance or interference from their children and grandchildren.

In terms of marital status, more than half of the adults in unmarried-couple households have never been married; one-third are divorced. The remainder are either married but separated, currently married to someone else, or widowed. About one-third of cohabiting couples have children living with them (U.S. Bureau of the Census 1990). These are usually children from a previous marriage. Most such heterosexual partners do not have children together unless they plan to marry (Bedard 1992).

Despite the widespread perception that cohabiting is most prevalent among the college population, it is more common among young people who are not attending college and those of lower socioeconomic status (Bumpass, Sweet, and Cherlin 1991). African-Americans have cohabitation rates three times greater than whites. Moreover, unmarried couples are more likely than married couples to be interracial. Nine percent of unmarried couples and 1.5 percent of married couples are interracial. "A reasonable speculation is that interracial couples violate strongly held

social norms; and, therefore, some of them may be reluctant to formalize their relationship by marriage" (Glick and Spanier 1980, p. 26).

Comparison of Cohabitors and Noncohabitors

Cohabitors tend to differ from noncohabitors in a variety of sociodemographic characteristics. For instance, they tend to see themselves as being more androgynous and more politically liberal, are less apt to be religious, are more experienced sexually, and are younger than married persons (Seccombe 1992).

Eleanor Macklin (1983) compared cohabiting couples with married couples and noncohabiting-engaged or going-steady couples. She found that nonmarried cohabitants indicated significantly less commitment than did married couples. When compared with engaged couples, the unmarried cohabitants tended to be less committed to their partners, to the relationship, and to the idea of marrying their partners. In regard to a division of labor, Macklin found cohabiting couples tended to mirror the society around them and engaged in gender-role behavior characteristic of other couples their age. While most believed in sexual freedom within the relationship, most voluntarily restricted their sexual activity as evidence of their commitment to the relationship. In terms of communication, satisfaction, and problems experienced, few differences were noted.

Many other factors differentiate cohabitors and noncohabitors. Individuals whose mothers married young and were pregnant at marriage enter into cohabitational unions (and marriage) at a substantially higher rate than other individuals (Thornton 1991). Background factors that increase the propensity to cohabit include not completing high school, growing up in a family that received welfare, and coming from a single-parent family (Bumpass and Sweet 1989).

Cohabitation and Marital Stability

Of particular interest is the difference in the quality and stability of married versus cohabiting relationships. Living with a potential spouse is perceived by many to be a critical stage in the transition from courtship to marriage. The belief that cohabitation is an important prelude to marriage rests on the assumption that this experience in domesticity serves to screen out potentially incompatible mates more effectively than do traditional dating and courtship. Although this proposition appears reasonable, there is a growing body of evidence that premarital cohabitation is more likely to be associated with a greater proneness for divorce (Thompson and Colella 1992). Those who cohabit prior to marriage have been shown to be significantly lower on measures of marital quality, to report a lower commitment to the institution of marriage, to have a more individualistic view of marriage, and to have a markedly higher risk of marital dissolution (DeMaris and Rao 1992). In short, people who have lived with one another before marriage are much less likely to have successful marriages than those who do not (Whyte 1992). Thus, cohabitation does not seem to serve the function of a trial marriage or of a system that leads to stronger marriages by weeding out unsuitable mates. For some, this suggests that without an essential commitment at the start, it is difficult to sustain the relationship over time (Popenoe 1993).

This proneness toward martial instability may in fact have little to do with cohabitation per se, but rather may be due to other differences in the personalities and expectations of marriage between cohabitors and noncohabitors (Seccombe 1992). Some scholars have suggested that, because cohabitation has historically been a nontraditional lifestyle, it has had the latent function of attracting individuals who are, from the beginning, more inclined to have unstable marriages. Such individuals have been variously described as those who, compared to noncohabitors, have higher expectations for marriage, adapt less readily to conventional marriage-role expectations, lean toward a more deviant lifestyle, or have a generally weaker commitment to the institution of marriage (DeMaris and Rao 1992).

Cohabitor Typologies

Several typologies have been created to try to capture the diversity of personal relationships found among cohabiting couples. Macklin (1983), for example, discusses four types that capture some of this variation: (1) temporary or casual alliances, in which the couple lives together for convenience or for pragmatic reasons; (2) going together, in which the couple is affectionately involved but has no definite plans for marriage; (3) transitional, in which the experience serves as a preparation for marriage; and (4) alternative to marriage, wherein the couple opposes marriage on ideological or other grounds.

Complications and Trends

While several states still have legal codes under which cohabitation is considered illegal, those laws are rarely, if ever, enforced. The legal controversy over cohabitation becomes salient when one partner dies or the couple separates. At this point, problems can and do arise regarding real estate, personal property, insurance, wills, estates, child custody, and other matters. The legal rights in such situations, particularly for women and children, are unclear. Traditionally, women in such unmarried-couple households acquired no property rights. If they contributed any service, they were not entitled to recover an interest in resulting property. Similar situations existed for children of unmarried partners; they were considered illegitimate and, on the death of the father, received no financial or property benefits.

Since the early 1970s, a trend has emerged toward granting increased legal protection for the "spouse" and children of cohabitants (Weitzman 1981). In 1973, a California appellate court held that opposite-sex live-in partners had the same property rights as married persons. Subsequently, that state's supreme court recognized the validity of an oral agreement between cohabitants by making it legally binding upon both parties. Following termination of the relationship, cohabitors may file suits to resolve disputes over property rights, the status of children, or other matters. They may ask the courts to require the former partner to fulfill written or implied obligations or to pay palimony (similar to alimony). The rulings or outcomes in such cases are not altogether predictable. Court decisions have reduced but not eliminated the potentially negative legal consequences of cohabitation for those involved. Wide variation still exists among state laws, and most states have yet to define the rights of cohabitors and their children.

Nevertheless, attitudes toward cohabitation have become increasingly positive, particularly among younger persons. Perhaps one indication of this shift in sentiments is the noticeable decline in using the term "shacking up" to describe this lifestyle, a sometimes disparaging reference common among earlier generations. In Sweden, cohabitation has become so common that it is considered a social institution in and of itself. It is a variant of marriage rather than of courtship; approximately one-fifth of all couples in that country who live together are unmarried. In other countries where this way of living is institutionalized, few distinctions are seen between it and marriage. Both are viewed as appropriate avenues for intimacy, and they resemble one another to a much greater degree than in the United States in terms of commitment and stability. If these trends continue, it is quite possible that the United States will move in a similar direction (Seccombe 1992).

BIBLIOGRAPHY

Bedard, M. E. (1992). *Breaking with Tradition.* New York: General Hall.

Bumpass, L. L., and Sweet, J. A. (1989). "National Estimates of Cohabitation: Cohort Levels and Union Stability." *Demography* 26:615–625.

Bumpass, L. L.; Sweet, J. A.; and Cherlin, A. (1991). "The Role of Cohabitation in Declining Marriage Rates." *Journal of Marriage and the Family* 53:913–927.

DeMaris, A., and Rao, K. A. (1992). "Premarital Cohabitation and Subsequent Marital Stability in the United States: A Reassessment." *Journal of Marriage and the Family* 54:178–190.

Glick, P. C., and Spanier, G. B. (1980). "Married and Unmarried Cohabitation in the United States." *Journal of Marriage and the Family* 42:19–30.

Kierman, K. (1990). "Ringing Changes." *New Statesman and Society* 3:25.

London, K. A. (1991). "Cohabitation, Marriage, Marital Dissolution, and Remarriage: United States, 1988." *Advance Data from Vital and Health Statistics*, no. 194. Hyattsville, MD: National Center for Health Statistics.

Macklin, E. D. (1983) "Nonmarital Heterosexual Cohabitation: An Overview." In *Contemporary Families and Alternative Lifestyles: Handbook on Research and Theory*, ed. E. Macklin and R. Rubin. Newbury Park, CA: Sage Publications.

Newcomb, P. R. (1979). "Cohabitation in America: An Assessment of Consequences." *Journal of Marriage and the Family* 41:597–602.

Popenoe, D. (1993). "American Family Decline, 1960–1990: A Review and Appraisal." *Journal of Marriage and the Family* 55:527–555.

Ridley, C.; Peterman, D. J.; and Avery, A. W. (1978). "Cohabitation: Does It Make for a Better Marriage?" *Family Coordinator* 27:129–136.

Seccombe, K. (1992). "Alternative Lifestyles." In *Encyclopedia of Sociology*, ed. E. F. Borgatta and M. L. Borgatta. New York: Macmillan.

Thompson, E., and Colella, U. (1992). "Cohabitation and Marital Stability: Quality or Commitment?" *Journal of Marriage and the Family* 54:259–267.

Thornton, A. (1991). "Influence of the Marital History of Parents on the Marital and Cohabitational Experiences of Children." *American Journal of Sociology* 96:868–894.

U.S. Bureau of the Census. (1992). "Marital Status and Living Arrangements: March 1990." *Current Population Reports.* Series P-20, no. 450. Washington, DC: U.S. Government Printing Office.

Weitzman, L. J. (1991). *The Marriage Contract: Spouses, Lovers, and the Law.* New York: Free Press.

Whyte, M. K. (1992). "Choosing Mates—The American Way." *Society* 29:71–77.

FELIX M. BERARDO

COMMITMENT

"...till death do us part." Although the common-sense understanding of the nature of commitment to a relationship is often confined to the simple image of dedication to the continuation of the relationship even in the face of adversity ("for richer or for poorer, in sickness and in health"), it is also often acknowledged that the forces that hold a relationship together over time can extend far beyond the personal dedication of the people involved (Fehr 1988). Everyone recognizes the difference between "I want this relationship so badly that I will do whatever I have to do to make it work," and "I am stuck in this relationship for now, whether I like it or not." The earliest social psychological work to focus on the identification of the various personal and social forces that produce relationship continuity was that of George Levinger (1965), who made a distinction between attractions to a relationship and barriers to leaving it. Although Levinger's cohesiveness framework was extremely influential in both theoretical work and in marital counseling throughout the 1960s and 1970s (Lewis and Spanier 1979), work shifted in the 1980s to the language of commitment and drew upon other theoretical traditions. Michael P. Johnson's (1973, 1982) elaboration of the concept of commitment is rooted in Howard S. Becker's (1960) symbolic interactionist analysis of the concept, and Caryl E. Rusbult's (1983) approach begins with the interdependence theories of Harold H. Kelley and John W. Thibaut (1978). The heart of all three approaches (Levinger, Johnson, Rusbult) is the recognition that there is more to relationship stability than personal satisfaction with the relationship.

Personal, Moral, and Structural Commitment

The distinctions among personal, moral, and structural commitment presented here are based upon the commitment framework developed by Johnson. At this point, a useful reminder is that, although much of the work on commitment to relationships has focused on romantic and marital relationships, commitments to other familial and nonfamilial relationships are also important. Commitments between children and their parents often maintain parent–child relationships throughout the life course, even in the face of considerable acrimony and great geographical and social distance. And although commitments to friends may not be as compelling as those to one's spouse, they are nevertheless important. The relative mix of personal, moral, and structural commitments is likely to differ considerably across the various types of personal relationships that enrich or burden people.

Personal commitment is the sense of *wanting* to continue a relationship, and flows from three major components: (1) attitude toward the relationship, (2) attitude toward the partner, and (3) relational identity. Although the first two components are likely to be highly correlated in the long run, the distinction is important; it is certainly possible to feel strong attraction to a person with whom one has a relationship that falls short of one's expectations. The third component of personal commitment, the extent to which the relationship has become a central part of one's self-concept, has received little attention in the relationship literature (cf. Aron, Aron, and Smollen 1992), but this component has long been a part of the symbolic interactionist analysis of self-concept (Kuhn and McPartland 1954). The psychological experience of relational identity is institutionalized in the tradition in which women legally take the name of their husbands (an asymmetry that has not, of course, gone unnoticed by feminists).

Moral commitment is the feeling that one *ought* to continue a relationship, often involving a sense of constraint, and in "I am not really doing what I wish to do, but what I should." There are three major sources of moral commitment. The first source is a general belief in the value of consistency, the morality of finishing what one starts. The second source of moral commitment is tied to particular types of relationships. For example, one's system of personal values may emphasize the immorality of divorce but place very little constraint on movement in and out of friendships throughout the course of one's life. The third source of moral commitment is tied to personal obligations to specific others in one's life. In some cases, such obligations may be explicit, as in one's promise to a significant other to stay with him or her forever, a promise that may be more or less public. In other cases, the obligation may not only be private, but implicit, for instance, "I feel that I should live up to my implied commitment to my roommate to continue to live with him until we graduate next year."

Structural commitment, the feeling that one *has* to continue a relationship, derives from factors that are experienced as external to the individual and constraining. These include irretrievable investments, social reaction, difficulty of termination procedures, and lack of attractive alternatives. First, the time, energy, and other resources that are consumed in the maintenance of a relationship are sometimes experienced as irretrievable investments that keep individuals from leaving relationships to which they are no longer personally or morally committed. If the resources were "invested" in the anticipation of the long-term payoffs of the relationship, and are not retrievable, then leaving the relationship early may be perceived to entail an unacceptable loss. A second source of structural commitment is social reaction. Relationships differ in the extent to which people other than the partners have feelings about the dissolution of the relationship, feelings that are founded either in moral orientations or in more pragmatic considerations. For example, a father's resistance to his child's impending divorce may flow from his beliefs about the morality of divorce, while the children's concerns about divorce have more to do with the fact that their lives are currently organized around the maintenance of their parents' relationship. The social pressure exerted by such others may be a major factor in the maintenance of some relationships. Third, termination procedures differ dramatically from relationship to relationship. One can terminate a casual dating relationship with virtually no cost whatsoever; the dissolution of a marriage is another story altogether. Finally, the lack of acceptable alternatives may be a major constraint. When one considers the ending of a relationship, one evaluates a broad range of possible consequences, including not only the possibility of a "replacement" for one's partner, but also the likely effects of relationship dissolution on one's social life, one's economic situation, and other matters. The alternatives available to a twenty-year-old college student considering the ending of a dating relationship are vastly different from those available to a forty-five-year-old mother of three who has given up participation in the labor force to raise her children.

Although all three forms of commitment contribute to relationship stability, they differ in both the cognitive and affective experiences associated with them. They also differ in the nature of their connection with the larger social system within which the relationship is embedded. Structural commitments, for example, are to a large extent a function of social and institutional arrangements external to the individual. One may thus be ignorant of structural commitments until one begins to explore the possible consequences of ending the relationship. Not until this point do the structural commitments have any emotional component. In contrast, personal commitments have much less to do with institutional structures (cf. Johnson 1991a, pp. 131-135); they involve a more immediately and generally accessible impact on one's emotional and cognitive experience.

Measuring Commitment

There have been three comprehensive efforts to develop measures of the various forms of relationship commitment, all of which involve relatively easy-to-administer questionnaire methodologies. Dennis A. Bagarozzi's questionnaire (Bagarozzi and Pollone 1983), designed for use in clinical settings, was stimulated by Levinger's cohesiveness framework but has been empirically demonstrated to break down into subscales that quite clearly correspond to personal, moral, and structural commitment. Mary Lund's (1985) work also provides a useful questionnaire approach to the measurement of commitment, although it tends to confound the various types distinguished above. Finally, Scott M. Stanley and Howard J. Markman (1992) have developed a comprehensive questionnaire measure that involves eleven subscales from which researchers and clinicians might pick and choose as they wish. All of these measures, however, suffer from the virtually unavoidable constraint that they can only assess *perceived* commitment. As the framework above suggests, relationships often involve commitments that are, from time to time, more or less unknown to the people involved. For example, a son may be quite unaware of how strongly his mother will react to the prospect of his divorce, and he may, furthermore, have little sense of the economic consequences of a relationship dissolution. Those commitments are real, nevertheless, and should he ever begin the process of disengagement, he will at some point encounter them, and perhaps have to reconsider his course of action in light of the new information.

Work by Catherine A. Surra (1985) suggests a more process-oriented approach to the assessment of commitment, one that combines the collection of data at different points in the development of the relationship with retrospective accounts of the causes of critical changes in commitment. As the awareness context of a relationship is altered (e.g., when one begins to consider dissolution seriously), changes may take place not only in one's awareness of current commitments, but also in one's understanding of the processes that produced those commitments.

Variations in Commitment

The strengths of the three basic forms of commitment differ, of course, across individual relationships, but they also differ systematically in relation to a number of other variables, such as relationship type, relationship stage, gender, and sexual orientation.

Relationship type. With regard to relationship type, consider a comparison of friendship, sibling, and marital relationships. Friendships are held together almost entirely by personal commitments; there is very little in the way of moral constraint to maintain friendships to which one is no longer personally committed, nor are there generally any serious structural commitments involved. Quite another pattern is characteristic of adult sibling relationships, which are held together by considerable moral commitment, accompanied by variable personal commitment, and very little structural commitment.

Marriages, in contrast, while showing considerable variability in personal commitment, almost inevitably involve major moral and structural commitments. As Kelley (1983) has observed, one of the important characteristics of moral and structural commitments is that they tend to fluctuate less dramatically than do personal commitments, helping to stabilize relationships over the inevitable ups and downs of personal life. Historical evidence suggests that the dramatic increase in the U.S. divorce rate since 1960 is due not to changes in marital satisfaction or personal commitment but to a decline in moral and structural commitment to marriage.

Relationship stage. As the adult sibling example would suggest, commitments to a relationship may also differ across different stages of the relationship. Consider, for instance, the virtually insurmountable structural commitment to one's siblings during childhood, in contrast with the generally trivial nature of such commitments in middle adulthood. Changes in the strength of various commitments with the development of a relationship affect not only the stability of the relationship but also the ties among the various types of commitment. For example, during the early and intermediate stages of romantic involvements, increases in personal commitment are likely to lead to actions such as announcements of steady dating, living together, or engagement, that increase moral and structural commitment and produce a strong correlation among the commitment types. After marriage, the three forms of commitment may be virtually unrelated to each other, with structural commitments fluctuating as a function of changes in employment status, moral commitment varying with the number and age of children, and personal commitment changing as a function of relationship quality. One of the consequences of such low correlations among forms of commitment is the "hollow shell marriage," in which the partners are no longer personally committed to the maintenance of the relationship but are held in it by moral and structural commitments.

Gender. Another important factor in the development of commitments to various types of family relationships is gender. One example involves the role of women as kinkeepers in families, due in part to women's personal commitment to the maintenance of kin ties, partly to a gendered sense of moral obligation, and partly to the structural commitments of social pressure for women to maintain those ties. Another important example is differential commitment to marriage, with women more likely than men to experience strong structural commitments to marriage, one of the most important of which is the degree of attractiveness or unattractiveness of alternatives. The standard of living of women declines dramatically following a divorce, while men's increases significantly (Witzmann 1985), and men are significantly more likely to remarry and to do so sooner than women. Since it is also the case that in roughly 90 percent of divorces involving children the mother receives physical custody of the children, the nature of the alternatives available to her affect both her and the children who depend upon her. These gender differences in commitment affect, among other things, the power differential in the marriage through the principle of least interest (Peplau 1984). They also affect the likelihood that a woman will be able to escape from an unsatisfactory or even abusive relationship (Strube and Barbour 1983).

Sexual orientation. The final example of systematic variations in commitment presented here involves the connections between sexual orientation and commitment to family relationships. Gay and lesbian couples do not enjoy the benefits (or constraints) of some of the structural commitments that buttress heterosexual unions. They are less likely to have kin who will put significant pressure on them to stay together, they are less likely to have the benefit of the moral commitment of religious sanction for their union, they do not have to undergo the vagaries of divorce court, and they are likely to be to a large extent economically independent. This means that large power differences within the relationship are less likely. It also means that such relationships are more vulnerable to dissolution in response to what otherwise might have been short-term declines in personal commitment.

Consequences of Commitment

One may divide the consequences of commitment into two general clusters: effects on the functioning of the intact relationship and effects on the stability of the relationship.

Rusbult and her colleagues (1991) present evidence that the nature of one's commitments affects one's reactions to "transgressions" in the relationship. Committed partners are more likely to react to their partner's mistakes with constructive communication ("voice" or "loyalty" in Rusbult's terminology) than with destructive communication ("exit" or "neglect").

The bottom line of the analysis of commitment, however, is relationship stability (Rusbult and Buunk 1993). Strong commitments of any sort contribute to the stability of relationships, a stability that may be a joy or a burden, depending on the particular mix of personal, moral, and structural commitment that keeps people together.

(*See also:* FAMILY THERAPY; FRIENDSHIP; INTIMACY; LOVE; MARITAL POWER; MARITAL QUALITY; PERSONAL RELATIONSHIPS; SIBLING RELATIONSHIPS; SYMBOLIC INTERACTIONISM; TRUST)

BIBLIOGRAPHY

Aron, A.; Aron, E. N.; and Smollen, D. (1992). "Inclusion of Other in the Self Scale and the Structure of Interpersonal Closeness." *Journal of Personality and Social Psychology* 9:21–50.

Bagarozzi, D. A., and Pollone, L. (1983). "A Replication and Validation of the Spousal Inventory of Desired Changes and Relationship Barriers (SIDCARB): Elaborations on Diagnostic and Clinical Utilization." *Journal of Sex and Marital Therapy* 9:303–315.

Becker, H. S. (1960). "Notes on the Concept of Commitment." *American Journal of Sociology* 66:32–40.

Fehr, B. (1988). "Prototype Analysis of the Concepts of Love and Commitment." *Journal of Personality and Social Psychology* 55:557–578.

Johnson, M. P. (1973). "Commitment: A Conceptual Structure and Empirical Application." *Sociological Quarterly* 14:395–406.

Johnson, M. P. (1982). "Social and Cognitive Feature of the Dissolution of Commitment to Relationships." In *Personal Relationships:* Vol. 4, *Dissolving Personal Relationships*, ed. S. Duck. New York: Academic Press.

Johnson, M. P. (1991a). "Commitment to Personal Relationships." In *Advances in Personal Relationships*, Vol. 3, ed. W. Jones and D. Perlman. London: Jessica Kingsley.

Johnson, M. P. (1991b). "Reply to Levinger and Rusbult." In *Advances in Personal Relationships*, Vol. 3, ed. W. Jones and D. Perlman. London: Jessica Kingsley.

Kelley, H. H. (1983). "Love and Commitment." In *Close Relationships*, ed. H. H. Kelley, E. Berschied, A. Christensen, J. H. Harvey, T. L. Huston, E. McClintock, L. A. Peplau, and D. L. Peterson. New York: W. H. Freeman.

Kelley, H. H., and Thibaut, J. W. (1978). *Interpersonal Relations: A Theory of Interdependence.* New York: Wiley.

Kuhn, M. H., and McPartland, T. S. (1954). "An Empirical Investigation of Self Attitudes." *American Sociological Review* 19:68–76.

Levinger, G. (1965). "Marital Cohesiveness and Dissolution: An Integrative Review." *Journal of Marriage and the Family* 27:19–29.

Levinger, G. (1991). "Commitment vs. Cohesiveness: Two Complementary Perspectives." In *Advances in Personal Relationships*, Vol. 3, ed. W. Jones and D. Perlman. London: Jessica Kingsley.

Lewis, R. A., and Spanier, G. B. (1979). "Theorizing about the Quality and Stability of Marriage." In *Contemporary Theories About the Family*, Vol. 1, ed. W. R. Burr, R. Hill, F. I. Nye, and I. L. Reiss. New York: Free Press.

Lund, M. (1985). "The Development of Investment and Commitment Scales for Predicting Continuity of Personal Relationships." *Journal of Social and Personal Relationships* 2:3–23.

Peplau, L. A. (1984). "Power in Dating Relationships." In *Women: A Feminist Perspective*, ed. J. Freeman. Palo Alto, CA: Mayfield.

Rusbult, C. E. (1983). "A Longitudinal Test of the Investment Model: The Development (and Deterioration) of Satisfaction and Commitment in Heterosexual Involvements." *Journal of Personality and Social Psychology* 45:101–117.

Rusbult, C. E. (1991). "Commentary on Johnson's 'Commitment to Personal Relationships': What's Interesting and What's New?" In *Advances in Personal Relationships*, Vol. 3, ed. W. Jones and D. Perlman. London: Jessica Kingsley.

Rusbult, C. E., and Buunk, B. P. (1993). "Commitment Processes in Close Relationships: An Interdependence Analysis." *Journal of Social and Personal Relationships* 10:175–204.

Rusbult, C. E.; Verette, J.; Whitney, G. A.; Slovick, L. F.; and Lipkus, I. (1991). "Accommodation Processes in Close Relationships: Theory and Preliminary Empirical Evidence." *Journal of Personality and Social Psychology* 60:53–78.

Stanley, S. M., and Markman, H. J. (1992). Assessing Commitment in Personal Relationships." *Journal of Marriage and the Family* 54:595–608.

Strube, M., and Barbour, L. S. (1983). "The Decision to Leave an Abusive Relationship: Economic Dependence and Psychological Commitment." *Journal of Marriage and the Family* 45:485–493.

Surra, C. A. (1985). "Reasons for Changes in Commitment: Variations by Courtship Type." *Journal of Personality and Social Psychology* 49:357–375.

Weitzman, L. (1985). *The Divorce Revolution.* New York: Free Press.

MICHAEL P. JOHNSON

COMMUNES

The contemporary communal movement emerged in the early 1960s in the Haight-Ashbury neighborhood of San Francisco, California, and by 1968 had spread throughout the United States to most major cities. The communal movement was both a rural and an urban phenomenon, concentrated along the coastal areas of the United States.

Trends in Communes

The first difficulty encountered when studying communes is a definitional one. Patrick W. Conover (1978) distinguishes among commune, intentional community, and collective. These three concepts are often used interchangeably by scholars when discussing the contemporary communal movement. A commune is a group of five or more adults who share housing, finances, labor, and meals, and who make the majority of their expenditures from a common purse. Intentional communities share some resources and rely on a common purse for only some important expenditures. A collective is an arrangement among those who share some living expenses. These three arrangements vary based on the degree of ideology or lifestyle sought by those who join the community.

Richard Fairfield (1972) differentiates among a commune, a collective, a cooperative, an intentional community, and an experimental community. Each of these is an arrangement of three or more people who are aligned with each other primarily through some form of sharing rather than through a blood or legal relationship. The level and degree of sharing vary from group to group. Some members share only in the legal ownership of land, while other members share all things in common (which was the practice of the early Christians). Cooperatives are the most conservative form; they maintain their own homes and jobs but share recreational land and gardens. Communes are the most radical form of communitarianism. Members share housing, income, expenses, child rearing, and sometimes even sex. Intentional communities are often referred to as planned utopian (ideal) communities; the end and the means for reaching that end are clearly articulated prior to the undertaking. Experimental communities are more flexible organizations that are open to change and ad hoc engineering.

Fairfield (1972) estimated that more than 2,000 communes existed during 1969 and 1970, plus an additional several thousand urban co-ops and collectives. Conover (1978) estimated that between 1971 and 1974 there were at least 3,000 communes, not counting traditional religious communes, with 30,000 to 40,000 members. Judson Jerome (1974) states that 750,000 people, or 3 percent of the American population, lived communally during the 1960s. Conservative estimates by scholars indicate that in 1991 there were 3,000 to 4,000 intentional communities in the United States and that information could be obtained from 300 to 400 of them. In addition, the *Directory of Intentional Communities: A Guide to Cooperative Living* (Fellowship for Intentional Community 1991) lists 359 North American communes and 57 international communes.

Brian J. L. Berry (1992) notes that 75 communes chose not to be listed in the directory. One hundred twenty of those listed were founded in the mid- to late 1980s, another 120 were founded between 1965 and 1975, and only 20 were founded before 1960. In addition to these communal groups there are 380 Hutterite colonies in North America (*Hutterite Address Book* 1992) with a combined population of 33,500. The largest communal movement outside North America comprises the Israeli *kibbutzim*. There are 275 *kibbutzim* in Israel, and together they have 125,000 members (Bowes 1989).

It is quite obvious based on this information that researchers have not agreed on the exact number of communes in the United States. It is impossible to report an exact number. Many functioning communes prefer to remain anonymous, while others are isolated and do not belong to associations such as the Fellowship for Intentional Community.

Even though William Kephart and William Zellner (1991) believe that the modern commune movement is dead or at least dormant, data provided by the Fellowship for Intentional Community (1991) and Yaacov Oved (1993) show that the communal movement is alive and well. Twin Oaks of Louisa, Virginia, a commune based on the principles of B. F. Skinner's *Walden Two*, is a good example of a contemporary commune; it celebrated its twenty-fifth anniversary in the spring of 1992.

Contemporary communes are not as visible as they were in the late 1960s. This visibility was due to the coverage provided by print and television media, but as Berry (1992, p. 245) states,

After a fifteen-year sag, the utopian urge thus has reappeared amid another primary trough. If the experience of previous primary troughs is any guide, the surge will not be massive, but communities that are being developed will be bellwethers of the utopian surge that will occur in the deflationary depression to come.

The troughs that Berry refers to are low points in the economy, the opposite of peaks. Fifty of the intentional communities listed by Berry were in the process of being formed in 1991, during this period of economic fluctuation.

Communal Types and Ideologies

Several useful models have been produced by scholars to classify communes. Benjamin Zablocki (1980) studied 120 communes (60 urban and 60 rural—37 religious and 83 secular) from 1965 to 1978. Figure 1 illustrates the two dimensions he used to distinguish among communal groups: (1) strategic philosophy (direct action and consciousness, otherwise known as nonaction) and (2) locus of attention (see Hall 1978, p. 202, for an alternate model).

Zablocki (1980) found the most significant differences regarding membership and social structure to be between the religious communes and the secular communes, not between consciousness-oriented groups and direct-action-oriented groups. This finding is consistent with the literature and supports the position that there are important differences in the cultural patterns of social organizations, specifically between religious and secular groups (Hall 1988).

Eastern religious communes were distinguished from each other based on religious tradition, whether it was Hindu, Buddhist, Sikh, or homegrown, while Christian communes were classified into four subtypes: evangelical youth, charismatic renewal, sectarian withdrawal, and social gospel. Among the secular

Locus of Attention	Strategic Philosophy		
	Consciousness	Direct Action	
spiritual world	Eastern	Christian	religious communes
individual self	psychological	rehabilitational	
primary group community	cooperative	alternative family	secular communes
secular society	countercultural	political	

Figure 1 Eight types of commune ideologies (Zablocki 1980, p. 205; reprinted by permission of the publisher).

commues, psychological commues are concerned with self-actualization and were classified into three groups—mystical, gestalt, and psychosexual—while rehabilitational commues had no subtypes because only four of them were found. Rehabilitational communes helped people with damaged and weak egos. Cooperative commues created a collective living situation and were classified as cooperative households, cooperative enterprises, "crashpad" commues, or devolved utopias. Alternative-family commue members believe that the traditional nuclear family is obsolete and seek a family structure that is not necessarily blood-related. Alternative-family commues can be classified as either patriarchal, matriarchal, fraternal, or group marriage. Countercultural commues are composed primarily of hippies and can be classified as cultural demonstration projects, hippie farms or houses, tribal settlements, or utopian reservations. Political commues are composed of members of the New Left who are striving to achieve a more anarchistic society or a socialistic one. Political commues can be classified as socialist, anarchist, or social democratic (Zablocki 1980).

Much has been written on the success and failure of contemporary commues. Rosabeth Moss Kanter (1972), studying nineteenth-century commues, developed a theory of commitment and concluded that those commues that were able to incorporate as many commitment-producing mechanisms as possible were more likely to survive and be successful (see Table 1). She identified three types of commitment that bind people to organized groups: continuance, cohesion, and control/moral. Kanter wanted to uncover the structural arrangements and organizational strategies that promote and sustain commitment. She found that nineteenth-century groups used transcendence and communion mechanisms the most, followed by sacrifice, renunciation, investment, and mortification. Hugh Gardner (1978) studied contemporary rural commues and found that commue members used fewer commitment mechanisms of all types than did nineteenth-century groups. Investment, renunciation, and mortification were strongly related to communal survival in contemporary rural commues, while sacrifice, communion, and transcendence were found to be weakly or negatively related to survival. William L. Smith (1986) investigated contemporary urban religious commues and found that communion, mortification, and transcendence mechanisms are used at moderate or higher levels, while sacrifice, investment, and renunciation are not widely present or used (see also Hall 1988).

Table 1 Commitment Mechanisms

Continuance
  Sacrifice: giving up something as a requirement for membership, such as alcohol and/or sex.
  Investment: committing resources to the group that frequently are not returned when one leaves the community, which makes leaving costly, such as bank accounts and other property.

Cohesion
  Renunciation: turning your back on the outside world; rarely leaving the physical boundaries of the community or not interacting with outside people.
  Communion: emphasizing the characteristics shared by group members, such as religion, education, race, or ethnicity, as well as labor, dwellings, meals, and clothing.

Control/moral
  Mortification: building a new identity and life that is partially based on rejecting one's previous identity and life. This process is enhanced when one is open to criticism.
  Transcendence: Instilling a strong ideology that stresses the importance of communal life and adherence to a fixed routine and conversion process.

Members of Communes

Communalists do not come solely from the upper-middle class. Approximately one-quarter of them come from working-class or lower-middle-class origins. Few communalists see themselves involved in building a new family form, and they do not reject the nuclear family in favor of communal alternatives (Aidala and Zablocki 1991).

The major thrust of contemporary communitarianism is not oriented to the specific goal of re-creating the family; in fact, communalists are estranged from most of the major social institutions—religious, political, familial, educational. Angela A. Aidala (1989) found support for the belief that commues attract those interested in "role moratorium" from marriage and other adult responsibilities—that is, commue members are interested in "stepping aside," for a period of time, from socially expected roles (primarily marital, parental, and breadwinner roles). A sizable number of ex-commue members have never married, although the majority have married. Many ex-commue members have chosen to live in multiadult households. Leigh Minturn (1984) found that communal social roles eventually evolve and become similar to those in extended families, with the exception of work roles, where male communal members do more cross-sex-type work. The reason most often given by communal members for joining communes is to live with people who have similar values and goals.

Conclusion

What is the future of communes? If history is an accurate predictor, the majority of communes in existence today will eventually disband, leaving those few that have been able to institutionalize commitment and conversion successfully. Does this mean that those communes that are no longer in existence have failed? No, not necessarily. How one measures failure and success is a relative issue. The major change related to communal living that will likely continue in the future is that communalists are selecting those things they value from mainstream society and are incorporating them into a communitarian lifestyle. Communes that dissolve are replaced by new ones, and the historical cycle continues.

(*See also:* COMMITMENT; UTOPIAN COMMUNITIES)

BIBLIOGRAPHY

Aidala, A. A. (1983). "Communes as Seeking Better Family? A Misleading Explanation." *Alternative Lifestyles* 6:115–139.

Aidala, A. A. (1989). "Communes and Changing Family Norms: Marriage and Lifestyle Choice Among Former Members of Communal Groups." *Journal of Family Issues* 10:311–338.

Aidala, A. A., and Zablocki, B. D. (1991). "The Communes of the 1970s: Who Joined and Why?" *Marriage and Family Review* 17:87–116.

Berry, B. J. L. (1992). *America's Utopian Experiments: Communal Havens from Long-Wave Crises.* Hanover, NH: University Press of New England.

Bowes, A. M. (1989). *Kibbutz Goshen: An Israeli Commune.* Prospect Heights, IL: Waveland.

Conover, P. W. (1978). "Communes and Intentional Communities." *Journal of Voluntary Action Research* 7:5–17.

Fairfield, R. (1972). *Communes USA: A Personal Tour.* Baltimore: Penguin Books.

Fellowship for Intentional Community. (1991). *Directory of Intentional Communities: A Guide to Cooperative Living.* Rutledge, MO: Communities Publications Cooperative.

Gardner, H. (1978). *The Children of Prosperity: Thirteen Modern American Communes.* New York: St. Martin's Press.

Hall, J. R. (1978). *The Ways Out: Utopian Communal Groups in an Age of Babylon.* London: Routledge & Kegan Paul.

Hall, J. R. (1988). "Social Organization and Pathways of Commitment: Types of Communal Groups, Rational Choice Theory, and the Kanter Thesis." *American Sociological Review* 53:679–692.

Hutterite Address Book. (1992). Great Falls, MT: Licini's Print Shop.

Jerome, J. (1974). *Families of Eden: Communes and the New Anarchism.* New York: Seabury.

Kanter, R. M. (1972). *Commitment and Community: Communes and Utopias in Sociological Perspective.* Cambridge, MA: Harvard University Press.

Kephart, W., and Zellner, W. (1991). *Extraordinary Groups.* New York: St. Martin's Press.

Minturn, L. (1984). "Sex-Role Differentiation in Contemporary Communes." *Sex Roles* 10:73–85.

Oved, Y. (1993). *Two Hundred Years of American Communes.* New Brunswick, NJ: Transaction.

Skinner, B. F. (1976). *Walden Two.* New York: Macmillan.

Smith, W. L. (1986). "The Use of Structural Arrangements and Organizational Strategies by Urban Communes." *Communal Societies* 6:118–137.

Zablocki, B. (1980). *Alienation and Charisma: A Study of Contemporary American Communes.* New York: Free Press.

WILLIAM L. SMITH

COMMUNICATION

Complicated and fascinating, marriages and families form the primary relationships of people's lives. An individual's first family has a great deal to do with creating a person, who in turn has the opportunity to participate in the creation of another family. What kind of family might be created and how will this challenging task be executed? How does gender influence the development of a family? What kind of communication supports the development of a successful marriage and family? Research, experiences, and communication that are central to marital and family life include the following:

- the role of communication in the changing face of marriage and family
- a receiver-oriented view of communication
- women's and men's differing approaches to communication
- how approaches to communication affect marital interaction
- developing effective communication patterns
- understanding the role of power and empowerment in marriage and families
- moving toward intimacy through communication.

The Changing Face of Marriage and Family

Right or wrong, there is a clear societal pressure to marry. This cultural push to be married and raise a family persists in spite of alternatives to marriage. Statistics project that between 90 and 95 percent of all Americans will get married (Fitzpatrick 1988).

Other societal trends in marriage and family affect the expectations and hopes of people beginning a new marriage or family. Culture has held the nuclear family as the ideal for quite a long time. In 1955, the model consisting of a working father, housewife mother, and two or more school-age children represented 60 percent of all families; now it represents 7 percent (Otto 1988). In addition to this significant change to the basic family model, population statistics show an increase since the early 1970s in the number of women in the work force. There has also been an increase in the number of divorces and children living with only one parent. Alternate lifestyle arrangements and same-sex households have become more common. The ethnic composition of American families has also changed. This increased diversity has had a significant effect on the quality and expectations of American family life (Richmond-Abbott 1992).

While pressure to be coupled has apparently increased, societal pressures to stay together have diminished. The societal sanctions against divorce have essentially disappeared. In the absence of these forces that keep a relationship together, couples have looked inward for relationship justification, appreciation, companionship, and emotional gratification (Fitzpatrick and Badinski 1985), creating a greater need for effective communication between partners and within families.

The changes in society have increased the complexity of marital and family relationships, but they have also increased the chances of making effective choices in these relationships. People now have more freedom to choose a mate and how to communicate with that person. Techniques and strategies that will make communication more effective in those relationships can be learned. Communication patterns in marriage and family that are more likely to lead to increased satisfaction, commitment, and stability can be established.

What makes a long-term relationship succeed? How can the chances of reaping the relational benefits and avoiding the pitfalls be increased? By becoming aware of the gender influences on communication and more fully understanding personal communication behavior, an individual can gain more control over the com-munication process. Many people go into marriage and parenthood with little more then romantic dreams and good intentions. They feel that if and when they find the right person, they will live happily ever after. Dreams of living happily ever after without awareness, understanding, and effective communication can lead to unmet expectations at the very least. In a complicated society, vague notions of marriage are inadequate. Significant amounts of time and energy need to be invested in marital and family relationships. Successful relationships do not just happen— they are created. They rely on communication based on awareness, understanding, and sensitivity.

Communication and Gender as Terms

As the methods (media, computers, voice mail, etc.) for communicating have expanded, so have problems in and meanings of the term "communication." Two communication theorists in the 1970s isolated 126 definitions of the term (Dance and Larson 1976). It is not necessary to review the many perspectives on human communication; the following perspective helps make communication in marriage and in the family more understandable.

Human communication is an ongoing and dynamic process of sending and receiving messages for the purpose of sharing meaning. To accomplish this purpose, people use both verbal and nonverbal communication (e.g., body movement, physical appearance, facial expression, touch, tone of voice). Communication flows back and forth simultaneously, both verbally and nonverbally, in a transactional fashion (DeVito 1988; Taylor et al. 1989). While both people are transacting communication, meaning that they are both sending and receiving verbal and nonverbal messages simultaneously, a conversation can be analyzed from a sender–receiver perspective.

While both roles of sender and receiver in the communication process are important, the receiver's interpretation of the sender's message is key to understanding successful communication. This view is termed the "receiver orientation" to communication. What a sender *intends* to convey is important, but it is less important than what a receiver *thinks is being conveyed*. Taking a receiver orientation means stopping to think about how the message will be understood by a listener. This can greatly enhance communicator skills.

When communication breaks down, the sender tends to think the receiver is at fault for not understanding the message. In a receiver-oriented view of communication, the sender is responsible for communicating in a manner that will be most easily understood by the receiver; the receiver's responsibility is to attempt to understand the intent of the sender. If people would spend more time figuring out how a listener will best hear, accept, understand, and retain a message and less time figuring out how they want to say something to please themselves, then their communication with others would vastly improve.

The following is an example to more vividly illustrate this notion of taking a receiver orientation to communication. After a visit to her parents, a wife says jokingly to her husband, "You know, you never did care for my mother." Feeling self-conscious and sensitive about his in-laws, he replies angrily, "We get along fine, but when are you going to start being nice to *my* mother?" This conversation is not going the way the wife intended. The husband took her statement as criticism, as though she were attacking him. Obviously, in this situation the message intended and sent did not equal the message received. Who is most responsible for the miscommunication in this situation?

From a receiver orientation to communication, it could be said that the sender, in this case the wife, should have used more caution in her message. If she had thought about the effect her humorous line might have had, she might have considered a different approach, one that would not appear to criticize. To say that the husband really overreacted is to adopt a sender orientation to communication, emphasizing what was *said* rather than how it was *taken*. The receiver-oriented person focuses on the other person. Considering in advance how a receiver will take or interpret a message will go a long way toward improving communicator skills.

"Gender," a complicated concept, is constructed, meaning that maleness or femaleness is more extensive than just being biologically male or female. Gender is not born; it is constructed or shaped by culture. Gender is also a combination of biological sex, psychological makeup, attitudes, beliefs, values, sexual orientation, and gender-role identity. Therefore, gender is a central aspect of identity and strongly influences communication. With this as a base, gender communication can be seen as communication about and between women and men. The front part of the statement—the "about" aspect—involves how the sexes are discussed, referred to, or depicted, both verbally and nonverbally. The "between" aspect is the interpersonal dimension of gender communication.

Communication becomes "gendered" when sex or gender begins to influence choices of what to say to others. For example, two students (both female, both

male, or opposite sexes) could be talking about a class project without necessarily involving gender communication. If the conversation topic shifts to a discussion of who the interactants are dating, or opinions regarding birth-control responsibilities, however, the awareness of genders may come into play; thus, gender communication is occurring.

Gender and gender-role expectations are a significant factor in many of the conversations that occur in the context of marriage and family. Before examining those two contexts, it is important to consider first *why* human beings communicate.

Functions of Communication

Do women and men communicate for similar purposes or to accomplish similar goals? What do men and women believe the *function* of talk, conversation, communication to be? Paul Watzlawick, Janet Helmick Beavin, and Don Jackson (1967) developed an influential set of axioms or rules about how human communication operates. One of these axioms contended that "every communication has a content and a relationship aspect" (p. 54). The content aspect of communication concerns what is actually said. The relational aspect tells the listener how the message should be interpreted. For instance, saying a simple "hello" to one's partner in a warm, friendly tone (the relational aspect) of voice conveys a sense of affection and familiarity, whereas a hollow, bland tone may suggest a problem in the relationship. In this example, the tone of voice indicates how the message should be interpreted and gives clues about the relationship. Most often the content element is conveyed verbally. The relational element is primarily communicated nonverbally, through the presence or absence of such behaviors as eye contact, facial expression, body movement and gesturing, tone of voice, and touch.

What does this information have to do with marriages and families? From Watzlawick, Beavin, and Jackson's axiom of communication, a fundamental difference exists in what women and men believe to be the function or purpose of conversation. Specifically, women often view conversation as a means of establishing and developing connections between persons. Many times women want to talk just to reinforce the fact that a relationship exists and is important. What someone says is of less concern than the fact that communication is occurring. Communication researchers Julia T. Wood and L. F. Lenze (1991, p. 5) suggest that, for women, "people are not considered as separate or separated individuals, but interdependent within web-like contexts of multiple human relationships. Thus, distance or separation from others tends to be threatening to female identity in the same way that close connections to others jeopardize male identity." Conversely, men tend to approach conversation more with the intent of imparting information (the content aspect) than to clue someone about the relationship (the relational aspect).

This does not mean that every time a man speaks, he is only conveying information or that women only communicate relationally without ever exchanging any real information. On the contrary, *every* message carries content and relational meanings. What this theory suggests is that men may use communication primarily for information exchange while women may view communication primarily as functioning to initiate and maintain relationships, exposing a fundamental sex difference before women and men even meet.

In *You Just Don't Understand*, sociolinguist Deborah Tannen (1990) describes male and female talk in ways that parallel the relational versus content supposition. She terms the female style "rapport talk" and the male style "report talk." Rapport talk is many women's "way of establishing connections and negotiating relationships. For many men, talk is primarily a means to preserve independence and negotiate and maintain status" (p. 77).

In research attempting to understand why people choose to interact, Rebecca B. Rubin, Elizabeth M. Perse, and Carole A. Barbato (1988) conducted a study with a primary goal of discovering a possible relationship between gender and the purpose of talk. The study addressed whether subjects communicated with other people for such purposes as wanting to be included by others, extending and receiving affection, for simple relaxation purposes, to meet their needs for companionship, or to control situations and people. The research produced a significant sex difference, in that female subjects were more likely to talk to others for pleasure, to express affection, to seek inclusion, and to relax. Men in this study reported communicating to exert control over a situation rather than express affection or seek inclusion from others.

Research results generally support the contention that, in many cases, men's and women's motives or purposes for engaging in conversation differ. This difference may lead to conflict during communication in opposite-sex relationships, especially in a relationship as significant as marriage.

Upon hearing an explanation of the relational versus content approach to communication, people have provided examples in which the female marital partner wanted to "stay home and talk" one evening, which led the male partner to wonder if something was wrong or if this was going to be "another one of those 'state of the marriage'-type discussions." Other conflicts have arisen when a wife interpreted her husband's silence to mean that something was wrong, he was mad about something and chose not to tell her, or his feelings for her had changed (for the worse). The husband's response was that he just did not have anything to say, but that obviously he must care about his wife because, "After all, I'm *here* aren't I?"

A married student, after hearing a class explanation on the relational versus content approach to communication, recalled a recent argument he had with his partner: "We'd been talking about something that happened a few nights before and it led to an argument. When I felt that I'd explained my side of the story sufficiently and that we'd argued enough, I simply said 'There's nothing more to say. End of discussion.' This made her furious and I couldn't figure out why. She wanted to continue talking about the incident, my side of it, her side of it, what the argument meant about our relationship, and I just wanted the conversation *over*."

These examples illustrate men's and women's different approaches to the uses or functions of communication. While men often think women talk on and on about nothing and women often think that men's relationships (and sometimes men themselves) are superficial, the truth is that in general, women and men are actually using communication for different purposes.

Which aspect of communication is more important—the content or the relational dimension? Which approach—male or female—is more appropriate or effective? The answer to both of these questions is "neither." Watzlawick, Beavin, and Jackson (1967) believed that a healthy relationship involved a balance of both content and relational aspects of talk. What is important to remember is that in every message—no matter how brief or trivial—both content and relational elements exist. The difference seems to lie in a person's view of the function or purpose of a given message. The message or benefit of this theory is that it can lead to the development of an integrated or balanced system of communication. Such a system draws from both the content and relational approaches, based on the realization that certain times, situations, and people may alter one's purpose in communicating. The skill comes in learning which communicative approach is best, given the dictates of the situation.

Communication, Satisfaction, and Marriage

In spite of the changing face of marriage, most people who do marry want that marriage to succeed not only in length of time but in the quality of its communication and the satisfaction derived from it.

Two points—patterns and intimacy—must be examined in terms of their relationship to gender, the improvement of marital communication, and the development of a wider repertoire of personal communication behaviors for both sexes that lead to greater effectiveness.

As a relationship develops, the communication begins to form into patterns. Understanding these patterns offers insights into a relationship and identifies areas for change. Communication patterns represent probably the single most useful tool in understanding the process of communication in marriage and family.

Judy C. Pearson (1989) defines patterns as "predictable and manageable sets of behaviors that are unique to the family and are distinctive from any one family member's own actions" (p. 34). Each relationship develops its own communication patterns that are usually based on a combination of societal norms and the needs and desires of the people involved in the relationship. The patterns are usually developed without conscious awareness; couples do not usually sit down and say, "Let's work out our pattern of communication."

While the concept is perhaps unusual, couples should hold periodic conversations about the quality of their relationships, examine the patterns that have developed, and discuss ways of changing the patterns for greater mutual satisfaction. In marriages, the sooner this occurs, the more likely it is that patterns will be formed purposefully rather than by accident. Talking about a relationship may seem forced and contrived at the onset, but it becomes easier with practice and reinforced through positive results. The quality of these patterns directly affects two major outcomes of marital communication—security and satisfaction.

Charles R. Berger and James J. Bradac (1982) have identified "uncertainty reduction" as a major motivation for communication. People who are uncertain about another person or about a relationship usually try to communicate to reduce that uncertainty. Reducing that uncertainty helps develop feelings of comfort, predictability, and security. One source of this security and one way to reduce uncertainty is through routine patterns of communication. Routine patterns of communication help lend predictability to a situation, and the predictability breeds security.

Security through predictability involves developing patterns that support the kind of communication and relationship quality the couple wishes to achieve and maintain in the relationship. As an example, one couple has a particular pattern that has supported their relational success. From their marriage ceremony through their children's teen years, they have had a weekly date. The date can be having a simple cup of tea late at night after the kids are in bed, working together on a household project, or taking a weekend getaway. The important thing is that these weekly dates are as regular as clockwork. They have become a predictable pattern, one that has created a strong sense of security and reduced the degree of uncertainty in this longstanding marriage.

Not all communication in a marriage should become routinized. However, these predictable patterns should be present in sufficient quality and quantity to support feelings of security on the part of both people in the marriage. Security is only the first step. Individuals usually want to feel secure in the relationship, but they also want to be satisfied with it as well. Research suggests that certain types of communication patterns are more likely to lead to feelings of relational satisfaction.

One study found that sharing tasks such as housework, keeping everyday interactions pleasant and positive, maintaining a high mutual level of self-disclosure, offering assurances of worth and love, and sharing time together were identified as important to satisfaction and to relationship maintenance (Dainton, Stafford, and McNeilis 1992). In other research, happily-married couples appear to have patterns with each other that are relaxed, open, friendly, flexible, and attentive (Honeycutt, Wilson, and Parker 1982). It is not an exaggeration to say that without healthy patterns that include some kind of regular talking about the relationship, this kind of mutual satisfaction would simply not exist. Other research has consistently found low correlations between husbands' and wives' judgments of marital satisfaction, so perhaps two people experience a marriage differently in terms of satisfaction (Bernard 1972; Fitzpatrick 1988). Satisfaction in a relationship is never guaranteed; the factors that enhance satisfaction must be talked about by the people involved.

A degree of courage is needed to sit down and examine the patterns of a relationship. Usually one person will feel the need for this first, but will also find difficulty in bringing it to the partner's attention. A technique called "I'm listening" often helps in this situation. The person who feels a need to bring up an uncomfortable topic can ask the other person to listen and respond simply with, "I'm listening." Physical response should be limited to nodding the head. When the partner initiating the encounter has said everything needed, they switch places. Often people simply need to be heard and encouraged to continue. By the time both people have had a chance to share openly in this matter, the fear and anger is generally reduced and a more level-headed, caring conversation can take place.

A further point on pattern change refers to time. The longer patterns are in existence, the harder they are to change. Therefore, it is important to establish the patterns early and evaluate them regularly. In spite of best efforts, however, problems may occur. Establishing, evaluating, and changing patterns within a relationship can be painful, but the long-term results are usually positive in that they enhance intimacy.

Intimacy established through consistent, open communication is central to successful relationships. The term "intimacy" can mean different things to different people, so researchers asked a variety of individuals, "What does intimacy mean to you?" The answers were organized around four themes: (1) sharing private thoughts, dreams, and beliefs; (2) sexuality, with an emphasis on affection and commitment; (3) having a personal sense of identity; and (4) absence of anger, resentment, and criticism (Waring et al. 1980). Lauri P. Arliss (1993) adds that spouses are supposed to be best friends and, at the same time, serve in a variety of pragmatic roles (e.g., maintaining a household).

Intimacy also seems to mean different things to the sexes. L. B. Feldman (1982) suggests that traditional sex-role conditioning has a negative effect on intimacy, encouraging male inexpressiveness and female nagging. Mary A. Fitzpatrick and Judy Indvik (1982, p. 196) report

> [T]he husbands in our sample perceived themselves as rarely nurturant, passive, or dependent, always dominant and task-oriented, and generally incapable of discussing or expressing their feelings. Consequently, it falls to the wives in these relationships to maintain some level of expressivity.... [W]hen wives cannot or refuse to be expressive, the relationship suffers. Wives may be said to bear the burden of expressivity in their marital relationships.

Men sometimes seem to be mystified by what women want, in terms of intimacy (McGoldrick 1989), while women complain that their husbands do not tell them what they are feeling (Rubin 1984). This is supported by research that shows that wives disclose more and value disclosure more than their husbands (Shimanoff 1985). Lillian B. Rubin (1984) also contends that women may fail to recognize their husbands' comments as self-disclosure and that men may feel intimacy just by being in physical proximity to their wives.

To achieve an increased level of satisfaction, balanced definitions of intimacy and satisfaction are critical. Kathy M. Galvin and Barry J. Brommel (1991) call the definitions "relational currencies." These are agreed-upon ways of conveying affection, information, caring, and other relational variables. The key is the mutual definition of the currency. For example, if a husband thinks he is expressing affection through an activity like tuning up his wife's car, but she does not see that act as affectionate, then these two have not yet agreed on the definition of the currency of affection. Developing shared definitions of relational currency is an important step.

Patterns and Power in Family Communication

In *Peoplemaking*, Virginia Satir (1972) likened the family to a "factory" where the person is made: "You, the adults, are the *people makers*" (p. 3). Gender is relevant since the gender identity of the individuals who begin a family will guide much of the family's communication and will influence the gender identity of the children.

Families have long been viewed as a "system" by researchers and writers concerned with family communication. As a system, each part affects the other parts; a change in one part will affect the rest of the system. The change can come from external factors (a change in job or a move to a new city), or members of a family can create their own change in the system. This view of communication is generally known as the "pragmatic" approach, as described by Watzlawick, Beavin, and Jackson (1967). In their view, any communication behavior is a reaction to other communication behaviors; understanding one person in a family or one communication act is only possible by understanding the communication pattern in which the act takes place. Communication behaviors are not the result of people, but the result of other communication behaviors. The pragmatic researcher believes that identification of recurrent communication patterns will help explain systems like families (Trenholm 1991). Because patterns of communication describe what is happening within a family, control of the patterns of communication within a family may provide control of the kind of people and satisfaction produced.

For example, at 8:30 on a Saturday morning, a six-year-old knocks on his parents' bedroom door, hears "Come on in," and runs into the room, where he is greeted with smiles and hugs. He then snuggles with his mom and dad. They all chat for a while, and then everyone gets up. This brief example speaks volumes about the interaction within the family. The child knows it is okay to go into the bedroom with permission, and he knows he will probably be warmly welcomed (though probably not all the time). Physical expressions of affection are apparent, as is talking with mom and dad.

The family plays a key role in the socialization of children, and families with traditional sex-role behaviors tend to develop children who stereotype the sexes (Repetti 1984). Research on parent–child patterns of interaction showed differences between parents and differential treatment based on the sex of the child. Parents do not speak the same way to daughters as they do to sons (Buerkel-Rothfuss et al. 1986). Both mothers and fathers took more conversational turns with sons than with daughters, and they had longer conversations with daughters (Golinkoff and Ames 1979).

In addition to conversational-pattern differences, communication patterns influence the development of the individuals within the family. Stephen T. Beebe and John T. Masterson (1986) describe the difference between person-centered and position-centered patterns of communication in a family. Position-centered patterns focus on the relatively stable position a person holds in a family. Person-centered families place a high value on the individuality of each member. The person-centered approach appears to encourage development of broader communication skills and the ability to communicate flexibility in various social situations. As Galvin and Brommel (1991, p. 122) state, "A key point in this process would be that the parents' view each child as naturally fitting somewhere within the broad range of gender communication patterns, rather than pressuring the child to fit the parents' own gender ideal."

One way to help generate broader communication skills on the part of children is through a form of empowerment. For instance, in researching the roots of schizophrenia, Robert White (1965) concluded that some aspects of the condition could be traced back to early childhood and to early language development. He noted that one symptom of schizophrenia is the belief on the part of the patients that their efforts do not matter, that no relationship exists between their actions and any effect in the outside world. White was interested in how this belief began

and the conclusion he came to has implications for family communication. He concluded that infants need to develop the connection early in life between their own actions and an effect in their outside world, to mold it to meet needs, and to begin to feel a sense of power.

The source of empowerment is the ability to use language effectively. Children should be able to use language to influence the world around them. They should see that their efforts to influence, through spoken language, would have some effect on other people, particularly parents. If a child gave a sufficiently good reason, parents could change their minds and go along with the request. At two years, the arguments may be very simple. At twenty-one years, the reasoning gets pretty elaborate. This one strategy is the sole contributor to developing effective children, but it helps. Children may learn that they will not always get what they want, but it is worth the effort to ask.

This is an example of a potentially consciously developed communication pattern that seems to work through empowerment. A person (in this case, a child) can develop a more positive self-image through positive reinforcement. As this develops, the person begins to feel greater control or influence over situations, greater responsibility, and eventually greater power.

Empowering someone else (especially a child) requires that someone give up power. In traditional families, this may be difficult. Galvin and Brommel (1991) describe examples of people who try to obtain power through the indirect and devious use of fear, guilt, helplessness, or intimidation. These are examples of "control power" (Steiner 1978). By way of contrast, Galvin and Brommel (1991, p. 151) describe "general power" as follows:

Gentle power sends the message: "I can give you what I feel and think. You can understand it and you can compare and decide." This makes people powerful. Ideally, to use communication effectively to counteract the negative aspects of power, there can be no power plays between the persons involved.

An understanding of the two variables of power and patterns can help develop effective family communication and influence the gender development of family members in positive ways. Ignoring these and other communication factors can have negative effects on the individuals within the system.

(*See also:* COMMITMENT; FAMILY GENDER ROLES; FAMILY SYSTEMS THEORY; FAMILY THERAPY; GENDER; INTIMACY; MARITAL

POWER; MARITAL QUALITY; MARRIAGE COUNSELING; PERSONAL RELATIONSHIPS; SELF-DISCLOSURE)

BIBLIOGRAPHY

Arliss, L. P. (1993). "First-Marriage Families: Gender and Communication." In *Women and Men Communicating: Challenges and Changes*, ed. L. P. Arliss and D. J. Borisoff. San Diego CA: Harcourt Brace Jovanovich.

Beebe, S. T., and Masterson, J. T. (1986). *Family Talk: Interpersonal Communication in the Family.* New York: Random House.

Berger, C. R., and Bradac, J. J. (1982). *Language and Social Knowledge: Uncertainty in Interpersonal Relationships.* London: Edward Arnold.

Bernard, J. (1972). *The Future of Marriage.* New York: World Publishing.

Buerkel-Rothfuss, N. L.; Covert, A. M.; Keith, J.; and Nelson, C. (1986). "Early Adolescent and Parental Communication Patterns." Paper presented at the annual meeting of the Speech Communication Association, Chicago.

Dainton, M.; Stafford, L.; and McNeilis, K. S. (1992). "The Maintenance of Relationships Through the Use of Routine Behaviors." Paper presented at the annual meeting of the Speech Communication Assocation, Chicago.

Dance, F. E. X., and Larson, C. E. (1976). *The Functions of Human Communication.* New York: Holt, Rinehart and Winston.

DeVito, J. A. (1988). *Human Communication: The Basic Course*, 4th edition. New York: Harper & Row.

Feldman, L. B. (1982). "Sex Roles and Family Dynamics." In *Normal Family Processes*, ed. F. Walsh. New York: Guilford.

Fitzpatrick, M. A. (1988). *Between Husbands and Wives: Communication in Marriage.* Newbury Park, CA: Sage Publications.

Fitzpatrick, M. A., and Badinski, D. (1985). "All in the Family: Communication in Kin Relationships." In *Handbook of Interpersonal Communication*, ed. M. L. Knapp and G. R. Miller. Newbury Park, CA: Sage Publications.

Fitzpatrick, M. A., and Indvik, J. (1982). "The Instrumental and Expressive Domains of Marital Communication." *Human Communication Research* 8:195–213.

Galvin, K. M., and Brommel, B. J. (1991). *Family Communication: Cohesion and Change*, 3rd edition. New York: HarperCollins.

Golinkoff, R. M., and Ames, G. J. (1979). "A Comparison of Fathers' and Mothers' Speech with Their Young Children." *Child Development* 50:28–32.

Honeycutt, J. M.; Wilson, C.; and Parker, C. (1982). "Effects of Sex and Degrees of Happiness on Perceived Styles of Communicating In and Out of the Marital Relationship." *Journal of Marriage and Family Counseling* 44:395–496.

McGoldrick, M. (1989). "The Joining of Families Through Marriage: The New Couple." In *The Changing Family Life Cycle*, 2nd edition, ed. G. Carter and M. McGoldrick. Boston: Allyn & Bacon.

Otto, H. (1988). "America's Youth: A Changing Profile." *Family Relations* 37:385–391.

Pearson, J. C. (1989). *Communication in the Family.* New York: HarperCollins.

Repetti, R. L. (1984). "Determinants of Children's Sex-Stereotyping: Parental Sex-Role Traits and Television Viewing." *Personality and Social Psychology Bulletin* 10:457–468.

Richmond-Abbott, M. (1992). *Masculine and Feminine: Gender Roles over the Life Cycle.* New York: McGraw-Hill.

Rubin, L. B. (1984). *Intimate Strangers: Men and Women Together.* New York: Harper & Row.

Rubin, R. B.; Perse, E. M.; and Barbato, C. A. (1988). "Conceptualization and Measurement of Interpersonal Communication Motives." *Human Communication Research* 14:602–628.

Satir, V. (1972). *Peoplemaking.* Palo Alto, CA: Science and Behavior Books.

Shimanoff, S. B. (1985). "Rules Governing the Verbal Expression of Emotions Between Married Couples." *Western Journal of Speech Communication* 49:85–100.

Steiner, C. (1978). "Problems of Power." Lecture delivered at the National Group Leaders Conference, Chicago.

Tannen, D. (1990). *You Just Don't Understand.* New York: William Morrow.

Taylor, A.; Meyer, A.; Rosegrant, T.; and Samples, B. T. (1989). *Communicating*, 5th edition. Englewood Cliffs, NJ: Prentice Hall.

Trenholm, S. (1991). *Human Communication Theory*, 2nd edition. Englewood Cliffs, NJ: Prentice Hall.

Waring, E.; Tillman, M.; Frelick, L.; Russell, L.; and Weisz, G. (1980). "Concepts of Intimacy in the General Population." *Journal of Nervous and Mental Disease* 168:471–474.

Watzlawick, P.; Beavin, J. H.; and Jackson, D. (1967). *Pragmatics of Human Communication.* New York: W. W. Norton.

White, R. (1965). "The Experience of Efficacy in Schizophrenia." *Psychiatry* 28:199–221.

Wood, J. T., and Lenze, L. F. (1991). "Gender and the Development of Self: Inclusive Pedagogy in Interpersonal Communication." *Women's Studies in Communication* 14:1–23.

PHIL BACKLUND
DIANA K. IVY

COMMUNITY PROPERTY *See* MARITAL PROPERTY AND COMMUNITY PROPERTY

CONCEPTION

This entry consists of the following two articles:

Medical Aspects
  Maxine J. Klein
Legal Aspects
  Gary N. Skoloff

Medical Aspects

Conception, by definition, refers to the joining of egg (from the female gonad, the ovary) and sperm (from the male gonad, the testicle) to create an embryo. Conception requires all elements of both male and female systems to work properly. There are many parts to the male and female reproductive systems.

The hypothalamus, a small area near the base of the brain, sends a releasing hormone called gonadotropin-releasing hormone to the female's pituitary gland (a small gland also at the base of the brain). The pituitary gland in turn releases two hormones—follicle-stimulating hormone (FSH), which causes growth of the egg, and luteinizing hormone (LH), which causes release of the egg (ovulation). The female human reproductive system is very sensitive to environmental and stress-related influences that can cause these hormones not to be secreted regularly, leading to menstrual irregularity. For ovulation to occur, the FSH and LH must be cyclically secreted. If the pituitary gland secretes FSH and LH at the right time, ovulation will occur approximately midcycle between menstrual periods; the first step in the conception process has occurred. The female reproductive system also includes the fallopian tubes, 10 to 12 centimeters in length, which transport the egg from the ovary to the uterus; the uterus, a muscular organ the size of a pear that supports implantation of the embryo and the growth of the fetus; the cervix, the opening to the uterus that holds the pregnancy in the uterus for the nine months; and the vagina, the sexual organ.

The male reproductive system, which is not on a hormonal cycle, includes testes (located in the scrotum), which produce testosterone (the male hormone) and sperm. Hormones similar to FSH and LH come from the pituitary gland to aid in sperm production and growth. The rest of the male reproductive system consists of the epididymis, a collection of small tubules attached to each testis, which store sperm; the vas deferens, which transports the sperm from the epididymis to the seminal vesicles where secretions making up the semen are provided; the prostate and Cowper's glands, which also add secretions; and the penis, the sex organ.

A woman is born with all the eggs she is ever going to have, while a man continually produces sperm in three-month cycles. There are 400,000 eggs left by the time puberty begins, so the majority of eggs degenerate or never develop. Therefore, as a woman gets older she finds it harder to become pregnant, and when the eggs eventually run out, she experiences menopause. The average reproductive lifespan in a female is approximately 500 menstrual cycles and the average number of sperm in a single ejaculate is 50 to 150 million per milliliter.

Physical conception takes place in the fallopian tube. An egg is released around midcycle between menstrual periods and takes about four days to traverse the fallopian tube, so a woman is fertile for about three days. When a man ejaculates during sexual intercourse, sperm in the semen are deposited into the vagina. The sperm are motile (i.e., mobile) and travel through the cervix and uterus into the fallopian tube, and if the egg is in the tube, conception takes place. Although sperm can be found in the fallopian tube in as little as four minutes, mucus in the cervix and uterus impede most of the sperm, so the amount of sperm that actually reaches the fallopian tube is greatly diminished. Therefore, for conception to take place, the ovary must be mobile so the fallopian tube can grab the egg, the tube cannot be blocked, and the sperm must be able to reach the egg. Once the egg is fertilized, it continues through the fallopian tube to the uterus and becomes implanted in the uterus about the seventh day after conception. If the lining of the uterus is not ready for the egg or if fertilization does not take place, a menstrual period ensues. Interference at any step of the process can prevent conception.

(*See also:* BIRTH CONTROL: CONTRACEPTIVE METHODS; CONCEPTION: LEGAL ASPECTS; INFERTILITY; PREGNANCY AND BIRTH)

BIBLIOGRAPHY

Mishell, D., Jr., and Davajan, V., eds. (1986). *Infertility, Contraception, and Reproductive Endocrinology*. Oradell, NJ: Medical Economics.

Visscher, H., and Rinehart, R., eds. (1990). *ACOG Guide to Planning for Pregnancy, Birth, and Beyond*. Washington DC: The American College of Obstetricians and Gynecologists.

Wisot, A., and Meldrum, D. (1990). *New Options for Fertility*. New York: Pharos Books.

MAXINE J. KLEIN

Legal Aspects

Traditionally, a couple who wanted children had two basic choices: (1) sexual intercourse leading to conception or (2) adoption. For couples who could not conceive because of physical problems, adoption was the only way to have a family. Yet, for many people, the ability to produce offspring who are genetically related was a powerful emotional need.

In the latter half of the twentieth century, technologies were developed that answer the emotional need and have made it possible for many infertile couples to have children. These technological developments have been welcomed with great eagerness by the prospective parents, but they have also created a legal minefield for the unwary. Terms that used to be easily defined, such as "mother," "father," and "parent," are called into question by the techniques used by science to afford couples an opportunity to have children. Unfortunately, science has moved far faster than the law, and no consistent policies or rules have been developed for these new "parents."

Medical Problems, High-Tech Solutions

Infertility is a growing problem in American society. An increase in toxins in the environment, venereal diseases, stress, and the decision of many women to delay childbearing beyond age thirty has led to a dramatic increase in the number of people who are unable to have children without assistance from medical technology (Andrews 1984).

When the male is infertile, or when a woman chooses to have a baby without assistance from a man, the woman can be artificially inseminated with the sperm of an anonymous donor.

If a woman is infertile, there are many possible solutions. If damage or blockage prevents her ova from reaching the womb, she may wish to select in vitro fertilization to overcome her problem. The process of in vitro fertilization requires the removal of her ova directly from her ovaries. The ova are then fertilized in a laboratory, and the embryo that develops is implanted in the woman's uterus. If the implantation is successful (most are not), she will give birth to a child who might be called a "test tube baby." The first successful use of this technique produced Louise Brown in 1978.

When a woman is unable to produce ova, however, she cannot produce a child genetically related to her. Nevertheless, several techniques, as discussed by Lori B. Andrews in *New Conceptions: A Consumer's Guide to the Newest Infertility Treatments* (1985), provide an opportunity for the woman to parent a child who is related to her partner, if not herself.

If there is no physical reason why the woman cannot carry a child to term, she may still be able to give birth to a child by either egg donation or embryo transfer. In egg donation, sperm provided by the woman's partner is used to fertilize the ovum removed from a fertile donor; the resulting embryo is then implanted in the infertile woman. In embryo transfer, an embryo (usually created by artificial insemination) is removed from the donor several days after she conceives and implanted in the infertile woman.

For the woman who is neither able to conceive nor to bear children, the above options are not available, and she may choose to turn to a surrogate to provide her with a child. The surrogate may be inseminated with the sperm of the infertile woman's partner or a donor, depending on whether the partner also has a fertility problem. The surrogate agrees to carry the child to term and then surrender the child for adoption by the infertile couple after the birth.

Theoretically, a child could have five "parents" shortly after his or her birth: the man who donated his sperm, the woman who donated her egg, another woman who gestated the child, and the man and woman who adopt the child and become the legal "parents."

Legal Issues

These technological advances have raised many new legal questions. Where is the borderline between black market baby selling and legitimate surrogacy? Does the biological parent have rights and responsibilities to the child? What are the rights of the potential adoptive parents? What if someone changes his or her mind after the child is conceived? All of these questions, and more, face legislators, lawyers, judges, and the people who are considering these alternative forms of conception. Unfortunately, no hard and fast rules have yet been developed, and there are no firm answers.

Most states have a legal presumption that a child born to married parents is the product of that marriage. In some states, the presumption is rebuttable, meaning that evidence can be used to prove that the child was not in fact conceived by his or her mother and her husband. Thus, if a married woman were to use either of the embryo transfer or egg donation techniques and give birth to a child, the law would presume that she and her husband were the biological parents of that child. On the other hand, this presumption would work against a couple using a married surrogate, since the law would presume that the surrogate's baby was the child of the surrogate and her husband (Goodwin 1992). Obviously, old legal definitions and ways of looking at parenthood do not fit well with the new technologies, and until the laws are changed, there may be legal problems for all parties involved.

In addition, traditional concepts of contract law do not necessarily apply to surrogacy or other donor contracts. The problem is particularly acute where there is a surrogate mother who carries a child to term. Even though she may have signed a contract that states she will give up her parental rights at the time of birth, a surrogate may change her mind and refuse to turn the child over. The potential parents then find themselves trying to enforce their contract, and in some states, they will not find sympathy in the courts. The leading case on this issue, *In re Baby M* (1988), was decided by the New Jersey Supreme Court, which found that the surrogate had to be given the opportunity to change her mind. The court found that this contract, which gave the surrogate $10,000, was an illegal contract for the sale of the baby. It is important to note, however, that the *Baby M* case was based very heavily on its particular facts and the law in New Jersey; another state court, with a different set of facts, might decide the question in an entirely different manner.

By the end of 1992, only a few states had enacted laws regarding surrogacy. New Hampshire requires prior court approval of a surrogacy contract. New Hampshire also imposes a time period within which the surrogate mother may change her mind. Many states with surrogacy laws require the adoptive parents to be married. In North Dakota, surrogacy contracts are void and have no legal effect (Goodwin 1992).

In vitro fertilization raises different problems. Due to the physical strain of surgery to remove the eggs, and the high failure rate of implantation, several embryos are generally kept in a lab for one couple at any given time. What if the genetic parents of these embryos die suddenly or decide to divorce? Are the embryos "property," and if so, who "owns" them? Are they human beings with rights of their own? Can or should they be implanted in someone else, or destroyed, or used for research? These questions, like the abortion issue, are highly controversial and are still being debated by people in all walks of life. The very few courts dealing with the issue have made different decisions, but as in *Baby M*, each case has

its own facts and each state has its own legal tradition. Louisiana has passed a law giving a frozen embryo "juridical personhood." The embryo is not a living human being, but neither is the embryo property of the genetic parents (Walther 1992).

Conclusion

As the world of reproductive technology moves ahead at a startling speed, laws seem to be forming slowly on a case-by-case, state-by-state basis in an attempt to balance and protect the rights of genetic parents, surrogates, adoptive parents, children conceived by these new technologies, and perhaps, the embryos themselves. Therefore, potential parents would be well advised to learn as much as possible about the techniques, risks, benefits, and legal ramifications before they enter into any contracts for one of the many artificial reproductive technologies.

(*See also:* ABORTION: LEGAL ASPECTS; ADOPTION; BIRTH CONTROL: LEGAL ASPECTS; CONCEPTION: MEDICAL ASPECTS; INFERTILITY; PREGNANCY AND BIRTH)

BIBLIOGRAPHY

Andrews, L. B. (1984). "Regulation of the New Reproductive Technologies." *Whittier Law Review* 6:789–798.

Andrews, L. B. (1985). *New Conceptions: A Consumer's Guide to the Newest Infertility Treatments.* New York: Ballantine.

Goodwin, A. (1992). "Determination of Legal Parentage in Egg Donation, Embryo Transplantation, and Gestational Surrogacy Arrangements." *Family Law Quarterly* 26:275–291.

Mazor, M. D., and Simons, H. F., eds. (1984). *Infertility: Medical, Emotional, and Social Considerations.* New York: Human Sciences Press.

Rust, M. (1987). "Whose Baby Is It? Surrogate Motherhood After Baby M." *American Bar Association Journal* 73:52–56.

Walther, D. K. (1992). "'Ownership' of the Fertilized Ovum In Vitro." *Family Law Quarterly* 26:235–256.

CASE

Baby M, In re, 109 N.J. 396 (1988).

GARY N. SKOLOFF

CONFLICT

Conflict is a natural and inevitable occurrence in families. Sibling rivalry, marital distress, and struggles between parents and their children are common manifestations of family life. This entry is confined to the two most obvious—and most researched—forms of family conflict: conflict between spouses and conflict between parents and their children.

The term "conflict" often conjures up perceptions of hostile disputes and "dysfunctional" families. However, scientific research has shown that the mere existence of conflict is not necessarily bad. In fact, some conflict produces positive outcomes, not just negative ones. Conflict allows family members to express important feelings and to devise creative solutions to problems. Further, successfully managed conflict can strengthen relational bonds and increase family cohesion and solidarity. Family conflict also contributes to the social development of children.

The intensity and seriousness of conflicts vary widely. Some conflicts reflect mild oppositions or complaints. These conflicts receive minimal attention and produce short-lived effects. Other conflicts represent ongoing struggles about personally significant issues that often produce intense personal anxiety and tension between partners.

An important finding in the conflict literature concerns how the mere frequency of disagreements reveals little about the overall health or stability of family relationships. Instead, the seriousness of family disputes and the manner in which they are managed more powerfully affect personal and relational outcomes (Gottman 1994; Prinz et al. 1979).

A fundamental feature of conflict management involves whether people engage or avoid each other to resolve the problem (Canary, Cupach, and Messman 1995; Sillars and Wilmot 1994). Engagement involves overt, verbal, and nonverbal confrontation. Avoidance can take many forms, such as withholding complaints, evading discussion of sensitive issues, and withdrawing from a conflict discussion in a defensive manner. Different families establish and maintain alternative norms regarding the frequency with which conflicts are engaged or avoided (Fitzpatrick 1988).

Perhaps the most important dimension of conflict management concerns its positivity or negativity (Gottman 1979; Sillars and Wilmot 1994). Some behaviors appear as relatively positive in emotional tone, such as conciliatory statements, supportive comments that validate the other's point of view, attempts to understand the other's position, and so on. Negative behaviors are disagreeable, inflammatory, and sometimes hostile. Examples include demands, threats, insults, and defensiveness. *How* thoughts are conveyed appears to be just as important as *what* thoughts are conveyed (Gottman 1979). People infer negative emotion primarily from nonverbal behavior,

especially facial and vocal cues. The negativity exhibited during conflict interactions constitutes one of the most important factors that predicts whether conflict between people will be constructive or whether it will be destructive.

Conflict Between Spouses

Determining how much conflict is "typical" or normal between spouses is difficult, although there are estimates (McGonagle, Kessler, and Schilling 1992). Indeed, averages of disagreements in various marriages are not very meaningful since different types of marriages exhibit different amounts of conflict. There are developmental patterns, however, that are fairly consistent. For example, older spouses who have been married for a longer period of time engage in fewer overt disagreements compared to younger newlyweds (Zietlow and Sillars 1988).

Ironically, conflict occurs most frequently with one's spouse, compared to other long-term relationships (Argyle and Furnham 1983). Marital relationships tend to be prone to conflict because spouses develop a great deal of shared intimacy, although there are some marriages wherein spouses prefer to avoid each other (Fitzpatrick 1988). Nevertheless, shared intimacy entails increasing interdependence between partners, which means the partners become more capable of influencing each other's behaviors and goals. At the same time, intimacy makes the partners more vulnerable to each other.

Some of the most frequent topics of conflict in marital relationships include communication, finances, sex, housework, jealousy, and in-laws (Gottman 1979; Mead et al. 1990). In addition, what appears to be a simple complaint on the surface often can reflect deeper relational struggles about power and intimacy (e.g., disagreements about spending time with particular people). Persistent conflicts about such relational issues have the greatest impact on relationship satisfaction (Kurdek 1994). A relationship in which partners cannot agree on such basic and important issues as trust, finances, and the like appears to be based on troublesome assumptions (Sillars and Wilmot 1994).

Studies of marital relationships have demonstrated that the ways in which spouses manage their conflict are connected to the quality and stability of the marriage. This connection is probably reciprocal—conflicts affect and are affected by one's relationship satisfaction, quality, and stability. Methods for confronting and avoiding conflict influence the extent to which spouses are satisfied in their marriage and ultimately affect the likelihood of separation and divorce. At the same time, the degree of happiness or unhappiness in a marriage affects communication during conflicts.

A rather sizable body of research has shown that conflict behaviors effectively discriminate between distressed and nondistressed married couples. Distressed couples refer to those in which partners report they are very unhappy with their marriage. In addition, distressed partners typically have sought marital counseling. The findings from this research yield three consistent conclusions (for reviews, see Cahn 1992; Canary, Cupach, and Messman 1995; Gottman 1994). First, distressed couples engage in more negativity during conflict interactions. Negativity includes attacks, criticisms, put-downs, belligerence, contempt, rejection, defensiveness, hostility, and so forth. Second, distressed marriages demonstrate less positivity, such as showing approval, using humor, making statements that validate the partner, seeking to understand the partner's point of view, and so on. In fact, John M. Gottman (1994) reports that stable marriages consistently exhibit about five times more positive behaviors than negative behaviors in conflict. Third, negative behaviors in distressed marriages are more likely to be reciprocated and become absorbing. Distressed spouses are more likely to get caught up in lengthy sequences of negative behaviors that are difficult to break. For example, one person makes a complaint, which is followed by the partner's counter-complaint in response, and so on.

Not all negative conflict behaviors are equally destructive, however. Based on more than two decades of extensive observation of marital interaction, Gottman (1994) has proposed a theory of behavioral patterns that predict divorce. Behaviors during conflict that erode satisfaction in a marriage also jeopardize the long-term stability of the marriage. Gottman refers to the most significant of these behaviors as the "Four Horsemen of the Apocalypse." Couples at greater risk for divorce repeatedly (1) engage in complaining and criticizing, which (2) leads to contempt, which (3) produces defensiveness, which (4) results in stonewalling (whereby the listener withdraws from interaction).

Behaviors alone do not account for all destructive consequences of conflict. When a spouse feels "flooded" by an emotional response to his or her partner's negative behavior, the spouse increasingly entertains negative assessments of the partner, the conflict, and the marriage itself. These thoughts further perpetuate the negativity of conflict behavior. For example, negative behaviors of the partner are increasingly blamed on the character of the partner (rather than circum-

stances), seen as global (rather than tied to a specific issue), and attributed to the selfish intent of the partner (Bradbury and Fincham 1990). Similarly, negative partner behavior is judged as incompetent and dissatisfying (Canary and Cupach 1988). The greater the frequency and duration of these perceptions over time, the more likely it is that marital partners experience distance and isolation from each other and move toward divorce.

Consequences of poor conflict management extend beyond the survival of the marriage. Increasingly, research suggests that conflict interactions can hurt one's health. For example, one research team found that negative conflict behaviors adversely affect blood pressure and immune systems (Kiecolt-Glaser et al. 1993). Although the long-term effects of conflict interaction on health are unknown, negative conflict behavior in one discussion can harm physical well-being for at least a day. If negative conflict occurs routinely, it appears that one's health would be adversely affected over time.

Ongoing hostilities between spouses can also adversely affect their children. Although separation and divorce are often blamed for child adjustment problems, parents' inability to manage conflict between themselves constructively is much more important (Amato and Keith 1991; Emery 1982, 1992). Hostile marital conflict adversely affects children by lowering their self-esteem, diminishing achievement in school, and increasing the likelihood of depression and antisocial behavior (Gottman 1994; Jenkins and Smith 1991; Montemayor 1983). Moreover, young children learn their own methods of managing conflict by observing their parents (Minuchin 1992). To the extent that parents are incompetent at managing differences, their children are at risk for being similarly incompetent at managing conflict as grown-ups in their own families. The damaging effects of divorce on a child can be somewhat nullified if parents constructively manage their relational problems and breakups and if parents provide positive support and do not use the child as a resource for winning the conflict.

Conflict Between Parents and Children

As with marital relationships, the average amount of conflict between parents and children is difficult to determine, although there are estimates (Montemayor 1986). Of particular importance, the occurrence of conflict is tied to child development. Among adolescents, for example, conflict interactions tend to increase until about age fifteen, then subside in late adolescence (Steinberg 1981). Parent–child conflict probably relates to parental development as well, though research is less definitive on this point. For example, the age of parents and their position in the life cycle may affect the issues that create arguments and the way parents deal with their adult children.

An important feature of parent–child relationships is that they are not voluntary. In other words, children do not usually pick their parents. Like marriage partners, parents and their offspring develop considerable intimacy. More so than spouses, however, parents and their children are "bound" in a family relationship, which can serve to intensify serious conflicts between them. It stands to reason that many family disputes represent underlying relational struggles regarding power or intimacy (Emery 1992).

Much of the research on parent–child conflict focuses on young children. Conflict between parents and toddlers in the two- to four-year-old range largely reflects the child's attempt to gain social control. Disagreements about rights of possession in particular are important for toddlers and young children (Hay and Ross 1982). Other common conflict issues concern caretaking, manners, destructive/hurtful actions, rules of the house, physical space, and independence (Dunn and Munn 1987; Eisenberg 1992).

Between ages four and seven, children become less concerned with possessions and the rightful use of objects and become more concerned with controlling the actions of others (Shantz 1987). For instance, five-year-olds can become quite distressed when the mother does not play in a preferred manner. Such struggles to gain the compliance of others are integral to the child's development of interpersonal competence. The child learns that cooperating with others is an important part of achieving one's own personally important goals. Engaging in conflict facilitates children's and adolescents' acquisition of social perspective-taking skills—that is, children learn how other people think and feel about the issue (Selman 1980).

Whereas younger children are concerned with gaining social control, adolescents attempt to gain personal control. Adolescents and parents often disagree about whether some forms of parental control and supervision over the adolescent are legitimate. Specifically, parents and adolescents have conflict about such day-to-day issues as responsibility for chores, doing schoolwork, observing a curfew, and respecting the adolescent's right to privacy (Smetana 1988, 1989; Smetana et al. 1991). Interestingly, the issues of parent–adolescent conflict persist across generations. Thus, today's "rebellious" adolescents mature into tomorrow's "controlling" parents (Montemayor 1983).

As with marital relationships, the perceived severity and communicative management of conflict appear to be more important than the mere frequency of conflict. Distressed families exhibit more negative conflict behaviors, greater reciprocation of negative emotions and behaviors, and a lower proportion of positive behaviors compared to nondistressed families (Montemayor 1986; Prinz et al. 1979; Robin and Foster 1989).

On balance, however, the consequences of parent–child conflict are most often positive. Oppositions between parents (usually mothers) and their small children are usually brief in duration and typically not emotionally charged. Although such conflicts can test the patience of both the parent and the child, they do not seriously affect the relationship.

Conflict interactions between parents and adolescents can be more intense and dramatic. Still, only 5 percent to 10 percent of families with adolescents experience detrimental effects on parent–child relationships due to conflict (Paikoff and Brooks-Gunn 1991). Thus, the overall context of most parent–child conflicts is one of support.

Considerable research portrays processes surrounding marital conflict, conflict between parents and their young children, and conflict between parents and their adolescent children. However, more research is needed to understand the nature of conflict between parents and their adult children and between adult friends. Still, it appears that how people communicate when they are in conflict can dramatically affect their relationships as well as their own personal development.

(*See also:* ATTRIBUTION IN RELATIONSHIPS; COMMUNICATION; EXCHANGE THEORY; FAMILY THERAPY; FAMILY VIOLENCE; IN-LAW RELATIONSHIPS; INTIMACY; JEALOUSY; MARITAL POWER; MARRIAGE COUNSELING; STRESS; TRUST)

BIBLIOGRAPHY

Amato, P. R., and Keith, B. (1991). "Parental Divorce and the Well-Being of Children: A Meta-Analysis." *Psychological Bulletin* 110:26–46.

Argyle, M., and Furnham, A. (1983). "Sources of Satisfaction and Conflict in Long-Term Relationships." *Journal of Marriage and the Family* 45:481–493.

Bradbury, T. N., and Fincham, F. D. (1990). "Attributions in Marriage: Review and Critique." *Psychological Bulletin* 107:3–33.

Cahn, D. (1992). *Conflict in Intimate Relationships.* New York: Guilford.

Canary, D. J., and Cupach, W. R. (1988). "Relational and Episodic Characteristics Associated with Conflict Tactics." *Journal of Social and Personal Relationships* 5:305–325.

Canary, D. J.; Cupach, W. R.; and Messman, S. J. (1995). *Relationship Conflict: Conflict in Parent–Child, Friendship, and Romantic Relationships*. Newbury Park, CA: Sage Publications.

Dunn, J., and Munn, P. (1987). "Development of Justification in Disputes with Another Sibling." *Developmental Psychology* 23:791–798.

Eisenberg, A. R. (1992). "Conflicts Between Mothers and Their Young Children." *Merrill-Palmer Quarterly* 38:21–43.

Emery, R. E. (1982). "Interparental Conflict and the Children of Discord and Divorce." *Psychological Bulletin* 92:310–330.

Emery, R. E. (1992). "Family Conflicts and Their Developmental Implications: A Conceptual Analysis of Meanings for the Structure of Relationships." In *Conflict in Child and Adolescent Development*, ed. C. U. Shantz and W. W. Hartup. New York: Cambridge University Press.

Fitzpatrick, M. A. (1988). "Negotiation, Problem Solving, and Conflict in Various Types of Marriages." In *Perspectives on Marital Interaction*, ed. P. Noller and M. A. Fitzpatrick. Philadelphia: Multilingual Matters.

Gottman, J. M. (1979). *Marital Interaction: Experimental Investigations*. New York: Academic Press.

Gottman, J. M. (1994). *What Predicts Divorce? The Relationship Between Marital Processes and Marital Outcomes*. Hillsdale, NJ: Lawrence Erlbaum.

Hay, D. F., and Ross, H. S. (1982). "The Social Nature of Early Conflict." *Child Development* 53:105–113.

Jenkins, J. M., and Smith, M. A. (1991). "Marital Disharmony and Children's Behavior Problems: Aspects of a Poor Marriage That Affect Children Adversely." *Journal of Child Psychology and Psychiatry and Allied Disciplines* 32:793–810.

Kiecolt-Glaser, J. K.; Malarkey, W. B.; Chee, M. A.; Newton, T.; Cacioppo, J. T.; Mao, H. Y.; and Glaser, R. (1993). "Negative Behavior During Marital Conflict Is Associated with Immunological Down-Regulation." *Psychosomatic Medicine* 55:395–409.

Kurdek, L. A. (1994). "Areas for Conflict of Gay, Lesbian, and Heterosexual Couples: What Couples Argue About Influences Relationship Satisfaction." *Journal of Marriage and the Family* 56:923–934.

McGonagle, K. A.; Kessler, R. C.; and Schilling, E. A. (1992). "The Frequency and Determinants of Marital Disagreements in a Community Sample." *Journal of Social and Personal Relationships* 9:507–524.

Mead, D. E.; Vatcher, G. M.; Wyne, B. A.; and Roberts, S. L. (1990). "The Comprehensive Areas of Change Questionnaire: Assessing Marital Couples' Presenting Complaints." *American Journal of Family Therapy* 18:65–79.

Minuchin, P. (1992). "Conflict and Child Maltreatment." In *Conflict in Child and Adolescent Development*, ed. C. U. Shantz and W. W. Hartup. New York: Cambridge University Press.

Montemayor, R. (1983). "Parents and Adolescents in Conflict: All Forms Some of the Time and Some Forms Most of the Time." *Journal of Early Adolescence* 3:83–103.

Montemayor, R. (1986). "Family Variation in Parent–Adolescent Storm and Stress." *Journal of Adolescent Research* 1:15–31.

Paikoff, R. L., and Brooks-Gunn, J. (1991). "Do Parent–Child Relationships Change During Puberty?" *Psychological Bulletin* 110:47–66.

Prinz, R. J.; Foster, S. L.; Kent, R. N.; and O'Leary, K. D. (1979). "Multivariate Assessment of Conflict in Distressed and Nondistressed Mother–Adolescent Dyads." *Journal of Applied Behavior Analysis* 12:691–700.

Robin, A. L., and Foster, S. L. (1989). *Negotiating Parent–Adolescent Conflict: A Behavioral Systems Approach*. New York: Guilford.

Selman, R. L. (1980). *The Growth of Interpersonal Understanding: Developmental and Clinical Analyses*. New York: Academic Press.

Shantz, C. U. (1987). "Conflicts Between Children." *Child Development* 58:283–305.

Sillars, A. L., and Wilmot, W. W. (1994). "Communication Strategies in Conflict and Mediation." In *Strategic Interpersonal Communication*, ed. J. A. Daly and J. M. Wiemann. Hillsdale, NJ: Lawrence Erlbaum.

Smetana, J. G. (1988). "Adolescents' and Parents' Conceptions of Parental Authority." *Child Development* 59:321–335.

Smetana, J. G. (1989). "Adolescents' and Parents' Reasoning About Actual Family Conflict." *Child Development* 60:1052–1067.

Smetana, J.; Yau, J.; Restropo, A.; and Braeges, J. L. (1991). "Adolescent–Parent Conflict in Married and Divorced Families." *Developmental Psychology* 27:1000–1010.

Steinberg, L. (1981). "Transformations in Family Relations at Puberty." *Developmental Psychology* 17:833–840.

Zietlow, P. H., and Sillars, A. L. (1988). "Life-Stage Differences in Communication During Marital Conflicts." *Journal of Social and Personal Relationships* 5:223–245.

WILLIAM R. CUPACH
DANIEL J. CANARY

CRISIS *See* CHRONIC ILLNESS; DEATH AND MOURNING; DISABILITIES; JUVENILE DELINQUENCY; SELF-HELP GROUPS; SUBSTANCE ABUSE; SUICIDE; UNEMPLOYMENT

D

DATE RAPE *See* RAPE

DATING *See* ATTRACTIVENESS; MATE SELECTION; PERSONAL RELATIONSHIPS

DEATH AND MOURNING

In any given year in the United States there are some 4 million births, and some 2 million deaths. Of those deaths, more than 16,000 will be children between the ages of 1 and 14, and almost 39,000 will be infants less than one year. There will be more than 38,000 youths between the ages of 15 and 24, and there will be more than half a million persons 75 and older who die that same year (National Center for Health Statistics 1991). Each of these deaths will have an effect on the survivors—parents, spouses, children, siblings, and countless other relatives.

Birth and death—the two extremities of the human condition—have a profound effect on families because the addition of a member, or the loss of a member, changes the structure and functional equilibrium of a family (Bowen 1978), in obvious and not so obvious ways. The varying effect this change has on families and on individuals might be summed up by the classic observation: "In some ways each man is like other men, and in some ways each man is like no other" (Gutmann 1987, p. 10). Although the effect of a child's birth on a family varies considerably (Rossi 1968), the effect of bereavement is even more varied. To be sure, there are common human responses to loss and grief, but there are enormous individual differences that make ready generalizations both suspect and potentially dangerous. Distinguishing between what is universal and what is idiosyncratic presents the social scientist with a formidable task.

A first step in gaining clarity is to "unpack" overlapping terms that are often used imprecisely. "Bereavement" is clearly a universal, in that the word refers to the fact of loss of a person to death. The term "grief," on the other hand, refers to the emotional and behavioral response to bereavement, and there are wide individual and cultural differences in the way such loss is handled. Finally, "mourning," a more generic term, refers to the expression of grief and the cultural response to death (Kastenbaum 1991, pp. 246–251).

This distinction has important implications for understanding the effect of death upon individuals and families. While bereavement, the objective loss of a family member, is a factual given, the response to this loss is highly varied and may involve crying, depression, and loss of appetite. However, grief is not the only response to the death of a family member; there may be anger, indifference, or denial, to name only a few. Care must be taken not to generalize how people "should" be expected to act. Understanding of grief can only occur on a person-to-person basis. Likewise, the cultural expression of mourning varies widely, whether it is the widow's black Victorian mourning dress, the Navajo's desertion of the hogan in which the family member died, or the modern industrial two-day excuse from work because of the death of "an immediate family member."

Thus, a man may grieve deeply but not mourn. His grief may be due to the fact that the man he lived with for the past ten years has died of AIDS, and the absence of mourning may be due to the fact that his lover's family does not want this relationship to be made public and, therefore, does not include him in the mourning ritual. A woman who is in grief over the loss of her father may not take part in the family mourning ritual because she has long been alienated from her subcultural background and does not feel comfortable conforming, even in this time of grief. On the other hand, a person may experience relief at the death of a loved one who has suffered through a long and painful illness and still engage in the culturally patterned expressions of mourning. Concerning these possibilities, Robert J. Kastenbaum (1991) observes: "The fact that the bereavement-grief-mourning sequence is subject to such variation suggests that the specific sense of each of these terms should be kept well in mind" (p. 250).

Stages of Grief

These distinctions serve as an important reminder that it is inappropriate to assume that observers "know" what is going on within an individual or in a family faced with death. However, it is useful to examine the aspects of grief that people are most likely to have in common. The work of Elisabeth Kübler-Ross is perhaps the best known scheme for conceptualizing the grief process. Her pioneering book, *On Death and Dying*, published in 1969, is credited with bringing death "out of the closet" in the United States and with providing a vocabulary that helped many people feel comfortable in discussing death and dying. Her five stages of anticipatory grief—denial, anger, bargaining, depression, and acceptance—have entered the popular vocabulary and have been looked on by many as *the* way to view the experience of grief. Additionally, it has been suggested that family members and friends go through the same stages in their care for terminally ill persons.

Death professionals and researchers have been quick to criticize Kübler-Ross's stage theory as being too linear and prescriptive. Research (Metzger 1979; Schulz and Aderman 1974) has not supported the existence of such discrete stages, nor has it been found that there is any predictable sequence of changes observable in the terminally ill and their families. In an overview of the field, Camille B. Wortman, Roxanne Cohen Silver, and Ronald C. Kessler (1993) conclude that "there is considerable variability in the specific kinds of emotions that are experienced, as well as in their sequence and intensity" (p. 351).

Yet these same authors note that among caregivers and helping professionals there is a "pervasive belief" that such stages exist, and they note that they themselves find the work of stage concept "to be extremely useful in a descriptive sense" (Wortman, Silver, and Kessler 1993, p. 352). Stephen R. Shuchter and Sidney Zisook (1993) suggest that as long as stages are seen as general guidelines and are not taken to prescribe where an individual "ought" to be in the grieving process, they can be quite useful. They postulate three overlapping phases (choosing the term "phase" instead of "stage") that probably summarize as well as any the consensus concerning how "normal" grief progresses. The first phase is one of shock, disbelief, and denial, followed by a phase of mourning, emotional discomfort, and social withdrawal. The final phase is "a culminating period of restitution" (Shuchter and Zisook 1993, p. 24). Robert S. Weiss (1990) uses the term "adaptation" for the final period, describing it as the time when the individual "gives new energy to establishing a new way of life" (p. 279).

Duration of Grief

Within these general guidelines there is, of course, enormous room for variation. In particular, it is difficult to find agreement among experts as to how long normal grief lasts. Early researchers, like Erich Lindemann (1944), suggested that grief is ordinarily resolved in a period of weeks to months, while later studies project much longer grief trajectories. Paul C. Rosenblatt (1983), in his analysis of nineteenth-century diaries, found evidence of grief appearing in "waves," and in some cases reemerging after years of absence. Others have found evidence that grief persists beyond what is normally thought of as the time of grief. Marcia Kraft Goin, R. W. Burgoyne, and John M. Goin (1979) noted that many people maintain a "timeless" emotional attachment with the deceased, and that this attachment in fact represents a healthy adaptation to loss. Zisook, Shuchter, and Lucy E. Lyons (1987) found features of grief that continued several years after the loss, leading to the conclusion that "aspects of grief work may never end for a significant proportion of otherwise normal bereaved individuals" (Shuchter and Zisook 1993, p. 25). But this permanent attachment to certain aspects of the bereaved relationship is not what is ordinarily meant by "grief."

Wortman and Silver (1990), after conducting an extensive review of the literature, concluded that not everyone experiences distress after a major loss. In fact, they note that a "substantial percentage" not only fail to experience distress in the first month after bereavement, but that those initial reactions appear to be highly predictive of long-term adjustment. The same authors, however, observe that those who do experience grief immediately following bereavement "may take far longer than . . . previously expected . . . to recover" (Wortman, Silver, and Kessler 1993, p. 356).

When studies are limited to the loss of a child, researchers, almost without exception, report intense grief, both immediately following the loss of the child and for extended periods afterward. Concerning the duration of such grief, Larry G. Peppers and Ronald J. Knapp (1980) coined the term "shadow grief" to capture the sorrow of a child's death that seems to follow a family like a shadow. The depth of the grief is suggested by the fact that the death of a child often leads to serious marital problems (Kaplan, Grabstein, and Smith 1976). Informal estimates suggest that divorce following the death of a child may be as high as 75 percent. Even when the death of a child does not lead to divorce, the impact can be profound. Weiss (1993), for example, tells of an eighty-eight-year-old widow who no longer grieved the death of her husband, even though she still grieved for her first child, who died some sixty years earlier.

Resolution of Grief

Such behavior leads to the question of not only how long grief lasts but how grief is resolved. Weiss (1993) suggests there are three processes involved in recovery. The first phase involves cognitive acceptance, which is achieved when the individual develops an acceptable account of the reason for the death. Historically, religious teachings have provided a cognitive framework for making sense of death, but with increasing secularization this source of understanding seems to be eroding. In their longitudinal study of motor-vehicle and SIDS (sudden infant death syndrome) deaths, Wortman, Silver, and Kessler (1993) found that almost three-quarters of the survivors were unable to find any meaning in their loss, even after several years had elapsed. They noted the importance of an individual's worldview in determining whether they can make sense of a loss, and this in turn proved to be highly predictive of the adequacy of their subsequent recovery.

The second phase of recovery, emotional acceptance, is closely related to the cognitive task of finding a meaning for the loss but entails the working through and acceptance of the realities of the loss. To use a more psychoanalytic term, it might be said that the person has to "decathect," or let go of the emotional bonds to the deceased, before making alternative emotional commitments. This is related to the third phase that Weiss postulated, that of appropriate identity change. In the new identity, bereaved people develop a new image of themselves in which they can view the attachment to the deceased as being part of a past self, rather than their present self.

As useful as Weiss's formulation is, especially in highlighting the importance of the cognitive component in the recovery process, it fails to indicate the indeterminacy of the end of grief. Murray Bowen (1978), working within a systems theory framework, uses the images of an earthquake to describe the effect of a death on a family. Like an earthquake, there is the initial trauma of an "emotional shock wave," and like a physical earthquake, there can be "aftershocks" that occur months or years after the original shock. These aftershocks come as the result of the "underground network of emotional dependence of family members on each other" (p. 339) and may not even be acknowledged as being related to the original death of a family member. In fact, Bowen has found that family members may resist acknowledging the relation of the aftershocks (which can take the form of illness, accidents, divorce, and other trauma) to the death of a family member.

The delayed, and often hidden, fallout from grief leads to the question of what, precisely, is resolution or recovery from grief. If resolution means simply the return to the original baseline of functioning, for most people resolution never occurs (Shuchter and Zisook 1993). Nor, on the other hand, is there often a complete failure to make progress in recovery from grief (Weiss 1993). Therefore, the ambiguity and diversity of human response to bereavement continues.

Conclusion

The ambiguity of these findings suggests that death is an inextricable part of the human condition. Just as life itself is never clear-cut and predictable, it is not surprising that personal responses to death are not any more predictable. The loss of a loved one makes a difference in the lives of most survivors, but the nature of that difference is far from predictable.

How one makes meaning of this loss is perhaps the key determinant of the grief experience. Viktor Frankl (1969), the founder of "logotherapy," believed that finding meaning is the central challenge of the human experience. Each person is faced with what Frankl terms the "tragic triad," consisting of pain, guilt, and death. Only as a person finds meaning in the face of these inevitable challenges will he or she be able to be fully human.

The loss of a member of a family system invariably changes the system and the lives of the remaining individual members as well. As playwright Robert

Anderson (1980) observes, "Death ends a life, but it does not end a relationship, which struggles on in the survivor's mind toward some final resolution, some clear meaning, which it perhaps never finds" (p. 55). Here lies the challenge of bereavement for the individual and the family, to determine whether there will be some resolved meaning. The outcome of the grief process hangs in the balance.

(*See also:* CHRONIC ILLNESS; ELDERS; HEALTH AND THE FAMILY; WIDOWHOOD)

BIBLIOGRAPHY

Anderson, R. (1980). "I Never Sang for My Father." In *Middle Age, Old Age: Short Stories, Poems, Plays, and Essays on Aging*, ed. R. G. Lyell. New York: Harcourt Brace Jovanovich.

Bowen, M. (1978). "Family Reaction to Death." In *Family Therapy: Theory and Practice*, ed. P. G. Gurin. New York: Gardner Press.

Frankl, V. (1969). *The Will to Meaning.* New York: New American Library.

Gutmann, D. (1987). *Reclaimed Powers.* New York: Basic Books.

Goin, M. K.; Burgoyne, R. W.; and Goin, J. M. (1979). "Timeless Attachment to a Dead Relative." *American Journal of Psychiatry* 136:988–989.

Kaplan, D.; Grabstein, R.; and Smith, A. (1976). "Predicting the Impact of Severe Illness in Families." *Health and Social Work* 1:71–82.

Kastenbaum, R. J. (1991). *Death, Society, and Human Experience*, 4th edition. New York: Macmillan.

Kübler-Ross, E. (1969). *On Death and Dying.* New York: Macmillan.

Lindemann, E. (1944). "The Symptomatology and Management of Acute Grief." *American Journal of Psychiatry* 101:141–148.

Metzger, A. M. (1979). "A Q-Methodological Study of the Kübler-Ross Stage Theory." *Omega, Journal of Death and Dying* 13:291–302.

National Center for Health Statistics. (1991). *Vital Statistics of the United States, 1988:* Vol. II-A, *Mortality.* Washington, DC: U.S. Government Printing Office.

Peppers, L. G., and Knapp, R. J. (1980). *Motherhood and Mourning: Perinatal Death.* New York: Praeger.

Rosenblatt, P. C. (1983). *Bitter, Bitter Tears: Nineteenth-Century Diarists and Twentieth-Century Grief Theories.* Minneapolis: University of Minnesota Press.

Rosenblatt, P. C. (1993). "Grief: The Social Context of Private Feelings." In *Handbook of Bereavement*, ed. M. S. Stroebe, W. Stroebe, and R. O. Hansson. New York: Cambridge University Press.

Rossi, A. S. (1968). "Transition to Parenthood." *Journal of Marriage and the Family* 30:26–39.

Schulz, R., and Aderman, D. (1974). "Clinical Research and the Stages of Dying." *Omega, Journal of Death and Dying* 5:137–144.

Shuchter, S. R., and Zisook, S. (1993). "The Course of Normal Grief." In *Handbook of Bereavement*, ed. M. S. Stroebe, W. Stroebe, and R. O. Hansson. New York: Cambridge University Press.

Weiss, R. S. (1993). "Loss and Recovery." In *Handbook of Bereavement*, ed. M. S. Stroebe, W. Stroebe, and R. O. Hansson. New York: Cambridge University Press.

Wortman, C. B., and Silver, R. C. (1990). "Successful Mastery of Bereavement and Widowhood: A Life Course Perspective." In *Successful Aging: Perspectives from the Behavioral Sciences*, ed. P. B. Baltes and M. M. Baltes. New York: Cambridge University Press.

Wortman, C. B.; Silver, R. C.; and Kessler, R. C. (1993). "The Meaning of Loss and Adjustment to Bereavement." In *Handbook of Bereavement*, ed. M. S. Stroebe, W. Stroebe, and R. O. Hansson. New York: Cambridge University Press.

Zisook, S.; Shuchter, S. R.; and Lyons, L. E. (1987). "Adjustment to Widowhood." In *Biopsychosocial Aspects of Bereavement*, ed. S. Zisook. Washington, DC: American Psychiatric Press.

L. EUGENE THOMAS

DECISION MAKING AND PROBLEM SOLVING

Decision making and problem solving are key management processes important to individuals and families. The effective implementation of these activities helps assure the productive use of resources and the potential achievement of individual and family goals. These activities pervade all aspects and all levels of human life. Most problematic situations in families result from the interplay between individual and family dynamics and factors in the environment. For that reason, problematic situations are described as having an interdependent nature. Since problems are unavoidable, humans spend a large portion of their time trying to solve them. Some of these attempts are successful and some are not. One of the purposes of studying these processes in individual and family contexts is to increase the probability of success.

Definitional issues have complicated the study of this key process. Five concepts have been confused: decision making, problem solving, conflict resolution, goal attainment, and coping. In the case of the confusion between decision making and problem solving, some view problem solving as the more general process, and decision making only the choice within the larger process, while others take the opposite view. Orville Brim and his colleagues (1962) have argued that the differences are more a matter of emphasis than of theory: Decision-making researchers have focused on their respondents' beliefs about the probability of success or failure of different alternatives, the desirability of different outcomes, the future consequences of actions, and use economic concepts such as probability, and costs and benefits of actions, while problem-solving researchers have studied a narrower and more artificial range of problems (e.g., puzzles, games, and contrived problems). Because these two processes differ mainly in terms of emphasis, Brim and his colleagues argue that the two concepts can be interchanged. Irving Tallman and Louis Gray (1990) take a different view of the differences and the importance of making a distinction between the concepts; they suggest that problem solving differs from decision making in that "the former always implies a process driven by a related series of decisions" (p. 424). These decisions might include deciding whether to make a problem-solving attempt or deciding whether to take any number of alternative actions. They argue that the distinctions between the concepts should be made to develop adequate theories of choice, decision making or problem solving.

Problem-solving behavior does not necessarily imply successfully achieving a goal or solving a problem. Problem solving is goal-striving behavior. Similarly, goal attainment may be accomplished through problem solving or habitual action. Viewing problem solving and goal attainment as the same process has two difficulties: (1) confusing the behavior designed to solve the problem with reaching a solution and (2) establishing a singular view of problem-solving outcomes. Other outcomes of interest besides goal attainment might include eliminating barriers to action, arriving at a goal for action, increasing resources for future action, increasing future conflict, accepting an inappropriate action, or rejecting an appropriate action.

Conflict resolution has many similarities to problem solving in that both involve the resolution of issues in which there are disagreements. Conflict resolution addresses disagreements that include antagonistic and highly emotional elements, whereas problem solving addresses disagreements that have less emotional aspects. Constructive conflict resolution as described by Morton Deutsch (1962) and Harold Raush and his associates (1974) is most similar to problem-solving interaction.

Problem solving and coping have emerged out of two different fields of study. Coping has tended to be associated with the more negative aspects of handling crises. It involves managing highly stressful situations in whatever way possible, given the situation. Prob-

lem solving, on the other hand, is viewed more positively in that problem situations are viewed as ones that are subject to control rather than management. Tallman (1993, p. 181) suggests that "coping refers to a stressful event, problem solving to changing the conditions that produce the stressful event."

Coping researchers tend to view problem-solving skills as a type of coping mechanism or resource used by individuals and families to handle crises; whereas problem-solving researchers see problem-solving skills as uniquely suited to handle the full range of life situations, including crises. David Klein (1983) argues that these two concepts and their streams of research and theory are really locations on a series of continuous dimensions. The object of study (crisis or problem) for coping and problem-solving researchers varies in its level of ambiguity, controllability, disruptiveness, and severity.

The purpose of identifying these conceptual issues is to note the potential connections and controversies that remain to be resolved in related fields of study. Tallman (1988) and Klein (1983) have argued that unless these definitional issues are attended to through greater collaboration among scholars in these different arenas, the growth of understanding of decision making and problem solving will continue to be impeded.

For purposes of this entry, problem solving will be defined as the general process and decision making subsumed as one step in the process. A problem is defined as "any situation involving an unachieved but potentially attainable goal in which the means for overcoming barriers to achieving the goal, though not immediately apparent, are considered feasible" (Klein and Hill 1979, p. 495). This definition captures the key elements of a problem that are generally agreed on by scholars (see Newell and Simon 1972; Tallman 1988; Tallman et al. 1974; Tallman and Miller 1974). These elements include a goal, some undesirable intrusion or barrier to attaining that goal, and some degree of uncertainty that the barriers can be overcome. Tallman (1988) argues that the essence of a problem is the notion of a barrier or obstacle that can potentially be avoided, overcome, or eliminated to reach a desired goal.

Most situations that humans handle are managed by routine and habitual behaviors that result from learning. Problem solving is necessary when routine is no longer effective. Problem solving is the complex and active process of developing a new response to those situations for which no existing response is available to achieve the desired goal. It involves a number of separate but interrelated steps and is not only based on previous learning but also may become a learning experience itself.

Nature of Family Problem Solving

Home management researchers as well as family studies researchers have suggested that there are generic aspects of problem solving that cut across the actions of completely independent persons and groups, including families. This position is based on the fact that for individuals and groups the problem-solving process involves situations in which there are resources, desired but unachieved goals, intrusive barriers, and the need for some type of personal or group action to resolve this disparity.

There is no doubt, however, that solving a problem in a group has an additional element. Klein and Reuben Hill (1979) argue that two major differences are of utmost importance: the nature of the goal structure and the organization of the behaviors of the group members. In groups, even groups like the family where goals are assumed to be shared, it is unlikely that the goals of group members are shared consistently. Thus, achieving goal consensus must be an additional element of the process in group problem solving. The balance of key activities involved in the process also differs. Individual problem solving depends more strongly on perception, cognition, and reflective thinking for action and success. Family problem solving also involves these aspects of individual action; however it is the interaction between and among members that makes the problem-solving action different. The organization and coordinated actions of family members as they clarify situations, establish or clarify goals, search out possible actions, divide up responsibilities, take action, and evaluate it are the critical aspects of family problem solving.

The nature of the family as a small problem-solving group cannot be ignored. If one were to design an ideal problem-solving group, it would probably not be based on a family model. The heterogeneous structure of familial groups and a continuous changing developmental context are two key elements of potential difficulty as a problem-solving unit. Karl Weick (1971) has identified other characteristics of family groups that may affect its operation as a problem-solving group. Characteristics such as problem solving under low energy levels, intentional masking of expert power, unequal access to essential information, the embedded nature of problem situations in families, and the predominance of unfinished business all create less than ideal conditions for arriving at effective solutions.

Key Family Problems

Literally anything can be problematic in a family. Many family problems are associated with accomplishing the functions typically associated with living in families: family continuity (e.g., making decisions about mate selection and parenthood, socialization of children, maintenance of intergenerational relationships); family commitment (e.g., developing family identity, maintaining commitment to the group); physical maintenance (e.g., providing for basic individual needs and maintaining health); maintaining group consensus (e.g., equitable handling of roles and responsibilities, maintaining marital and family morale, establishing conflict resolution processes); and attending to boundary maintenance (e.g., maintaining the security and integrity of the group in relation to pressures from the outside world). These problematic situations are not uniformly important for all families. While most families handle the physical maintenance issues in a routine manner, families living in poverty must spend an inordinate amount of time and energy on these issues. Family groups determine the importance of a problem based on a range of factors including a current assessment of family resources, the implications of lack of attention to the situation, and the potential for success in resolving the issue. Since problems result from the complex interrelationships among individual, family, and environmental factors, families differ in their definitions of what are key issues at any given time.

Family problems may be categorized in a number of ways. Brim and his colleagues (1962) noted that prior work on classifying decisions and problems could be divided into those dealing with formal properties, as opposed to substantive characteristics of the decision. Formal properties relate to theoretical and abstract characteristics of decision that are independent of content or the substantive nature of the problem. Formal properties include such aspects as the amount of risk involved, the amount of information necessary, and whether the decision is irrevocable. Substantive properties are associated with the content of the problem (e.g., economic problems, mate selection, planned parenthood, marital relations, and parenting). Substantive classifications often are based on the social context or role in which the problem solving occurs. Marvin Shaw (1971), Bert N. Adams (1971), and Tallman and his colleagues (1974) have all developed typologies of family problems based on formal characteristics. Klein and Hill (1979) noted that ten intrinsic characteristics were the bases of these typologies: difficulty or complexity, solution multiplicity, requirement for coordination, pervasiveness, intellectual versus manipulative requirements, external versus internal source, requisite time for solving, object versus interpersonal barrier, extent to which the problem is governed by preexisting rules, and degree of control family members have to influence the course of events leading to a solution. These typologies are important in that the situational features of problems are expected to affect both the likelihood and degree of effective problem solving, and the interaction patterns displayed by families. The situational features of the problems also provide the conditions that can either promote or enhance the achievement of family problem-solving effectiveness (Klein and Hill 1979). The careful study of the impact of these different problem characteristics on problem solving has not been completed.

Theories of Family Problem Solving

In contrast to many other areas of family studies, family problem solving has generated more creative work in the area of theory than it has verification research. During the 1970s, a group of partial theories of problem solving were developed. The development of these theories benefited from scientific work in five substantive areas: family crises, normal family development, small group problem solving, family and social problems, and organizational decision making. Key theorists included Murray Straus (1968), Tallman (1970, 1971), Tallman and Gary Miller (1974), Rosalyn Cohen (1974), Ralph Turner (1970), Joan Aldous (1971), Mary Ellen Oliveri and David Reiss (1971), and Weick (1971). Tallman has since written revisions of his original theory (Tallman 1988; 1993; Tallman et al. 1993).

Such a rich grounding in theory, with the potential of application to a wide substantive area, should have generated a large number of empirical studies. Unfortunately, the fact that these separate theories were largely unintegrated and unsystematic may have limited their impact. Of these theorists, only Reiss has consistently maintained a research program designed to test his theory. Early work by Tallman, Straus, Aldous, and Cohen at the University of Minnesota held the promise of major breakthroughs; however, integrated research programs based on this work have not been sustained.

In 1979, Klein and Hill published a major paper that attempted to integrate these partial theories and provide a model and structure of a proposed theory. This was intended to stimulate integration and empirical testing of the major components of the model. After analyzing the theoretical propositions of each of the partial theories, Klein and Hill first put the variables under several umbrella concepts. These concepts included social placement, member characteristics, cultural orientations, group structural properties, problem-solving interaction, and characteristics of problems. Second, definitions were proposed for key concepts, and relationships among variables within each block were explored. For example, in the case of problem-solving interaction, the key aspects of interaction during problem solving were identified as the amount of various types of interaction (e.g., the frequency of such activities as questioning, information gathering, alternative generation, decisions), the distribution of these activities (e.g., leadership patterns, power, patterns of receiving and sending messages), the sequencing of these activities (e.g., steps, phasing) and the normativity of these activities (e.g., conformity to family or societal norms). Third, causal relationships among entire blocks of variables were proposed. Family problem-solving effectiveness, composed of both quality and satisfaction elements, was the dependent variable in the proposed theoretical structure. The model captures the complexity of the family problem-solving process by demonstrating that the effectiveness of problem solving in families results from the interaction of a number of factors. While this theoretical structure has contributed to some new empirical tests of several aspects of the model (see Aldous and Ganey 1989; Kieren and Hurlbut 1986; Rueter 1992; Riemenschneider 1986), much remains to be explored.

Conclusion

Given the importance of problem solving in achieving individual and group goals, it is surprising that so little attention has been given to the study of family problem solving in a variety of situations. Problem solving in groups like the family remains a largely uncharted process. Several reasons contribute to this dearth of information. First, problems and problem solving have been interpreted negatively in family contexts. Second, the process itself is difficult to observe and study, particularly in the natural environment of the family. Since every form of behavior can be interpreted as involving problem solving, it is often embedded and confused with other behaviors such as thinking, task performance, communication, and information processing. This makes it difficult to identify when and if families are actually engaging in problem solving.

To unlock the mysteries of this key family process, greater attention needs to be given to collaborative and integrated studies of related processes, such as decision making, coping, and conflict negotiation, to benefit from the cross fertilization of ideas. In addition, increased attention to developing methodologies that capture both the quantitative and qualitative aspects of family problem solving is necessary to help develop a broad understanding of this complex process and distinguish effective from ineffective family problem solving units.

(*See also:* CONFLICT; MARITAL POWER; MARITAL QUALITY; RESOURCE MANAGEMENT)

BIBLIOGRAPHY

Adams, B. N. (1971). *The American Family: A Sociological Interpretation*. Chicago: Markham.

Aldous, J. (1971). "A Framework for the Analysis of Family Problem Solving." In *Family Problem Solving: A Symposium on Theoretical, Methodological, and Substantive Concerns*, ed. J. Aldous, T. Condon, R. Hill, M. Straus, and I. Tallman. Hinsdale, IL: Dryden.

Aldous, J., and Ganey, R. (1989). "Families' Definition Behavior of Problematic Situations." *Social Forces* 67:871–897.

Brim, O.; Glass, D.; Lavin, D.; and Goodman, N. (1962). *Personality and Decision Processes*. Stanford, CA: Stanford University Press.

Cohen, R. (1974). "Social Class Differences in the Problem-Solving Process: An Integration of Social Organization, Language, and Nonverbal Communication." Ph.D. diss. University of Minnesota.

Deutsch, M. (1962). "Conflicts: Productive and Destructive." *Journal of Social Issues* 25:7–41.

Kieren, D.; and Hurlbut, N. (1986). "Methodological Issues in the Measurement of Nonrandom Family Problem-Solving Interaction." Edmonton: University of Alberta. (ERIC Document Reproduction Service, no. CG019615).

Klein, D. (1983). "Family Problem Solving and Family Stress." In *Social Stress and the Family*, ed. H. McCubbin, M. Sussman, and J. Patterson. New York: Haworth Press.

Klein, D., and Hill, R. (1979). "Family Problem-Solving Effectiveness." In *Contemporary Theories About the Family*, Vol. 1, ed. W. Burr, R. Hill, F. I. Nye, and I. L. Reiss. New York: Free Press.

Newell, A., and Simon, H. (1972). *Human Problem Solving*. Englewood Cliffs, NJ: Prentice Hall.

Nickell, P.; Dorsey, J.; and Budolfson, M. (1961). *Management in Family Living*, 3rd edition. New York: Wiley.

Oliveri, M. E., and Reiss, D. (1971). "A Theory-Based Empirical Classification of Family Problem-Solving Behavior." *Family Process* 20:409–418.

Raush, H.; Barry, W.; Hertel, R.; and Swain, M. (1974). *Communication, Conflict, and Marriage*. San Francisco: Jossey-Bass.

Reiss, D. (1971a). "Varieties of Consensual Experience: I. A Theory for Relating Family Interaction to Individual Thinking." *Family Process* 10:1–28.

Reiss, D. (1971b). "Varieties of Consensual Experience: II. Dimensions of a Family's Experience of Its Environment." *Family Process* 10:28–35.

Reiss, D. (1971c). "Varieties of Consensual Experience: III. Contrasts Between Families of Normals, Delinquents, and Schizophrenics." *Journal of Nervous and Mental Disease* 152:73–95.

Reiss, D. (1981). *The Family's Construction of Reality*. Cambridge, MA: Harvard University Press.

Rueter, M. (1992). "The Relationship Between Family Problem-Solving Interaction and Family Problem-Solving Effectiveness." *Family Perspective* 26:331–339.

Riemenschneider, D. (1986). *Problem-Solving Effectiveness: The Effect of Family System Variables and Family Interaction Variables*. Ph.D. diss. Michigan State University.

Shaw, M. (1971). *Group Dynamics: The Psychology of Small Group Behavior*. New York: McGraw-Hill.

Straus, M. (1968). "Communication, Creativity, and Problem-Solving Ability of Middle- and Working-Class Families in Three Societies." *American Journal of Sociology* 73:417–430.

Tallman, I. (1971). "Family Problem Solving and Social Problems." In *Family Problem Solving: A Symposium on Theoretical, Methodological, and Substantive Concerns*, ed. J. Aldous, T. Condon, R. Hill, M. Straus, and I. Tallman. Hinsdale, IL: Dryden.

Tallman, I. (1970). "The Family as a Small Problem-Solving Group." *Journal of Marriage and the Family* 32:94–104.

Tallman, I. (1988). "Problem Solving: A Revisionist View." In *Social Stress and Family Development*, ed. D. Klein and J. Aldous. New York: Guilford.

Tallman, I. (1993). "Theoretical Issues in Researching Problem Solving in Families." *Marriage and Family Review* 18:155–186.

Tallman, I., and Gray, L. (1990). "Choices, Decisions, and Problem Solving." *Annual Review of Sociology* 16:405–433.

Tallman, I., Klein, D.; Cohen, R.; Ihinger, M.; Marotz, R.; Torsiello, P.; and Troost, K. (1974). "A Taxonomy of Group Problems and Implications for a Theory of Group Problem Solving." Minneapolis: University of Minnesota Press.

Tallman, I.; Leik, R.; Gray, L.; and Stafford, M. (1993). "A Theory of Problem-Solving Behavior." *Social Psychology Quarterly* 56:157–177.

Tallman, I., and Miller, G. (1974). "Class Differences in Family Problem Solving: The Effects of Verbal Ability, Hierarchical Structure, and Role Expectations." *Sociometry* 37:13–37.

Turner, R. (1970). *Family Interaction*. New York: Wiley.

Weick, K. (1971). "Group Processes, Family Processes, and Problem Solving." In *Family Problem Solving: A Symposium on Theoretical, Methodological, and Substantive Concerns*, ed. J. Aldous, T. Condon, R. Hill, M. Straus, and I. Tallman. Hinsdale, IL: Dryden.

DIANNE K. KIEREN

DEMOGRAPHY

The composition of American families changed dramatically throughout the second half of the twentieth century in ways that have important implications for the well-being of all persons, from the very young to the oldest old. Young adults are increasingly choosing to delay or forgo marriage, and those who do marry face a high likelihood of divorce. As a result, men and women are spending fewer of their adult years with a spouse, and children are spending a greater proportion of their childhood living with a single parent or in stepfamilies than ever before.

This entry focuses on the years since 1960 and documents trends in family and household composition and their underlying demographic components. Where possible, demographic rates and trends in these rates for the United States are compared with those of other countries.

It is important to point out that using 1960 as a starting point for a study of family change in the United States can be somewhat distorting (Cherlin 1981; Goldscheider and Waite 1991). The reason for this is that the period covering the late 1940s and 1950s, commonly referred to as the "baby boom" era, was quite unusual with respect to patterns of marriage and childbearing. Many of the trends reviewed here are not new but are rather continuations of patterns that extend back into the early 1900s (Cherlin 1981). Hence, to place later patterns in a more proper perspective, figures from years prior to 1960 will be cited in some instances.

Family Formation and Dissolution

While it is true that a large majority of men and women continue to marry at some point in their lives, the timing and duration of marriage have changed substantially (Bianchi and Spain 1986). More and more young men and young women are opting to delay marriage, and for those who do marry, the risk of divorce has increased dramatically. In addition, those who have experienced divorce or widowhood are remarrying at lower rates. The net result has been a reduction in both the average duration of marriage and the total proportion of an individual's life that is shared with a spouse. One study suggests that American men and women who reach adulthood around the end of the twentieth century can expect to spend more than half of their lives unmarried (Schoen et al. 1985).

Marriage patterns. A number of important changes have occurred in the marriage patterns of women and men in the United States since World War II that have led to a general decline in marriage rates. Researchers use several different types of marriage rates (e.g., Pollard, Yusuf, and Pollard 1983; Shryock and Siegel 1976); however, one measure commonly used for examining trends over time is expressed as the ratio of the number of marriages occurring in a

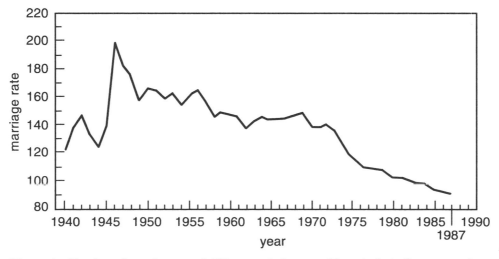

Figure 1   Number of marriages per 1,000 unmarried women fifteen to forty-four years of age in the United States from 1940 to 1987 (National Center for Health Statistics 1991a).

given year to the number of unmarried women between ages fifteen and forty-four. Based on this definition, the marriage rate peaked at 199.0 marriages per 1,000 unmarried women age fifteen to forty-four in 1946 (see Figure 1), coinciding with the end of World War II and the return of many thousands of young American soldiers. Since that time, the marriage rate has fluctuated somewhat, but it showed a gradual decline to 141.3 in 1972, after which it dropped sharply to 92.4 in 1987. Marriage rates for men showed a similar decline during this period (National Center for Health Statistics 1991a). The general decline in marriage rates observed since World War II reflects, in part, an increasing tendency by both women and men to postpone marriage temporarily or to forgo marriage altogether.

First marriage. While marriage is still highly valued by Americans and a large majority of young persons in the United States expect to marry at some time during their lives (Bumpass 1990; Thornton and Freedman 1983), young men and women are increasingly opting to delay the start of their married lives. As illustration of this trend, the median age at first marriage (i.e., the age by which exactly half of all persons marrying for the first time in the specified year were married), has increased steadily since 1960 for both men and women. For women, the median age at first marriage increased from 20.3 in 1960 to 24.1 in 1991. The median age at first marriage for men, which is typically higher than that for women by about two years, also increased during this period, from 22.8 in 1960 to 26.3 in 1991 (U.S. Bureau of the Census 1991b; U.S. Bureau of the Census 1992a).

Another way of looking at this trend is to observe the proportion of persons within specific age groups who have never married over time. As shown in Table 1, the

Table 1 Percent Never Married (United States)

Sex, Age	1960	1970	1980	1990
Women				
20–24	28.4	35.8	50.2	62.8
25–29	10.5	10.5	20.9	31.1
30–34	6.9	6.2	9.5	16.4
35–39	6.1	5.4	6.2	10.4
Men				
20–24	53.1	54.7	68.8	79.3
25–29	20.8	19.1	33.1	45.2
30–34	11.9	9.4	15.9	27.0
35–39	8.8	7.2	7.8	14.7

source U.S. Bureau of the Census (1991b).

Table 2 Percent Never Married (Age 45 to 49 Years)

Country (Year)	Men	Women
Japan (1985)	4.7	4.3
United States (1988)	5.7	5.1
Canada (1988)	7.1	5.9
Netherlands (1988)	7.8	5.1
United Kingdom (1988)	8.8	4.9
France (1988)	9.1	6.8
Finland (1987)	13.4	9.6
Ireland (1988)	14.8	9.0
Sweden (1988)	15.4	9.1

source United Nations (1992).

proportion of young adults who have not yet married has increased dramatically since 1960. Among persons twenty to twenty-four years of age, the proportion never married increased from 28.4 percent in 1960 to 62.8 percent in 1990 for women, and from 53.1 percent to 79.3 percent during this same period for men. The trend was equally striking among persons twenty-five to twenty-nine years of age, for whom the proportion never married tripled for women and more than doubled for men between 1960 and 1990. Men and women age thirty to thirty-four and thirty-five to thirty-nine years also experienced increases in the percentage never married during this period.

This rise in the proportion of adults in their twenties and thirties who have never married reflects the increasing tendency of persons to delay marriage and suggests the potential for future increases in the proportion of persons who choose to remain single throughout their lives. In 1992, the proportion of older Americans who have never married was extremely small: Roughly 5 percent of women age seventy-five years or over, and 4 percent of men in this age group had never married (U.S. Bureau of the Census 1993). As a result of the sustained decline in marriage rates, however, researchers have projected that the proportion of persons born in 1980 who never marry will reach 11 percent for women and 13 percent for men (Schoen et al. 1985).

Despite sharp declines in marriage rates since World War II, the United States still has one of the highest rates relative to other countries at similar levels of social and economic development. Table 2 shows the proportion of men and women forty-five to forty-nine years of age who had never married, for selected countries. With the exception of Japan, which has traditionally placed a great deal of emphasis on familial relations and obligations, all of the countries have higher proportions of men who have never married by ages forty-five to forty-nine compared to the United States. The figures for women are more variable; however, the proportion of American women who were never married at this age in 1988 was among the lowest of all countries considered here.

Remarriage. As is true for patterns of first marriage, rates of remarriage (expressed as the ratio of the number of marriages involving persons who were previously married to the number of previously married persons in any given year) have declined for both men and women. For example, between 1973 and 1987, the remarriage rate declined from 133.3 to 90.8 for men and from 40.6 to 35.8 for women (National Center for Health Statistics 1991a). Throughout this period, rates of remarriage for men remained considerably higher than those for women, although the differential narrowed somewhat due to the much sharper decline in rates for men compared to women.

Part of the decline in rates of remarriage is attributable to the fact that persons who have experienced marital dissolution through divorce or widowhood are less likely to remarry than they once were (Bumpass 1990). In addition, just as women and men have delayed the timing of first marriage, they have also extended the length of time between marriages. For example, the median interval to remarriage (i.e., the length of time within which half of all persons remarrying in a given year have remarried) doubled between 1970 and 1987, from 1.3 to 2.6 years for women and from 1.0 to 2.2 years for men (National Center for Health Statistics 1991a).

Divorce. Perhaps no other demographic trend has raised more concern than the increasing prevalence of divorce among American couples. Divorce is not a new phenomenon in this country, however; in fact, divorce rates have been increasing in the United States since as far back as 1860 (Cherlin 1981). What is unique about the present era is the pace at which divorce rates have increased.

Following a century characterized by a slow but steady rise, divorce rates increased dramatically during the 1960s and 1970s, to reach an all-time high in 1979. The divorce rate (expressed as the number of divorces per 1,000 married women fifteen years of age or older) more than doubled between 1960 and 1979, from 9.2 to 22.8 (see Figure 2). During the 1980s and early 1990s, the trend leveled off, and divorce rates actually declined slightly to 21.2 in 1992 (National Center for Health Statistics 1993a). Unless divorce rates decline substantially, however, researchers estimate that as many as 60 percent of first marriages occurring since the late 1980s will end in divorce (Bumpass 1990).

Women and men who marry at a young age have a particularly high risk of divorce. For example, in 1985, nearly one-third of all women who first married before age twenty had divorced, compared to 18 percent among women who married for the first time between ages twenty and twenty-four (U.S. Bureau of the Census 1989b). The percentage divorced was even lower for women who first married at age twenty-five or above. Although the increased risk of divorce among young newlyweds is not new, the disparity has grown since 1970 as persons marrying at ages under twenty-four have experienced much greater increases in divorce rates than those who marry for the first time at

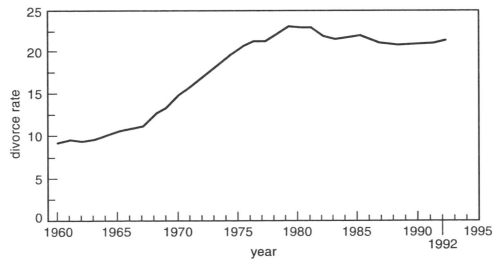

Figure 2 Number of divorces per 1,000 married women fifteen years of age or over in the United States from 1960 to 1992 (National Center for Health Statistics 1991a, 1993a).

153

age twenty-five or above (U.S. Bureau of the Census 1989b).

The United States is not alone in experiencing an increase in divorce rates. Table 3 presents divorce rates for ten-year intervals between 1960 and 1990 for several countries. The trends in divorce rates were especially striking for Canada, the Netherlands, and the United Kingdom, all of which experienced at least a fourfold increase in rates during this period. With the exception of Japan, for which the increase was very modest, all of the other countries experienced increases similar in magnitude to that of the United States. Although the United States was the only country to experience a decline in rates between 1980 and 1990, divorce rates in the other countries appeared to level off somewhat during this period.

Of additional interest, however, is that the United States has a substantially higher rate of divorce compared to other countries. In most of these years, the U.S. rates were nearly double those of any other country shown in Table 3.

Widowhood. Ultimately, all marriages dissolve—if not through divorce, then through the death of a spouse. Indeed, throughout the history of the United States, widowhood, not divorce, was the more common outcome for married persons. However, beginning in the mid-1970s this balance shifted, such that the number of marriages ending in divorce each year actually exceeded the number ending through the death of a spouse (Cherlin 1981). Although the increase in the prevalence of divorce is largely responsible, part of this pattern can be attributed to declines in adult mortality throughout the twentieth century, which have served to postpone widowhood (for figures on trends in mortality, see National Center for Health Statistics 1991b). The net result has been a

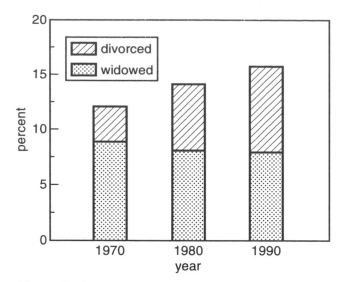

Figure 3 Percent widowed and divorced among all persons eighteen years of age or older in the United States from 1970 to 1990 (U.S. Bureau of the Census 1993).

marked change in the composition of the formerly married population.

Figure 3 presents data on the proportion of the population who were widowed and divorced in 1970, 1980, and 1990. As shown here, the percentage widowed declined slightly during this period, from approximately 9 percent in 1970 to just over 7 percent in 1990. At the same time, the percentage divorced increased substantially, leading to an increase in the total proportion of formerly married persons. More importantly, however, is that divorced persons made up an increasingly large share of the group across the three time points. For example, whereas in 1970 approximately one-quarter of formerly married persons were divorced, this proportion had increased to more than one-half by 1990.

Cohabitation. The practice of men and women living together as an unmarried couple (i.e., cohabitation) became increasingly common during the latter half of the twentieth century. Defined as households containing only two adults with or without children under fifteen years of age present, the number of unmarried-couple households increased from 523,000 in 1970 to 2.9 million in 1990 (U.S. Bureau of the Census 1991b). This substantial increase in actual numbers translates into nearly a 400 percent increase in the proportion of all households that were comprised of unmarried couples, from 0.8 percent in 1970 to 3.1 percent in 1990.

While the 1990 percentage is quite small, it is important to note that the proportion of persons cohabiting in any given year is substantially smaller than the

Table 3 Number of Divorces per 1,000 Married Women

Country	1960	1970	1980	1990
Netherlands	2	3	8	8
United Kingdom	2	5	12	12*
Canada	2	6	11	12
France	3	3	6	8†
Japan	4	4	5	5
Sweden	5	7	11	12
Denmark	6	8	11	13
United States	9	15	23	21

* Figure is from 1988.

† Figure is from 1989.

SOURCE U.S. Bureau of the Census (1993).

proportion who have cohabited at some point during their lives. Based on the 1988 National Survey of Family Growth, which surveyed a nationally representative sample of women fifteen to forty-four years of age, researchers found that although only 5 percent of the women were cohabiting at the time of the survey, a full one-third reported that they had cohabited at some time (London 1991).

Cohabitation before first marriage is more common among young adults than among older adults (London 1991; U.S. Bureau of the Census 1991b). For example, whereas 39 percent of women age twenty-five to twenty-nine reported having cohabited prior to their first marriage, this percentage dropped sharply with age to 12 percent among those age forty to forty-four (London 1991). This age pattern suggests that cohabitation has become more common over time, and therefore further increases in the proportion of persons who cohabit can be expected in the future.

Childbearing

Children have always been and continue to be a central part of the American family. Despite the profound changes that have occurred since World War II with respect to patterns of marriage and divorce, the vast majority of young women (more than 90%) still expect to give birth to at least one child at some point in their lives (U.S. Bureau of the Census 1991a). This does not imply that patterns of childbearing (or fertility) have remained unchanged, however. In fact, with the exception of a brief but dramatic increase in fertility rates during the postwar "baby boom," family size has declined fairly steadily throughout the nineteenth and twentieth centuries (Cherlin 1981).

The most notable aspects of childbearing patterns in recent decades are the pace at which fertility declined during the 1960s and 1970s, and the fact that fertility rates reached an all-time low during this period. A number of factors contributed to this decline, including an increasing tendency by young couples to delay the start of childbearing, to have fewer children in total, or to remain childless altogether. In addition to the general decline in fertility rates, the context in which childbearing takes place also changed during this period, as the proportion of births occurring outside of marriage increased dramatically.

Fertility trends. The Total Fertility Rate (TFR) is a measure of fertility that is commonly used to represent the average number of children per woman. More specifically, the TFR indicates how many children a woman would bear during her lifetime, on average, assuming that fertility rates did not change over time.

As shown in Figure 4, the TFR fluctuated considerably during the middle decades of the twentieth century. Following World War II, during the period known as the "baby boom," the average number of births per woman increased rapidly, from 2.5 in 1945 to a high of 3.7 in 1960. During the 1960s and early 1970s, however,

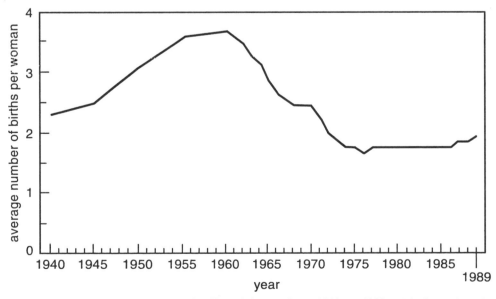

Figure 4 Total fertility rates in the United States from 1940 to 1989, with data given in five-year intervals for 1940 to 1955 and in single years for 1960 to 1989 (National Center for Health Statistics 1993c).

155

the TFR underwent a dramatic and equally rapid decline, to reach an unprecedented low of 1.7 in 1976. Since then there has been little change in the TFR, except for a slight increase in the years immediately preceding 1989, when the level reached 2.0. Although the 1989 TFR was low relative to the baby boom period (1945–1970), it was similar in magnitude to the 1940 rate and somewhat higher than rates for a number of European and Asian countries (for international comparisons, see U.S. Bureau of the Census 1993).

The decline in fertility rates following the baby boom and later sustained low rates result from several factors. These include a delay in the start of childbearing and longer spacing between children, as well as an increased tendency by women (or couples) during this time to have only one child or to remain childless permanently. Because most births still occur within marriage, the changes in marriage and divorce discussed previously, which have shortened the average length of time men and women spend in marriage, have also played a role in reducing fertility rates (Bianchi and Spain 1986).

As women and men are increasingly delaying marriage, so too are they delaying the birth of their first child. The median age at first birth rose nearly two years between 1960 and 1989, from 21.8 to 23.7 years (National Center for Health Statistics 1993c). During this same period, the proportion of women in their twenties who had not yet had a child increased substantially. Among ever-married women twenty to twenty-four years of age, the proportion who were

childless increased from 24 percent in 1960 to 39 percent in 1990; among ever-married women age twenty-five to twenty-nine years, this proportion more than doubled, from 13 percent in 1960 to 29 percent in 1990 (Bianchi and Spain 1986; U.S. Bureau of the Census 1992b).

In addition to delaying the onset of childbearing, an increasing proportion of couples are choosing to have only one child or no children at all. It is still too early to tell what consequences the sustained low fertility levels of the 1970s and 1980s will have for completed fertility levels, because women who entered their childbearing years during that period are only now starting to complete their childbearing. However, the experiences of women who had their children toward the end of the baby boom and who have now completed their families lend some insight into what might happen in the future. For example, the proportion of women age fifty to fifty-four who had only one child increased slightly between 1985 and 1991, from 9.6 percent to 11.1 percent. The percentage of women in this age group who were childless also increased slightly during the late 1980s, from 8.4 percent in 1987 to 9.3 percent in 1991 (National Center for Health Statistics 1993b). This latter figure is expected to increase rapidly, however, and researchers have projected that the proportion of women who remain childless may reach as high as 25 percent among women who will be completing their childbearing early in the twenty-first century (Bloom and Trussell 1984).

Another factor related to the fertility decline is that, for those opting to have more than one child, the interval between births has lengthened. Between 1970 and 1989, the mean number of months between first and second births increased from thirty-seven months to forty-six months (National Center for Health Statistics 1975, 1993c).

Births to unmarried women. Childbearing in the United States has become increasingly separated from marriage. Sexual activity outside marriage, particularly premarital sexual activity, has risen dramatically among women since the 1960s, and women are becoming sexually active at younger ages on average than ever before (National Center for Health Statistics 1987). These trends, coupled with the fact that women are delaying marriage and spending a smaller portion of their reproductive years in marriage, have led to an increase in the number and proportion of births that occur to unmarried women. In 1960, there were 73,000 never-married women between ages eighteen and thirty-four who had children; just twenty years later, in 1980, this figure topped 1 million (Sweet and Bumpass 1987), and by 1990, it had risen to approximately 3.7

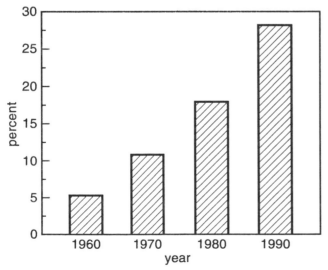

Figure 5 Percentage of births occurring to unmarried women in the United States from 1960 to 1990 (National Center for Health Statistics 1993c; U.S. Bureau of the Census 1993).

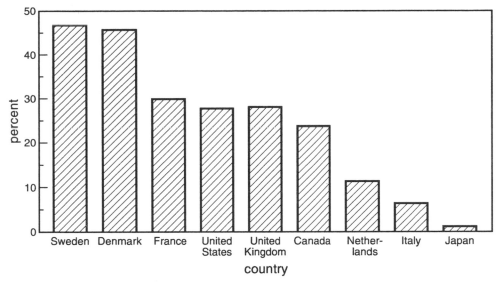

Figure 6 Percentage of births occurring to unmarried women in selected countries in 1990 (U.S. Bureau of the Census 1993).

million (U.S. Bureau of the Census 1991a). In addition to absolute numbers of premarital births, rates of childbearing among unmarried women have increased. Expressed as the number of births occurring to unmarried women per 1,000 unmarried women age fifteen to forty-four years, the birth rate for unmarried women increased from 26.4 in 1970 to 43.8 in 1990 (U.S. Bureau of the Census 1993).

This marked increase in birth rates among unmarried women has taken place at the same time that overall fertility rates have been declining. As a result, the proportion of all births occurring to unmarried women increased substantially during this time, as shown in Figure 5. In 1960, approximately 5 percent of all births occurred to unmarried women, whereas by 1990 the percentage of births occurring to unmarried women had increased sixfold, to nearly 30 percent of all births.

The United States is not the only country to experience high rates of childbearing among unmarried women. As shown in Figure 6, the percentage of births occurring to unmarried women in 1990 was higher in at least three other countries than in the United States. Sweden and Denmark showed the highest percentages, with just under one-half of all births in 1990 occurring to unmarried women. The percentages for France, the United States, the United Kingdom, and Canada ranged between 25 percent and 30 percent, whereas those for the Netherlands and Italy were somewhat lower. The relatively low percentage of nonmarital births in Japan is likely due, at least in part, to continued high rates of marriage in that country.

Changing Family and Household Composition

The net result of the demographic and social trends outlined above is that the family experience of Americans, both old and young, has changed significantly. Changes in patterns of family formation and dissolution and childbearing have translated into profound shifts in family and household composition for children and adults. The once-dominant family model of breadwinner-husband and homemaker-wife raising their own children together in their own home is increasingly being replaced by a mosaic of alternative family types, including single-parent families, remarried-parent or stepfamilies, married couples with no children, and unmarried couples with children (Ahlburg and De Vita 1992). In addition, households comprised of persons living alone or with nonrelatives are becoming increasingly common.

Figure 7 shows the composition of households in the United States between 1960 and 1990. Taken together, the top two portions represent the percentage of all households comprised of families of various types, while the bottom three portions represent the percentage of all households comprised of nonfamily groups. As defined by the U.S. Bureau of the Census, a family household is composed of a householder and at least one other person who is related to the householder by marriage, birth, or adoption. A nonfamily household consists of a householder who either lives alone or exclusively with persons unrelated to the householder (U.S. Bureau of the Census 1989a).

As more and more women and men are opting to live alone or with nonrelatives, the proportion of all households comprised of family groups has decreased. As shown in Figure 7, the percentage of nonfamily households doubled between 1960 and 1990, from 15 percent to 30 percent. At the same time, the proportion of households comprised of families with dependent children (i.e., children under eighteen years of age) declined, whereas the proportion of families without dependent children remained fairly constant.

Perhaps more striking are changes that have occurred in the composition of the family groups themselves. As shown in Figure 8, the percentage of families with dependent children that are maintained by two parents declined since 1970. The proportion maintained by a single parent (either mother or father) more than doubled during this period, from approximately 13 percent in 1970 to just under 30 percent in 1990. Single-parent families are much more likely to be maintained by a mother than a father. Although this pattern is starting to change somewhat, even in 1990 the vast majority of single-parent families (87%) were maintained by women (U.S. Bureau of the Census 1991b).

What the rise in single parenthood means from a child's perspective is that an increasing number and proportion of children are spending at least part of their childhood with only one parent. In 1992, more than one-quarter of all children under eighteen years of age (representing a total of 17.6 million children) were living in a single-parent family, up from 9 percent (or 5.8 million) in 1960 (U.S. Bureau of the Census 1991b, 1993). These figures relate to living arrangements at a given point in time; however, the proportion of chil-

dren who have experienced or will ever experience living in a single-parent home is somewhat higher. Based on trends in marital dissolution and nonmarital fertility described earlier, researchers have estimated that the proportion of children expected to live in a single-parent household at some time before reaching adulthood will range between one-half and three-quarters (Bumpass 1984; Hofferth 1985). For some children this arrangement is only short-term, followed quickly by the parent's remarriage and the arrival of a stepparent; however, many children may spend a large part of their childhood years living with a single parent, because the parent either never remarries or experiences multiple marital disruptions (Sweet and Bumpass 1987).

Stepfamilies are also becoming much more prevalent in American family life, and it is important to keep in mind that children who are reported as living with two parents do not necessarily live with their biological parents. In 1985, just under 7 million children were living with a stepparent. This number represented 15 percent of all children under eighteen years of age who were living with two parents in 1985, a slight increase from 13 percent in 1980 (U.S. Bureau of the Census 1989b). The proportion of children in stepfamilies is expected to increase further, and one estimate is that at least 25 percent of all children will live with a stepparent at some time before they reach sixteen years of age (Zill 1988).

With respect to the population as a whole, it has been estimated that one of every three Americans is either a stepparent, stepchild, stepsibling, or some other member of a stepfamily, and that by the year 2000 more than half of all Americans will be part of a stepfamily (Larson 1992). The union of two or more

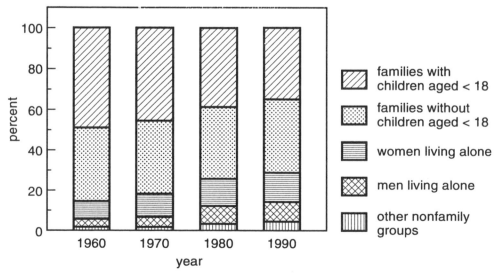

Figure 7 Household composition in the United States from 1960 to 1990 (U.S. Bureau of the Census 1987, 1990).

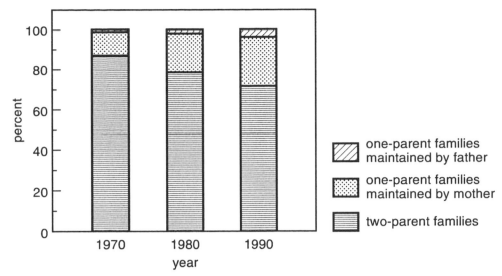

Figure 8 U.S. family groups with children under age eighteen for 1970, 1980, and 1990 (U.S. Bureau of the Census 1990).

families into a stepfamily introduces a complex set of interrelationships among both the immediate and the extended family. Unfortunately, little research has been conducted to obtain benchmark figures on the prevalence of stepfamilies, much less their impact on the lives of family members, so the dynamics of stepfamilies are not well understood.

Conclusion

The underlying social and economic factors that have motivated the changes reported in this entry are complex and varied. A number of explanations have been proposed, ranging from changes in economic conditions that are thought to affect the timing and propensity of marriage, childbearing, and divorce to transformations in women's roles that have led to greater autonomy among women and focused attention on opportunities available to them outside the family.

There is a great deal of uncertainty about what the future will bring for the American family, as well as what the consequences of changes experienced thus far will be for individuals, family groups, and society at large. Demographic trends since the mid-1980s suggest a somewhat slower pace of change for the beginning of the twenty-first century. Furthermore, despite profound changes in its composition and function, the family continues to be highly valued in U.S. society, and the vast majority of young Americans expect to marry and have children at some point in their lives. Because the changes that have occurred have been so far-reaching, however, it seems unlikely that there will ever be a return to what Dennis A. Ahlburg and Carol

J. De Vita referred to as the "seemingly well-ordered family world of the 1950s" (1992, p. 38). Hence it will be important to continue to focus efforts on developing a better understanding of the "new realities" of family life.

(*See also:* COHABITATION; DIVORCE: EMOTIONAL AND SOCIAL ASPECTS; HISTORY OF THE FAMILY; MARRIAGE DEFINITION; REMARRIAGE; STEPPARENTING; WIDOWHOOD)

BIBLIOGRAPHY

Ahlburg, D. A., and De Vita, C. J. (1992). "New Realities of the American Family." *Population Bulletin* 47(2):1–43.

Bianchi, S. M., and Spain, D. (1986). *American Women in Transition.* New York: Russell Sage Foundation.

Bloom, D. E., and Trussell, J. (1984). "What Are the Determinants of Delayed Childbearing and Permanent Childlessness in the United States?" *Demography* 21:591–611.

Bumpass, L. L. (1984). "Children and Marital Disruption: A Replication and Update." *Demography* 21:71–82.

Bumpass, L. L. (1990). "What's Happening to the Family? Interactions Between Demographic and Institutional Change." *Demography* 27:483–498.

Cherlin, A. J. (1981). *Marriage, Divorce, Remarriage.* Cambridge, MA: Harvard University Press.

Goldscheider, F. K., and Waite, L. J. (1991). *New Families, No Families? The Transformation of the American Home.* Berkeley: University of California Press.

Hofferth, S. L. (1985). "Updating Children's Life Course." *Journal of Marriage and the Family* 47:93–115.

Larson, J. (1992). "Understanding Stepfamilies." *American Demographics* 14:36–40.

London, K. A. (1991). "Cohabitation, Marriage, Marital Dissolution, and Remarriage: United States, 1988." *Advance Data from Vital and Health Statistics*, no. 194. Hyattsville, MD: National Center for Health Statistics.

National Center for Health Statistics. (1975). *Vital Statistics of the United States, 1970*: Vol. I, *Natality*. Washington, DC: U.S. Government Printing Office.

National Center for Health Statistics; Bachrach, C. A.; and Horn, M. C. (1987). "Married and Unmarried Couples: United States, 1982." *Vital and Health Statistics*. Series 23, no. 15, PHS 87-1991. Washington, DC: U.S. Government Printing Office.

National Center for Health Statistics. (1991a). *Vital Statistics of the United States, 1987*: Vol. III, *Marriage and Divorce*. Washington, DC: U.S. Government Printing Office.

National Center for Health Statistics. (1991b). *Vital Statistics of the United States, 1988*: Vol. II-A, *Mortality*. Washington, DC: U.S. Government Printing Office.

National Center for Health Statistics. (1993a). "Annual Summary of Births, Marriages, Divorces, and Deaths: United States, 1992." *NCHS Monthly Vital Statistics Report*. Vol. 41, no. 13. Hyattsville, MD: Public Health Service.

National Center for Health Statistics. (1993b). *Health, United States, 1992*. Hyattsville, MD: Public Health Service.

National Center for Health Statistics. (1993c). *Vital Statistics of the United States, 1989*: Vol. I, *Natality*. Washington, DC: U.S. Government Printing Office.

Pollard, A. H.; Yusuf, F.; and Pollard, G. N. (1983). *Demographic Techniques*, 2nd edition. Rushcutters Bay, Australia: Pergamon.

Schoen, R.; Urton, W.; Woodrow, K.; and Baj, J. (1985). "Marriage and Divorce in Twentieth-Century American Cohorts." *Demography* 22:101–114.

Shryock, H. S., and Siegel, J. S. (1976). *The Methods and Materials of Demography*. San Diego: Academic Press.

Sweet, J. A., and Bumpass, L. L. (1987). *American Families and Households*. New York: Russell Sage Foundation.

Teachman, J. D.; Polonko, K. A.; and Scanzoni, J. (1987). "Demography of the Family." In *Handbook of Marriage and the Family*, ed. M. B. Sussman and S. K. Steinmetz. New York: Plenum.

Thornton, A., and Freedman, D. (1983). "The Changing American Family." *Population Bulletin* 38(4):1–43.

United Nations. (1992). *1990 Demographic Yearbook*. New York: Author.

U.S. Bureau of the Census. (1989a). "Changes in American Family Life." *Current Population Reports*. (Special Studies) Series P-23, no. 163. Washington, DC: U.S. Government Printing Office.

U.S. Bureau of the Census. (1989b). "Studies in Marriage and the Family." *Current Population Reports*. Series P-23, no. 162. Washington, DC: U.S. Government Printing Office.

U.S. Bureau of the Census. (1990). "Household and Family Characteristics: March 1990 and 1989." *Current Population Reports*. Series P-20, no. 447. Washington, DC: U.S. Government Printing Office.

U.S. Bureau of the Census. (1991a). "Fertility of American Women: June 1990." *Current Population Reports*. Series P-20, no. 454. Washington, DC: U.S. Government Printing Office.

U.S. Bureau of the Census. (1991b). "Marital Status and Living Arrangements: March 1990." *Current Population Reports*. Series P-20, no. 450. Washington, DC: U.S. Government Printing Office.

U.S. Bureau of the Census. (1992a). "Marital Status and Living Arrangements: March 1991." *Current Population Reports*. Series P-20, no. 461. Washington, DC: U.S. Government Printing Office.

U.S. Bureau of the Census. (1992b). *Statistical Abstract of the United States*, 112th edition. Washington, DC: U.S. Government Printing Office.

U.S. Bureau of the Census. (1993). *Statistical Abstract of the United States*, 113th edition. Washington, DC: U.S. Government Printing Office.

Zill, N. (1988). "Behavior, Achievement, and Health Problems Among Children in Stepfamilies: Findings from a National Survey of Child Health." In *The Impact of Divorce, Single Parenting, and Stepparenting on Children*, ed. E. M. Hetherington and J. D. Arasteh. Hillsdale, NJ: Lawrence Erlbaum.

MARY BETH OFSTEDAL

DISABILITIES

Disability does not just happen to an individual; it happens to the whole family. Disability affects families in many different ways, depending on the type of disability, the age of the person, and the type of family. Disability does not go away like acute illness does. It is always there; it is chronic. It changes the life course of the family as a unit and often changes the life course of some family members. Reciprocally, how the family responds to the disability and its challenges affects the life course and development of the person with the disability. Some families cope and adapt very well; they even become stronger by learning to live with disability. Other families struggle and experience more problems when they are not able to discover the resources they need to manage. These two perspectives—the impact of disability on the family and the family's response to the disability—are part of a continuous cycle of effects. These effects are diagrammed in Figure 1.

This way of thinking about the reciprocal effects of the disability on the family and the family on the person with disability is called a family systems perspective (Patterson 1991a). This perspective has become increasingly important for those who develop policies

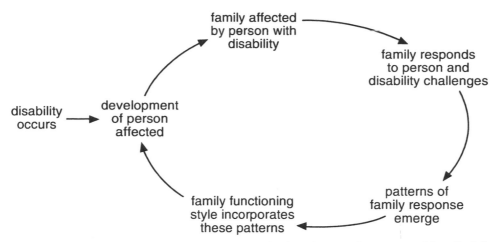

Figure 1 Circular pattern of effects between the functioning of a person with a disability and family functioning.

and design programs and interventions to support persons with disability and their families to have a full and complete life (Dunst et al. 1993; Singer and Powers 1993; Turnbull and Turnbull 1986). From this perspective it is no longer enough to focus only on the person with the disability. Rather, the goals of programs and interventions are to support and empower the families of persons with disabilities so they all can adapt successfully and have a high quality of life (Dunst, Trivette, and Deal 1988).

Definition and Prevalence

Disabilities have become a major health-related issue for an increasing number of people in the United States. Based on data from the 1988 National Health Interview Survey, it is estimated that 35 million Americans have a disability (Pope and Tarlov 1991). Furthermore, the overall prevalence of disabilities has been increasing in the United States, primarily because of biomedical advances that are able to keep people alive longer. This is the case for all ages across the lifespan, from very premature infants to the elderly. However, maintaining life does not always mean cure. Many more individuals live with the residue of what cannot be cured; they live with chronic conditions, and many chronic conditions create disability or gradually lead to disability over time. By definition, disability is the inability to engage in any substantial gainful activity by reason of some medically determined physical or mental impairment that can be expected to last or has lasted for a continuous period of not less than twelve months. Disability is the gap between a person's capabilities and what the environment expects a person to be able to perform in personal, fa-

milial, and social roles (Pope and Tarlov 1991). When estimates of the prevalence of disabilities are made, primary social roles are defined as follows: "playing" for children under five years; "going to school" for children ages five to seventeen; "working or keeping house" for adults ages eighteen to sixty-nine; and "living independently" for adults over seventy.

The main causes of activity limitation leading to disability are mobility impairments (38%); chronic diseases (32%); sensory impairments (8%); and intellectual impairments, including mental retardation (7%) (LaPlante 1988). Both the prevalence and the severity of disabilities increase with age. The percent of each age group with a disability is 2 percent of children under five years, 8 percent of children ages five to seventeen years, 10 percent of adults eighteen to forty-four years, 23 percent of adults forty-five to sixty-four years, 36 percent of adults sixty-five to sixty-nine years, and 38 percent of adults over seventy (National Center for Health Statistics 1989). For children under 18 years, intellectual limitations and chronic diseases are the major causes. Above eighteen years, mobility impairments are the primary cause. For those between eighteen and forty-four years of age, accidents and injuries are a major contributing factor to mobility impairment; among older ages, mobility impairment is more the result of chronic disease, such as arthritis.

Not all chronic conditions are associated with disability. Some chronic conditions cause no limitations. For those that do, the degree of limitation varies from minor to being unable to perform a major activity, such as working. For those conditions associated with disability, families increasingly have taken over a major role in providing assistance and care for their members who are disabled (Chilman, Nunnally, and

Cox 1988). Very few families can expect to go through their life course without caring for at least one member with a disability. In many instances, however, the onset and severity of disability can be prevented or postponed, especially those related to chronic diseases. This is influenced by the person's lifestyle, access to regular medical care, and willingness to take an active role in managing his or her health condition. The family, of course, is a critical social context influencing how an individual responds to a chronic condition, as well as how an individual responds to physical, intellectual, and sensory impairment. In this way the family can have a major impact on the course of chronic conditions, if and when disability emerges, and how severe the disability is.

Impact of Disabilities on Families

Disability places a set of extra demands or challenges on the family system; most of these demands last for a long time (Murphy 1982). Many of these challenges cut across disability type, age of the person with the disability, and type of family in which the person lives. There is the financial burden associated with getting health, education, and social services; buying or renting equipment and devices; making accommodations to the home; transportation; and medications and special food. For many of these financial items, the person or family may be eligible for payment or reimbursement from an insurance company and/or a publicly funded program such as Medicaid or Supplemental Security Income. However, knowing what services and programs one is eligible for and then working with a bureaucracy to certify that eligibility (often repeatedly) is another major challenge faced by families. Coordination of services among different providers (such as a physician, physical therapist, occupational therapist, dietician, social worker, teacher, and counselor) who often are not aware of what the other is doing and may provide discrepant information is another challenge faced by families (Sloper and Turner 1992). While care coordination or case management is often the stated goal of service programs, there are many flaws in implementation. Families experience the burden of this lack of coordination.

The day-to-day strain of providing care and assistance leads to exhaustion and fatigue, taxing the physical and emotional energy of family members. There are a whole set of issues that create emotional strain, including worry, guilt, anxiety, anger, and uncertainty about the cause of the disability, about the future, about the needs of other family members, about

whether one is providing enough assistance, and so on. Grieving over the loss of function of the person with the disability is experienced at the time of onset, and often repeatedly at other stages in the person's life.

Family life is changed, often in major ways. Caretaking responsibilities may lead to changed or abandoned career plans. Female family members are more likely to take on caregiving roles and thus give up or change their work roles. This is also influenced by the fact that males are able to earn more money for work in society. When the added financial burden of disability is considered, this is the most efficient way for families to divide role responsibilities.

New alliances and loyalties between family members sometimes emerge, with some members feeling excluded and others being overly drawn in. For example, the primary caregiver may become overly involved with the person with disability. This has been noted particularly with regard to mothers of children with disabilities. In these families, fathers often are underinvolved with the child and instead immerse themselves in work or leisure activities. This pattern usually is associated with more marital conflict. It is important to note, however, that there does not appear to be a greater incidence of divorce among families who have a child with a disability, although there may exist more marital tension (Hirst 1991; Sabbeth and Leventhal 1984).

The disability can consume a disproportionate share of a family's resources of time, energy, and money, so that other individual and family needs go unmet. Families often talk about living "one day at a time." The family's lifestyle and leisure activities are altered. A family's dreams and plans for the future may be given up. Social roles are disrupted because often there is not enough time, money, or energy to devote to them (Singhi et al. 1990).

Friends, neighbors, and people in the community may react negatively to the disability by avoidance, disparaging remarks or looks, or overt efforts to exclude people with disabilities and their families. Despite the passage of the Americans with Disabilities Act in 1990, many communities still lack programs, facilities, and resources that allow for the full inclusion of persons with disabilities. Families often report that the person with the disability is not a major burden for them. The burden comes from dealing with people in the community whose attitudes and behaviors are judgmental, stigmatizing, and rejecting of the disabled individual and his or her family (Knoll 1992; Turnbull et al. 1993). Family members report that these negative attitudes and behaviors often are characteristic of their friends, relatives, and service providers as well as strangers (Patterson and Leonard 1994).

Overall, stress from these added demands of disability in family life can negatively affect the health and functioning of family members (Patterson 1988; Varni and Wallander 1988). Numerous studies report that there is an increased risk of psychological and behavioral symptoms in the family members of persons with disabilities (Cadman et al. 1987; Singer and Powers 1993; Vance, Fazan, and Satterwhite 1980). However, even though disability increases the risk for these problems, most adults and children who have a member with a disability do not show psychological or behavioral problems. They have found ways to cope with this added stress in their lives. Increasingly, the literature on families and disabilities emphasizes this adaptive capacity of families. It has been called family resilience (Patterson 1991b; Singer and Powers 1993; Turnbull et al. 1993). Many families actually report that the presence of disability has strengthened them as a family—they become closer, more accepting of others, have deeper faith, discover new friends, develop greater respect for life, improve their sense of mastery, and so on.

While there are many commonalities regarding the impact of disabilities on families, other factors lead to variability in the impact of disability on the family. Included in these factors are the type of disability, which member of the family gets the disability, and the age of onset of the disability.

Disabilities vary along several dimensions, including the degree and type of incapacitation (sensory, motor, or cognitive); the degree of visibility of the disability; whether the course of the condition is constant, relapsing, or progressive; the prognosis or life expectancy of the person; the amount of pain or other symptoms experienced; and the amount of care or treatment required. John Rolland (1994) has outlined a typology of chronic conditions based on some of these factors and has described the psychosocial impact on families based on these factors. His argument, and that of several others (Perrin et al. 1993; Stein et al. 1993), is that the variability in the psychosocial impact of chronic conditions is related more to characteristics of the condition than to the diagnosis per se.

Consider the course of the condition. When it is progressive (such as degenerative arthritis or dementia), the symptomatic person may become increasingly less functional. The family is faced with increasing caretaking demands, uncertainty about the degree of dependency and what living arrangement is best, as well as grieving continuous loss. These fam-

ilies need to readjust continuously to the increasing strain and must be willing to find and utilize outside resources. If a condition has a relapsing course (such as epilepsy or cancer in remission), the ongoing care may be less, but a family needs to be able to reorganize itself quickly and mobilize resources when the condition flares up. They must be able to move from normalcy to crisis alert rapidly. An accumulation of these dramatic transitions can exhaust a family. Disabilities with a constant course (such as a spinal cord injury) require major reorganization of the family at the outset and then perseverance and stamina for a long time. While these families can plan, knowing what is ahead, limited community resources to help them may lead to exhaustion.

Disabilities where mental ability is limited seem to be more difficult for families to cope with (Breslau 1993; Cole and Reiss 1993; Holroyd and Guthrie 1986). This may be due to greater dependency requiring more vigilance by family members, or because it limits the person's ability to take on responsible roles, and perhaps limits the possibilities for independent living. If the mental impairment is severe, it may create an extra kind of strain for families because the person is physically present in the family but mentally absent. This kind of incongruence between physical presence and psychological presence has been called boundary ambiguity (Boss 1993). Boundary ambiguity means that it is not entirely clear to family members whether the person (with the disability in this case) is part of the family or not because the person is there in some ways but not in others. Generally, families experience more distress when situations are ambiguous or unclear because they do not know what to expect and may have a harder time planning the roles of other family members to accommodate this uncertainty.

In addition to cognitive impairment, other characteristics of disabilities can create ambiguity and uncertainty for families. For example, an uncertain life expectancy makes it difficult to plan future life roles, to anticipate costs of care, or to make decisions about the best living arrangements for adults requiring assistance in the activities of daily living. For example, from 1970 to 1991, survival for children with cystic fibrosis increased 700 percent, to a life expectancy of twenty-six years in the United States (Fitzsimmons 1991). These young adults now face difficult family decisions, such as whether to marry and whether to have children. In more extreme cases related to severe medical conditions, persons may have their lives extended by using advances in biomedical science and technology. When this happens, families can be faced with very difficult decisions about what techniques and equipment should be used, for how long, with what expected gains, at what cost, and so on. Society is facing new issues in biomedical ethics, but there is no social consensus about how aggressively to intervene and under what circumstances. Family members who bear the emotional burden of these decisions do not always agree on a course of action and, furthermore, may be blocked by hospitals and courts from carrying out a particular course of action. While these kinds of cases may not yet be widespread, they have sparked intense debate and raised the consciousness of many families about issues they may face.

In addition to type of impairment, there is variability in the severity of impairment. The degree to which a person with disability is limited in doing activities or functions of daily living (e.g., walking, feeding oneself, and toileting) can be assessed and is called functional status. The lower the person's functional status, the more assistance he or she will need from other people and/or from equipment and devices. Family members are a primary source of this needed assistance (Biegel, Sales, and Schulz 1991; Stone and Kemper 1989). Providing this assistance can create a burden for family caregivers, which may result in physical or psychological symptoms of poor health. For example, parents, especially mothers, experience more depression when their children with disabilities have lower functional status (Patterson, Leonard, and Titus 1992; Singer et al. 1993). For elderly caregivers, physical strain may be a limiting factor in how much and for how long assistance can be provided for the disabled individual (Blackburn 1988).

The age of the person when the disability emerges is associated with different impacts on the family and on the family's life course, as well as on the course of development for the person with disability (Eisenberg, Sutkin, and Jansen 1984). When conditions emerge in late adulthood, in some ways this is normative and more expectable. Psychologically it is usually less disruptive to the family. When disability occurs earlier in a person's life, this is out of phase with what is considered normative, and the impact on the course of development for the person and the family is greater. More adjustments have to be made and for longer periods of time.

When the condition is present from birth, the child's life and identity are shaped around the disability. In some ways it may be easier for a child and his or her family to adjust to never having certain functional abilities than to a sudden loss of abilities later. For example, a child with spina bifida from birth will adapt differently than a child who suddenly becomes a paraplegic in adolescence due to an injury.

The age of the parents when a child's disability is diagnosed is also an important consideration in how the family responds. For example, teenage parents are at greater risk for experiencing poor adaptation because their own developmental needs are still prominent, and they are less likely to have the maturity and resources to cope with the added demands of the child. For older parents there is greater risk of having a child with certain disabilities, such as Down syndrome. Older parents may lack the stamina for the extra burden of care required, and they may fear their own mortality and be concerned about who will care for their child when they die.

The course of the child's physical, psychological, and social development will forever be altered by the chronic condition. Since development proceeds sequentially, and since relative success at mastering the tasks of one stage is a prerequisite for facing the challenges of the next stage, one could anticipate that the earlier the onset, the greater the adverse impact on development (Eisenberg, Sutkin, and Jansen 1984).

There are many ways in which the accomplishment of development tasks is complicated for persons with disabilities. This, in turn, has an effect on their families as well as on which family roles can be assumed by the person with disability (Perrin and Gerrity 1984). For example, in infancy, disability may frighten parents, or the infant may be unresponsive to their nurturing efforts such that attachment and bonding necessary for the development of trust are compromised. The parent may feel inadequate as a caregiver, and parenting competence is undermined. For a toddler, active exploration of the social environment, needed to develop a sense of autonomy and self-control, may be restricted because of the child's motor, sensory, or cognitive deficits. Parents, fearing injury or more damage to their young child, may restrict their child's efforts to explore and learn, or they may overindulge the child out of sympathy or guilt. If other people react negatively to the child's disability, parents may try to compensate by being overly protective or overly solicitous. These parent behaviors further compromise the child's development of autonomy and self-control.

As children with disabilities move into school environments where they interact with teachers and peers, they may experience difficulties mastering tasks and developing social skills and competencies. Although schools are mandated to provide special education programs for children in the least restrictive environment and to maximize integration, there is considerable variability in how effectively schools do this.

Barriers include inadequate financing for special education; inadequately trained school personnel; and, very often, attitudinal barriers of other children and staff that compromise full inclusion for students with disabilities. Parents of children with disabilities may experience a whole set of added challenges in assuring their children's educational rights. In some instances, conflict with schools and other service providers can become a major source of strain for families (Walker and Singer 1993). In other cases, school programs are a major resource for families.

Developmental tasks of adolescence—developing an identity and developing greater autonomy—are particularly difficult when the adolescent has a disability. Part of this process for most adolescents generally involves some risk-taking behaviors, such as smoking and drinking. Adolescents with disabilities take risks too, sometimes defying treatment and procedures related to their condition, such as skipping medications or changing a prescribed diet. Issues related to sexuality may be particularly difficult because the person with disability has fears about his or her desirability to a partner, sexual performance, and worries about ever getting married or having children (Coupey and Cohen 1984). There is some evidence that girls may be at greater risk for pregnancy because of their desire to disavow their disability and prove their normalcy (Holmes 1986). Teens with mental impairment may be subjected to sexual exploitation by others.

When disability has its onset in young adulthood, the person's personal, family, and vocational plans for the future may be altered significantly. If the young adult has a partner where there is a long-term commitment, this relationship may be in jeopardy, particularly if the ability to enact adult roles as a sexual partner, parent, financial provider, or leisure partner are affected (Ireys and Burr 1984). When a couple has just begun to plan a future based on the assumption that both partners would be fully functional, they may find the adjustment to the disability too great to handle. The development of a relationship with a significant other *after* the disability is already present is more likely to lead to positive adjustment. Young adulthood is that critical transition from one's family of origin to creating a new family unit with a partner and possibly children. When disability occurs at this stage, the young adult's parents may become the primary caregivers, encouraging or bringing the young person home again. The risk is that the developmental course for the young adult and his or her parents may never get back on track. This is influenced in part by the extent to which there are independent living op-

tions for persons with disabilities to make use of in the community.

When the onset of disability occurs to adults in their middle years, it is often associated with major disruption to career and family roles. Those roles are affected for the person with the disability as well as for other family members who have come to depend on him or her to fulfill those roles. Some kind of family reorganization of roles, rules, and routines is usually required. If the person has been employed, he or she may have to give up work and career entirely or perhaps make dramatic changes in amount and type of work. The family may face a major loss of income as well as a loss in health and other employee benefits. If the person is a parent, childrearing responsibilities may be altered significantly. The adult may have to switch from being the nurturer to being the nurtured. This may leave a major void in the family for someone to fill the nurturing role. If the person is a spouse, the dynamics of this relationship will change as one person is unable to perform as independently as before. The partner with the disability may be treated like another child. The sexual relationship may change, plans for having more children may be abandoned, lifestyle and leisure may be altered. Some spouses feel that their marital contract has been violated, and they are unwilling to make the necessary adjustments. Children of a middle-aged adult with a disability also experience role shifts. Their own dependency and nurturing needs may be neglected. They may be expected to take on some adult roles, such as caring for younger children, doing household chores, or maybe even providing some income. How well the family's efforts at reorganization work depends ultimately on the family's ability to accommodate age-appropriate developmental needs. In families where there is more flexibility among the adults in assuming the different family roles, adjustment is likely to be better.

The onset of disability in old age is more expectable as bodily functions deteriorate. This decline in physical function is often associated with more depression. An older person may live for many years needing assistance in daily living, and the choices of where to get that assistance are not always easily made. Spouses may be unable to meet the extra caretaking needs indefinitely as their own health and stamina decline (Blackburn 1988). Adult children are often in a position of deciding where their elderly parent or parents should live when they can no longer care for themselves. Having their parents move in with them or having them move to a nursing home or seniors' residence are the most common options. However, each of these choices carries with it emotional, financial, and social costs to the elderly person as well as to his or her adult children. This responsibility for elderly parents is not always shared among adult children. Adult daughters are more likely than adult sons to be involved in providing direct care for their elderly parents (Brody 1985). The many decisions and responsibilities can be sources of tension, conflict, and resentment among extended family members. This period of disability in old age can go on for a very long time, given the medical capability to sustain life. While the practice is still not widespread, more elderly people are preparing a living will, which is a legal document preventing extraordinary means from being used to prolong their lives.

Family Response to Disabilities

How do families respond to the challenges of disabilities? Some of the more common responses will be discussed, although it is important to emphasize that there are many different ways by which families can successfully adapt. Response to disability can be divided into three phases: crisis, chronic, and terminal (Rolland 1994).

The initial response of most families to the sudden onset of disability is to pull together and rally around the person affected and provide support to each other (Steinglass et al. 1982). Some or all family members may suspend their daily routines for a period of time as they focus on the immediate crisis. They gather more information about the condition, its course, treatment options, and where to get services. Often there are new behaviors to be learned, including how to provide care and treatment to the person with the disability, how to interact with health care and other service providers, and how to access needed information. There is also a whole set of emotional issues that confronts family members, including grief over the loss of abilities; worry about the future and the costs; feelings of guilt, blame, or responsibility; and trying to find a cause and a meaning for this event. Families are more variable in how they deal with these emotional challenges. Some avoid them altogether and stay focused on gathering information and learning new behaviors. Other families are split, with some members having intense emotional reactions and others avoiding them. Even though there is the expectation that family members should provide support to each other in times of crisis, this is often unrealistic when members are out of sync with each other and each person needs so much. This is a place where health-care providers could be more helpful to families—both in validating their strong emotional reactions and in providing support or finding other resources, as well as in recognizing and not judging family members who have different responses. This is a very vulnerable time for most families, and those who make the diagnosis and provide the initial care are powerful in influencing how the family responds. In many ways their early response sets the stage for how the family will adapt to the disability over the long run (Rolland 1994).

Following this crisis phase, there is the chronic phase of living with a disability. This phase varies in length depending on the condition, but it is essentially the "long haul," when the family settles into living with the disability. The ultimate challenge to the family is to meet the disability-related needs and simultaneously to meet the needs of the family and its members of having a normal life. A metaphor used to describe this challenge is "finding a place for the disability in the family, but keeping the disability in its place" (Gonzalez, Steinglass, and Reiss 1989).

The terminal phase is when the inevitability of death is clear. Of course, not all conditions signal a terminal phase, but for those that do, the patient and family are faced with a set of choices about how directly they wish to face death and saying good-bye. Families vary in their responses at this phase as well. In some cases, it is an occasion of healing and of celebration of what the person's life has meant for a family. In other cases, it can be a tremendous relief and an escape from a burden that was resented and never acknowledged. Family members who respond in this way usually need healing after the death. In still other families, the death creates a void in the family's lifestyle that may never be filled because the person's disability was the cornerstone around which family life was organized.

How the family organizes itself for the chronic phase of a disability is particularly important in understanding how the course of development for the person, the disability, and the family will evolve (see Figure 1, lower left quadrant). The central issue seems to be the degree to which the condition takes over family life and becomes the centerpiece around which all other activities are organized. David Reiss, Peter Steinglass, and George Howe (1993) have emphasized that a family's identity can be subsumed within and around the disability: "We are an 'asthmatic family.'" Important aspects of family life such as routines, rituals, leisure activities, and friends may be changed or given up to accommodate the disability-related needs. One person's needs take precedence over the needs of the whole family system to mature and for other members to progress along their developmental course. This "skew toward the disability" can evolve into a larger pattern of family responses (Gonzalez, Steinglass, and Reiss 1989). There is the tendency for family members to hold back from discussing any strong negative feelings they may have about their situation. It is as though they have no right to feel angry or resentful since, after all, they are not the one with the disability. This can lead to general repression of feelings in the family—an emotional shutdown. The overall climate in the family may frequently be tense, as though "walking on eggshells." When no one wants to upset the balance, there is a tendency to try to maintain control by becoming rigid and fixed in daily routine and activity. The flexibility that is generally adaptive for families may be given up. If families get to this point, they usually are resistant to help from the outside, including advice from friends and relatives. They tend to become socially isolated. Families can stay locked in this pattern for a very long time. A crisis related to the chronic condition or even related to another family member may be the occasion for such a pattern to change (since crisis, by definition, disrupts the status quo) and could put the family in contact with professional or informal resources that could help them. This particular pattern of family response, which is based on clinicians' experiences working with families coping with disability, has been elaborated to illustrate one way in which a family's response patterns could be problematic for the person with the disability and for the family unit. However, there are many other ways by which families respond.

There is a growing body of research that emphasizes the many positive ways by which families adapt to disability. Several aspects of family functioning patterns have been associated with good adjustment in the person with the disability and in other family members. This approach emphasizes resilience, or the ability of families to discover resources and overcome challenges. Nine aspects of resilient family process have been described based on the findings from numerous studies of successful family coping with disabilities (Patterson 1991b).

Balancing the condition with other family needs. Because there is a tendency to let the disability dominate daily life, many families learn to meet the normative developmental needs of the person with the disability as well as their disability needs (Cappelli et al. 1989). They plan for and take time for other family needs as well as those associated with the chronic condition (Beavers et al. 1986; Spinetta et al. 1988). They also try to maintain their normal family routines and rituals as a way to preserve their identity and lifestyle (Newbrough, Simpkins, and Maurer 1985; Steinglass and Horan 1987).

Maintaining clear family boundaries. A boundary is that psychological line that sets a system, such

as a family, apart from its context. While families need to develop connections to the service delivery system to meet the needs of the person with a disability, they also need to maintain their own integrity and sense of control over their lives and not allow themselves to be overdirected by what professionals want them to do. In this way the family maintains its external boundary and improves the likelihood that the family will stay intact. Inside the family, it is usually best for family functioning when the parents work together to manage the family. This is called a generational boundary. When it is clear, children know that parents are in charge, and they function better (Beavers et al. 1986; Foster and Berger 1985). It reduces the likelihood of overinvolvement of one parent with the child, and it helps to maintain marital quality (Cappelli et al. 1989).

Developing communication competence. When disability is present, there are often more decisions to be made and more problems to be solved. Many families living with disability become more effective in learning to work through these issues (Newbrough, Simpkins, and Maurer 1985). Because there are so many intense feelings associated with living with disability, families do better over the long run when they are able to express feelings openly and respectfully, even when the feelings are negative and seem unjustified (Daniels et al. 1987; Kupst and Schulman 1988).

Attributing positive meanings to the situation. In addition to being able to talk openly, families who are able to think positively about their situation and develop positive attitudes manage better (Austin and McDermott 1988; Cowen et al. 1985; Krause and Seltzer 1993). Family members often acknowledge the positive contributions that the person with disability brings to family life (Behr and Murphy 1993) and how they have developed a new outlook on life that has more meaning (Frey, Greenberg, and Fewell 1989; Venters 1981).

Maintaining family flexibility. Flexibility is one of those family resources that benefits all families, particularly when chronic demands are present and when day-to-day life is not predictable. Being able to shift gears, change expectations, alter roles and rules, and try new things all contribute to better outcomes (Watson, Henggeler, and Whelan 1990).

Maintaining a commitment to the family unit. Of all the family resources studied, cohesion, or the bonds of unity and commitment linking family members, is probably the single most important protective factor that has consistently been reported in well-functioning families when a member has a chronic condition (Daniels et al. 1987; Kazak 1989;

Spinetta et al. 1988; Thompson et al. 1992; Varni and Setoguchi 1993). These families cooperate with and support each other in their efforts to manage the disability. One member does not have a disproportionate burden of caregiving. A sense of teamwork prevails. Good family relationships provide a buffer from the stress of caregiving (Evans, Bishop, and Ousley 1992).

Engaging in active coping efforts. Many different aspects of coping have been studied relating to families' responses to chronic conditions. Those families who actively seek information and services (Donovan 1988); who actively work to solve problems and express feelings (Timko, Stovel, and Moos 1992); and who balance their personal, family, and illness needs (Patterson et al. 1993) show better adaptation than do families who engage in passive resignation.

Maintaining social integration. The ability to maintain supportive relationships with people in the community is another important protective factor for the family (Frey, Greenberg, and Fewel 1989; Kazak 1989; Jessop, Riessman, and Stein 1988). It is also a resource that often is threatened by the presence of disability in the family. There may be less time for maintaining social connections, and in some cases, friends and relatives are not supportive in their responses and old networks are abandoned. Support from other families who have a member with a chronic condition has become a major resource to many families, as evidenced in the many parent-to-parent support programs (Santelli et al. 1993).

Developing relationships with professionals. In addition to informal support from friends and relatives, the quality of the relationships that families have with professionals who provide services to the member with a disability becomes another protective factor for them (Walker and Singer 1993). Family members, of course, are only half of these dyads and cannot solely determine the quality of the relationship. Taking time to share information, working together to make decisions about care, respecting differences, avoiding attempts to control the other, and sharing risks associated with outcomes are factors that contribute to satisfaction on both sides (Chesler and Barbarin 1987).

Programs and Interventions

The unit of care and support when a person has a disability should be the family or caregiving system, not just the individual (McDaniel, Hepworth, and Doherty 1992). As already noted, the family is both affected by the disability and is a major source of capa-

bilities for responding to it. Within the United States, there is a strong emphasis on family support initiatives as a way to improve the quality of life for people with disabilities (Dunst et al. 1993). Family support has been articulated in the philosophy of the Maternal and Child Health Bureau with regard to children with special health needs: Care should be family-centered, community-based, coordinated, comprehensive, and culturally competent (Hutchins and McPherson 1991).

Family support is also being implemented in early intervention programs for children with disabilities. Federal legislation has mandated states to develop systems of care that integrate health, education, and social services for these children and their families. One component of this legislation calls for an individual family service plan (McGonigel and Garland 1988). There is a meeting of family members and professionals serving the child to develop a comprehensive plan for meeting the needs of the child and the family. Families have a key role in identifying the needs and in identifying their strengths. The intent of the legislation is that parents should be included as an equal partner and full collaborator in deciding about and managing their child's care.

At the heart of the family support movement is the concept of family empowerment, which is defined as enabling an individual or family to increase their abilities to meet needs and goals and maintain their autonomy and integrity (Patterson and Geber 1991). Rather than the helper doing everything for the person being helped, thus maintaining dependency, a process is begun whereby the help-seeker discovers and builds on his or her own strengths, leading to a greater sense of mastery and control over his or her life.

Professionals who provide services to persons with disabilities and their families are being challenged to use this orientation when working with families. Training programs have curricula for developing these skills in new professionals. The emphasis is on the *process* of providing services and not just the *outcomes.* Empowerment involves believing in and building on the inherent strengths of families; respecting their values and beliefs; validating their perceptions and experiences as real; creating opportunities for family members to acquire knowledge and skills so they feel more competent; mobilizing the family to find and use sources of informal support in the community; and developing a service plan together and sharing responsibility for it (Dunst et al. 1993; Knoll 1992).

Coordination is another important way by which service delivery can be improved for persons with disabilities. Many persons need a multiplicity of services, and often they do not know what they are eligible for or where to find it. Case management or care coordination is needed to provide this information, to create linkages among these providers, and to assure that families are given complete and congruent information (Sloper and Turner 1992). In some instances, families are able to function as their own case managers, but this requires a high level of knowledge as well as skill in dealing with a bureaucratic system. Furthermore, it consumes a lot of time that many family members would prefer to devote to meeting other family needs. High-quality care coordination can reduce costs, relieve family stress, and improve the quality of life for persons with disabilities.

Another strategy to facilitate family coping and adaptation is linking persons with disabilities and their families together in support programs. There are many support groups for specific conditions (epilepsy, spina bifida, etc.) across the country that meet regularly to provide information and emotional support to those living with disability. In other instances, someone who has lived with the disability for a long time is paired with someone newly diagnosed (Santelli et al. 1993). These informal connections (in contrast to professional therapy services) are particularly effective because people feel they are not alone and are not abnormal in their struggles. There is the opportunity both to give and to receive support, which benefits both sides.

While family members are the primary source for providing care and assistance to a person with a disability, many families are unable to do this for an extended period of time without help from other community sources (Nosek 1993). Many persons with disability now use personal assistance services on a regular basis, which relieves the family of these tasks and allows them to interact with the person with a disability in more normative ways. In addition, personal assistants contribute to an adult's ability to make independent choices about where he or she will live. It makes it possible to transition from the family home and to live as an adult in the community.

Respite care is another community resource that can give families a break from caretaking and prevent total burnout and exhaustion (Folden and Coffman 1993). Respite care is usually provided on an as-needed basis, in contrast to personal assistants, who are usually available every day. When these kinds of resources are available to support families in their caregiving efforts, the families are better able to keep the persons with disability at home, and they do not have to turn to institutional placement.

Many different types of interventions have been developed by psychologists, social workers, and other mental health professionals for families who have members with disabilities (Singer and Powers 1993). These psychoeducational interventions are designed with a variety of goals in mind. They may be designed to support families in dealing with their emotional responses or to teach skills and strategies for managing difficult behavior. Programs may teach techniques for managing stress more effectively, or they may teach family members how to interact with professional providers of services. Some programs target one individual in the family, such as the primary caregiver; in other instances the whole family is the unit of intervention (Gonzalez, Steinglass, and Reiss 1989). Many families with members with disabilities are reluctant to use psychological resources because they cannot find time to go or they may interpret use as a judgment that they are not competent. Generally, persons from lower socioeconomic groups are more likely to view therapy as stigmatizing and so do not participate. Given the evidence that disability increases stress in families and increases the chance that someone will experience psychological or behavioral problems, programs and services to help families cope could prevent many of these secondary problems.

With increasing numbers of persons experiencing disability in the United States and with the reality that families are their primary source of care, it is important that public policies are designed so that families are given the support they need to fulfill this important role. Most families want to provide assistance to their members. However, community resources are also needed to augment their contributions. This kind of family-community collaboration will ultimately contribute to the best quality of life for persons with disabilities, members of their families, and the people in their communities.

(*See also:* Chronic Illness; Elders; Family Systems Theory; Health and the Family; Psychiatric Disorders; Stress)

BIBLIOGRAPHY

Austin, J., and McDermott, N. (1988). "Parental Attitude and Coping Behavior in Families of Children with Epilepsy." *Journal of Neuroscience Nursing* 20:174–179.

Beavers, J.; Hampson R.; Hulgus, Y.; and Beavers, W. (1986). "Coping in Families with a Retarded Child." *Family Process* 25:365–378.

Behr, S., and Murphy, D. (1993). "Research Progress and Promise: The Role Perceptions in Cognitive Adaptation to Disability." In *Cognitive Coping, Families, and Disability*, ed. A. Turnbull, J. Patterson, S. Behr, D. Murphy, J. Marquis, and M. Blue-Banning. Baltimore: Paul H. Brookes.

Biegel, D.; Sales, E.; and Schulz, R. (1991). *Family Caregiving in Chronic Illness.* Newbury Park, CA: Sage Publications.

Blackburn, J. (1988). "Chronic Health Problems of the Elderly." In *Chronic Illness and Disability,* ed. C. Chilman, E. Nunnally, and F. Cox. Newbury Park, CA: Sage Publications.

Boss, P. (1993). "The Reconstruction of Family Life with Alzheimer's Disease: Generating Theory to Lower Family Stress from Ambiguous Loss." In *Sourcebook of Family Theories and Methods: A Contextual Approach,* ed. P. Boss, W. Doherty, R. LaRossa, W. Schumm, and S. Steinmetz. New York: Plenum.

Breslau, N. (1993). "Psychiatric Sequelae of Brain Dysfunction in Children: The Role of Family Environment." In *How Do Families Cope with Chronic Illness?,* ed. R. Cole and D. Reiss. Hillsdale, NJ: Lawrence Erlbaum.

Brody, E. (1985). "Parent Care as a Normative Family Stress." *Gerontologist* 25:19–29.

Cadman, D.; Boyle, M.; Szatmari, P.; and Offord, D. (1987). "Chronic Illness, Disability, and Mental and Social Well-Being: Findings of the Ontario Child Health Study." *Pediatrics* 79:805–812.

Cappelli, M.; McGrath, P.; MacDonald, N.; Katsanis, J.; and Lascelles, M. (1989). "Parental Care and Overprotection of Children with Cystic Fibrosis." *British Journal of Medical Psychology* 62:281–289.

Chesler, M., and Barbarin, O. (1987). *Childhood Cancer and the Family: Meeting the Challenge of Stress and Support.* New York: Brunner/Mazel.

Chilman, C.; Nunnally, E.; and Cox, F., eds. (1988). *Chronic Illness and Disability.* Newbury Park, CA: Sage Publications.

Cole, R., and Reiss, D. (1993). *How Do Families Cope with Chronic Illness?* Hillsdale, NJ: Lawrence Erlbaum.

Coupey, S. M., and Cohen, M. I. (1984). "Special Considerations for the Health Care of Adolescents with Chronic Illnesses." *Pediatric Clinics of North America* 31:211–219.

Cowen, L.; Corey, M.; Keenan, N.; Simmons, R.; Arndt, E.; and Levison, H. (1985). "Family Adaptation and Psychosocial Adjustment to Cystic Fibrosis in the Preschool Child." *Social Science and Medicine* 20:553–560.

Daniels, D.; Moos, R.; Billings, A.; and Miller, J. (1987). "Psychosocial Risk and Resistance Factors Among Children with Chronic Illness, Healthy Siblings, and Healthy Controls." *Journal of Abnormal Child Psychology* 15:295–308.

Donovan, A. (1988). "Family Stress and Ways of Coping with Adolescents Who Have Handicaps: Maternal Perceptions." *American Journal of Mental Retardation* 92:502–509.

Dunst, C.; Trivette, C.; and Deal, A. (1988). *Enabling and Empowering Families: Principles and Guidelines for Practice.* Cambridge, MA: Brookline Books.

Dunst, C.; Trivette, C.; Starnes, A.; Hamby, D.; and Gordon, N. (1993). *Building and Evaluating Family Support Initiatives.* Baltimore: Paul H. Brookes.

Eisenberg, M. G.; Sutkin, L. C.; and Jansen, M. A., eds. (1984). *Chronic Illness and Disability Through the Lifespan: Effects on Self and Family.* New York: Springer-Verlag.

Evans, R.; Bishop, D.; and Ousley, R. (1992). "Providing Care to Persons with Physical Disability: Effect on Family Caregivers." *American Journal of Physical Medicine and Rehabilitation* 71:140–144.

Fitzsimmons, S. C. (1991). *Cystic Fibrosis Foundation Patient Registry Pulmonary Data 1990.* Bethesda, MD: Cystic Fibrosis Foundation.

Folden, S., and Coffman, S. (1993). "Respite Care for Families of Children with Disabilities." *Journal of Pediatric Health Care* 7:103–110.

Foster, M., and Berger, M. (1985). "Research with Families with Handicapped Children: A Multilevel Systemic Perspective." In *The Handbook of Family Psychology and Therapy,* Vol. II, ed. L. L'Abate. Homewood, IL: Dorsey Press.

Frey, K.; Greenberg, M.; and Fewel, R. (1989). "Stress and Coping Among Parents of Handicapped Children: A Multidimensional Approach." *American Journal of Mental Retardation* 94:240–249.

Gonzalez, S.; Steinglass, P.; and Reiss, D. (1989). "Putting the Illness in Its Place: Discussion Groups for Families with Chronic Medical Illnesses." *Family Process* 28:69–87.

Hirst, M. (1991). "Dissolution and Reconstitution of Families with a Disabled Young Person." *Developmental Medicine and Child Neurology* 33:1073–1079.

Holmes, D. M. (1986). "The Person and Diabetes in Psychosocial Context." *Diabetes Care* 9:194–206.

Holroyd, J., and Guthrie, D. (1986). "Family Stress with Chronic Childhood Illness: Cystic Fibrosis, Neuromuscular Disease, and Renal Disease." *Journal of Clinical Psychology* 42:552–561.

Hutchins, V., and McPherson, M. (1991). "National Agenda for Children with Special Health Needs." *American Psychologist* 46:141–143.

Ireys, H., and Burr, C. (1984). "Apart and A Part: Family Issues for Young Adults with Chronic Illness and Disability." In *Chronic Illness and Disability Through the Life Span: Effects on Self and Family,* ed. M. G. Eisenberg, L. C. Sutkin, and M. A. Jansen. New York: Springer-Verlag.

Jessop, D.; Riessman, C.; and Stein, R. (1988). "Chronic Childhood Illness and Maternal Mental Health." *Journal of Developmental and Behavioral Pediatrics* 9:147–156.

Kazak, A. (1989). "Family Functioning in Families with Older Institutionalized Retarded Offspring." *Journal of Autism and Developmental Disorders* 19:501–509.

Knoll, J. (1992). "Being a Family: The Experience of Raising a Child with a Disability or Chronic Illness." *Monographs of the American Association on Mental Retardation* 18:9–56.

Krause, M., and Seltzer, M. (1993). "Coping Strategies Among Older Mothers of Adults with Retardation: A Lifespan Developmental Perspective." In *Cognitive Coping, Families, and Disability,* ed. A. Turnbull, J. Patterson, S. Behr, D. Murphy, J. Marquis, and M. Blue-Banning. Baltimore: Paul H. Brookes.

Kupst, M., and Schulman, J. (1988). "Long-Term Coping with Pediatric Leukemia: A Six-Year Follow-Up Study." *Journal of Pediatric Psychology* 13:7–22.

LaPlante, M. P. (1988). *Data on Disability from the National Health Interview Survey, 1983–1985: An InfoUse Report*. Washington, DC: National Institute on Disability and Rehabilitation Research.

McDaniel, S.; Hepworth, J.; and Doherty, W. (1992). *Medical Family Therapy*. New York: Basic Books.

McGonigel, M., and Garland, C. (1988). "The Individualized Family Service Plan and the Early Intervention Team: Team and Family Issues and Recommended Practices." *Infants and Young Children* 1:10–21.

Murphy, M. A. (1982). "The Family with a Handicapped Child: A Review of the Literature." *Developmental and Behavioral Pediatrics* 3:73–82.

National Center for Health Statistics. (1989). "Current Estimates from the National Health Interview Survey, 1988." *Vital and Health Statistics*. Series 10, no. 166, PHS 89–1501. Washington, DC: U.S. Government Printing Office.

Newbrough, J.; Simpkins, C.; and Maurer, M. (1985). "A Family Development Approach to Studying Factors in the Management and Control of Childhood Diabetes." *Diabetes Care* 8:83–92.

Nosek, M. (1993). "Personal Assistance: Its Effect on the Long-Term Health of a Rehabilitation Hospital Population." *Archives of Physical Medicine and Rehabilitation* 74:127–132.

Patterson, J. (1988). "Chronic Illness in Children and the Impact on Families." In *Chronic Illness and Disability*, ed. C. Chilman, E. Nunnally, and F. Cox. Newbury Park, CA: Sage Publications.

Patterson, J. (1991a). "A Family Systems Perspective for Working with Youth with Disability." *Pediatrician* 18:129–141.

Patterson, J. (1991b). "Family Resilience to the Challenge of a Child's Disability." *Pediatric Annals* 20:491–496.

Patterson, J.; Budd, J.; Goetz, D.; and Warwick, W. (1993). "Family Correlates of a Ten-Year Pulmonary Health Trend in Cystic Fibrosis." *Pediatrics* 91:383–389.

Patterson, J., and Geber, G. (1991). "Preventing Mental Health Problems in Children with Chronic Illness or Disability." *Children's Health Care* 20:150–161.

Patterson, J., and Leonard, B. (1994). "Caregiving and Children." In *Family Caregiving Across the Lifespan*, ed. E. Kahana, D. Biegel, and M. Wykle. Newbury Park, CA: Sage Publications.

Patterson, J.; Leonard, B.; and Titus, J. (1992). "Home Care for Medically Fragile Children: Impact on Family Health and Well Being." *Developmental and Behavioral Pediatrics* 13:248–255.

Perrin, E., and Gerrity, P. S. (1984). "Development of Children with a Chronic Illness." *Pediatric Clinics of North America* 31:19–31.

Perrin, E.; Newacheck, P.; Pless, I.; Drotar, D.; Gortmaker, S.; Leventhal, J.; Perrin, J.; Stein, R.; Walker, D.; and Weitzman, M. (1993). "Issues Involved in the Definition and Classification of Chronic Health Conditions." *Pediatrics* 91:787–793.

Pope, A., and Tarlov, A., eds. (1991). *Disability in America: Toward a National Agenda for Prevention*. Washington, DC: National Academy Press.

Reiss, D.; Steinglass, P.; and Howe, G. (1993). "The Family's Reorganization Around Illness." In *How Do Families Cope with Chronic Illness?*, ed. R. Cole and D. Reiss. Hillsdale, NJ: Lawrence Erlbaum.

Rolland, J. (1994). *Families, Illness, and Disability: An Integrative Treatment Model*. New York: Basic Books.

Sabbeth, B., and Leventhal, J. (1984). "Marital Adjustment to Chronic Childhood Illness: A Critique of the Literature." *Pediatrics* 73:762–768.

Santelli, B.; Turnbull, A.; Lerner, E.; and Marquis, J. (1993). "Parent-to-Parent Programs." In *Families, Disability, and Empowerment*, ed. G. Singer and L. Powers. Baltimore: Paul H. Brookes.

Singer, G., and Powers, L., eds. (1993). *Families, Disability, and Empowerment*. Baltimore: Paul H. Brookes.

Singer, G.; Irvin, L.; Irvine, B.; Hawkins, N.; Hegreness, J.; and Jackson, R. (1993). "Helping Families Adapt Positively to Disability." In *Families, Disability, and Empowerment*, ed. G. Singer and L. Powers. Baltimore: Paul H. Brookes.

Singhi, P.; Goyal, L.; Pershad, D.; Singhi, S.; and Walia, B. (1990). "Psychosocial Problems in Families of Disabled Children." *British Journal of Medical Psychology* 63: 173–182.

Sloper, P., and Turner, S. (1992). "Service Needs of Families of Children with Severe Physical Disability." *Child: Care, Health, and Development* 18:259–282.

Spinetta, J.; Murphy, J.; Vik, P.; and Day, J. (1988). "Long-Term Adjustment in Families of Children with Cancer." *Journal of Psychosocial Oncology* 6:179–191.

Stein, R. E. K.; Bauman, L. J.; Westbrook, L. E.; Coupey, S. M.; and Ireys, H. T. (1993). "Framework for Identifying Children Who Have Chronic Conditions: The Case for a New Definition." *The Journal of Pediatrics* 122:342–347.

Steinglass, P., and Horan, M. (1987). "Families and Chronic Medical Illness." *Journal of Psychotherapy and the Family* 3:127–142.

Steinglass, P.; Temple, S.; Lisman, S.; and Reiss, D. (1982). "Coping with Spinal Cord Injury: The Family Perspective." *General Hospital Psychiatry* 4:259–264.

Stone, R., and Kemper, P. (1989). "Spouses and Children of Disabled Elders: How Large a Constituency for Long-Term Care Reform?" *Milbank Quarterly* 67:485–506.

Thompson, R.; Gustafson, K.; Hamlett, K.; and Spock, A. (1992). "Stress, Coping, and Family Functioning in the Psychological Adjustment of Mothers of Children and Adolescents with Cystic Fibrosis." *Journal of Pediatric Psychology* 17:573–585.

Turnbull, A.; Patterson, J.; Behr, S.; Murphy, D.; Marquis, J.; and Blue-Banning, M., eds. (1993). *Cognitive Coping, Families, and Disability*. Baltimore: Paul H. Brookes.

Turnbull, A. P., and Turnbull, H. R. (1986). *Families, Professionals, and Exceptionalities: A Special Partnership.* Columbus, OH: Charles E. Merrill.

Vance, J.; Fazan, L.; and Satterwhite, B. (1980). "Effects of Nephrotic Syndrome on the Family: A Controlled Study." *Pediatrics* 65:948–956.

Varni, J., and Setoguchi, Y. (1993). "Effects of Parental Adjustment on the Adaptation of Children with Congenital or Acquired Limb Deficiencies." *Developmental and Behavioral Pediatrics* 14:13–20.

Varni, J., and Wallender, J. (1988). "Pediatric Chronic Disabilities: Hemophilia and Spina Bifida as Examples." In *Handbook of Pediatric Psychology*, ed. D. Routh. New York: Guilford.

Venters, M. (1981). "Familial Coping with Chronic and Severe Childhood Illness: The Case of Cystic Fibrosis." *Social Science and Medicine* 15A:948–956.

Walker, B., and Singer, G. (1993). "Improving Collaborative Communication Between Professionals and Parents." In *Families, Disability, and Empowerment*, ed. G. Singer and L. Powers. Baltimore: Paul H. Brookes.

Watson, S.; Henggeler, S.; and Whelan, J. (1990). "Family Functioning and the Social Adaptation of Hearing-Impaired Youths." *Journal of Abnormal Child Psychology* 18:143–163.

JOÄN M. PATTERSON

DISCIPLINE

Parental discipline of children has long been a controversial topic. In the leading parenting book of the 1930s, *Psychological Care of Infant and Child* (1928), John B. Watson argued that mothers should avoid being nurturant with their children. However, nurturance made a comeback with Benjamin Spock's *Pocket Book of Baby and Child Care* (1946).

Parental education materials of the 1990s also differ from each other and from earlier perspectives, sometimes dramatically. Since there is little hard evidence supporting any of the popular parenting programs, this summary of parental discipline is based primarily on evidence from social scientific research.

There are two major groups of social scientists that have studied parental discipline. The first, cognitive developmental psychologists, have studied typical families and the kinds of parental discipline associated with appropriate or inappropriate child behavior. The second, behavioral parent trainers, have developed the most effective treatment for overly aggressive preadolescents (McMahon and Wells 1989). In so doing, they have tried to discover the best ways for parents to help children improve their conduct.

Cognitive developmentalists have drawn on theories about how children form opinions and how parents can influence their children to adopt moral behavior. This process is called moral internalization, the process of making a set of moral values one's own. Parent trainers, on the other hand, have drawn on modern behavioral theories that address how best to change children's behavior.

Goals of Discipline

Cognitive developmentalists focus on internalization, moral behavior, and the development of autonomy as important socialization goals. Autonomy refers to children's growing sense of themselves as capable, independent persons. Consequently, developmentalists are concerned about the possible negative effects of oversocialization when children become too compliant with parental requests.

Parent trainers, in contrast, have focused on problems associated with noncompliance. Their goals for unruly children have been to increase compliance with parental requests while decreasing the rate of problem behaviors, such as antisocial aggression.

Discipline by parents should reduce or prevent serious misbehaviors and still allow children to exercise their skills of independent acting and decision making as they grow toward becoming independent adults. A suitable balance in discipline should allow for appropriate disagreements with adults and fair and reasonable negotiations of differences of opinion.

The objectives of discipline should also take into consideration the importance of fostering a positive parent–child relationship. Therefore, discipline methods need to be evaluated not only in terms of their ability to achieve an appropriate balance between compliance and autonomy, but also in terms of their effect on the closeness of the existing parent–child relationship.

Parental Foundations for Discipline

Several characteristics of the parent–child relationship have been shown to increase both the appropriateness of a child's behavior and the effectiveness of discipline responses to misbehavior.

The most important foundation for effective discipline is parental nurturance. Discipline responses have been shown by some researchers to be more effective to the extent that a parent is loving toward the child in nondiscipline situations (Sears, Maccoby, and Levin 1957). Other researchers have suggested that parental nurturance by itself has a major influence on moral development (Rollins and Thomas 1979; Shaffer and Brody 1981). Specific aspects of parental nurturance that improve child behavior directly or indirectly have been identified.

Sensitivity to an infant's cues and timely, appropriate responsiveness are important for developing a secure attachment to the parents by twelve months of age. Because the parents are able to act as a secure base from which the toddlers can begin to explore the world around them, this secure attachment aids in the development of new skills and appropriate independence while maintaining a close parent–child relationship. A secure attachment at twelve months has also been shown to predict problem-solving ability, social competence with peers, resilience, independence, compliance, and cooperation with adults in later childhood (Erickson, Sroufe, and Egeland 1985), along with greater mother–toddler harmony in handling conflict (Bates, Maslin, and Frankel 1985).

During the preschool years, parents spending more time in play and conversation with their children is associated with better behavior (Gardner 1989). The Good Behavior Game has been demonstrated to improve child behavior by training parents to respond positively to their children's behavior rather than trying to direct it (Parpal and Maccoby 1985). Parents designate twenty minutes each day for special child-directed play, responding to what the child is doing by describing his actions (sometimes like a sportscaster) and praising specific behaviors (Barkley 1987). Directing the child's behavior during this twenty-minute period is prohibited.

Another prerequisite for effective parental discipline is the development of self-regulation in the child. Claire Kopp (1982) has identified three stages in the development of self-regulation. The first stage, control, typically occurs from about twelve to twenty months of age. During this time, toddlers begin to comply with commands and modify their behavior accordingly. These modifications usually depend on adult influence, such as concrete reminders, because toddlers have a limited capacity to remember past events and abstract rules for conduct.

Self-control, Kopp's second stage, normally begins at about twenty-four months of age and includes new capabilities for delaying an action when requested and behaving according to clear expectations when not directly supervised. These new capabilities are linked to newly emerging mental abilities, best illustrated by language development, that allow for mental representation of objects. During this phase, however, children still have only a limited ability to delay prohibited behavior and modify their actions to meet the expectations of new situations. They have limited ability to predict the consequences of an action, monitor their own behavior, and modify their ongoing behavior. Conduct rules are easily overridden by attractive objects, such as a ball rolling into the street.

Kopp's final stage, self-regulation, begins at about thirty-six months of age. Self-regulation involves an increased ability to apply moral rules for behavior in a wide variety of situations, monitor one's own behavior, and modify behavior according to expectations. Although little is known about the gradual shift from self-control to self-regulation, parental discipline probably plays a role in the transition.

Proactive Discipline

Following the old adage that "an ounce of prevention is worth a pound of cure," proactive discipline consists of parental strategies to promote appropriate behavior and prevent inappropriate behavior in their children.

George Holden (1983, 1985) studied mothers who were shopping with their preschool-age children. Proactive strategies that mothers reported included shopping when the store was not so busy and the child was not hungry or tired; giving the child instructions ahead of time; providing the child with a toy or a piece of fruit; placing the child in the seat of the shopping cart; having the child hold the shopping list or look for a particular item; diverting attention away from tempting items; bypassing troublesome aisles; staying in the center of the aisle; and initiating conversation with the child. Holden studied two of the most common strategies in depth: initiating conversation and providing fruit or a toy. Both strategies were found to reduce children's misbehaviors in the supermarket.

Adult monitoring of children's activities is another important preventive measure. Such supervision tends to prevent delinquency and drug abuse while enhancing popularity and scholastic achievement (Chamberlain and Patterson 1994; Rubin and Mills 1992; Rutter and Giller 1984). Monitoring takes different forms depending on the child's age. During the preteen years, the important dimensions of monitoring seem to include parental involvement and responsiveness. Later, knowing an adolescent's whereabouts and activities becomes a more important aspect of monitoring, reflecting an appropriate balance between parental influence and that teenager's growing independence.

Proactive discipline also involves teaching positive skills and abilities, not merely preventing inappropriate behavior. A major study by Diana Baumrind (1973) compared authoritative, authoritarian, and permissive parents. The children of authoritative parents tended to outperform children of the other parents in terms of self-control, self-reliance, explorativeness, and contentment. The authoritative parents combined nurturance and firm control with a more active teaching role than did the parents with the other parenting styles. They encouraged their children to develop new skills and to use age-appropriate levels of independence.

In 1934, Lev Vygotsky used the label "zone of proximal development" to identify a child's area of readiness to learn new abilities (Rieber and Carton 1987). He noted that new abilities are not learned as one complete package, but bit by bit. Parents can facilitate children's learning by first demonstrating a new skill, asking leading questions, introducing the first parts of the new skill, and then gradually giving the children growing independence in performing the new skill by themselves. What children are able to do with help at first, they will later become able to do by themselves.

"Catching them being good" is another important aspect of proactive discipline. The parents of well-behaved children tend to praise appropriate behavior much more than do the parents of problem children (Bates, Maslin, and Frankel 1985; Forehand and McMahon 1981; Grusec and Goodnow 1994).

Parents can also prevent behavior problems by using appropriate commands and requests. For young children, it is especially important to get their attention first; use clear, simple commands; and then wait several seconds for them to respond (Forehand and McMahon 1981; Roberts et al. 1978).

Discipline Responses

It would be wonderful if the quality of the parent–child relationship and proactive discipline could be so effective that parents never had to deal with misbehavior. Even among the highly educated, this happy result occurs in only about 6 percent of families by the time the child is four years of age (Baumrind 1971). Opinions differ about how the other 94 percent should respond to misbehavior. Cognitive developmentalists recommend maximal use of reasoning and minimal use of negative consequences. In contrast, behavioral parent trainers recommend the systematic use of time-out in response to selected misbehaviors.

The major support for the cognitive developmental viewpoint comes from studies showing that parents of well-behaved children tend to rely mostly on reasoning, whereas parents of poorly behaved children tend to rely much more on punishment of various kinds, especially physical punishment (Grusec and Goodnow 1994).

Attribution theory provides an explanation of why less severe discipline responses are related to better moral development. If children stop their misbehavior because of obvious parental influence, then they are likely to account for their own appropriate behavior in terms of parental intervention. In contrast, if appropriate behavior occurs without obvious parental influence, then children are more likely to account for their own behavior with self-originating reasons, such as "I want to behave appropriately." To the extent that children see themselves behaving appropriately for their own reasons, they are more likely to do so when their parents are not around. According to this perspective, the least obvious parental pressure will lead to the greatest internalization of appropriate moral standards (Lepper 1983).

Martin Hoffman (1977, 1994) has recommended that parental reasoning should emphasize how other people are hurt by inappropriate behavior, thereby increasing the child's empathy for others. At least two studies have found that other-oriented reasons are more effective in promoting moral internalization (Eisenberg-Berg and Neal 1979; Kuczynski 1982). Reasoning should also clarify why the behavior is suitable (or not) to help the child apply the lesson appropriately in other situations. Reasoning may also modify the child's emotional reaction to a discipline response from anger and bitterness toward empathy and better understanding.

Cognitive developmentalists have not sufficiently explained how parents can socialize their child so that less severe discipline responses, such as reasoning, will be effective in obtaining the desired compliance. The lack of a firm explanation leads to the implication that parents should use as much reasoning as possible as early as possible in the child's development. However, parents who use reasoning without negative consequences with a child of two or three years of age tend to see an increase in the child's oppositional behavior over the next year or two (Sather 1992). Frequent reasoning without clear negative consequences for misbehavior can develop into a pattern where negative parental comments are overused, a common pattern in families with aggressive children (Patterson 1982). Reasoning can be an effective discipline response with a child as young as two and a half years of age, but it must be used with sufficient firmness to get the attention of the child (Larzelere and Merenda 1993). Reasoning with toddlers is most effective as a discipline response if it is backed up with negative consequences when necessary (Larzelere and Schneider 1991; Sather 1992).

Whereas cognitive developmentalists have emphasized reasoning as a disciplinary tool, behavioral parent trainers have emphasized effective negative consequences for misbehavior. The best-documented parent-training programs teach parents to use a carefully prescribed time-out procedure as a negative consequence for important misbehaviors (Barkley 1987; Christopherson 1988; Forehand and McMahon 1981). Gerald Patterson (1982), for example, says that the most important component of treatment for antisocial children is to teach their parents how to use negative consequences more effectively. Typical guidelines for time-out include (1) start with only a few types of misbehavior; (2) make sure children understand what is expected of them; (3) use one, and only one, warning; (4) take the child immediately to the time-out location, such as a chair in a room near the parent's whereabouts; (5) set a timer for a maximum of five minutes for the time-out period; (6) require the child to be quiet and still for a small period of time (e.g., fifteen seconds) before ending the time-out; and (7) require the child to follow the original instruction upon completion of the time-out.

Children sometimes refuse to follow the time-out procedure when it is first used. Practicing the entire procedure before beginning to use it often helps. Some children also need a back-up to time-out at first. The most effective forms of backup have been either two slaps with an open hand to the buttocks (for children from two to six years of age) or putting the child in a room with the door held shut for one minute (Roberts and Powers 1990). Withdrawing privileges or adding chores are more suitable backup strategies for older children (Forgatch and Patterson 1989; Patterson and Forgatch 1987). If a child does not begin complying with the time-out procedure after four to six successive backup repetitions, then the parents may want to seek help from a mental health professional experienced in behavioral parent training.

Although few attempts have been made to combine the best of both the cognitive developmental and parent-training perspectives, the following is one attempt to do so. A parent's first goal should be to establish reasoning as an effective discipline response by the time the child is seven years old. By that age, children begin making attributions similar to adults, an ability relevant to children's internalization of parental values and moral standards. Negative consequences should be used primarily to enforce verbal corrections and rationales as effective discipline responses, beginning at least by two and a half years of age.

One possible sequence of discipline responses to a preschooler's misbehavior might consist of issuing a verbal directive, getting the child's attention; presenting an age-appropriate rationale; warning about time-out; using time-out; warning about the backup for time-out; and then using the backup. For targeted or serious misbehaviors, the sequence would be followed until appropriate compliance occurred. Research has shown that the later steps in this sequence improve the effectiveness of the earlier steps by themselves in later discipline encounters (Roberts and Powers 1990; Sather 1992).

There are several considerations relevant to the effectiveness of this sequence of discipline responses. First, the sequence needs to be used flexibly, adapting it to the situation and the child. Second, parents should avoid overusing negative consequences because they become less effective the more frequently they are used. Parents who reserve negative consequences for more important misbehaviors tend to get better results than those who use them for minor misbehaviors as well. Third, children need to be allowed to negotiate what they do in an appropriate way whenever possible. The best place to allow negotiation in the discipline sequence would be prior to the first warning. For example, a child might be allowed to ask politely whether it is acceptable to take five minutes to complete a play activity before coming to eat dinner. Fourth, parents need to be sober (i.e., not drunk or stoned) and in control of their emotions. Explosive, irritable discipline responses are consistently associated with negative child characteristics (Chamberlain and Patterson 1994). Finally, if spanking is used (e.g., as a backup for time-out), it should never be hard enough to leave marks.

Conclusion

Parental discipline is a complex responsibility. Parents need to develop an appropriate foundation for discipline, use good strategies for proactive discipline, and provide effective but nonabusive discipline responses. Use of the conclusions reached in this summary, based on findings from two major psychological perspectives on parental discipline, should be limited to the conditions carefully prescribed herein. It would be totally inappropriate to use this summary as general evidence for punitive parenting or physical punishment outside these conditions.

(*See also:* ATTACHMENT; ATTRIBUTION IN RELATIONSHIPS; CHILD ABUSE AND NEGLECT: SOCIOLOGICAL ASPECTS; CHILD CARE; PARENT EDUCATION; PERSONALITY DEVELOPMENT)

BIBLIOGRAPHY

Barkley, R. A. (1987). *Defiant Children: A Clinician's Manual for Parent Training.* New York: Guilford.

Bates, J. E.; Maslin, C. A.; and Frankel, K. A. (1985). "Attachment Security, Mother–Child Interaction, and Temperament as Predictors of Behavior-Problem Ratings at Age Three Years." In *Monographs of the Society for Research in Child Development: Growing Points of Attachment Theory and Research,* ed. I. Bretherton and E. Waters, 50(1-2, Serial no. 209):167–193. Chicago: University of Chicago Press.

Baumrind, D. (1971). "Harmonious Parents and Their Preschool Children." *Developmental Psychology* 4:99–102.

Baumrind, D. (1973). "The Development of Instrumental Competence Through Socialization." In *Minnesota Symposia on Child Psychology,* ed. A. D. Pick, 7:3–46. Minneapolis: University of Minnesota Press.

Chamberlain, P., and Patterson, G. R. (1994). "Discipline and Child Compliance." In *The Handbook of Parenting,* Vol. 4, ed. M. Bornstein. Hillsdale, NJ: Lawrence Erlbaum.

Christopherson, E. R. (1988). *Little People: Guidelines for Commonsense Child Rearing,* 3rd edition. Kansas City, MO: Westport.

Eisenberg-Berg, N., and Neal, C. (1979). "Children's Moral Reasoning About Their Own Spontaneous Prosocial Behavior." *Developmental Psychology* 15:228–229.

Erickson, M. F.; Sroufe, L. A.; and Egeland, B. (1985). "The Relationship Between Quality of Attachment and Behavior Problems in Preschool in a High-Risk Sample." In *Monographs of the Society for Research in Child Development: Growing Points of Attachment Theory and Research,* ed. I. Bretherton and E. Waters, 50(1-2, Serial no. 209):147–166. Chicago: University of Chicago Press.

Forehand, R. L., and McMahon, R. J. (1981). *Helping the Non-Compliant Child: A Clinician's Guide to Parent Training.* New York: Guilford.

Forgatch, M. S., and Patterson, G. R. (1989). *Parents and Adolescents Living Together: Family Problem Solving.* Eugene, OR: Castalia.

Gardner, F. E. M. (1989). "Inconsistent Parenting: Is There Evidence for a Link with Children's Conduct Problems." *Journal of Abnormal Child Psychology* 17:223–233.

Grusec, J. E., and Goodnow, J. J. (1994). "Impact of Parental Discipline Methods on the Child's Internalization of Values: A Reconceptualization of Current Points of View." *Developmental Psychology* 30:4–19.

Hoffman, M. L. (1977). "Personality and Social Development." *Annual Review of Psychology* 28:295–321.

Hoffman, M. L. (1994). "Discipline and Internalization." *Developmental Psychology* 30:2–28.

Holden, G. W. (1983). "Avoiding Conflict: Mothers as Tacticians in the Supermarket." *Child Development* 54:233–244.

Holden, G. W. (1985). "How Parents Create a Social Environment via Proactive Behavior." In *Children Within Environments: Toward a Psychology of Accident Prevention,* ed. T. Garling and J. Valsinger. New York: Plenum.

Kopp, C. B. (1982). "Antecedents of Self-Regulation: A Developmental Perspective." *Developmental Psychology* 20:1061–1073.

Kuczynski, L. (1982). "Intensity and Orientation of Reasoning: Motivational Determinants of Children's Compliance to Verbal Rationales." *Journal of Experimental Child Psychology* 34:357–370.

Larzelere, R. E., and Merenda, J. (1993). "A Test of Hoffman's Socialization Theory Using Toddlers." Paper presented at the annual meeting of the American Psychological Association, Toronto.

Larzelere, R. E., and Schneider, W. N. (1991). "Does Parental Punishment Reduce Misbehavior in Toddlers? Testing Predictions from Behavioral vs. Survey Research." Paper presented at the annual meeting of the American Psychological Association, San Francisco.

Lepper, M. R. (1983). "Social Control Processes and the Internalization of Social Values: An Attributional Perspective." In *Social Cognition and Social Development: A Sociocultural Perspective,* ed. E. T. Higgins, D. N. Ruble, and W. W. Hartup. Cambridge: Cambridge University Press.

McMahon, R. J., and Wells, K. C. (1989). "Conduct Disorders." In *Treatment of Childhood Disorders,* ed. E. J. Mash and R. A. Barkley. New York: Guilford.

Parpal, M., and Maccoby, E. (1985). "Maternal Responsiveness and Subsequent Child Compliance." *Child Development* 56:1326–1344.

Patterson, G. R. (1982). *Coercive Family Process.* Eugene, OR: Castalia.

Patterson, G. R., and Forgatch, M. S. (1987). *Parents and Adolescents Living Together: The Basics.* Eugene, OR: Castalia.

Rieber, R. W., and Carton, A. S., eds. (1987). *The Collected Works of L. S. Vygotsky: Problems of General Psychology.* New York: Plenum.

Roberts, M. W., and Powers, S. W. (1990). "Adjusting Chair Timeout Enforcement Procedures for Oppositional Children." *Behavior Therapy* 21:257–271.

Roberts, M. W.; McMahon, R. J.; Forehand, R.; and Humphreys, L. (1978). "The Effect of Parental Instruction-Giving on Child Compliance." *Behavior Therapy* 9:793–798.

Rollins, B. C., and Thomas, D. L. (1979). "Parental Support, Power, and Control Techniques in the Socialization of Children." In *Contemporary Theories About the Family,* Vol. 1, ed. W. R. Burr, R. Hill, F. I. Nye, and I. L. Reiss. New York: Free Press.

Rubin, K. H., and Mills, R. S. L. (1992). "Parents' Thoughts About Children's Socially Adaptive and Maladaptive Behaviors: Stability, Chance, and Individual Differences." In *Parental Belief Systems: The Psychological Consequences for Children,* 2nd edition, ed. I. E. Sigel, A. V. McGillicuddy-Delisi, and J. J. Goodnow. Hillsdale, NJ: Lawrence Erlbaum.

Rutter, M., and Giller, H. (1984). *Juvenile Delinquency: Trends and Perspectives.* New York: Guilford.

Sather, P. R. (1992). "Negative and Positive Side Effects of Alternative Parental Discipline Responses to Toddler Misbehavior." Ph.D. diss. Biola University, La Mirada, CA.

Sears, R. R.; Maccoby, E. E.; and Levin, H. (1957). *Patterns of Child Rearing.* New York: Harper & Row.

Shaffer, D. R., and Brody, G. H. (1981). "Parental and Peer Influences on Moral Development." In *Parent–Child Interaction: Theory, Research, and Prospects*, ed. R. W. Henderson. New York: Academic Press.

Spock, B. (1946). *The Pocket Book of Baby and Child Care.* New York: Pocket Books.

Watson, J. B. (1928). *Psychological Care of Infant and Child.* New York: W. W. Norton.

ROBERT E. LARZELERE

DISORDERS *See* CODEPENDENCY; EATING DISORDERS; PSYCHIATRIC DISORDERS; SEXUAL PROBLEMS

DIVISION OF LABOR

Families provide love and support to adults and children, but homes are also workplaces, and households are important parts of the larger economy. Even when families do not directly produce or sell goods and services, they keep the economy running by supporting and maintaining adult workers, buying and consuming products, and reproducing the work force by having babies and socializing children. These domestic activities require labor. The total amount of time and effort put into feeding, clothing, and caring for family members rivals that spent in all other forms of work.

Every home is a combination of hotel, restaurant, laundry, and often child-care and entertainment center. The mundane work that goes into these activities is usually invisible to the people who benefit from it, especially children and husbands, who are the equivalent of nonpaying customers. Cleaning and cooking definitely require work, but even fun activities like parties or holiday gatherings require planning, preparation, service, cleanup, and other behind-the-scenes work. Most of this family labor is performed by women, even though men do the same things outside the home for pay as chefs, waiters, or janitors.

Although people tend to think of domestic activities as "naturally" being women's work, there is enormous variation in who does what both inside and outside the home. Every society has restrictions on what kinds of work men and women do, but there is no global content to these roles, and studies show that divisions of labor are influenced by specific environmental and social conditions. Activities often associated with women, such as nurturance, domestic chores, and child care, are sometimes performed by men, and activities often associated with men, such as warfare, hunting, and politics, are sometimes performed by women (Coltrane 1992). Thus, although gender is often used to divide labor, there is no universal set of tasks that can be defined as "women's work" or "men's work."

Historical Trends

During the late 1800s, a belief in separate spheres for men and women gained popularity in the United States. Before the nineteenth century, men, women, and children tended to work side by side in family-based agricultural production, often doing different chores, but cooperating in the mutual enterprise of running a farm or family business. After the rise of industrialization, most men entered the paid labor force and worked away from home. A romantic ideal of separate spheres emerged to justify the economic arrangement of women staying home while men left home to earn wages. Women came to be seen as pure, innocent, and loving, traits that made them ideally suited to the "private" sphere of home and family. The "cult of true womanhood" that became popular at this time elevated mothering to a revered status and treated homemaking as a full-time profession. Men who were previously expected to be intimately involved in raising children and running the home were now considered temperamentally unsuited for such duties and were expected to find their true calling in the impersonal "public" sphere of work (Degler 1980; Welter 1966). This simplified account of the historical emergence of separate spheres ignores the partial and uneven pace of industrialization, the continual employment of working-class and minority women, and the many families that deviated from the ideal, but it underscores the importance of cultural myths in creating a rigid division of family labor (Bose 1987).

Household work has changed. Before the twentieth century, running the typical American household was more physically demanding; most houses lacked running water, electricity, central heating, and flush toilets. Without water heaters, gas stoves, washing machines, and other modern conveniences, people had to do everything by hand, and tasks like carrying water, tending fires, and preparing food were arduous and time-consuming. In the nineteenth century, most middle- and upper-class households in the United States also included servants, so live-in maids, cooks, and housekeepers did much of this work. In the twentieth century, indoor plumbing and electricity became widely available and the invention and distribution of labor-saving appliances changed the nature of housework. By mid-century, the suburbs had multiplied, home ownership had become the norm, and the number of household servants had dropped dramatically.

In spite of the introduction of modern conveniences, the total amount of time that American women spent on housework was about the same in 1960 as it was in 1920 (Cowan 1983). This is because standards of comfort rose for most families. When laundry was done by hand, people changed clothes infrequently, unless they had servants to do the washing. With the advent of the washing machine, the average housewife began to wash clothes more often, and people began to change clothes more frequently. Similarly, standards for personal hygiene, diet, and house cleanliness increased as conveniences such as hot running water, refrigerators, and vacuum cleaners became available. Although women's total housework time changed little, there were shifts in the types of tasks performed, with food preparation and meal cleanup consuming somewhat less time and shopping, direct child care, and household management taking up more.

Contemporary Divisions of Household Labor

Before the 1970s, most family researchers accepted the separate spheres ideal and assumed that wives would do the housework and child care and that husbands would limit their family contributions to being a "good provider." As more women entered the paid labor force, and as women's issues gained prominence, studies of household labor became more common. Sociologists, psychologists, economists, and anthropologists began asking who was more likely to perform various tasks, who performed them last week, or how many hours each family member spent doing particular chores. Depending on the method and sample used, researchers arrived at different estimates of the absolute and relative amounts of time men and women spent on various tasks. There are problems interpreting results from these studies because of sampling limitations, because the same questions were not asked for everyone, and because

people's answers tend to reflect what they think they should be doing as much as what they are actually doing. Nevertheless, these studies provide a rough estimate of who does what in American families.

The few household labor studies that included men before the 1970s found that wives did virtually all of the repetitive inside chores associated with cooking and cleaning, whereas husbands spent most of their household work time doing repairs, paying bills, or performing outside chores like mowing the lawn or taking out the trash. If American men contributed to other forms of routine housework, it was usually in the area of meal preparation, where husbands averaged just over one hour each week, compared to an average of more than eight hours per week for wives (Robinson 1988). Even when cooking, however, husbands tended to limit their contributions to gender-stereotyped tasks like barbecuing on the weekend, rather than contributing substantially to the preparation of daily meals. In the mid-1960s, husbands contributed less than a tenth of the time spent in cleaning up after meals or washing dishes in the average household and only about a twentieth of the time spent doing housecleaning. Married men were extremely unlikely to do laundry or iron clothes, averaging about five hours per *year* in the 1960s, compared to more than five hours per *week* for married women. Overall, husbands contributed only about two hours per week to the combined tasks of cooking, meal cleanup, housecleaning, and laundry, compared to an average of almost twenty-five hours per week for their wives (Robinson 1988).

Studies conducted in the United States during the 1970s and early 1980s showed that wives continued to perform more than two-thirds of the total household labor, even though by then about half of married women were in the paid labor force. Household work continued to be divided according to gender, with women performing 80 percent to 90 percent of the repetitive indoor housework tasks. Most men persisted in focusing their efforts on outside chores or playing with children. According to national surveys, husbands increased their hourly contributions to the inside domestic chores of cooking, cleaning, and laundry only slightly, but because employed women were performing fewer domestic chores, men's proportionate contributions to household tasks rose (Berk 1985; Pleck 1983; Robinson 1988; Thompson and Walker 1989).

Researchers investigating divisions of family labor also discovered that psychological distress was greatest among wives with husbands who did little to assist with household chores (Ross, Mirowsky, and

Huber 1983). This was primarily the result of the amount and type of labor for which wives and mothers were responsible. Not only did women spend many more hours on household labor than men, but they tended to do the least pleasant tasks, such as cleaning bathrooms, and most of their tasks were relentless, obligatory, and performed in isolation. The lonely and never-ending aspects of women's housework contributed to the increased risk of depression observed for American housewives from the 1950s through the 1970s. Men's household chores, in contrast, have tended to be infrequent or optional, and when they do inside chores, they often get help or concentrate their efforts on relatively fun activities like playing with the children or cooking (Berk 1985; Collins and Coltrane 1991; Robinson 1988; Thompson and Walker 1989).

Because responsibility for child care is difficult to measure with simple surveys, household labor studies have tended to reduce parenting to the number of hours spent directly feeding, bathing, dressing, instructing, or putting children to bed. Studies have consistently found that mothers spend more time than fathers in these activities, although men did increase their time with children slightly during the 1970s, especially in conventional gender-type activities like physical play (Parke and Tinsley 1984). However, effective parenting also includes meeting emotional needs, providing encouragement, anticipating problems, facilitating social and intellectual learning, and enforcing discipline. Few time-use studies are sensitive enough to explore these sorts of issues, but most in-depth family studies show that mothers are primarily responsible for these activities as well. Even if couples share housework before they have children, they often shift to a more conventional gender-based allocation of chores when they become parents (Cowan and Cowan 1992).

Getting married and having children have, therefore, been events that increased women's domestic labor, whereas men's domestic labor has remained more stable. Still, most women consider their divisions of household labor to be fair. According to survey research conducted in the 1970s and 1980s, the majority of wives had low expectations for help with housework. Although many women expressed a desire for husbands to spend more time parenting, it was framed in terms of benefiting the children rather than substituting for their own time. Women rarely seek help with behind-the-scenes attentive and coordinative family work, such as overseeing child care, managing emotions and tension, sustaining conversations, or maintaining contact with kin. Wives and mothers derive considerable satisfaction and self-worth from caring for loved ones and enjoy autonomy in these activities. Women feel less entitled to domestic services than do most men and view husband's help as a gift that requires appreciation. Women who try to share domestic tasks often find that it threatens the harmony of the family relationship they work so hard to foster (Hochschild 1989; Thompson and Walker 1989).

Researchers studying families in the late 1980s reported some modest changes in the division of household labor. Men's average hourly contributions to inside housework had almost doubled since the 1970s, whereas women's contributions had decreased by about a third. In the earlier period, men in dual-earner households were doing only about 10 percent of the inside chores, but by the late 1980s, they were averaging 20 percent to 25 percent. Husbands with employed wives now do more housework than husbands with nonemployed wives, but even single-earner families show an increase in the husband's percent of housework. Although most husbands still do far less than their wives, the trend is toward more sharing of more tasks, and a few studies find that the total hours spent on paid and unpaid labor (not including child care) is now about equal between husbands and wives (Ferree 1991).

The household tasks that husbands are doing more of include child care, shopping, and meal preparation. Studies of dual-earner couples using representative samples show men contributing 25 percent to 40 percent of the time devoted to these activities, averaging almost 33 percent. Meal cleanup and housecleaning continue to lag behind, with men contributing 15 percent to 30 percent, averaging about 25 percent. Finally, men doing laundry is still relatively rare, but husbands in dual-earner families now contribute 10 percent to 25 percent of the hours spent in clothes care, compared to the 2 percent to 5 percent they contributed in the 1960s (Ferree 1991; Gershuny and Robinson 1988; Shelton 1992).

Although men are putting in more hours on housework tasks, responsibility for noticing when tasks should be performed or setting standards of their performance is still most often assumed by wives. In the majority of families, husbands notice less about what needs to be done, wait to be asked to do various chores, and require explicit directions if they are to complete the tasks successfully. In line with this division of responsibility for management of household affairs, most couples continue to characterize husbands' contributions to housework or child care as "helping" their wives (Berk 1985; Coltrane 1989;

Thompson and Walker 1989). Because men benefit from women's domestic services, they can be expected to resist more equal divisions of labor.

Child care is the area marked by the most apparent change in the past decade, and it may presage more sharing of housework in the future. Studies show that men are contributing close to a third of the child-care hours in dual-earner couples (Goldscheider and Waite 1991; Pleck 1987). Women still put in more hours supervising children and typically act as overseers when others watch them, but parents are increasingly likely to work different shifts and to alternate child care between them. One in four preschool children of employed mothers were cared for by their fathers in 1991, up more than 25 percent from the 1977–1987 period (O'Connell 1993). These figures demonstrate that women are still responsible for most family work but there has been a slow shift toward more sharing of both child care and housework.

Children and other family members also perform household labor, though their contributions have varied as much as those of women and men. Children participate in household labor for several reasons. In some households, their domestic contributions are sorely needed; they are required to participate for practical and financial reasons. In other households, children are expected to assume responsibility for household chores as part of their training and socialization or because it expresses a commitment to the family. For children, as for adults, household tasks are divided by gender, with girls putting in more hours and performing more of the cooking and cleaning. Children's housework is typically conceived of as helping the mother, and young people's contributions tend to substitute for the father's (Goodnow 1988).

Theoretical Explanations

Various theories have been advanced to explain why women perform most household labor and to predict the conditions under which divisions of household labor might change. The theories can be grouped into four general categories according to the primary causal processes thought to govern the allocation of domestic labor: nature, culture, economy and practicality, and gender inequality.

Nature. Biological and religious arguments suggest that women, as a whole, are physically or spiritually predisposed to take care of children and husbands; housework is assumed to follow naturally from the nurturance of family members. Similarly, functionalist theories suggest that the larger society needs women to perform expressive roles in the fam-

ily while men perform instrumental roles connecting the family to outside institutions. However, feminist critiques claim that these theories have flawed logic and methods and cite historical and cross-cultural variation to show that divisions of labor are socially constructed (Thorne and Yalom 1992); only women can bear and nurse children, but the gender of the people who cook or clean is neither biologically fixed nor preordained.

Culture. Theories that consider the division of labor to be culturally fashioned tend to emphasize the importance of socialization and ideology. Historical analyses of the ideal of separate spheres fall into this category, as do anthropological explanations that rely on rituals, customs, myths, and language to explain divisions of labor (Rosaldo 1980). Socialization theories suggest that children and adults acquire beliefs about appropriate roles for men and women and that they fashion their own family behaviors according to these gender scripts (Bem 1981). Some sociocultural and psychological theories suggest that exclusive mothering encourages girls to develop personalities dependent on emotional connection, which, in turn, propels women into domestic roles. Boys also grow up in the care of mothers, but to establish a masculine identity, they reject things feminine, including nurturance and domestic work (Chodorow 1978).

The basic idea in most cultural theories is that values and ideals shape people's motivations and cause them to perform gender-typed activities. Empirical tests of hypotheses derived from these theories on contemporary U.S. populations yield mixed results. Some researchers conclude that abstract beliefs about what men and women "ought" to do are relatively inconsequential for actual behavior (Thompson and Walker 1989), whereas others conclude that there is a consistent, though sometimes small, increase in sharing when men and women believe that housework or child care should be shared (Pleck 1983).

Economy and practicality. Theories that consider the division of labor by gender to be a practical response to economic conditions are diverse and plentiful. New home economics theories suggest that women do the housework because labor specialization maximizes the efficiency of the entire family unit. Women are assumed to have "tastes" for doing housework, and their commitments to childbearing and childrearing are seen as limiting their movement into the marketplace (Becker 1981). Resource theories similarly assume that spouses make cost–benefit calculations about housework using external indicators such as education and income. Family work is treated as something to be avoided, and women end up doing more of it because their time is worth less on the economic market and because they have less marital power due to lower earnings and education (Geerken and Gove 1983).

Educational differences between spouses are rarely associated with divisions of labor, and men with more education often report doing *more* housework, rather than less, as resource theories predict. (It may be that well-educated men are simply reporting more sharing because they think they should do more.) Similarly, total family earnings have little effect on how much housework men do, though middle-class men talk more about the importance of sharing than working-class men. There may be more actual sharing among working-class families because men's and women's incomes are more similar than in middle-class families. Some studies show that spouses with more equal incomes share more household labor, but women still do more than men when they have similar jobs. Thus, relative earning power is important, but there is no simple trade-off of wage work for housework (Gerson 1993; Hochschild 1989; Thompson and Walker 1989). Most studies find that the number of hours spouses are employed is more important to the division of household labor than simple earnings. Time demands and time availability—labeled by researchers as practical considerations, demand–response capability, or situational constraints—undergird most people's decisions about allocating housework and child care (e.g., England and Farkas 1986; Peterson and Gerson 1992; Spitze 1988).

Gender inequality. The final set of theories also focuses on power and practicality, but more emphasis is placed on conflict and gender inequality. Women are compelled to perform household labor because economic market inequities keep women's wages below those of men (Hartmann 1981). Unlike the new home economics, these theories do not assume a unity of husband's and wife's interests, and unlike many resource theories, they do not posit all individuals as utility maximizers with equal chances in a hypothetical free market. Other versions of theories in this tradition suggest that social institutions like marriage, the legal system, the media, and the educational system also help to perpetuate an unequal division of labor in which women are forced to perform a "second shift" of domestic labor when they hold paying jobs (Chafetz 1990; Hochschild 1989). Some versions draw on the same insights but focus on the ways that the performance of housework serves to demarcate men from women, keeps women dependent on men, and serves to construct the meaning of gender in everyday interaction (Berk 1985; Coltrane

1989). In empirical tests, hypotheses derived from these gender-inequality theories receive moderately strong support (Ferree 1991; Petersen and Gerson 1992; Thompson and Walker 1989).

Household-labor theories are often complementary or overlapping. The theories in the last three categories suggest that a more equal division of household labor could exist if more women move into the paid labor market; if men's and women's educations, incomes, and work schedules converge; if cultural images portray parenting as a shared endeavor; if governments and businesses promote sharing through programs and policies; and if more children are exposed to egalitarian practices and ideals. Related trends (e.g., continued high levels of cohabitation, divorce, and remarriage, along with postponement of marriage and parenthood) also imply that more sharing of household labor is probable in the future. Changes are likely to be modest, however, as many of the conditions that brought about the unequal division of labor still exist. More men will share child care and housework, but most women will remain responsible for family work.

(*See also:* CHILD CARE; DUAL-EARNER FAMILIES; FAMILY GENDER ROLES; HISTORY OF THE FAMILY; RESOURCE MANAGEMENT; WORK AND FAMILY)

BIBLIOGRAPHY

Becker, G. S. (1981). *A Treatise on the Family.* Cambridge, MA: Harvard University Press.
Bem, S. (1981). "Gender Schema Theory: A Cognitive Account of Sex-Typing." *Psychological Review* 88:354–364.
Berk, S. F. (1985). *The Gender Factory: The Apportionment of Work in American Households.* New York: Plenum.
Bose, C. E. (1987). "Dual Spheres." In *Analyzing Gender: A Handbook of Social Science Research,* ed. B. Hess and M. M. Ferree. Newbury Park, CA: Sage Publications.
Chafetz, J. (1990). *Gender Equity.* Newbury Park, CA: Sage Publications.
Chodorow, N. (1978). *The Reproduction of Mothering.* Berkeley: University of California Press.
Collins, R., and Coltrane, S. (1991). *Sociology of Marriage and the Family: Gender, Love, and Property.* Chicago: Nelson-Hall.
Coltrane, S. (1989). "Household Labor and the Routine Production of Gender." *Social Problems* 36:473–490.
Coltrane, S. (1992). "The Micropolitics of Gender in Nonindustrial Societies." *Gender and Society* 6:86–107.
Cowan, R. S. (1983). *More Work for Mother.* New York: Basic Books.
Cowan, C. P., and Cowan, P. A. (1992). *When Partners Become Parents: The Big Life Change for Couples.* New York: Basic Books.

Degler, C. N. (1980). *At Odds: Women and the Family in America from the Revolution to the Present.* New York: Oxford University Press.

England, P., and Farkas, G. (1986). *Households, Employment, and Gender.* New York: Aldine.

Ferree, M. M. (1991). "The Gender Division of Labor in Two-Earner Marriages: Dimensions of Variability and Change." *Journal of Family Issues* 12:158–180.

Geerken, M., and Gove, W. (1983). *At Home and at Work: The Family's Allocation of Labor.* Newbury Park, CA: Sage Publications.

Gershuny, J., and Robinson, J. (1988). "Historical Changes in the Household Division of Labor." *Demography* 25:537–552.

Gerson, K. (1993). *No Man's Land: Men's Changing Commitments to Family and Work.* New York: Basic Books.

Goldscheider, F. K., and Waite, L. J. (1991). *New Families, No Families? The Transformation of the American Home.* Berkeley: University of California Press.

Goodnow, J. (1988). "Children's Household Work: Its Nature and Functions." *Psychological Bulletin* 103:5–26.

Hartmann, H. (1981). "The Family as the Locus of Gender, Class, and Political Struggle: The Example of Housework." *Signs* 1:366–394.

Hochschild, A. R. (1989). *The Second Shift: Working Parents and the Revolution at Home.* New York: Viking Press.

O'Connell, M. (1993). *Where's Papa? Fathers' Role in Child Care.* Washington, DC: Population Reference Bureau.

Park, R. D., and Tinsley, B. R. (1984). "Fatherhood: Historical and Contemporary Perspectives." In *Lifespan Developmental Psychology: Historical and Generational Effects,* ed. K. A. McCluskey and H. W. Reese. New York: Academic Press.

Peterson, R. R., and Gerson, K. (1992). "Determinants of Responsibility for Child-Care Arrangements Among Dual-Earner Couples." *Journal of Marriage and the Family* 54:527–536.

Pleck, J. (1983). "Husbands' Paid Work and Family Roles: Current Research Issues." In *Research in the Interweave of Social Roles,* ed. H. Lopata and J. Pleck. Greenwich, CT: JAI Press.

Pleck, J. H. (1987). "American Fathering in Historical Perspective." In *Changing Men: New Directions in Research on Men and Masculinity,* ed. M. Kimmel. Newbury Park, CA: Sage Publications.

Robinson, J. (1988). "Who's Doing the Housework?" *American Demographics* 10:24–28, 63.

Rosaldo, M. (1980). "The Use and Abuse of Anthropology." *Signs* 5:389–417.

Ross, C. E.; Mirowsky, J.; and Huber, J. (1983). "Dividing Work, Sharing Work, and In-Between: Marriage Patterns and Depression." *American Sociological Review* 48:809–823.

Shelton, B. A. (1992). *Women, Men, Time.* New York: Greenwood Press.

Spitze, G. (1988). "Women's Employment and Family Relations: A Review." *Journal of Marriage and the Family* 50:595–618.

Thompson, L., and Walker, A. J. (1989). "Gender in Families." *Journal of Marriage and the Family* 51:845–871.

Thorne, B., and Yalom, M. (1992). *Rethinking the Family: Some Feminist Questions,* 2nd edition. Boston: Northeastern University Press.

Welter, B. (1966). "The Cult of True Womanhood: 1820–1860." *American Quarterly* 18:151–174.

SCOTT COLTRANE

DIVORCE

This entry consists of the following four articles:

Legal Aspects
   J. Thomas Oldham
Economic Aspects
   Barbara R. Rowe
Emotional and Social Aspects
   Peggy Sudol
Effects on Children
   Lawrence A. Kurdek

Legal Aspects

The United States has a federalist legal system; some matters are regulated solely by the federal government, some are regulated solely by individual state governments, and others are regulated by both state and federal law. Although Canada, which also has a federalist system, has regulated divorce solely at the federal level, the United States has left regulation of divorce to the individual states.

History of Divorce

Each one of the original American colonies was founded predominantly by people who had emigrated from a particular country or were members of a particular group. Because of these settlement patterns, the countries of origin, and therefore the cultural heritages, of the settlers often varied from one colony to another. As a result, there were many inconsistent policies among colonies. The policies that the individual colonies adopted regarding divorce were no exception.

Before the American Revolution, England and the countries of Western Europe had by no means reached a consensus about divorce acts either. In eighteenth-century England, an absolute divorce required, among other things, a bill to be passed by Parliament. This was a remedy available only to the very wealthy, and only thirteen divorce acts were passed by Parliament between 1760 and 1769 (Phillips 1991). A "divorce from bed and board" was easier to obtain but had a number of disadvantages. Such a "divorce" (what might actually be called a legal separation) allowed a couple to live separately, but the marriage was not formally ended; the man still had to support the woman, and neither could remarry. The right to a judicial absolute divorce was not created in England until 1857.

At the Council of Trent in 1563, the Catholic Church rejected the concept of divorce, although annulments remained possible (Phillips 1991). Therefore, countries where Catholicism was the predominant religion, such as France (until the revolution), Italy, and Spain, did not accept divorce. In contrast, countries that were predominantly Protestant, such as Germany, Switzerland, the Netherlands, and Denmark, adopted the views of Martin Luther and John Calvin that absolute divorce should be possible (Phillips 1991).

Given this history of European divorce policy, perhaps it is not surprising that it was not easy for America to develop a consensus regarding divorce. The colonies in the Northeast, such as Connecticut, Massachusetts, and Rhode Island, permitted absolute divorce. Most southern colonies did not permit absolute divorce, but divorce from bed and board was possible (Riley 1991). During the period after the American Revolution, an increasing number of states created a procedure for absolute divorce. Many states initially followed the English practice of allowing a legislative body to hear the evidence and decide whether to grant a divorce.

During the nineteenth century, as the number of people seeking a divorce increased, legislators decided that they did not want to be the body charged with hearing each divorce petition. By the time of the American Civil War, almost all state legislatures had delegated to a state court the power to hear divorce cases and to grant a divorce. Most states accepted that absolute divorce should be possible, but only if appropriate "grounds" for divorce were established. A fundamental assumption of divorce law during this period was that marriage was a lifetime commitment; a person could be released from these ties while his or her spouse was alive only if it could be established that the spouse had "breached" the marriage contract. Most states at this time accepted adultery or desertion as an appropriate ground for divorce. Less of a consensus existed regarding "cruelty"; critics worried that such a ground was too vague and would permit a

too lenient standard for divorce. By 1886, however, all states but six had accepted this ground, and most states construed cruelty broadly. States with more lax rules also accepted neglect or mental suffering as an acceptable ground.

A somewhat obvious corollary of the fault-based divorce system is that a married person could not always obtain a divorce, even if he or she was unhappy. A divorce was possible only if an acceptable ground could be established. However, this requirement was not always strictly enforced. If both parties desired a divorce, they could agree to fabricate grounds for divorce. For example, one spouse could agree to be in bed with a third party at an appointed time, and the other spouse would then arrive and "catch" them together, thereby establishing adultery, grounds for divorce. So if both parties wanted the divorce, divorce was not difficult to obtain. During the nineteenth century, however, the "guilty" spouse frequently was banned from remarrying, while the "innocent" spouse was free to remarry.

The growing mobility of American society and the delegation of divorce regulation to the individual states significantly affected American divorce policy during the nineteenth and twentieth centuries. Because Americans seemed inclined to move frequently (particularly during the period when the American frontier was being settled), a person in an unhappy marriage could, with relative ease, merely leave the marital home, settle in a new place, and remarry. Desertion, the "poor man's divorce," followed by remarriage to another, was probably quite common, even though it was not legally permitted (Riley 1991).

Although all states until 1970 required a petitioner to prove fault to obtain a divorce, the possibilities of desertion or de facto consensual divorce made American divorce policy in practice much less restrictive than it appeared from the statutory rules. Unhappily married people living in states with "strict" divorce laws sometimes were tempted to move for a short while to a state with a "lax" law, obtain a divorce, and then return to the former home. During the nineteenth century and the early twentieth century, South Dakota, North Dakota, and Indiana enjoyed brief periods of prosperity as "divorce mills" because of their lax grounds for divorce and short residency requirements (Riley 1991). Nevada eventually prevailed in this struggle and became the domestic divorce mill of choice for much of the twentieth century; this monopoly ended only after all states adopted no-fault divorce laws (Blake 1962; Phillips 1991). In *Williams* v. *North Carolina* (1942), the U.S. Supreme Court decided that all states had to honor divorces granted by another state, as long as the person petitioning for the divorce was a bona fide resident of the issuing state at the time the divorce was granted.

Even ignoring desertion, the American divorce rate has been among the highest in the industrialized world for more than a century. For example, in 1886 there were 400 divorces in England; in the United States, a country with a significantly smaller population, about 18,000 couples divorced that year. Similarly, fewer than 600 English couples divorced in 1904, compared to more than 72,000 American couples in 1906. In 1910, a total of 83,045 American couples divorced, compared to the total of 20,329 divorces granted in England, Scotland, France, Belgium, the Netherlands, Switzerland, Norway, Denmark, and Sweden. The U.S. divorce rate increased from 0.3 per 1,000 individuals in 1870 to 0.7 per 1,000 in 1900 to 0.9 per 1,000 just before World War I. No European country had a divorce rate higher than 0.5 per 1,000 before World War I. Between 1867 and 1907, there were 431 divorces in Canada and 1,274,341 in the United States (Phillips 1991). Even adjusting for the difference in population, this reflects a substantial difference in divorce rates between the United States and Canada.

Trends in Divorce Rates After 1945

By the end of World War II, most states had enacted relatively broad "fault" divorce systems. Both parties to the divorce could remarry, even the party at fault. South Carolina was the last holdout; absolute divorce was not accepted there until 1949.

Although the American divorce rate in the nineteenth century was relatively high compared to that of other industrialized countries, the U.S. divorce rate rose dramatically in the half century after World War II. As might be expected, at the end of the war a very large number of divorces occurred, due in part to hasty marriages before enlistment and estrangement caused by long separation. The divorce rate then stabilized for a short while, but at a rate higher than the prewar rate. The divorce rate then climbed again, from 1960 to 1990. By 1985, the U.S. divorce rate reached about 5 per 1,000 individuals (Phillips 1988). It has been estimated that about 5 percent of all marriages celebrated in 1860 ended in divorce, and about one-third of all marriages entered into in 1960 have ended in divorce. It has been further estimated that 50 percent of marriages celebrated in the early 1990s will end in divorce (Cherlin 1992). A number of explanations have been offered for this trend, including high marital expectations, longer life expectancies (so people are married much longer, unless they divorce), the

increasing difficulty of deserting rather than divorcing, and the expansion of employment options outside the home for women. Critical reaction to this trend in the American divorce rate has been mixed. Some decry the increasing prevalence of divorce, due to the low standard of living of many women and children in divorced households and the damage that could result to children due to the divorce. Others applaud couples who, rather than resign themselves to an unhappy marriage, separate and attempt to create better, more satisfying marriages with others. Proponents of this view also express concern that rates of spousal abuse and child sexual abuse would increase if more unhappy couples were forced to stay together.

No-Fault Divorce

In the 1960s, a consensus did develop that the "fault" divorce system was too adversarial and probably based on the erroneous assumption that only one party causes an unhappy marriage. Drafters of U.S. family policy concluded that in most instances both parties are responsible for the success of a relationship. In addition, fault divorce was perceived to exacerbate the hostility frequently exhibited by divorcing couples. Also, many concluded that all parties would be better off if unhappy spouses were able to separate. Because of these concerns, almost all states accepted some version of no-fault divorce between 1969 and 1989.

Under this procedure, a married person could allege that there were "irreconcilable differences" between the spouses, and a divorce would be possible. This procedure was envisioned as one that would be less adversarial; it also would no longer require parties to manufacture evidence of fault dishonestly, as occurred in many instances under the fault regime. No-fault divorce has another very significant, if less apparent, effect: It lets either party obtain a divorce for no reason, even if the other spouse resists the idea of divorce. This trend toward acceptance of no-fault divorce has been a worldwide movement. For example, a number of European countries as well as Australia, New Zealand, and Canada accepted no-fault divorce between 1960 and 1990 (Phillips 1991).

Uniform Marriage and Divorce Act

A uniform American divorce law was promulgated in 1970. This law, the Uniform Marriage and Divorce Act (UMDA), incorporated the prevailing views of divorce policy commentators at the time. For example, no-fault divorce (irreconcilable differences) was proposed as the ground for divorce. This uniform law also attempted to address other important matters that should be addressed at divorce. For example, under UMDA if a couple has a minor child at divorce, the court is directed to consider various possible custody options and to choose the one that would be "in the best interests of the child." No gender-based preference was adopted; neither parent was presumed to be the better custodial parent merely based on the parent's sex.

When a couple divorces, property owned by either spouse needs to be divided. The drafters of UMDA proposed two different statutes: one for community property states (Texas, Louisiana, New Mexico, Arizona, Nevada, California, Washington, and Idaho) and one for the rest of the country. The community property provision limited the scope of divisible property to that acquired by either spouse during marriage, other than a gift or inheritance received by one spouse from a third party. The other provision authorized a divorce court to divide in an equitable manner all property owned by either spouse at divorce, regardless of how or when the property was acquired.

Spousal support was also permitted in some circumstances under UMDA (e.g., if the paying spouse could afford it and the other spouse could not be self-supporting either due to limited career options or child-care responsibilities). The noncustodial parent was expected to contribute a reasonable amount of child support to the custodial parent as support of any children of the marriage until the children reached adulthood.

Divorce Procedures

Although the drafters of UMDA hoped that no-fault divorce would be less adversarial, divorce proceedings continue to be hotly contested in many instances, even with the acceptance of no-fault divorce. This probably results from a number of factors. Divorcing couples tend to be very angry at some stages of the divorce process, and this can cause the spouses to react in a hostile and destructive manner. Lawyers sometimes compound the problem with excessively adversarial tactics in the divorce. The litigation in cases where both parents want custody of their children can also be very adversarial.

Mediation. An adversarial divorce process has a number of drawbacks. A number of divorcing parties have found the process very unpleasant and their legal fees very high. Children can also be harmed by an adversarial divorce. An increasing number of divorcing couples are trying to reach a settlement themselves with the help of a mediator, rather than delegating the negotiating job to their lawyers. The mediator meets with the parties, sometimes with lawyers present and sometimes with the lawyers available via telephone, and explores whether the parties can reach a negotiated agreement. The mediator does not dictate the terms of any agreement; a settlement occurs only if the parties themselves agree.

Compared to a trial, mediation in many instances offers a number of advantages. Mediation is an informal process, normally conducted in an office, not a courtroom. Many believe it is a more humane and less damaging process than a trial. Many parties reach agreement through mediation relatively quickly and incur lower legal fees. Some mediation outcomes are quite creative, at least in part because mediators are trained to suggest various alternatives to the parties. In addition, parties seem more willing to comply with an agreement they negotiated, compared to one dictated by a judge (Folberg and Milne 1988).

Although mediation has advantages for many couples, it may not be a good idea for all couples. Research suggests that if parties to a mediation have unequal bargaining power, an unfair agreement may result, particularly if lawyers are not involved. So mediation probably is more appropriate for couples with relatively equal bargaining power.

Settlement agreements. If parties can reach an agreed settlement, either through mediation or via lawyers, courts generally accept these terms without a very thorough review. Particularly if both parties have retained attorneys, many judges assume that each spouse and the children have been adequately protected.

Equitable distribution. Every state now permits a divorce court to divide property owned by the parties at divorce. Under the law of many states, the court may not divide property owned by a spouse before marriage or acquired by gift or inheritance during marriage. In contrast, some states permit a divorce court to divide all property owned by either spouse at divorce, regardless of when or how it was acquired. In most states, the court divides the property equitably after considering a number of factors; the division does not have to be equal (Oldham 1994).

In the past, courts construed the term "property" fairly narrowly in divorce proceedings, generally limiting the term to tangible property. Now, most courts include other types of property, such as pensions.

Spousal support. All states other than Texas permit a court to order one spouse to pay spousal support to the other after divorce. The support can be either for a fixed term (rehabilitative support) or for an indefinite duration. Rehabilitative support is ordered to enable a spouse to pursue some type of training or education so the spouse can thereafter be economically self-sufficient. In most instances, the latter type of support award occurs only when parties divorce after a long marriage and one spouse has a relatively high income (Clark 1988). In a majority of divorces, no spousal support is ordered.

Custody and child support. If the spouses have a minor child at the time of divorce, they need to agree on a custody arrangement. The most common arrangement in most jurisdictions is for one parent to have primary custody; this means that the child lives with that parent. The other parent normally then has the right to take the child for short periods (e.g., every other weekend) and is expected to contribute a reasonable amount of child support.

When custody is disputed, a court attempts to determine what custody arrangement would be in the best interests of the child. Some states utilize the presumption that the parent who was the "primary caretaker" of the child during marriage (i.e., the parent who looked after the child by fulfilling such duties as providing transportation to school, scheduling medical appointments, and preparing nutritious meals) would be the best custodial parent.

An alternate custody arrangement is "joint custody," whereby each parent is a legal custodian and thereby has some power to make decisions affecting the child (for things such as choice of school and medical care). Under this arrangement the parents may divide physical custody, so that the child lives at both parents' homes for a portion of the year (sometimes called split custody); more frequently, the parents agree that the child should live primarily with one parent. Child support may still be ordered if the parents are awarded joint custody.

Contested divorces. A divorce may be contested or uncontested. An uncontested divorce is one where there are no disputed issues. In a contested divorce, there are disputed issues, such as the value of the divisible marital estate, how the property should be divided, the appropriate custody arrangement, or the reasonable amount of spousal or child support.

Pro se divorce. Divorce is a legal procedure; a divorce decree issued by a judge must be obtained. Lawyers are not required, but many find some legal advice helpful, particularly if a spouse has a significant amount of property or the couple has a child. Some couples divorce without being represented by a lawyer; this is referred to as a pro se divorce.

Divisible divorce. Any U.S. state has the power to grant a divorce to a person who resides there. However, to do anything else, more complicated jurisdictional rules apply. To order a parent to pay child support, this court must have "personal jurisdiction" over that parent. This means that there must be some significant contact between that parent and the state. Likewise, to divide marital property located outside the state, that state must have personal jurisdiction over both spouses. If the spouses have a child, the state where the court is located must have significant contact with the child to make a custody determination. This normally arises when the child lives in that state.

If a state has the power to grant a divorce but does not have the power to divide marital property, order support, or make a custody determination, the court still may grant a divorce. This "divisible divorce" terminates the marriage but leaves the other issues involved unresolved.

Property located outside the state. If a court has personal jurisdiction over both spouses, the court may divide all property divisible under that state's law, regardless of where the property is located. To divide realty located outside the state, the better practice is to order the record owner to sign a deed conveying title and to record the deed in the appropriate office where the realty is located, instead of merely relying on the court's order to change title.

Conclusion

The U.S. divorce rate has increased substantially since World War II. Despite this fact, however, marriage does not appear to be a declining institution for most people. It has been estimated that three-quarters of all divorced men and two-thirds of all divorced women will remarry (Cherlin 1992). This suggests that most Americans, even those who have been unsuccessful in their first attempt at marriage, have a sufficiently strong interest in marriage to try again. Apparently, most Americans continue to believe that marriage is the most desirable domestic arrangement.

This is not to say that divorce does not have its costs. Some writers argue that divorce can significantly harm children. In addition, many studies document the substantial decrease in the standard of living of women and children after divorce. A significant decrease in the divorce rate seems unlikely, so it will be important to consider what new policies can be implemented to reduce the harm stemming from divorce.

(*See also:* ALIMONY AND SPOUSAL SUPPORT; ANNULMENT; CHILD CUSTODY; CHILD SUPPORT; DIVORCE: ECONOMIC ASPECTS;

Divorce: Emotional and Social Aspects; Divorce: Effects on Children; Marital Property and Community Property)

BIBLIOGRAPHY

Blake, N. M. (1962). *Road to Reno.* Westport, CT: Greenwood Press.

Cherlin, A. (1992). *Marriage, Divorce, Remarriage.* Cambridge, MA: Harvard University Press.

Clark, H. (1988). *The Law of Domestic Relations in the United States.* St. Paul, MN: West Publishing.

Folberg, J., and Milne, A. (1988). *Divorce Mediation: Theory and Practice.* New York: Guilford.

Oldham, J. T. (1994). *Divorce, Separating, and the Distribution of Property.* New York: New York Law Journal Seminars-Press.

Phillips, R. (1988). *Putting Asunder.* Cambridge, Eng.: Cambridge University Press.

Phillips, R. (1991). *Untying the Knot.* Cambridge, Eng.: Cambridge University Press.

Riley, G. (1991). *Divorce: An American Tradition.* Oxford, Eng.: Oxford University Press.

CASE

Williams v. *North Carolina*, 317 U.S. 287 (1942).

J. THOMAS OLDHAM

Economic Aspects

By studying the available data relevant to the economic consequences of divorce, researchers have established that women and their children suffer a dramatic decline in income and standard of living following divorce proceedings, with older homemakers and mothers of young children experiencing the greatest hardships. For men, on the other hand, divorce often leads to an improved economic standard of living. Divorce law, then, is said to be a primary contributor to the increase in impoverished women and children, referred to as the "feminization of poverty."

Property

Traditionally, in most of the eight community property states, each spouse had a vested, undivided, one-half interest in all property acquired during the marriage; property owned prior to marriage, or acquired as a gift or inheritance, was deemed separate property and not subject to division (deFuniak and Vaughn 1974; Greene 1979). In the other states, which formed the majority and were known as common law states, property was owned by the husband or wife whose name appeared on the title, unless the marital property were jointly owned or a property distribution had been previously agreed upon. The divorce courts in these common law states could not or would

not require the property-owning spouse to divide these assets (Kulzer 1975; Parkman 1992).

The introduction of equitable distribution in common law states expanded the pool of property subject to division by allowing judges to look beyond title when allocating property at divorce and to include assets such as pensions, goodwill, and professional degrees and licenses (Garrison 1991). Some states now include all assets of the couple as subject to division, regardless of when or how the assets were acquired. Other states restrict divisible assets to those deemed marital property—assets acquired during the marriage through the joint efforts of both spouses. Most statutes authorize courts to divide property as deemed "just and fair," although there may be a presumption in favor of equal distribution. Most statutes also recognize the contribution of a homemaker's services to be of equal value to wage earning when allocating property at divorce.

Researchers have found that in equitable distribution states, divorced wives, on average, receive at least half, and in some instances the majority, of the net family assets (Baker 1987; Garrison 1991; McLindon 1987; Rowe and Lown 1990; Rowe and Morrow 1988). However, divorcing couples generally have few assets to divide in terms of tangible property, such as homes, other real estate, businesses, savings, and marketable securities. In most states, the median net value of marital assets does not exceed $30,000 (Garrison 1991). Typically, the family home is the couple's most important asset. Without enough other property of value, it is impossible to give the family home to the custodial parent, usually the wife, and award an equal amount of assets to the husband. As a result, in an effort to equalize property settlements, there has been an increase in the forced sale of the family home upon divorce (Garrison 1991; McLindon 1987).

Although women who divorce in equitable distribution states have been shown to receive more property than those who divorce in states with equal distribution rules, it is important to realize the nature and limited value of these assets. Usually the couple's net worth is all tied up in the family home, cars, and furniture—assets that are not liquid and thus are difficult to use for current consumption (Garrison 1991; Rowe and Lown 1990). Retaining the family home, with its attendant mortgage obligation, tends to limit geographic mobility and employment opportunities. When they exist, income-producing assets (e.g., businesses, stocks and bonds, and pensions) are almost always retained by husbands.

Some studies have suggested that when the value of marital property increases, the percentage awarded to the wife declines. In New York, Marsha Garrison (1991) found that wives in the group with the lowest net worth received almost double the percentage share of assets of wives with the highest net worth. Similar results have been found in Connecticut and Utah (McLindon 1987; Rowe and Lown 1990).

Alimony

Except in Texas, courts can award alimony to dependent spouses of either gender. The justification for alimony under no-fault rules is to provide support for spouses who temporarily or permanently have compelling economic need (Krauskopf 1988; Weitzman 1985). Alimony statutes reflect this goal by directing judges to consider factors such as a spouse's age, health, custody of minor children, and ability to earn income (Reynolds 1988).

Although the percentage of women awarded spousal support or alimony varies from state to state, only 15.5 percent of all divorcing women nationwide are awarded alimony (U.S. Bureau of the Census 1991). Nor have many women historically received post-divorce support; from 1822 to 1922, only 9 percent to 15 percent of all divorces included provisions for alimony (Weitzman 1985).

Several state research reports have demonstrated that since the divorce reforms of the 1970s there has been a change in the duration of alimony awards from permanent (until the death of either spouse, remarriage/cohabitation of the recipient, or a substantial change in the economic circumstances of either party) to short-term rehabilitative awards (Garrison 1991; McLindon 1987; Weitzman 1985). Several factors prompted this legal trend: a rising divorce rate, an increasing number of women with children in the labor market, and the idea that the wife was to become self-sufficient after marriage. Theoretically, limited-duration alimony awards are structured to give the recipient time in which to find employment or to gain the skills, training, or education necessary for self-support. However, rehabilitative awards in many states are so short-term and the amounts so low that they are insufficient to cover the cost or the actual time required to complete a vocational or professional training program or to find employment (Baker 1987). Reports show that the average alimony award is about $337 a month and ranges in duration from an average of 4.7 years in New York to one year in Alaska (Baker 1987; Garrison 1991).

Full-time homemakers married for twenty years or longer are more likely to receive an alimony award than women married for a shorter time and are more

likely to receive a permanent award rather than a time-limited award. However, nonpayment of alimony and support obligations is a widespread problem. Either no payment is made at all, or payments are not made on time and arrearages build up. Even when payments are made for the first year or two, they often stop or tail off with the passage of time. Frequently it is not economically feasible for women to enforce the order. For example, where the typical award is about $4,400 per year for two years (i.e., a total award of only $8,800), legal fees and other costs incurred in enforcing such an award could easily exceed the amount of the total award itself (California Senate Task Force on Family Equity 1987).

The absence of adequate alimony awards for a reasonable length of time is particularly harsh for older women who were full-time homemakers throughout the marriage and for young mothers who interrupted their employment or advanced education for child rearing. At divorce they are forced to compete in a labor market where their job skills are increasingly obsolete and their earning capacity is permanently impaired.

Child Support

Passage of the Child Support Enforcement Amendments of 1984 was the federal response to a spiraling poverty rate among women and children. The key provision of this legislation was a requirement that each state must develop and implement uniform guidelines for determining the amount of child support in divorce and paternity cases. Congress took this action for several reasons. First, national data on child support awards indicated that of the 8.8 million women raising children whose fathers were not living in the household, only about 60 percent had an order or agreement to receive child support (Goldfarb 1987). Second, of the women supposed to receive child support, less than half (48.9 percent) received the full amount due. About a quarter received partial payment, and more than a quarter received no payment at all (U.S. Bureau of the Census 1991). Third, even when nonresidential fathers paid support, the amount was generally set at levels too low to meet children's actual needs, even at the poverty level. A Colorado researcher found that two-thirds of the fathers in her study were ordered to pay less per month for child support than they were spending on car payments (Yee 1979).

In some instances, a father's ability to support is stretched to the limit by his remarriage and assumption of the financial burdens of a new family. In other cases, the father's income is simply too low to share; nothing divided by two is still nothing. However, two frequently cited studies found that many fathers do have the financial ability to pay more. According to these studies, fathers, in general, can afford to pay two and one-half times the amount of their current support orders and more than three times what they are actually paying (Garfinkel and Oellerich 1989; Haskins et al. 1985).

Over time, single mothers bear more and more of the economic costs of children alone, since support awards are rarely indexed to the cost of living or increases in the obligor's income (McLanahan 1991). Even fewer awards recognize that child-rearing costs increase as children grow older. One study of parental expenditures on children found that older children increased expenses 23.6 percent, while estimates calculated for the U.S. Department of Agriculture suggest a 23.1 percent increase (Williams 1987).

In all but a few states, support orders end on the child's eighteenth birthday. Child support is for minors. In the wake of the passage of the Twenty-sixth Amendment to the U.S. Constitution, which reduced the voting age from twenty-one to eighteen, most states passed statutes allowing children to achieve adult status at eighteen. They are no longer entitled to parental support after that time unless physically or mentally disabled and unable to provide for themselves (Horan 1987).

However, the years after eighteen are the years of highest cost, especially if the child enters college. This dilemma is further complicated if the nonresidential parent's income becomes a factor for eligibility for financial aid. If the nonresidential parent's income is adequate to support the children during college, financial aid may be denied even if the nonresidential parent is not, in fact, supplying child support (Wallerstein and Corbin 1986). This effectively deprives many children in divorced families of the chance to go to college and forces them prematurely into the labor market (Eden 1987).

Fourteen states permit court-initiated awards of postminority support. Another seven states will uphold an order for postminority support if there is a voluntary agreement to do so by the parents (Horan 1987). The argument against postminority support is that it imposes a duty on divorced parents when married parents have no similar obligation.

Inadequate and poorly paid support orders led Congress to insist that states enact numeric guidelines for setting child support. Unfortunately, competing political agendas and lobbying efforts by nonresidential parents' groups have resulted in many states adopting guidelines that have only modestly increased awards or kept the situation at status quo. One three-state research project found that the average postguidelines child support award was only 15 percent higher than the preguidelines average (Pearson, Thoennes, and Tjaden 1989). In another study, which analyzed 1988 and 1991 data from all fifty states, it was found that nominal and inflation-adjusted support awards declined in many states between 1988 and 1991 (Pirog-Good 1993).

Economic Well-Being After Divorce

The disparity between the postdivorce economic well-being of husbands and wives has been well documented. Numerous studies have shown that after divorce, husbands' financial well-being increases, while that of wives decreases. Precise estimates of the decline in women's income vary among studies, but the range is reported to be 30 percent to 50 percent (Burkhauser and Duncan 1989; Duncan and Hoffman 1985). Divorced men may experience an immediate decline in income due to the loss of earnings of their former spouses, but when income relative to needs is compared, divorced men actually improve their level of economic well-being even after deductions for alimony and child support payments (Duncan and Hoffman 1985; Rowe and Lown 1990).

The economic impact of divorce affects children also. Census data show that 90 percent of children living in single-parent families live with their mothers (U.S. Bureau of the Census 1991); thus, women's economic decline as a result of divorce directly affects their dependent children. There is a large body of research showing that children from poor, mother-only homes are less likely to receive adequate nutrition and health care, less likely to complete high school, more likely to have babies out of wedlock, and more likely to commit delinquent behavior than their two-parent counterparts. Moreover, those who marry are more likely to divorce (Danziger 1990; McLanahan 1991).

Some decline in economic well-being can be expected when the income adequate for one household has to cover the expenses of two. The problem is that the cost is being disproportionately borne by women and the children in their custody. Critics contend that no-fault divorce laws have hurt women because an equal division of marital assets and limited amounts of support have been instituted at a time when equality is lacking in areas of employment opportunity, child-rearing responsibilities, and career preparation (Holden and Smock 1991; Weitzman 1985).

Proposals for Reform

There is growing recognition of the need to reform the financial arrangements made at divorce because of their undesirable results. Some critics suggest a return to fault-based criteria for dividing property and awarding support, thus restoring a balance of negotiating power between husbands and wives (Sugarman 1990). Several comparative studies, however, show that the prior fault system did not do better (Garrison 1991; Melli 1986).

Several other policy proposals that have been suggested include giving the custodial parent a special preference in the family home; using alimony to equalize the postdivorce standard of living of husbands and wives; and basing child support on the true costs of custody, including the reduced social and employment opportunities available to the custodial parent (Parkman 1992; Weitzman 1985).

Some legal scholars have called for expanding the definition of the property divided at divorce to include "career assets" (e.g., health insurance coverage, wage-continuation programs such as disability and worker's compensation payments, advanced education, professional or career development, and increased future earnings resulting from joint marital efforts), but because so few couples own these career assets, their division will do little overall to lessen the poverty among women and children after divorce (Baker 1987; Garrison 1991; McLindon 1987).

Most reform efforts have focused on expanding the list of items treated as property to include human capital. The value of an individual's human capital would be based on anticipated future earnings. To the extent that a husband or wife's human capital has increased or decreased during the marriage, adjustments would be required in the property settlement at divorce. If earning capacity has increased over the duration of the marriage, human capital has been increased, and it should be divided like any other marital property. Alternatively, if expected earnings have decreased, the spouse incurring such loss should be compensated for the reduced value of his or her human capital (Parkman 1992). Critics of this proposal say it creates disincentives to work for the recipient spouse and incentives to stop working for the payer spouse. In addition, both parties may have made career decisions during the marriage such as passing up advanced training, refusing job transfers, or limiting overtime and overnight travel that can affect future earnings.

Other commentators have noted that the problem is that divorce terminates women's access to men's wages that were available to them through marriage. Women's earnings do not make up the difference because of women's reduced labor market experience and occupational concentration in low-paying, low-skill jobs. Child custody and the cost of child care constrain the time women have available for market work at the same time that they bear a disproportionate share of their children's expenses (Holden and Smock 1991). Advocates call for continued sharing after the end of marriage in the form of payments from husband to wife through revised alimony and child support laws (Garrison 1991).

None of the alternative approaches to the divorce laws produce perfect outcomes. Divorce laws cannot correct women's disadvantages in the labor market, nor can they completely reduce the numbers of children living in poverty when parents' resources are inadequate. It will take broader initiatives in the areas of employment, welfare, health, pension, child care, and family subsidies to effect any meaningful reform agenda.

(*See also:* ALIMONY AND SPOUSAL SUPPORT; CHILD SUPPORT; DIVORCE: LEGAL ASPECTS; DIVORCE: EMOTIONAL AND SOCIAL ASPECTS; DIVORCE: EFFECTS ON CHILDREN; MARITAL PROPERTY AND COMMUNITY PROPERTY; SINGLE PARENTS)

BIBLIOGRAPHY

Baker, B. (1987). *Family Equity at Issue: A Study of the Economic Consequences of Divorce on Women and Children.* Anchorage: Alaska Women's Commission.

Brett, L. J.; Shepela, S. T.; and Kniffin, J. (1990). *Women and Children Beware: The Economic Consequences of Divorce in Connecticut.* Hartford: Connecticut Women's Education and Legal Fund.

Burkhauser, R. V., and Duncan, G. J. (1989). "Economic Risks of Gender Roles: Income Loss and Life Events over the Life Course." *Social Science Quarterly* 70:3–23.

California Senate Task Force on Family Equity. (1987). *Final Report.* Sacramento: Joint Publications.

Danzinger, S. (1990). "Antipoverty Policies and Child Poverty." *Social Work Research and Abstracts* 26:17–24.

deFuniak, W. Q., and Vaughn, M. J. (1974). "Why Community Property Is So Misunderstood—Knowing Its Origins Is the Key." *Community Property Journal* 1:97–116.

Duncan, G. J., and Hoffman, S. D. (1985). "A Reconsideration of the Economic Consequences of Marital Dissolution." *Demography* 22:485–497.

Eden, P. (1987). "Critique of Interim Report, Development of Guidelines for Establishing Child Support Orders." In *Critical Issues, Critical Choices: Special Topics in Child Support Guideline Development.* Washington, DC: Women's Legal Defense Fund.

Garfinkel, I., and Oellerich, D. (1989). "Noncustodial Fathers' Ability to Pay Child Support." *Demography* 26:219–233.

Garrison, M. (1991). "Good Intentions Gone Awry: The Impact of New York's Equitable Distribution Law on Divorce Outcomes." *Brooklyn Law Review* 57:621–754.

Goldfarb, S. F. (1987). "What Every Lawyer Should Know About Child Support Guidelines." *Family Law Reporter (BNA)* 13:3031–3037.

Greene, S. (1979). "Comparison of the Property Aspects of the Community Property and Common-Law Marital Property Systems and Their Relative Compatibility with the Current View of the Marriage Relationship and the Rights of Women." *Creighton Law Review* 13:71–119.

Haskins, R.; Schwartz, J. B.; Akin, J. S.; and Dobelstein, A. W. (1985). "How Much Child Support Can Absent Fathers Pay?" *Policy Studies Journal* 14:201–222.

Holden, K. C., and Smock, P. J. (1991). "The Economic Costs of Marital Dissolution: Why Do Women Bear a Disproportionate Cost?" *Annual Review of Sociology* 17:51–78.

Horan, K. C. (1987). "Postminority Support for College Education—A Legally Enforceable Obligation in Divorce Proceedings?" *Family Law Quarterly* 20:589–612.

Krauskopf, J. M. (1988). "Rehabilitative Alimony: Uses and Abuses of Limited Duration Alimony." *Family Law Quarterly* 21:573–589.

Kulzer, B. A. (1975). "Law and the Housewife: Property, Divorce, and Death." *University of Florida Law Review* 28:1–55.

McLanahan, S. S. (1991). "The Long-Term Economic Effects of Family Dissolution." In *When Families Fail . . . the Social Costs*, ed. B. J. Christensen. New York: New York University Press.

McLindon, J. B. (1987). "Separate but Unequal: The Economic Disaster of Divorce for Women and Children." *Family Law Quarterly* 20:351–409.

Melli, M. (1986). "Constructing a Social Problem: The Postdivorce Plight of Women and Children." *American Bar Foundation Research Journal* 4:759–797.

Parkman, A. C. (1992). *No-Fault Divorce: What Went Wrong?* Boulder, CO: Westview Press.

Pearson, J.; Thoennes, N.; and Tjaden, P. (1989). "Legislating Adequacy: The Impact of Child Support Guidelines." *Law & Society Review* 23:569–590.

Pirog-Good, M. (1993). "Child Support Guidelines and the Economic Well-Being of Children in the United States." *Family Relations* 42:453–462.

Reynolds, S. (1988). "The Relationship of Property Division and Alimony: The Division of Property to Address Need." *Fordham Law Review* 54:827–916.

Rowe, B. R., and Lown, J. M. (1990). "The Economics of Divorce and Remarriage for Rural Utah Families." *Journal of Contemporary Law* 16:301–322.

Rowe, B. R., and Morrow, A. M. (1988). "The Economic Consequences of Divorce in Oregon After Ten or More Years of Marriage." *Willamette Law Review* 24:463–484.

Sugarman, S. D. (1990). "Dividing Financial Interests on Divorce." In *Divorce Reform at the Crossroads*, ed. S. D. Sugarman and H. H. Kay. New Haven, CT: Yale University Press.

U.S. Bureau of the Census. (1991). *Child Support and Alimony: 1989*. Washington, DC: U.S. Government Printing Office.

Wallerstein, J. S., and Corbin, S. B. (1986). "Father–Child Relationships After Divorce: Child Support and Educational Opportunity." *Family Law Quarterly* 20:109–128.

Weitzman, L. J. (1985). *The Divorce Revolution: The Unexpected Social and Economic Consequences for Women and Children in America*. New York: Free Press.

Williams, R. G. (1987). "Guidelines for Setting Levels of Child Support Orders." *Family Law Quarterly* 21:281–324.

Yee, L. M. (1979). "What Really Happens in Child Support Cases: An Empirical Study of Establishment and Enforcement of Child Support Orders in the Denver District Court." *Denver Law Journal* 57:21–68.

BARBARA R. ROWE

Emotional and Social Aspects

Divorce is one of the major crises in the family life cycle. The effects of this event are often traumatic and are felt on an individual basis as well as throughout the family and social network of the separating couple. While legally divorce is a single event that terminates a marriage contract between two people, emotionally it sets off a sequence of events that permanently change the lives of those involved. Some couples may legally end their marriages while remaining emotionally tied to each other for years. Relationships seldom end in the divorce court; they merely change. Much of the available literature on divorce examines the phenomenon from a middle-class perspective and tends to be gender-biased.

Initial Emotional Crisis

Divorce is usually initiated by one member of the couple as a solution to individual discontent in the relationship. The discontent can be a result of issues such as increased emotional distance due to changes in one or both persons, or it may result from other dynamics that render the union intolerable. The period of greatest anguish for the initiator is usually in deciding to end the marriage and is most often experienced in private. While changes in the relationship may be apparent, it is not unusual for the other spouse to be surprised when the decision to leave the marriage is announced.

Shock, disbelief, sadness, and humiliation are among the many feelings expressed by the unsuspecting spouse, while the initiator often remains calm and steadfast in what may appear to be an impulsive decision. Strong recurring guilt feelings regarding the decision to end one's marriage may influence decisions such as those made during the distribution of property and resources. Some individuals take a self-reproaching position in an effort to alleviate their guilt feelings by making atonement through giving in to the other's settlement demands, which usually creates more anger and resentment in the long run.

Dissolution of a relationship frequently starts as a process of one seeking self-worth outside the union. As discoveries of self-esteem and validation from outside sources increase, so does the distance with spouse, children, and family. The dissatisfied partner forges an identity independent of the relationship, often experiencing ambivalence while entertaining fantasies of reconciliation. Increased stress, arguing, and blaming are common characteristics of this phase of the separation process.

Social Reactions

The word "divorce" conjures up different meanings for different people. Some people, when confronted with divorce, assume that it is an inherently adversarial process. This perception usually comes from having watched friends or coworkers go through hostile conflicts in and out of the courtroom. Others equate divorce with the ultimate in personal failure, believing that they should have somehow been able to make the marriage work. There is an intense sense of social stigma experienced in watching couples operate in the world while standing alone in fear of what others will think. Divorced individuals frequently report feelings of embarrassment and humiliation about being alone. Divorced individuals no longer fit into the married social scene. They are often regarded as a threat, either of enticing another's married partner, or of spreading the perceived contagion of divorce. Couple friends (friends who are still married, as opposed to friends who are single) tend to choose sides and socialize with only one member of the divorcing couple. The social network is gradually replaced with single, more casual relationships.

The dissolution of a marriage challenges beliefs about families. Despite the advances in women's place in society, there remains a common belief that a woman is successful if she has a satisfying marriage. Many women blame themselves for not living up to the belief that it is up to them to keep the family together. Even in an unhappy marriage, some women secretly wish that their husbands would die, removing

the responsibility and abating guilt feelings for wanting to end the relationship. Society continues to hold the intact biological nuclear family up as the ideal, implying that other family configurations are deviant.

Some men experience intense turmoil when faced with the loss of their identity as head of household and protector of the family. Other men have relied on women to fill their dependency needs and lack peer friendships and social connections. The loss of home, children, friends of the couple, shared social activities, and the change in status occur simultaneously and can have an overwhelming effect. After relying on his wife to coordinate his personal life, the divorced man is faced with learning new skills and building new relationships with family as well as seeking new social contacts.

Emotional Reactions

In the United States, more women initiate divorce than men. Men are more likely to focus on pragmatic and financial aspects, while women tend to view the process with greater emotional emphasis. The range of emotions for both sexes varies from relief to intense anger, loneliness, and feelings of personal failure. The fluctuation in these moods often causes individuals to have difficulty sleeping, concentrating, eating, and in general daily functioning. This transition increases people's risk of accidents, physical and emotional illness, and substance abuse. During the initial crisis stage of divorce, these emotions change unpredictably, causing individuals to fear that the pain will last indefinitely.

Depression is a major consequence of divorce. There is a deep sense of disorientation and hurt surrounding the dissolution of the marriage, the loss of supportive companionship of the spouse and/or children, and guilt feelings from a profound sense of failure. The divorce process is permeated by loss. Similar to loss experienced by the death of a loved one, anger and self-blame can become consuming. Feelings of hopelessness can result, with suicide often being perceived as the only alternative to cope with the increasing level of depression and hopelessness. Both death and divorce involve loss of a love object, structure, identity in extended family relationships, loyalties, and expectations for family life. In divorce, however, these elements still exist, but they are unavailable to the partners in ways that they once were. Many authors have outlined stages of grieving, similar to those used in explaining death, in an effort to help individuals heal from the emotional trauma involved in the dissolution of marriage.

Changes in status also contribute to depression and emotional instability. One spouse tends to benefit more than the other as a result of the divorce. Persons who experience substantial stress in daily living, such as individuals in a lower socioeconomic status, can become overwhelmed and unable to cope with normal day-to-day stress when faced with the realities that accompany the divorce process. Loss of income, parenting children alone, and other added stresses cause extreme anxiety, which can interfere with cognitive functioning and contribute to erratic behavior. While the partner who sought the divorce usually improves the quality of his or her life, the other is in a position that that person did not necessarily choose to be in. This situation produces in the latter feelings of loss of control and diminished self-confidence.

There are individuals and families who benefit from divorce. Ongoing alcohol and/or drug abuse, violence, and chronic conflict that have not responded to helping interventions are a few of the situations in which family members experience relief and an increased sense of well-being following dissolution of the marriage. Individuals who have changed through maturity, personal growth, education, or other personal endeavors can find that they no longer have common interests or life goals with their mate. They may also benefit from discontinuing a relationship that no longer fits their changing needs.

The fear of isolation and loneliness can be paralyzing throughout the divorce process. There is frequently a perception of being overwhelmed and unable to cope with the reality of the situation. Some people have developed a dependency on others by never having lived alone, having gone from their parents' nest directly into marriage. The thought of being alone can be devastating. These feelings tend to come in waves, lasting throughout the divorce process, usually diminishing in frequency and intensity over time.

Other people experience a sense of liberation, leaping immediately into the dating arena. A series of brief sexual relationships can ensue as a means of validating one's desirability or as an attempt to regain youthful feelings. Once the initial exhilaration of being single subsides, less and less energy is expended in the endeavor. Improvement in physical appearance becomes important, with many newly single people losing weight and improving their overall body image. This can also be a time for emotional and/or spiritual growth as people expand their horizons through education, therapy, or other self-help activities.

Emotional Adjustment

One of the elements determining emotional adjustment following divorce is the degree of attachment to the former spouse. Couples who share continued intimacy remain positively attached, often experiencing emotional disturbance and an idealized view of their former mate. Those involved in ongoing conflict with their former partners hold strong negative images and feelings. It is not uncommon for individuals to alternate between positive and negative attachment. Resolution of attachment issues leading to reduction in emotional distress occurs when individuals can achieve a balanced perception of the positive and negative attributes of their ex-spouse and respond to them with little emotional reactivity.

It takes women an average of three to three and one-half years and men two to two and one-half years to reorganize and establish an externalized sense of control over their lives following divorce. Adjustments to differences in relationships, identities, physical relocations, and social networks result in a life that can be very different from the life experienced previously. The inability to resolve attachments to the former mate often results in continued mood disturbance and individuals being emotionally unavailable to embark on new relationships. Postdivorce adjustment can also be influenced by education, social activities and supports, occupation, personal maturity, and financial assets.

Outside stressors also play an important role in postdivorce adjustment. Issues such as child custody and child support can weigh heavily on the psychological well-being of all involved. A mother who is the noncustodial parent may hold a more negative stereotype than the mother with traditional arrangements in child custody. A father who is no longer part of the family must make arrangements to visit the children, coordinating with schedules of the children and the former spouse. A majority of single-parent families are at a disadvantage in society relative to other family groups. Typically, such families are characterized by a high rate of poverty, a high percentage of minority representation, lower education, and a higher rate of mobility. American culture views single-parent families as unconventional and somewhat deviant.

As extended family relationships shift to accommodate the changing nuclear family, issues of blame and alliances can arise, straining formerly comfortable ties. Some newly single individuals return to live with their families of origin as an oasis of emotional and perhaps financial support, while others cut off from their families to protect themselves from real or imagined sanctions.

Even after a seemingly successful adjustment process, attachment issues can reemerge following the announcement of remarriage of the former spouse. This can spark latent ambivalence or a secret reconciliation fantasy, unleashing a whole new wave of feelings and emotions. A potential stepparent raises a myriad of issues, including loyalty, financial complications, and possible child custody disputes. As in the original crisis of divorce, the entire extended family is shaken.

The adjustment from living with a child on a daily basis to being with the child only on weekends and occasional holidays is not easy for parents or children. Greater geographical distances between children and their biological fathers that limits the amount of direct contact may intensify the father's feelings of estrangement, loneliness, and sadness. When fathers do not pay court-ordered child support, visitation becomes difficult, and they further alienate themselves from their families.

The custodial parent faces many increased stressors, including role confusion and blurring of boundaries with the children. Usually out of a sense of loneliness, the custodial parent takes the child or children into confidence, sharing adult thoughts and feelings and creating a peerlike relationship. Children frequently respond to this new communication with a pseudo-maturity, encouraging the parent to continue building more of a friendship than an appropriate parent–child situation. The tendency many single parents have to isolate themselves from peer relationships contributes to their excess focus on their children's behavior, taking to heart everything they say and do. At its extreme, this can result in role reversal, leaving both parent and child angry and bitter, being overwhelmed by the inherent lack of clarity and complexities of the postdivorce situation.

Many couples take an adversarial stance in the legal arena, increasing the emotional tension and resulting in years of animosity and distrust. In these situations children can be used as currency in the power struggle or as weapons with which parents inflict excruciating pain on each other. Even the most well-meaning parents can become motivated by pain and revenge, losing sight of what is in the best interest of their child.

Parents who have not successfully resolved attachment issues toward their former mates frequently involve their children in their struggles. Withholding child support, visitation, chronic conflict in scheduling, and differences in parenting are some of the ways in which parents continue their attachment through their offspring. The cycle may dissipate when parental energies are redirected to new relationships, career, or educational pursuits.

It is common for emotional tension to increase during transition times such as remarriage or developmental milestones of children. Men tend to remarry sooner, choosing younger wives, and women with young children tend to marry sooner than their childless counterparts. Remarried couples are more likely to divorce than first-time partners due to issues related to parenting each others' children. In most first marriages there is some time for the couple to adjust to one another before children enter the union. Remarried couples often bring children into the marriage, clinging to a myth of instant family unity. The confusion involved in merging extended families and ex-extended families can be overwhelming, despite a good marital relationship. The developmental stage of the families and the cultural backgrounds and practices are issues that are relevant but rarely discussed by the couple, often leading to open conflict following remarriage. Stepfamily integration requires a minimum of two years to establish a workable new structure that will enable the individuals to progress emotionally.

Conclusion

As individuals integrate all of the changes that have occurred throughout the divorce process, there is potential for immeasurable self-growth and discovery. Letting go of attachments, expectations, and fantasies toward one's ex-spouse allows room for new direction in one's own life. Reinvesting energy in one's self by exploring interests, expanding personal horizons, and planning for the future can begin to replace feelings of anger and resentment.

(*See also:* ALIMONY AND SPOUSAL SUPPORT; CHILD CUSTODY; CHILD SUPPORT; DIVORCE: LEGAL ASPECTS; DIVORCE: ECONOMIC ASPECTS; DIVORCE: EFFECTS ON CHILDREN; MARITAL PROPERTY AND COMMUNITY PROPERTY; REMARRIAGE; STEPPARENTING)

BIBLIOGRAPHY

Belli, M., and Krantzler, M. (1988). *Divorcing.* New York: St. Martin's Press.

Broder, M. (1988). *The Art of Living Single.* New York: Avon Books.

Bruce, M. L. (1992). "Differences in the Effects of Divorce on Major Depression in Men and Women." *American Journal of Psychiatry* 149:914–917.

Dreyfus, E. A. (1979). "Counseling the Divorced Father." *Journal of Marital and Family Therapy* 5:77–86.

Everett, C., and Volgy, S. (1991). "Treating Divorce in Family-Therapy Practice." In *Handbook of Family Therapy*, Vol. II, ed. A. Gurman and D. Kniskern. New York: Brunner/Mazel.

Glenwic, N., and Mowerey, J. (1968). "When Parent Becomes Peer." *Family Relations* 35:57–62.

Glick, P. C., and Lin, S. L. (1986). "Recent Changes in Divorce and Remarriage." *Journal of Marriage and the Family* 48:433–441.

Goldsmith, J. (1982). "The Postdivorce Family System." In *Normal Family Processes*, ed. F. Walsh. New York: Guilford.

Grief, G. (1986). "Mothers Without Custody and Child Support." *Family Relations* 35:78–93.

Herz, F. (1989). "The Postdivorce Family." In *The Changing Family Life Cycle: A Framework for Family Therapy*, 2nd edition, ed. B. Carter and M. McGoldrick. Boston: Allyn & Bacon.

Isaacs, M. B.; Montalvo, B.; and Abelsohn, D. (1986). *The Difficult Divorce: Therapy for Children and Families*. New York: Basic Books.

Kaslow, F. (1981). "Divorce and Divorce Therapy." In *Handbook of Family Therapy*, Vol. I, ed. A. Gurman and D. Kniskern. New York: Brunner/Mazel.

Krantzler, M. (1974). *Creative Divorce: A New Opportunity for Personal Growth*. New York: Signet Books.

Norton, A., and Glick, P. C. (1986). "One-Parent Families: A Social and Economic Profile." *Family Relations* 35:9–17.

Sabalis, R. F., and Ayers, G. W. (1977). "Emotional Aspects of Divorce and Their Effects on the Legal Process." *Family Coordinator* 26:391–394.

Sager, C. J.; Brown, H. S.; Crohn, H.; Engle, T.; Rodstein, E.; and Walker, L. (1983). *Treating the Remarried Family*. New York: Brunner/Mazel.

Stack, S. (1980). "The Effects of Marital Dissolution on Suicide." *Journal of Marriage and the Family* 42:83–92.

Triere, L., and Peacock, R. (1982). *Learning to Leave*. Don Mills, Ontario, Canada: Beaverbooks.

Tschann, J.; Johnston, J.; and Wallerstein, J. (1989). "Resources, Stressors, and Attachment as Predictors of Adult Adjustment After Divorce." *Journal of Marriage and the Family* 51:1033–1046.

Vaughn, D. (1986). *Uncoupling: Turning Points in Intimate Relationships*. New York. Oxford University Press.

Visher, E., and Visher, J. (1982). "Stepfamilies and Stepparenting." In *Normal Family Processes*, ed. F. Walsh. New York: Guilford.

Wallerstein, J. S., and Blakeslee, S. (1990). *Second Chances: Men, Women, and Children a Decade After Divorce*. New York: Ticknor & Fields.

Walsh, F. (1991). "Promoting Healthy Functioning in Divorced and Remarried Families." In *Handbook of Family Therapy*, Vol. II, ed. A. Gurman and D. Kniskern. New York: Brunner/Mazel.

Walsh, F., and McGoldrick, M. (1991). "Loss and the Family: A Systemic Perspective." In *Living Beyond Loss: Death in the Family*, ed. F. Walsh and M. McGoldrick. New York: W. W. Norton.

PEGGY SUDOL

Effects on Children

Estimates indicate that every year more than 1 million children in the United States experience the divorce of their parents (U.S. Bureau of the Census 1989). Because the home environment provided by both parents is thought to be important for the healthy development of the children, parental divorce has been proposed to place children at risk for short- and long-term problems (Amato and Keith 1991).

Parental Divorce As a Risk Factor

Many professionals concerned about children's healthy development have argued that children who experience a parental divorce will develop less well than children who live continuously with both of their biological parents. There are nine basic reasons why they think this is so.

Parental divorce is a stressor. Children consistently rate parental divorce as one of the most stressful life experiences they encounter (Brown and Cowen 1988). In general, adjustment problems are thought to occur when stressors exceed coping resources. With regard to divorce, adjustment problems happen when the difficulties related to the divorce become too much for the child to handle.

Children who experience parental divorce are likely to be exposed to parent conflict. The link between parent conflict and child behavior problems is one of the most consistent findings in the clinical child psychology literature (Grych and Fincham 1990). Most divorces occur because husbands and wives cannot find ways to solve the problems they face. Children exposed to a lot of parental fighting are thought likely to develop adjustment problems because they have a history of becoming anxious and upset when parents fight and because they have not had parents who show them how to solve problems with other people in constructive ways, such as negotiating and compromising (Grych and Fincham 1990).

Parental divorce involves some degree of loss of the parent who moves out of the house. Because parental divorce involves one parent—typically the father—physically leaving the child's home, the child experiencing a parental divorce is likely not to see this parent as much as in the past. Some fathers even stop seeing their children altogether (Furstenberg and Nord 1985). If the child and the father were close before the divorce, diminished contact after the divorce is likely to cause the child distress because of the separation and because the father is not around to provide comfort, support, and direction. Some scholars think that the loss of time spent with a father is likely to result in the child experiencing some problems in trusting other people and in learning rules of how men in general are supposed to behave (Kalter 1987; Stevenson and Black 1988).

Parental divorce results in money problems. Divorce frequently means that the parent with whom the child lives—usually the mother—has a lot less money to spend (Weiss 1984). For some children, money problems become so bad that in addition to problems associated with the divorce there are problems associated with poverty. These children may not be sure that they will have a roof over their heads, may not have enough food to eat, and may have to live in neighborhoods where crime and violence are prevalent. Often, a mother who has never worked outside of the home must get a job, sometimes even more than one. In many instances, a mother's employment means that the mother herself will not be around to make sure that her child feels cared for and is supervised. Because the divorce has probably resulted in the father not being around very frequently to attend to the child, the increased time the mother has to spend outside of the family in employment means that some children actually experience some loss of contact with *both* parents.

Parental divorce may involve children developing faulty beliefs regarding their role in why the divorce happened. Because some parents mistakenly think that young children cannot understand many divorce-related experiences, they provide no explanations or inappropriate explanations for why the divorce happened (Waldron, Ching, and Fair 1986). Because children actively try to make sense out of what happens to them even in the absence of information geared to their age level, they are likely to develop faulty beliefs regarding their role in the divorce, such as blaming themselves for their parents not being together anymore (Kurdek and Berg 1987). These beliefs, in turn, may provide a basis for problem behaviors.

Parental divorce involves many changes in the settings in which children develop. When parents divorce, children are likely to experience many changes in their usual routines (Stolberg and Anker 1983). These may include moving to a new residence, a new school, and a new neighborhood. These changes may pose problems for children because relatives, friends, teachers, and neighbors that the child used to count on for help will not be there anymore and no one is available to take their places (Wolchik, Sandler, and Braver 1987).

Parental divorce may affect quality of parenting. Because parents are likely to be dealing with their own adjustment to the divorce, they may have little time and energy to be good parents (Hetherington 1993). When they are caught up with their own problems, they may have difficulty meeting their children's nutritional and emotional needs, supervising their children's academic and social activities, helping their children feel good about themselves and in control of their lives, and providing structured home routines and consistent discipline. The longer the parents focus on their own problems, the more likely the child will experience some form and degree of neglect.

Parental divorce may result in children assuming roles and responsibilities that are beyond them. Due to money problems and the limited availability of both parents, some children may be given child-care and household responsibilities that are more appropriate for older children and even adults. Although it is generally good for children to be given some responsibility, too much responsibility is not a good thing (Weiss 1979). If children spend most of their free time doing things around the house or taking care of younger brothers and sisters, they may not be able to learn important social skills that generally come from being with other children of the same age.

Parental divorce may result in negative reactions from others. Although the fairly high frequency of divorce may have reduced some of its stigma, children growing up in a family that includes anyone other than both biological parents may be perceived negatively by others (Bryan et al. 1986). Thus, common behavioral problems experienced by such children may be perceived to be worse than they actually are (Santrock and Tracy 1978).

Meta-Analysis of Divorce Literature

Given these nine reasons why parental divorce places children at risk for adjustment problems, one would think that studies that have compared the well-being of children of divorce with that of children who have always lived with both biological parents would be unanimous in concluding that parental divorce has very large negative effects on children's well-being. Before discussing whether this conclusion is true, however, some comments need to be made about the kind of research done with regard to the effects of divorce on children.

In general, although many studies have compared the well-being of children living continuously with both biological parents to that of children who have experienced parental divorce, the majority of these studies are limited in two ways. First, most of them have used small, white, middle-class, volunteer samples that may not represent the larger group of children affected by parental divorce. Second, many of these studies have not examined whether effects due to parental divorce hold across children of different ages, across boys and girls, and across different types of well-being.

However, scholars have come up with a way of dealing with these problems of single studies by examining patterns of findings taken from *the entire collection* of studies. If someone wants to review findings from all of the studies that have compared the well-being of children who have and who have not experienced parental divorce, they would do a meta-analysis.

In a meta-analysis, existing studies are reviewed to see if they meet certain criteria. For example, studies might be included in a meta-analysis only if they contain (1) a group of children living in single-parent families resulting from separation or divorce, (2) a group of children continuously living with both biological parents, and (3) information on the well-being of children in each of the two groups.

If a given study meets these three criteria, then the person doing the meta-analysis searches the study for information to calculate a number—the effect size—that provides an index of the extent to which the well-being of children of divorce differs from that of children who have lived continuously with both biological parents. The most direct way to derive such an effect size is to subtract the average well-being score for the continuous-parent group from that of the parental-divorce group and divide it by a number that represents the variability of well-being scores in the two combined groups (usually the pooled within-group standard deviation). The effect size resulting from this calculation represents an estimate of the relative well-being of the two groups: An effect size of 0 indicates no difference between the parental-divorce and the continuous-parent groups; a negative effect size indicates a lower level of well-being for children in the parental-divorce group; and a positive effect size indicates a higher level of well-being for children in the parental-divorce group.

One key feature of a meta-analysis is that an overall effect size is derived across *all* available studies, and statistical procedures are used to assess whether the overall effect size is significantly different from 0. (If the absolute value of the effect size is different from 0, then effect sizes of 0.80 or greater are considered large, those around 0.50 moderate, and those around 0.20 small.) Another key characteristic is that one can also use effect sizes to identify factors linked to especially strong effect sizes. For example, one can compare effect sizes obtained for samples of boys with those obtained for samples of girls to see if the gender of the child influences the extent to which children are affected by parental divorce.

A meta-analysis matching this description was conducted by Paul Amato and Bruce Keith (1991), who derived 284 effect sizes from 92 studies involving more than 13,000 children. Two findings from this meta-analysis are of note. The first finding deals with the overall size of the difference in well-being between children in the parental-divorce group and those in the continuous-parent group. The second finding deals with factors that affect the size of the difference in the well-being of children in these two groups. Each set of findings is discussed in turn.

With regard to the overall size of the difference in well-being between children in the parental-divorce group and those in the continuous-parent group, Amato and Keith (1991) reported a mean overall effect size of -0.17. Although this value was statistically different from 0, it is regarded as a small effect size (because it is less than 0.20). In fact, an effect size of -0.17 indicates that the well-being scores of children in the parental-divorce group were less than one-fifth of a standard deviation below those of children in the continuous-parent group.

With regard to factors that affected how large effect sizes were, Amato and Keith (1991) found that the size of differences of well-being between children in the parental-divorce group and those in the continuous-parent group depended on (1) the type of well-being score, (2) who provided information regarding well-being, and (3) the age of the child. There was little evidence that parental divorce affected boys and girls differently.

Concerning the type of well-being score, of the seven such types identified (school achievement, conduct, psychological adjustment, self-concept, social adjustment, mother–child relationships, and father–child relationships), the two largest effect sizes were obtained for father–child relationships (an effect size of -0.26 based on 18 effect sizes) and conduct (an effect size of -0.23 based on 56 effect sizes). Again, however, these effect sizes can be considered to be small, with children in the parental-divorce group having well-being scores that were on average about only one-fourth of a standard deviation below those of children in the continuous-parent group.

Concerning who provided information regarding well-being, of the effect sizes based on information obtained from children, parents, teachers, and researchers, those from parents and teachers tended to be smaller (mean effect size of 0.16) than those from the other sources (mean effect size of about 0.20), suggesting that parents and teachers may underestimate and others, including the children themselves, may overestimate the negative nature of children's well-being.

Concerning the development level of the child, of the seven domains of well-being identified, effect sizes for grade level of the sample varied for psychological adjustment, social adjustment, mother–child relationships, and father–child relationships. Overall, effect sizes were largest for children of primary school and high school age (compared to preschool- and college-age groups), with specific effect sizes ranging from -0.12 to -0.66.

Finally, with regard to gender of the child, of the seven domains of well-being, effect sizes for boys and for girls differed only for one. With regard to social adjustment, the difference between the parental-divorce and the continuous-parent groups was larger for boys than for girls (effect sizes of -0.57 and -0.16, respectively).

In sum, despite the nine somewhat compelling reasons listed earlier that suggest that children of divorce should have lower well-being than those who live continuously with both parents, most studies report that children in these two groups are more similar to each other than they are different. Further, when differences in well-being between these two groups of children are found, they tend to be small and to depend on the dimension of well-being, who provides information regarding well-being, and the age of the child.

Family Process Versus Family Structure

Based partially on the rather low effect sizes associated with comparisons between children who have experienced parental divorce and those who have not, there is a growing movement to focus less on with whom children live (family structure) and to focus more on what kinds of things happen between children and the people with whom they live (family process). Two important reasons for this shift from family structure to family process are that (1) studies that have looked at the same group of children before and after the divorce have found that some of the problems experienced by children after the divorce were present *beforehand* (Cherlin et al. 1991) and (2) children whose well-being seems most at risk are those who have experienced multiple parental divorces (Capaldi and Patterson 1991; Kurdek, Fine, and Sinclair 1994).

The emphasis on family processes is based on the idea that differences in well-being associated with family structure (e.g., living with a divorced single parent versus living with both biological parents) are explained by changes caused by divorce-related events that influence the extent to which the family is a setting for healthy development. For example, parents who are unhappy with and lack commitment to their marriages are likely to negatively influence their children's well-being in the predivorce period because they expose their children to a rather steady diet of unresolved conflict; because their preoccupation with their own concerns limits the time and energy they have to provide age-appropriate levels of warmth and supervision for their children; and because conflict between parents may result in inconsistent discipline.

As a result of the focus on family process, there has been increasing support for the view that processes that occur in families, regardless of the specific family structure (e.g., one parent, two parents, or stepparents), can help or hinder the development of children's well-being (Kurdek and Sinclair 1988; Lamborn et al. 1991). Simply living continuously with both biological parents is no guarantee for healthy development, nor is living with a single divorced parent a guarantee of unhealthy development.

(*See also:* CHILD CUSTODY; CHILD SUPPORT; DIVORCE: LEGAL ASPECTS; DIVORCE: ECONOMIC ASPECTS; DIVORCE: EMOTIONAL AND SOCIAL ASPECTS; GUARDIANSHIP; REMARRIAGE AND CHILDREN; STEPPARENTING)

BIBLIOGRAPHY

Amato, P. R., and Keith, B. (1991). "Parental Divorce and the Well-Being of Children: A Meta-Analysis." *Psychological Bulletin* 110:26–46.

Brown, L. P., and Cowen, E. L. (1988). "Children's Judgments of Event Upsettingness and Personal Experiencing of Stressful Events." *American Journal of Community Psychology* 16:123–135.

Bryan, L. R.; Coleman, M.; Ganong, L. H.; and Bryan, S. H. (1986). "Person Perception: Family Structure as a Cue for Stereotyping." *Journal of Marriage and the Family* 48:169–174.

Capaldi, D. M., and Patterson, G. R. (1991). "Relation of Parental Transitions to Boys' Adjustment Problems." *Developmental Psychology* 27:489–504.

Cherlin, A. J.; Furstenberg, F.; Chase-Landsdale, L.; Kiernan, K.; Robins, P.; Morrison, D. R.; and Teitler, J. (1991). "Longitudinal Studies of Effects of Divorce on Children in Great Britain and the United States." *Science* 252:1386–1389.

Furstenberg, F. F., and Nord, C. W. (1985). "Parenting Apart: Patterns of Child Rearing After Marital Disruption." *Journal of Marriage and the Family* 47:893–904.

Grych, J. H., and Fincham, F. D. (1990). "Marital Conflict and Children's Adjustment: A Cognitive-Contextual Framework." *Psychological Bulletin* 108:267–290.

Hetherington, E. M. (1993). "An Overview of the Virginia Longitudinal Study of Divorce and Remarriage with a Focus on Early Adolescence." *Journal of Family Psychology* 7:39–56.

Kalter, N. (1987). "Long-Term Effects of Divorce on Children: A Developmental Vulnerability Model." *American Journal of Orthopsychiatry* 57:587–600.

Kurdek, L. A., and Berg, B. (1987). "Children's Beliefs About Parental Divorce Scale: Psychometric Characteristics and Concurrent Validity." *Journal of Consulting and Clinical Psychology* 55:712–718.

Kurdek, L. A.; Fine, M. A.; and Sinclair, R. J. (1994). "The Relation Between Parenting Transitions and Adjustment in Young Adolescents: A Multi-Sample Investigation." *Journal of Early Adolescence* 14:412–431.

Kurdek, L. A., and Sinclair, R. J. (1988). "Adjustment of Young Adolescents in Two-Parent Nuclear, Stepfather, and Mother-Custody Families." *Journal of Consulting and Clinical Psychology* 56:91–96.

Lamborn, S. D.; Mounts, N. S.; Steinberg, L.; and Dornbusch, S. (1991). "Patterns of Competence and Adjustment Among Adolescents from Authoritative, Authoritarian, Indulgent, and Neglectful Families." *Child Development* 62:1049–1065.

Santrock, J. W., and Tracy, R. L. (1978). "Effects of Children's Family Structure Status on the Development of Stereotypes by Teachers." *Journal of Educational Psychology* 70:753–757.

Stevenson, M. R., and Black, K. H. (1988). "Parental Absence and Sex-Role Development: A Meta-Analysis." *Child Development* 59:793–814.

Stolberg, A. L., and Anker, J. M. (1983). "Cognitive and Behavioral Changes in Children Resulting from Parental Divorce and Consequent Environmental Changes." *Journal of Divorce* 7:23–41.

U.S. Bureau of the Census. (1989). *Statistical Abstract of the United States*, 109th edition. Washington, DC: U.S. Government Printing Office.

Waldron, J. A.; Ching, J. W. J.; and Fair, P. H. (1986). "A Children's Divorce Clinic: Analysis of 200 Cases in Hawaii." *Journal of Divorce* 9:111–121.

Weiss, R. S. (1979). "Growing Up a Little Faster: The Experience of Growing Up in a Single-Parent Household." *Journal of Social Issues* 35:97–111.

Weiss, R. S. (1984). "The Impact of Marital Dissolution on Income and Consumption in Single-Parent Households." *Journal of Marriage and the Family* 46:115–128.

Wolchik, S. A.; Sandler, I. N.; and Braver, S. L. (1987). "Social Support: Its Assessment and Relation to Children's Adjustment." In *Contemporary Topics in Developmental Psychology*, ed. N. Eisenberg. New York: Wiley.

LAWRENCE A. KURDEK

DOMESTIC VIOLENCE   *See* CHILD ABUSE AND NEGLECT: SOCIOLOGICAL ASPECTS; ELDER ABUSE; FAMILY VIOLENCE; SPOUSE ABUSE AND NEGLECT

DUAL-EARNER FAMILIES

Throughout history, both husbands and wives have been important economic producers. In all preindustrial societies through the eighteenth century, women and men had both "family" and "economic" jobs. In addition to caring for infants and young children, women gathered food, plowed fields, processed roots or grains, sheared sheep, spun wool, made clothes, or processed candles. They turned milk into butter, wool into yarn, and yarn into clothes. Young children also helped their parents with chores. Until modern times, therefore, all families were "dual-earner" families, but most husbands and wives "worked" in or near their households (Cancian 1987; Mintz and Kellogg 1988).

The Contemporary Dual-Earner Family

With the Industrial Revolution, people began to move from family farms to cities, where they could work in factories and offices. This change was something quite unique for family life; people had to leave their households to go to work. Caring for young children and working in the economy at the same time became more difficult. In addition, machinery was so efficient that there were not enough paid jobs for all adults. Therefore, a belief system developed that justified a quite new and radical distinction between men's and women's lives and fostered the principle of separate spheres for men and women. Men were supposed to leave their households to work in paid labor; women were supposed to remain at home to specialize in child care and housewifery. For the first time, women as a group were *supposed* to work only at child care and domestic chores.

Despite this new belief system, only the wives of wealthy men could afford the luxury of specializing in housewifery during the early decades of the industrial era. Poorer women, immigrant women, and most women of color had no choice but to work in the paid labor force. By the end of World War II, however, the majority of married American women remained outside the paid labor force, and men who could not solely support their families were judged harshly. Most married couples had only a single earner (i.e., only one spouse received a paycheck) by the middle of the twentieth century, and this seemed beneficial to corporations and businesses. They could expect male workers to ignore the family needs that the wives were supposed to handle. Single-earner families continued to be the norm for several decades, until as recently as the 1970s.

The norm of single-earner families was destined to be short-lived, however, for many reasons. First, the mid-twentieth century was the only time in history that women were expected to work exclusively at child care. Second, during this same time, the average family size fell to fewer than two children per couple, so many women had young children at home for less than a decade. Third, housing costs began to require two incomes. Finally, many women became more educated and wished to use their professional training.

Since the mid-1970s there has been a phenomenal rise in the number of two-earner families (i.e., families in which both husbands and wives earn money). Married women have returned to the labor force in large numbers. By 1990, fewer than 16 percent of American households fit the definition of a family as an employed husband, a homemaker wife, and dependent children (Thorne 1992). In 1988, more than 50 percent of all women with infants were in the paid labor force (Greenstein 1993).

Dual-Earner Family Research

Researchers are usually interested in understanding the effect of this return of married middle-class women to the labor force on family life and child development. Therefore, most research compares married couples where mothers are employed with those families where mothers work only in the home.

The earliest studies of dual-earner families were really studies of dual-career families. The difference is that any family in which both spouses earn a paycheck is a dual-earner family, but a dual-career family is one in which both the husband and the wife hold professional or managerial jobs. Studies of dual-career families were popular in the 1970s, when middle-class women were only beginning to reenter the work force. These studies are less useful now that so many women with all different kinds of jobs are in the labor force.

Much of the past research on dual-earner families has several shortcomings. Most studies simply categorize mothers as employed or not employed (e.g., Barnett and Baruch 1987; Paulson, Koman, and Hill 1990; Pleck and Staines 1985), while other studies categorize mothers as employed full-time, part-time, or not at all. In addition, most studies simply assume that fathers work full-time and do not measure their hours of employment or their work schedules at all. However, it is very likely that the combination of total hours during which husbands and wives are employed and their work schedules affect their children and their marriage (Crouter et al. 1987). After all, a family with a male physician employed full-time and a wife who works in his office a few hours a week when

their children are in school has a considerably different family life than one in which both spouses are flight attendants. Yet both families would, unfortunately, be similarly categorized as dual earners in much of this research.

Another problem is that much of this research ignores any effects of the father's employment on the family. This omission is particularly serious because there are indications that fathers exert important influences on the social and cognitive functioning of their children (Radin and Russell 1983). In addition, the concentration of studies on the possibly negative outcomes for children as a consequence of maternal employment supports the modern cultural ideology of motherhood (but not fatherhood) as a full-time occupation (Silverstein 1991). This ideology ignores, of course, the historical reality that until the twentieth century mothers had always done economic work while they raised their children.

Historically, minority families have been more likely to be poor and thus include wives who work for pay out of necessity. For example, among African-American married couples, wives are more likely to be in the paid labor force than wives in any other group, and they are more likely to work full-time year-round (McAdoo 1988). African-American women also are more likely than white women to remain continuously employed throughout their lives (Belgrave 1988). Ironically, most of the literature about dual-earner families is based on studies using samples of predominantly middle-class white American families (Spitze 1988). Few studies have offered comparisons between dual-earner families on the basis of race or ethnicity. Consequently, relatively little is known about dual-earner families of ethnic or racial groups other than white Americans. The findings that follow, therefore, must be considered preliminary rather than definitive. Despite the problems with past research, there is still much useful information available.

Effects on Marriage

Much research describes how marriage is different when wives are employed than when they focus exclusively on family work. The literature on dual-earner families and marriage can be discussed in terms of attitudes toward women's equality, division of household labor, and marital satisfaction. It is often hard to know, however, whether couples who differ on these points are more likely to choose for the wife to be employed on the basis of their attitudes or whether wives' employment changes attitudes and behaviors.

Attitudes toward women's equality. There does not seem to be a very strong relationship between wives' employment and attitudes toward women's equality. Most research (Komarovsky 1987; Rubin 1977) finds that the gender beliefs of working-class husbands and wives remain traditional despite the fact that a majority of wives are in the labor force. That is, husbands and wives usually work for the same reasons—for money; an employed wife does not necessarily indicate that she is a proponent of egalitarianism between the sexes. African-American couples do tend to support such egalitarian norms in terms of employment more than do their white counterparts, perhaps because wives have a long history of labor force participation in the African-American community (Staples and Mirande 1980; Willie 1981). Dual-career couples also are likely to support women's equality because career-oriented people tend to be college-educated and education is strongly related to egalitarian beliefs.

Research also suggests, however, that whatever their beliefs about equality, women with their own paychecks have more power in their marriages (Blumstein and Schwartz 1983; Scanzoni and Scanzoni 1988). Therefore, while employment may not directly change attitudes about egalitarianism between the sexes, it does seem to help women gain more equality in their own marriages.

Division of household labor. Perhaps the most consistent finding in the research about dual-earner families is that even when the wife works as many hours as her husband, she continues to do most of the household and child care (Berardo, Shehan, and Leslie 1987; Pleck 1983). This can best be understood by thinking of the wife as simply keeping her old job as housewife and taking on a second job as a paid worker. This is partially explained by the male belief that sharing the family work would not be "masculine"—that is, to do dishes or diaper babies might make them effeminate (West and Zimmerman 1987). Some wives also feel that successfully running a home by themselves is an essential part of being a woman, even if it must be done before and after a paid job. Another part of the explanation is that even when women want to share the work with their spouses, they do not have enough power in their marriages to insist that their husbands act accordingly. Some research (e.g., Ferree 1990) suggests that only when wives earn as much as or more than their husbands do they gain enough leverage to insist on sharing the household chores.

There is contradictory evidence as to whether the more egalitarian attitudes of African-American cou-

ples toward employment translate into a more equitable division of household labor. In an early review of studies that examined the effects of race on sharing of household responsibilities, Joseph Pleck (1983) reported two studies that suggest that African-American husbands did more household work than white husbands and two studies in which they did less. Similar inconsistencies appear with respect to racial differences in responsibility for child care. Elizabeth Maret and Barbara Finlay (1984) found that African-American women had less sole responsibility for family work than did white women. As some research (Cherlin 1992; Stack 1974) suggests, however, family members other than husbands, such as grandparents, may be the ones who share this family work.

There is much less research on social class variations among dual earners. In an early, important study of working-class couples, Lillian Rubin (1977) described marriages in which husbands were largely traditional in their beliefs and behavior. Later research provides some indication that, despite traditional values, many working-class men may actually participate in more housework duties than do middle-class and upper-class husbands (Komarovsky 1987; Presser 1988). Peter Stein (1984) suggests that husbands of working-class and lower-income families may be more likely to participate in household tasks out of necessity, as they lack the financial resources to hire household help. Myra Marx Ferree (1984) argues that when working-class wives need assistance with household tasks, they may be more likely to get it because their employment is an undeniable economic necessity. In addition, as many as one-third of all young married dual-earner parents engage in shift work (Presser 1988). This usually means that one parent works nights and the other works days. In these families, parents may "split the shift" of child care, often saving on child-care expenses. Therefore, such families share child care, if not housework, more equally.

Dual-earner couples in the upper-middle and upper social classes have been examined in depth by Rosanna Hertz (1986) and Lisa Silberstein (1992), who conducted intensive interviews with married dual-career couples. In both of these studies, such couples were employed in professional (e.g., physician, attorney, scientist) or corporate managerial positions. Although these couples believe in sexual equality, only one-third of them shared the household labor equally (Silberstein 1992). Family responsibilities remained primarily with the wives in many cases (Hertz 1986), although most wives hired housekeepers and child-care providers to do the bulk of the work involved.

These findings show that dual-career couples rely on working-class women to provide the services for hire that neither the husband nor the wife has the time to provide personally.

This evidence suggests that while working-class men probably do more housework than middle-class professional men or husbands in dual-career families, none of them does very much. This leads to the final and perhaps most important conclusion concerning the division of household labor: When paid work and family work are both considered, wives work a full extra month a year more than their husbands. Arlie Hochschild and Anne Machung (1989) have labeled wives' extra family work their "second shift" after a full day on the job. They suggest that this extra work has created an ever-growing emotional tension between husbands and wives, perhaps decreasing the quality and stability of American marriages.

Marital satisfaction. A number of factors associated with employment have been thought to affect marriage negatively. For example, the increase in stress from work has been thought to "spill over" into the marriage. However, it appears that trying to meet the demands of *both* paid work and family work produces a negative effect on marriage quality. Wives whose husbands share this "second shift" with them are happier in their marriages than those who do the extra work alone. Husbands with egalitarian beliefs about gender share this work without decreasing their marital satisfaction. Husbands preferring a traditional breadwinner–homemaker arrangement tend to be less satisfied with their marriages if their wives work, particularly if they see it as a reflection of their own failure to provide adequately for their families (Kessler and McRae 1982; Perry-Jenkins and Crouter 1990; Rosin 1990). However, marital satisfaction is affected by a wide variety of factors in addition to the employment status of wives.

Effects on Children

Intense debate has taken place about the effect of nonparental care on the development of children under two years of age. One type of research focuses on the attachment between mothers and infants and is often based on an investigative technique called the "strange situation procedure" (Ainsworth et al. 1978). In this experiment, mothers leave their infants for a brief time and then return. Despite some contradictory findings, most research reveals no significant differences between the reactions of the infants who have employed mothers and the ones who have stay-at-home mothers (Hoffman 1989).

Another way that researchers have approached the issue of nonparental care is to compare the development of children who spent their infancy and toddler years at home with their parents (usually mothers) to those who were in supplemental care—that is, in day-care centers or with baby-sitters (e.g., Belsky 1988; Clarke-Stewart 1988; Baydar and Brooks-Gunn 1991).

There are indeed quite mixed findings concerning the effects of having an employed mother on a child's academic competence. Some studies indicate that there may be certain negative effects on school performance and/or cognitive development for boys with employed mothers (Baydar and Brooks-Gunn 1991; Hoffman 1979). However, positive effects of maternal employment on cognitive achievement have been reported by others (Clarke-Stewart 1989). Among blue-collar and lower-income families, for instance, maternal employment appears to increase rather than decrease school competence (Hoffman 1979; Vandell and Ramanan 1992).

Children with two employed parents hold less gender-stereotyped views than those with homemaker mothers (Hoffman 1989; Weinraub, Jaeger, and Hoffman 1988). Daughters, in particular, appear to benefit from having employed mothers in that they tend to exhibit higher levels of self-esteem and self-confidence than do girls whose mothers remain outside the labor force (Hoffman 1989; Weinraub, Jaeger, and Hoffman 1988).

Jay Belsky (1988) suggests that full-time employment of mothers during their children's infancy poses significant risks to their children's social development. He finds that, among elementary school children, boys who attended day-care centers full-time during their first year of life were significantly more troubled than their peers. Susan Crockenberg and Cindy Litman (1991) and Ellen Greenberger and Robin O'Neill (1992) also suggest that children with employed mothers may show increased aggression and noncompliance. However, K. Alison Clarke-Stewart (1989) and Deborah Phillips and her colleagues (1987) report no such risks. Louise Silverstein (1991) suggests that what some researchers might call "noncompliance" may be better defined as the early development of independence. In an analysis of a large sample of four- and five-year-olds, Theodore Greenstein (1993) reports that "early and extensive maternal employment does not seem to have generally adverse effects" (p. 349). Therefore, these data seem to suggest that there may be both positive and negative outcomes of full-time parental care or supplemental care. What seems to matter most is the *quality* of the child care.

Studies have generally been concerned with the effects of maternal employment on preschool-age or school-age children and have focused relatively little attention on adolescents. However, some studies have examined, for example, the effects of mothers' employment on adolescents' self-reports of stress and psychological adjustment. The majority of studies report no association between mothers' employment status and adolescents' psychological well-being (Bird and Kemerait 1990; Galambos and Maggs 1990; Orthner 1990) or academic adjustment (Armistead, Wierson, and Forehand 1990; Gottfried, Gottfried, and Bathurst 1988).

Conclusion

The industrial economy originally developed with the presumption that successful workers would be men with homemaker wives and that these men would have no responsibility for running their households, raising their children, or caring for elders. Despite this ideal, many working-class women struggled to be both family caretakers and workers. Not until the middle of the twentieth century were middle-class women in a position to specialize entirely in family work and remain outside the labor force.

However, the whole notion of separate spheres for men and women is becoming something for historians rather than sociologists to study. Most men and women will spend the majority of their lifetimes in paid work. Research suggests that during this transition in family life, the dual-earner family has both advantages and disadvangages. Among the advantages of the dual-earner family are the opportunity for wives to be economically independent. The primary problem dual-earner families face, a "time crunch" that affects the quality of family life, affects wives in particular because of the inequitable distribution of family responsibilities between most husbands and their wives.

To help increase the overall quality of family life, a better understanding of how to reshape the postindustrial economy to make it more supportive of contemporary families is needed. Businesses must begin to realize that many workers, men and women, have family responsibilities that go beyond merely bringing home a paycheck. It is to everyone's advantage for today's employees to raise happy, healthy, and socially productive children; to do so takes time, sometimes even time away from the job. The potential emotional estrangement of husbands and wives in dual-earner marriages will also remain a hazard until the division of household labor is more equitable.

More information is needed to help identify those conditions that promote a fair division of family work. The future of dual-earner families—and that means most families headed by married couples—depends on more successful and equitable integration of paid labor and family work for both men and women.

(*See also:* CHILD CARE; CHILDHOOD; DIVISION OF LABOR; FAMILY GENDER ROLES; HISTORY OF THE FAMILY; MARITAL QUALITY; SUBSTITUTE CAREGIVERS; WORK AND FAMILY)

BIBLIOGRAPHY

Ainsworth, M. D. S.; Blehar, M. C.; Waters, E.; and Wall, S. (1978). *Patterns of Attachment: Observations in the Strange Situation and at Home.* Hillsdale, NJ: Lawrence Erlbaum.

Armistead, L.; Wierson, M.; and Forehand, R. (1990). "Adolescents and Maternal Employment: Is It Harmful for a Young Adolescent to Have an Employed Mother?" *Journal of Early Adolescence* 10:260–278.

Barnett, R. C., and Baruch, G. K. (1987). "Determinants of Fathers' Participation in Family Work." *Journal of Marriage and the Family* 49:29–40.

Baydar, N., and Brooks-Gunn, J. (1991). "Effects of Maternal Employment and Child-Care Arrangements on Preschoolers' Cognitive and Behavioral Outcomes: Evidence from the Children of the National Longitudinal Survey of Youth." *Developmental Psychology* 27:932–945.

Belgrave, L. L. (1978). "The Effects of Race Differences in Work History, Work Attitudes, Economic Resources, and Health on Women's Retirement." *Research on Aging* 10:383–398.

Belsky, J. (1988). "The Effects of Infant Day Care Reconsidered." *Early Childhood Research Quarterly* 3:235–272.

Berardo, D. H.; Shehan, C. L.; and Leslie, G. (1987). "A Residue of Tradition: Jobs, Careers, and Spouses' Time in Housework." *Journal of Marriage and the Family* 49:381–390.

Bird, G. W., and Kemerait, L. N. (1990). "Stress Among Early Adolescents in Two-Earner Families." *Journal of Early Adolescence* 10:344–365.

Blumstein, P., and Schwartz, P. (1983). *American Couples: Money, Work, Sex.* New York: Pocket Books.

Cancian, F. (1987). *Love in America: Gender and Self-Development.* New York: Cambridge University Press.

Cherlin, A. (1992). "Race and Poverty." In *Marriage, Divorce, Remarriage,* ed. A. Cherlin. Cambridge, MA: Harvard University Press.

Clarke-Stewart, K. A. (1988). " 'The "Effects" of Infant Day Care Reconsidered' Reconsidered: Risks for Parents, Children, and Researchers." *Early Childhood Research Quarterly* 3:293–318.

Clarke-Stewart, K. A. (1989). "Infant Day Care: Maligned or Malignant?" *American Psychologist* 44:266–273.

Crockenberg, S. B., and Litman, C. (1991). "Effects of Maternal Employment on Maternal and Two-Year-Old Behavior." *Child Development* 62:930–953.

Crouter, A. C.; Perry-Jenkins, M.; Huston, T. L.; and McHale, S. M. (1987). "Processes Underlying Father Involvement in Dual-Earner and Single-Earner Families." *Developmental Psychology* 23:431–440.

Ferree, M. M. (1984). "The View from Below: Women's Employment and Gender Equality in Working Class Families." *Marriage and Family Review* 7:57–75.

Ferree, M. M. (1990). "Beyond Separate Spheres: Feminism and Family Research." *Journal of Marriage and the Family* 52:866–884.

Galambos, N. L., and Maggs, J. L. (1990). "Putting Mothers' Work-Related Stress in Perspective: Mothers and Adolescents in Dual-Earner Families." *Journal of Early Adolescence* 10:313–328.

Gottfried, A. E.; Gottfried, A. W.; and Bathurst, K. (1988). "Maternal Employment, Family Environment, and Children's Development: Infancy Through the School Years." In *Maternal Employment and Children's Development: Longitudinal Research*, ed. A. E. Gottfried and A. W. Gottfried. New York: Plenum.

Greenberger, E., and O'Neill, R. (1992). "Maternal Employment and Perceptions of Young Children: Bronfenbrenner et al. Revisited." *Child Development* 63:431–448.

Greenstein, T. N. (1993). "Maternal Employment and Child Behavior Outcomes: A Household Economics Analysis." *Journal of Family Issues* 14:323–354.

Hertz, R. (1986). *More Equal Than Others: Women and Men in Dual-Career Marriages.* Berkeley: University of California Press.

Hochschild, A., and Machung, A. (1989). *The Second Shift.* New York: Penguin Books.

Hoffman, L. W. (1979). "Maternal Employment: 1979." *American Psychologist* 34:859–865.

Hoffman, L. W. (1989). "Effects of Maternal Employment in the Two-Parent Family." *American Psychologist* 44:283–292.

Kessler, R. C., and McRae, J. A., Jr. (1982). "The Effect of Wives' Employment on the Mental Health of Married Men and Women." *American Psychological Review* 47:216–227.

Komarovsky, M. (1987). *Blue-Collar Marriage*, 2nd edition. New Haven, CT: Yale University Press.

Maret, E., and Finlay, B. (1984). "The Distribution of Household Labor Among Women in Dual-Earner Families." *Journal of Marriage and the Family* 46:357–364.

McAdoo, H. P. (1988). *Black Families.* Newbury Park, CA: Sage Publications.

Mintz, S., and Kellogg, S. (1988). *Domestic Revolutions: A Social History of American Family Life.* New York: Free Press.

Orthner, D. K. (1990). "Parental Work and Early Adolescence: Issues for Research and Practice." *Journal of Early Adolescence* 10:246–259.

Paulson, S. E.; Koman, J. J., III; and Hill, J. P. (1990). "Maternal Employment and Parent–Child Relations in Families of Seventh Graders." *Journal of Early Adolescence* 10:279–295.

Perry-Jenkins, M. A., and Crouter, A. C. (1990). "Men's Provider-Role Attitudes: Implications for Household Work and Marital Satisfaction." *Journal of Family Issues* 11:136–156.

Phillips, D.; McCartney, K.; Scarr, S.; and Howes, C. (1987). "Selective Review of Infant Day Care Research: A Cause for Concern." *Zero to Three* 7:18–21.

Pleck, J. H. (1983). "Husbands' Paid Work and Family Roles: Current Research Issues." In *Research in the Interweave of Social Roles:* Vol. 3, *Families and Jobs*, ed. H. Z. Lopata and J. H. Pleck. Greenwich, CT: JAI Press.

Pleck, J. H., and Staines, G. L. (1985). "Work Schedules and Family Life in Two-Earner Couples." *Journal of Family Issues* 6:61–82.

Presser, H. B. (1988). "Shift Work and Child Care Among Young Dual-Earner Parents." *Journal of Marriage and the Family* 50:133–148.

Radin, N., and Russell, G. (1983). "Increased Father Participation and Child Development Outcomes." In *Fatherhood and Family Policy*, ed. M. E. Lamb and A. Sagi. Hillsdale, NJ: Lawrence Erlbaum.

Rosin, H. M. (1990). "The Effects of Dual-Career Participation on Men: Some Determinants of Variation in Career and Personal Satisfaction." *Human Relations* 43:169–182.

Rubin, L. (1977). *Worlds of Pain: Life in the Working-Class Family.* New York: Basic Books.

Scanzoni, L. D., and Scanzoni, J. (1988). *Men, Women, and Change.* New York: McGraw-Hill.

Silberstein, L. R. (1992). *Dual-Career Marriage: A System in Transition.* Hillsdale, NJ: Lawrence Erlbaum.

Silverstein, L. B. (1991). "Transforming the Debate About Child Care and Maternal Employment." *American Psychologist* 46:1025–1032.

Spitze, G. (1988). "Women's Employment and Family Relations: A Review." *Journal of Marriage and the Family* 50:595–618.

Stack, C. B. (1974). *All Our Kin: Strategies for Survival in a Black Community.* New York: Harper & Row.

Staples, R., and Mirande, A. (1980). "Racial and Cultural Variations Among American Families." *Journal of Marriage and the Family* 42:887–903.

Stein, P. J. (1984). "Men in Families." *Marriage and Family Review* 7:143–162.

Thorne, B. (1992). *Rethinking the Family: Some Feminist Questions.* Boston: Northeastern University Press.

Vandell, D. L., and Ramanan, J. (1992). "Effects of Early and Recent Maternal Employment on Children from Low-Income Families." *Child Development* 63:938–949.

Weinraub, M.; Jaeger, E.; and Hoffman, L. (1988). "Predicting Infant Outcome in Families of Employed and Nonemployed Mothers." *Early Childhood Research Quarterly* 3:361–378.

West, C., and Zimmerman, D. H. (1987). "Doing Gender." *Gender and Society* 1:125–151.

Willie, C. V. (1981). *A New Look at Black Families*, 2nd edition. New York: General Hall.

DANETTE JOHNSON SUMERFORD

BARBARA J. RISMAN

DYSFUNCTIONAL FAMILY

The family structure is constantly under pressure from economic and sociological changes. Divorce, remarriage, and both parents working outside the home are some of the challenges that families face. Families do not become dysfunctional from these situations but from how they operate to address these and other challenges.

Prior to the 1980s, family therapists used the terms "troubled family" or "multiproblem family" to describe the connection between problems of an individual and family functioning. The term "dysfunctional family" emerged through the self-help movement of Alcoholics Anonymous (AA); many adults from alcoholic families discovered that they had significant problems as adults even though they were not addicted to alcohol or drugs. The realization that their family life did not prepare them for adulthood led to the formation of the Adult Children of Alcoholics (ACOA) movement. The term dysfunctional family was used to describe the source of their difficulties. Janet Woititz (1983) is generally credited with being the first to write about dysfunctional families. Since then, the term has been applied in psychiatry, family therapy, and the popular press. Sometimes the application has been inappropriate.

For the purpose of this entry, a family is defined as any group of people where adults are responsible for raising the children in the group with the goal of creating independent and productive adults. Generally, a dysfunctional family is not child-centered. A family that is child-centered nurtures the emotional needs of children, helps them develop a sense of self-worth, self-reliance, and self-esteem, and provides appropriate limits on their behavior. When a family fails to do this, the children are more prone to difficulty in later adult relationships, are more susceptible to emotional problems, and are less likely to raise their own children effectively.

Families fail when there is dysfunction in the hierarchy, rules, and communication of the family over an extended period of time. Most families have difficulties in one or all of these areas at various times without becoming a dysfunctional family. These families are flexible and adaptive; they adjust to the developmental needs of each member. Dysfunctional families have limited problem-solving skills and use old solutions for new problems. They may also deny that problems exist.

The hierarchy of a family refers to who is in charge and who organizes, plans, and sets the rules. In a dysfunctional family, either there is confusion over who is in charge or the parents have relinquished responsibility to the children, leaving the children to raise themselves as best they can. Typically, an older child parents the younger siblings or may serve as counsel to a parent. The children may take care of the parents or be overinvolved in the marital relationship, sacrificing their development for the needs of the parent. In the process, important developmental tasks are missed or delayed, which may lead to difficulty in adult life.

The rules of the family determine how the family operates, and in a dysfunctional family, there is either extreme rigidity or chaos. Planning is determined by one person without involvement from others or the family follows prescribed rules that do not change. In either case, the rules are often covert and not open for discussion. Families that operate in chaos, on the other hand, have no organization or planning and usually move from one crisis to another. Personal boundaries are unclear and often violated.

Communication in a dysfunctional family is not clear and leads to confusion and guessing. There is inconsistency between what is stated and what is implied, leading to double messages, confused behavior, shame, and blame. Denial of problems and feelings can cause children to doubt their worth because they cannot discuss and understand their experiences.

Dysfunctional family rules and poor communication serve to maintain secrets that can be harmful. Family members may not acknowledge serious problems such as sexual abuse, alcoholism, and emotional damage.

These dysfunctional interactions are generational and arise from chronic problems such as addiction and mental or physical illness. They are behaviors parents usually learned as children in dysfunctional families and continue to practice because either they know no other way to behave or they are loyal to family traditions. Low self-esteem and self-worth or emotional problems may also prevent them from functioning as adequate parents. Loyalty, shame, denial, and the need to keep secrets prevent families from effectively using help from outside the family.

Many alcoholics and drug abusers cannot function effectively in a family situation because of their addiction. Lack of awareness about their drug-induced behavior and their attention to addiction behaviors prevent them from attending to the needs of others. The results of their addiction, such as job loss and mental and physical deterioration, also prevent them from functioning well as parents. The presence of a family history of addiction may indicate a generational foundation of learned dysfunctional behavior. Parents who have chronic mental or physical illness may not be able to attend to the needs of their children for some of the same reasons.

Families that consistently repress feelings, deny problems, do not seek help outside of the family, and have children acting the roles of responsible adults are in danger of becoming dysfunctional, if they are not dysfunctional already.

(*See also:* CODEPENDENCY; COMMUNICATION; FAMILY THERAPY; SELF-ESTEEM; SELF-HELP GROUPS; SUBSTANCE ABUSE)

BIBLIOGRAPHY

Bowen, M. (1978). "The Differentiation of Self from One's Own Family." In *Family Therapy in Clinical Practice*, ed. M. Bowen. New York: Jason Aronson.

Bradshaw, J. E. (1987). *Bradshaw on the Family: A Revolutionary Way of Self-Discovery.* Deerfield Beach, FL: Health Communications.

Carter, E. A., and McGoldrick, M. (1980). *The Family Life Cycle: A Framework for Family Therapy.* New York: Gardner Press.

Forward, S. (1989). *Toxic Parents.* New York: Bantam.

Kaminer, W. (1993). *I'm Dysfunctional, You're Dysfunctional.* New York: Vintage.

LaMar, D. F. (1992). *Transcending Turmoil: Survivors of Dysfunctional Families.* New York: Plenum.

Minuchin, S. (1974). *Families and Family Therapy.* Cambridge, MA: Harvard University Press.

Satir, V. (1967). *Conjoint Family Therapy*, revised edition. Palo Alto, CA: Science and Behavior Books.

Woititz, J. G. (1983). *Adult Children of Alcoholics.* Deerfield Beach, FL: Health Communications.

Woititz, J. G. (1992). *Healthy Parenting.* New York: Simon & Schuster.

DAVID ZEMKE

EATING DISORDERS

Eating disorders have become a major public health problem in the United States, directly and indirectly affecting the lives of many young people.

In anorexia nervosa, people refuse to maintain a minimally normal body weight, engage in a relentless pursuit of thinness, have a distorted body image, and suffer physical side effects such as amenorrhea (loss of the menstrual cycle), decreased interest in sexuality, impaired bone density and hormonal functioning, and cardiac abnormalities secondary to hypometabolism and muscle wasting.

People with bulimia nervosa may not lose weight or be at a dangerous weight, but they engage in overeating (binging) and purging (via laxatives, diuretics, vomiting, and excessive exercise). Like people with anorexia, they are preoccupied by their weight and base their self-esteem and identity on it. Bulimia also results in serious medical side effects, including cardiac abnormalities, gastrointestinal problems, liver and kidney damage, and erosion of dental enamel.

Both anorexia and bulimia are starvation states. Many people exhibit a combination of anorectic and bulimic behaviors, while a substantial number may also demonstrate some but not all of the symptoms and may be diagnosed as having an atypical eating disorder.

Binge-eating disorder, which has also been proposed as a psychiatric diagnosis, is characterized by consuming excessive amounts of food accompanied by a lack of control and marked distress, with a minimum frequency of twice a week for six months.

Who Develops Eating Disorders

Women are more likely to develop eating disorders than men. In fact, 90 to 95 percent of cases occur in females. Conversative estimates suggest that between 1 percent and 4 percent of high school and college-age women suffer from anorexia or bulimia (APA 1994). The number of females in this age group who may episodically engage in these symptoms to maintain an artificially low body weight and are chronically malnourished is unknown but substantial, perhaps as high as 20 percent. Although women are more likely to develop these problems, men are certainly affected when their mothers, sisters, girlfriends, and peers have these symptoms. Thus, it is important for men to understand how and why eating disorders develop.

In the past, eating disorders in the United States were most likely to occur in white, upper-middle-class female adolescents. However, incidence patterns are changing. Eating disorders are now found in any race, ethnicity, social class, culture, age, and sex. Children as young as eight years old can develop eating disorders and increasing cases are appearing in adults. More males are also developing eating disorders, although due to the tendency to see these disorders as a woman's problem, the men may not be promptly diagnosed.

Many women who develop eating disorders have been abused sexually or physically. In fact, some studies indicate that well over half of adult women with eating disorders have been victimized in this way (Wooley 1993). An eating disorder may be a way to deal with the anger, guilt, rage, depression, and other powerful emotions evoked by trauma. It may also be a way to set boundaries and to deal with sexuality by trying to become more or less attractive, with the misguided notion that this will protect them from future trauma. Effective treatment must address the issues related to trauma and empower the individuals to deal more directly with their feelings. If the abuse involved family members, its impact may be particularly harmful and the individual will need much support to address these issues.

The countries reporting the most significant number of eating disorders are the advanced technological nations, such as the United States, Canada, the United Kingdom, other Western European countries, and Japan. However, some women from Third World countries and Eastern Europe have also developed eating disorders. These women usually have been influenced by Western culture.

Males or females participating in sports or other pursuits that emphasize low body weight are at special risk for developing eating disorders. Participation in activities such as ballet, cheerleading, gymnastics, track, and wrestling often pressures young people to keep their weight below their set point (a genetically predetermined weight range), thereby placing participants at additional risk to engage in the symptoms of eating disorders. When people restrict their dietary intake excessively, the risk of binge eating is high. Purging symptoms relieve the guilt about eating and give a maladaptive and temporary sense of control. The demands that sports place on the body actually increase nutritional needs, so the pathogenic weight-control measures of anorectic and bulimic symptoms are especially dangerous. Since those most at risk for eating disorders are adolescents, who are undergoing important physical processes such as growth and organ and bone maturation, the potential health consequences are severe.

How Culture Contributes

The causes of eating disorders are complicated; no single factor leads to these illnesses. Instead, the disorders result from complex interactions among numerous forces. One such factor is the barrage of social and cultural messages young people receive about body image, appearance, and the importance of weight. These exert more pressure on women than men because advertising and the media target the female market, seducing them to buy diet books, products, or programs. Estimates indicate that Americans spend more than $50 billion on diet products. Most of this money is spent by women, who are taught from early on to please others by being cute, pretty, coy, or neat, and to put others' desires before their own. The bombardment of media and advertising messages to change their bodies or to win affection through their appearance, thus, hits females much harder than it does males.

The ideal body being promoted, also, is an unrealistic one, as it is significantly taller and thinner than the average healthy woman. The difference between the real and the ideal is increasing. In the 1970s, the average fashion model weighed 8 percent less than the average American woman. In the 1990s, the difference rose to 23 percent. As girls grow up, they unfortunately are sold on an ideal that few can realistically reach. However, this does not keep women from trying, and many of them will inadvertently develop eating disorders.

Another risk factor making girls more vulnerable to eating disorders is the confusion about the role women should have in society. Since the advances made by the feminist movement in the last quarter of the twentieth century, many opportunities have become available to women. This has transformed the female role by adding new responsibilities and pressures; women are now expected to perform and succeed in their roles both at home and in the workplace, while looking beautiful and thin at all times. As women have expanded their role in the world outside of the home, a world long dominated by men, they are not necessarily confident nor do they feel welcomed or supported. In fact, a backlash against women's power has resulted in increased emphasis on the female employee's appearance, and a particular standard of appearance may be required, whether stated (e.g., by television or the airline industries) or unstated (in many other vocations). Therefore, women battle their natural bodies and their weight to please others and to succeed in the workplace. Many of them develop eating disorders as a result.

In addition to the impact of role changes and pressures, women's relationships to their bodies and to food also create a risk for eating disorders. Women are closer to food both socially and biologically than are men. In all cultures studied by anthropologists, women are the feeders of their family or social group. They have traditionally organized their lives around feeding others and have done so for as long as is known. Women also can nurture a fetus and feed an infant; the female body functions to nurture others. The combination of biological capacity and long-term social role makes the experience of food a complex, very intimate one for women. As they experience more pressure to be thin and to diet, women may become more conflicted about food and may engage in starving themselves. The overly restricted nutritional intake involved in severe dieting may lead to anorexia and dramatic weight loss. It may also, however, contribute to the binging behaviors of bulimia (followed by purging) or to compulsive overeating. Sociocultural forces, thus, are major contributors to eating disorders.

The Family's Role

The family also contributes to eating disorders. Although often more than one family member develops these problems, the family's contribution is much more social and environmental than genetic. Also, eating disorders, though not physically communicable diseases, are certainly socially spread. For example, when a parent obsesses about food, weight, and body shape and overemphasizes the importance of these to self-acceptance or self-esteem, a child easily develops similar attitudes (Maine 1991). Increasing numbers of men and women are dieting and unhappy with their bodies. The messages they impart to their children echo those of advertising and the media by tying appearance to self-worth and by suggesting that extremely thin bodies, devoid of fat, are natural or healthy.

Family, food, and feelings. The children of parents or grandparents who espouse the belief that weight and food intake are critical to self-worth are quite likely to develop eating disorders. What parents do is as important as what they say. If they model excessive dieting or exercise and judge themselves harshly due to their weight or shape, their children will apply these same standards to themselves, no matter what positive messages the parents may also be communicating. When approval is tied to appearance, whether the standard is for oneself or for others, the risk of an eating disorder is high.

Families also set the stage for how children will relate to food, regardless of issues related to weight. For instance, many parents use food to reward or punish, and their children then learn that food is more than a substance of nourishment. For some, eating or not eating will become a way to reward, punish, comfort, or soothe oneself. If families do not help children develop other ways to deal with feelings, food may be the only means of self-expression. Similarly, some parents ignore their young children's cues and feed them according to parental needs, schedules, or beliefs about how much the child should eat. This does not allow the individual to develop awareness of appetite, hunger, or fullness. For some, this denial of their needs early in childhood will result in a lifelong liability.

Since eating is the first interaction between parents and children and so much of early childhood revolves around this activity, it lays the groundwork for how children deal with food and their bodies' needs for the rest of their lives. Parents must help children learn how to self-regulate or how to tune in to their bodies and meet their own needs. When this process does not begin early, children do not develop sufficient self-awareness and may be more at risk to eat according to social or external demands and to be unable to figure out if they are hungry or full. People with eating disorders show consistently poor internal awareness both of body states and of feelings. They have to learn how to listen to their bodies, feed them, and express their feelings and needs. This remedial work is often done in family therapy if the other family members are willing or able to participate.

Individual therapy is also a positive experience for people as they try to learn about early development and about how their family issues contributed to an eating disorder. Group therapy is also very useful, since people with eating disorders have such common experiences but tend to be socially isolated.

Conflict and communication. Often the families of people with eating disorders have had difficulty managing conflicts and communicating directly. Food and weight become the way the eating-disordered individual resolves this, since direct communication seems impossible.

The "anorectic family" typically differs from the "bulimic family" in the way conflicts and communication occur. Usually, the anorectic family is constricted, expressing little emotion; they can be described as in denial about many issues, since the unspoken rules do not allow people to talk freely, particularly about difficult subjects. For the individuals who develop anorexia, there appears to be no other way to express themselves; their bodies will show their pain, their confusion, and their sadness. The bulimic family generally is more open about its problem. However, these families are often chaotic environments and the problems are never explored in a helpful way and are never resolved. Frequently, other family members have difficulties with alcohol or drug use, so expressing oneself indirectly through harmful behaviors can be the norm.

In many cases, the parents have marital issues that they are not addressing directly. Sometimes the individual with the eating disorder has served as the peacemaker, best friend, or confidant to one or both parents. While the eating-disorder symptoms may begin as a way to deal with feelings the individual cannot otherwise express, the eating disorder may eventually become a way to keep the family together. As the individual becomes increasingly ill, parents often pay attention to the individual in a way that is reassuring and comforting; a couple in conflict may rally together to try to help their child, especially if they know how serious the side effects of the illness are.

The challenge of growing up. Families help children to grow up successfully by providing a secure, loving, and understanding environment that cherishes the child but tolerates, without inducing guilt, the steps the child takes to be separate. Parents must welcome and reward the child's uniqueness and differences. Thus, parents need to acknowledge that the child's feelings can be different from their own and that their needs cannot all be met within the family. Often, people with eating disorders had family environments that did not respect or encourage them to grow but instead conveyed that they needed to put themselves subservient to the family's wishes. This sort of environment makes the normal steps of growing up and becoming more independent and more involved with friends; developing one's own opinions, beliefs, and interests; and gradually getting ready to leave the family very difficult. The message in such families is that "we need you and won't be able to function without you."

For some, an eating disorder is the only way to say the words all adolescents need to say: "I'm a separate person and I have control of my life." Being in control of what they eat, what they do to their bodies, and what they weigh may be the only ways they can express their individuality.

Eating disorders may develop in adolescence and early adulthood when the family has not been able to foster healthy separation. As the individual tries to become more independent, guilt, fear, confusion, and sadness become overwhelming. An eating disorder may keep the individual tied to the family, as it gradually impairs health and performance. The symptoms paradoxically are both the way to be separate and in charge of one's own body and to stay connected with the family.

Roles and relationships. Families need to be flexible and to change to meet the unique demands of each member. The typical family has changed; many children are raised in single-parent homes, have experienced divorce, or have both parents working outside the home. Therefore, the roles within the family must adapt to these new demands. For example, when both parents are employed full-time, they should share some of the responsibilities at home. However, most couples grew up in more traditional families, so they do not have a model for this. People suffering from eating disorders often come from homes where responsibilities and roles were not shared. Usually, the mothers felt full responsibility for the families and got little help from their husbands. In these families, female children may wonder how they will be able to have more personal power, more satisfaction in their

roles, and more shared responsibility. Girls who develop eating disorders often report that they did not want to have a life similar to their mothers. Boys with eating disorders often have been overly close to their mothers due to their concerns about their mother's unhappiness and burdens in the family.

The family relationships of men and women who develop eating disorders are quite similar. Usually, the individual who develops the problem has had a special role, often as an auxiliary parent taking care of their parents and their siblings. They have assumed much responsibility for the family and have not been allowed to be children. In most cases, the fathers have been emotionally distant, preoccupied, and unavailable. This intensifies the relationship with the mother for both sexes. Often the child becomes too close to the mother, but sometimes, particularly in the case of girls, the child becomes very open about anger toward and rejection of the mother. Understanding and reworking the relationships with the family are usually important parts of recovery.

Families as problem and solution. While families contribute to eating disorders, they also are affected by them. Many professionals have described the tendency of the family to overprotect, to control, and to intrude on the privacy of the individual with an eating disorder. However, some of this behavior is evoked by concern that their loved one might die. Therapists need to support and direct the concerns of parents and other family members so they promote recovery rather than take over the person's life. Family members may sometimes need their own therapy as they struggle with their anxiety about their loved one or with their guilt for the problems the family has experienced. Individual or family therapy may be useful, as is participation in support groups for family members and friends.

When family members become involved in treatment and openly explore the issues and problems contributing to the eating disorder, it helps the "patient" to feel less guilty and less abnormal. This leads to more self-worth and self-confidence and encourages work toward recovery. Thus, although families may be part of the problem, they are equally important as part of the solution.

Conclusion

Eating disorders are potentially life-threatening, resulting in death for at least 10 percent of those individuals who develop the disorders (APA 1994). Psychologically, eating disorders rob a person of self-worth, self-confidence, and happiness. Interpersonally, important relationships erode as the eating disorder requires more time, energy, self-absorption, and distance from others. While each case develops for different reasons, the roles of the culture and of the family are particularly critical. An eating disorder is frequently an attempt to gain power, control, success, self-confidence, or admiration, but it often results in the opposite. Due to the powerful influence of the culture and the family and the potential loss of health, well-being, and life, prevention of eating disorders is very critical to assuring the health of the next generation.

(*See also:* ADOLESCENCE; MASS MEDIA; SELF-ESTEEM)

BIBLIOGRAPHY

American Psychiatric Association (APA). (1994). *Diagnostic and Statistical Manual of Mental Disorders*, 4th edition. Washington, DC: American Psychiatric Press.

Kano, S. (1989). *Making Peace with Food: Freeing Yourself from the Diet/Weight Obsession.* New York: Harper & Row.

Kinoy, B. P., ed. (1994). *Eating Disorders: New Directions in Treatment and Recovery.* New York: Columbia University Press.

Maine, M. (1991). *Father Hunger: Fathers, Daughters, and Food.* Carlsbad, CA: Gurze Books.

Siegel, M.; Brisman, J.; and Weinshel, M. (1988). *Surviving an Eating Disorder: Strategies for Families and Friends.* New York: Harper & Row.

Wolf, N. (1991). *The Beauty Myth: How Images of Beauty are Used Against Women.* New York: William Morrow.

Wooley, S. C. (1993). "Sexual Abuse and Eating Disorders: The Concealed Debate." In *Feminist Perspectives on Eating Disorders*, ed. P. Fallon, M. A. Katzman, and S. C. Wooley. New York: Guilford.

Zerbe, K. J. (1993). *The Body Betrayed: Women, Eating Disorders, and Treatment.* Washington, DC: American Psychiatric Press.

MARGO MAINE

EDUCATION *See* HOME SCHOOLING; PARENT EDUCATION; SCHOOL; SEXUALITY EDUCATION; TRUANCY

ELDER ABUSE

Although conflict between older and younger generations in families has been a consistent theme in world literature since ancient times, elder abuse did not surface as a social problem until the mid-1970s.

The "discovery" of child abuse a decade earlier, followed by the emergence of the battered women's movement, helped pave the way for the public disclosure of elder abuse. Through congressional hearings and the media, the nation learned of the unspeakable and horrifying conditions endured by some older persons at the hands of family members (U.S. House of Representatives, Select Committee on Aging 1979, 1981, 1985). In response, the states passed elder abuse legislation or amended existing adult protection statutes. Three-quarters of the states now mandate certain professional groups (physicians, social workers, nurses, etc.) to report cases of suspected abuse. Once a case is reported, the situation is investigated; if substantiated, an assessment is conducted, and needed services are provided to resolve the problem.

Each state system operates with its own set of definitions. The inconsistency among the states has made it almost impossible to learn the extent of the problem on the national level or to compare state experiences. However, there is general agreement about the basic concept. Elder mistreatment is an act of commission (abuse) or omission (neglect), intentional or unintentional, and of one or more types: physical, psychological (emotional), and/or financial. Whether the behavior is labeled as abusive or neglectful may depend on its frequency, duration, intensity, severity, or consequences. Some researchers have questioned the legal and professional basis of definitions and suggest that it is the older person's perception of the behavior that is meaningful (Hudson 1994; Johns, Hydle, and Aschjem 1991). Others have noted the importance of cultural traditions, values, and attitudes in defining what is acceptable and what is unacceptable behavior (Griffin 1994; Moon and Williams 1993).

Prevalence

The lack of national data has hampered policy and program development. Only one prevalence study has been reported in the United States. A research team (Pillemer and Finkelhor 1988), using a methodology validated in two national family violence studies, interviewed more than 2,000 noninstitutionalized persons sixty-five years or older in the Boston metropolitan area. They found that 3.2 percent had been physically abused, verbally abused, and/or neglected since their sixty-fifth birthday. Spouse abuse (58%) was more common than abuse by adult children (24%), men were as likely as women to be victims, and economic status and age were not related to the risk of abuse. This profile differs markedly from statistics produced by the state reporting systems (Tatara 1990), which show victims more likely to be female, very old, and dependent, and perpetrators more apt to be adult children than spouses.

When the Boston metropolitan area survey was repeated in Canada (Podnieks 1992) with questions on financial abuse added, 4 percent of the national representative sample stated that they had been abused recently, more often financially than physically or through neglect. Similar questions added to a British population survey resulted in a positive response rate of 5 percent for verbal abuse and 2 percent for physical abuse (Ogg and Bennett 1992). One other prevalence study has been reported. Based on questionnaires and clinical examinations, researchers (Kivelä et al. 1992) found that 5.4 percent of the retired population of a small Finnish town had been physically, psychologically, or financially abused or neglected since they had reached retirement age. These studies suggest a prevalence rate of about 5 percent, which, for the United States, translates into almost 2 million cases.

Risk Factors and Interventions

Many risk factors for elder abuse and neglect have been proposed, ranging from "violence as a way of life" to "ageism in society." The most likely risk factors are victim–perpetrator dependency, perpetrator deviance, victim disability, caregiver stress, and social isolation. The "cycle of violence" theory closely associated with child abuse and spouse abuse has not been substantiated in elder abuse cases. As with other forms of domestic violence, however, alcohol is present in a large proportion of cases (Wolf and Pillemer 1989).

Certain characteristics tend to be identified with specific types of abuse. For instance, perpetrator deviance and dependency are more often associated with physical abuse; caregiver stress and victim disability with neglect; and social isolation (victim) with financial abuse.

When elder abuse was thought to be primarily a result of caregiver stress, reducing the dependency of the victim was the treatment of choice, such as bringing services into the home (e.g., skilled nursing, homemaker assistance, personal care, meals-on-wheels, chore services, and respite care) or providing adult day care, as well as offering behavior management training, counseling, and skills building for the caregiver. However, if the mistreatment, particularly physical abuse, is related to the financial and emotional dependency of the perpetrator, then vocational counseling, job placement, housing assistance, alcohol and drug treatment, and mental health services may be successful interventions. In cases where it is necessary to take emergency action, the courts are called on for orders of protection, mental health commitment papers, guardianship proceedings, and financial management arrangements. When a civil or criminal offense has been committed, law enforcement and the criminal justice system become involved, resulting possibly in prosecution and incarceration.

Conclusion

Some progress has been made in trying to treat and prevent elder abuse. All fifty states have systems for reporting and investigating elder abuse cases. The National Center on Elder Abuse has been established in the culmination of a ten-year effort to pass federal legislation. Public awareness campaigns and professional training programs have multiplied. Increasing numbers of elder abuse coalitions and multidisciplinary teams are being organized by communities to develop a more coordinated approach for handling the complicated issues represented by elder abuse and neglect cases. Despite these advances, knowledge of the nature, cause, and scope of elder mistreatment is still very incomplete. Intervention strategies remain untested, and primary prevention programs have yet to be incorporated into most adult protective service departments' strategic plans.

(*See also:* ELDERS; FAMILY VIOLENCE; FILIAL RESPONSIBILITY)

BIBLIOGRAPHY

Griffin, L. W. (1994). "Elder Maltreatment Among Rural African Americans." *Journal of Elder Abuse and Neglect* 6:1–28.

Hudson, M. F. (1994). "Elder Abuse: Its Meaning to Middle-Aged and Older Adults; Part II, Pilot Results." *Journal of Elder Abuse and Neglect* 6:55–82.

Johns, S.; Hydle, I.; and Aschjem, D. (1991). "The Act of Abuse: A Two-Headed Monster of Injury and Offense." *Journal of Elder Abuse and Neglect* 3:53–64.

Kivelä, S.-L.; Köngäs-Saviaro, P.; Kesti, E.; Pahkala, K.; and Ijäs, M.-L. (1992). "Abuse in Old Age—Epidemiological Data from Finland." *Journal of Elder Abuse and Neglect* 4:1–18.

Moon, A., and Williams, O. J. (1993). "Perceptions of Elder Abuse and Help-Seeking Patterns Among African-American, Caucasian-American, and Korean-American Elderly Women." *Gerontologist* 33:386–395.

Ogg, J., and Bennett, G. (1992). "Elder Abuse in Britain." *British Medical Journal* 305:998–999.

Pillemer, K., and Finkelhor, D. (1988). "Prevalence of Elder Abuse." *Gerontologist* 28:51–57.

Podnieks, E. (1992). "National Survey on Abuse of the Elderly in Canada." *Journal of Elder Abuse and Neglect* 5:5–58.

Straus, M. A., and Gelles, R. J. (1986). "Societal Change and Change in Family Violence from 1975 to 1985 as Revealed by Two National Surveys." *Journal of Marriage and the Family* 48:465–479.

Tatara, T. (1990). *Summaries of National Elder Abuse Data: An Exploratory Study of State Statistics Based on a Survey of State Adult Protective Service and Aging Agencies.* Washington, DC: National Aging Resource Center on Elder Abuse.

U.S. House of Representatives, Select Committee on Aging. (1979). *Elder Abuse: The Hidden Problem.* Washington, DC: U.S. Government Printing Office.

U.S. House of Representatives, Select Committee on Aging. (1981). *Elder Abuse: An Examination of a Hidden Problem.* Washington, DC: U.S. Government Printing Office.

U.S. House of Representatives, Select Committee on Aging. (1985). *Elder Abuse: A National Disgrace.* Washington, DC: U.S. Government Printing Office.

Wolf, R. S., and Pillemer, K. A. (1989). *Helping Elderly Victims: The Reality of Elder Abuse.* New York: Columbia University Press.

ROSALIE S. WOLF

ELDER CARE   *See* CHRONIC ILLNESS; DISABILITIES

ELDERS

Any definition of "elders" reveals cultural variations about what it means to be an elder in different societies. In some traditional societies, to be old is to be respected, considered wise, and looked up to as a teacher of traditions. "Elder" is a term of respect reserved for the people who are older or higher in rank. Within the diversity of modern American society, specific variations on aging also exist in families, communities, and in identified ethnic and cultural groups.

One of the most exciting and challenging realities of contemporary American society is the increase in individual life expectancy. A child born in 1991 can expect to live seventy-five and one-half years, about twenty-eight years longer than a child born in 1900 (AARP 1993), and life expectancy at birth may be ninety years for white females by the year 2080 (Faber and Wilkin 1981). Not only are individuals experiencing greater longevity, but societies as a whole are also aging. The percentage of seniors in American society

increased from 2 percent in 1790 to 12.5 percent in 1990 (Atchley 1994).

A second important demographic factor is that the elderly population (all people sixty-five or older) is itself aging. Individuals eighty-five or older are expected to compose 14.7 percent of all elderly by the year 2000, as compared to 9.6 percent in 1990 (AARP 1993).

A third important characteristic of the population of elders is the increasing racial-ethnic diversity among the population. By the year 2050, 20 percent of people over age sixty-five are expected to be nonwhite (U.S. Department of Health and Human Services 1990). Fernando M. Torres-Gil (1992, p. 19) notes that "the elderly of the next several decades will have fewer [white] members and be less English-speaking than ever before." This change has important implications for future services and resources available to elders. Robert Butler (1975) wrote that when people talk about living longer, they are really talking about their own future.

Many facets of American life are affected by these three demographic trends. Most elders are experiencing better health than previous age cohorts (Fries 1994) and consequently can look forward to greater activity in later years. Families as well as older individuals themselves are challenged by the new phenomenon of twenty to thirty years of life after retirement. Harry Moody (1988) raises issues about how individuals will use this time in later life and how quality of life can be maintained.

The issue of at what chronological age an individual should be considered an elder is being raised. Elders can have several careers; take many roles in families and the community; and maintain good health through disease prevention, healthy diet, exercise programs, and increased medical technology. New and unexpected roles for later life are emerging for elders. These include volunteer activities, nontraditional student roles, caring for grandchildren in parental roles, and creative artistic and athletic pursuits. Learning to cope with changing physical and mental abilities is also new at this time of life.

Butler coined the word "ageism" in 1968 to describe the process of systematic stereotyping of and discrimination against people because they are old. Ageism is a term that parallels other "isms" in society such as racism, sexism, and classism. "Ageism allows [other] generations to see older people as different from themselves; thus they subtly cease to identify with their elders as human beings" (Butler 1975, p. 12). All people, including adolescents and elders, can be discriminated against based on age. Common myths and stereotypes about elders that form the basis for ageism include invisibility, "senility," disrespect, cartoons and jokes, and avoidance of older persons. The popular media can promote negative attitudes and images of elders based on ageism for young and old alike.

Most elders continue to perform in roles as they always have: They are sexual beings; they continue to participate in hobbies and other activities; they are parents, spouses, and friends; and they maintain most of the patterns and characteristics of earlier times in the life cycle. Sometimes, because of life situations, individuals may change in unexpected ways: They may begin to drink alcohol to cope with difficulties; they may seem to change personality traits because of medications or mental or physical changes in their bodies; or they may become sad or depressed because of unexpected losses or changes in their lives. When these responses occur, they can be treated in many of the same ways as they are diagnosed and treated in younger persons. These situational changes should not be assumed to be an inevitable part of the aging process.

Political and policy debates have captured the aging of society issue as a theme with respect to intergenerational equity concerns. The need for personal care and for other resources in later life is becoming more evident. While some social scientists raise a specter of competition and unrest between generations based on limited resources (Hewitt and Howe 1988), others stress the intergenerational solidarity and interdependence that occurs through family networks (Pollack 1988). Meredith Minkler (1991) and other social policy analysts argue that society needs to look at inequality in distribution among socioeconomic classes rather than focusing on generational inequality.

Overall, the opportunity to have a longer life with increasingly productive roles is, for the first time, possible. Society is challenged to change the negative attitudes toward the aging process and look for better ways to integrate its aging population fully as a strong and contributory force for the future. Another important challenge is to find new, compassionate ways to meet the needs of elderly individuals who require care.

Both culture and context are important for understanding what it means to be an elder. Jay Sokolovsky (1993) highlights the importance of understanding the nature of the aging experience within an appropriate cultural context. He states that the context of the aging experience includes such things as kinds and amount of family support,

socioeconomic class position, and gender. Younger members of society are socialized to the elder experience by cultures that structure social boundaries between generations, distribute power between genders over the life cycle, and perpetuate stories and mythology.

(*See also:* ELDER ABUSE; FILIAL RESPONSIBILITY; GRANDPARENTHOOD; LATER-LIFE FAMILIES; RETIREMENT; WIDOWHOOD)

BIBLIOGRAPHY

American Association of Retired Persons (AARP). (1993). *A Profile of Older Americans: Based on Data from U.S. Bureau of the Census.* Washington, DC: Author.

Atchley, R. C. (1994). *Social Forces and Aging*, 7th edition. Belmont, CA: Wadsworth.

Butler, R. (1975). *Why Survive?* New York: Harper & Row.

Faber, I. F., and Wilkin, I. C. (1981). *Social Security Area Population Projections, 1981.* Washington, DC: U.S. Social Security Administration.

Fries, I. F. (1994). "The Sunny Side of Aging." In *Aging: Concepts and Controversies,* ed. H. R. Moody. Thousand Oaks, CA: Pine Forge Press.

Hewitt, P. S., and Howe, N. (1988). "Future of Generational Politics." *Generations* 7:10–13.

Minkler, M. (1991). " 'Generational Equity' and the New Victim Blaming." In *Critical Perspectives on Aging: The Political and Moral Economy of Growing Old,* ed. M. Minkler and C. L. Estes. Amityville, NY: Baywood.

Moody, H. R. (1988). *Abundance of Life: Human Development Policies for an Aging Society.* New York: Columbia University Press.

Pollack, R. F. (1988). "Serving Intergenerational Needs, Not Intergenerational Conflict." *Generations* 7:14–18.

Schneider, E. J., and Brody, J. (1994). "Aging, Natural Death, and the Compression of Morbidity: Another View." In *Aging: Concepts and Controversies,* ed. H. R. Moody. Thousand Oaks, CA: Pine Forge Press.

Sokolovsky, J. (1993). "Images of Aging: A Cross-Cultural Perspective." *Generations* 17:51–54.

Torres-Gil, F. M. (1992). *The New Aging.* New York: Auburn House.

U.S. Department of Health and Human Services. (1990). *Minority Aging: Essential Curricula Content for Selected Health and Allied Health Professions.* Washington, DC: Author.

PAMELA K. METZ
ENID O. COX

EMPTY-NEST SYNDROME *See* FAMILY DEVELOPMENT THEORY; MIDDLE AGE

ENTITLEMENTS

The United States operates a multibillion-dollar social welfare system of enormous size and complexity. Dozens of federal and state programs provide social welfare assistance for retirement, disability, health, education, housing, public assistance, employment, and other needs. Indeed, some seventy-five federal programs, such as Aid to Families with Dependent Children (AFDC) and Medicaid, provide assistance just to low-income individuals (National Commission for Employment Policy 1991). Still other programs, such as Social Security and Medicare, provide assistance to virtually all individuals. The vast majority of these programs transfer cash or in-kind benefits (e.g., food or medical care) directly to individuals. Millions of Americans receive benefits under such transfer programs. Indeed, the federal government alone spent more than $650 billion on these programs in 1994 (U.S. Congress 1993, p. 1767).

Government also provides social welfare benefits through numerous special income tax deductions, exclusions, and credits known as "tax expenditures." Most of these social welfare tax expenditures provide benefits indirectly to individuals via reduced taxes. For example, the federal income tax deduction for home mortgage interest helps individuals buy houses. Similarly, the federal dependent care credit helps workers pay for employment-related child care. Millions of Americans take advantage of these social welfare tax expenditures, and the revenue loss attributable to all the tax expenditures in the federal income tax that are designed to improve the social welfare exceeded $175 billion in 1994 (U.S. Congress 1993, pp. 984–985).

These social welfare transfer programs and tax expenditures are all creatures of statutes enacted by federal and state governments. An individual who meets the statutory criteria for a given social welfare benefit is said to be entitled to the benefit; hence, such benefits have come to be called entitlements.

Individuals do not have a constitutional right to any minimum level of social welfare benefits (*Harris* v. *McRae* 1980). Rather, the scope and reach of social welfare benefits are matters of legislative grace. Generally, a legislature may design an entitlement program in almost any way it desires, as long as the legislature acts rationally and the entitlement program does not invidiously discriminate against those racial, religious, and other groups protected by the Constitution (*Dandridge* v. *Williams* 1970). For example, the U.S. Supreme Court held that providing different Social Security benefits for men and women violated the due process clause of the Fifth Amendment (*Weinberger* v. *Wiesenfeld* 1975).

On the other hand, once an entitlement program has been created by statute, the due process clauses of the Fifth and Fourteenth amendments to the U.S. Constitution protect an individual's entitlement from arbitrary governmental action (*Flemming* v. *Nestor* 1960). For example, an AFDC beneficiary is entitled to a hearing if a governmental agency plans to terminate or suspend those benefits (*Goldberg* v. *Kelly* 1970).

Social welfare policy analysts generally differentiate between social welfare transfer programs that are "means-tested" and programs that are not. For means-tested transfer programs (e.g., AFDC, Medicaid, and food stamps), eligibility and benefits depend on an individual's need, as measured by the individual's income and assets. For nonmeans-tested transfer programs (e.g., Social Security, Medicare, and veteran benefits), eligibility is based on other criteria, such as age, work history, and military service.

Means-Tested Transfer Programs

AFDC provides cash assistance (through states) to needy families with dependent children and helps those families become self-sufficient (U.S. Congress 1993, pp. 615–739). AFDC provides cash welfare payments for (1) needy children who have been deprived of parental support or care because their father or mother is absent from the home continuously, incapacitated, deceased, or unemployed; and (2) certain others in the household of such a child.

States define "need," set their own benefit levels, establish (within federal limitations) income and resource limits, and administer the program or supervise its administration. The federal government pays 50 percent to 80 percent of AFDC costs. AFDC payments vary dramatically from state to state. For example, in January 1993, the maximum monthly grant that an AFDC family of three could receive ranged from $120 in Mississippi to $923 in Alaska.

In 1992, the AFDC program had an average monthly caseload of almost 4.8 million households (13.6 million people). The AFDC program delivered some $22.2 billion in benefits in 1992 and had total administrative costs of some $2.7 billion. In 1992, monthly AFDC benefits averaged $136 per person and $388 per family. In addition to AFDC, many states also provide short-term emergency assistance or general assistance to persons not covered by AFDC.

Supplemental Security Income (SSI) is a federal program that provides cash benefits to needy persons who satisfy the program criteria for age, blindness, or disability (U.S. Congress 1993, pp. 813–867). In 1994, the maximum federal benefit for an individual was $446 per month, and the maximum federal benefit for couples was $669 per month; however, some states provide small additional supplements (U.S. Department of Health and Human Services 1993). In 1992, some 5.6 million people received some $22.2 billion in SSI benefits. In September 1992, the average monthly benefit paid to an SSI recipient was about $350.

Medicaid is a federal-state matching entitlement program that provides medical assistance for needy persons who are aged, blind, disabled, members of families with dependent children, and certain other pregnant women and children (U.S. Congress 1993, pp. 1633–1666). States design and administer their programs within federal guidelines, and the federal government reimburses them for 50 percent to 83 percent of their costs. In 1991, the Medicaid program served 28.3 million people at a total cost of $95 billion. The average expenditure per person was $2,725.

Several social welfare programs provide food assistance to needy households (U.S. Congress 1993, pp. 1605–1632). The largest of these, the food stamp program, is administered by state agencies operating under the supervision of the U.S. Department of Agriculture. The federal government fully finances food stamp benefits and reimburses one-half of state administrative expenses. In general, food stamp benefits are issued in the form of booklets of coupons that participating households use to buy food items for home preparation and consumption. Food stamp benefits are a function of a household's size, its counted monthly income, and a maximum monthly benefit level. In 1992, the food stamp program served 26.9 million people at a total cost of $24.9 billion. Monthly food stamp benefits averaged $68.50 per person and about $170.00 per household.

The Special Supplemental Food Program for Women, Infants, and Children (WIC) provides food assistance and nutritional screening to needy pregnant and postpartum women and their infants, as well as to needy children up to age five. This program is federally funded, but it is administered by the states. WIC has categorical, income, and nutritional risk requirements for eligibility, and it does not serve all who are eligible. In 1992, the federal government spent about $2.6 billion to assist some 5.4 million women, infants, and children. In 1991, the average monthly cost of a WIC food package was $31.67 per participant.

Also, the National School Lunch Program and the School Breakfast Program provide subsidized meals to children at participating public and private schools and nonprofit residential institutions. Free and reduced-price meals are targeted to help children who live in needy households. For 1992, the federal government spent about $5.3 billion on these two programs.

A number of programs administered by the U.S. Department of Housing and Urban Development and the U.S. Farmers Home Administration provide housing assistance for low-income households (U.S. Congress 1993, pp. 1667–1676). Most housing assistance is provided in the form of traditional rental assistance or traditional homeowners' assistance. Traditional rental assistance is provided through two basic approaches: (1) project-based aid, such as the public housing program and the Section 8 new construction and substantial rehabilitation program; and (2) household-based subsidies, such as Section 8 rental certificates and vouchers. Traditional homeowners' assistance is provided in the form of mortgage-interest subsidies. Federal housing assistance has never been provided as an entitlement to all eligible low-income households. Nevertheless, the federal government spent almost $20 billion in 1993 to provide housing assistance to some 5.7 million households. The average subsidy per participating household was $4,240.

The Low-Income Home Energy Assistance Program (LIHEAP) helps low-income families meet their energy-related expenses (U.S. Congress 1993, pp. 1692–1698). In 1992, the federal government allotted almost $1.5 billion to the states for distribution to eligible low-income households to pay their heating or cooling bills, for low-cost weatherization, and to assist households during energy-related emergencies. Some 5.8 million households received heating assistance benefits.

Non-Means-Tested Transfer Programs

The Social Security system is by far the largest and most important social welfare transfer system operating in the United States (U.S. Congress 1993, pp. 3–136). It consists of two key programs. The Old-Age and Survivors Insurance (OASI) program provides monthly cash benefits to retired workers and their dependents and to survivors of insured workers. The Disability Insurance (DI) program provides monthly cash benefits for disabled workers under age sixty-five and their dependents.

Workers build protection under these programs by working in employment that is covered by the Social Security system and paying the applicable payroll taxes. Roughly 96 percent of the work force is in covered employment. In 1994, workers and their employers paid Social Security taxes equal to 7.65 percent of the first $60,600 in wages paid to that worker and 1.45 percent of wages in excess of $60,600 (U.S. Department of Health and Human Services 1993).

At retirement, disability, or death, monthly Social Security benefits are paid to insured workers and to their eligible dependents and survivors. In December 1992, there were 41.5 million beneficiaries in the OASI and DI programs. In 1993, the total cost of the OASI and DI programs was almost $305 billion. The average payment to a retired worker was $653 per month, and the average payment to a disabled worker was $626 per month. Additional amounts were paid on behalf of dependents of these covered workers.

In general, OASI and DI benefits are related to the earnings history of the insured worker. For example, workers over age sixty-two generally are entitled to OASI benefits if they have worked in covered employment for at least ten years. Benefits are based on a measure of the worker's earnings history in covered employment known as the average indexed monthly earnings (AIME). Basically the AIME measures the worker's career-average monthly earnings in covered employment.

The AIME is linked by a formula to the monthly retirement benefit payable to the worker at normal retirement age, a benefit known as the primary insurance amount (PIA). A worker's normal retirement age is the earliest age at which unreduced retirement benefits can be received. A worker's normal retirement age is sixty-five, but the normal retirement age is scheduled to increase gradually to sixty-seven after the year 2000, so that the normal retirement age will be set at sixty-seven for workers reaching sixty-two in 2022 (sixty-seven in 2027).

For a worker reaching age sixty-two in 1994, the worker's PIA was equal to 90 percent of the first $422 of the worker's AIME, plus 32 percent of the worker's AIME over $422 and through $2,545 (if any), and plus 15 percent of the worker's AIME over $2,545 (if any) (U.S. Department of Health and Human Services 1993). On its face, the benefit formula is progressive, meaning it is designed to favor workers with relatively low career-average earnings.

A worker's benefits may be increased or decreased for several reasons. Most importantly, benefits are indexed each year for inflation. Also, benefits payable to workers who choose to retire after their normal retirement age are actuarially increased through the delayed retirement credit. On the other hand, workers who retire before age sixty-five have their benefits actuarially reduced. Moreover, the so-called retirement earnings test can reduce the benefits of individuals who continue to work after retirement. For example, in 1994, workers age sixty-five through sixty-nine lost $1 of benefits for each $3 of annual earnings in excess of $11,160.

Dependents and survivors of workers may also receive monthly Social Security benefits. These so-called auxiliary benefit amounts are also based on the worker's PIA. For convenience, worker and auxiliary benefits are generally combined into a single monthly check. Table 1 summarizes the principal types of auxiliary benefits.

For example, the sixty-five-year-old wife or husband of a retired worker is entitled to a monthly spousal benefit equal to 50 percent of the worker's PIA. Consequently, a retired worker and spouse generally can claim a monthly benefit equal to 150 percent of what the retired worker alone could claim. Alternatively, the sixty-five-year old widow or widower of a worker is entitled to a monthly surviving spouse benefit equal to 100 percent of the worker's PIA. Auxiliary beneficiaries can begin receiving actuarially reduced benefits before age sixty-five.

These auxiliary benefit amounts are subject to a variety of limitations. For example, the retirement earnings test also limits the benefits paid to auxiliary beneficiaries who continue to work. Also, the maximum monthly benefit that can be paid with respect to any worker is limited to 150 percent to 188 percent of the worker's PIA. Moreover, under the so-called dual entitlement rule, when an individual is entitled to both a worker's benefit and a benefit as an auxiliary of another worker, only the larger of the two benefits is paid.

Medicare is a federal health care program for the aged and certain disabled persons (U.S. Congress 1993, pp. 137–222). It consists of two parts: the hospital insurance (HI, or Part A) program, and the supplementary medical insurance (Part B) program. Persons

Table 1 Percentage of Primary Insurance Amount (PIA) Generally Paid for Auxiliary Benefits

Type of Monthly Benefit	Percent of PIA
Dependents	
Wives, husbands—age 65	50.0
Mothers, fathers, children, grandchildren	50.0
Survivors	
Widows, widowers—age 65	100.0
Dependent parent—age 62	82.5
Widows, widowers, disabled—age 50	71.5
Mothers, fathers, children	75.0

age sixty-five or older are automatically entitled to protection under Part A (i.e., hospital care) if they are "fully insured" under Social Security. Part B is a voluntary program: Paying a premium of $36.60 per month (as of January 1, 1992) provides insurance coverage for physician and certain other medical services. People under age sixty-five who are receiving monthly Social Security disability benefits are also eligible for Medicare after a two-year wait.

In 1993, some 31.3 million aged persons and 3.7 million persons with disabilities were covered by Medicare Part A, and 30.8 million aged persons and 3.4 million persons with disabilities were covered under Part B. The total program costs were projected to reach $149.5 billion in 1993. The average annual benefit per person enrolled under Part A was $2,567, and the average annual benefit per person enrolled under Part B was $1,598.

Unemployment compensation is a joint federal–state program that provides cash benefits to individuals who have recently become unemployed (U.S. Congress 1993, pp. 474–523). States administer their programs within federal guidelines. Some 99 percent of all wage and salaried workers and 90 percent of all employed persons are covered by unemployment compensation, about 105 million individuals in all.

Benefits are financed through Federal Unemployment Tax Act (FUTA) taxes, a gross tax of 6.2 percent on the first $7,000 paid annually by covered employers to each employee. States set the benefit amounts as a fraction of the individual's weekly wage, up to some state-determined maximum. Unemployed persons usually receive unemployment benefits for twenty-six weeks; however, the federal–state extended benefits program provides for up to thirteen additional weeks. In 1992, the national average weekly benefit amount was $173 and the average duration was 15.9 weeks, making the average total benefits $2,751.

Workers' compensation programs provide cash and medical benefits to workers with job-related disabilities and to survivors of workers who are killed in work-related accidents or illness (U.S. Congress 1993, pp. 1702–1706). Most workers' compensation programs are state-run and state-financed, but the federal government provides similar benefits through a number of programs (e.g., black lung benefits for coal miners). Some 95.1 million workers were covered by workers' compensation laws during an average month in 1990. Workers' compensation benefits vary dramatically from program to program. For example, in July 1988, the maximum weekly benefit level ranged from $175 in Georgia to $1,094 in Alaska, with a median amount of $340.50. In 1990,

total workers' compensation benefit payments exceeded $38 billion.

The U.S. Department of Veterans Affairs provides a wide variety of benefits and services to veterans of the U.S. Armed Forces (U.S. Congress 1993, pp. 1699–1701). Veterans who have incurred injuries or illness while in the service are entitled to service-connected compensation based on the extent of their disability, and war veterans who become disabled from non-service-connected causes are entitled to pensions. Additional benefits are available for survivors of these veterans. Other veterans programs include readjustment and rehabilitation benefits, education and job training programs, medical care services, and housing and loan guarantee programs. The federal government spent more than $33 billion on veterans programs in 1992.

Tax Provisions Related to Social Welfare

A significant portion of the federal budget consists of direct payments (expenditures) to individuals for retirement, health, public assistance, employment, and disability benefits provided pursuant to entitlement programs. One may also view the federal government as providing indirect payments to individuals by means of special income tax deductions, exclusions, and credits related to health and other social policy objectives.

The federal income tax is imposed on a taxpayer's taxable income. In general, a taxpayer's taxable income is equal to the taxpayer's gross income less certain allowable deductions. Gross income includes most valuable economic benefits that a taxpayer receives during the year, including but not limited to wages, salary, tips, dividends, interest, rents, and royalties received. Certain economic benefits are excluded from gross income by statute. For example, the value of employer-provided health care is excluded from the gross income of employees. Child support received by a taxpayer is also excluded from gross income.

As for deductions, most taxpayers simply claim a standard deduction and personal exemptions. Many taxpayers, however, claim certain itemized deductions instead of the standard deduction. For example, homeowners may claim itemized deductions for the mortgage interest and state and local real property taxes they pay.

Certain other deductions are allowed without regard to whether the taxpayer chooses to itemize. For example, alimony paid in connection with a divorce or separation may be deducted without regard to whether a taxpayer itemizes. Child support is never deductible.

A taxpayer's tentative tax liability (if any) is determined by applying 15 percent, 28 percent, 36 percent, and 39.6 percent rates to taxable income. The amount that the taxpayer must actually pay with his or her tax return or, alternatively, will receive as a refund is equal to the taxpayer's tentative tax liability minus allowable credits. The principal credits used by families are the credit for child and dependent care and the earned income credit.

Each year, the U.S. Department of the Treasury indexes the standard deduction amounts, the personal exemption amounts, the maximum earned income credit, and the income tax rate tables for inflation (U.S. Department of the Treasury 1993). For 1994, the basic standard deduction amounts were $6,350 for married couples filing jointly and surviving spouses; $5,600 for heads of households; $3,800 for unmarried individuals; and $3,175 for married individuals filing separately. Aged or blind taxpayers generally are entitled to claim an additional standard deduction amount of $750, except that aged or blind single individuals can claim an additional standard deduction amount of $950.

The personal exemption amount for 1994 was $2,450. The rate tables were also modified so that, for 1994, the 15 percent marginal tax rate extended to all taxable incomes up to $38,000 for married couples filing jointly and surviving spouses; $30,500 for heads of households; $22,750 for unmarried individuals; and $19,000 for married individuals filing separately. For taxable incomes above those amounts, marginal tax rates of 28 percent, 31 percent, 36 percent, and 39.6 percent are applicable.

The earned income credit is a refundable credit available to low- and moderate-income taxpayers with earned income. In 1994, taxpayers with one qualifying child were entitled to an earned income credit of up to $2,038, and taxpayers with two or more qualifying children were entitled to an earned income credit of up to $2,527. For the first time ever, starting in 1994, the earned income credit was available to certain low-income taxpayers without children. These taxpayers were entitled to an earned income credit of up to $306 in 1994.

The dependent care credit is a nonrefundable credit for up to 30 percent of employment-related dependent care expenses incurred by an individual who maintains a household that includes one or more qualifying individuals. A qualifying individual is a dependent under age thirteen or a physically or mentally incapacitated dependent or spouse. The maximum 30 percent credit rate is reduced, but not below 20 per-

cent, by 1 percentage point for each $2,000 (or fraction thereof) of adjusted gross income above $10,000. Eligible employment-related expenses are limited to $2,400 if there is one qualifying individual (maximum credit of $720 is 30 percent of $2,400), or $4,800 if there are two or more qualifying individuals (maximum credit of $1,440 is 30 percent of $4,800).

Table 2 provides estimates of the revenue losses in 1993 that were attributable to all of the income tax expenditures related to retirement, health, poverty, employment, and disability (U.S. Congress 1993, pp. 984–985). Among the most costly were the net exclusion for pension plan contributions and earnings; the exclusion of employer contributions for medical insurance premiums and medical care; and the various tax expenditures related to housing. The consolidated revenue loss attributable to all the income tax expenditures in Table 2 was $176.6 billion.

Problems with Entitlements

The system of social welfare programs and tax expenditures developed largely as the result of piecemeal social policymaking. Consequently, there is little coordination among the mishmash of social welfare entitlement programs and tax expenditures. Four of the most frequently cited problems resulting from this lack of coordination are that the current system is inequitable, inefficient, overly complicated, and expensive to administer.

A number of strategies have been suggested to help improve synchronization among the various social welfare transfer programs and tax expenditures (Forman 1993). For example, if different programs had synchronized eligibility criteria, (1) a single, multipurpose application form could be used for all programs; (2) a single verification by one program should suffice for others; and (3) centralized eligibility determinations could be made for all programs. Different programs could also better synchronize their benefit-computation formulas.

Some of the greatest gains could come from consolidating programs with similar missions. Combining such programs could reduce duplication, improve program management, and reduce administrative costs. For example, it might make sense to combine AFDC and food stamps, Medicare and Medicaid, or Social Security and SSI.

Many analysts have concluded that comprehensive welfare reform can come only from combining as many transfer programs and tax expenditures as possible into a single, rational, and unified program, perhaps administered by a state or local welfare agency

Table 2 Estimates of the Revenue Loss in Fiscal Year 1993 in Billions of Dollars

Item	Amount
Tax expenditures related to retirement	
Net exclusion of private retirement plan contributions and earnings	66.3
Exclusion of Social Security and railroad retirement benefits	24.5
Tax expenditures related to health	
Exclusions of employer contributions for medical insurance premiums and medical care	46.4
Exclusion of Medicare benefits	12.0
Deductibility of medical expenses	3.1
Tax expenditures related to poverty	
Earned income tax credit	10.9
Credit for child medical insurance premiums	.7
Exclusion of public assistance and SSI payments	.4
Tax expenditures related to employment	
Dependent care credit	2.8
Exclusion of employer-provided dependent care	.4
Exclusion for benefits provided under cafeteria plans	2.9
Other	1.0
Tax expenditures related to elderly and disabled	
Exclusion of workers' compensation and special benefits for disabled coal miners	3.3
Additional standard deduction for elderly and blind	1.8
Tax credit for the elderly and for people with disabilities	.1
Tax expenditures related to housing	
Deductibility of mortgage interest	44.2
Deductibility of property tax on owner-occupied housing	13.3
Deferral of capital gains on sale of principal residence	13.2
Exclusion of capital gains on sale of residence of persons 55 or over	4.6
Other	5.4

(Stoetz and Karger 1992). Another way to integrate the social welfare transfer program and tax expenditures would be to replace them all with a negative income tax (Green and Lampman 1967). Basically, a negative income tax gives cash to low-income families, and the less income a family has, the more cash it gets from the government. In that regard, to help alleviate child poverty, the National Commission on Children has called for the creation of a $1,000 refundable tax credit for all children (National Commission on Children 1991).

High cost is another problem with the system of social welfare transfer programs and tax expenditures, particularly as the federal government is running annual budget deficits of $200 billion or more. Conservative thinkers generally have suggested curtailing means-tested transfer programs (Gilder 1981; Murray 1984). They argue that giving poor people money saps their incentive to work. Hence, cutting means-tested programs would spur the poor to work their way out of poverty.

Liberal thinkers, on the other hand, often have argued for expansion of the entitlement system—for example, by adding a national health care program. Liberals also have tended to support proposals for government-provided child care, job training, and full employment programs. To the extent that liberals have been willing to think about cuts in entitlement programs, they usually have suggested cuts in non-means-tested programs—for example, by means-testing Social Security and Medicare benefits (Ford Foundation 1989). Along those lines, starting in 1994, high-income individuals were required to pay federal income tax on as much as 85 percent of their Social Security benefits.

Liberals have also expressed concern about the distributional aspects of various tax expenditures (Surrey 1973). For example, the deduction for home mortgage interest provides large tax savings to wealthy Americans with mansions but no tax savings whatsoever for poor apartment renters. Tax expenditure analysts have often recommended repealing such upside-down tax expenditures and/or replacing them with means-tested transfer programs.

Many entitlement programs contain disincentives for marriage (Abramowitz 1988; Miller 1990). For example, if each of two elderly individuals qualified for Supplemental Security Income (SSI), each could receive as much as $446 per month from the federal government. If they decided to get married, however, the maximum total SSI they could receive would be $669. Thus there is a disincentive for them to marry.

Similarly, a welfare recipient could lose both Aid to Families with Dependent Children (AFDC) and Medicaid benefits by marrying someone with a moderate income. Disincentives for marriage exist in many other transfer programs and in the federal income tax. Worse still, these so-called marriage penalties can lead married couples to divorce. Unfortunately, marriage penalties seem to be the inevitable consequence of efforts to keep costs down and to target benefits to the most needy beneficiaries.

Conclusion

The role of government in the lives of its citizens has grown dramatically since the enactment of the Social Security Act in 1935. Now, millions of Americans benefit from social welfare entitlement programs and tax expenditures. However, control needs to be established over the cost and complexity of the social welfare system.

(*See also:* Family Policy; Health and the Family; Homeless Families; Poverty; Retirement; Unemployment; Work and Family)

BIBLIOGRAPHY

Abramowitz, M. (1988). *Regulating the Lives of Women: Social Welfare Policy from Colonial Times to the Present.* Boston: South End Press.

Ford Foundation Project on Social Welfare and the American Future. (1989). *The Common Good: Social Welfare and the American Future.* New York: Ford Foundation.

Forman, J. B. (1993). "Administrative Savings from Synchronizing Social Welfare Programs and Tax Provisions." *Journal of the National Association of Administrative Law Judges* 13:5–76.

Gilder, G. (1981). *Wealth and Poverty.* New York: Basic Books.

Green, C., and Lampman, R. J. (1967). "Schemes for Transferring Income to the Poor." *Industrial Relations* 6:121–153.

Miller, D. C. (1990). *Women and Social Welfare: A Feminist Analysis.* New York: Praeger.

Murray, C. (1984). *Losing Ground.* New York: Basic Books.

National Commission on Children. (1991). *Beyond Rhetoric: A New American Agenda for Children and Families.* Washington, DC: U.S. Government Printing Office.

National Commission for Employment Policy. (1991). *Coordinating Federal Assistance Programs for the Economically Disadvantaged: Recommendations and Background Materials, Special Report No. 31.* Washington, DC: U.S. Government Printing Office.

Regan, J. J. (1992). *Entitlements.* Los Angeles: American College of Trust and Estate Counsel Foundation.

Stoetz, D., and Karger, H. J. (1992). *Reconstructing the American Welfare State.* Boston: Rowman & Littlefield.

Surrey, S. S. (1973). *Pathways to Tax Reform.* Cambridge, MA: Harvard University Press.

U.S. Congress, Staff of the House Committee on Ways and Means. (1993). *Overview of Entitlement Programs: 1993 Green Book: Background Material and Data on Programs Within the Jurisdiction of the Committee on Ways and Means,* 103d Cong., 1st sess. Washington, DC: U.S. Government Printing Office.

U.S. Department of Health and Human Services. (1993). "1994 Cost-of-Living Increase and Other Determinations." *Federal Register* 58:58,004-58,008.

U.S. Department of the Treasury, Internal Revenue Service. (1993). "Revenue Procedure 93-49." *Internal Revenue Bulletin* 42:18–23.

CASES

Dandridge v. *Williams,* 397 U.S. 471 (1970).
Flemming v. *Nestor,* 363 U.S. 603 (1960).
Goldberg v. *Kelly,* 397 U.S. 254 (1970).
Harris v. *McRae,* 448 U.S. 297 (1980).
Weinberger v. *Wiesenfeld,* 420 U.S. 636 (1975).

Jonathan Barry Forman

EQUITY AND CLOSE RELATIONSHIPS

Issues of equity or fairness arise in even the most intimate of relationships. A wife feels taken advantage of when her husband does not help with the housework. A young college female, deciding which of two men she should date, chooses the one she believes will offer as much to the relationship as she will. Two women in a lesbian relationship have had a very satisfying and conflict-free relationship until one of them, after losing her job and gaining weight, feels guilty because she might not be able to offer as much to the relationship as she once did.

In every close relationship, behaviors and resources are exchanged, and consciously or unconsciously, the partners attempt to achieve a balance in what is exchanged. Individuals offer certain desirable attributes (looks, good family background, intelligence) and engage in positive behaviors (doing dishes, engaging in sexual activities, loading software onto a partner's new computer). Of course, they also have a negative trait or two with which a partner must deal. In return for all that individuals offer the relationship, they get back partners who offer their own desirable traits and behaviors (and annoying habits). If people select their friends, lovers, and spouses wisely, relationships are usually "fair" or "equitable" from the beginning, and each partner gets out of the relationship about the same amount that is put into the relationship. In the best of all worlds, the relationship is equitable *and* very rewarding to both partners from the beginning until the end. However, things do not always work as they should. People sometimes enter mismatched liaisons where one partner offers more to the relationship than the other. Relationships sometimes become inequitable over time.

Background to Equity Theory

Most research examining the effects of equity on close relationships is based on principles of equity theory presented by Elaine Hatfield and her colleagues (Walster, Walster, and Berscheid 1978; note that Hatfield and the first Walster are the same person). Based on but also extending the earlier justice theories of George C. Homans (1961), J. Stacy Adams (1965), and Peter M. Blau (1964), this version of equity theory contains the following propositions:

Proposition 1: Individuals will try to maximize their outcomes (where outcomes equal rewards minus punishments).

Proposition 2a: Groups (or rather the individuals comprising these groups) can maximize collective reward by evolving accepted systems for equitably apportioning resources among members. Thus, groups will evolve such systems of equity and will attempt to induce members to accept and adhere to these systems.

Proposition 2b: Groups will generally reward members who treat others equitably and generally punish members who treat others inequitably.

Proposition 3: When individuals find themselves participating in inequitable relationships, they will become distressed. The more inequitable the relationship, the more distress they will feel.

Proposition 4: Individuals who discover they are in inequitable relationships will attempt to eliminate their distress by restoring equity. The greater the inequity that exists, the more distress

they will feel, and the harder they will try to restore equity.

In a general sense, equity refers to the degree of perceived balance in the partners' inputs and outcomes. More specifically, "an equitable relationship exists when the person evaluating the relationship—who could be Participant A, Participant B, or an outside observer—concludes that all participants are receiving equal *relative gains* from the relationship" (Hatfield and Traupmann 1981, p. 166). Inputs are defined as the positive and negative contributions to the exchange that entitle each participant to reward or punishment. Outcomes are defined as the rewards and punishments each participant receives in the relationship. Total outcomes are defined as rewards minus punishments.

Two types of inequity can be experienced in a close relationship: underbenefiting inequity and overbenefiting inequity. An underbenefited partner in a relationship is the victim of inequity. When comparing what is put into and what is gained from the relationship, this person concludes that the relationship is not a good deal. However, an overbenefited partner, who benefits from inequity, believes that the relationship is a good deal. Because equity is "in the eye of the beholder," the two partners in the relationship may not have the same perceptions about the equity in the relationship; both could feel underbenefited. Furthermore, outside observers (friends, parents) may have a completely different perception of the situation than the members of the relationship.

Equity theorists predict that both underbenefited and overbenefited partners will feel distress but that the underbenefited will feel more distress than the overbenefited. According to the theory, underbenefited individuals should feel angry, and overbenefited individuals should feel guilt. Although there is some support that these emotions of anger and guilt are experienced in reaction to inequities, research also suggests that depression and frustration are common emotional reactions to underbenefiting inequity (Sprecher 1986, 1992).

Because inequity is distressing, relational partners who are experiencing inequity are likely to want to restore equity to the relationship. There are two possible ways to restore equity. Individuals may engage in actual equity restoration by changing their own contributions or by convincing the partners to change. Psychological equity restoration involves the ability to create the mental conviction that the inequity does not really exist. If neither of these strategies works, a final alternative is to "leave the field," end the relationship. It is assumed, and some supporting evidence exists, that individuals choose the equity-restoring action that is least costly (e.g., Sprecher 1992).

Equity theory is part of the larger literature on social exchange. Because researchers have compared the importance of equity with the importance of other exchange variables for predicting which couples will be satisfied in a relationship and stay together, a brief theoretical background to other social exchange variables is needed.

Distributive justice norms. Equity and equality are considered to be distributive justice norms. According to this justice rule, relationships will be more satisfying and last longer if both partners receive the same level of outcomes regardless of level of inputs. Some theorists (e.g., Deutsch 1975; Steil and Turetsky 1987) argue that equality is the distributive justice norm that is most conducive for building intimate relationships.

Outcome interdependence theory. A distinction is often made between the theory of distributive justice (e.g., equity) and general social-exchange theory as represented by outcome interdependence theory. The major variables included in the interdependence theory of John W. Thibaut and Harold H. Kelley (1959) are rewards, costs, comparison level (general expectations of what one deserves), and comparison level for alternatives (expectations of rewards one could obtain in other relationships). Using these variables, Caryl E. Rusbult (1980, 1983) developed the investment model of relationships. She defined investments as the direct and indirect resources one gives to the relationship that cannot be retrieved if the relationship were to end and argued that they act to bind one to the relationship. The investment model distinguishes between predictors of satisfaction (positive experiences in the relationship) and commitment (intent to maintain and feel psychologically attached to the relationship). Satisfaction is expected to increase with greater rewards and lower costs as compared to one's comparison level. Commitment is expected to increase with greater satisfaction, a lower comparison level for alternatives, and greater investments in the relationship. Greater commitment is expected to increase the likelihood that the person remains in the relationship.

Measurement of Equity

Equity has been measured in a number of ways for research on close relationships. In many studies, a global measure is used to assess perceptions of relationship equity. Such a measure is called global because respondents are asked to think about everything exchanged in the relationship and provide their overall assessment of the equity or inequity in the relationship. The Hatfield Global Measure (Hatfield, Utne, and Traupmann 1979), which may be the most frequently used measure of equity, is

Considering what you put into your relationship, compared to what you get out of it . . . and what your partner puts in compared to what he or she gets out of it, how does your relationship stack up?

1. I am getting a much better deal than my partner.
2. I am getting a somewhat better deal.
3. I am getting a slightly better deal.
4. We are both getting an equally good . . . or bad . . . deal.
5. My partner is getting a slightly better deal.
6. My partner is getting a somewhat better deal.
7. My partner is getting a much better deal than I.

In some studies, subjects give their perceptions of the equity or inequity for each of several important areas of the relationship, and the responses to these items are summed or averaged in the calculation of a final equity score. For example, Hatfield and her colleagues created a detailed measure, the Traupmann-Utne-Hatfield Equity Scale (Traupmann et al. 1981), which includes items from four areas of the relationship—personal concerns, emotional concerns, day-to-day concerns, and opportunities gained or lost. Subjects rate their own inputs in twenty-two areas and their own outcomes in twenty-four areas. They also rate their perceptions of their partner's inputs and outcomes in the same areas. Other research measures the equity of a few important roles in the relationship. For example, Robert B. Schafer and Patricia M. Keith (1980) examined perceived equity in the marital roles of cooking, housekeeping, earning income, companionship, and caring for children.

Effects of Equity

For most of the research on the effect of equity in close relationships, the dependent variable has been a measure of effect (e.g., distress, relationship satisfaction), although the effect of equity on commitment and actual relationship stability has also been examined.

Satisfaction and feelings. Equity theory (e.g., Adams 1965; Walster, Walster, and Berscheid 1978) was initially proposed as a general social psychological theory concerned with fairness primarily in casual relationships (employer–employee, helper–helpee). Beginning in the mid-1970s, Hatfield and her colleagues extended equity theory to the area of intimate relationships. This application of equity theory was accompanied with a theoretical debate as to whether equity *should* apply to such relationships (see Hatfield et al. 1985 for a summary of this debate).

The initial research that extended equity to intimate relationships (see Hatfield and Traupmann 1981; Hatfield et al. 1985) was focused on testing the third proposition of equity theory, which states that perceived inequity leads to distress. Distress was measured in most of this research by the Austin Contentment/Distress Measure (Austin 1974), which asks "When you think about your relationship—what you put into it, and what you get out of it—how does that make you feel?" Subjects were then asked to indicate how content, happy, angry, and guilty they felt.

In a number of studies (e.g., Traupmann, Hatfield, and Wexler 1983; Utne et al. 1984; Walster, Walster, and Traupmann 1978), Hatfield and her colleagues demonstrated that dating and married individuals who perceive themselves to be equitably treated in the relationship experienced more positive and less negative effect than individuals who perceived themselves to be inequitably treated. Furthermore, over-benefited individuals generally did not experience as much distress as underbenefited individuals, although they generally experienced more guilt. Hatfield and her colleagues also found that the distress experienced as a result of inequities puts a strain on the overall relationship so that inequity, particularly underbenefiting inequity, is likely to result in decreased satisfaction and happiness with the entire relationship. They were also able to show that individuals who feel inequitably treated in a relationship are less committed to the relationship and less certain that the relationship will remain stable over time.

Rewards and other social-exchange variables. The early research conducted by Hatfield and her colleagues showed that perceptions of equity and inequity affected how people felt about their relationships. However, the early research did not tell how important equity was relative to other aspects of the exchange in the relationship. For example, maybe what mattered most was that the relationship was very rewarding.

By the early 1980s, researchers began to examine the role of equity relative to other social-exchange variables. In one study, Rodney M. Cate and his colleagues (1982) examined how important equity was relative to equality and reward level in predicting re-

lationship satisfaction. They found a high association between equity and equality (relationships that were equitable also tended to be equal) and concluded that "reward level is more 'predictive' (in terms of the unique amount of variance accounted for) than either equity or equality" (p. 180). A few other studies were conducted that also demonstrated that equity was not as important as the absolute level of reward in contributing to the general quality of the relationship (Cate, Lloyd, and Long 1988; Martin 1985; Michaels, Acock, and Edwards 1986; Michaels, Edwards, and Acock 1984).

Susan Sprecher (1988) compared equity with three investment model variables—satisfaction, investments, and alternatives—and with the degree of social network support for the relationship. In her study, comparison level for alternatives was found to be the strongest predictor of commitment to the romantic relationship, but satisfaction, perceived social support, and equity were also found to be positive predictors.

The importance of equity relative to other types of variables has also been considered in some research. For instance, with a sample of married individuals, Ronald M. Sabatelli and Erin F. Cecil-Pigo (1985) found that perceived equity was a more important predictor of commitment to the relationship than any of the other variables measured, which were satisfaction, perceived barriers to the dissolution of the relationship, presence of children, and religious beliefs. In a study of young adults who were dating, Sprecher (1986) compared the effect of inequity to two other relationship variables, personal dependence and structural dependence, and two individual factors, gender and self-esteem. She examined underbenefiting inequity and overbenefiting inequity and looked at their effects on both negative and positive emotions experienced by the couple during the previous month. Underbenefiting inequity was found to be the strongest predictor of negative emotions and also a strong predictor of positive emotions. Overbenefiting inequity was also a significant predictor of both positive and negative emotions, although it was a less important predictor of emotions than most of the other variables.

Behaviors. Although most of the research on equity in close relationships has focused on the effect of equity on feelings, such as distress, satisfaction, commitment, and marital adjustment, equity is also likely to affect how intimate partners behave toward each other. Two types of behaviors that have been found to be influenced by the equity in the relationship are sexual behaviors and maintenance behaviors.

Couples who are distressed because their relationship is inequitable are likely to be less intimate sexually than couples who perceive their relationship to be equitable. In one study (Walster, Walster, and Traupmann 1978), undergraduate students who described their dating relationships as equitable reported going further sexually than students in inequitable dating relationships. In addition, the individuals who perceived themselves to be equitably treated were more likely than the inequitably treated individuals to report that they had sexual intercourse because both partners wanted it (e.g., "we are or were in love"). In later studies, Hatfield and her colleagues also found that dating and married individuals experienced less sexual satisfaction in their relationship when they were underbenefited (Hatfield et al. 1982; Traupmann, Hatfield, and Wexler 1983).

Sex outside of the relationship may also be used as a way to restore equity to the primary relationship. Evidence for this was found in a sample of cohabiting and married couples who responded to a *Psychology Today* survey (Walster, Traupmann, and Walster 1978). Individuals who were underbenefited in their primary relationship were more likely to report that they had an extramarital affair. Another study (Prins, Buunk, and Van Yperen 1993) found that, for women, inequity was associated with actual extramarital behavior and the desire to engage in extramarital sex, controlling for other predictors (e.g., marital dissatisfaction). The same relationship was not found for men, however.

Maintenance strategies and activities are those behaviors engaged in once a relationship has developed that keep it maintained or prevent it from beginning to deteriorate. Dan J. Canary and Laura Stafford (1991) found that married individuals who perceived their relationship to be equitable were more likely to engage in maintenance activities than individuals who perceived their relationship to be inequitable.

Breakup. Almost one in two marriages ends in divorce. Moreover, only a small proportion of cohabiting and dating relationships move to marriage. Does inequity play a role in the breakup of relationships?

Although the research shows that equity influences partners' commitment to their relationship, there is very little evidence to indicate that inequity causes a relationship to break up (or that equity causes a relationship to remain intact). For example, Harold Lujansky and Gerold Mikula (1983) compared, over a period of five months, the equity scores between a group of male students who remained in their dating relationship and a group who did not. No significant differences were found between the two groups on a variety of equity measures. A longitudinal study of couples who had only recently begun to date (Berg and McQuinn 1986) showed that some social-exchange variables predicted which relationships remained together and which broke up, but equity was found to be insignificant. Another study (Felmlee, Sprecher, and Bassin 1990) found that equity and inequity did not affect the rate at which dating relationships broke up over a three-month period, controlling for several other variables. Although equity may be a more important predictor of the breakup of marital relationships, no longitudinal studies have been conducted to examine whether equity or inequity predicts marital disruption.

Perceived inequity in one or two very central areas of the relationship can possibly lead to the breakup of a relationship. For instance, the degree to which the relationship partners are equal or equitable in their love or attachment may be all that matters in determining whether they stay together. In the classic Boston Dating Couples study (Hill, Rubin, and Peplau 1976), dating couples who were equally involved in the relationship were much more likely to remain together over time than couples in which at least one member reported that they were not equally involved. Further, the same study reported that it was not only the less involved partners who ended relationships; more involved partners, particularly women, also ended relationships.

Although researchers interested in the role of equity in the breakup of relationships have focused on how perceptions of equity or inequity lead a relationship to end, there is another way perceptions of equity and inequity may be involved in the breakup of the relationship. Once one partner in the relationship decides to end the relationship, perceptions of inequity may follow. In many cases, individuals who are in the process of breaking up need to justify the breakup—to themselves and to others—and it may help to get over a breakup if they can find fault with the partner and the relationship ("Well, now that I think about it, I was treated unfairly").

Furthermore, equity issues are very salient in divorce proceedings as ex-spouses divide up the assets, debts, and rights to the children. Ex-spouses are likely to get along better if they perceive that the divorce settlement was equitable (Arditti and Allen 1991).

Conclusion

There have always been some theorists skeptical of the application of equity theory to close relationships. Certainly, equity theory has not provided the general theory social psychologists so badly need. Based on the research conducted since the mid-1980s, however, equity can be concluded to play an important role in intimate relationships for *most* people *some* of the time and for *some* people *most* of the time.

It is still to be discovered which people are most concerned with equity issues and under what conditions equity becomes a salient issue. For example, some types of individuals may get extremely upset when their relationship becomes inequitable, whereas others may be able to exist comfortably with a perception of injustice, or may tend to redefine reality to suit their psychological and practical needs. Research has shown that some individuals are high in "exchange orientation" and these individuals are more likely to become distressed in response to inequities than individuals low in exchange orientation. Many other types of variables may also affect how inequities affect the relationship. These other variables include individual difference variables (e.g., gender, religiosity, gender-role orientation), reward level (perhaps people get upset over inequities only when their reward level is low), relationship length or intimacy (people may get more upset over inequities early in the relationship than later), and relationship type (people may get more upset over inequities in friendship than in marriage or familial relationships).

(*See also:* CONFLICT; DIVISION OF LABOR; DUAL-EARNER FAMILIES; EXCHANGE THEORY; FAMILY GENDER ROLES; MARITAL POWER; MARITAL QUALITY)

BIBLIOGRAPHY

Adams, J. S. (1965). "Inequity in Social Exchange." In *Advances in Experimental Social Psychology*, Vol. 2, ed. L. Berkowitz. New York: Academic Press.

Arditti, J. A., and Allen, K. R. (1991). "Understanding Distressed Fathers' Perceptions of Legal and Relational Inequities Postdivorce." Paper presented at the annual meeting of the National Council on Family Relations, Denver.

Austin, W. G. (1974). "Studies in 'Equity with the World': A New Application Equity Theory." Ph.D. diss., University of Wisconsin, Madison.

Berg, J. H., and McQuinn, R. D. (1986). "Attraction and Exchange in Continuing and Noncontinuing Dating Relationships." *Journal of Personality and Social Psychology* 50:942–952.

Blau, P. M. (1964). *Exchange and Power in Social Life.* New York: Wiley.

Canary, D. J., and Stafford, L. (1991). "Maintenance Strategies, Equity, and Locus of Control in the Preservation of Relational Characteristics." Paper presented at the International Network on Personal Relationships Conference, Bloomington, IL.

Cate, R. M.; Lloyd, S. A.; Henton, J. M.; and Larson, J. H. (1982). "Fairness and Reward Level as Predictors of Relationship Satisfaction." *Social Psychology Quarterly* 45:177–181.

Cate, R. M.; Lloyd, S. A.; and Long, E. (1988). "The Role of Rewards and Fairness in Developing Premarital Relationships." *Journal of Marriage and the Family* 50:443–452.

Deutsch, M. (1975). "Equity, Equality, and Need: What Determines Which Value Will Be Used as the Basis of Distributive Justice?" *Journal of Social Issues* 31:137–150.

Felmlee, D.; Sprecher, S.; and Bassin, E. (1990). "The Dissolution of Intimate Relationships: A Hazard Model." *Social Psychology Quarterly* 53:13–30.

Hatfield, E.; Greenberger, D.; Traupmann, J.; and Lambert, P. (1982). "Equity and Sexual Satisfaction in Recently Married Couples." *Journal of Sex Research* 18:18–32.

Hatfield, E., and Traupmann, J. (1981). "Intimate Relationships: A Perspective from Equity Theory." In *Personal Relationships*, Vol. 1, ed. S. W. Duck and R. Gilmour. London: Academic Press.

Hatfield, E.; Traupmann, J.; Sprecher, S.; Utne, M.; and Hay, J. (1985). "Equity and Intimate Relations: Recent Research." In *Compatible and Incompatible Relationships*, ed. W. Ickes. New York: Springer-Verlag.

Hatfield, E.; Utne, M. K.; and Traupmann, J. (1979). "Equity Theory and Intimate Relationships." In *Social Exchange in Developing Relationships*, ed. R. L. Burgess and T. L. Huston. New York: Academic Press.

Hill, C. T.; Rubin, Z.; and Peplau, L. A. (1976). "Breakups Before Marriage: The End of 103 Affairs." *Journal of Social Issues* 32:147–168.

Homans, G. C. (1961). *Social Behavior.* New York: Harcourt, Brace & World.

Lujansky, H., and Mikula, G. (1983). "Can Equity Theory Explain the Quality and Stability of Romantic Relationships?" *Journal of Social Psychology* 22:101–112.

Martin, M. W. (1985). "Satisfaction with Intimate Exchange: Gender-Role Differences and the Impact of Equity, Equality, and Rewards." *Sex Roles* 13:597–605.

Michaels, J. W.; Acock, A. C.; and Edwards, J. N. (1986). "Social Exchange and Equity Determinants of Relationship Commitment." *Journal of Social and Personal Relationships* 3:161–175.

Michaels, J. W.; Edwards, J. N.; and Acock, A. C. (1984). "Satisfaction in Intimate Relationships as a Function of Inequality, Inequity, and Outcomes." *Social Psychology Quarterly* 47:347–357.

Prins, K. S.; Buunk, B. P.; and Van Yperen, N. W. (1993). "Equity, Normative Disapproval, and Extramarital Relationships." *Journal of Social and Personal Relationships* 10:39–53.

Rusbult, C. E. (1980). "Commitment and Satisfaction in Romantic Associations: A Test of the Investment Model." *Journal of Experimental Social Psychology* 16:172–186.

Rusbult, C. E. (1983). "A Longitudinal Test of the Investment Model: The Development (and Deterioration) of

Satisfaction and Commitment in Heterosexual Involvements." *Journal of Personality and Social Psychology* 45:101–117.

Sabatelli, R. M., and Cecil-Pigo, E. F. (1985). "Relational Interdependence and Commitment in Marriage." *Journal of Marriage and the Family* 47:931–937.

Schafer, R. B., and Keith, P. M. (1980). "Equity and Depression Among Married Couples." *Social Psychology Quarterly* 43:430–435.

Sprecher, S. (1986). "The Relationship Between Inequity and Emotions in Close Relationships." *Social Psychology Quarterly* 49:309–321.

Sprecher, S. (1988). "Investment Model, Equity, and Social Support Determinants of Relationship Commitment." *Social Psychology Quarterly* 51:318–328.

Sprecher, S. (1992). "How Men and Women Expect to Feel and Behave in Response to Inequity in Close Relationships." *Social Psychology Quarterly* 55:57–69.

Steil, J. M., and Turetsky, B. A. (1987). "Is Equal Better?" In *Family Processes and Problems: Social Psychological Aspects*, ed. S. Oskamp. Newbury Park, CA: Sage Publications.

Thibaut, J. W., and Kelley, H. H. (1959). *The Social Psychology of Groups*. New York: Wiley.

Traupmann, J.; Hatfield, E.; and Wexler, P. (1983). "Equity and Sexual Satisfaction in Dating Couples." *British Journal of Social Psychology* 22:33–40.

Traupmann, J.; Petersen, R.; Utne, M.; and Hatfield, E. (1981). "Measuring Equity in Intimate Relationships." *Applied Psychological Measurement* 5:467–480.

Utne, M. K.; Hatfield, E.; Traupmann, J.; and Greenberger, D. (1984). "Equity, Marital Satisfaction, and Stability." *Journal of Social and Personal Relationships* 1:323–332.

Van Yperen, N. W., and Buunk, B. P. (1991). "Equity Theory, Exchange and Communal Orientation from a Cross-National Perspective." *Journal of Social Psychology* 131:5–20.

Walster, E.; Traupmann, J.; and Walster, G. W. (1978). "Equity and Extramarital Sexuality." *Archives of Sexual Behavior* 7:127–141.

Walster, E.; Walster, G. W.; and Berscheid, E. (1978). *Equity: Theory and Research*. Boston: Allyn & Bacon.

Walster, E.; Walster, G. W.; and Traupmann, J. (1978). "Equity and Premarital Sex." *Journal of Personality and Social Psychology* 36:82–92.

SUSAN SPRECHER

ETHNICITY

The word "ethnic" is derived from the Greek *ethnikos*, the adjective form of *ethnos*, meaning a nation or race. The word was applied originally to heathens, pagans, and to outsiders as a class. From an original biological context, it was broadened to include cultural characteristics and political structures (Petersen 1980).

The use of the word "ethnicity" and the more common term "ethnic groups" is relatively new; they did not appear in standard English dictionaries until the 1960s. In the broadest sense of their original meanings, all human groups belonged to ethnic groups, but because the definitions have narrowed, some human groups can no longer be classified as ethnic groups (Glazer and Moynihan 1975).

Michael Banton (1983) indicates that one of the first studies to use ethnic as a term to denote the lower classes was W. Lloyd Warner's 1941 study of Yankee City. He classified Greek, Irish, Italian, Jewish, and Polish Americans as ethnics, while immigrants from England, Scotland, and Northern Ireland were not.

The terms ethnicity, ethnic groups, ethnic consciousness, and ethnic identity now appear regularly in both social science writings and in the mass media. However, as with many popular terms, there is a great deal of difficulty in defining ethnicity and what constitutes an ethnic group.

The *Harvard Encyclopedia of American Ethnic Groups* (Thernstrom, Orlov, and Handlin 1980), in developing criteria for inclusion under ethnicity, considered some of the following features:

1. common geographic origin
2. migratory status
3. race
4. language and dialect
5. religious faith or faiths
6. ties that transcend kinship, neighborhood, and community boundaries
7. shared traditions, values, and symbols

The definition of ethnicity, or its more functional term, ethnic group, is individuals and families who are members of national, religious, cultural, and racial groups that do not belong to the dominant group in a society. They can be differentiated from both the dominant and other ethnic groups by some combination of their values, expectations, attitudes, customs, lifestyles, rituals, and celebrations. In addition, their ethnicity and sense of peoplehood are recognized by themselves and by others.

A number of other terms, such as "minority" and "racial groups," are related to the term ethnic group. Minorities are differentiated on the basis of power and resources, so that to be a member of a minority group is to share a status relationship with a dominant group. To be a member of a racial group is to be defined on the basis of both physical and cultural characteristics. The same individual can be a member of a minority group, a racial group, and an ethnic group (Mindel, Habenstein, and Wright 1988).

Origins and Importance of Ethnicity

Nathan Glazer and Patrick Moynihan (1975) contrast two major conceptions of ethnicity—the "primordialists" and the "circumstantialists." The primordial approach emphasizes history and experiences and may even include genetic transmission, so ethnicity is viewed as a basic identity that may be both overt and latent. It implies the existence of a distinct culture or subculture, so that members feel themselves bound together by a number of commonalities, including history, visibility, values, norms, and behaviors. There is a strong sense of ethnic identity and peoplehood, and the distinctiveness of the group is also recognized by other members of the society (Yetman 1985). The identity is more likely to be ascribed, rather than voluntary.

The circumstantialist, or instrumentalist, view is a functional one, with ethnicity serving the economic and political interests of individuals. An ethnic group uses traditional beliefs, symbols, and ceremonials in order to develop an informal political organization in its struggle for power (Cohen 1969). As such, it is less permanent and may vary in terms of time, place, and situation.

A third perspective emphasizes the role of marginality in the development and maintenance of ethnicity. Groups that are placed on the fringes and labeled as "outsiders" (either through their own volition or through barriers such as prejudice, discrimination, and segregation) with seemingly little chance of ever being accepted by the dominant society as equals are most likely to develop an ethnic perspective. The more marginal a group, the higher the possibility of developing and maintaining a strong ethnic identity. Conversely, the more accepted a group, the less likely it is to develop a strong ethnic identity.

Ethnic groups can last over long periods, but they can also change, merge, or disappear. Assimilation is one outcome for groups with weak ethnic identities. The term describing the process of developing new ethnic groups is "ethnogenesis."

Ethnic identification and membership in an ethnic group are important because they control, limit, and enhance opportunities for well-being in society. Conversely, it would only be of limited interest if they just described some passing variations (Mindel, Habenstein, and Wright 1988).

The diversity between and within ethnic families defies simple generalizations. The historical background—what they were, why they came, what they brought with them, and their reception by both the ethnic and the dominant community—offers clues for understanding the ethnic family. Their expectations and goals, coupled with their exposure and interaction with American society, provide the impetus for possible conflict and change.

It is impossible to present the full spectrum of ethnic groups and their families; therefore, the divisions developed by Charles Mindel, Robert Habenstein, and Roosevelt Wright (1988) provide useful categories. The divisions include (1) European families, (2) Hispanic families, (3) Asian families, and (4) historically subjugated families. There are also socioreligious groups, such as the Amish, Jews, Arabs, and Mormons. There are both differences and a degree of overlap in the categories between and within groups.

European Ethnic Minorities

Examples of European ethnic groups include immigrants from Europe, such as the Poles, the Italians, the Greeks, and the Irish. Basic differences between the European families and those in the other categories were visibility and racial similarity, so that in the final analysis, ethnicity was more voluntary than ascribed. There are a number of models that analyze the European experience.

Straight line theory (Sandberg 1974) assumes there is a decline in ethnicity with each generation so that each group becomes more American as it is exposed, socialized, and influenced by the dominant culture. Robert Park's (1950) race relations cycle of immigration, contact, competition, accommodation, and eventual assimilation and Milton Gordon's (1964) assimilation model are also based on the European experience. Immigrants arrive voluntarily in the new world with "old-world" family patterns. Exposure to American society changes, or acculturates, the ethnic family to more American models. There may be instances of conflict during this process.

Helen Lopata (1988) indicates that the role of many of the early Polish male immigrants was to work hard, putting in long hours, which meant little time for their children. Their primary family role was to serve as disciplinarians. Girls were expected to work with their mothers, so that learning to keep house, sew, cook, and take care of younger children was their primary role. There was also a fear of sexuality, of girls becoming pregnant before marriage, and the development of bad reputations. Some common themes included religious identification as Catholics, a strong family orientation, and an emphasis on courtesy and etiquette (Lopata 1976).

It is difficult to assess the ethnicity of third- and fourth-generation Poles, since many do not identify with the ethnic group when they answer census or survey questions. Geographic dispersion, economic mobility, higher education, and high rates of intermarriage have created new generations that are less likely to identify with Polish or Polish-American culture (Lopata 1988).

The experiences of Italian, Greek, and Irish families also followed a similar pattern. George Kourvetaris (1988) sees the transformation of the Greeks from a rural, traditional, immigrant family to a Greek-American urban middle class. He concludes that the family has moved away from the traditional, and taken on the new, which includes the loss of family traditions, parental respect, and cooperation among family units. The erosion of the family and the emphasis on individualism are reflected in growing consumerism and rising divorce rates, presenting a threat to previously cohesive communities.

The Italian family also started with "traditional" family structures and values. The necessity of family ties was of such importance that the highest shame was to be without a family. Men who violated family codes became outcasts, while loyal kin were rewarded by having a place in the family. The aged were cared for by the family and only those without family ties ended up in poorhouses or on public charity (Squier and Quadagno 1988). Increased education and mobility have decreased the importance of family units, especially the extended family, so that there has been a drop in the degree of ethnicity. However, one study indicated that third-generation Italians were more likely to think of themselves as ethnics than the first and second generations (Goering 1971). However, other studies indicated that the straight line model was appropriate. The highest levels of ethnicity were found among those with the fewest years of schooling and lower occupational levels (Roche 1984; Squier and Quadagno 1988).

Irish families were generally Catholic, and their experiences were similar to the other European ethnic groups. Sibling loyalty, loyalty to the family unit, and extended kinship gatherings were part of family life. However, life in America brought about changes, so that even though fathers assumed the role of head of the family, many wives began to work outside of the home. The Catholic family remained strong, so that the Irish were more culturally pluralistic than many of the other European groups (Horgan 1988).

Differences do exist between and within the European groups in terms of generation, social class, sex, urban–rural areas, and mobility. However, there is a lack of empirical research concerning these specific differences.

Acculturation has led to a weakening of "old-world" family styles. Each succeeding European generation has become more like the dominant society, so that ethnic identity has lost its focus in culture, family structure, and social behavior. What remains as ethnicity in the lives of the children of European immigrants is what Herbert Gans (1985) refers to as symbolic ethnicity, so that it is not a critical factor in their lives.

Hispanic Ethnic Minorities

Hispanic ethnic minorities include the Mexican-American, the Cuban-American, and the Puerto Rican-American family. The general background of each of these groups is that of foreign influences in their homelands, first by Europeans, primarily the Spanish, then by the United States. The geographic closeness of their homelands has also meant continued ties between their place of origin and the United States.

Mexican-American families consist largely of descendants of unskilled immigrants who worked in the low-wage sectors of American economy (Becerra 1988). They concentrated initially in the Southwest, especially New Mexico and Southern California, but have also moved to the Midwest.

Mexican Americans are currently a heterogeneous population. Some are descendants of early Spanish and Mexican settlers who inhabited the Southwest and were "conquered" by the Americans; others came from various parts of Mexico at different historical periods. There has been a continuous flow of these immigrants, including an unknown number of undocumented cases.

The traditional structure of the Mexican family, or *familia*, was based on the socioeconomic needs of the agrarian and craft economies of Mexico. It meant an extended, multigenerational group of persons with special ascribed roles. The division of roles and functions, which included mutual support, enabled the family to survive during difficult times. The family, in both work and leisure times, was the most important structure in traditional Mexican society (Becerra 1988).

A popular stereotype concerning the role of the Mexican-American male is that of machismo. It is often equated with the absolute power of the male, including excessive aggression, and sexual prowess,

229

and a secondary role for women. Rosina Becerra (1988) indicates that genuine machismo is characterized by true bravery, valor, courage, generosity, and a concern for others. It serves to protect and provide for the family, and includes the use of just authority and a respect for wife and children.

Figures indicate the Mexican-American family income is low, that fertility is high, and that there has been a move toward the urban centers. Mexican-American families are less likely to have extended kin residing in the same household, and the traditional family system is more characterized by voluntary interaction than by the necessity of family survival.

Because of the various patterns of immigration, Mexican Americans span a variety of generations and a wide continuum of those who have been affected by acculturation and assimilation. Ethnicity has been reinforced by the Chicano movement, especially in Los Angeles, which has awakened a political identity. The Mexican-American family, then, represents a wide spectrum, ranging from the traditional *familia* to the acculturated American, with points in between that are neither totally Mexican nor totally American. The continued influx of newcomers, the numerical growth of the population, and the maintenance of language, food, and lifestyles indicate the importance of ethnicity in the bilingual, bicultural adaptation of Mexicans to American society.

The Cuban family is also related to its immigration history. Although there was already a small number of Cubans in the United States, the bulk of immigration came in a number of waves after the takeover of Cuba by Fidel Castro in 1959.

Jose Szapocznik and Roberto Hernandez (1988) indicate that the traditional extended family of Cuba had already began its change toward a more nuclear family structure before 1959. The tightly knit nuclear family had allowed for the inclusion of relatives and godparents (*padrinos*). There was a strong emphasis on lineal, family relations, so that it was expected that children show absolute obedience to their parents, and wives to husbands.

Cuban women became much more prominent in the labor market upon arrival in the United States. As a result, the traditional patriarchal structure of the family began to change. Younger families are usually comprised of husbands and wives who, having grown up in the United States, find the more egalitarian roles of men and women less stressful.

The process of adaptation and adjustment has resulted in the disruption of the traditional, closely knit family. Parents who expect children to carry out the traditions of family values and interactions brought from Cuba may become alienated from their highly Americanized children, just as their children may turn away from their old-fashioned parents.

The conflict between first-generation immigrant families and their American-born, second-generation children is a familiar theme and is not unique to any one group. Szapocznik and Hernandez (1988) indicate that individuals who live in bicultural environments are better off in developing a bicultural style. Those who adapt a monocultural style, either solely Cuban or solely American, may lack the flexibility and balance necessary to live in a bicultural world. Therefore, parental tendencies to hang tenaciously onto traditional Hispanic family and cultural values, including strong family cohesion and controls, may exacerbate the conflict between generations. To avoid the detrimental effects of adaptation to a new culture, individuals living in bicultural communities, such as in Miami, may find it more useful to develop a bicultural perspective. It means learning and communicating in different cultural contexts and maintaining a Cuban and an American identity.

Puerto Ricans are similar to the Mexicans and Cubans in terms of traditional family structures and values. Their major migration took place after World War II and has been to the East Coast, especially New York City. The reasons for this migration include rapid population growth and high rates of unemployment on their island and the prospect for employment and higher wages in the United States.

The traditional Puerto Rican family was described as an extended family, with the primary responsibility for child rearing vested in the nuclear family. Although husbands were the traditional source of family authority, child rearing was the major responsibility of the wives (Steward 1956). Kinship bonds were strong, and interdependence was a major theme among family and kinship members. *Compadrazgo* (coparenthood) and the practice of *hijos de crianza* (informal adoption of children) were two components of extended kinship (Sanchez-Ayendez 1988).

Joseph Fitzpatrick (1971) provides four variations of the household composition, reflecting the need to cope in different economic and social circumstances. There is the modified extended family, which includes families with frequent interaction and interdependence patterns among several generations and other kin members; the nuclear family, with weak bonds to other family and extended family members; parents with both their own children and children from another union; and single-parent families.

The interactions of a variety of factors have made Puerto Ricans relatively unique among immigrant groups. They are conscious of their American citizenship, they are extremely close to their homeland so that there is constant contact with friends and relatives, and there is a continuity of shared meaning and communication, including family interdependence. Generations born and reared in the United States rely less on Spanish, yet few see themselves as exclusively American. As with the majority of the other two Hispanic groups discussed here, emphasis is on a bicultural approach, rather than total assimilation into the dominant culture.

Asian Ethnic Minorities

Asian groups include the Chinese, Japanese, Koreans, and Filipinos. There is a remarkable diversity between and within the groups in terms of history, time of immigration, demographic variables, and reasons for migration. There are also some similarities, including Asian ancestry and a Confucian value system, with the exception of the Filipino.

The Chinese were the earliest immigrant group from Asia, the first wave arriving after the discovery of gold in California in 1848. The majority were young male laborers who, because of discrimination, lived segregated lives in menial occupations. Many returned to China; very few were able to bring wives from China to start a family.

Morrison Wong (1988) indicates that the Chinese family, which takes many forms, is the product of the complex interaction of immigration; social, legal, political, and economic factors; culture; and generations. Among the many family types are the traditional; the "mutilated," in which husbands and wives were separated for long periods of time; the small producer, in which the entire family formed self-contained units in a family business; the "normal," which followed the more American model of a family; and the ghetto and professional families.

The majority of Asian-American families can trace their roots to the traditional family structure of China, which included (1) patriarchal rule, with clearly defined roles of male dominance; (2) patrilocal residence patterns, where married couples lived with the husband's parents; and (3) extended families, in which many generations lived with their offspring under one roof.

Because ancestor worship was emphasized, having sons to carry on the family name was a cherished value. Another important value was filial piety: duty, obligation, importance of the family name, self-sacrifice for the good of the elders, and respect for status characterized family relations, even in marriage (Hsu 1971). Love was not a common element in choosing martial partners; arranged marriages were common. As one consequence, migration patterns included husbands leaving for distant lands for extended periods of time, while the wife and children remained at the home of the husband's parents in the village (Nee and Wong 1985).

The Japanese were the second major Asian immigrant group and their early experiences were similar to those of the Chinese. However, their primarily single, male, young adult population called for wives, often called "picture brides," from Japan, so when the 1924 Immigration Act forbade the immigration of all Asians, the Japanese already had wives and were able to start families. One consequence of their interrupted migration pattern and the beginning of family life was the importance of generations. The Issei, or first-generation immigrants, arrived between 1890 and 1924, and the remaining survivors comprise the very elderly. Their American-born children, the Nisei, now are the bulk of the older adult and elderly population. The Sansei, or third generation, make up the bulk of the adult population.

Each generation has its unique features. The Issei represents the culture of Meiji Japan with its emphasis on vertical family structure with male dominance, interaction with kin and ethnic community, minimal interaction with the dominant community, and retention of a strong ethnic identity.

Nisei, born in the United States, were exposed to American society, but they faced the same severe prejudice and discrimination as the Issei. The hostility toward Japanese Americans peaked during World War II with their incarceration in "relocation centers," a euphemism for concentration camps. This forced a reexamination of their ethnicity, since even the most acculturated had to face the consequences of their "Japaneseness." The Sansei and later American-born generations are almost thoroughly American, with only their physical features distinguishing them from the dominant society.

The Japanese family reflects generational lines. Marriage is one example of the changes by generation; Sansei rates of marrying non-Japanese are well over 50 percent, whereas Issei and Nisei rates of outmarriage are significantly below these figures (Kitano and Daniels 1988).

However, ethnicity remains a critical variable for most Japanese Americans, regardless of generation, since many Americans have difficulty in differentiating between Japanese Americans and Japanese from Japan (as evidenced by the internment of Japanese Americans during World War II). "Japan-bashing" serves as a continued reminder to Japanese Americans of their ancestry.

Other Asian-American groups have arrived in the United States at different times with different family compositions. The early Filipino experience was similar to that of the Chinese and Japanese; family life was often delayed. However, the Koreans did not arrived in significant numbers until after the 1965 Immigration Act. Much of their migration has been with intact families so that the maintenance of large Korean communities has strengthened ethnic identity. (Kitano and Daniels 1988). The Vietnamese immigrated to the United States primarily as refugees. The move was made by individuals as well as families and extended families. Although initially scattered throughout the United States, many have relocated to California and formed communities with names such as "Little Saigon," preserving their ethnic identity.

Although there is a wide diversity between and within the various Asian-American groups, there are also similar processes, depending on the time of arrival. Because of race, they have faced and continue to face prejudice, discrimination, and segregation. One response has been to form local ethnic communities, which has tended to reinforce an ethnic culture. In addition, each American-born generation has been exposed to American models, leading to a variety of adaptations, including Americanization, the retention of ethnic ways, and a bicultural mode. Family styles reflect these differences.

Subjugated Minorities

The two most prominent subjugated minorities are the African American and the Native American. As with the Asian Americans, they are visible minorities, and their historical experiences have deeply affected their family lives. They were also involuntary immigrants: the Native Americans, though already here, were forced to move off their lands; and African Americans arrived as slaves. Therefore, the desire to "become American," a motivating force for European groups, was lacking.

A combination of four cultural traits distinguished African Americans from other immigrants: (1) they came from countries with norms and values that were dissimilar to the American way of life; (2) they were from many different tribes, each with its own language, culture, and traditions; (3) in the beginning they came without women; and (4) they came in bondage (Billingsley 1968).

Many of the writings concerning the African-American family have dealt with their problems, fo-

cusing on the lower-income strata (with terms such as deviance, pathology, and the like), while ignoring stable black families. It should be noted that, although an ethnic group's families may not fit into the normative model of the dominant society, it often has its own functional organization that meets the needs of the group (Billingsley 1970).

Nevertheless, ethnicity, in terms of visibility and racism, has been the dominant factor affecting African-American family life. It has affected the employment and attrition of black men in the labor force; created an imbalance of female-only households; affected rates of divorce and out-of-wedlock births; and created crisis conditions in many black families. The disintegration of the family is a symptom of the larger problem, the institutional decimation of black males. Although there are many children who overcome the handicap of poverty and one-parent households, the odds are against them.

> Large numbers of them, especially the males, will follow their biological fathers to an early grave, prison, and the ranks of the unemployed. Only by resolving the problems of the black male can we restore the black family to its rightful place in our lives [Billingsley 1968, p. 321].

As Andrew Billingsley is quick to point out, however, there are also many stable, two-parent, middle-class families that have survived racism and have been contributing members of society.

Native Americans are different in that they were America's original inhabitants and were conquered. At the time of their contact with the Europeans, there were several hundred ethnolinguistic groups (John 1988).

John Red Horse (1978) offers a typology of three family patterns; the traditional, the bicultural, and the pan-traditional. He further delineates structural patterns of family life in four settings: (1) small reservation communities; (2) interstate extended families; (3) families in urban areas; and (4) families in large metropolitan areas, including nonkin who assume family roles (Red Horse 1980).

Old Indian ways include extended family households, the use of Indian language, and participation in tribal religious practices. There is low educational attainment and little value is placed on education. The economy is a communal family economy, and there is minimal participation in wage labor. The supervision of children is little and tolerant, stressing the importance of grandparents' participation in child rearing. (John 1988).

New Indian ways include nuclear family households with high educational attainment. There are more material possessions, and steady employment in wage labor. The Christian religion is practiced, and supervision of children is strict. Contact with whites is increased, and there is increased intermarriage outside tribal boundaries (John 1988).

Conclusion

The Hispanics, the Asians, the Native Americans, and the African Americans were, at one time or another, specified as ethnics by the government for exclusionary purposes. Ethnicity meant pariah status; there were anti-immigration laws, laws against intermarriage, and barriers toward gaining citizenship. Opportunities for housing, education, and employment were limited, and social equality was a distant dream. Developing a healthy ethnic identity has been a constant issue.

These groups, most marginalized from the mainstream through visibility, race, and culture, have retained a strong ethnic identity, while groups more similar to the mainstream have seen the weakening of an ethnic identity.

In addition, immigrants with traditional family orientations and a cohesive ethnic community maintain ethnicity and customary ways. Less cohesive ethnic communities, especially those that are more accepted by the dominant community, are prone to lose their ethnicity and to assimilate.

(*See also:* EXTENDED FAMILY; FAMILY RITUALS; FAMILY STORIES AND MYTHS; FAMILY VALUES; FICTIVE KINSHIP; FILIAL RESPONSIBILITY; INTERGENERATIONAL RELATIONS; INTERMARRIAGE; KINSHIP; NUCLEAR FAMILY)

BIBLIOGRAPHY

Banton, M. (1983). *Racial and Ethnic Competition*. Cambridge, Eng.: Cambridge University Press.

Becerra, R. (1988). "The Mexican American Family." In *Ethnic Families in America*, ed. C. H. Mindel, R. W. Habenstein, and R. Wright, Jr. New York: Elsevier.

Billingsley, A. (1968). *Black Families in White America*. Englewood Cliffs, NJ: Prentice Hall.

Billingsley, A. (1970). "Black Families and White Social Science." *Journal of Social Issues* 26:127–142.

Brass, P. R. (1991). *Ethnicity and Nationalism*. Newbury Park, CA: Sage Publications.

Cohen, A. (1969). *Custom and Politics in Urban Africa*. London: Routledge & Kegan Paul.

Fitzpatrick, J. (1971). *Puerto Rican Americans*. Englewood Cliffs, NJ: Prentice Hall.

Gans, H. H. (1985). "Symbolic Ethnicity: The Future of Ethnic Groups and Cultures in America." In *Majority and Minority*, 4th edition, ed. N. R. Yetman. Boston: Allyn & Bacon.

Glazer, N., and Moynihan, P. (1975). *Ethnicity: Theory and Experience*. Cambridge, MA: Harvard University Press.

Goering, J. (1971). "The Emergence of Ethnic Interests: A Case of Serendipity." *Social Forces* 50:379–384.

Gordon, M. (1964). *Assimilation in American Life*. New York: Oxford University Press.

Horgan, E. (1988). "The American Catholic Irish Family." In *Ethnic Families in America*, ed. C. H. Mindel, R. W. Habenstein, and R. Wright, Jr. New York: Elsevier.

Hsu, F. (1971). *Under the Ancestors' Shadow: Chinese Culture and Personality*. Stanford, CA: Stanford University Press.

John, R. (1988). "The Native American Family." In *Ethnic Families in America*, ed. C. H. Mindel, R. W. Habenstein, and R. Wright, Jr. New York: Elsevier.

Kitano, H., and Daniels, R. (1988). *Asian Americans*. Englewood Cliffs, NJ: Prentice Hall.

Kourvetaris, G. A. (1988). "The Greek American Family." In *Ethnic Families in America*, ed. C. H. Mindel, R. W. Habenstein, and R. Wright, Jr. New York: Elsevier.

Lopata, H. Z. (1976). "Polish Immigration to the United States of America." *Polish Review* 21:85–108.

Lopata, H. Z. (1988). "The Polish American Family." In *Ethnic Families in America*, ed. C. H. Mindel, R. W. Habenstein, and R. Wright, Jr. New York: Elsevier.

Mindel, C.; Habenstein, R.; and Wright, R., Jr., eds. (1988). *Ethnic Families in America*. New York: Elsevier.

Nee, V., and Wong, H. (1985). "Asian-American Socioeconomic Achievements: The Strength of Family Bond." *Sociological Perspectives* 28:281–306.

Park, R. (1950). *Race and Culture*. New York: Free Press.

Petersen, W. (1980). "Concepts of Ethnicity." In *Harvard Encyclopedia of American Ethnic Groups*, ed. S. Thernstrom, A. Orlov, and O. Handlin. Cambridge, MA: Harvard University Press.

Red Horse, J. (1978). "Family Behavior of Urban American Indians." *Social Casework* 59:67–72.

Red Horse, J. (1980). "Family Structure and Value Orientation in American Indians." *Social Casework* 61:462–467.

Roche, J. (1984). "Social Factors Affecting Cultural, National, and Religious Ethnicity: A Study of Suburban Italian Americans." *Ethnic Groups* 6:27–45.

Sanchez-Ayendez, M. (1988). "The Puerto Rican Family." In *Ethnic Families in America*, ed. C. H. Mindel, R. W. Habenstein, and R. Wright, Jr. New York: Elsevier.

Sandberg, N. C. (1974). *Ethnic Identity and Assimilation: The Polish American Community*. New York: Praeger.

Squier, D. A., and Quadagno, J. (1988). "The Italian American Family." In *Ethnic Families in America*, ed. C. H. Mindel, R. W. Habenstein, and R. Wright, Jr. New York: Elsevier.

Steward, J. H. (1956). *The People of Puerto Rico*. Urbana: University of Illinois Press.

Szapocznik, J., and Hernandez, R. (1988). "The Cuban American Family." In *Ethnic Families in America*, ed. C. H. Mindel, R. W. Habenstein, and R. Wright, Jr. New York: Elsevier.

Thernstrom, S.; Orlov, A.; and Handlin, O., eds. (1980). "Introduction." In *Harvard Encyclopedia of American Ethnic Groups*. Cambridge, MA: Harvard University Press.

Wong, M. G. (1988). "The Chinese American Family." In *Ethnic Families in America*, ed. C. Mindel, R. W. Habenstein, and R. Wright, Jr. New York: Elsevier.

Yetman, N. (1985). "Introduction: Definitions and Perspectives." In *Majority and Minority: The Dynamics of Race and Ethnicity in American Life*, ed. N. Yetman. Boston: Allyn & Bacon.

HARRY H. L. KITANO

EXCHANGE THEORY

The idea that social relationships are organized around the exchange of valued resources has been a central theme among some philosophers and social scientists for almost 200 years. Its origins lie in the writings of the utilitarian philosophers and classical economists of the early nineteenth-century (Turner 1978, pp. 201–204). The principle advanced by these scholars was that human behavior was driven by the desire or need of individuals to maximize their benefits (sometimes referred to as rewards or gains) and minimize costs (which include losses or punishments). This principle has had a profound influence on modern economic theory.

The impact of these ideas, however, extended beyond economics to include the other social sciences. In the beginning of the twentieth century a group of anthropologists, notably Sir James George Frazer, Bronislaw Malinowski, Marcel Mauss, and Claude Lévi-Strauss, used ethnographic data to demonstrate how the exchanges of different kinds of goods and services (including human beings) were central in the organization of social life (Turner 1978).

It was not until the 1960s and 1970s that family scholars became seriously interested in using social exchange theories as a way of explaining family behavior. This interest was sparked by the publication of three books: John Thibaut and Harold H. Kelley's *The Social Psychology of Groups* (1959), George Homans's *Social Behavior: Its Elementary Forms* (1961, revised 1974), and Peter M. Blau's *Exchange and Power in Social Life* (1964).

Two basic ideas underlie all three books: (1) the important things people want can only be gained through exchanges with other people and (2) people will attempt to obtain the things they desire with as little effort or cost as possible. Thus, at least in situations in which there is free choice, people engage in interactions or join groups because they consider it to be in their best interests. The parallels to the economic notion of a free marketplace are apparent. Human beings are thought to engage in interpersonal relationships to make a profit or, under some conditions, to keep their losses at a minimum.

There are, however, important differences between economic and social exchanges. For one thing, the resources exchanged in social relationships are more extensive than those traded in the economic marketplace. Furthermore, some social resources are not as easily quantified as economic goods and services. For example, in addition to exchanging quantifiable resources such as money, goods, and services, people also exchange qualitative phenomena such as love, status, and information (Foa and Foa 1974). Another key difference is that the exchanges that take place in interpersonal relationships tend to increase the partners' dependency on one another (Thibaut and Kelley 1959; Kelley and Thibaut 1978). Unlike economic market transactions in which every exchange is considered to be a new deal that is evaluated on its own merits, social and interpersonal exchanges, if they are successful, will tend to be repeated with the same partners—thereby limiting the range of possible partners and continually increasing each partner's dependency on the other (Emerson 1981).

Given the subjective nature and qualitative character of many of the resources that are exchanged in social relationships, the question arises as to how people determine if the outcomes of exchanges are profitable. Thibaut and Kelley (1959) introduce the concept of comparison level (CL) as one possible answer to this question. CL represents the acceptable level of benefit a person expects on the basis of past experience. Thus, the willingness of a wife to tolerate apparent mistreatment by her husband may be attributable to her prior experiences and observations of marital relationships. Her decision to remain or leave is based on the comparisons available to her. Another determining factor in such an evaluation is the individual's awareness of existing alternatives. Thibaut and Kelley refer to this assessment as "comparison level alternatives" (CLalt). It may be that the wife described is unhappy but does not leave the relationship because her perception of her alternatives ap-

234

pears worse than her present condition. Much of the effort in assisting abused wives can be interpreted as seeking to alter their CLalt.

Homans's (1961, revised 1974) version of exchange theory draws heavily from B. F. Skinner's (1938) theory of operant conditioning, with occasional assists from economic theories of rational choice. Homans views human exchanges as resulting from persons either being rewarded (reinforced) or punished. His propositions assert that exchanges that are rewarded will be repeated, that people learn from prior experience the conditions (stimuli) under which certain behaviors will be rewarded, and consequently people expect that if they behave in a certain way in a given situation they will be rewarded. Therefore, individuals find themselves attracted to some people and not others because these people are associated in the individual's minds with previous successful encounters and they believe they know how to act with such people to elicit positive rewards.

However, if a given reward comes too frequently or too easily, an individual becomes satiated and each successive unit of the reward is valued less. The converse is also true: The more a person has been deprived of a reward, the more highly it will be valued. Hence, a wife who is constantly told how attractive she is by her husband may pay little notice when her husband tells her she looks pretty, but she may feel considerable pleasure if she is told this by a friend whom she seldom sees. Homans (1961, revised 1974) also proposes, following Skinner's research on animals, that humans who do not receive the rewards they expect will experience feelings of anger. For instance, if a husband works hard to prepare a dinner, he may expect an expression of gratitude or affection from his wife as reward for his investment of time and effort. If the wife expresses no such appreciation, the husband is likely to feel angry.

These relatively simple propositions about elementary behaviors have provided the foundation for Homans and others to develop theoretical explanations for such phenomena as group formation, social stratification, authority and power structures, cooperation and competition, negotiations and bargaining, the assessment of justice or fairness, commitment to long-term relationships, and even altruism.

The appeal of exchange theory for family scholars lies in its potential for explaining a great deal of family-related behavior with relatively few logically consistent concepts. F. Ivan Nye (1978) shows how diverse explanations for such family phenomena as dating, decline in kinship ties, wife and child abuse, marital satisfaction, and marital power can be incorporated within a parsimonious set of social exchange principles.

Explanation of dating and mate selection have probably received the most attention from researchers who employ an exchange orientation. These behaviors fit neatly into exchange notions. Dating and mate selection are viewed in market terms; they take place in a competitive arena in which the possibility exists of gaining considerable pleasure and status, but there is also the danger of considerable pain of rejection. Since both parties want to avoid the costs while deriving the benefits associated with the relationship, it has been hypothesized that there will be a tendency for those who form successful relationships to be matched on key criteria (Huston 1973; Murstein 1972). If the partners are sufficiently similar in attractiveness, for example, they minimize the chances that one of the partners will be rejected or exploited. For instance, if Andy believes Betty is more attractive than he, he is not likely to seek a date because he anticipates rejection, which is psychologically very costly; he might also fear that if they do go on a date Betty could use her greater attractiveness to demand more from him in the way of services or affection than she is willing to give in return. Andy would be more likely to seek a date with Carol, who is similar to him in attractiveness and therefore perceived as more willing to go out with him. A number of studies have supported the prediction that romantically involved couples tend to be matched on physical attractiveness. Elaine Hatfield, Mary K. Utne, and Jane Traupmann (1979) report data indicating matching also occurs using criteria such as mental health, physical health, intelligence, and education.

Exchange theories have also been used to explain the developing processes in an evolving love relationship, including the conditions under which partners are willing to make long-term commitments (Rusbult and Buunk 1993; Tallman, Gray, and Leik 1991; Walster, Walster, and Berscheid 1978). Although these explanations differ in a number of ways, they share a central premise: The more people invest in a given relationship, the greater their dependence on it and, therefore, the greater the costs to them of getting out. Consequently, the greater the dependence, the stronger the commitment the individual is willing to make.

George Levinger (1979) reports research that suggests marriage partners in stable relationships resist thinking in cost-benefit terms. It appears that when a marriage is going well or is stable, those involved have less need to engage in continual monitoring of the relationship. At the very least, the time frame for such an evaluation is greatly extended (see also Leik and Leik 1977). According to Levinger, cost-benefit assessments are more likely to take place (1) when marriage is contemplated and (2) when the relationship is dissolving. In the beginning of a relationship, such an assessment is linked to determining the probability that the marriage will be satisfying and happy. When a marriage is in trouble, the parties involved are likely to consider the personal and material costs of remaining married against those involved in dissolving the union.

Implicit in the calculation of costs and benefits in a marriage is the question of fairness or justice. What is fair distribution of family resources? To what extent should the benefits accruing to a family member correspond with personal investment of time, effort, status, and resources? Homans's (1961, revised 1974) conception of distributive justice is based on the principle of "equity." An equitable exchange is one in which the rewards are commensurate with the investment the individual makes in the exchange. When such rewards are not forthcoming, Homans predicts the disadvantaged person will experience feelings of anger. Elaine (Hatfield) Walster, G. William Walster, and Ellen Berscheid (1978) developed a general theory of equity that has been applied to marital relationships (Hatfield, Utne, and Traupmann 1979). However, a number of investigators have reported that equity is not the only norm used in assessing the fairness of resource distributions (Jasso 1989; Meeker and Elliot 1987; Tallman and Ihinger-Tallman 1979). The most common distinction drawn is between norms of equality and equity (Meeker and Elliot 1987; Tallman and Ihinger-Tallman 1979). Equality refers to the equal distribution of resources across a group regardless of the members' input; equity refers to the rewards being proportionate to effort. In general, poor or deprived persons or groups advocate norms of equality, while those who are better off support equity (Hegtvedt 1992; Tallman and Ihinger-Tallman 1979). Others have reported that "need" is an important, if underrepresented, norm of distributive justice, especially in family relationships (Prentice and Crosby 1987).

The determination of what is fair in family relationships is linked to the distribution of power within the family system (Scanzoni 1979). Essentially, it can be assumed that inequitable distributions of resources produce inequitable power, which results in unjust treatment of persons in weak power positions (Blau 1964). Thus, within the exchange framework, power is not viewed as an attribute of a person but as an element of relationships between people. Perhaps the clearest formulation of this relationship is provided by Richard Emerson (1962, 1972). Emerson describes power as a function of one person's dependency on another. The more John is dependent on Debbie for some resource such as love, the greater the power Debbie has over John. Willard Waller's (1938) "principle of least interest" parallels Emerson's idea of power/dependence. Waller claims that the spouse who loves least has the most power in the relationship, primarily because that individual has the least to lose.

A key element in Emerson's theory pertains to the degree to which the power/dependence in a relationship is balanced. If Debbie loves John as much as he loves her, their power/dependence is balanced and the relationship may be relatively stable. If, on the other hand, John's dependency is greater than Debbie's, the possibility exists that Debbie can exploit her advantage by demanding more from John than she is willing to give in return. According to Emerson, such imbalance will result in efforts to restore balance. The weaker person (A) will attempt to increase the stronger person's (B) dependency on A, or A will lower dependency on B. Failure to attain balance can lead to exploitative relationships.

Irving Tallman, Ramona Marotz-Baden, and Pablo Pindas (1983), in a comparative study of Mexican and U.S. families, used power/dependence theory to explain the greater observed use of power among Mexican peasant wives as compared to Mexican middle-class and U.S. blue- and white-collar wives. Colleen Johnson (1975) uses this type of explanation to account for the discrepancy between the authority vested in Hawaiian Japanese-American husbands and the greater daily decision-making power found in their wives. The theory has also been used to explain the persistent gender inequalities in the household division of labor (Hiller 1984; Brines 1993).

Clearly, any theory based on the assumption that human beings are motivated by self-interest is going to attract critics (see Ekeh 1974; Beutler, Burr, and Bahr 1989). The theory is also charged with being tautological (Turner 1978); excessively individualistic and therefore inappropriate for explaining social systems and social relationships (Ekeh 1974); and overly rational and therefore incapable of dealing with such key emotional elements as warmth and love (Beutler, Burr, and Bahr 1989; Denzin 1990). Exchange theorists have mounted reasonable defenses against most of these attacks. There does seem to be one area of general agreement regarding the limitations of this perspective, however. Exchange theory is limited to structural explanations of social relationships; that is, it focuses on the distribution of resources and the opportunities to obtain those resources. In this sense, it does not offer a complete explanation of social relationships, which also must be influenced at a minimum by cultural, personality, genetic, and ecological factors.

(*See also:* ATTRACTIVENESS; DIVISION OF LABOR; EQUITY AND CLOSE RELATIONSHIPS; MARITAL POWER; MATE SELECTION; RESOURCE MANAGEMENT)

BIBLIOGRAPHY

Beutler, I. F.; Burr, W. R.; and Bahr, K. S. (1989). "The Family Realm: Theoretical Contributions for Understanding Its Uniqueness." *Journal of Marriage and the Family* 51:805–816.

Blau, P. M. (1964). *Exchange and Power in Social Life*. New York: Wiley.

Brines, J. (1993). "The Exchange Value of Housework." *Rationality and Society* 5:302–340.

Denzin, N. K. (1990). "Reading Rational Choice Theory." *Rationality and Society* 2:172–189.

Ekeh, P. P. (1974). *Social Exchange Theory*. Cambridge, MA: Harvard University Press.

Emerson, R. M. (1962). "Power-Dependence Relations." *American Sociological Review* 27:31–41.

Emerson, R. M. (1972). "Exchange Theory, Parts I and II." In *Sociological Theories in Progress*, ed. J. Berger, M. Zelditch, Jr., and B. Anderson. Boston: Houghton Mifflin.

Emerson, R. M. (1981). "Social Exchange Theory." In *Social Psychology: Sociological Perspectives*, ed. M. Rosenberg and R. H. Turner. New York: Basic Books.

Foa, U. G., and Foa, E. D. (1974). *Societal Structures of the Mind*. Springfield, IL: Charles C Thomas.

Hatfield, E.; Utne, M. K.; and Traupmann, J. (1979). "Equity Theory and Intimate Relationships." In *Social Exchange in Developing Relationships*, ed. R. L. Burgess and T. L. Huston. New York: Academic Press.

Hegtvedt, K. A. (1992). "When Is a Distribution Rule Just?" *Rationality and Society* 4:308–331.

Hiller, D. V. (1984). "Power Dependence and Division of Family Work." *Sex Roles* 10:1003–1018.

Homans, G. C. (1961, revised 1974). *Social Behavior: Its Elementary Forms*. New York: Harcourt Brace Jovanovich.

Huston, T. L. (1973). "Ambiguity of Acceptance, Social Desirability, and Dating Choice." *Journal of Experimental Social Psychology* 9:32 42.

Jasso, G. (1989). "Self-Interest, Distributive Justice, and the Income Distribution: A Theoretical Fragment Based on St. Anselm's Postulate." *Social Justice Research* 3:251–276.

Johnson, C. (1975). "Authority and Power in Japanese-American Marriage." In *Power in Families*, ed. R. Cromwell and D. Olson. New York: Wiley.

Kelley, H. H., and Thibaut, J. W. (1978). *Interpersonal Relations: A Theory of Interdependence*. New York: Wiley.

Leik, R. K., and Leik, S. A. (1977). "A Transition to Interpersonal Commitment." In *Behavioral Theory in Sociology*, ed. R. L. Hamblin and J. H. Kunkel. New Brunswick, NJ: Transaction.

Levinger, G. (1979). "A Social Exchange View on the Dissolution of Pair Relationships." In *Social Exchanges in Developing Relationships*, ed. R. L. Burgess and T. L. Huston. New York: Academic Press.

Meeker, B. F., and Elliot, G. C. (1987). "Counting the Costs: Equity and the Allocation of Negative Group Products." *Social Psychology Quarterly* 50:7–15.

Murstein, B. I. (1972). "Physical Attractiveness and Marital Choice." *Journal of Personality and Social Psychology* 32:465–481.

Nye, F. I. (1978). "Is Choice and Exchange Theory the Key?" *Journal of Marriage and the Family* 40:219–233.

Nye, F. I. (1982). *Family Relationships: Rewards and Costs*. Newbury Park, CA: Sage Publications.

Prentice, D. A., and Crosby, F. (1987). "The Importance of Context in Assessing Deserving." In *Social Comparison, Social Justice, and Relative Deprivation*, ed. J. C. Masters and W. P. Smith. Hillsdale, NJ: Lawrence Erlbaum.

Rusbult, C. E., and Buunk, B. P. (1993). "Commitment Processes in Close Relationships: An Interdependent Analysis." *Journal of Social and Personal Relationships* 10:175–204.

Scanzoni, J. (1979). "Social Processes and Power in Families." In *Contemporary Theories About the Family*, Vol. 1, ed. W. R. Burr, R. Hill, F. I. Nye, and I. Reiss. New York: Free Press.

Skinner, B. F. (1938). *The Behavior of Organisms*. New York: Appleton-Century-Crofts.

Tallman, I.; Gray, L.; and Leik, R. K. (1991). "Decisions, Dependency, and Commitment: An Exchange-Based Theory of Group Formation." In *Advances in Group Processes*, Vol. 8, ed. E. J. Lawler, B. Markovsky, C. Ridgeway, and H. Walker. Greenwich, CT: JAI Press.

Tallman, I., and Ihinger-Tallman, M. (1979). "Values, Distributive Justice, and Social Change." *American Sociological Review* 44:216–235.

Tallman, I.; Marotz-Baden, R.; and Pindas, P. (1983). *Adolescent Socialization in Cross-Cultural Perspective*. New York: Academic Press.

Thibaut, J. W., and Kelley, H. H. (1959). *The Social Psychology of Groups*. New York: Wiley.

Turner, J. H. (1978). *The Structure of Sociological Theory*. Homewood, IL: Dorsey Press.

Waller, W. (1938). *The Family: A Dynamic Interpretation*. New York: Cordon.

Walster, E. (Hatfield); Walster, G. W.; and Berscheid, E. (1978). *Equity: Theory and Research*. Boston: Allyn & Bacon.

IRVING TALLMAN
BROWYN CONRAD

EXTENDED FAMILY

Any discussion of the extended family must of necessity make a distinction between extended family households and extended family ties. By definition, the term "extended family" has been applied to the kinship network of social and economic ties composed of the nuclear family (parents and children) plus other "extended" family members. Extended family members typically include the household heads' brothers and sisters, the grandparents and grandchildren, and depending on the society, the aunts and uncles. In some societies, the extended family may commonly share residence, and it is in these circumstances that the social and economic importance of extended family can most readily be seen. Alternatively, nuclear family households may predominate within a network of social and economic codependence where extended family members rely on each other to assist with basic day-to-day activities and provide emotional and economic support. For example, married brothers or sisters with their own households may farm their separate landholdings jointly, families may share child care, and a grandson or granddaughter working in the capital city may send money home every month. All societies have a concept of extended family. What varies is its relative importance, its structure, and its specific functions.

The extended family household as a cultural idea has characterized the majority of documented human history. In fact, the contemporary Western household model, in which the nuclear family household is the prominent ideal and the importance of extended family minimized, is a relatively recent concept. This innovation was associated with many factors, but chief among them were the Industrial Revolution, the associated rise of class influences in social networks, the increasing importance of individualism brought about by Western political change and education, the decline of kinship in defining social networks, and the replacement of government services for those traditionally associated with the family. However, it would be a mistake to believe that all historical societies were characterized by extended family households, or that all contemporary societies are dominated by the nuclear family. Quite the contrary. Extended family households, even in societies where they were the ideal, may still have actually constituted only a minority of households. Household formation is a cycle in which both nuclear and extended family households may appear. Extended family households in non-Western societies have proved remarkably resil-

ient in the face of otherwise pervasive economic and social change toward Western cultural models.

Extended Family Structures and Functions

The importance of extended family ties is most easily seen in settings where there is common residence. Such households may be broadly divided into two major categories. The first type is based on polygyny and composed of several wives and their children cohabiting in the same house or household compound. Despite lack of acceptance in the Western world, such households are extremely common elsewhere, particularly in Africa.

The second type of extended family household is based on common descent. This type of extended family continues to exist in Western culture and also remains prevalent throughout Europe, Asia, and the Americas. Every household with a grandparent, as is common among urban African Americans in the United States, is an extended family household by this definition. In much of Asia, the stem family household still represents an important cultural norm (De Vos and Lee 1973: Foster 1978; Liu and Yu 1977; Tsui 1989). This household form, made up of three generations of related nuclear families, is sometimes considered to be in a class by itself. Stem family households are common in agricultural societies where inheritance is based on primogeniture and all land is passed from father to first-born son. One popular theory, although widely contested, is that stem family households resulted from land scarcity and were an adaptation for keeping landholdings intact (Verdon 1979). An alternative view is that stem family households provide secure retirement environments for the elderly.

From another perspective, households may be extended either lineally (e.g., containing grandparents or grandchildren), laterally (e.g., aunts or uncles, nephews, and nieces), or combinations of the two. While there is no steadfast rule, contemporary extended family households based on common descent usually show more lineal than lateral extension.

Kinship is primary to social structure in all preindustrial societies. In hunter-gatherer, horticultural, and agricultural societies, both past and present, it is no exaggeration to say that kinship is the mechanism through which nearly all social networks are organized. How people are related to one another often determines interpersonal rules of conduct, status in the community, whom one can and cannot marry, and the boundaries that separate the "us" from the "them." In societies emphasizing descent as an organizing principle, extended family groups often form "corporations" of individuals who function in concert as a single social and economic unit.

Extended family ties that reach across households provide important social and economic advantages in terms of shared labor, socialization of children, and support for the elderly. In preindustrial societies, labor cooperation is often essential, and kinship is the primary means of defining the composition of groups. Extended family ties spread both risks and benefits—important especially in settings with scarce resources. One traditional example is in contemporary hunter-gatherer societies, where resources are often uncertain and the success of individuals in obtaining these resources is low. In these settings, there are often highly elaborate rules, based in concepts of extended family, for sharing kills or distributing other resources. In this way, the success of an individual benefits the group.

Nonetheless, the universe that constitutes extended family varies widely across cultures. Societies in which the extended family network is defined primarily through relationships between males are patrilineal. This type of descent system, where membership is passed from father to son, is most common cross-culturally. The Tiv of Nigeria, for example, live in extended polygynous family compounds consisting of the household head, several wives, and perhaps the household head's married brother, wives, and children. However, several such compounds linked by blood ties between males occupy a common contiguous territory and form a corporate economic unit more important than the household (Bohannan and Bohannan 1968).

In matrilineal systems, membership in an extended family group is defined through women. Matrilineal descent systems are most often found in sedentary agricultural cultures where women perform the majority of agricultural tasks. Both the Hopi Indians of North America and the Trobriand Islanders off eastern New Guinea are prominent examples of cultures with matrilineal systems. Unlike patrilineal systems where daughters usually leave the extended family group to marry, in matrilineal systems it is usually the son who moves to his wife's household. However, matrilineages are far from the reverse of patrilineages. Matrilineal systems, not usually definable as matriarchies, nonetheless provide women with a degree of control over property and politics that is not found elsewhere.

In cognatic descent systems, any combination of male and female kin may be used to define who constitutes the extended family network. This type of descent system is the most flexible in allowing individuals to define their own universe of extended family members.

If the extended family network relationships can all be traced through a common known ancestor, this network may be said to constitute a lineage, particularly if the members function together as a single corporate unit. For example, all the members of a Tiv patrilineage can trace their relationship to a single known ancestor. If such links are not exactly known, or if they are based less in fact than in myth, the extended family network constitutes a clan.

Study of the Extended Family

Study of the extended family has been integrated into a number of disciplines; chief among them are anthropology, demography, history, sociology, and social work. Understanding of the extended family and extended family ties has been defined as essential to a wide array of policy concerns including economic development policies, effective health-care delivery (e.g., Pilisuk and Froland 1978), and assimilation of immigrants (e.g., Benson 1990; Chavez 1985). From a historical perspective, extended family households have been studied extensively for their role in shaping the direction of social, economic, and demographic change. From a sociological/anthropological orientation, extended family ties form much of the basis for understanding social networks in both traditional and contemporary societies.

Historical perspective. Critical to understanding the historical study of extended families is the distinction between extended family ties and extended family households. Historical study is almost exclusively limited to examining the form and function of extended family households whose structures can be determined from census records, tax lists, and other widely available written sources. Understanding the historical importance of extrahousehold extended family ties from a social perspective is a more difficult task, and the available sources limited. Researchers are dependent on surviving family diaries, journals, and letters in attempting to understand how extended family networks functioned across households. Oral traditional societies, nineteenth-century British colonies in Africa for example, often had surviving census and tax documents but little other written data.

Interest in the history of the extended family households was kindled in the 1940s and 1950s as an aspect of population and development studies. The idea was simple: The extended family household, prominent in many non-Western societies, stood as a barrier to economic modernization. One popular position suggested that women living in extended families were likely to marry earlier and have more children, the resultant large families being defined as an obstacle to economic and social development. An alternative perspective held that Western industrialization had, in effect, "caused" the emergence of the nuclear family household. Both perspectives made a better understanding of historical family forms important.

It now seems clear that neither position in its extreme adequately reflects the historical record. There are numerous examples of the resiliency of extended family networks despite pervasive economic and social change toward Western models. Extended family networks and households are still important in Taiwan (Stokes, Leclere, and Yeu 1987), Japan (Morgan and Kiyosi 1983), and China (Tsui 1989), to cite only a few examples. In Africa, researchers have portrayed the persistence of extended family networks as cultural bridges in modernization rather than impediments (Silverstein 1984). From this perspective, economic diversification within an extended family network is viewed as a mechanism for dealing with the uncertainties created by change.

Alternatively, it seems clear that nuclear family households were often prevalent prior to industrialization. Even in societies where large extended family households were the ideal, such households may have constituted only a minority or simple majority of households. Household formation is a process. Nuclear family households may "mature" into extended family households as children grow up and marry. This type of evolution is particularly evident in stem family household cycles. On the other hand, an extended family household may disappear with the death of the grandparent. In short, it is rarely accurate to talk about the disappearance of extended family households. Instead, from a historical perspective, the issue is more often one of frequency and transformation of structure.

One well-documented example that demonstrates these concepts is the Balkan *zadruga*. The *zadruga*, or South Slavic rural extended family household, was important in shaping the central Serbian frontier during the nineteenth century. In its classic sense, the *zadruga* consisted of married brothers and their families living in a single household and functioning as a single agricultural economic unit. *Zadrugas*, based on male bonds of kinship, were rigidly patriarchal and sometimes contained twenty or thirty members.

After World War II, the *zadruga* lost much of its historical economic importance with the increasing industrialization of the region. However, the resultant change is better described as one of transformation rather than disappearance. With increasing longevity, decreasing fertility, and increased nonagricultural economic opportunities, ties between brothers have been replaced by ties between grandfathers and grandsons. Laterally extended households have been replaced by lineally extended ones. Agricultural cooperation has been superseded by economic diversification. Sons may live away from the village, but a pattern of sending remittances home is common. Historical research on a small village in central Serbia shows that the number of households containing extended family members has varied little since the midnineteenth century, remaining constant at about 70 percent (Halpern and Anderson 1970).

Nevertheless, when researchers discuss the demise or evolution of the extended family, several factors are commonly cited. Industrialization and its correlates most often take prominence. By removing kinship from the economic arena, industrialization is said to have made the viability of nuclear family households possible. From this perspective, extended family households are portrayed as inherently unstable, fraught with internal conflict, and ready to come apart given favorable circumstances. Indeed, the potential for conflict is greater within extended family households, but this is often overstated as a problem.

Equally important in the evolution of the extended family is the proliferation of Western political and education models over the last century. Western education and politics, with their emphasis on individualism, are said to have produced value changes in direct opposition to extended family life. Education for women, by altering the balance of power in the household, also contributes to the potential for household dissolution. Meanwhile, the growth of government services has made extended family life less important for the care of the elderly.

Contemporary perspective. As noted, extended family ties and households have often proved remarkably adaptable to changing socioeconomic conditions. However, in other settings, circumstances have also given rise to new extended family forms. One such example is the growing importance of extended family households and networks among low-income urban African Americans; considerable research points to the benefits of grandmothers in single-parent households and extrahousehold extended family networks as important mechanisms for coping with inadequate financial resources (e.g., Aschenbrenner 1973; Ford and Harris 1991; Pearson et al. 1990).

Other researchers have noted the importance of extended family networks in assisting immigrants to assimilate (Chavez 1985). Support from the extended family has been portrayed, for example, as a significant factor in the successful integration of Vietnamese refugees into American life (Benson 1900), and extended family ties are viewed as providing a basis for this support.

Some medical evidence further suggests that loss of extended family support is correlated with increased incidence of heart disease, ulcers, and other stress-related disorders (Pilisuk and Froland 1978).

Other types of extended family ties. No discussion of the extended family is complete without including reference to fictive kinship. Fictive kinship often elaborates the body of people considered to be extended family members. In much of Mexico and Latin America, *compadrazgo* (godparenthood) is as important a relationship as any tie of blood or marriage. Other examples occur in many diverse settings, including a comparable pattern of godfatherhood among Yugoslavs (*kumstvo*).

Social and economic changes have also given rise to new family forms based on fictive kinship. These family forms can best be described as "extended" and include same-sex couples with children living in extended family arrangements (Ainslie and Feltey 1991) and the Israeli kibbutz (Talmon 1972).

(*See also:* DIVISION OF LABOR; ETHNICITY; FICTIVE KINSHIP; GRANDPARENTHOOD; KINSHIP; NUCLEAR FAMILY)

BIBLIOGRAPHY

Ainslie, J., and Feltey, K. M. (1991)."Definitions and Dynamics of Motherhood and Family in Lesbian Communities." *Marriage and Family Review* 17:63–85.

Aschenbrenner, J. (1973). "Extended Families Among Black Americans." *Journal of Comparative Family Studies* 4:257–268.

Benson, J. E. (1990). "Households, Migration, and Community Context." *Urban Anthropology* 19:9–29.

Bohannan, L., and Bohannan, P. (1968). *Tiv Economy.* Evanston, IL: Northwestern University Press.

Byrnes, R. F., ed. (1976). *Communal Families in the Balkans: The Zadruga.* Notre Dame, IN: University of Notre Dame Press.

Castillo, G. T.; Wiesblat, A. M.; and Villareal, F. R. (1968). "The Concept of the Nuclear and Extended Family." *International Journal of Comparative Sociology* 9:1–40.

Chavez, L. R. (1985). "Households, Migration, and Labor Market Participation: The Adaptation of Mexicans to Life in the United States." *Urban Anthropology* 14:301–346.

Chen, X. (1985). "The One-Child Population Policy, Modernization, and the Extended Chinese Family." *Journal of Marriage and the Family* 47:193–202.

De Vos, S., and Lee, Y. J. (1993). "Change in Extended Family Living Among Elderly People in South Korea, 1970–80." *Economic Development and Cultural Change* 41:377–393.

Ford, D. Y., and Harris, J. J. (1991). "The Extended African-American Family." *Urban League Review* 14:71–83.

Foster, B. L. (1978). "Socioeconomic Consequences of Stem Family Composition in a Thai Village." *Ethnology* 17:139–156.

Gunda, B. (1982). "The Ethnosociological Structure of the Hungarian Extended Family." *Journal of Family History* 7:40–51.

Halpern, J. M., and Anderson, D. (1970). "The Zadruga: A Century of Change." *Anthropologia* 12:83–97.

Laslett, P., and Wall, R., eds. (1972). *Household and Family in Past Time.* Cambridge, Eng.: Cambridge University Press.

Liu, W. T., and Yu, E. S. H. (1977). "Variations in Women's Roles and Family Life Under the Socialist Regime in China." *Journal of Comparative Family Studies* 8:201–215.

Mere, A. A. (1976). "Contemporary Changes in Igbo Family System." *International Journal of Sociology of the Family* 6:155–160.

Morgan, S. P., and Hirosima, K. (1983). "The Persistence of Extended Family Residence in Japan: Anachronism or Alternative Strategy?" *American Sociological Review* 48:269–281.

Pearson, J. L.; Hunter, A. G.; Ensminger, M. E.; and Kellam, S. G. (1990). "Black Grandmothers in Multigenerational Households: Diversity in Family Structure and Parenting Involvement in the Woodlawn Community." *Child Development* 61:434–442.

Pilisuk, M., and Froland, C. (1978). "Kinship, Social Networks, Social Support, and Health." *Social Science and Medicine* 12:273–280.

Silverstein, S. B. (1984). "Igbo Kinship and Modern Entrepreneurial Organization: The Transportation and Spare Parts Business." *Studies in Third World Societies* 28:191–209.

Stokes, C. S.; LeClere, F. B.; and Yeu, S. H. (1987). "Household Extension and Reproductive Behavior in Taiwan." *Journal of Biosocial Science* 19:273–282.

Talmon, Y. (1972). *Family and Community in the Kibbutz.* Cambridge, MA: Harvard University Press.

Tsui, M. (1989). "Changes in Chinese Urban Family Structure." *Journal of Marriage and the Family* 51:737–747.

Verdon, M. (1979). "The Stem Family: Toward a General Theory." *Journal of Interdisciplinary History* 10:87–105.

Wall, R.; Robin, J.; and Laslett, P., eds. (1983). *Family Forms in Historic Europe.* New York: Social Science Research Council.

RICHARD A. WAGNER

EXTRAMARITAL SEX

Where there is but one basic term for marriage and one for love, there is a plethora of ways to describe a breach of *the* fundamental rule of marriage—that it is a sexually exclusive relationship. These terms include "extramarital sex," "adultery," "an affair," "being unfaithful," "cheating," "having another relationship," "playing around," "having a bit on the side," and then descriptions of type—the "casual affair," the "serious affair," the "one-night stand." This is by no means an exhaustive list, and not all describe only a sexual relationship that occurs when at least one of the partners is already married. People may speak of an affair, of a one-night stand, or of having another relationship when they are not married. But from the base of a marriage, each takes on a specific connotation—a step over the boundary around the couple and their marriage.

While marriage has until very recent times been lawful only as a heterosexual relationship, throughout the world and in all societies being celebrated between a man and a woman (or more than one man/woman), in rare instances now (e.g., in some states of the United States) gay and lesbian couples may form unions, while many more consider themselves in the equivalent of a sexually faithful marriage. For such couples, extramarital sex and its various other names may also be a breach of their relationship rules. In addition, there has been a highly significant increase since the mid-1970s in cohabitation between committed heterosexual couples who have children without marrying. Sexual fidelity is usually central to such relationships, and the affair becomes as significant a breach as it is in marriage.

Meanwhile, some married couples formulate different rules for themselves; they may set out to have a marriage that permits each spouse additional sexual partners, or they may arrive at this arrangement over time and because of specific circumstances; such marriages are generally known as open. This does not mean that they are without rules. Usually the rules relate to what is to be said about other relationships to the spouse and the degree to which the third party is to remain excluded from the marital couple's life. In this context, "infidelity" is an inappropriate term. There is no breach of faith because no vows of fidelity have been sworn, or, if they once were made, the couple has changed faith and new contracts have been forged. Such couples may also dislike the term "extramarital" sex, preferring "comarital."

To speak of "extramarital sex" or an "extramarital relationship" is a way of expressing what is going on

without condemnation—they are the terms preferred by medical and social scientists in an effort to distance themselves from the long history of this ancient triangular relationship known as adultery and condemned as a sin in the Judeo-Christian and Islamic worlds and often also as a crime. Indeed, individuals only use these terms with doctors, lawyers, and researchers, or in similar more formal settings. Stigma for those involved is much more commonly avoided by talking about "an affair." To use the term "adultery" is precisely to remember not only the history involved but also to enable clear thinking about the different implications for women and men, wives and husbands.

In Hebraic law, and despite the fact that the "Thou shalt not commit adultery" Commandment does not distinguish between men and women, adultery was an act only of a married woman. Leviticus (20:10) speaks of a man, but he shall be punished only if he commits adultery with another man's *wife:* "And the man that committeth adultery with another man's wife, even he that committeth adultery with his neighbor's wife, the adulterer and the adulteress shall surely be put to death."

The meaning of the different terms varies both by whether the person speaking has had an extramarital relationship ("adulterous liaison," "affair," or whatever term those in the relationship choose) and according to whether they are male or female.

In Morton Hunt's (1969) study, respondents were asked whether a married person having sexual relations with someone picked up in a bar would constitute an extramarital affair. While half of the "faithful" did think so, only a third of those who had been "unfaithful" thought it did. There were also differences between the men and women: "A third to a half more men than women classify as an extramarital affair a situation in which two married strangers meet at a party, swiftly develop emotional rapport, and have sexual relations that same night" (p. 9).

Women, said Hunt, require a certain depth of feeling to classify something as an "affair," preferring more pejorative terms such as "cheating" or "running around" for the swift, spontaneous sexual encounter. Men, too, thought it was not "real" infidelity to have sex with a call girl while away from home on business. They needed to care for another woman, see a good deal of her, and spend part of the family income on her for this to amount to infidelity.

Of the 130 people in Annette Lawson's (1988) adultery study who said they had actually used the term "committing adultery" to describe their own actions, 62 percent were women and 38 percent were men.

While both women and men participants in the study preferred to describe their liaisons as "serious affairs" or to use the word "relationship" either on its own or in "extramarital relationship," women much less often than men said their liaisons were "one-night stands," "brief encounters," or "casual affairs." In this way, the greater breach implied by a wife's adultery compared with that of a husband's is emphasized.

People also frequently discount relationships that occur in particular contexts—on vacation, away on business, at a conference, when one partner is sick, and so forth. These contexts have a long history of being perceived differently. In some European societies, when men were away fighting wars, they made their wives wear chastity belts, while in some parts of Africa, the warriors, perhaps aware that making dire threats of death or magical illnesses to follow any infidelity of their wives during their absence were likely to be ineffective, arranged for a brother or other "safe" relative to have access to her. It would seem that the wives had little say in such arrangements.

Finally, it is important to note that people not infrequently consider that "lusting after someone in your heart" is equivalent to adultery; in one study, more than 40 percent said they had had a relationship that they considered adulterous even though they "had never made love" (Lawson 1988, p. 37).

Prevalence

No one knows how many individuals have extramarital sex. Partly this is because the range of terms and meanings is so great that it is hard to find a good way to ask questions. Partly this stems from the difficulty in defining what one really wants to know. The figures would be quite different if one asked a sample who had been married only two years, as opposed to a sample of those who had been married twenty years. First marriages might differ from second or later marriages. Some people would consider themselves to be having extramarital sex if they were living apart but were not yet divorced; others would not. In addition, because the subject is still relatively taboo, and because people fear for their marriages if a secret extramarital relationship becomes known, they may be unwilling to tell the truth.

Perhaps because for men an ideal of virility leads them to exaggeration, while for women the ideal of chastity leads them to minimize their encounters, every study of extramarital sex finds not only a smaller proportion of married women having extramarital affairs than married men, but also that the adulterous woman has fewer liaisons than does the adulterous man. Paul Gebhard (1980) in the United States and Lawson (1988) in the United Kingdom found very similar patterns in this respect. Gebhard suggests that about half of married men but one-third of married women altogether might have extramarital sex; of these women, half have only one and the other half two to five liaisons. Lawson found that only 15 percent of men had just one liaison compared with a quarter of women, and while half of the women had no more than three liaisons, 40 percent of the men had at least four. Indeed, twice as many men as women had six or more liaisons. However, while the youngest and most recently married women are less likely overall to be unfaithful (perhaps because their marriages are so relatively new that they are less "at risk"), those who are unfaithful are taking more lovers.

Much lower figures have been found in broad-based statistical samples examining sexual behavior without paying particular attention to meaning and focusing on the prevention of AIDS. For example, a British sample of 18,876 adults between 16 and 59 years of age reported the number of sexual partners they had had in different time periods before completing the questionnaire (Johnson et al. 1994). Only 4.5 percent of married men and 1.9 percent of married women reported an additional sexual partner to their spouse in the preceding year. While this could still amount to high figures over a long-term marriage, the effect of monogamous values was considerable, with single, divorced, or widowed people reporting far more sexual partners in the same time period.

Tom Smith, in the October 1993 issue of the *Economist* (p. 6), reported the results of a U.S. survey by the University of Chicago National Opinion Research Center. This survey also had the overwhelming majority of married people saying not only that they believed in fidelity (found repeatedly in surveys around the world) but also that they were faithful; only 15 percent admitted to having had sex with someone other than a spouse during marriage.

Nonetheless, women's behavior and their willingness to admit to earlier and more active sex lives have changed since the mid-1960s. Both in the United States and in the United Kingdom, studies show the mean age of first intercourse to be about seventeen years, a fall, since 1960, of about two full years. There is also a powerful relationship between premarital and extramarital sex. Of course, this does not mean that all those who are virgins at marriage will not take lovers or that those who have active premarital sex lives will also have extramarital affairs; it does mean that they are more likely to do so.

The youngest women in Lawson's sample had extramarital relationships earlier in their first marriages than had older women and had "overtaken" similar aged men in the speed with which this occurred (Lawson 1988, pp. 172–174). Table 1 shows the mean length of time "waited" before a first liaison (for women and men who have had at least one liaison) according to the date of first marriage. Those who married before the 1960s averaged over forty-five years of age, those marrying in the 1960s averaged thirty-five to forty-five, and those marrying in the 1970s were under thirty-five at the time of the study.

This does not mean that young women as a whole are any more likely than men to have extramarital sex, only that if they are unfaithful, their pattern is now much closer to the male pattern, and they have changed more than men.

Reasons for Extramarital Sex

Biologists take the view that males have an interest in spreading their genes as widely as possible to ensure their continuity, while females have an interest in finding males who will not only give their children good genes but also provide protection for them during the long period of child rearing.

Such theories fail to explain the range of behaviors for human beings whose actions are always meaningful in relation to particular cultures and historical periods as well as to each person's unique psychological needs. In modern times, with effective contraception and a norm of small family size, it has little explanatory power.

In the Judeo-Christian tradition of the West, when people enter into marriage, or a long-term committed relationship, they are pursuing a moral quest—one held out to them in myth and legend, in literature and film, and reiterated and strengthened on a daily basis in the media. This quest is for true love—a relationship in which one both gives and is given to. Over the centuries the guiding myth or narrative has developed to reflect changing gender roles within new economic systems and has become somewhat distanced from the religious ideal of marriage as a sacrament, wherein wives were more subservient and dutiful. While there has always been a tension between the economic and the romantic or companionate relationships involved, in modern times, whatever private reasons are being played out, only love is considered a good enough *public* reason for marriage. Furthermore, the love envisaged is both erotic and caring, a mixture of the Greek *eros* and *agape*. This guiding myth could be termed the "romantic myth of marriage." It might equally be called the "myth of romantic love." (It should be noted that the term "myth" is used not to suggest any truth or falsity. Rather, these are story lines or scripts highlighted in cultures. As creative actors in their own societies, people rewrite and play the roles in the dramas.)

In modern times, this myth is further confused because it contains within it the ancient story of adulterous love that was always disastrous in its ending, having not (as in marriage) a creative but a tragic outcome. Usually, the lovers died; certainly, the adulterous woman or scheming mistress does so. Examples include *Tristan and Isolde*; *Anna Karenina*; and *Fatal Attraction*.

There is another potent myth that also guides the modern woman or man, and it has been especially powerful as women have become more liberated. This encourages everyone to fulfill his or her potential and sees each human being as equally entitled—it stresses an egalitarian partnership. This could be called the "myth of me," but it might also be termed the "myth of partnership."

Given the high commitment expressed around the world to the ideal of fidelity in marriage (above 80 percent is the common finding that extramarital sex is always or almost always wrong), it is clear that people who have an affair have to do a good deal of emotional work or labor (Hochschild 1983) to avoid overwhelming guilt. But what is sought in an affair depends on what part the marriage is expected to play. Janet Reibstein and Martin Richards (1992) point to three types of marriage—for everything, for the growth of the individual, or segmented by function. Public, practical, emotional, and sexual dimensions are divided out by each spouse privately or in discussion. Such different expectations affect how people explain their need for the affair.

Lawson (1988) found some individuals putting forward a "myth of me" argument. They believe that the extramarital affair will meet their own need for self-expression and fulfillment and view it as an entitlement—indeed, obligation—to pursue the moral goal of finding true love, while others speak a more hedo-

Table 1 Duration of First Marriage Before First Liaison

	Mean Years	
	Women	Men
All marriages	8.9	8.2
Those married before 1960	14.6	11.3
1960–1969	8.2	7.9
1970 or later	4.2	5.3

nistic language. Some people stress the absences—that they have not found the egalitarian partnership they were seeking; sex (erotic love) was poor; or they failed to meet their own ideals because of particular circumstances, such as a spouse's illness or their own absence from home. Some individuals disclaim full responsibility, as in "I was drunk at the time." A few who have a pact with their spouse that does not include sexual fidelity point out that they are not being "unfaithful" but simply fulfilling their own special contracts that permit them to meet sexual and emotional needs outside and in addition to their primary relationships.

The absence of good communication stressed by modern psychology and its attendant professions (counseling, therapy, and self-help guides) provides a further reason for seeking something better. Essentially all such reasoning is arguing that the marital relationship is not good enough.

Without taking gender into account, however, the reasons people give for additional sexual partners cannot be understood. While much is shared, the substantial difference lies in the greater feeling of entitlement among men, especially older men, and the greater sense of emotional need among women of all ages.

What Is Achieved?

An examination of what people say they get from extramarital relationships shows that sex is important for both women and men, but while men place sexual fulfillment at the top of their list, well above friendship and emotional satisfaction, women place these factors so closely together that it is necessary to speak of "sex'n'friendship" in one word. Both are pursuing their different scripts, playing the roles in the ancient drama, and gaining enormous pleasure. Woman: "For the first time, I felt alive." Woman: "I not only felt I was alive but also knew why I was alive." Man: "I felt ten foot tall, a man." The majority say, even when the outcome was bad for the marriage or unhappy for them, that "it was worth it," and most would do the same again.

Types of Extramarital Affairs

Researchers use a range of typologies to study extramarital affairs. Reibstein and Richards (1992) relate their typology to the variations in expectations of marriage and to vulnerable points such as the early years, when children arrive, midlife, and when children leave home. Frank Pittman (1989) sees affairs as signs of the unhealthiness of a marriage and classes

them as "accidental," "philandering," "romantic," or "marital arrangements." Emily Brown (1991) employs a system useful for therapy: They may be "out-the-door," "conflict-avoiding" (to avoid facing and resolving conflict), "intimacy-avoiding," or a "sexual addict affair." Lawson (1988) sees three major types, all of which may work either to support or to be dangerous to the marriage and some of which may be transitional—seeking a way to move out and on. They are

- Parallel: husbands keeping mistresses in parallel with, perhaps known to, and condoned by, wives.
- Traditional: a considered breach of the marriage, usually kept secret at least at first; common for wives.
- Recreational: satisfying a need to play; sometimes irrelevant or unimportant to the marriage, usually short in duration; frequent in the open marriage.

Affairs are also usefully classified by duration and importance for the individuals involved.

Responses to the Affair

Many, perhaps most, affairs are not known to the spouse. His or her response depends in part on how the affair is discovered. While modern culture, especially in North America, welcomes openness and good communication (almost everyone thinks "honesty is the cornerstone of a good marriage"), it is hard to keep an affair secret. Traditionally it has been far too dangerous for women to tell their husbands; economic dependency—their possession as chattels of their husbands—and the long tradition of women's virtue worked against this, but men, too, usually thought it important to keep their "bit on the side," or their mistress tucked securely away from the eyes and knowledge of family, friends (except perhaps a trusted family lawyer), and community. This was especially important when the man was an upright, churchgoing pillar of the community.

Within this context, as many as 40 percent of the women in Lawson's (1988) study, compared with 30 percent of the men, were clear that telling their spouses themselves had had adverse consequences. By contrast, more than one-quarter of the men but only one-tenth of the women believed there had been no effect on the marriage. It seems that men do not think it makes much difference, so they might as well tell her. Indeed, if women have become more sexually adventurous since the 1970s, men have tried to be more communicative—at least in telling their wives about their extramarital lives.

In the course of the marriage, there is a growth of shared knowledge that might be called the communal knowledge capital of the couple, some of which is also shared with children. This, perhaps, is what makes the shock of discovery about a spouse's affair lead to the cry, "But I was the last to know! It's not the fact that she (or he) slept with him (or her) but that they lied; that everyone else knew, that I didn't know; that I was deceived; that they know things about me, about us, that I thought were private, just for us. . . ." What is unexpressed is the feeling that the body has been stolen or given.

Men expressed surprise at the powerful responses of their wives and also sometimes at how shocked they themselves were to learn of a wife's extramarital relationship, even when they had given her permission to go ahead. Such reactions may be linked to the long history of the male's possession of the woman's body.

People in open marriages usually make rules that they *must* know, stressing even further the widely expressed value placed on good communication and the absence of secrets, especially sexual secrets.

Nonetheless, some (especially men) are able to admit their response is a gut one: "I could kill him [the lover]." Lawson (1988) has classified typical responses on discovery. Wives usually move from self-blame, "What have I done wrong?" to "I could kill her [lover]!" to "The b——, how could he do this to me?" On the other hand, the husbands generally move from "The b——, how could she do this to me?" to "I could kill him [lover]!" to "I wonder if I had something to do with it?" Such responses represent the different gender roles and psychological development of men and women.

Effects on the Marriage

Most affairs do not lead to divorce; most are not known about or are condoned, and some are symptoms of a separation that is coming or has already begun. Some affairs, however, lead immediately to the breakdown of the marriage; others eventually do so. People say something has been "spoiled," and they speak about the abuse of "trust." Betrayal leads to a deep sense of low self-esteem, fury, and sometimes even murder or suicide.

Some individuals recognize that there is a problem, and they attempt to come to terms with it by altering the rules of their marriage to permit other partners. Too often it is only one partner who desires such a change, usually the husband, for such compartmen-talization of the self and of the marriage tends to be harder for women, whose tasks remain to keep the emotional oil pouring on troubled waters and to ensure the smooth running of the family's relationships. Yet, when asked about fidelity and how important it is "now," both women and men who have had at least one liaison and are still in that marriage say it is not a central concern. Some couples seek counseling or marital therapy and may claim that the marriage is stronger as a result.

The effects on friends and relatives of the couple are more tenuous and difficult to explore. Friends may feel insecure in their own relationships, especially, as is not uncommon, when the adulterous pair is known to them. If the marriage breaks down and there are children, all the consequences of divorce have to be faced, and it may be more difficult for the children, grandparents, and friends if a new marriage, with the adulterous partner, is forged, for there is no one to be blamed who remains outside the magic family circle.

Conclusion

Extramarital sex needs to be understood in the context of constantly changing roles for women and men and in the variety of family forms. Most married women now work outside the home, even when children are small. Their opportunities for self-development and for engagement with others, sometimes in great intimacy at work, may make clear divisions between home and work hard to sustain. Men have kept a range of boundaries around their activities and tried to ensure that they also controlled those around their wives and children. This is no longer possible. Nor is it desirable. It has already led to a continuing renegotiation of relationships, and the stressing of different aspects of them. It is hard to know what it means to be a "proper" man or a "proper" woman. But it is clear that the roles people fulfill may be as important as their gender: Women in traditional male jobs (accountancy, law, business) show a pattern of extramarital sex that is typical of men; men in traditional female roles (teachers, nurses, social workers) show a pattern of extramarital sex that is typical of women. Neither previous personality nor greater opportunity adequately explains both trends.

(*See also:* COMMITMENT; COMMUNICATION; FAMILY GENDER ROLES; GENDER; LOVE; MARITAL SEX; MARRIAGE COUNSELING; SEXUALITY; TRUST)

BIBLIOGRAPHY

Brown, E. (1991). *Patterns of Infidelity and Their Treatment.* New York: Brunner/Mazel.

Gebhard, P. (1980). "Sexuality in the Post-Kinsey Era." In *Changing Patterns in Sexual Relations*, ed. W. Armytage, R. Chester, and J. Peel. New York: Academic Press.

Hochschild, A. (1983). *The Managed Heart: The Commercialization of Human Feeling.* Berkeley: University of California Press.

Hunt, M. M. (1969). *The Affair: A Portrait of Extra-Marital Love in Contemporary America.* New York: World Publishing.

Hunt, M. M. (1974). *Sexual Behavior in the 1970s.* New York: Dell.

Johnson, A.; Wadsworth, J.; Wellings, K.; and Field, J. (1994). *Sexual Attitudes and Lifestyles.* Oxford, Eng.: Blackwell Scientific Publications.

Lawson, A. (1988). *Adultery.* New York: Basic Books.

Lawson, A., and Samson, C. (1988). "Age, Gender, and Adultery." *British Journal of Sociology* 39:408–439.

Pittman, F. (1990). *Private Lies: Infidelity and the Betrayal of Intimacy.* New York: W. W. Norton.

Reibstein, J., and Richards, M. (1992). *Sexual Arrangements: Marriage and Affairs.* London: Heinemann.

ANNETTE LAWSON

FAMILY DEVELOPMENT
THEORY

Family development theory focuses on the systematic and patterned changes experienced by families as they move through their life course. The term "family" as used here represents a social group containing at least one parent–child relationship. The family group is organized and governed by social norms. The general notion of a family life cycle has a long history that dates back to 1777 (Mattessich and Hill 1987). A more recent formulation known as family development theory began after World War II with work on family stress by Reuben Hill (1949) and a later textbook by Evelyn Duvall (1957). The first systematic statement of the approach characterized family development as proceeding through life-cycle stages such as early marriage, families with young children, the launching of children out of the home, and the empty nest (Hill and Rodgers 1964). Family stages can be studied on three levels of analysis: the individual-psychological, the interactional-associational, and the societal-institutional.

In the decades following the initial formulation of family development theory, there has been a conscious departure from the life-cycle concept. Roy H. Rodgers (1973) suggests abandoning the family life-cycle concept in favor of a more life-course-oriented concept that he calls "the family career." Joan Aldous (1978) argues that the family career contains subcareers, most notably the sibling career, the marital career, and the parental career. These in turn are strongly influenced by careers external to the family, such as educational and occupational careers. Paul Mattessich and Hill (1987) maintain that family development unfolds through invariant, universal stages, a conception that is very similar to the aging process. However, the conception of invariant and universal

family stages continues to attract criticism (e.g., White 1991; Bengston and Allen 1993). Aldous (1990) believes the major difference between the life-course and family development perspectives is that the life-course perspective focuses on the individual, whereas the family developmental approach focuses on the family as a group. She maintains that neither approach can properly be called a "scientific theory."

In contrast to Aldous, James M. White (1991) proposes that family development is a "scientific theory" because it offers general propositions derived from a mathematical model that describes the process of family development. Rodgers and White (1993) suggest that the "old" perspective of families moving through deterministic, invariant stages invites a stagnant and less productive understanding of family dynamics. Family development theorists Rodgers and White have revised and simplified some of the following key concepts.

Position in the kinship structure is defined by gender, marriage or blood relations, and generational relations. The basic positions within the family are husband, wife, father, mother, son, daughter, brother, and sister.

Norms are social rules that govern group and individual behavior. For example, the incest taboo is a strong and pervasive social rule forbidding mating between family members.

Role is defined as all the norms attached to one of the kinship positions. For instance, in most societies the role of mother entails the norm of nurturance of the young. However, because the positions are defined structurally, the content of a role (the norms) may change from society to society or ethnic subculture to ethnic subculture.

Family stage is defined as the period of time in which the structure and interactions of role relationships are noticeably distinct from other periods. The stage is usually inferred from events that indicate a change in the membership of the family or the way in which members are spatially and interactionally organized. For example, launching a child does not mean the end of the parental role but a change based on the spatial and interactional organization of the family members.

Transitions from one family stage to another are indicated by the events between stages. Family stages are experienced as "on time" or "off time" in terms of the expected timing for these events. For instance, having another child when post-adolescent children are leaving home would be "off time."

Family career is composed of all the events and periods of time (stages) between events traversed by a family. At the societal level, the stage-graded norms are indicated by the sequence of events followed by most families. For example, a premarital birth is considered "out of sequence" for most people. Variations in families indicate the strength of the norms within any given birth cohort and historical period.

Deviation by large numbers of families from a career sequence is viewed as a source of social change. Social change comes about because families seek to align their sequencing of stages with the sequencing and timing norms of nonfamily institutions (e.g., education and occupation). For instance, as the time required for education rises, the age at which a person marries rises and the period of fertility available to a couple is reduced. Cross-institutional norms, such as finishing one's education before marriage, create the need for systematic deviation in family career and, hence, social change.

Basic propositions proposed by Aldous (1978) lead to the definition of the process of family development. Rodgers and White (1993), in defining the process, claim the probability for a family to move to a new stage of family development is dependent on the old stage they were in and how long they had been in that stage. They further suggest the process can be mathematically modeled as a semi-Markov process (e.g., Coleman 1981; Tuma and Hannan 1984). Two examples of propositions derived by Rodgers and White (1993) are that "normative demands of any given institution must be in line with the stage of the family, otherwise the family is strained" and "institutional normative adaptation is preceded by systematic behavioral deviance" (p. 244).

Debate continues as to the usefulness of concepts such as "developmental tasks" and the amount of emphasis on structure rather than interaction. Family researchers using family development concepts have produced only modest empirical correlations with de-pendent variables such as marital satisfaction. Developmental scholars argue that these disappointing results are due to a lack of appropriate measurement of the concepts. Critics respond that this is because the concepts are too vague or ambiguous. In addition, the focus on the modal (center point of all variations) career has been criticized as concealing cohort, ethnic, racial, and gender variability.

Application of the theory has been undertaken in the study of stress (e.g., Klein and Aldous 1988). As a result, the theory is seen as a therapeutic tool to assist in the analysis of "on-time" and "off-time" careers and events (Carter and McGoldrick 1988; Falicov 1987).

Future improvements of family development theory may bring the possibility of integration between the life-course perspective and family development theory (Aldous 1990; Bengston and Allen 1993). Such an integration might pave the way for ever-wider scope and application.

(*See also:* ADOLESCENCE; CHILDHOOD; ELDERS; FAMILY LIFE EDUCATION; FAMILY SYSTEMS THEORY; FAMILY THEORY; RETIREMENT; STRESS)

BIBLIOGRAPHY

Aldous, J. (1978). *Family Careers.* New York: Wiley.

Aldous, J. (1990). "Family Development and the Life Course: Two Perspectives." *Journal of Marriage and the Family* 52:571–583.

Bengston, V. L., and Allen, K. R. (1993). "The Life Course Perspective Applied to Families over Time." In *Sourcebook of Family Theories and Methods: A Contextual Approach*, ed. P. Boss, W. Doherty, R. LaRossa, W. Schumm, and S. Steinmetz. New York: Plenum.

Carter, E. A., and McGoldrick, M., eds. (1988). *The Changing Family Cycle: A Framework for Family Therapy*, 2nd edition. New York: Gardner Press.

Coleman, J. S. (1981). *Longitudinal Data Analysis.* New York: Basic Books.

Duvall, E. M. (1957). *Family Development.* Philadelphia: Lippincott.

Falicov, C., ed. (1987). *Family Transitions.* New York: Guilford.

Hill, R. (1949). *Families Under Stress.* New York: Harper & Row.

Hill, R., and Rodgers, R. H. (1964). "The Developmental Approach." In *Handbook of Marriage and the Family*, ed. H. T. Christensen. Chicago: Rand McNally.

Klein, D. M., and Aldous, J., eds. (1988). *Social Stress and Family Development.* New York: Guilford.

Mattessich, P., and Hill, R. (1987). "Life Cycle and Family Development." In *Handbook of Marriage and the Family*, ed. M. B. Sussman and S. K. Steinmetz. New York: Plenum.

Rodgers, R. H. (1973). *Family Interaction and Transaction: The Developmental Approach.* Englewood Cliffs, NJ: Prentice Hall.

Rodgers, R. H., and White, J. M. (1993). "Family Development Theory." In *Sourcebook of Family Theories and Methods: A Contextual Approach*, ed. P. Boss, W. Doherty, R. LaRossa, W. Schumm, and S. Steinmetz. New York: Plenum.

Tuma, N. B., and Hannan, M. T. (1984). *Social Dynamics.* New York: Academic Press.

White, J. M. (1991). *Dynamics of Family Development: A Theoretical Perspective.* New York: Guilford.

JAMES M. WHITE

FAMILY GENDER ROLES

The concept of role is widely used inside and outside academic literature. The term derives from theater, suggesting that persons play their parts on life's stage, working out their roles amid an array of expectations. "Scripting" also is used to emphasize social prescriptions in human activities (Strong and DeVault 1992). Some people criticize role concepts because "role playing" suggests superficial and conforming behavior (playacting) rather than true expression of feeling and emotion. Nonetheless, social role concepts continue to be useful to researchers describing family and other relationships.

Role Concepts

Family gender roles derive from different reproductive activities of males and females. The concept of social role is useful in examining prescriptive and behavioral differences associated with gender, since it has diverse applications. Role theory permits the examination of family behavior from both personal and social perspectives. Social roles include not only how persons behave in families but also how persons interpret, through language, others' expectations about how they ought to behave. Consequently, the family is an important arena for persons forming ideas about themselves (Thompson 1993). This interaction between self and family places social role concepts in the context of symbolic interaction, since language and communication are the bases for understanding oneself in relation to others (Charon 1989).

Family gender roles are not isolated from gender roles in the rest of society. Earlier and in some contemporary societies, the kinship system was primary in defining and sustaining family roles, but it was closely integrated with political, economic, educational, and religious systems. Therefore, one's survival was closely tied to conforming to prescribed roles. Leaving the family by choice or force meant being cut off from the primary source of survival. The family's ability to control role behavior diminished as economic options increased. This permitted change to occur in such important matters as spouse selection and adherence to the laws and norms governing inheritance (de Rougemont 1956).

The family's control over social roles lessened as economic, political, and other institutions became more specialized and expanded their jurisdiction (Grbich 1992). The movement toward less gender discrimination in jobs, arguments about the ordination of women, and concern for getting more women in public office are examples of these changes. Gender roles outside the family influence family roles in such areas as authority and equity in taking care of the home and children (Li and Currie 1992).

Social roles pivot on assigned and attained places in various social settings, including work, politics, religion, and family activities. An important assigned social location among these is gender. In the past, "sex role" was the common designation for activities based on being male or female (Astin, Parelman, and Fisher 1975). However, "gender role" has become more frequently used since it seems less restrictive than "sex role" (Ferree 1990). Both terms continue to be used interchangeably.

Social role applies to family in a number of ways, but examining adult roles is complicated by the kind of living arrangement; family roles vary importantly among one-parent, two-parent, and multiple-parent families, depending on the combination of persons by gender. In the United States, this number is defined by state laws, since the U.S. Constitution makes no mention of the family per se. These laws, which exist in *all* states, define that one male and one female, at a time, comprise the married unit. Preindustrial cultures more commonly prescribed, or permitted, a marital unit with one male and more than one female, with one female and more than one male being less common (Lee and Whitbeck 1990). The status of a male or female reflected, in part, how many spouses one would have (Cassidy and Lee 1989). Higher-status males tended to have more wives. The social context of these different family living arrangements dictates different rights and responsibilities based on gender. The modernization of cultures seems to be related to growing equalization of gender status and power (Mir-Hosseini 1989).

A number of terms identify basic social role dimensions, and an extensive body of literature discusses these dimensions (Biddle 1992; Farmer 1992; Sarbin and Allen 1968). One dimension is role location or status. Common titles identify family role location, such as "mother," "father," "daughter," "son," "uncle," and "aunt." These titles identify the general relationship of the persons within the family and the gender of the actor. Hence, these titles reflect gender rights and responsibilities, duties and privileges, power and authority. Gender is important in making social distinctions, since families often transmit wealth and property by gender, making gender identity a factor in determining family status (de Riencourt 1974; Stone 1979). Role status varies widely among cultures and ethnic groups (Davidson and Gordon 1979).

Cultures and Role Restriction

Cultures vary considerably in their degree of governing family gender roles. Some cultures allow one set of paired adult family roles and others allow a variety of roles. Descriptions of wife–husband roles emerging from the nineteenth century assumed a male provider role and a female mediator-nurturant role. Talcott Parsons and Robert Bales (1955) elaborate these assumptions in portraying the father as performing instrumental activities such as providing the means of livelihood and dealing with the social system external to the family. The mother performs expressive activities in caring for the children, mediating feelings, and caring for the home. Crossing gender lines, such as women working in defense plants, was tolerated and expected during World War II, but reversion to traditional gender roles was expected when peace resumed. Deviance from gender roles meets with overt and covert punishments and in some cultures may include death. Generally punishments are more harshly applied to women than to men (Stephens 1963).

Cultures that strictly enforce one gender role for men and one for women are meeting with considerable criticism nearly worldwide because they assume a division of labor based on political and economic conditions no longer suitable for industrial or postindustrial societies (McLanahan 1988). Even though loosened roles might focus on lessening female restrictions, both males and females usually see personal advantages in moving toward more role options. Some persons wish to incorporate role dimensions not currently assigned to their gender, such as males wanting to be more expressive and nurturant and fe-

males more job-oriented. Role assumptions and behavior do not, however, necessarily coincide, as was noted by Eleanor Maccoby and Carol Jacklin (1974), who found limited or no evidence for a number of assumed gender differences, such as females being more nurturant than males.

Industrial and postindustrial cultures tend to permit husbands and wives more role latitude (Popenoe 1993). These cultures ease role restrictions by allowing women to emulate men's greater freedom in the marketplace and by inducing men to have greater domestic responsibilities. Single parenting requires even more flexibility in both female and male parenting roles. Even though cultures permit multiple parenting roles, they are based on gender identity (Charles and Hopflinger 1992; Kingsbury and Scanzoni 1989).

There are signs that married roles are becoming even more flexible, as reflected in the individualized vows spoken in marriage ceremonies. These individualized agreements may elaborate traditional norms or reflect innovative lifestyles. It is possible to conceive of a culture with nearly as many self-prescribed married roles as there are married couples.

Personal Identity and Roles

Persons may advocate that married roles ought not to be gender-distinctive at all (androgyny), though persons may have understandings about their married responsibilities and privileges (Hendrick and Hendrick 1992). However, these would not be governed by gender identity. Conceivably, this is possible in all but specific reproductive activities; females continue to become pregnant and have babies, and males do not. Hence, one may think of cultures aligned along a continuum, with one wife and husband role at one end and no gender-based family roles at the other. Role conflict occurs in a single-gender role system because of limited role options. However, a lack of clear roles creates role ambiguity. When roles are not clearly delineated but gender distinctions continue to be made, roles become ambiguous. Persons respond either by developing new roles or having a confused identity. This latter condition occurred in China when the older Confucian ideals were supplanted by more equalitarian family codes during the establishment of the People's Republic of China (de Riencourt 1974).

Elaborate sets of norms, or role prescriptions, delineate behavior appropriate to gender role status. Depending on gender and age, the child differentially defers to either the father or the mother. In the family setting, daughters expect to perform a variety of activities imitative of the mother's status. Similarly, the son is expected to defer to the father and imitate the father's behavior. A family often experiences role conflict when children do not conform to their gender status.

Self-identity is an important dimension of the social role (Forisha 1978). Another kind of conflict occurs when cultural norms strictly enforce gender roles but gender identity does not match the norms. Its resolution commonly includes finding ways around these prescriptions. In the family setting, the mother or the father may reject aspects of their role assignment— for instance, the father accepting the mother as being the better provider. An extreme resolution includes surgical intervention, changing the bodies' morphology to conform to the self's gender identity. The self-identity conflicts derive from general societal norms or from the inability of persons to conform to each other's expectations. Societies often restrict the behavior of one gender more than the other. In most cases, it is the female who is more severely restricted under what is called the "double standard" (Hendrick and Hendrick 1992).

Role stereotypes introduce another source of role conflict (Alperson and Friedman 1983). Stereotypes are shorthand assumptions about how persons in different social categories behave, such as husbands and wives. Conflict occurs in the failure to distinguish between stereotypical assumptions and actual behavior, causing misunderstanding and misinterpretation between men and women. Much literature discusses communication used to diminish marital conflict derived from gender stereotypes.

Role Expectations and Demands

It is clear that gender roles, as they pertain to the family, are interactive. Being a daughter implies that there is a mother or a father. It suggests that being a daughter entails expectations about a female's behavior vis-à-vis a parent and vis-à-vis the daughter. A daughter or a son reasonably expects physical care and emotional support to a certain age, and parents might expect increasing domestic responsibility and self-direction with their child's physical maturation. Societies usually codify in general terms these responsibilities, though precise rights and responsibilities are often interpreted through specific cases channeled through the legal system and welfare agencies, particularly for those families needing public assistance. These responsibilities extend in other ways, as by employed offspring caring for their elderly parents through a modified extended family (Gerstel and Gallagher 1993).

Role anticipation is associated with becoming an adult as children mature in the family (Giele 1978). Role anticipation assumes that a particular role will exist in the future, and self-anticipation assumes that the person will someday occupy that role. For example, role anticipation occurs when a daughter assumes that in the future there will be working mothers. If she also assumes that she will be a working mother someday, she engages in self-anticipation. Children emulate the behavior of the parent they identify with, usually the same-gender parent. In this case, the mother becomes an important referent for the daughter's learning the anticipated working mother role. However, children may also develop closer affectional ties with a crossgender parent.

The assumption is that role learning for the son will be more difficult if the father is missing. However, daughters also experience different learning experiences with absent fathers in that crossgender parental experiences are missing, and she may experience earlier domestic responsibility because of a need to share the heavier workload placed on the mother. Families with missing mothers occur less frequently in modern societies, but role effects do occur with greater impact if the loss occurs during a child's early years (Spanier and Thompson 1984).

Role compatibility is important in a society that permits a number of different role sets for wives and husbands, as when a wife expects her role to include employment outside the home and her husband does not. These kinds of incompatibilities produce role conflict, in this case between the female's self-expectations and the male's role prescriptions. Therefore gender roles become an important part of premarital assumptions and anticipations. Such incompatibilities require various forms of negotiation if conflict reduction is accomplished. Various theories address the communication and negotiation process, which may include external mediation and counseling (Grbich 1992; Noller and Fitzpatrick 1990). Role overload and role conflict are closely related. A wife who is employed and does a large part of domestic chores experiences role overload. This produces role strain in that not all tasks can be performed in the time available. Consciously realizing this imbalance leads to arguments and, if not resolved, to divorce.

Work role and other demands external to the family heighten both role strain and conflict (Bolger et al. 1989). The wife's employment introduces a competing set of role demands, which increases role strain and may increase conflict through social power adjustments (Menaghan and Parcel 1990; Standing 1991). The Parsonian model (Parsons and Bales 1955) has the male dealing with the external system and the female with the internal system, a system assuming female economic dependency. This role division may now be nearly extinct (Popenoe 1993). When the female enters the marketplace, she derives status benefits from her direct contribution to the family income. She might also gain family bargaining power (Williams 1990). Also, if the husband assumes greater domestic responsibility, he may gain bargaining power because of his greater domestic investment. These imbalances require role negotiations to reduce role conflict. With the wife's lowered economic dependency she is more likely to sever the relationship if bargaining does not produce a more favorable outcome (Booth et al. 1984). However, dual-earner families may be more independent of external controls because they have more than one source of income, permitting greater latitude in role selection and employment choices. For example, the husband may elect to spend more or all of his time in domestic duties while the wife pursues her career goals.

The feminist movement, not a homogeneous entity in either its historical roots or its current organization, also influences gender role change both in and outside the family (Ferree 1983). Broadly speaking, the movement may be viewed as a social process focusing on female role identities and prescriptions. Its considerations affect the family in a number of ways. Its basic premise is that gender ascriptions produce power inequities in the traditional family system, where the male is the primary bread earner and the wife a domestic and caregiver of children. Domestic work is viewed as important but not well rewarded in money or status. Feminism points out inequities and suggests strategies for their modification. Educational processes are to examine gender role inequities (consciousness raising) and challenge traditional gender roles (Forisha 1978). This dialogue enters the age-old debate of nature versus nurture by determining precisely what aspects of role behavior are tied to genetic differences and what are culturally derived. In consequence, these discussions tend to weaken the gender-based roles, leading to more individualized family roles.

(*See also:* CONFLICT; DIVISION OF LABOR; EQUITY AND CLOSE RELATIONSHIPS; GENDER; GENDER IDENTITY; MARITAL POWER; MEASURES OF FAMILY CHARACTERISTICS; SYMBOLIC INTERACTIONISM; WORK AND FAMILY)

BIBLIOGRAPHY

Alperson, B., and Friedman, W. (1983). "Some Aspects of the Interpersonal Phenomenology of Heterosexual Dyads with Respect to Sex-Role Stereotypes." *Sex Roles* 9:453–474.

Astin, H.; Parelman, A.; and Fisher, A. (1975). *Sex Roles: A Research Bibliography*. Rockville, MD: National Institute of Mental Health.

Biddle, B. (1992). "Role Theory." In *Encyclopedia of Sociology*, ed. E. Borgatta and M. Borgatta. New York: Macmillan.

Bolger, N.; DeLongis, A.; Kessler, R. C.; and Wethington, E. (1989). "The Contagion of Stress Across Multiple Roles." *Journal of Marriage and the Family* 51:175–183.

Booth, A.; Johnson, D.; White, L.; and Edwards, J. (1984). "Women, Outside Employment, and Marital Instability." *American Journal of Sociology* 90:567–583.

Cassidy, M., and Lee, G. (1989). "The Study of Polyandry." *Journal of Comparative Family Studies* 20:1–11.

Charles, M., and Hopflinger, F. (1992). "Gender, Culture, and the Division of Household Labor." *Journal of Comparative Family Studies* 23:375–387.

Charon, J. (1989). *Symbolic Interactionism*, 3rd edition. Englewood Cliffs, NJ: Prentice Hall.

Davidson, L., and Gordon, L. (1979). *The Sociology of Gender*. Chicago: Rand McNally.

de Riencourt, A. (1974). *Sex and Power in History*. New York: Dell.

de Rougemont, D. (1956). *Love in the Western World*. New York: Pantheon.

Farmer, Y. (1992). "Role Models." In *Encyclopedia of Sociology*, ed. E. Borgatta and M. Borgatta. New York: Macmillan.

Ferree, M. (1983). "The Women's Movement in the Working Class." *Sex Roles* 9:493–505.

Ferree, M. (1990). "Beyond Separate Spheres: Feminism and Family Research." *Journal of Marriage and the Family* 52:866–884.

Forisha, B. (1978). *Sex Roles and Personal Awareness*. Morristown, NJ: General Learning Press.

Gerstel, N., and Gallagher, S. (1993). "Kinkeeping and Distress: Gender, Recipients of Care, and Work–Family Conflict." *Journal of Marriage and Family* 55:598–608.

Giele, J. (1978). *Women and the Future: Changing Sex Roles in Modern America*. New York: Free Press.

Grbich, C. (1992). "Societal Response to Familial Role Change in Australia." *Journal of Comparative Family Studies* 23:79–94.

Hendrick, S., and Hendrick, C. (1992). *Liking, Loving, and Relating*, 2nd edition. Pacific Grove, CA: Brooks/Cole.

Kingsbury, N., and Scanzoni, J. (1989). "Process Power and Decision Outcomes Among Dual-Career Couples." *Journal of Comparative Family Studies* 20:231–246.

Lee, G., and Whitbeck, L. (1990). "Economic Systems and Rates of Polygyny." *Journal of Comparative Family Studies* 21:13–24.

Li, S., and Currie, D. (1992). "Gender Differences in Work Interruptions as Unequal Effects of Marriage and Child-bearing." *Journal of Comparative Family Studies* 23:217–229.

Maccoby, E. E., and Jacklin, C. N. (1974). *The Psychology of Sex Differences*. Stanford, CA: Stanford University Press.

McLanahan, S. S. (1988). "Family Structure and Dependency." *Demography* 25:1–16.

Menaghan, E. G., and Parcel, T. L. (1990). "Parental Employment and Family Life." *Journal of Marriage and the Family* 52:1079–1098.

Mir-Hosseini, Z. (1989). "Some Aspects of Changing Marriage in Rural Iran." *Journal of Comparative Family Studies* 20:215–229.

Noller, P., and Fitzpatrick, M. (1990). "Marital Communication in the Eighties." *Journal of Marriage and the Family* 52:832–843.

Parsons, T., and Bales, R. (1955). *Family, Socialization, and Interaction Process*. New York: Free Press.

Popenoe, D. (1993). "American Family Decline, 1960–1990: A Review and Appraisal." *Journal of Marriage and the Family* 55:527–542.

Sarbin, T. R., and Allen, V. (1968). "Role Theory." In *The Handbook of Social Psychology*, Vol. I, ed. G. Lindzey and E. Aronson. Reading, MA: Addison-Wesley.

Spanier, G., and Thompson, L. (1984). *Parenting: The Aftermath of Separation and Divorce*. Newbury Park, CA: Sage Publications.

Standing, H. (1991). *Dependence and Autonomy: Women's Employment and the Family in Calcutta*. London: Routledge & Kegan Paul.

Stephens, W. N. (1963). *The Family in Cross-Cultural Perspective*. New York: Holt, Rinehart and Winston.

Stone, L. (1979). *The Family, Sex, and Marriage in England, 1500–1800*. New York: Harper & Row.

Strong, B., and DeVault, C. (1992). *The Marriage and Family Experience*, 5th edition. St. Paul, MN: West Publishing.

Thompson, L. (1993). "Conceptualizing Gender in Marriage: The Case of Marital Care." *Journal of Marriage and the Family* 55:557–569.

Williams, L. (1990). "Marriage and Decision Making: Intergenerational Dynamics in Indonesia." *Journal of Comparative Family Studies* 21:55–66.

LAURENCE L. FALK

FAMILY LAW

Virtually all American law schools offer one or more courses in family law, sometimes referred to as domestic relations law. Family law involves a myriad of legal issues concerning the relationships between husbands and wives; parents and children; and, more recently, nontraditional families consisting of unmarried cohabitants of the same or the opposite sex. Basic introductory family law courses provide the foundation for more advanced specialized courses and seminars. Separate courses on juvenile law focus on issues involving children, such as parental control over children, child abuse and neglect, and delinquency. The content of family law courses varies considerably because family law has changed dramatically since the early 1960s and continues to evolve at a rapid pace.

Historically, family law has been regulated by the laws of the individual states rather than by federal laws. However, the federal government has become increasingly involved in family law matters, especially in the areas of child support enforcement and child custody. State laws that govern families differ considerably from one jurisdiction to another, even though many states have adopted all or parts of various recommended, standardized laws such as the Uniform Marriage and Divorce Act, the Uniform Child Custody Jurisdiction Act, and the Uniform Reciprocal Enforcement of Support Act. Despite its diversity throughout the United States, the subject matter of family law can be grouped into three categories: creation of families, regulation of families, and dissolution of families.

Creation of Families

American law has always manifested a strong preference for establishing families by means of the institution of marriage. States regulate entry into formal marriage by enacting procedural requirements, such as licensure and ceremony, and substantive restrictions that dictate who is eligible to marry whom, such as monogamy constraints, prohibitions against same-sex marriages, minimum age qualifications, and prevention of marriages between certain relatives. A marriage that violates a state restriction may be deemed void and of no legal effect or merely voidable and subject to annulment, a judicial declaration of invalidity.

The U.S. Supreme Court has held that the rights to marry, raise a family, and enjoy individual privacy are important constitutional rights. Therefore, state restrictions on marriage may be invalid if they unduly infringe on those rights. For example, the Court declared prohibitions on interracial marriages unconstitutional in the case of *Loving* v. *Virginia* (1967) and recognized an unwed father's right to continue raising his children in *Stanley* v. *Illinois* (1972).

Approximately fourteen states authorize an informal form of marriage known as common-law marriage, which requires an agreement to be husband and wife. Some states also require that the parties live together and hold themselves out to the public as being married. States that do not otherwise permit common-law marriages generally will recognize marriages that were validly entered into in another state or country. Common-law marriage is a substitute method for attaining the status of legal spouse without participating in a formal marriage. However, no state recognizes a common-law divorce, and once a common-law marriage is established, the parties must obtain a legal divorce to terminate the relationship.

A number of states recognize the "putative spouse" doctrine, which preserves certain marital rights and benefits, usually of an economic nature, for a person who does not otherwise qualify as a legal spouse. The putative spouse doctrine protects a person who innocently enters into an invalid marriage while he or she continues to hold a good-faith belief in the legality of the marriage. Some federal statutes, such as the Social Security Act, also give limited recognition to the putative spouse doctrine.

Until the 1970s, the legal system generally refused to recognize any rights or obligations of unmarried cohabitants. The courts even denied enforcement of an unmarried couple's explicit agreements to share acquired property or to provide for support of one another due to the belief that these relationships were illicit and immoral. Since the widely publicized California case of *Marvin* v. *Marvin* (1976), most states will uphold legal contracts between unmarried cohabitants, at least with respect to property rights, although some impose high standards for proving such agreements. Some jurisdictions also recognize additional remedies to protect the legitimate expectations of unmarried cohabitants upon the death of one of the partners or the dissolution of the relationship. None, however, extends the same recognition afforded married partners.

In theory, the same analysis applies to homosexual as well as to heterosexual cohabitation, although the case law reveals a greater continuing bias against gay and lesbian couples. Specifically, antigay ordinances have been enacted in certain cities. Conversely, however, a number of municipalities and private businesses have granted some recognition and benefits to unmarried domestic partners.

Family law also deals with issues surrounding procreation. The U.S. Supreme Court's recognition of privacy rights has defeated much state regulation of birth control and sterilization. Thus, individuals have considerable freedom to choose whether and when to have children. Abortion remains a controversial issue

and, according to the Supreme Court's opinion in *Roe* v. *Wade* (1973), a woman's right to choose to terminate a pregnancy may be restricted by the state's countervailing interests in health, safety, and the unborn child. Restrictions include parental or judicial consent requirements for minors seeking abortions. Also, public funding for abortions has been severely limited since the early 1980s.

Historically, the law treated children born outside of marriage very harshly and restricted nonmarital children from most rights to support and inheritance. During the twentieth century, the legal treatment of such children improved considerably; most discrimination against nonmarital children has been constitutionally prohibited. Nonetheless, proof of paternity and legitimization remain problematic, although they have been facilitated by the development of more accurate scientific procedures.

The parent–child relationship may be established by adoption as well as by biological means. Adoption usually terminates a child's relationship with the birth family and transplants the child into the adoptive family. Adoption requires extinguishing the birth parents' relationship by consent or involuntary termination for unfitness. Adoption may be accomplished by private placement or through agencies. Both procedures are highly regulated to safeguard the best interests of the child.

Advances in medical technology now enable various types of alternative reproductive methods, such as artificial insemination, fertilization outside the human body, embryo donation, and surrogate motherhood. These technological advances have generated new legal problems regarding the respective rights of the multiple parties involved and safeguards for the interests of the children so conceived.

Regulation of Families

The American legal system respects family autonomy and intervenes in the functioning of intact families only when severe conflicts threaten the health, safety, or well-being of family members. Historically, the husband, as the head of the family, was entitled to the services, earnings, and obedience of the wife and children, who had few legal rights. In turn, the husband and father owed his dependents a duty of support. The law refused, however, to dictate the level of that support beyond the basic necessities. Today, both the spousal and parental duties of support are usually gender-neutral, and all states have laws to protect family members from nonsupport, abuse, and neglect.

The majority of American states historically have applied English common-law "title theory" property principles to allocate ownership of earnings and assets acquired during marriage. Title theory traces ownership of property to the party who earned the funds for its acquisition, who historically was, and to a significant extent still is, the husband. Absent a gift to the other spouse, the property owner has the right to manage and control the asset during marriage, retain it upon divorce, or transfer it to a third party on death. However, a number of legal doctrines have developed for protecting the other spouse on dissolution of the marriage.

Eight states have traditionally followed the community property system of marital property ownership, which is based on partnership theories of marriage developed in Spain and France. Community property deems the assets acquired by either or both spouses during marriage to be owned equally by the husband and wife. In addition, it allows either spouse to have separate property. Separate property typically is defined to include assets acquired prior to marriage, gifts or inheritances received by one spouse alone during marriage, and property designated as separate by a court decree or mutual agreement of the spouses. When the marriage dissolves by death or divorce, each spouse (or a deceased spouse's estate) is entitled to one-half of the community property as well as all of his or her own separate property. By adopting the Uniform Marital Property Act, a common-law property state may become, in effect, a community property state.

Society's perspective of intrafamily relationships has also changed. While parents are afforded considerable decision-making authority and disciplinary power over their children, and whereas personal disputes between or among family members are generally resolved privately, domestic violence has become an issue of public concern. In response, most states have enacted protective legislation to deal with family violence. In extreme situations, parents' relationships with their children may be severed, either temporarily or permanently, for child abuse or neglect. Children outside of parental control may become involved in the juvenile court system and be placed in reformatory institutions or foster homes.

Dissolution of Families

Divorce traditionally required proof that a spouse had committed some serious type of marital fault such as adultery, abandonment or desertion, or cruelty. The court would deny a divorce if a defense existed or if both parties caused the breakdown of the marriage, even if both desired a divorce. As a result, individuals frequently resorted to perjury or traveled to other states with more lenient divorce laws. These alternatives undermined the legal system, and divorce law underwent dramatic and rapid changes beginning in the late 1970s.

Consequently, all states have since adopted some form of no-fault divorce to supplement or replace the traditional fault grounds by substituting grounds that simply acknowledge that a marriage is no longer functional. No-fault grounds frequently are framed in terms of "incompatibility" or "irreconcilable differences," or authorize divorce based on a specified period of physical separation.

While divorce itself severs the bonds of marriage and frees the parties to remarry, a divorce action generally also resolves the economic incidents of marriage either by agreement or court order. Most states base division of marital property on principles of equitable distribution rather than a strict tracing of ownership. Difficulties continue with respect to ownership and division of intangible or speculative assets such as educational degrees, professional licenses, pensions, and professional goodwill.

Divorce may also include claims for alimony, frequently called maintenance or spousal support. Traditionally, alimony was awarded only to wives who successfully proved the marital fault of their husbands. Alimony typically was awarded as "permanent" or "periodic," payable in installments for an indefinite period of time, although it could be awarded as a lump-sum payment. Periodic alimony terminated on the death of either spouse or the remarriage of the wife and could be modified upon proof of a substantial change in circumstances of either party.

Today, both husbands and wives are eligible to receive alimony. Because of the decline of fault-based divorce, the primary focus has shifted from marital fault to balancing the needs of the dependent spouse with the ability of the supporting spouse to pay, in light of the marital standard of living. Awards of periodic alimony are infrequent. When alimony is granted at all, it is usually in the form of short-term, "rehabilitative" alimony intended to supplement the income of the spouse during a period of transition and retraining to become self-supporting. A number of states have recognized new forms of alimony such as "restitutional" or "reimbursement" alimony to compensate a spouse for contributions to the education or career of the other spouse.

If the divorcing couple has minor children of the marriage, the divorce action will also involve child custody and child support. Because the state has an interest in protecting minor children, courts are more actively involved with issues regarding custody and child support. Courts scrutinize private agreements more closely and retain jurisdiction to modify child custody or support orders when the circumstances of the parties involved change.

Custody entails the legal authority of a parent to make important decisions concerning the child's upbringing as well as the child's residence. Usually, one parent will have primary or sole custody, while the other is granted reasonable visitation privileges. In determining which of two otherwise fit parents should be awarded primary custody of the children, all factors relating to the child's best interests are relevant. However, consideration of factors such as a parent's race, religion, or handicap may raise constitutional issues, and the parent's sexual practices and orientation should not influence a custody decision unless the child is directly and detrimentally affected. In the past, courts applied the "tender years" presumption, a maternal preference that awarded custody of young children to their mothers. However, changed attitudes toward child development and claims of discrimination against fathers have prompted most courts to adopt gender-neutral standards for child custody.

Similarly, the legal duty of child support is now imposed on both parents. Traditionally, child support was calculated on an ad hoc basis by balancing the resources of the parent against the needs of the child, which resulted in awards that lacked uniformity and predictability. Since the 1980s, federal legislation has stimulated state enactment of child support guidelines. Some states have adopted schedules that base child support awards on a percentage of the noncustodial parent's income, while other states apply complex formulas that consider the financial situations of both parents.

Enforcement of child support entails additional problems. Collection remedies include potential jail sentences for contempt of court, as well as conventional methods of debt collection from the property or wages of the delinquent parent. Federal intervention in child support enforcement has encouraged states to employ additional, more effective methods, including expedited procedures for withholding wages and income tax refunds and the use of new tracing mechanisms. Moreover, all states have adopted some version of the revised Uniform Reciprocal Enforcement of Support Act, which facilitates interstate collection of child support.

The tax implications of the financial incidents of divorce can raise additional dilemmas. Likewise, if a bankruptcy action is filed, the original financial obligations arising from the divorce may be altered.

Jurisdictional issues may also complicate family law matters. In general, if a marriage was valid where it took place, other states will recognize it unless some strong public policy would be violated. Jurisdiction for divorce usually is based on the domicile of either spouse, and an absent spouse must be given proper notice of the proceeding and the opportunity to be heard. When a court has jurisdiction over only one spouse, it may terminate the marriage, but it may not alter economic rights such as property division or spousal support of the out-of-state spouse. Similarly, to order or modify child support, the state court must have sufficient connections with the parent, although interstate processes available through the Uniform Reciprocal Enforcement of Support Act simplify obtaining jurisdiction over an absent party. Special jurisdictional rules have been established for custody litigation in an attempt to safeguard the best interests of children, to prevent parental child-snatching, and to restrict multiple lawsuits seeking more favorable laws in other states. The Uniform Child Custody Jurisdiction Act, which has been adopted by all states, sets out several bases for authorizing custody jurisdiction that focus on the optimal location for litigating placement of a particular child. Similarly, the federal Parental Kidnapping Prevention Act dictates the type of child custody decrees that must be recognized and enforced by other states. It also deals with the circumstances under which a state may validly modify an earlier custody order of another state. Additionally, the United States has joined a number of other nations in ratifying the Hague Convention on the Civil Aspects of International Child Abduction in an attempt to facilitate the return of children wrongfully removed to other countries.

Conclusion

Most family law courses also examine ethical issues and the role of lawyers. Law schools are placing an increased emphasis on alternate forms of dispute resolution, such as negotiation, mediation, and arbitration, to replace the traditional adversarial system of litigation in the family law context.

(*See also:* ABORTION: LEGAL ASPECTS; ADOPTION; ALIMONY AND SPOUSAL SUPPORT; ANNULMENT; BIRTH CONTROL: LEGAL ASPECTS; CHILD ABUSE AND NEGLECT: LEGAL ASPECTS; CHILD CUSTODY; CHILDREN'S RIGHTS; DIVORCE: LEGAL ASPECTS; INHERITANCE; MARITAL PROPERTY AND COMMUNITY PROPERTY; PREMARITAL AGREEMENTS; PRIVACY AND CONFIDENTIALITY)

BIBLIOGRAPHY

Areen, J. (1992). *Family Law*, 3rd edition. Westbury, NY: Foundation.

Blumberg, G. G. (1987). *Community Property in California*. Boston: Little, Brown.

Clark, H. H., Jr. (1980). *Domestic Relations*, 3rd edition. St. Paul, MN: West Publishing.

Clark, H. H., Jr. (1988). *The Law of Domestic Relations in the United States*, 2nd edition. St. Paul, MN: West Publishing.

Ellman, I. M.; Kurtz, P. M.; and Bartlett, K. T. (1991). *Family Law*, 2nd edition. Charlottesville, VA: Michie.

Foote, C.; Levy, R. J.; and Sander, F. E. A. (1985). *Cases and Materials on Family Law*. Boston: Little, Brown.

Gregory, J. D. W.; Swisher, P. N.; and Scheible, S. L. (1993). *Understanding Family Law*. New York: Matthew Bender.

Krause, H. D. (1986). *Family Law in a Nutshell*, 2nd edition. St. Paul, MN: West Publishing.

Krause, H. D. (1990). *Family Law*, 3rd edition. St. Paul, MN: West Publishing.

Mnookin, R. H., and Weisberg, D. K. (1989). *Child, Family, and State: Problems and Materials on Children and the Law*, 2nd edition. Boston: Little, Brown.

Reppy, W. A., and Samuel, C. A. (1994). *Community Property in the United States*. Detroit: Lupus.

Swisher, P. N.; Miller, H. A.; and Weston, W. I. (1990). *Family Law: Cases, Materials, and Problems*. New York: Matthew Bender.

CASES

Loving v. *Virginia*, 388 U.S. 1 (1967).

Marvin v. *Marvin*, 577 P.2d 106 (1976).

Roe v. *Wade*, 410 U.S. 113 (1973).

Stanley v. *Illinois*, 405 U.S. 645 (1972).

STATUTES

Hague Convention on the Civil Aspects of International Child Abduction, 19 I.L.M. 1501 (1980).

Parental Kidnapping Prevention Act, 28 U.S.C. §1738A (1980).

Uniform Child Custody Jurisdiction Act, 9 U.L.A. 116 (1988).

Uniform Marital Property Act, 9A U.L.A. 97 (1983).

Uniform Marriage and Divorce Act, 9A U.L.A. 147 (1987).

Uniform Reciprocal Enforcement of Support Act, 9A U.L.A. 643 (1987).

SHERYL L. SCHEIBLE WOLF

FAMILY LIFE EDUCATION

Preparing individuals and families for the roles and responsibilities of family living is nothing new. Because human beings have no built-in knowledge about human development, interpersonal relationships, and family living, they must obtain this knowledge from somewhere. Societies have thus developed different ways through which they may transmit the wisdom and the experience of family living from one generation to succeeding generations. In some societies, knowledge about these matters may be transmitted through formal events such as puberty or initiation rites. For the most part, however, individuals have learned about family living in the family setting itself as they observe and participate in family activities and interactions in their own families and sometimes in other families around them.

In complex and changing societies, however, this pattern of informal learning about living in families may be inadequate. Changes in the broader society such as the development of new knowledge, advances in technology, and changing social and economic conditions may create situations in which the teachings of previous generations may no longer be appropriate or sufficient. In such circumstances, societies must find or create new ways through which to prepare individuals for their family roles and responsibilities. One of these ways has been the movement called family life education.

Family life education developed as an educational specialty around the turn of the twentieth century in response to some of the changing social conditions of the time (Darling 1987; Lewis-Rowley et al. 1993). Changes such as urbanization, industrialization, and the changing roles of women were perceived to have negative impacts on families, resulting in negative repercussions for the broader society. Certain family difficulties (e.g., an increased divorce rate, increased parent–child strife, shifts in marital and familial roles) have commonly occurred in societies as they become industrialized and urbanized. Because families often have appeared to be inadequately prepared to deal with these and other social changes, attempts have been made over time to strengthen families through the efforts of outside agencies. The early founders of the family life education movement believed that through the development of formalized family life education programs, family-related social problems such as delinquency or divorce would be ameliorated or reduced and family living would be improved.

Purpose and Content of Family Life Education

The major purpose of family life education is to strengthen and enrich individual and family well-being (Arcus, Schvaneveldt, and Moss 1993; Thomas and Arcus 1992). Although many different goals and objectives have been identified, some of the most

259

common include (1) gaining insight into one's self and others, (2) learning about human development and behavior in the family setting over the life course, (3) learning about the patterns and processes of marriage and family living, (4) acquiring personal and interpersonal skills essential for family living, (5) developing the potentials of individuals and families in their present and their future family roles, and (6) building strengths in individuals and families (Arcus and Thomas 1993). The underlying assumption appears to be that if these and other similar objectives are met through family life education, then families will be better able to deal with or prevent problems, and they will be empowered to live their family lives in ways that are both personally satisfying and socially responsible.

The focus taken in family life education is educational rather than therapeutic, that is, family life education is intended to *equip* individuals for their family roles rather than to *repair* family dysfunction (Arcus, Schvaneveldt, and Moss 1993; Thomas and Arcus 1992). Several different dimensions of learning are central to family life education: acquiring knowledge about concepts and principles relevant to family life education; exploring attitudes and values (both one's own and those of others); and developing personal and interpersonal skills that will likely contribute to individual and family well-being. Family life education programs differ in the emphasis placed on each of these dimensions.

Family life education is a broad, multidisciplinary area of study encompassing many different subject matter or content areas (Arcus 1987; Darling 1987). This content is drawn from diverse disciplines and fields of study such as anthropology, biology, economics, education, home economics, law, medicine, philosophy, psychology, social work, sociology, and theology (Arcus, Schvaneveldt, and Moss 1993). Each of these fields contributes important concepts and principles to the study of family life and approaches this study from different perspectives.

The content of family life education has been described in the Framework for Lifespan Family Life Education, developed under the auspices of the National Council on Family Relations, the major international organization for family scholars and family professionals (National Council on Family Relations 1984). This framework identifies seven topic areas (human development and sexuality; interpersonal relationships; family interaction; family resource management; education about parenthood; ethics; and family and society) and three processes (communication, decision making, and problem solving) that

together specify the content of family life education. In the framework, each topic area is further clarified by listing some of the important knowledge, attitudes, and skills relevant to that topic. For example, the interpersonal relationships topic area includes knowledge, such as the factors that influence mate selection and the changes in marital relationships over time; attitudes and values, such as respecting self and others and accepting responsibility for one's actions; and skills, such as communicating effectively and initiating, maintaining, and ending relationships.

Although the content areas listed in the framework can be seen as distinct areas of study and are sometimes a focus of specialized areas of practice in family life education (e.g., sexuality education, parent education), it is generally believed that meeting the educational needs of individuals and families requires integration across the topic areas (Arcus 1987; National Council on Family Relations 1984). Education about the development of sexual relationships, for instance, should not only include content from the topic areas of human development and sexuality and interpersonal relationships, but also appropriate content from other topic areas such as ethics (e.g., respect for person, nonexploitative behaviors, social responsibility) and family interaction (e.g., effects of the family on the self-concepts of its members, lifestyle choices) and the processes of communication, decision making, and problem solving (Thomas and Arcus 1992).

Lifespan Perspective in Family Life Education

It is both an underlying assumption and a principle of family life education that it is relevant to individuals of all ages and to all families whatever their structure, their stage of the life course, or their special circumstances (Arcus, Schvaneveldt, and Moss 1993; Darling 1987). The impetus for some programs may be related to the various normative developments for individuals and families, such as getting married, becoming a parent, or retiring from a job (Hennon and Arcus 1993). These normative developments may be age-related (attaining puberty), event-related (the loss of a family member), or a combination of age and event (first marriage during young adulthood). Other programs may be based on nonnormative developments, that is, they focus on the special needs and transitions that affect some but not all individuals and families (parenting children with special needs, getting divorced, facing unemployment or underemployment). The response of family life educators to both the normative and nonnormative events and transitions of families has resulted in a number of new specialty areas within family life education, with some specialties well established (parent education, sexuality education, marriage preparation) and others emerging (parent education for adolescent parents, sexual abuse education and prevention, marriage the second time around).

The Framework for Lifespan Family Life Education illustrates that although each topic area is relevant to people of all ages, the focus and complexity of each topic vary for children, adolescents, and adults. In the topic area of ethics, for example, family life education for children focuses on taking responsibility for actions; that for adolescents broadens to include the development of a personal ethical code; while for adults, it expands even further to include (at least for some adults) assisting in the formation of ethical concepts and behavior in others. In addition to these differences in content, there are also some differences in the focus and emphasis of family life education programs depending on the age group for which the programs are intended.

Family life education for children. During childhood, there are many important concepts, attitudes, and skills to be learned that are relevant for living in families: developing self-esteem, making and keeping friends, understanding family similarities and differences, learning to make choices and to use resources wisely, taking responsibility for one's actions, and understanding the importance of families and communities (Hennon and Arcus 1993). Although some of this learning occurs as a result of socialization within the family setting some families may be unwilling or unable to provide appropriate socialization, or their efforts at socialization may be unsuccessful or incorrectly timed.

Most formal family life education programs for children are provided in school settings rather than by community agencies. Although there has been no systematic review of these programs (Hennon and Arcus 1993), most appear to be organized around individual development needs rather than family development, that is, children of the same age or development stage are taught the same things regardless of their particular family situation. This focus on the normative needs and interests of children is generally viewed as appropriate, as children of like ages indeed do have many similar developmental needs. However, some important needs of children may be nonnormative ones related to their particular family circumstances, such as being raised by grandparents rather than by parents or being the oldest child in a single-parent family and taking on adult responsibilities. Family life

education programs that ignore these nonnormative family situations may miss the opportunity to meet some of the real educational needs of children in these families.

Concerns about child sexual abuse have resulted in the development of sexual-abuse prevention programs for young children. These programs focus on concepts of personal safety such as good and bad touch, saying no, and telling someone you trust about the abuse. Little is known, however, about program effectiveness. There is some evidence that sexual abuse education does increase knowledge, but acquiring knowledge per se does not appear to prevent abuse or to change behaviors (Engel, Saracino, and Bergen 1993). Despite the need for sexual-abuse prevention programs, concerns have been expressed about their potential negative side effects. For those programs that have been studied, there is no evidence that such education increases a child's fears or damages their relationships with parents or other significant adults. Still, in the absence of positive sexuality education, it is of concern that children may learn only negative messages about sexuality (Engel, Saracino, and Bergen 1993).

Family life education for adolescents. There appear to be more family life education programs provided for adolescents than for children. Most of these programs are found in school settings, although some may be offered through youth organizations, community agencies, and churches. Programs for adolescents typically focus on the normative needs of adolescents (self-understanding, forming and maintaining relationships, making choices about sexuality, becoming an adult within one's family) and on anticipatory socialization for potential future family roles, specifically education for marriage and parenthood (Hennon and Arcus 1993). As most adolescents have not yet selected a marital partner, anticipatory education for marriage tends to focus on gaining general knowledge about marriage and relationships, learning or improving general relationship skills in communication and problem solving, and exploring personal attitudes and values regarding marriage, marital expectations, and marital roles (Stahmann and Salts 1993). Those programs that provide anticipatory education for parenthood focus on acquiring knowledge about child development and about different patterns of child rearing and may include field or other experiences involving the study and observation of children (Brock, Oertwein, and Coufal 1993). Despite considerable school-based family life education for adolescents and the availability of numerous curriculum guides, there is little systematic knowledge about these programs and little information regarding their effectiveness (Hennon and Arcus 1993). Many programs appear to be hampered in their efforts by the lack of time, resources, and other support, and by limitations in the preparation of teachers for family life education.

Important questions have been raised about what has been called "the promise" of anticipatory family life education for adolescents, that is, the underlying assumption that if young people are prepared specifically for their potential future family roles, then their adult family life experiences in these roles will be more successful (Hennon and Arcus 1993). According to Vladimir de Lissovoy (1978), for example, the goal of better prepared parents is a sound one, but he questions whether adolescents are an appropriate target group for parent education. In his view, adolescents are not maturationally ready to understand and to prepare for the specific developmental tasks of parenthood. He believes instead that the best parent education for adolescents would be preparent education that focuses on the precursors of successful parenting, such as self-understanding and the development of interpersonal relationships and skills.

Most schools provide some form of sexuality education for adolescents, although many curricular guides are out-of-date and programs may not be comprehensive. With the emergence of AIDS as a health and social issue, substantial attention is now directed toward prevention of sexually transmitted diseases (STDs), including AIDS (Engel, Saracino, and Bergen 1993). In addition to providing information about STDs and AIDS, these programs also address issues of personal values and responsibility, communication and decision making, and the reduction of risk-taking behaviors. Research on the effectiveness of AIDS prevention programs is not conclusive, with only some studies reporting positive outcomes. There is some evidence, however, that AIDS prevention programs for gay males are particularly successful (DeMayo 1991).

Concerns about the increasing incidence of adolescent pregnancy have led to the development of specific programs designed to prevent these pregnancies. Most focus on increasing knowledge about sexuality, improving communication and assertiveness skills, influencing attitudes and motivations, and/or increasing access to contraceptive and other health services. Research on the effectiveness of these programs is limited, and although there is some evidence of increased knowledge, findings typically do not report any changes in adolescent sexual and contraceptive behavior, which are complex issues with many factors

unrelated to and unaffected by the education system. Most adolescent pregnancy prevention programs encourage abstinence, but those programs that confine themselves to this goal alone seem to have limited effectiveness (Engel, Saracino, and Bergen 1993).

Some family life education programs for adolescents may be related to nonnormative developments, that is, becoming an adolescent parent. Parent education programs for adolescent parents may be home-based; center-based, provided either in schools or in hospitals; or a combination of both home-based and center-based elements (Clewell, Brooks-Gunn, and Benasich 1989). The major purpose of these programs is to develop or improve parenting skills, but attention is also given to the completion of education and to job training. Many programs also provide health and social services for the family. Center-based programs appear to be more effective, especially for high-risk adolescents.

Family life education for adults. Two characteristics distinguish family life education for adults from that for children and adolescents: (1) It is more complex and more varied, as adults must not only meet their own needs for family living but may also bear some responsibility for the family socialization of the next generation(s), and (2) it is more likely to be related to family life tasks and transitions than to age or developmental level, that is, getting married or becoming parents is more likely to serve as the focal point for programs rather than the age at which these transitions might occur (Hennon and Arcus 1993).

The earliest family life education programs for adults were parent education programs (Brock, Oertwein, and Coufal 1993). These early programs were general in nature and were provided primarily for mothers who met in groups specifically organized for the purpose of improving parent understanding and parenting practices (Lewis-Rowley et al. 1993). Most parenthood education programs are also provided in group settings, and although fathers are increasingly involved, most participants are mothers. Many of the early generic programs have now been adapted to specific target groups, such as parents with different backgrounds, with different parenting needs, and with children of different ages. Although many different kinds of parent education programs have been developed, nearly all are based on the authoritative model of parenting, on effective communication practices, and on the principles of behavior modification.

The most widely used parent education program is Systematic Training for Effective Parenting (STEP) (Dinkmeyer and McKay 1976, 1989). STEP is also the most widely researched program, with at least some studies indicating that it leads to positive changes in parent–child interactions, in parental attitudes, in child behaviors, and in parental perceptions of child behaviors (Brock, Oertwein, and Coufal 1993). There appears to be greater improvement in family climate when both parents participate in the program, but despite the diversity of programs available, research suggests that no one parent education program is more effective than the others (Medway 1989).

Education for marriage is also a major focus in family life education for adults. Becoming a couple is one of the most complex and difficult transitions of the family life cycle, as it involves the negotiation of many individual and family-of-origin issues (Stahmann and Salts 1993). Because the interpersonal patterns that are developed during courtship have an impact on marital success, considerable attention has been given to the preparation of adults for their marital roles. Many different models and approaches for the education of prospective mates have been developed and are provided either to groups of couples or to individual couples through educative counseling (Bagarozzi and Rauen 1981). Regardless of the approach or the format used, the purposes of marriage preparation are to provide the premarital couple with opportunities to gain knowledge about and discuss the critical issues and tasks of marriage, to acquire behavioral skills and problem-solving strategies that might enhance the marital relationship, and to evaluate their own relationship (Bagarozzi and Rauen 1981). Marital preparation is also designed to combat the romanticism of many premarital couples and to assist them in examining their untested assumptions and unrealistic expectations (Hennon and Arcus 1993). Originally, marriage preparation was provided primarily for young adult couples. However, in recent years, versions of these programs have also been developed for couples marrying for the second time or for those marrying during the later years.

Several studies indicate that marriage-preparation programs are effective, with couples reporting significant gains in couple adjustment and commitment (Buckner and Salts 1985) and perceived improvement in sexual understanding and communication skills (Fournier, Olson, and Druckman 1983). However, one study that found little or no benefit from the general premarital interviews conducted by clergy suggested that postmarital education might be more effective than premarital education (Guldner 1971).

This raises important questions about what counts as success in marriage preparation and when this success is best measured. Most contemporary studies rely almost exclusively on self-reports of couple satisfaction, either immediately after taking the program or shortly after the wedding. Few studies have examined any long-term effects of marriage-preparation programs. One exception is the research carried out by Edward Bader and his associates (Bader et al. 1980a, 1980b; Bader, Riddle, and Sinclair 1980). They compared couples who did and who did not take marriage preparation, obtaining information at several different time periods (prior to the program; before postwedding sessions; near the couple's first anniversary; five years after the wedding). Those couples who participated in marriage preparation reported less conflict over interpersonal topics, an increased ability to resolve hypothetical conflict situations, and less help-seeking behavior. Differences in the two groups were still evident five years later.

Another form of marriage education (marriage enrichment) emerged during the 1960s, based on the premise that all relationships have a need for growth and that under appropriate conditions all persons can learn to maintain significant interpersonal relationships (Hof and Miller 1980). The marriage enrichment philosophy is based on a dynamic view of relationships and emphasizes the strengths of relationships rather than their problems. Programs are designed to increase awareness of self and others, to explore and express thoughts and feelings with honesty and empathy, and to develop and use skills important in relationships (communication, problem solving, conflict resolution). They are typically delivered either through a series of weekly meetings or in intensive weekend retreats (Mace 1982). Reviews indicate that marriage enrichment programs are effective, although their effects appear to diminish over time (Stahmann and Salts 1993).

While not as numerous or as well developed as parent education and marriage preparation/marriage enrichment, other family life education programs that address important adult needs have emerged. Some of these needs include adjusting to divorce, providing caregiving for aging family members, being grandparents, preparing for retirement, and dealing with loss, grief, and bereavement. However, little is known about the effectiveness of the diverse programs that are involved.

Issues in Family Life Education

Since the inception of the family life education movement at the beginning of the twentieth century, there has been considerable growth in the number and the kinds of programs available for individuals and families of all ages and in the number of individuals and families who are served by these programs (Hennon and Arcus 1993). Over time, the dynamic nature of family life education has been reflected in the modification of existing programs and the emergence of new specializations to better respond to contemporary circumstances and needs.

Despite the growth and apparent success of this movement, however, several issues require attention. Most family life education participants are white, female, and middle class. Although this is slowly changing, important issues of diversity (gender, class, ethnicity) need to be seriously addressed to ensure that programs reflect the real diversity of contemporary society and better meet the needs of those who are currently neglected or underserved. Despite their importance and centrality, values have often been problematic and sometimes ignored in family life education (Arcus and Daniels 1993). Attention needs to be given not only to the diversity of personal and cultural values but also to shared and socially beneficial values, such as respect for persons, justice and equity, social responsibility, and so on.

Some important issues are related to the delivery of family life education programs. It may be time to target families as whole units in family life education rather than separate individuals. It may also be time to provide family life education in nontraditional settings such as the workplace, particularly for adults. Because the body of evidence on the effects of family life education is limited, more and better research on these programs is needed. More attention also needs to be given to the preparation of the family life educators, as they bear the major responsibility for shaping the programs and the nature of the educational experience.

Underlying the practice of family life education is a basic belief in the importance of family living and a basic respect for persons that recognizes their abilities to take charge of their own lives in satisfying ways. These issues need to be addressed to expand and improve family life education efforts and thus help to strengthen families as they fulfill their significant role as the basic unit of society.

(*See also:* ADOLESCENCE; CHILDHOOD; COMMUNICATION; DECISION MAKING AND PROBLEM SOLVING; PARENT EDUCATION; PERSONALITY DEVELOPMENT; SEXUALITY EDUCATION; SEXUALITY IN THE LIFE CYCLE; TEENAGE PARENTING)

BIBLIOGRAPHY

Arcus, M. E. (1987). "A Framework for Lifespan Family Life Education." *Family Relations* 36:5–10.

Arcus, M. E. (1992). "Family Life Education: Toward the 21st Century." *Family Relations* 41:390–393.

Arcus, M. E., and Daniels, L. B. (1993). "Values and Family Life Education." In *Handbook of Family Life Education, Foundations of Family Life Education*, Vol. 1, ed. M. E. Arcus, J. D. Schvaneveldt, and J. J. Moss. Newbury Park, CA: Sage Publications.

Arcus, M. E.; Schvaneveldt, J. D.; and Moss, J. J. (1993). "The Nature of Family Life Education." In *Handbook of Family Life Education, Foundations of Family Life Education*, Vol. 1, ed. M. E. Arcus, J. D. Schvaneveldt, and J. J. Moss. Newbury Park, CA: Sage Publications.

Arcus, M. E., and Thomas, J. (1993). "The Nature and Practice of Family Life Education." In *Handbook of Family Life Education, The Practice of Family Life Education*, Vol. 2, ed. M. E. Arcus, J. D. Schvaneveldt, and J. J. Moss. Newbury Park, CA: Sage Publications.

Bader, E.; Microys, G.; Sinclair, C.; Willett, E.; and Conway, B. (1980a). *Do Marriage Preparation Programs Help? A Five Year Study.* Toronto: University of Toronto Department of Family and Community Medicine.

Bader, E.; Microys, G.; Sinclair, C.; Willett, E.; and Conway, B. (1980b). "Do Marriage Preparation Programs Really Work? A Canadian Experiment." *Journal of Marital and Family Therapy* 6:171–179.

Bader, E.; Riddle, R.; and Sinclair, C. (1980). *Do Marriage Preparation Programs Help? A Five-Year Study.* Toronto: University of Toronto Department of Family and Community Medicine.

Bagarozzi, D. A., and Rauen, P. (1981). "Premarital Counseling: Appraisal and Status." *American Journal of Family Therapy* 9:13–28.

Brock, G. W.; Oertwein, M.; and Coufal, J. D. (1993). "Parent Education: Theory, Research, and Practice." In *Handbook of Family Life Education, The Practice of Family Life Education*, Vol. 2, ed. M. E. Arcus, J. D. Schvaneveldt, and J. J. Moss. Newbury Park, CA: Sage Publications.

Buckner, L., and Salts, C. (1985). "A Premarital Assessment Program." *Family Relations* 34:513–520.

Clewell, B. C.; Brooks-Gunn, J.; and Benasich, A. A. (1989). "Evaluating Child-Related Outcomes of Teenage Parenting Programs." *Family Relations* 38:201–209.

Darling, C. A. (1987). "Family Life Education." In *Handbook of Marriage and the Family*, ed. M. B. Sussman and S. K. Steinmetz. New York: Plenum.

de Lissovoy, V. (1978). "Parent Education: White Elephant in the Classroom?" *Youth and Society* 9:315–338.

DeMayo, M. (1991). "The Future of HIV/AIDS Prevention Programs: Learning from the Experiences of Gay Men." *SIECUS Report* 20(October-November):1–7.

Dinkmeyer, D., and McKay, G. (1976). *Systematic Training for Effective Parenting: Parent's Handbook.* Circle Pines, MN: American Guidance Service.

Dinkmeyer, D., and McKay, G. (1989). *Parenting Young Children.* Circle Pines, MN: American Guidance Service.

Engel, J. W.; Saracino, M.; and Bergen, M. B. (1993)."Sexuality Education." In *Handbook of Family Life Education,*

The Practice of Family Life Education, Vol. 2, ed. M. E. Arcus, J. D. Schvaneveldt, and J. J. Moss. Newbury Park, CA: Sage Publications.

Fournier, D.; Olson, D.; and Druckman, J. (1983). "Assessing Marital and Premarital Relationships: The PREPARE-ENRICH Inventories." In *A Sourcebook in Marriage and Family Assessment*, ed. E. Filsinger. Newbury Park, CA: Sage Publications.

Guldner, C. (1971). "The Postmarital: An Alternate to Premarital Counseling." *The Family Coordinator* 20:115–119.

Hennon, C. B., and Arcus, M. E. (1993). "Lifespan Family Life Education." In *Family Relations: Challenges for the Future*, ed. T. H. Brubaker. Newbury Park, CA: Sage Publications.

Hof, L., and Miller, W. R. (1980). "Marriage Enrichment." *Marriage and Family Review* 3:1–17.

Lewis-Rowley, M.; Brasher, R. E.; Moss, J. J.; Duncan, S. F.; and Stiles, R. J. (1993). "The Evolution of Education for Family Life." In *Handbook of Family Life Education, Foundations of Family Life Education*, Vol. 1, ed. M. E. Arcus, J. D. Schvaneveldt, and J. J. Moss. Newbury Park, CA: Sage Publications.

Mace, D. (1982). *Close Companions: The Marriage Enrichment Handbook.* New York: Continuum.

Medway, F. (1989). "Measuring the Effectiveness of Parent Education." In *The Second Handbook on Parent Education: Contemporary Perspectives*, ed. M. J. Fine. San Diego: Academic Press.

National Council on Family Relations. (1984). *Standards and Criteria for the Certification of Family Life Educators, College/University Curriculum Guidelines, and Content Guidelines for Family Life Education: A Framework for Planning Programs Over the Lifespan.* Minneapolis: Author.

Stahmann, R. F., and Salts, C. J. (1993). "Education for Marriage and Intimate Relationships." In *Handbook of Family Life Education, The Practice of Family Life Education*, Vol. 2, ed. M. E. Arcus, J. D. Schvaneveldt, and J. J. Moss. Newbury Park, CA: Sage Publications.

Thomas, J., and Arcus, M. (1992). "Family Life Education: An Analysis of the Concept." *Family Relations* 41:3–8.

MARGARET EDWARDS ARCUS

FAMILY PLANNING

Family planning is defined as the act of making a conscious plan about the number and timing of children. Timing may include the time of the first birth, the amount of space between births, and the time of the final birth. Family planning is more than birth control because it includes the positive aspects as well as the negative aspects. Planning takes place at both the societal level and the level of the individual or couple.

Methods and Effectiveness

People have consciously or unconsciously engaged in family planning throughout history. Abstinence, either lifelong or temporary, and prohibitions during certain times in the year curtail the fertility rate (the number of live births for each woman during her lifetime). Separation of husbands and wives for long periods of time by war or business trips also curtails the fertility rate.

Abortion was often used to limit family size, and favored methods can be cited from the folklore of women and midwives of most societies. The deliberate abandonment of infants and children, even killing of newborns, is written about in the literature of ancient Greece and Rome. The Christians outlawed infanticide but emphasized the stigma of illegitimacy, so out-of-wedlock infants were brought to overcrowded orphanages and monasteries, where the majority of them died of starvation and/or disease within a few months.

Prolonged lactation was also an important method for spacing births. Lactation and the stimulus of the infant suckling ordinarily suppresses ovulation and menstruation. It is highly effective as a birth control mechanism only when the total food supply of the infant is breast milk, or when abstinence during lactation is the norm. As partial weaning takes place—as early as four to six months—the menstrual cycle returns in most women who are adequately nourished, and pregnancy is again possible.

Numerous devices such as condoms and IUDS are used in family planning. Alternate methods of intercourse, including withdrawal and anal intercourse, also lessen the chance of pregnancy. One of the earliest results of the use of broad-scale methods sufficient to affect national fertility was the decline in the French birth rate from the end of the eighteenth century, a decline attributed to the widespread use of coitus interruptus (Van de Walle 1978). The use of such a wide variety of techniques emphasized an almost universal desire for humans to gain some control over the number and spacing of births.

The effectiveness of family planning is measured by the fertility rate. In the industrial countries of the 1990s, population remains stable over the long run, with a fertility rate of slightly under 2 (Green 1992). However, this rate will still result in population increase because of the potential of greater longevity and the existence of several generations of a family at the same time. In determining potential rates of increase, demographers use the married Hutterite women as their maximum standard for potential. The Hutterites are members of a religious sect (in the northern United States and southern Canada) who do not use any method of family planning. Their living standard is not luxurious, but their food supply is more than adequate and they are regarded as very healthy. The average number of children born to a Hutterite woman in the early part of the nineteenth century was 12 (Coale 1971), and this is considered the maximum for a totally uninhibited rate of fertility. Modern fertility rates in some countries of the Third World, such as Saudi Arabia, Malawi, and Rwanda, are between 7 and 8 (Green 1992). These rates are lower than the Hutterite rate because the women are not as well nourished and because national family planning policies as well as the work of international family planning agencies have brought even these rates down.

Social Regulation

Organized efforts at family planning date primarily from the nineteenth century. Such efforts were started by individuals concerned with the poverty and malnutrition that seemed to be endemic among large families. Governmental bodies initially paid little attention to such efforts, and among those that did, the effort was to increase family size rather than decrease it. In the United States, governmental agencies such as the post office classified family planning materials as pornography. At the beginning of the twentieth century, President Theodore Roosevelt compared women who avoided pregnancy to men who refused to serve in the armed forces. He argued that having children was the patriotic duty of American women. It was not until the last part of the twentieth century that governments in general took direct or indirect action to encourage family planning. This concern came primarily because of a growing concern about overpopulation.

At the beginning of the industrial revolution in the eighteenth century, the world population was estimated at 750 million. With growing urbanization and industrialization, growth escalated rapidly, reaching 1 billion in 1830, 2 billion in 1930, 3 billion in 1960, 4 billion in 1975, and more than 5 billion by 1990 (McKeown 1976; Green 1992). If such rates were to continue it has been anticipated that the number will reach 8.2 billion by 2020. This growth can be attributed to declining mortality as the standard of living was raised, sanitation was improved, and communi-

cable diseases were controlled. However, the most rapid growth has not been in the highly industrialized countries but in the countries that have not yet industrialized. As the standard of living has been raised in Western Europe, the United States, and the other industrialized countries, the fertility rate has fallen below 2.0, and in some is as low as 1.3 (Green 1992).

Most countries have relied on education in family planning to lower fertility rates, although more drastic means have been used. In some areas of India, for example, it was alleged that sterilization was being forced on the less educated peasants. Such allegations resulted in a slowdown in the campaign.

On a world scale, fertility rates have been declining. The problem is that in many underdeveloped countries, the largest segment of the population is in the childbearing years. Therefore, even with the lowering of fertility ratios, population will continue to grow unless the birth rate can be radically decreased. This problem has plagued the People's Republic of China.

With a population of 1.2 billion, China has become the first country in the world to embark on a deliberate and comprehensive course to reach zero population growth by the year 2000 or as soon after that as possible (Bullough and Bullough 1983–1984). To achieve this, the Chinese government called on the people to limit their families to one child. The limitations are enforced by *danwei*, collectives that are used to organize factories, farms, or even blocks in cities. In addition to facilitating birth control, abortions, and sterilizations, these groups provide rewards at work and better schooling for the child if the couple has complied with the one-child norm.

Although the Chinese government has allowed many more exceptions in recent years, the family planning policy was further emphasized in 1993. At that time, the Communist Party Congress approved a bill to forbid marriages of persons with hepatitis, venereal disease, or mental illness to reduce the number of congenitally disabled persons and limit population growth (Tempest 1993). China's problems emphasize the difficulty that even authoritarian states have in encouraging family planning, and these difficulties are compounded in democratic states that rely on education. Although the United States has a fertility rate of 1.8, half of the pregnancies are unplanned or unwanted, a higher rate than in most other industrialized countries (Jones et al. 1989). In addition, the United States has a high abortion rate, with approximately one-third of the pregnancies (29.7%) ending in an abortion (Jones et al. 1989) Among the industrialized countries only Italy, Japan, and the states that make up the former Soviet Union have abortion rates that are higher than or comparable to the abortion rate in the United States.

A study published in 1989 compared the countries with low rates of unplanned pregnancies with the United States to identify the factors that might explain this situation (Jones et al. 1989). Most of the unintended pregnancies in the United States occurred to women who came from disadvantaged backgrounds and were under age twenty-five. Moreover, most of the countries with low rates of unintended pregnancies have comprehensive national health plans that made family planning services readily available to all women regardless of their income and age, something that has not yet occurred in the United States. In addition, media restrictions against advertising and open discussion of contraceptives traditionally have been problems in the United States, although television networks have accepted advertisements for condoms because of the AIDS epidemic.

The high rate of unplanned pregnancies also suggests that group norms in the United States have not yet fully changed to fit the belief in an overpopulated world. How much they should change is a matter of public discussion. The fact that not all states allowed the dissemination of contraception until 1965 and abortions were prohibited until 1973 emphasizes the difficulty family planning had in being accepted (Bullough and Bullough 1977). Still, barriers to effective family planning have slowly been removed. One barrier to effective family planning, the dependence of the older generation on their children, was considerably lessened by the passage of various types of Social Security legislation. Equal opportunities acts have also allowed greater freedom to women in making choices about family size or even whether to have children. The growing tolerance of homosexuality and lesbianism is also an indicator of changing public attitudes toward pronatalism.

Premarital and Out-of-Wedlock Pregnancies

In the eighteenth century, where 30 percent of pregnancies occurred at least two months before marriage, pregnancy usually led to marriage. In the late twentieth century, however, pregnancy does not necessarily lead to marriage, particularly among those in the fifteen- to nineteen-year-old age group. Each year, approximately one of every ten American teenagers becomes pregnant. This constitutes about 800,000 pregnancies each year; 53 percent result in live births and 47 percent in abortions or spontaneous miscarriages (Trussell 1988). It is important to point out that this is a much lower pregnancy rate among

fifteen- to nineteen-year-olds than existed in the past. The difference is that in the past most young women, who married at a younger age, were already married when they became pregnant, or they married before delivery.

Some people see teenage pregnancy as a moral failure, while others see it as a failure in family planning. Evidence for moral failure is controversial, since sexual intercourse among teenagers is not new; they just are not being sanctified by marriage after pregnancy occurs. Moreover, in the past, the double standard for sexual activity supported young men in their teens having sexual experience, but young women were supposed to remain celibate. Norms of the late-twentieth century do not support the double standard, and two-thirds of American women have had sexual experience during their teen years (Janus 1993).

It is difficult to see the decline of the double standard and decrease in forced marriages as moral failures. However, there seem to be very real planning failures. Contraception options are better than they have ever been. An abortion can be a traumatic experience, while having a baby during the teen years cuts down a woman's options and opportunities. Most households headed by a single female are poverty households; such women earn only about 71 percent as much as men (Filer 1989). White women and women with more education typically seek abortions, while African-American women and women from disadvantaged backgrounds are more likely to carry to term and raise the baby alone. Better contraceptive information and better planning for teenagers certainly seem like necessities.

Individual Regulation

The optimal situation for family planning involves both members of the couple, is initiated before sex is started, and includes a sharing of mutual hopes and desires to make sure they are sufficiently congruent to make a good marriage or partnership. All aspects of planning (whether marriage will occur and when, whether children are planned and when, and the number and spacing of children) should be included.

Consideration of whether the individual man or woman wants to have children should occur early in the discussion. Most young people want at least one child, although this opinion can change over time. A 1991 study of undergraduate students reported that 95 percent wanted children (Seccombe 1991). However, a national sample of married adults of childbearing age and from a wider variety of socioeconomic backgrounds found that 19 percent of the wives and 13 percent of the husbands did not want to have children, a significant increase from the past and indicative of the pace of change in attitudes (Seccombe 1991).

If the couple decides to have children, the number of children is then an item for planning. People make these decisions in the context of the norms of their individual group, although these norms can change. Religious men and women who belong to pronatal churches indicate that they want more children than other persons. At the height of the baby boom in the 1950s, a study of college women indicated that the average woman wanted 4.4 children. However, women in Catholic schools wanted 5 or more, while women in nonsectarian schools averaged 3.5 to 3.8 These statistics are reflective not only of the religious influence but also of the influence of the era. Since that time, the desired family size has fallen to 2.2, with only slight differences between Catholic and other women. Men's conception of the desirable family size is similar to that of women (Seccombe 1991).

How much additional change there will be is unclear, since society is based on the assumption that most adults will have children. Whole industries are built upon serving the needs of children, not the least of which is the educational system. Children are certainly interesting, make life more complex, and can give a focus for the future. Large numbers of people feel that having children gives their life meaning, broadens their concern away from themselves, and gives them a feeling of creativity. Women, especially, perceive motherhood and children as part of their female role, with many believing they are not fully a woman unless they have children. Men for their part regard children as proof of their manhood. They not infrequently speak of their commitment to preserving the family name and see their children as a way of sharing continuity with the future.

The timing of children is also an important part of planning. There is evidence that being too young or too old is not advantageous to the health of the mother and infant. Teenage mothers who are still growing themselves are more likely to have low-birthweight infants and other complications. However, the most significant problem for the mother who is still in her teens is the fact that she often does not finish high school, a significant problem for her in the job market for the rest of her life.

The problems are different for the woman who is at the end of her fertility cycle, a problem that is increasing because many people have put off having families.

The incidence of Down syndrome and other congenital abnormalities starts to increase at age thirty-five and is greater each year after that (Maheady 1992). Pregnancy in older women can also complicate other existing chronic diseases, such as diabetes. Therefore, good planning for the older woman who decides to have a pregnancy late in her reproductive years includes amniocentesis. Men past fifty face the worry of being able to work long enough to raise their child, and this can create a great deal of stress.

Infertility

Perhaps the best indicator of the American desire for children is the current concern with infertility, something that is also part of the family planning. Approximately 10 percent to 15 percent of all couples have difficulty conceiving, with the causes about equally divided between men and women (Freeman and Bullough 1993). Major causes include venereal infections, failure to ovulate, low sperm counts, obstructions in either the male or female reproductive organs, or impenetrable cervical mucus. Sometimes these problems can be treated with antibiotics, surgery, or hormones. If these methods fail, artificial insemination or in vitro fertilization can sometimes be used. These approaches have been successful for many couples and have brought them great joy. However, there is a down side to their use. The fact that these technological approaches to conception are now possible makes some couples feel obligated to try to have a baby, but the elaborate approaches, including in vitro fertilization, are expensive, time-consuming, and often disappointing.

Conclusion

Ideal family planning includes consideration of the timing of marriage, number and spacing of children, and when the first and last births will occur. It necessitates discussions of sexuality, contraception, and other plans such as schooling or work plans that affect births. Americans still do little of this planning, and teenagers are inadequately taught about these topics. Family planning should be an important part of the modern lifestyle. If individuals do not take on this responsibility, there is always the potential that the government, as in the case of China, will see a need to intervene.

(*See also:* ABORTION: MEDICAL AND SOCIAL ASPECTS; ADOPTION; BIRTH CONTROL: SOCIOCULTURAL AND HISTORICAL ASPECTS; BIRTH CONTROL: CONTRACEPTIVE METHODS; CONCEPTION:

Medical Aspects; Demography; Genetic Counseling; Infertility; Pregnancy and Birth)

BIBLIOGRAPHY

Bullough, V., and Bullough, B. (1977). *Sin, Sickness, and Sanity: A History of Sexual Attitudes.* New York: New American Library.

Bullough, V., and Bullough, B. (1983–1984). "Population Control vs. Freedom in China." *Free Inquiry* 3:12–15.

Cleland, J., and Hobcraft, J., eds. (1985). *Reproductive Change in Developing Countries: Insights from the World Fertility Survey.* Oxford: Oxford University Press.

Coale, A. J. (1971). "The Decline of Fertility in Europe from the French Revolution to World War II." In *Fertility and Family Planning: A World View*, ed. S. J. Behrman, L. Corsa, Jr., and R. Freedman. Ann Arbor: University of Michigan Press.

Filer, R. K. (1989). "Occupational Segregation, Compensating Differentials, and Comparable Worth." In *Pay Equity*, ed. R. T. Michael, H. I. Hartman, and B. O'Farrel. Washington, DC: National Academy Press.

Freeman, S., and Bullough, V. L. (1993). *The Complete Guide to Fertility Family Planning.* Buffalo, NY: Prometheus.

Green, C. P. (1992). *The Environment and Population Growth: Decade for Action.* Supplement to *Population Reports*, Series M, no. 10, Vol. 20. Baltimore: Population Information Program, Johns Hopkins University.

Janus, S. S., and Janus, C. L. (1993). *The Janus Report on Sexual Behavior.* New York: Wiley.

Jones, E. F.; Forrest, J. D.; Henshaw, S. K.; Silverman, J.; and Torres, A. (1989). *Pregnancy, Contraception, and Family Planning Services in Industrialized Countries.* New Haven, CT: Yale University Press.

Maheady, D. C. (1992). "Nursing Care of Children with Disabling Conditions." In *Child Health Care: Process and Practice*, ed. P. T. Castiglia and R. E. Harbin. Philadelphia: Lippincott.

McCammon, S. I.; Knox, D.; and Schacht, C. (1993). *Choices in Sexuality.* St. Paul, MN: West Publishing.

McKeown, T. (1976). *The Modern Rise of Population.* New York: Academic Press.

Seccombe, K. (1991). "Assessing the Costs and Benefits of Children: Gender Comparisons Among Childfree Husbands and Wives." *Journal of Marriage and the Family* 53:191–202.

Tempest, R. (1993). "China Denies Plan for Forced Abortions." *Los Angeles Times*, December 30, p. A6.

Trussell, J. (1988). "Teenage Pregnancy in the United States." *Family Planning Perspectives* 20:262–271.

U.S. Bureau of the Census. (1992). *Statistical Abstract of the United States*, 112th edition. Washington, DC: U.S. Government Printing Office.

Van de Walle, E. (1978). "Alone in Europe, The French Fertility Decline Until 1850." In *Historical Studies of Changing Fertility*, ed. C. Tilly. Princeton, NJ: Princeton University Press.

Westoff, C. F., and Potvin, R. H. (1967). *College Women and Fertility Values.* Princeton, NJ: Princeton University Press.

Bonnie Bullough
Vern L. Bullough

FAMILY POLICY

The term "family policy" as used in the United States is relatively new. The concept was first mentioned in the social science literature in the 1960s, but it did not receive expanded discussion until the mid- to late 1970s. Much of the writing concerning family policy since the mid-1980s has focused on defining what the term means, developing a conceptual framework for understanding family policy, and applying the concept to real policy advocacy efforts at either the state or federal level. A benefit from these scholarly efforts has been an increased level of attention given to family issues in the policymaking arena.

Meaning of Family Policy

To understand family policy it is important to know the meaning of social policy. Social policy has been defined as a system of interrelated principles and actions that shape the quality of life or the well-being of members of a society. Such policy can determine the nature of all societal relationships among individuals, social groups, and society as a whole. Social policy would include all courses of action that affect human relationships and the quality of life in society, in an attempt to intervene and regulate what otherwise might be a random social system (Zimmerman 1976).

Richard Titmuss (1969) suggested that social policy consists of acts of government that are undertaken for a variety of political reasons to provide for a range of needs that the economy does not or cannot satisfy for certain segments of the population. These needs, whether financial, social, educational, or medical, relate to perceived problems and challenges experienced by certain disparate groups of society, such as children, women, the poor, the elderly, or the handicapped. The needs change as a reflection of a changing society; thus, social policy is determined to be ever evolving.

The main traditions that have influenced social policy in the United States are individualism, a minimum of government intervention, and negotiation among interest groups. The relationship between family and government has been uneasy. Unlike most Western democracies, the founding fathers chose not to mention family in the Constitution of the United States, which does not assume protection of family life. The reigning philosophy of that time celebrated individualism and focused on removing constraints on individual freedom. The strongly held belief was that if one worked hard, that person could aspire and rise to whatever level of success he or she chose, which could be much more than that person's family had achieved. Political quarrels about family policy can be traced to a conflict between concern for the individual and concern for the well-being of the family group.

Understanding social policy is important for those interested in the social sciences and those working or planning to work in human services because, to a large extent, social policy shapes the form of practice professionals use, and social policy determines the client systems available as well as which clients may use these systems. For example, social policy can shape the form of practice used by dictating the kinds of programs that will be funded. Within these programs, guidelines often state the criteria for the type of individual who may use the program. Thus, the demand for services such as family therapy, employment counseling, or community day-care centers, among other forms of human services, result in part from the choices that are shaped and made available by social policies.

How does family policy differ from social policy? It is important first to discuss the definition of family in this presentation. Theodora Ooms and Steven Preister (1988) define family as two or more persons related by blood, marriage, or adoption. This definition is more encompassing than that of the U.S. Bureau of the Census, which defines a family as two or more persons related by blood, marriage, or adoption who reside in the same household. Ooms and Preister's definition highlights that families are multigenerational units; therefore, family relationships and responsibilities at different stages of the life cycle, not households, should be a policy focus to enable issues such as child support, custodial visitation, and the support of relatives to elderly family members living independently to be addressed accurately. Second is the importance of maintaining open contacts among family members. Families serve their functions best when each individual in the family is able to have access to every other member, including contact between generations. Social policy can foster, limit, or cut off contact among family members. Every public

policy must involve some clear consideration of how the various alternative policies either foster family contact or discourage such contact. Although this definition does not include any group of persons living together and caring for one another and defining themselves as a family, sometimes in service delivery some of the rights of family are extended to individuals living in "family-like" situations, such as foster care.

Ooms and Preister (1988) define family policy broadly to include decisions made and implemented at the federal, state, and local levels, and in the executive, legislative, and judicial branches of government. Sheila B. Kamerman and Alfred J. Kahn (1976) define family policy as everything that government does to or for the family. Janet Z. Giele (1979) defines family policy as any social policy with clear, important consequences for families, generally oriented either to helping target groups of individuals or to supporting family functions.

All of these definitions recognize the role of government in determining policies that are to benefit families. Some would consider family policy to be a more specific example of social policy—family policy began to be explored in the context of social policy as one approach to achieving a series of societal objectives for families. Family policy is espoused as providing a strategy for supporting the family in their caring role.

Historically, under the Tenth Amendment to the U.S. Constitution, powers not assigned to the federal government are delegated to the various states. Issues related to family matters, such as marriage, divorce, property distribution, and child welfare, are relegated to the individual states. Thus, state laws and judicial actions, differing from state to state, created the structure that regulated families and were, in effect, the first family policies (Anderson 1989).

When state regulation failed to resolve certain family problems, the federal government was willing to step in on occasion. For example, government began to assume responsibility for the care of children and dependents who could not be cared for properly by their own families. However, once again, social policy emphasizing concern for the individual rather than for the total family dominated government activity.

By the mid-1970s, there was a small but significant press for government policy to focus more directly on the well-being of the American family and its members. American demographics were beginning to indicate that family life was changing, and many people were concerned that family was being destroyed. Efforts were made to develop policies to accommodate such family trends as women's growing presence in the workplace, the need for child-care services, divorce, teenage single parenthood, and elderly dependents, as well as problems such as teenage suicide, substance abuse, and family violence. The 1980 White House Conference on Families focused attention on the relationship between government and family life, and the groundswell needed to form an American consensus on family policy was begun.

Although the 1980s did not witness the development of any cohesive and comprehensive family policy, political dialogue increasingly included discussion of the potential impact of proposed legislation on family life. The consequences from the Reagan administration's dismantling during the 1980s of many of the accomplishments of the New Deal welfare support net, as well as many of the programs developed during the Johnson administration's "Great Society" efforts, increased societal attention to the important role that family plays in society. Social service reform, industrial benefits, and child welfare legislation have been some of the legislative areas in which the needs of families have been considered. The pluralism of families has begun to be recognized and ethnic diversity understood. Political campaigns at both the state and federal levels that introduced the 1990s were often waged on redeeming the plight of America's families. Therefore, any social policy developed in response to a crisis must consider increasingly the potential implications for families and their members.

Legislative Initiatives

Several major family policy legislative initiatives occurred at the state and/or federal level during the 1980s and the 1990s.

Family leave. Family leave refers to a leave of absence from work to care for a newborn, sick, or adopted child, or to care for an ill adult such as a spouse or elderly parent. This term contrasts with maternal leave that is provided to females during their pregnancy. The Pregnancy Discrimination Act of 1978 was one of the first formalized attempts to provide some protection against discrimination for pregnant working women. Congress stated that pregnancy and pregnancy-related conditions should be treated similarly to other medical conditions (Monroe and Garand 1991), yet no maternity or family leave was guaranteed.

Until 1987, neither the federal nor any state government passed a family leave policy. During the 1987 legislative session, family leave legislation was introduced in twenty-eight states but passed in only four

(Wisensale and Allison 1989). The bills that passed differed on the number of weeks of leave, whether employee benefits would be paid during the leave, appropriate reasons for the leave, and who was eligible for leave. Yet all agreed that the leave would be unpaid, and those companies to which the bill applied were mandated to offer the leave. Hence, this legislative session was a benchmark year in the efforts to pass federal legislation.

By late 1990, sixteen states had passed some form of family and parental leave legislation (Monroe and Garand 1989), and another twenty-four had considered such legislation. This family policy initiative was clearly one whose time had arrived. The U.S. Congress also had been struggling to pass such legislation since 1986. During the summer of 1990, Congress passed a parental leave measure, but President George Bush vetoed the bill primarily because of Republican opposition to mandating the private sector to implement such a law versus providing tax breaks and other incentives for reluctant businesses.

The final federal legislative output for the family leave act revolved around the 1992 presidential election. Clearly this family policy issue was one of the major family areas discussed repeatedly throughout the campaign. Following the 1990 presidential veto, Democratic presidential nominee Bill Clinton vowed during his campaign that family leave would be one of the first bills he would sign into law if elected president. After his inauguration, family leave was one of the first bills introduced in Congress and passed into law; in February 1993, President Clinton signed the Family and Medical Leave Act, his first law signed as the new president. Because family leave legislation is so relatively new, the long-term effects of this family policy will need to be explored further.

Child care. Child care in the United States is regulated primarily by the states (Morgan 1987). Federal involvement is limited to requiring that federally funded programs meet state standards. Programs falling under these requirements mostly are targeted to low-income families. The federal government first became involved in the 1930s in assisting parents with child care, due to the inability of state and local agencies to meet the needs of poor families. The Great Depression created the need for several emergency programs to meet the needs of families suffering economic loss. These "emergency nurseries" ended as the economy improved at the start of World War II. However, some of the nurseries were transformed into child-care centers in 1941 to enable mothers to work in war industries. At the end of the war, federal legislators expressed the belief that jobs should go to men returning from the war and children should be returned to their mothers at home. Most of the child-care centers were dismantled in 1946.

Not until the 1960s was there renewed federal involvement in child care. To reduce welfare dependency, legislation was proposed for child care to enable welfare parents to work or obtain job training. Subsequently, the establishment of child-care programs under Aid to Families with Dependent Children (AFDC), child welfare, the Elementary and Secondary Education Act, and Work Incentive Now (WIN) occurred (Steiner 1976). These programs required that child-care centers receiving federal funds have a state license, so states established licensing standards (Weintraub and Furman 1987). In 1968, the Federal Interagency Day Care Requirements (FIDCR) were passed, specifying staff–child ratios, group size, staff qualifications, health and safety requirements, educational and social services to be provided, and parental involvement. Compliance was neither mandated nor enforced, and opposition to federal involvement in child care and concern about costs resulted in the suspension of the FIDCR in 1980 (Weintraub and Furman 1987).

Attempts had been made in the early 1970s to pass comprehensive child-care legislation. President Richard Nixon in 1971 vetoed such measures because of concern about "communal approaches to child rearing" (Steiner 1976). This action virtually ended child-care legislation for the next decade. However, with the increasing numbers of women entering the job market and the rise in single-parent households, congressional interest surged around child-care legislation by the mid-1980s. More than one hundred child-care-related bills were introduced in Congress from 1987 to 1989.

The culminating legislation, the Act for Better Child Care (ABC bill), was introduced in 1987 as a result of the efforts of a broad coalition called the Alliance for Better Child Care. The policy proposed that a national advisory committee establish minimum health and safety standards, with all state-licensed programs required to meet these standards (Ooms and Herendon 1989). The ABC bill did not pass Congress in 1988 but was reintroduced in 1989. In 1989, passage did not occur because of criticism over the bill's cost: $2.5 billion for the first year (Weintraub and Furman 1987).

A compromise bill passed in 1990 and was signed into law by President Bush. This policy omitted the federal standards of quality but expanded parental choice of care by relatives, neighbors, or church or other private centers. While this family policy legislation was the first major congressional child-care mea-sure passed in twenty years, it is important to remember that about 5,000 American parents must reject work daily because they cannot find adequate or affordable child care (Thomas and Thomas 1990).

Child support. As the number of single-parent, female-headed households has increased, and as the "feminization of poverty" has become a popular term for the consequences of this demographic change, concern about the rising rates of childhood poverty has also become paramount. These two economic realities have brought about a growing sentiment in favor of mandating that noncustodial parents contribute to their children's support.

Federal laws were first passed in 1975 and 1984 to increase markedly the level of child support paid by absent fathers (Chilman 1991). In 1975, Congress added Part D to Title IV of the Social Security Act to create the federal Office of Child Support Enforcement and required each state to establish a corresponding agency to help enforce child support for all children dependent on AFDC. Since 1980, IV-D services have been available in non-AFDC cases when requested by the custodial parent. In 1984, legislation extended the period during which paternity action could be taken to a child's eighteenth birthday. Additionally, all states were required to develop guidelines for court use in determining the amount of child support awards. Finally, states were required to adopt income withholding for child support after a one-month lapse in payment.

Against the backdrop of increasing rates of child poverty, the Family Support Act of 1988 was passed. This legislation requires that states withhold court-ordered child support payments from the wages of all absent fathers whose paternity has been legally established and whose families are welfare-dependent. By 1994, it had been ordered that states must provide, unless otherwise arranged, immediate wage withholding for all support orders regardless of whether IV-D services are used or payments are in arrears. How effective this family policy is depends on the administration and enforcement of the legislation and importantly on whether absent parents are employed with wages sufficient to provide financial assistance (Chilman 1988).

Health policy. The Department of Health and Human Services, after three years of conferences, debate, and work, published *Healthy People 2000* in 1991. The goals stated are to increase the healthy lifespan, reduce health disparities, and achieve access to preventive services for all Americans (Feldman 1992). Some have argued that this document should have been titled *Healthy Families 2000;* it is time to stop thinking of health policy only from an individual perspective and at least place this discussion in the context of the family. It is in families that individuals are shaped and supported in their health behaviors; cared for in their illnesses; and, at times, subjected to deleterious influences such as abuse that require some form of medical or mental health intervention (Campbell 1991).

This line of argument summarizes to a certain extent the stage of the debate over family health policy. Should the health-care policy preserve the rights of the individual yet simultaneously help or require families to fulfill their responsibilities in the care of their members? A good example of this dilemma is adolescent pregnancy. In 1978, the federal government established the first federal grant program under the Office of Adolescent Pregnancy Programs in the Department of Health, Education, and Welfare. By the mid-1980s, most policy initiatives had passed to the states. A wide range of activities to reduce the rates of teenage pregnancy developed (Ooms and Golonka 1990).

The early 1970s targeted pre- and postnatal care to the mother and her infant. The late 1970s included more comprehensive services, such as schooling, income support, counseling, family planning, child care, and sometimes housing. By the mid-1980s, programs began to address the male partner and various family involvement strategies, working with the girl's family. The late 1980s emphasized long-term teen parent dependency on welfare. Hence, the Family Support Act of 1988 focused on school and job training for mothers' and fathers' financial responsibility.

Congressional action on adolescent health was focused primarily through the enactment in 1981 of the Adolescent Family Life Program under Title XX of the Public Health Service Act. This legislation places strong emphasis on serving adolescents in their family context, promotes self-discipline and abstinence, and emphasizes adoption. Many believe that the controversies about abortion, contraceptives, parental notification for family planning, and abstinence have stymied much federal legislation and limited the comprehensiveness of most state initiatives.

Regardless of the ages of the family members or their health concerns, recognition that the family unit is the primary context in which health-promoting activities occur must be emphasized. Nearly 80 percent of the diseases in industrialized countries result from lifestyle behaviors involving diet, exercise, smoking, lack of seat belt use, alcohol and substance abuse, and from not using available services (Anderson and Feldman 1993). In health policy reform, the role of

family must be given a central position. The family policy outcomes from this debate remain to be seen.

Long-term care. Long-term care has been a family policy issue receiving much discussion but little legislative initiative. Eleven million people in the United States need some form of assistance for daily living, with two-thirds of these more than sixty-five years of age. Four million of those cannot complete three of the five basic living skills—dressing, eating, bathing, toileting, and getting out of a chair (Scanlon 1991). Eighty-four percent of the people needing long-term care live in the community. Fifty-nine percent live at home, and 75 percent of these people receive 100 percent of their care from family. Family efforts in caring for the elderly and disabled are heroic.

Seven of ten informal caregivers—family members and friends—bear the major responsibility for care, and one of three is a sole provider (Stone, Cafferata, and Sangl 1987). Eight of ten caregivers provide unpaid assistance averaging four hours a day, seven days a week. The burden falls overwhelmingly on women; three-quarters of informal caregivers are females. One-third of these caregivers have family incomes in the poor or near-poor category.

The legislative conceptual framework for policies concerning long-term care for the elderly has been based predominantly on a crisis approach. For example, Social Security resulted from the Great Depression, and Medicare and Medicaid resulted from the health-care crisis of the 1960s (Ford 1989; Kerschner and Hirschfield 1975). Attempts to redistribute the cost of care for the elderly to the private sector—namely, family members—may be the result of budgetary constraints of the 1990s. However, such efforts lack a clear philosophy for designing family policy. The implications for family well-being may be catastrophic.

Long-term care across the lifespan is funded by more than eighty federal programs providing cash, in-kind transfers such as housing and transportation, or goods and services (O'Shaughnessy, Price, and Griffiths 1987). The major sources of support are Medicaid (Title XIX), Medicare (Title VIII), and Social Services of the Social Security Act (Title XX). Policies on long-term care have been dominated by opponents of state welfare who want to shift cost and care responsibility for the elderly back to the private sector (Goodin 1986). Family responsibility has become the mainstay behind policies on long-term care. Although family certainly is important for the well-being of elders, and often is critical in halting their institutionalization, family members alone cannot maintain sole responsibility for the aging population.

It is particularly important for policymakers to consider the social environment of the elderly. Older individuals are most dependent on their social networks for assistance in handling later-life events such as illness, retirement, limited income, and the death of spouse or friends (Ford 1991; Hayslip et al. 1980). Therefore, their informal network is a primary source of support for dependent elderly.

Increasingly, it should be evident to policymakers that the health and functional well-being of the elderly is not only dependent on their adaptation to biological and other physical constraints but also to their social and cultural environment. One's social environment is indicative of past, present, and future events for an elderly person. Thus, policies addressing long-term care must depart from a strictly medical perspective and incorporate a family environment framework. Lack of a clear perspective on long-term care will continue to increase the cost, financially as well as psychologically, to individual families and society as a whole.

Conclusion

There appears to be growing consensus that government should strive to promote family well-being. It is a myth to believe that families can be totally self-sufficient in performing their basic responsibilities. A major goal for adopting a family perspective in policymaking could be to strengthen the partnership between families and social institutions.

Regardless of one's political perspective, past legislative efforts suggest that concern for family can move beyond opposing political ideology. Furthermore, the deterioration of the standard of living for many families, particularly women and children, demonstrates the continuing immediacy of action by family policy decision makers.

(*See also:* CHILD CARE; CHILDREN'S RIGHTS; CHILD SUPPORT; ELDERS; ENTITLEMENTS; FAMILY LAW; FILIAL RESPONSIBILTY; HEALTH AND THE FAMILY; HISTORY OF THE FAMILY; POVERTY)

BIBLIOGRAPHY

Anderson, E. A. (1989). "Implications for Public Policy: Towards a Pro-Family AIDS Social Policy." *Marriage and Family Review* 13:187–228.

Anderson, E. A., and Feldman, M. (1993). "Family-Centered Health Policy." In *Vision 2010: Families and Health Care*, ed. S. Price and B. Elliott. Minneapolis, MN: National Council on Family Relations.

Campbell, T. L. (1991). "Healthy Families 2000: The Role of the Family in Meeting the Nation's Health Objectives." Proceedings of the 1991 Public Health Conference on Records and Statistics. Washington, DC: National Center for Health Statistics.

Children's Defense Fund. (1991). *The State of America's Children, 1991.* Washington, DC: Author.

Chilman, C. (1988). "Never-Married, Single, Adolescent Parents." In *Families in Trouble*, ed. C. Chilman, E. Nunnally, and F. Cox. Newbury Park, CA: Sage Publications.

Chilman, C. (1991). "Working Poor Families: Trends, Causes, Effects, and Suggested Policies." *Family Relations* 40:191–198.

Feldman, M. (1992). "Health-Care Reform: How Do Women, Children, and Teens Fare?" Statement submitted to the House Select Committee on Children, Youth, and Families on behalf of the National Council on Family Relations. Washington, DC: U.S. Government Printing Office.

Ford, D. (1989). "Translating the Problems of the Elderly into Effective Policies: An Analysis of Filial Attitudes." *Policies Studies Review* 8:704–716.

Ford, D. (1991). "Translating the Problems of the Elderly into Effective Policies: Filial Responsibility." In *The Reconstruction of Family Policy*, ed. E. A. Anderson and R. C. Hula. Westport, CT: Greenwood Press.

Giele, J. Z. (1979). "Social Policy and the Family." *Annual Review of Sociology* 5:275–302.

Goodin, R. E. (1986). "Defining the Welfare State." *American Political Science Review* 1:952–954.

Hayslip, B.; Ritter, M. L.; Ottman, R. M.; and McDonnel, C. (1980). "Home Care Services and the Rural Elderly." *Gerontologist* 20:192–198.

Kamerman, S. B., and Kahn, A. J. (1976). "Explorations in Family Policy." *Social Work* 21:181–186.

Kerschner, P. A., and Hirschfield, I. S. (1975). "Public Policy and Aging: Analytic Approaches." In *Aging: Scientific Perspective and Social Issues*, ed. D. S. Woodruff and J. E. Birren. New York: Van Nostrand.

Monroe, P. A., and Garand, J. C. (1989). "Parental Leave Legislation in Congress and the States: Development of a Model." Paper presented at the meeting of the National Council on Family Relations, New Orleans.

Monroe, P. A., and Garand, J. C. (1991). "Parental Leave Legislation in the U.S. Senate: Toward a Model of Roll-Call Voting." *Family Relations* 40:208–217.

Morgan, G. (1987). *The National State of Child-Care Regulation, 1986.* Watertown, MA: Work/Family Directions.

Ooms, T., and Golonka, S. (1990). "Evolving State Policies on Teen Pregnancy and Parenthood: What More Can the Feds Do to Help?" Washington, DC: AAMFT Research and Education Foundation.

Ooms, T., and Herendon, L. (1989). "Federal Child-Care Policy: Current and Proposed." Washington, DC: AAMFT Research and Education Foundation.

Ooms, T., and Preister, S., eds. (1988). *A Strategy for Strengthening Families: Using Family Criteria in Policymaking and Program Evaluation.* Washington, DC: AAMFT Research and Education Foundation.

O'Shaughnessy, C.; Price, R.; and Griffiths, J. (1987). "Financing and Delivery of Long-Term Care Services for the Elderly." Washington, DC: Congressional Research Service.

Scanlon, W. (1991). "An Overview of Long-Term Care Needs." *Long-Term Care*. Washington, DC: B'nai B'rith Women.

Sidel, R. (1986). *Women and Children Last: The Plight of Poor Women in Affluent America*. New York: Viking Press.

Steiner, G. Y. (1976). *The Children's Cause*. Washington, DC: Brookings Institution.

Stone, G.; Cafferata, L.; and Sangl, J. (1987). "Caregivers of the Frail Elderly." *Gerontologist* 27:616.

Thomas, J. E., and Thomas, L. T. (1990). "ABCs of Child Care: Building Blocks of Competitive Advantage." *Sloane Management Review* 2:31–40.

Titmuss, R. (1969). "The Social Division of Welfare." *Essays on the Welfare State*. Boston: Beacon Press.

Weintraub, K. S., and Furman, L. N. (1987). "Child Care: Quality, Regulation, and Research." *Social Policy Report*. Washington, DC: Society for Research in Child Development.

Wisensale, S. K., and Allison, M. D. (1989). "Family Leave Legislation: State and Federal Initiatives." *Family Relations* 38:182–189.

Zimmerman, S. (1976). "The Family and Its Relevance for Social Policy." *Social Casework* 57:547–554.

ELAINE A. ANDERSON

FAMILY RITUALS

Family rituals have been identified as powerful organizers of family life (Bossard and Boll 1950). However, one of the problems in discussing family rituals is that every family may have its own definition of what constitutes a ritual. For some families, regularly attended mealtimes may be a ritual, whereas for other families mealtime may be less predictable and ritual practices are centered around Saturday afternoon sporting events. It is the meaning attached to predictable family interactions that provides the foundation for family rituals.

Family rituals are practiced in different settings and are composed of different dimensions. Steven J. Wolin and Linda A. Bennett (1984) have identified three types of family rituals that differ in setting and the degree to which they are connected to cultural practices. Family celebrations are holidays practiced and prescribed by the culture, such as Passover Seders, and rites of passage such as weddings. Family traditions are linked to family activities such as birthday customs, family vacations, or special anniversaries and are less culture-specific. Patterned routines, the third category of family rituals, are the least consciously planned but may occur on a regular basis (i.e., dinnertime, bedtime routines, or the type of greeting made when someone returns home). Family rituals involve not only the practice of routines, but also the representations and beliefs of the family's identity (Bennett, Wolin, and McAvity 1988; Reiss 1989). The reporting of family ritual activities reflects how family members feel about being together, the degree to which symbolic significance is attached to family gatherings, and the belief that family rituals provide meaning to family life.

Drawing upon the work of Wolin and Bennett (1984) and cultural anthropologists such as Victor Turner (1967), Barbara H. Fiese and her colleagues have identified eight dimensions to family rituals: (1) occurrence defined as how often the activity occurs, (2) attendance defined as the expectation of whether attendance is mandatory, (3) affect defined as the emotional investment in the activity, (4) symbolic significance defined as the attachment of meaning to the activity, (5) continuation defined as the perseverance of the activity across generations, (6) deliberateness defined as the advance preparation and planning associated with the activity, (7) roles defined as the assignment of roles and duties during the activity, and (8) routine defined as the degree of rigidity or flexibility associated with the activity (Fiese 1992; Fiese and Kline 1993).

Two general factors have been identified to summarize the dimensions of family rituals: a routine factor composed of roles and routines and a meaning factor composed of occurrence, affect, symbolic significance, and deliberateness. The routine factor describes the degree to which roles are rigidly adhered to and how flexibly the family practices their rituals. The meaning factor captures the symbolic aspect of family rituals, highlighting how families make sense of family interactions and gatherings.

Janine Roberts (1988) has identified six typologies of family rituals. Underritualized families rarely practice family rituals, often ignoring important family milestones such as anniversaries or birthdays. Rigidly ritualized families prescribe strict rules for conduct and hold high expectations for attendance by all family members. Skewed ritualization is evident when the ritual practices are linked primarily to one member of the family or one aspect of a family's life, such as religion or ethnic heritage. Families that practice hollow rituals are characterized by a lack of meaningful affect in their rituals, emphasizing the routine aspect of family rituals without the symbolic component. Some families experience interrupted rituals due to sudden changes in the family such as illness or death. Families that practice flexible rituals maintain the symbolically meaningful aspect of family rituals and are able to adapt the roles and routines across the life cycle of the family.

Assessment of Family Rituals

One method used in assessing the presence and strength of family rituals is the interview format. Family members are asked to identify two family life areas that are carried out mainly by members of the immediate family and two that are carried out with relatives or friends. An open-ended interview is then conducted and coded across four areas: (1) level of ritualization, (2) evidence of developmental changes, (3) comparison of the same events in family of origin, and (4) role of drinking in rituals. The interview format allows for an in-depth evaluation of family rituals and may be used to identify areas of family life that may be modified when the family is experiencing problems (Wolin, Bennett, and Jacobs 1988).

Family rituals can also be assessed through the use of a questionnaire. The Family Ritual Questionnaire (FRQ) is a 56-item forced-choice questionnaire based on the Wolin and Bennett Family Ritual Interview. The FRQ assesses the degree to which rituals are practiced in seven different settings (dinnertime, weekends, vacations, annual celebrations, special celebrations, religious holidays, and cultural and ethnic traditions) and across eight different dimensions (occurrence, roles, flexibility, attendance, affect, symbolic significance, continuation, and deliberateness). Two factors have been identified in the FRQ, a family ritual routine factor and a family ritual meaning factor. The family ritual meaning factor has been demonstrated to be related to family well-being measures such as self-esteem and marital satisfaction (Fiese 1992; Fiese et al. 1993; Fiese and Kline 1993).

Research on Family Rituals

Systematic research on family rituals has focused on family risk conditions such as alcoholism and points of family transition such as becoming parents. Family rituals may prove to have the strongest effect on adults and children during times of stress or transition. In this regard, family rituals may serve a protective function (Garmezy 1985). That is, when the family is experiencing stress, either normative or nonnormative, family rituals may serve to protect family members from the negative effects associated with the stressor. The protective functions of family rituals have been most clearly outlined in studies of alcoholism and transition points in the family life cycle.

Family rituals and alcoholism. Beginning in the 1970s, Wolin and Bennett began a series of studies examining the relation between family rituals and alcoholism. In the first study, the relationship between ritual disruption and alcohol transmission was examined. The researchers hypothesized that families with more intact rituals would be less likely to transmit alcoholism in the next generation. Ritual disruption was assessed using the family ritual interview, focusing on the impact of the alcoholic parent's drinking behavior on family rituals. "Subsumptive" families, in which alcohol use had overridden and effectively controlled the practice of family rituals, were identified, as were "distinctive" families, in which the practice of family rituals remained distinct from alcohol use. The families in which alcohol had subsumed family ritual practice were more likely to have children who developed problematic drinking or married individuals with alcohol problems (Wolin et al. 1980).

Furthermore, protective factors were identified in the study of individuals raised in alcoholic households. When children of alcoholics chose spouses with highly developed nonalcoholic family rituals, there was less likelihood of developing an alcoholic family identity. The second protective factor was a distinctive dinner ritual in which children from alcoholic families whose parents preserved the dinner ritual had a higher likelihood of a nonalcoholic outcome (Bennett et al. 1987).

Fiese (1993) found similar evidence for the role of family rituals in protecting children from the effects of family alcoholism. Using the FRQ and self-report measures of problematic drinking and health symptomatology, it was noted that the adolescents who reported meaningful family rituals in addition to parental problematic drinking were less likely to develop anxiety-related health symptoms than adolescents reporting parental problematic drinking and relatively hollow family rituals.

The results from these studies suggest that under potentially stressful child-rearing conditions, such as parental alcoholism, family rituals may serve a protective function. In setting aside family gatherings as distinct from alcoholic behavior and in imbuing meaning and deliberateness in the practice of patterned family interactions such as dinnertime, the child may develop an identity of the family that is separate from the disruptions associated with alcoholism.

Family transitions and rituals. Family rituals may also serve a protective function during periods of normative family transitions. The transition to parenthood and becoming a family has been identified as a potentially stressful period for adults, particularly in their material relationships (Belsky and Pensky 1988). Family rituals may be a potent factor in preserving relationships during times of transition and therefore should protect couples from increasing levels of marital dissatisfaction as their children reach preschool age. A study of 115 married couples found that couples with preschool-age children reported more meaning associated with their family rituals than couples whose oldest child was less than a year old. Furthermore, couples with preschoolers who were able to practice meaningful family rituals reported more marital satisfaction than those who reported relatively hollow family rituals (Fiese et al. 1993). Irving Goffman (1971) has proposed that supportive rituals are practiced to renew relationships. These rituals may aid in renewing relationships that have been weakened by neglect and boredom (Cheal 1988). For the couple with a preschool-age child, family rituals may offer an opportunity to renew a partnership that has been neglected during the intense care-giving period of infancy.

Therapeutic Use of Family Rituals

Initially, rituals conducted in a therapeutic setting focused on the enactment of the ritual (Selvini-Palazzoli 1974), because the *practice* of the ritual was considered an important element in effecting therapeutic change. However, Onno van der Hart (1983) later proposed that the prescription of rituals must involve a symbolic element lest they become hollow activities. From the family therapist's perspective, rituals may link observed family interaction patterns with symbolic meaning experienced in the family (Roberts 1988). Central to the therapeutic literature on family rituals is the idea that rituals are intimately connected to the group's shared construct of reality (van der Hart, Witztum, and de Voogt 1989).

Rituals have been used in couples therapy (Imber-Black 1988). For couples unhappy with their relationship, an evaluation of past and current ritual practices may be warranted. Through a consultation interview, the degree to which couples have either given up or ignored meaningful rituals may illustrate how the partners have lost touch with each other and are in need of a revitalized relationship. The renewal of wedding vows, deliberateness in planning a couple vacation, or creating a ritual to facilitate forgiveness and healing are examples of therapeutic rituals.

Rituals may be used therapeutically with families undergoing life-cycle transitions. For example, when adolescents begin to exert their independence, rituals formed during early and middle childhood may prevent the development of autonomy. Increased attention to allowing the adolescent to design and contribute to the practice of family rituals may be explored in consultation with the family. An example is offered by William D. Lax and Dario J. Lussardi (1988) in which a teenage daughter was receiving the message that she should "act older" from her mother and "be younger" from her father. The therapist prescribed a ritual in which on alternate days the daughter was to be treated as either younger or older. After a short period of time, the parents reported that the ritual allowed them to see how they held conflicting expectations for their daughter's behavior. They were then able to recognize that their daughter was receiving confusing messages about her role in the family. Subsequently, the family was able to choose deliberately which of the old roles associated with being a young child could be retained (e.g., being a playful sibling) and what new roles and young-adult responsibilities (e.g., preparing the family meal once a week) could be added.

Therapeutic rituals have also been used during the transitions associated with remarriage (Whiteside 1988). As children are faced with moving in with a new parent and siblings, the role of previous rituals may become particularly poignant. How to celebrate holidays and birthdays and even how regular meals are to be conducted are subject to change. Therapeutic intervention with remarried families is less likely to involve a direct prescription of rituals by the therapist. Rather, an assessment by the family as to which rituals they have practiced in the past and how practices from the various families may be integrated in the newly formed family may be the subject of their discussion.

Conclusion

There has been a renewed interest in the study and therapeutic use of family rituals. Although it is possible that family rituals are indirect measures of broader family system variables such as organization, warmth, and flexibility, the study of family rituals is ecologically valid. Rituals are easily recognized by family members, they can be talked about, and they can be planned. Rituals cut across socioeconomic and ethnic backgrounds. In addition, family rituals offer a way to examine family meaning as distinct from family roles and routines. The force of family rituals is not that the interaction took place but that the family has come to place meaning on their patterned interactions. The practice and meaning of a family ritual are not traits possessed by the family but a process that changes with new demands of family life. Family rituals may be protective and have their greatest influence under stressful or transition conditions. They also appear to have a strong generational component. Efforts should be directed toward charting the developmental course of family rituals across key points of the family life cycle and identifying how families come to create more meaningful practices in the face of adversity. The recognition that family rituals are most effectively designed and interpreted by each family fosters a respect for the diverse ways in which families face the challenges of forming and maintaining close family relationships.

(*See also:* Family Stories and Myths; Family Therapy; Marriage Ceremonies; Marriage Definition; Religion; Remarriage and Children; Stress; Substance Abuse)

BIBLIOGRAPHY

Belsky, J., and Pensky, E. (1988). "Marital Change Across the Transition to Parenthood." *Marriage and Family Review* 12:133–156.

Bennett, L. A.; Wolin, S. J.; and McAvity, K. J. (1988). "Family Identity, Ritual, and Myth." In *Family Transitions*, ed. C. J. Falicov. New York: Guilford.

Bennett, L. A.; Wolin, S. J.; Reiss, D.; and Teitelbaum, M. (1987). "Couples at Risk for Transmission of Alcoholism: Protective Influences." *Family Process* 26:111–129.

Bossard, J., and Boll, E. (1950). *Ritual in Family Living.* Philadelphia: University of Pennsylvania Press.

Cheal, D. (1988). "Relationships in Time: Ritual, Social Structure, and the Life Course." *Studies in Symbolic Interaction* 9:83–109.

Fiese, B. H. (1992). "Dimensions of Family Rituals Across Two Generations: Relation to Adolescent Identity." *Family Process* 31:151–162.

Fiese, B. H. (1993). "Family Rituals in Alcoholic and Non-Alcoholic Households: Relation to Adolescent Health Symptomatology and Problem Drinking." *Family Relations* 42:187–192.

Fiese, B. H.; Hooker, K. A.; Kotary, L.; and Schwagler, J. (1993). "Family Rituals in the Early Stages of Parenthood." *Journal of Marriage and the Family* 55:633–642.

Fiese, B. H., and Kline, C. A. (1993). "Development of the Family Ritual Questionnaire (FRQ): Initial Reliability and Validation Studies." *Journal of Family Psychology* 6:290–299.

Garmezy, N. (1985). "Stress-Resistant Children: The Search for Protective Factors." In *Recent Research in Developmental Psychopathology*, ed. J. E. Stevenson. Oxford: Pergamon.

Goffman, I. (1971). *Relations in Public.* New York: Basic Books.

Imber-Black, E. (1988). "Normative and Therapeutic Rituals in Couples Therapy." In *Rituals in Families and Family Therapy*, ed. E. Imber-Black, J. Roberts, and R. Whiting. New York: W. W. Norton.

Lax, W. D., and Lussardi, D. J. (1988). "The Use of Rituals in Families with an Adolescent." In *Rituals in Families and Family Therapy*, ed. E. Imber-Black, J. Roberts, and R. Whiting. New York: W. W. Norton.

Reiss, D. (1989). "The Represented and Practicing Family: Contrasting Visions of Family Continuity." In *Relationship Disturbances in Early Childhood*, ed. A. J. Sameroff and R. N. Emde. New York: Basic Books.

Roberts, J. (1988). "Setting the Frame: Definition, Functions, and Typology of Rituals." In *Rituals in Families and Family Therapy*, ed. E. Imber-Black, J. Roberts, and R. Whiting. New York: W. W. Norton.

Rogers, J. C., and Holloway, R. L. (1991). "Family Rituals and the Care of Individual Parents." *Family Systems Medicine* 9:249–259.

Selvini-Palazzoli, M. (1974). *Self Starvation: From the Intrapsychic to the Transpersonal Approach to Anorexia Nervosa.* London: Chaucer.

Turner, V. (1967). *The Forests of Symbols: Aspects of Ndembu Ritual.* Ithaca, NY: Cornell University Press.

van der Hart, O. (1983). *Rituals in Psychotherapy: Transition and Continuity.* New York: Irvington.

van der Hart, O.; Witztum, E.; and de Voogt, A. (1989). "Myths and Rituals: Anthropological Views and Their Application in Strategic Family Therapy." In *Family Myths: Psychotherapy Implications*, ed. S. A. Anderson and D. A. Bagarozzi. New York: Haworth Press.

Whiteside, M. F. (1988). "Creation of Family Identify Through Ritual Performance in Early Remarriage." In *Rituals in Families and Family Therapy*, ed. E. Imber-Black, J. Roberts, and R. Whiting. New York: W. W. Norton.

Wolin, S. J., and Bennett, L. A. (1984). "Family Rituals." *Family Process* 23:401–420.

Wolin, S. J.; Bennett, L. A.; and Jacobs, J. (1988). "Assessing Family Rituals in Alcoholic Families." In *Rituals in Families and Family Therapy*, ed. E. Imber-Black, J. Roberts, and R. Whiting. New York: W. W. Norton.

Wolin, S. J.; Bennett, L. A.; Noonan, D. L.; and Teitelbaum, M. A. (1980). "Disrupted Family Rituals: A Factor in the Generational Transmission of Alcoholism." *Journal of Studies of Alcohol* 41:199–214.

Barbara H. Fiese

FAMILY STORIES AND MYTHS

Humans are storytelling beings who, personally and collectively, lead storied lives. The study of stories provides insight into how individuals and families experience the world. Storytelling takes place in American families whenever they come together, during ordinary activities such as mealtime and at special occasions such as holiday celebrations, graduations, and funerals.

Storytelling is one of the most important ways in which families give life meaning beyond the immediate present. A family's past is reshaped and personalized over time according to its needs and desires. As raw experiences are transformed into stories, myths, customs, rituals, and routines, they are codified in forms that can be easily recollected (Martin, Hagestad, and Diedrick 1988; Zeitlin, Kotkin, and Baker 1982). Almost any bit of lore about a family member or experience qualifies as a family story—as long as it is significant and has worked its way into the family canon to be told and retold (Stone 1988, p. 5). Without family storytelling, the past remains past and can never be brought into simultaneity with the present.

The family canon is the creative expression of a common history transformed into stories for present and future generations. These stories are as likely to be about the "black sheep" in the family as they are to be about those who have led exemplary lives. Despite the fact that the main character is often a man, women in families are the primary keepers of the canon (Diedrick, Martin, and Hagestad 1986; Martin, Hagestad, and Diedrick 1988; Stone 1988).

Family stories, as with all stories, are told after the fact. This is important because each family can be selective about the events or incidents it chooses to remember and preserve. Steven Zeitlin, Amy Kotkin, and Holly Baker (1982, p. 16) noted that "in this way, each narrative becomes not a rehash of an event, but a distillation of experience" unique to each family.

The power of family stories, which are allegorical in nature, may be due to the context in which they are told. Elizabeth Stone (1988, p. 101) explains that

families believe in their myths for reasons more compelling than respect for the versatility of metaphor. What the family tells us has a force and power that we never quite leave behind. What they tell us is our first syntax, our first grammar, the foundation onto which we later add our own perceptions and modifications. We are not entirely free to challenge the family's beliefs as we might challenge any other system of belief. And even when we do challenge, we half disbelieve ourselves.

Myths and stories are meant to offer "possible, if not always plausible, explanations for emotional cataclysms within the family" (Stone 1988, p. 98). They are a blend of fact and fiction preserving important themes, special events, and notable personalities in the history of each family (Anderson and Bagarozzi 1983; Bagarozzi and Anderson 1982). However, to family members, "veracity is never the main point—what's important is what could be rather than what actually was" (Stone 1988, p. 129).

The stories a family tells differentiate it from other families. This idiosyncratic nature of family stories underscores, in a way invariably clear to the members of a particular family, the essentials of being a part of that family (Stone 1988; Zeitlin, Kotkin, and Baker 1982).

Family stories and myths have a unique ability to attract the attention of individuals in the family. Stone (1988, pp. 98–99) pointed out that family stories

are well equipped to lull us. We accede to the nature of the genre, and enter into it on its own terms. As part of the oral tradition, family stories do not easily encompass intricate analyses or explanations of the many causes for an event. In fact, they obey the conventions of the oral tradition, reducing complex phenomena to single comprehensible causes. Because they are casually told and even more casually heard, we hear without alerting our more critical faculties. And so we may believe emotionally without truly assenting intellectually.

Through family stories and myths, individual family members make sense of the world and simplify the complexities of family life into an easily remembered, easily communicated narrative (Bagarozzi and Anderson 1982; Zeitlin, Kotkin, and Baker 1982).

Family myths are the most secret and intimate genre of storytelling. They offer "an explanation and justification of family members' roles, self-images, and shared consensual experience" (Anderson and Bagarozzi 1983, p. 153). Family myths are stories that communicate about the most idiosyncratic family convictions, convictions that existed prior to the stories meant to exemplify them, convictions the family is most reticent to surrender (Stone 1988).

Family stories and myths are influential in three specific ways. First, they shape the personalities of individual family members. Zeitlin, Kotkin, and Baker (1982) labeled this notion the character principle of family stories. Families are complicated, especially in their messages to the individuals who comprise them. Powerful messages about who each person in the family is, what each member is to do, and how each life is to be lived are transmitted through the medium of family stories and myths. In other words, these stories serve as the family's most important instructions to, and perhaps covert ground rules for, its members—what they ought to be like. The nature of the family definition of each individual and the stories used to buttress that definition give clues to the family's organization and its power center.

Second, family stories go a step further than simply telling the individual family members about themselves. The stories constitute a chronicle of the way a particular family thinks of itself. Family stories define the family as a unit that encounters numerous transitions together over time. These stories can include marriage, family feuds, great accomplishments, the birth and welcoming of children into the family fold, and tragic losses. This is called the transition principle in family stories (Zeitlin, Kotkin, and Baker 1982). Furthermore, family stories describe "the decorum and protocol of family life—what we are and to whom, what we can expect and from whom, in time or in money or emotion" (Stone 1988, p. 18). They also enrich the perspectives family members have regarding intergenerational relationships (Zeitlin, Kotkin, and Baker 1982).

Finally, family stories are interpretive. They offer guidance, based on the collective experience of the family, to individual members as they make sense of the world outside the family. Every family has a vision of what the world is like and a set of implicit and explicit rules for survival. "It is the first job of the family, through its stories, to explain to its members where they are positioned socially" (Stone 1988, p. 145).

Family myths and stories can be adaptive by providing a sense of cohesion and direction in the face of adversity and tragedy. They may, on the other hand, be dysfunctional, like the myths of many abusive or alcoholic families, and pass a legacy of anger, shame, and inadequacy from one generation to another. Nevertheless, the family myths will be prized and protected because of their role in preserving family structure and organization (Anderson and Bagarozzi 1983).

Family stories and myths are difficult to verify or quantify according to the scientific paradigm (Bruner 1987; Connelly and Clandinin 1990; Reason and Hawkins 1988). This difficulty in quantification is one reason why little research has been done by social scientists. Family therapists, literature and folklore scholars, and others more inclined toward qualitative methods have offered most of what is known about the salience of myths and stories to contemporary family life. Their research has done much to elaborate on the subtle yet important dynamics at the heart of family interaction.

(*See also:* FAMILY RITUALS; FAMILY THERAPY; FAMILY VALUES; HISTORY OF THE FAMILY; INTERGENERATIONAL RELATIONS; MASS MEDIA)

BIBLIOGRAPHY

Anderson, S., and Bagarozzi, D. (1983). "The Use of Family Myths as an Aid to Strategic Therapy." *Journal of Family Therapy* 5:145–154.

Bagarozzi, D., and Anderson, S. (1982). "The Evolution of Family Mythological Systems: Considerations for Meaning, Clinical Assessment, and Treatment." *Journal of Psychoanalytic Anthropology* 5:71–90.

Bruner, J. (1987). "Life as Narrative." *Social Research* 54:11–32.

Connelly, F., and Clandinin, D. (1990). "Stories of Experience and Narrative Inquiry." *Educational Researcher* 19:2–14.

Diedrick, P.; Martin, P.; and Hagestad, G. (1986). "Gender Differences as Reflected in Family Stories." ERIC Document Reproduction Service #ED279929. Washington, DC.

Martin, P.; Hagestad, G.; and Diedrick, P. (1988). "Family Stories: Events (Temporarily) Remembered." *Journal of Marriage and the Family* 50:533–541.

Reason, P., and Hawkins, P. (1988). "Storytelling as Inquiry." In *Human Inquiry in Action*, ed. P. Reason. Newbury Park, CA: Sage Publications.

Stone, E. (1988). *Black Sheep and Kissing Cousins*. New York: Times Books.

Zeitlin, S.; Kotkin, A.; and Baker, H. (1982). *A Celebration of American Family Folklore*. New York: Pantheon.

JAMES J. PONZETTI, JR.

FAMILY SYSTEMS THEORY

Family systems theory, also known as family process theory, grew out of the experience of early family therapists who sought a system of explanation for the patterns of family interaction they observed. As they developed their ideas, they found it useful to think of families as social systems fitting well within the conceptual framework provided by general systems theory as developed by the biologist Ludvig von Bertalanffy and the mathematician and engineer Norbert Weiner. More than other family theories do, the family systems approach deals with family activity in real time (seconds, minutes, hours, and days). It also shares with other theories a concern for the long-term outcome of various styles of family socialization processes over developmental time (years, decades). Over the years, many have contributed to the development of family systems theory, and today there are a number of distinct versions and applications, each with its own constituency and distinctive vocabulary. What follows is an attempt to represent the core concepts common to most versions.

In categorizing systems, it has proved useful to distinguish between closed mechanical systems and open living systems that exchange energy and information with their environment and that are self-regulating. Among living systems, it is often useful to distinguish between mere biological systems and social systems that depend on self-awareness and interpersonal awareness, communication, and the construction of shared meanings to operate. Finally, it is important to distinguish the unique features of that subset of social systems identified as family systems.

Family systems are living systems and as such share a number of features with all other living systems. They receive inputs of energy, material, and information from their environment and generate output to the environment in all three categories. Moreover, they are self-regulating, which means that they are sufficiently complex in their structures to be able to receive and interpret changes in their own status or in their immediate environment, resulting from their output as feedback, which may be utilized to correct future outputs. For example, each living system maintains a boundary between itself and its environment. As already noted, this boundary must be permeable, permitting energy, information, and material to flow back and forth across its borders. Through the mechanism of feedback, it is able to be selective in its permeability. On the one hand, if it is to survive, it must identify and screen out threatening or toxic elements while admitting and, when necessary, seeking out those environmental elements vital to its well-being. On the other hand, it must also rid itself of its own toxic wastes while simultaneously retaining its essential component parts.

As with all social systems, the protective boundaries of families are not literal membranes, but social rules that determine who has the right and the obligation to be in or out of the family and the conditions of entering and exiting. These rules are typically reflected in physical structures, such as the fences and walls that separate the family residence from the nonfamily environment. Families employ locks and sometimes even alarm systems and devices for monitoring incoming phone calls to increase their control over their socially defined boundaries. Of course, they also employ doors, telephones, and television sets to admit desirable visitors, conversations, or stimuli.

Like all living systems, family systems are in constant flux. Not only do they typically go through a daily dispersal (to school, work, market, etc.) and in-gathering, but also over developmental time they experience the addition of new members through birth, adoption, or marriage and the loss of members through death, divorce, or leaving. For this reason systems theorists tend to focus less on the structural features of families—their anatomy, as it were—and more on the processes that seem to link the members to each other and to the external world. Internal re-

lations are referred to as interactions, while relations between family members and the outside world are called transactions. By careful observation, it may be deduced that these complex ongoing relationships are by no means structured randomly but are patterned according to discoverable rules. These rules themselves can be organized from the most concrete (you must not hit your sister; whoever is closest to the phone should answer it when it rings) to the abstract general principles that may be seen as shaping the whole operation of the family (the outside world is a very hostile and dangerous place; we must all stick closely together and resist any outside influence or incursion). Systems theorists speak of rules as being hierarchically structured, with the more concrete rules nested under the umbrella of increasingly more general policies until at the top of the pyramid are the most comprehensive policies of all. These overarching sets of principles at the top of the rules hierarchy are observed to shape and color all of a particular family's interactions and transactions and are referred to as family paradigms.

One of the features of social systems that distinguishes them from other living systems is that their component parts are people, sentient beings, each with his or her own history, perceptions, and needs, and each capable of making independent and interdependent decisions. Consequently, social systems can be not only self-regulating (as all living systems are) but also self-directing. In his pioneering book on social systems, Walter Buckley (1967, p. 56) noted that to be self-directing a system must have hierarchically ordered goals and "must continue to receive a full flow of three kinds of information: (1) information from the world outside; (2) information from the past with a wide range of recall and recombination; and (3) information about itself and its own parts." The decision-making processes employed are often complex and differ among families, but every family can use these types of information in making a decision to move, to take a joint vacation, or to establish a common eating hour.

Systems theorists have focused a lot of attention on the processes by which systems maintain the equilibrium or change and, if they change, whether the change does or does not challenge the basic family paradigm. First-order changes, such as moving from one place to another or marrying off a daughter, need not disturb the basic operating procedures in a family. On the other hand, changing religious affiliation or going through a divorce or remarriage or even family therapy may trigger second-order change—that is, a fundamental restructuring of how the family does business. The processes of resisting change in the face of shifting circumstances is called "morphostasis"; the processes of undergoing second-order change is called "morphogenesis."

Among the substantive issues that have been addressed within this framework are such matters as the rhythms of emotional distance regulation among family members, the processes of decision making and of avoiding decision making (which is far more common), and the mechanisms according to which differences in individual needs, opinions, and perceptions are accommodated or become the subject of conflict. There has also been a great deal of interest in constructing typologies of family paradigms and investigating the correlates of each, particularly the implications for successful child rearing.

The question of whether a particular social system meets the qualifications to be identified as a family system has become politicized. Over the years, most systems theorists have followed the convention that defines a system as a family only if the members are related by blood or marriage and share a common residence. This definition has been criticized as unduly restrictive, and it may be that a more expansive and flexible definition will emerge.

Family systems theory, like all living theory, is still in the process of evolution and refinement, but it appears already to have established itself as one of the more generative conceptual approaches to the understanding of family behavior.

(*See also:* COMMUNICATION; DECISION MAKING AND PROBLEM SOLVING; FAMILY DEVELOPMENT THEORY; FAMILY THEORY; MARITAL TYPOLOGIES; SYMBOLIC INTERACTIONISM)

BIBLIOGRAPHY

Bouchner, A. P., and Eisenberg, E. M. (1987). "Family Process: Systems Perspectives." In *Handbook of Communication Science*, ed. C. R. Berger and S. H. Chaffee. Newbury Park, CA: Sage Publications.

Broderick, C. B. (1993). *Understanding Family Process: Basics of Family Systems Theory.* Newbury Park, CA: Sage Publications.

Buckley, W. (1967). *Sociology and Modern Systems Theory.* Englewood Cliffs, NJ: Prentice Hall.

Kantor, D., and Lehr, W. (1975). *Inside the Family.* New York: Harper & Row.

Watzlawick, P.; Weakland, J. H.; and Fisch, R. (1974). *Change: Principles of Problem Formation and Problem Resolution.* New York: W. W. Norton.

Whitchurch, G. G., and Constantine, L. L. (1993). "Systems Theory." In *Sourcebook of Family Theories and Methods: A Contextual Approach,* ed. P. G. Boss, W. J. Doherty, R. LaRossa, W. R. Schumm, and S. K. Steinmetz. New York: Plenum.

CARLFRED B. BRODERICK

FAMILY THEORY

Suppose a couple is recently divorced. A friend may wonder why this happened and develop several hunches. Perhaps they argued a lot, and one or both may have frequently seemed upset. The friend may begin thinking about why the couple got married in the first place. Perhaps their dating relationship was unusual, or perhaps their upbringing as children offers clues. Using information about their past, the friend might develop a theory, a speculative argument about factors contributing to the couple's divorce. The word "theory" derives from the Greek verb *theorein*, meaning to behold or contemplate. People have contemplated the nature and operation of human families at least since the ancient Greeks, and they continue to do so today. All individuals may wonder how their own or other families work and about the problems involved.

Theorizing about a particular event or a particular marriage or family seems natural in everyday life. Social scientists, however, are not interested in explaining single events or how one marriage or family works. Instead, social scientists want to know how marriages and families work in general. This does not mean that every divorce will have the same cause, only that the emphasis is on a broad understanding of many marriages and families. If they know what generally is true by examining many different marriages and divorces, they come closer to developing a useful theory about divorce. A useful theory provides a general understanding of what has happened in the past, and it enables the scientists to make predictions about what might happen to other couples in the future.

Furthermore, if social scientists want to help other couples deal effectively with their relationships, they need to have confidence that information about a particular couple is not unique. They need to know what makes marriages similar to one another and especially what makes some marriages different from others.

Why is it impossible to have a scientifically useful theory about one event, such as a particular divorce? Suppose it is strongly believed that certain factors in a couple's past are responsible for their divorce. To be sure of this, the social scientists would have to argue that if the couple's pasts had been different in certain ways then they would not have gotten divorced. Something that actually did not happen might have prevented the divorce. The problem is that scientists cannot know about things that did not happen. Such unknown circumstances are called "counterfactuals." Theories containing counterfactuals may be plausible, but they cannot be proven true.

Social scientists want to have theories capable of being generally true for as many marriages and families as possible. When exceptions are found, they can explore why the exceptions occur. Good theories also must be capable of disproof. If there is no way to disprove them, outrageous claims can be made, and there is no effective way to argue against them. Because a couple cannot turn back the clock and behave differently, it will never be known what caused their divorce.

Family scientists base their theories on information enabling comparisons across many cases. If many similar couples can be found, and all of them get divorced, scientists might be closer to a general understanding of the causes of divorce. Moreover, if many couples who are similar in all respects but a few are found, and those with the differing circumstances do not divorce, scientists might form an even more useful theory about divorce. Instead of relying on arguments about what did not happen, they compare different couples who have different experiences, some ending in divorce and some staying married.

In this way, family scientists have developed many theories to guide their thinking (Boss et al. 1993). These theories differ from each other in several fundamental ways.

Philosophies of Family Science

Theorizing can be based on different ideas about how a science works. Three primary approaches can be distinguished. A positivistic philosophy of family science makes several assumptions:

1. There is a real world of family life. This world is a natural one, and it operates according to a set of general principles. Truth is a matter of discovery.
2. The world of family life is ultimately knowable. Through careful study of how individual families work, scientists can increase their understanding of family life.
3. The best way to study families is by using standard methods useful in other domains of scientific inquiry. Reliable and valid evidence, or factual information, must be collected, based on observing families.

4. With increasing knowledge based on the facts, social scientists can intervene or assist others to intervene to improve family life.

This positivistic or optimistic approach was dominant throughout the twentieth century. It arose to help family studies gain stature as a scientific enterprise not unlike the other more established sciences. It also helped to distinguish scientific theories about the family from other kinds of contemplation, based on theological principles or other beliefs about the "appropriate" ways of being a family. Social science should be conducted in a spirit of free inquiry, without interference from governments or other nonscientific authorities.

On the other hand, the critical philosophy of family science starts with the idea that all beliefs and practices are political. Families, as well as the scholars who study them, are engaged in a struggle for domination and respect.

Historically, it can be observed that certain kinds of families and family members have been dominated and oppressed by those who are in more powerful positions in society. The less powerful usually have been females, persons of relatively low socioeconomic status, members of racial and ethnic minority groups, children, and sometimes elderly members of society. Any person or group different from the image of a "normal" family is considered to be abnormal or deviant by members of dominant groups. Those people in power not only control material resources but also intellectual resources, the way society thinks about families. Most members of the scientific "establishment," including family researchers and theorists, have been members of dominating social groups and categories.

The critical perspective challenges not only the content of positivistic theories, but also the assumptions upon which positivism rests. There is no natural world of family life to be discovered. Instead, what seems natural is the product of political forces, and of the domination of thinking and acting by some privileged families, family members, and family scientists. Truth is not a discovery, but a weapon. The proper goals of science are not the accumulation of facts and theories based on them, but instead are enlightenment and emancipation. Theories should be used to expose domination, and to assist the transformation of society and of science itself into more humane entities, resulting in a better world. Such a world will be one in which diversity of both lifestyles and modes of thinking will be equally respected and allowed to flourish. Some feminist theories and social conflict theories of family life rely on a critical philosophy of science (Farrington and Chertok 1993; Osmond 1987; Osmond and Thorne 1993).

A third philosophy of science influencing family theory is the interpretive approach. This view claims that all reality is a human construction. There is no objective truth about families, only a variety of subjective views that are developed through a dialogue with others in an effort to achieve a shared and workable understanding. Whatever is claimed to be known is tentative, always in process, and always just one point of view within a stream of alternative and evolving views. Whatever entity is called a family, the members of that entity are principally engaged in negotiating a sense of meaning, one that enables them to better understand who they are and how they fit into the environment.

Interpretive family theorists tend to reject positivism as naive, as making ideas seem firmer, more factual, or more stable than they really are. Truth is not a discovery, but an invention. The purpose of theorizing about the family is to make a personal statement based on an inevitably limited view. Instead of finding theories that will stand the test of time, the best theories are about the search for meaning in which families participate. These understandings and the processes by which they are created should be part of the content as well as the method used by family theorists. Interpretive theorists and researchers let family members speak and act for themselves and observe how reality is socially constructed. The theories of scholars then emerge and change as the theories created by families emerge and change. Symbolic interaction theory and phenomenological theory usually rely on an interpretive philosophy of science (Gubrium and Holstein 1993; LaRossa and Reitzes 1993).

All three philosophies influenced family scholars throughout the twentieth century. Because they are philosophies, there is no positivistic way of deciding which is best. The preferences of family theorists relate to the way they were trained, the acceptance by their colleagues of the alternatives, and the personal lives and other professional experiences of those in the scientific community (Klein and Jurich 1993; Thomas and Wilcox 1987).

These philosophies do not represent entirely incompatible viewpoints. Some family theorists accept the usefulness of more than one philosophy, even if they rely on only one of their own theories. Others combine features of two or more philosophies of science when they theorize.

Purposes of Family Theory

Theories about the family also differ in terms of the purposes that theorists have in formulating them. The most common goal is to provide a general description of how families work. In order to achieve a useful description, theories contain concepts. These concepts, such as cohesiveness, size, or patriarchy, help to compare families, and commonly have technical definitions. Family theorists usually strive for clear and precise definitions, so that they may measure what happens when families are directly observed or when members report their ideas, feelings, and behaviors. Many concepts are treated as variables, properties with different quantities on some scale. For example, families may be more or less cohesive, larger or smaller, and more or less patriarchal.

Different types of concepts are used in family theories. Some point to the structure of a family, its composition or the way it is organized. Some concepts describe patterns of social interaction, the quality of relationships, or processes that occur in families. Some theoretical concepts show how other concepts are related to each other. For example, if a family has five members and one descriptive concept refers to how flexible each member is, the family itself may be flexible if it meets a certain level of flexibility in its members. Perhaps all members must be at least halfway flexible, or perhaps some of the five must be very flexible to compensate for the inflexibility of the others. Whatever concepts are used, it is impossible to have a family theory unless there is a fairly detailed vocabulary for describing what makes families similar to and different from each other.

Most family theories go beyond description and provide an explanation. To explain something, it is essential to argue why it occurs. There are two basic ways to explain family life (Burr et al. 1979).

One type of explanation uses a deductive argument. This begins with a small number of premises (or axioms), statements individuals are willing to assume are true. Then, other statements (or theorems) are logically derived from the premises. Consider the following illustration:

1. All social systems are goal-directed. (Axiom 1)
2. All families are social systems. (Axiom 2)
3. One goal of all social systems is survival. (Axiom 3)
4. All families direct energy toward survival. (Theorem 1)

The theorem may be true, but only if all three axioms are true, in which case an explanation for why families direct energy toward survival exists; they do so because of the meanings inherent in the axioms. If the illustration were a real deductive explanation, additional information would have to be provided. The meaning of social system, goal, family, and energy would have to be defined, and more theorems would be derived. Deductive explanations are usually considered to be powerful if many theorems can be derived from a small set of axioms.

Notice how an explanation is achieved in this example. Families are treated as one type of social system, and survival is treated as one type of goal. Subsuming one phenomenon under a broader phenomenon is a common way of making a deductive argument. Another common way is to link statements in a chain. For example:

1. If parents encourage their children to explore the environment, children will explore the environment. (Axiom 4)
2. If children explore the environment, they will have high self-esteem. (Axiom 5)
3. If children have high self-esteem, they will effectively solve their problems later in life. (Axiom 6)
4. If parents encourage their children to explore the environment, children will effectively solve their problems later in life. (Theorem 2)

Here, effective problem solving for some people has been explained by referring to a chain of events that produces it. Furthermore, it has been argued that these axioms are transitive. That is, by having a series of statements with "then" in one becoming "if" in the next, it is possible to see a link between two ideas (in this case, what parents do and how children solve problems), a link that previously may have gone unnoticed. The argument may require elaboration before it is satisfactory, however. Simple "if/then" statements may hold only under special conditions. For instance, it may be argued that other things must be present, such as a willingness on the part of children to do what parents encourage them to do, before they will act as Axiom 4 argues.

While deductive explanations tend to be clear about the logic underlying an argument, family theorists have found them to be of limited value. The main reason is that it must be assumed that the premises are true. It often is difficult to make a convincing case that they are true. Different premises might be created that lead to the same conclusions, which would raise doubt about the original premises, or further research might prove that some theorems are false. Either of these situations would indicate that something is wrong with the original deductive explanation, but it would not pinpoint the problem.

The most popular way to explain family life uses a causal argument, which starts by assuming that everything that happens has some cause. The way families are or the actions they take cannot just be accidental. Some actions or conditions in the past exert influence on the current situation. An explanation is achieved by first showing how families are different from each other and then showing how differing prior circumstances are responsible for the differences to be explained.

In its simplest form, a causal argument is deterministic. It is assumed that there is one primary causal factor and it completely determines the result. In practice, however, family scholars have realized that causes are seldom so simple. Causal explanations generally employ several antecedent factors or conditions, working together or as alternatives, and all of them are included in the argument. Each causal element only works to increase the probability that a particular outcome will occur.

Causal explanations may show several factors converging to influence one outcome. They may show several separate paths, with several intervening steps, before an outcome is reached. They may even specify the conditions necessary before one variable can have an influence on another variable. In any case, causal explanations require fairly stable and strong connections between variables. Causal factors must happen chronologically before the effects occur, and the connections must not be just coincidental, byproducts of something else that is the "true" cause.

While causal explanations in family science have been popular, they are often viewed cautiously. Even the best ones tend to explain only a modest fraction of the differences between families. To improve them, there often is a temptation to make causal arguments more complex. If they grow too complex, however, they begin to lose their intuitive appeal. It is a challenge to understand what a very complex casual argument is really claiming. Part of the attraction of causal arguments in family theories is that the technology for using them to conduct empirical research is well developed. This technology involves statistical skills that sometimes seem remote from the family lives the researchers are trying to understand.

One problem with causal explanations is the frequent requirement that scientists follow families over time, because the families are supposed to change due to causal forces. Quite often, however, researchers compare different families at one time, and changes within families are not observed. Thus, researchers may be tempted to think that they have found causes, when they really have only found associations between variables.

Another problem with causal explanations is the mistaken belief that it is possible to explain what usually happens causally. Suppose it is discovered that 30 percent of all children in the United States are born to single mothers. Researchers may want to know the cause of this percentage. Then, they may identify a possible cause, perhaps the advantages of staying single. When this idea is included, the problem of counterfactuals is faced again. Single mothers may have common experiences suggesting the advantages of singlehood. But social scientists must compare single mothers with other mothers, and they must also compare all of the mothers with regard to the proposed cause. Family scientists can never causally explain what often or always happens in families or the average family experience. Instead, causal explanations can only explain differences, in this example why some mothers are married when they bear children while other mothers are not.

Some critics of causal explanations argue that the entire enterprise is misguided because scientists never can prove that something is a cause or part of a cause. Nevertheless, theories that rely on causal explanations remain popular in the family field, even if they cannot provide complete explanations. Causal explanations provide a useful way to think about family life, and the challenge is to make them better than rival causal explanations, not to assume that they ever will provide the final word or the perfect theory.

Most family theorists who provide descriptions and explanations believe these are the two most important purposes to achieve. Some family theorists, however, want to show how to change families by intervening to do something for their benefit. This goal is based on the idea that some families are not functioning well and that it is important to solve family problems or prevent them from occurring.

Interventions to change families must be based on an evaluation of the current situation and a decision that some families should be altered to reach an objective not now being met. Because people often disagree about goals and standards, any intervention relies on a point of view. Families themselves may determine that they are not meeting their own goals. A theorist may have goals for families that do not correspond with a family's own goals or values. The

standard selected may be some notion of what is generally acceptable in society at large.

Whose goals should direct an intervention is often controversial. Consider the discovery that physical abuse of children by parents is fairly common in the United States. A scholar may develop a good theory about why some parents abuse their children and others do not. Perhaps one causal factor in the theory is the extent to which parents feel they have the right to punish children as they see fit. Those parents who feel that severe physical punishment is acceptable then use this form of punishment. A good theory should allow the theorist to determine what needs to be done to reduce the likelihood of child abuse. In this example, what is needed is a change in the belief by some parents that their behavior is acceptable. The problem is that parents may not feel that their punishing behaviors are unacceptable. The only way to avoid controversy surrounding the use of family theories to change families is to identify a goal that everyone accepts.

Even if there is no controversy over goals and values, it may be difficult to implement the desired change. If the theory implies that families must be changed, a program of action must be developed to reach families and change them. Sufficient confidence in the theory must exist so that a change in the causal factors has a good chance of producing the desired effect. This often requires careful research, because undesirable consequences of well-intentioned changes may occur. Finally, the required change in the cause may be difficult in principle to produce. If, for example, a theory argued that the basic fabric of society must be changed in order to reduce child abuse, figuring out how to change the fabric of society would be a tall order.

If a theory explains well what has happened in the past, it should provide a good prediction about the future. Another purpose of family theory is to enable accurate estimates of what families will be like in the future. Therefore, once a theory has been formulated, further research must be conducted to see if the theory remains useful. The connection between past and future, however, depends on a fairly stable environment. Some family theories do not survive events that take place after they have been formulated. This usually means that the original theory must be revised to reflect changes in families and in their environments more accurately. If a theory cannot be revised, it tends to be discarded.

Difficulty predicting family life may not be a serious deficit. The future is difficult to predict in many areas of science. Nevertheless, it is important to notice when a family theory was developed, and to find out what has happened subsequently. If an older theory about the family is encountered that no longer seems popular, newer literature can be examined to see if this loss of popularity is due to faulty prediction or a failure to revise the theory. Family theories usually are not static entities. They tend to change as families and their environments change, and as new theorists with new insights join the field.

Meaning of Family

Another important difference among family theories is in the way their central topic, the family, is defined and used. While all theories have a descriptive purpose, not all family theorists view families identically. In fact, they view families according to four different meanings of the term "family."

One way to look at families is based on structural features. Families contain varying numbers of persons who are related in particular ways, including such persons as mothers, fathers, and children. This view may be extended to include grandparents, in-laws, step-relations, and perhaps even former relatives. Structural definitions of family focus on the composition of its membership. They may indicate that family members are related by blood, marriage, or some other legal bond such as adoption. Sharing a household may be another structural feature. With a structural definition, the theorist is able to determine which kinds of social groups do not qualify as families and which individuals are in a particular family.

Structural definitions of family also attend to the types of relationships that create social bonds between members. Important bonds are created by communication, power, and affection, as well as the daily work and leisure performed by family members. Scientists can observe how patterns of social interaction among the members are structured, and they can specify the various rules or principles that families use to organize their activities. Families may be structured by such characteristics as gender, age, and generation, as well as their connections to the outside world. These structures also are useful for distinguishing families from other kinds of social groups and organizations.

Theories about the family usually focus on some limited structural form. For example, they may apply only to married couples or to mothers and daughters. Sometimes theories compare different family structures. A theory might deal with how parent–child relations differ when two-parent families are compared to mother-led families.

A second way to look at families is based on functional elements. Why do families exist in the first place? Every human society has families, so they must serve some generally recognized purpose or function. Most functional definitions of the family focus on the importance of human reproduction and the necessity of nurturing dependent children for a relatively long period of time. Functional family theories often address the structural variety of families, with assertions about how effective each structure is in accomplishing the requisite functions that families everywhere have. From this perspective, if a certain structure does not fulfill some family function, families with that structure may be considered to be dysfunctional families.

A third meaning of family is based on interactional features, that is, it emphasizes repeatable processes of social interaction within families. Such interaction may be patterned or structured, but the focus is on the ongoing activity within the family, often conducted jointly by the members or otherwise coordinated. Family theories that rely on an interactional definition include concepts and variables describing what each participant is doing, how the members influence each other, and the quality of their relationships. From this perspective, a group need not have any particular structure to be counted as a family. Any social group that acts like a family would qualify as being a family. Social exchange theories often adopt an interactional view of family relationships (Sabatelli and Shehan 1993).

The fourth meaning of family is based on symbolic elements. Focus is on the meanings, perceptions, and interpretations that people have about family experiences. Only by watching how persons communicate or use dialogue to construct, challenge, and alter meanings do social scientists come to understand what a family is. Often this expression is verbal. The symbols people use to create and recreate family go beyond spoken words, however. Other important symbols are nonverbal intonations, bodily gestures, practices of dress and grooming, written statements, and visual images such as photographs and the spatial arrangement and condition of possessions in the home. Family theories based on the symbolic perspective emphasize various languages used to communicate, as well as the many artifacts with symbolic meaning created by families.

These four meanings of family are not always used separately. Two combinations are especially common. A combined structural and functional perspective informs structure-functional theory (Kingsbury and Scanzoni 1993). A combined interactional and symbolic perspective informs symbolic interaction theory (LaRossa and Reitzes 1993).

Each of the four meanings of family can be used alone, however. For example, it is possible to have a structural theory about some aspect of family life, perhaps offering structural causes of some limited family activity, without implying anything about the functionality of what is explained. For instance, the size of families or the size of communities in which they live might influence the amount of companionship among family members. It is also possible to use patterns of interaction as a cause or as the outcome in a family theory, without incorporating any ideas about the symbolic significance of the interaction to the family's members. For example, how often family members argue may influence how household chores are performed.

Level or Scope of Family Theories

Theories about the family differ in terms of their breadth of vision, level of analysis, and scope. Microscopic theories tend to focus on the internal workings of families, viewed as small groups of people in fairly intense relationships.

Mesoscopic theories focus on the transactions between families and people in the near environment who represent other groups and organizations. At this level, family theories are concerned with such things as friendships between members of different families, and the linkages between families and schools, churches, places of employment, the mass media, retail firms, and other public or private facilities and organizations.

Macroscopic theories concentrate on how the family as a social institution is embedded in society at large or in the nonhuman environment. They may, for instance, address how contemporary ways of family living emerged from significant changes in the economy, in national politics, or in technological developments. Structural and functional theories tend toward the macroscopic end of the spectrum, while symbolic and interactional theories tend toward the microscopic end.

Scope is a relative matter. For theorists of the human family, the social unit called family is roughly at the center of the spectrum, so that moving outward makes a particular theory more macro and moving inward makes it more micro.

Some family theorists focus on a fairly narrow range of the spectrum and formulate all of their ideas at one level or another. Other family theorists deliberately bridge levels, creating a transcopic theory.

These multilevel theories often argue that phenomena at one level are the causes of phenomena at another level. Among such theories, the most common is a top-down approach. Societies affect families, and families in turn affect the individual persons in them. Increasingly popular are bottom-up theories that simply reverse the direction of causation, and reciprocating transcopic theories that emphasize mutual causation between levels in either alternating or simultaneous patterns. Family theories based on ecological principles currently are popular among those that are transcopic (Bubolz and Sontag 1993).

The scope of a theory helps scientists see the amount of causal agency attributed to families, as opposed to other factors outside or inside the family. Some theorists argue that families are primary causal agents. What they do has important consequences, and what makes them act may be important but is not addressed in the theory. Other theorists take exactly the opposite approach. Phenomena at the family level are to be explained by forces external or internal to them. If a theory remains entirely at the family level, it will explain something about family life in terms of causes elsewhere at the family level. A causal theory must have at least some cause or some effect at the family level to really be a theory about families. Some theories are called family theories even if they deal with only parts of a family, such as a theory about divorce or about the relationship between grandparents and grandchildren.

Time Perspectives

All theories about the family deal with the flow of chronological time, and sometimes with the social and psychological organization of time. Four principal time perspectives are common: static, episodic, biographical, and epochal.

In some theories, time is suspended or relegated to the margins. The idea is to craft a theory that is timeless. This static picture may be useful, especially if it is a general description. Given the previously noted problems associated with change, however, static family theories are themselves not very durable.

Often, the image of time is episodic. A process is being described and perhaps explained, and it is temporary. The entire process may last a few moments, a few days, or several months. If scientists trace what is happening over the course of events contained in the theory, everything can be observed with moderate effort when the theory is tested.

Another image of time is biographical. This perspective usually considers the entire span or course of life. Family phenomena begin at birth, develop through time, change along the way, and end when life ends. The idea of a "life" comes from the study of individual organisms, and it must be adjusted to speak meaningfully about the lifetime of a social group containing several organisms.

One adjustment is to consider the "birth" of the group to occur when the group itself forms, with the "death" of the group corresponding to the dissolution of the group. Some of the members will be alive before the group forms, after it dissolves, or both. New members may be added after the family forms, and some may be lost before the family ends. Families may endure even with great turnover in membership, as for example a lineage that survives over many generations. Individual persons may have experiences as members of several different families over the course of their own lives. Becoming a widow, getting divorced, remarrying, and giving birth to or adopting a child are among the events marking the course of both an individual's life and the life of the group.

Because it is usually impractical for one scholar to study large numbers of families from their formation to their dissolution, many theories that deal with biographical time concentrate on a shorter time segment. Some describe and explain what is happening during a particular stage of family life, such as when children are adolescents or after all of the children have become adults and left their parental homes. Another common alternative is to focus on a particular transition period. For instance, some theories focus on the process by which couples get married, or why some get married and others do not, tracing events from first meeting to the early years after marriage or until a breakup before marriage. Other time-limited biographical theories concern the transition to parenthood, the transition to the "empty nest," and so on. Family development is the most common name for the theories that treat families in biographical time (Rodgers and White 1993).

The other image of time is epochal. Fairly broad sweeps of history may be examined and categorized into periods. Families in ancient Greece, families in the American colonies, families during the early industrial era, and families during the Great Depression represent some of the historical categories that may give focus to a family theory. Other theories take a more sweeping historical perspective. Theorists may wish, for example, to explain how human families evolved from primate families, or how the contemporary family emerged from forces at work over several centuries. While many family theories using an epochal image of time are descriptive, evolutionary or biosocial theories of family life usually are explanatory as well (Troost and Filsinger 1993).

Forms of Expressing Theory

One useful way to differentiate theories about the family concerns the way they are expressed by their authors. Some theories are written in narrative form. They use prose expressed in commonly understood language. Other family theories are somewhat more formalized and are called propositional. A theorist identifies a set of well-bounded, declarative statements that serve as the theory's core propositions. Many of the concepts in these statements have technical meanings, and definitions are included. Often, the propositions assert how two or more variables are related, how strong the connections are and when they happen, and whether or not causal influence is implied. Theories that use shorthand, technical expressions are even more formalized. They contain mathematical symbols, diagrams with arrows, flow charts, or figures with classifications into types.

All forms of expression have virtues and limitations. More formalized theories are precise, and they are easy to distinguish from other theories with similar content. If a theory is imprecise or fuzzy, it is difficult for the scientific community to agree on what is meant, and extremely difficult to demonstrate that some of the arguments may be incorrect. Formalized theories require specialized training to be fully interpreted, however. Because technical expressions are arbitrary and may require intricate rules, some family theorists avoid them. Some avoid highly formalized theories because they can dehumanize the subject matter and place more emphasis on the structure of an argument than on its content. A truly good theory may be one that either combines forms of expression or can be translated from one form to another without changing its meaning.

Methods of Creating Theories

Theories about families usually develop over time as theorists incorporate prior knowledge and new experience. At first, there may be only fragments, enough of an argument to share the basic shape of a theory with an audience. If a particular theory has been discussed for a period of time and a consensus has been established, the theory may be named and only brief mention made of its details, on the assumption that colleagues understand what is involved. Working to produce a family theory, however, usually takes place in one of two ways.

Deductive theory is produced by starting with fairly abstract ideas and without particular regard for the way families can be observed to operate in the "real" world. Some of the ideas may be borrowed from other areas of study, and some may represent the integration or modification of existing ideas about family. Portions may be entirely new, but more often the theorist is just reshaping or recombining ideas that have appeared in other scholarly works. Theorists may work deductively even when they are not creating deductive explanations.

Once the new theory is given a clear structure, the theorist or a colleague who is attracted to the theory conducts empirical research to test some of the arguments. If the theory is supported by research data, gathered and analyzed using suitable methods, the theory is provisionally accepted. This acceptance is provisional because it takes repeated tests, often by different groups of researchers using somewhat different methods, before a great deal of confidence in the theory is warranted. If the theory is unsupported or refuted by research data, it is revised or discarded in favor of a superior alternative. Ideally, two rival theories with different explanations and predictions are pitted against each other in a single study or a carefully managed series of studies. This enables scholars to determine which of the two theories is better.

Some family scientists object to the deductive process. While they acknowledge that it is the usual textbook approach, they offer either of two arguments. The "weak theory" objection is that scholars really do not use the deductive method. Instead, they are guided by hunches derived from the direct experiences they have, either as handlers of empirical data or as participants in family life. The "strong theory" objection is that every judgment and decision a scholar makes is based on preconceived ideas to which that scholar has very strong attachments. Because all social scientists have ideas and beliefs about families, the theories they create are biased in ways that escape the attention of even the most impartial theorist.

To take advantage of both objections, some family scientists use an inductive method to create their theories. In its pure form, the scientist disregards all previous knowledge and speculation about the topic of interest. Research with minimal biases is conducted, and the participating families and the results they produce are taken at face value. A useful theory is developed either after the research is concluded or slowly during the process of study. A "grounded" theory emerges.

Much family theorizing is transductive, with elements of both deduction and induction. The two extreme approaches provide models for how to work, but there is room for an intermediate approach.

Many participants are involved in the process of creating any theory. Even if only one author receives credit, that person builds on the ideas of others. If a particular theory has many acknowledged contributors and if it endures sufficiently long, it becomes recognized as a theoretical tradition or school of thought. The family members who participate in the creation of family theory may be recognized as coauthors, but often they are not.

Other Differences

Family theories can be distinguished in additional ways. Some theories are relatively abstract and speculative, while others are more concrete and stated in language closer to observable phenomena.

Some family theories are quite general, while others are much more context-specific. General theories are claimed to hold regardless of time or place, or apply to broadly encompassed times and places. Context-specific theories tend to focus on restricted populations, such as one culture or society, the families in one social class, a segment of families with a narrow age structure, one gender, or one racial or ethnic group. Some family theories entail comparisons across contexts, but without covering all of the possibilities. The context of time also varies between family theories. Whether they adopt episodic, biographical, or epochal images of time, most family theories concerned with processes of change carve out a limited span of time for their arguments.

Theories about the family also differ in terms of the breadth of content they cover and which particular subunits within the family are addressed. Theories may be narrow, middle-range, or broad in their content. Relatively speaking, a theory about the effectiveness of communication by husbands is narrow, while a theory of marital quality is middle-range, and a theory of family functioning is broad. In this example, not only does the subject matter become broader with the move from narrow to broad theories, but the relevant units also become broader.

Family theories differ considerably in complexity. Simple theories may involve no more than two or three concepts and two or three relationships among them. Complex theories contain a large number of concepts or variables, and many links exist among the concepts.

Finally, family theories differ according to how coherent a picture of family life they present. Some theories represent families as fairly atomistic collections of elements; scientists understand families if they understand how their elements work, and understanding is impeded if elements are combined that really do not go together. Other theories are more holistic, because they focus on the family as a totality; while families may have elements or features, scientists do not understand how families work unless they see how the features are connected and how these connections produce something unique. Family systems theory is an example of a popular holistic theory (Broderick 1993; Whitechurch and Constantine 1993).

The ways family theories differ in their abstractness, generality, breadth, complexity, and the coherence of their imagery are all matters of degree. While there is much diversity, there also are unifying efforts. Abstract theories can be made more concrete, context-specific theories can be made more general, and complex theories can be simplified, among other possibilities. Part of the ongoing excitement about theorizing in the family field is that there is an endless array of projects for enterprising theorists.

Conclusion

There are several reasons for the diversity among family theories. One is the growing number of scholars who have taken family life as an area of serious investigation and the rapidly expanding library of works they have produced. Family theorists also represent a large number of academic and applied disciplines, in and beyond the social sciences. Their ideas are shaped by the specialized training they receive and the different missions established in each discipline. Finally, some questions seem to be answered more satisfactorily if one type of theory is used instead of another.

As long as families remain a central domain in the way people think about the world, and as long as family life is sometimes viewed as troubled or problematic, there will be a sense of urgency about increasing understanding of families. The result is predictable: more theories, more research, and more programs proposed to change what can be changed and to accept what cannot.

(*See also:* DYSFUNCTIONAL FAMILY; EXCHANGE THEORY; FAMILY DEVELOPMENT THEORY; FAMILY SYSTEMS THEORY; MARITAL TYPOLOGIES; MEASURES OF FAMILY CHARACTERISTICS; RESEARCH METHODS; SYMBOLIC INTERACTIONISM)

BIBLIOGRAPHY

Boss, P. G.; Doherty, W. J.; LaRossa, R.; Schumm, W. R.; and Steinmetz, S. K., eds. (1993). *Sourcebook of Family Theories and Methods: A Contextual Approach.* New York: Plenum.

Broderick, C. B. (1993). *Understanding Family Process: Basics of Family Systems Theory.* Newbury Park, CA: Sage Publications.

Bubolz, M. M., and Sontag, M. S. (1993). "Human Ecology Theory." In *Sourcebook of Family Theories and Methods: A Contextual Approach,* ed. P. G. Boss, W. J. Doherty, R. LaRossa, W. R. Schumm, and S. K. Steinmetz. New York: Plenum.

Burr, W. R.; Hill, R.; Nye, F. I.; and Reiss, I. L., eds. (1979). *Contemporary Theories About the Family:* Vol. 1, *Research-Based Theories.* New York: Free Press.

Farrington, K., and Chertok, E. (1993). "Social Conflict Theories of the Family." In *Sourcebook of Family Theories and Methods: A Contextual Approach,* ed. P. G. Boss, W. J. Doherty, R. LaRossa, W. R. Schumm, and S. K. Steinmetz. New York: Plenum.

Gubrium, J. F., and Holstein, J. A. (1993). "Phenomenology, Ethnomethodology, and Family Discourse." In *Sourcebook of Family Theories and Methods: A Contextual Approach,* ed. P. G. Boss, W. J. Doherty, R. LaRossa, W. R. Schumm, and S. K. Steinmetz. New York: Plenum.

Kingsbury, N., and Scanzoni, J. (1993). "Structural-Functionalism." In *Sourcebook of Family Theories and Methods: A Contextual Approach,* ed. P. G. Boss, W. J. Doherty, R. LaRossa, W. R. Schumm, and S. K. Steinmetz. New York: Plenum.

Klein, D. M., and Jurich, J. A. (1993). "Metatheory and Family Studies." In *Sourcebook of Family Theories and Methods: A Contextual Approach,* ed. P. G. Boss, W. J. Doherty, R. LaRossa, W. R. Schumm, and S. K. Steinmetz. New York: Plenum.

LaRossa, R., and Reitzes, D. C. (1993). "Symbolic Interactionism and Family Studies." In *Sourcebook of Family Theories and Methods: A Contextual Approach,* ed. P. G. Boss, W. J. Doherty, R. LaRossa, W. R. Schumm, and S. K. Steinmetz. New York: Plenum.

Osmond, M. W. (1987). "Radical-Critical Theories." In *Handbook of Marriage and the Family,* ed. M. B. Sussman and S. K. Steinmetz. New York: Plenum.

Osmond, M. W., and Thorne, B. (1993). "Feminist Theories: The Social Construction of Gender in Families and Society." In *Sourcebook of Family Theories and Methods: A Contextual Approach,* ed. P. G. Boss, W. J. Doherty, R. LaRossa, W. R. Schumm, and S. K. Steinmetz. New York: Plenum.

Rodgers, R. H., and White, J. M. (1993). "Family Development Theory." In *Sourcebook of Family Theories and Methods: A Contextual Approach,* ed. P. G. Boss, W. J. Doherty, R. LaRossa, W. R. Schumm, and S. K. Steinmetz. New York: Plenum.

Sabatelli, R. M., and Shehan, C. L. (1993). "Exchange and Resource Theories." In *Sourcebook of Family Theories and Methods: A Contextual Approach*, ed. P. G. Boss, W. J. Doherty, R. LaRossa, W. R. Schumm, and S. K. Steinmetz. New York: Plenum.

Sprey, J., ed. (1990). *Fashioning Family Theory: New Approaches.* Newbury Park, CA: Sage Publications.

Thomas, D. L., and Wilcox, J. E. (1987). "The Rise of Family Theory: A Historical and Critical Analysis." In *Handbook of Marriage and the Family*, ed. M. B. Sussman and S. K. Steinmetz. New York: Plenum.

Troost, K. M., and Filsinger, E. (1993). "Emerging Biosocial Perspectives on the Family." In *Sourcebook of Family Theories and Methods: A Contextual Approach*, ed. P. G. Boss, W. J. Doherty, R. LaRossa, W. R. Schumm, and S. K. Steinmetz. New York: Plenum.

Whitechurch, G. G., and Constantine, L. L. (1993). "Systems Theory." In *Sourcebook of Family Theories and Methods: A Contextual Approach*, ed. P. G. Boss, W. J. Doherty, R. LaRossa, W. R. Schumm, and S. K. Steinmetz. New York: Plenum.

DAVID M. KLEIN

FAMILY THERAPY

Family therapy has been conducted on an informal basis from the beginning of time. Starting with families helping each other and including priests and physicians who advise people on family matters, society has supported family unity. As society changed, life became more complex, and family life became more conflicted. This conflict was compounded by changing moral values, increasing divorce rate, increasing life span, and economic change. Support for families decreased as society became more mobile and as families moved away from extended family members.

From these changes, family therapy emerged with the help of many agents. Social workers contributed to the field of family therapy as they worked with the problems of the poor at the turn of the twentieth century. As early as 1910, psychiatrists Alfred Adler and Carl Jung explored the effects of family on an individual's mental illness. Harry Stack Sullivan explored the illness of schizophrenia and expanded on the connection between family interaction and a client's illness. In the early 1900s, the family life education movement provided homemaking and parenting classes for women to promote family health, both physical and emotional. Before 1932, Havelock Ellis of Great Britain and Magnus Hirschfeld of Germany recognized a need for practical information regarding sexual practices and birth control, and the field of sex

therapy was established. In 1934, Ernest Groves led a conference on marriage and the family at the University of North Carolina (The Chapel Hill Conference), and began teaching courses in marriage and family relations. Groves's work pulled together the biological, psychological, and social elements of marriage in a practical manner and began a trend of looking at marriage and family life from a holistic perspective.

Theories of Family Therapy

Formal theories of family therapy began in the 1950s. John Bell, a professor of psychology at Clark University, met with John Sutherland, medical director of the Tavistock Clinic in England. From a comment by Sutherland about meeting with a whole family, Bell began to work with the family as a whole, not just with the identified client. He continued to work in this way and began to present his findings in both the academic and therapeutic communities.

During this time, Murray Bowen, a child psychiatrist working at the Menninger Clinic in Topeka, Kansas, and later at the National Institute of Mental Health (NIMH) in Bethesda, Maryland, worked with families of children with schizophrenia. His work with these families led to the theory known as intergenerational family therapy. Bowen's theory proposes that dysfunction in families occurs when family members of different generations are too emotionally entangled with each other. The goal of therapy is to help individuals become more emotionally independent, to differentiate from their family of origin so they can function successfully. Bowen advises the therapist to be aware of a triangle in the family and in the therapeutic system. This triangle is described as two people who pull in a third party (or work, or alcohol, or the therapist) so they do not have to deal with a problem between themselves. A family system can have many different, overlapping triangles.

At the same time that Bowen was doing his work on the East Coast, a group of therapists known as the Palo Alto Group were developing other theories of family therapy at the Mental Research Institute (MRI) in California. There, Gregory Bateson began assessing communication styles in schizophrenic families. From his work, strategic family therapy developed. Looking at dysfunctional sequences of behaviors in a family rather than intergenerational relationships, strategic family therapists suggest direct changes in behavior and terminate therapy when the presenting problem has been resolved.

Structural family therapy began with the work of Salvador Minuchin at the Wiltwyck School for Boys.

Working with poor families in New York City in the 1960s, Minuchin developed an active therapy designed to place parents in charge of children and to establish a hierarchy in the family where each generation has its place. Structural therapy considers the life cycle of a family, including births, deaths, and marriages, as part of normal family life, and the therapist works with these milestones to promote healthy functioning within the family.

Systemic family therapy recognizes the life cycle of the family as a process of continuing evolution or change as individuals mature. Influenced by the work of Gregory Bateson, systemic family therapy uses the therapist as a neutral party who hypothesizes about the presenting problem and discusses it with the family by means of circular questioning—asking one family member to comment on the behavior of two or more other members, to determine a way to intervene in the family system.

Contextual family therapy evolved in the late 1950s from the work of Ivan Boszormenyi-Nagy. Seeing family dysfunction as the product of loyalty issues to members of one's family of origin, contextual therapy tries to rebalance the family scale and free the individual to participate in his or her new family.

In the late 1970s, brief therapy was developed at the MRI in California. This theory places the focus on brief solutions to family problems without looking for pathology in each issue. It deals with the problem presented by the family, reflects on what has not worked to solve the issue, and teaches problem-solving methods to modify the complaint.

Family therapy is not just a group of theories. Theories are the baseline used to work with problems of living, which change in some way with each generation. Each theory proposes a position for the therapist to take with the family—supportive, directive, or collaborative—and views the client as part of a family system.

From these theories, many different ways of working with families evolved. Existential, experiential, behavioral, art and drama, play, and group therapies are all used in family therapy. Family therapists adopt a theory that fits their ability to work with clients. Family therapy has become one of the support systems used to improve the quality of family life as therapy in general has lost some of its stigma of being only for people who are mentally ill.

Definitions

The definition of "family" has changed since the late 1800s. Biological or nuclear families account for fewer than half of today's families. A biological family is defined as two people who marry each other, stay married for their lifespan, and have children of this marriage.

Single-parent families result from a choice made by a person to have and to raise a child alone, or they are due to divorce or the death of one biological parent. "Stepfamily" has become a common name for families who have lost one biological parent and the remaining parent has remarried. Children who are adopted either into an existing family or by a childless couple create another form of family.

Each type of family brings to the therapist a unique set of strengths and weaknesses. In biological or nuclear families, the couple has a commitment to each other and to their family. The commitment to stay together to raise their children in a society where it is easier to get a divorce than to work out the problems is a challenge. Lack of parent education, different parenting styles, drug and alcohol use, financial stress, and many other factors combine to separate couples from their commitment to each other.

Single-parent families are sometimes created from loss, sometimes from choice. The loss of a parent by death or divorce can be a mixed blessing, creating confusing emotions for both children and parent. When a parent leaves, either by death or divorce, children often feel guilty or blame themselves for this. If the loss has been after a long period of illness or abuse, the feeling of relief is confused with feelings of remorse and guilt. Depending on the age of the parent and children, their respective stages of development, and their economic status, a single-parent family may remain intact for a long time.

Single-parent families created from choice include single men and women adopting a child or becoming biological parents and remaining alone. The problems unique to these families are the reaction of family and friends and the perceived need of an opposite-sex role model for the child. For those single mothers who did not get pregnant by choice or plan, family therapy is available to support them while making the decision to abort or maintain the pregnancy, keep the child, or place the child for adoption.

Stepfamilies are not a new phenomenon. In prior generations, men were killed in farm or industrial accidents, and women often died in childbirth. The remaining spouse often remarried as a means of raising children from the original marriage. In today's society, stepfamilies are more often the result of divorce. Created from loss, they present issues of divided loyalties of parents and children. The separation of children from one biological parent and the union of two households, often each with children, are not always thought out beforehand. Premarital counseling and preplanning do much to make this transition go smoothly. The age of parents and children, the decision where to live, and contact with former families and spouses all contribute to the chaos of this family system.

Adoption creates its own set of unique circumstances. Prior to adoption, a couple may have tried many resources to have a biological child. Much thought and counseling may have gone into their decision to adopt, and much time may have elapsed prior to the actual receiving of a child. In prior generations, adopted children often came from family members who had children out of wedlock. Single women who became pregnant did not have access to abortion, so the child was placed for adoption after the birth. In today's society, more single mothers are choosing abortion rather than continuing an unplanned pregnancy, but some are keeping their children. This may lead couples who want to adopt to explore foreign adoption agencies, interracial adoption, adopting special-needs children, or the use of surrogate mothers. The choice to have or adopt a child in a lesbian or gay relationship is also more common in today's society. The process of identifying themselves as a couple or family is a struggle for some gay or lesbian couples, knowing the rejection and anger they may face.

A family does not exist alone. This microsystem is part of a larger macrosystem, which includes the health-care, welfare, legal, educational, or work environments. The family therapist may include members of these systems in therapy to enhance family unity and promote wellness. The boundaries of family therapists are often challenged in regard to confidentiality and the safety of children and parents. A family therapist is bound by law to report suspected or known cases of child abuse. One is also bound by an ethic of confidentiality not to reveal information presented by a client in a therapy session unless there is a danger of harm to the client or to others. These legal and ethical issues are thoroughly explored in the therapist's educational process.

Therapist Education

To meet the many challenges presented by families, therapists receive formal education and training and integrate this learning with their own value system. The therapist's own family issues; socioeconomic status; and religious, ethnic, and moral values all influence his or her ability to work with clients. The

strengths, weaknesses, biases, and ethical dilemmas presented by clients often make family therapists aware of their own issues and how they have or have not been addressed.

In 1978, the American Association for Marriage and Family Therapists (AAMFT) evolved from the American Association of Marriage and Family Counselors. AAMFT sets standards for education and provides ongoing supervision and training for its members and for members of other professional groups who choose to learn more about family therapy. As a professional organization, AAMFT does ongoing research, holds annual conferences on state and national levels, and promotes state certification of qualified therapists.

Education is specialized in a master's degree program and includes theories of family therapy, stages of physical and emotional development of individuals, the life cycle of the family, the impact of chronic illness on the family system, and awareness of different ethnic family values and of the many changes in lifestyles that affect relationships in families. Ethical and legal implications for the therapist, the family system, and the megasystem with which they interact are all part of this education.

Integration of Theory and Practice

For family therapy to be effective, theory, legal and ethical issues, and the problems presented by families in the real world must be integrated by the therapist.

Acknowledging individual stages of development helps the family therapist assign age-appropriate tasks to each family member. When delayed development or retardation is present, understanding normal development helps the family therapist assess the special needs of the child and family, being empathic with the fears of both children and adults. Feelings of blame, anger, shame, and fear may go unspoken and be acted out in unhealthy ways or can be better managed with therapeutic help. The therapist can refer the family to appropriate sources of support and help for their specific medical or educational needs.

The family life cycle can be defined as the stages a family goes through as each individual member of the family grows and moves on in life. As young adults begin the natural process of separating from their families of origin, differences of opinions and lifestyles challenge the family. Many of these challenges are healthy and normal, yet difficult for parents to accept. When children marry and begin their own families, both they and their parents must adopt a new way of relating to each other. If these new families choose to separate or divorce, family values are chal-

FAMILY VALUES

lenged. As each generation grows older, couples retire; their children mature; the effects of aging, illness,
and the death of parents affect the family system.

Chronic illness at any stage of family development,
and for any family member from youngest to oldest,
places stress on individuals in the family and on the
family system at large. Loss, fear of possible contagion, issues of a disease, financial pressures, and social stigmas all create barriers to family unity.

Awareness of the way different cultures view their
family systems helps the family therapist to understand the way this family is or is not working. Families new to a country bring with them cultural
traditions and biases that can create difficulty for
them both within their families and within their new
communities. Traditional family values, culture, and
language may be rejected by children trying to assimilate into a new school and community, causing family disruption and distress.

The family life cycle repeats itself with each generation, yet each generation must meet it with new
knowledge of self and the world, changes in social
and economic development, and traditional and new
resources.

(*See also:* Child Abuse and Neglect: Emotional and Psychological Aspects; Codependency; Divorce: Emotional
and Social Aspects; Divorce: Effects on Children; Dysfunctional Family; Family Life Education; Marriage Counseling; Psychiatric Disorders; Remarriage; Remarriage
and Children)

BIBLIOGRAPHY

Bernard, J. M., and Hackney, H. (1983). *Untying the Knot: A Guide to Civilized Divorce.* Minneapolis, MN: Winston Press.

Boszormenyi-Nagy, I., and Framo, J., eds. (1965). *Intensive Family Therapy: Theoretical and Practical Aspects.* New York: Harper & Row.

Boszormenyi-Nagy, I., and Ulrich, D. (1981). "Contextual Family Therapy." In *Handbook of Family Therapy,* Vol. I, ed. A. S. Gurman and D. P. Kniskern. New York: Brunner/Mazel.

Bowen, M. (1978). *Family Therapy in Clinical Practice.* New York: Jason Aronson.

Brodzinski, D. M. (1992). *Being Adopted: A Lifelong Search for Self.* New York: Doubleday.

Carter, B., and McGoldrick, M., eds. (1989). *The Changing Family Life Cycle: A Framework for Family Therapy,* 2nd edition. Boston: Allyn & Bacon.

De Shazer, S. (1982). *Patterns of Brief Family Therapy.* New York: Guilford.

Gurman, A. S., and Kniskern, D. P., eds. (1991). *Handbook of Family Therapy,* Vol. II. New York: Brunner/Mazel.

Haley, J. (1976). *Problem Solving Therapy.* San Francisco: Jossey-Bass.

Kaplan, H. S. (1979). *Disorders of Sexual Desire.* New York: Brunner/Mazel.

Lebow, J. (1987). "Developing a Personal Integration in Family Therapy: Principles for Model Construction and Practice." *The Journal of Marital and Family Therapy* 13:1–14.

McDaniel, S.; Weber, T.; and McKeever, J. (1983). "Multiple Theoretical Approaches to Supervision: Choices in Family Therapy Training." *Family Therapy Training* 2:491–500.

Minuchin, S. (1976). *Families and Family Therapy.* Cambridge, MA: Harvard University Press.

Nichols, W. C. (1992). *Fifty Years of Marital and Family Therapy.* Washington, DC: American Association for Marriage Family Therapists.

O'Hanlon, W. H., and Weiner-Davis, M. (1989). *In Search of Solutions: A New Direction in Psychotherapy.* New York: W. W. Norton.

Piercy, F. P., Sprenkle, D. H. (1986). *Family Therapy Sourcebook.* New York: Guilford.

Rofes, E., ed. (1982). *The Kid's Book of Divorce: By, for, and About Kids.* New York: Vintage Books.

Schorr, L. B. (1988). *Within Our Reach: Breaking the Cycle of Disadvantage.* New York: Doubleday.

Storm, C. L. (1993). "Supervision That Considers Context Creates Competence in Supervisees." *Family Therapy News* 24:20, 26.

Sue, D. W., and Sue, S. (1982). *Counseling the Culturally Different.* New York: Wiley.

Wallerstein, J. S., and Kelly, J. B. (1980). *Surviving the Breakup: How Children and Parents Cope with Divorce.* New York: Basic Books.

CAROLYN L. SCHOLZ

FAMILY TYPES   See Cohabitation; Communes;
Dual-Earner Families; Dysfunctional Family; Extended
Family; Gay and Lesbian Parents; Military Families; Nu-
clear Family; Polandry; Polygyny; Single Parents

FAMILY VALUES

Are America's family values in decline? Debate
erupted over the state of American family values during the 1992 U.S. presidential campaign. The sometimes contentious discourse was sparked by Vice
President Dan Quayle's comments concerning a television situation comedy in which the fictional charac-

ter Murphy Brown gave birth to a child without benefit of marriage. Quayle chastised Hollywood writers for story lines such as the *Murphy Brown* segment, which, he argued, encouraged irresponsible sexual behavior and glorified single parenting. The vice president's comments drew a mixed bag of responses. Conservative policymakers and scholars extolled what they perceived to be Quayle's profamily stance. Liberal thinkers and single parents, on the other hand, interpreted Quayle's speech as an indictment of millions of women who struggle to support their families single-handedly. This entry provides a discussion of some of the arguments and prevailing myths about family values and their alleged demise. Further, it argues that a major shift has taken place in the twentieth century—not in family values, but in the economic sphere, which continues to alter family roles and relationships.

Family Values Undefined

What is instructive about the family values debate is the failure, by writers and politicians who have jumped into the fray, to articulate what they mean by family values. For the most part, public dialogue has carefully sidestepped a definition of the term. More frequently the focus has shifted from a discussion about values to one about family structure. All too often, nostalgic references to the breadwinner/homemaker family model that was emblazoned on television screens in the 1950s are evoked. Generally, the implication is that normative (though neither identified nor specified) family values can be passed on to America's younger generation in two-parent families only. The mother-father-child family form is touted as the solution for poverty, welfare, urban violence, and crime. Such a perspective maintains that family structures that deviate from the nuclear family model are undesirable and dysfunctional for society. However, other scholars view the nuclear family as one of many possible family forms. Proponents of this school characterize the family as a social construct shaped and altered by the social, political, and economic environment in which it exists (Collier, Rosaldo, and Yanagisako 1992).

Three themes are central to the family values debate: the increase in the divorce rate, the growing proportion of teen births, and the younger age at which premarital sex is initiated. The first issue—the divorce rate—is cited as a major factor contributing to the extinction of the nuclear family and, consequently, family values. Those writing in this vein view the increase in divorce as an indication of a lack of

solemnity regarding marriage—that is, a tendency for individuals entering marriage not to take their marriage vows seriously. However, an argument can be made that the significant proportion of remarriages that occur in the United States demonstrate a commitment to the ideology of marriage. Divorced individuals return to the altar because the married state is normative and the divorced state is deviant. Coming from another perspective, Stephanie Coontz (1992) questions whether, as nostalgia suggests, there was greater commitment to marriage at other time periods than there is today. She contends that a hundred years ago marital separation occurred, but the split took place within households, concealed from outsiders. Today it is merely out in the open.

The second issue cited as symptomatic of declining collective morality—the increasing incidence of teen births—began with the 1960s sexual revolution, according to the family values proponents. However, one would have to look to the 1950s, the decade of low divorce rates and high marriage rates, to find the highest rate of teen births. In 1957, to be exact, the birth rate was 97 live births for every 100 young women aged 15 to 19 years; the figure for the early 1990s is half that (Coontz 1992).

In citing their distress about the young age at which sexual intercourse is initiated, the "just say no" contingency within the family values camp ignores the premarital sexual behavior pattern established by America's forefathers and foremothers, long before this century's "sexual revolution." Specifically, in the two decades preceding the American Revolution, one-third of all births occurred without benefit of marriage, and in the decades following the Revolution, one-third of the brides in rural New England were pregnant at the time of their wedding (Larkin 1988). These statistics provide evidence that America's changing sexual mores of the 1960s were neither new nor revolutionary. The question then becomes: Which era should policymakers use as an example to "restore" America's mythical morality to its rightful place?

There are those who would argue that the issue of premarital sex has more to do with biological and sociological dissonance than with values—that is, the initiation of female menses occurs on average at a younger age than it did in the nineteenth century because of improved nutrition and a higher standard of living, while the age at first marriage has continued to rise in response to economic and social instability. Consequently, young women are physiologically capable of mating at earlier ages and are doing just that, but the means to provide sustenance for the young born of such mating becomes problematic in an increasingly unstable economic environment.

Television Characters as Role Models

Generally, those writing within the family values framework ignore the economic dimensions of family foundation. Instead, idealized images of the 1950s are offered as icons of family values. Television series such as *Ozzie and Harriet, Father Knows Best,* and *Leave It to Beaver* are treated as paragons of bygone family virtues that beg to be "reinstated" at the societal level. But these series were not docudramas. Using fictional characters is tantamount to regarding the family "through a murk of sentimentality" (Collins 1975, p. 225). The monolithic fictional families of the 1950s "devalue [the] rich variety of kinship stories" (Stacey 1992, p. 109) that have always been part of the American landscape. If fantasy families are not valid paradigms, can the "real" 1950s be used as the basis for examining the myriad changes the institution of the family has experienced?

The 1950s: Reality Versus Reverie

Social demographers provide evidence that the decade of the 1950s was a blip, an aberration, a reversal of trends that had been occurring for more than a century (Coontz 1992; Kain 1990). Marriage and parenthood had been declining steadily for more than 150 years, and the 1950s created a minor reversal in that course. For the first time in 100 years, the age for marriage and motherhood fell, fertility increased, and the divorce rate declined (Coontz 1992; Kain 1990). The major impetus for the demographic changes was the American economy, which surged worldwide after two decades of being sidetracked, first by the Depression and then by World War II. Real wages increased by more than they had in the preceding fifty years. With governmental assistance, home ownership became a reality for millions of families; about one-half of suburban homes were acquired through some form of federal funding (Coontz 1992).

Although the 1950s was a decade of American hegemony, unparalleled prosperity, and economic opportunity that became accessible for many, it offers memories of political, economic, and social inequality for millions. It was a time when 20 percent of the population was defined as poor. It was a period when half of Americans had no savings and 25 percent had no liquid assets. For African Americans, the situation in the pre-civil rights 1950s was catastrophic. Fifty-two percent of two-parent African-American families

were in poverty, even though 40 percent of African-American women with small children worked outside the home. Clearly, the astigmatic yearning of politicians and scholars for the white, male-dominated, privileged 1950s ignores the devalued existence that millions endured. Yet, it continues to be the decade Americans are encouraged to emulate.

Although the poverty rate has declined overall since that ten-year period, economic well-being continues to be elusive for millions of families. In the early 1990s, the average hourly wages of private workers were lower than they had been since 1966, after adjusting for inflation (Coontz 1992). Families with adults in their twenties, whether two-parent or single-parent, were more likely to be poor than such families in the 1960s and 1970s. By the 1980s, more than 40 percent of wages went to cover housing costs, compared with 15 percent in the 1950s (Coontz 1992). The 1950s were economic boom years, and millions of American families flourished. During the 1980s and early 1990s, the economy stagnated, and millions of American families suffered. Could it be that alteration in family formation is less connected to values than to family finances?

Women's Economic Contribution

To offset the financial strain on families, female labor force participation has increased dramatically since the early 1960s. The majority of women have gone to work not as a result of the women's movement, nor because they have turned their back on their families, as some suggest (Popenoe 1993), but out of a sense of responsibility for their families. Economic necessity, as noted, and the creation of traditionally female-type jobs have pulled women into the labor market. Even with women's financial contribution to their families, a majority of the increase in family poverty since 1979 has occurred in two-parent families, while more than one-third of the increase in poverty has occurred in families in which only one parent is present (Coontz 1992).

Men as Breadwinners

In response to criticism concerning his "single-mother comments," Quayle declared his respect for female heads of households, while chiding absent fathers; Quayle argued that delinquent fathers need "to be reminded that they have a responsibility for the children they have fathered" ("Trying to Redefine Debate" 1992). Quayle is not alone in his denunciation of absent fathers. Others—David Popenoe (1993), for one—maintain that one measure of "divestiture" of the family unit (i.e., the decline of the family) is the proportion of fathers who fail to support their children. On the other hand, people such as Judith Stacey (1992) argue that as men's ability to live up to their provider role declines so too do the roles that are intricately intertwined with the provider role, such as husband and father. The evidence suggests that fewer men will be able to take on the traditional male provider role in the future. At least one study estimated that only one-third of men between ages twenty-five and thirty-four will be likely to have a better job than their fathers had (Coontz 1992).

The situation is worse for African-American men—the group that is disproportionately targeted by the policymakers' moralizing about personal responsibility. African-American men are more likely than white men to losse their jobs due to economic restructuring, with younger African-American men suffering the greatest losses (Coontz 1992). In one study of five Great Lakes cities, conducted between 1979 and 1984, researchers found that 50 percent of African-American male workers lost their jobs as manufacturing occupations declined in the area (Baca-Zinn 1992).

If there is a link between economic well-being and family formation, African-American men are least likely to be financially able to take on familial responsibilities. And if marriage is an exchange between partners (Becker 1973), African-American men are limited in what they can offer in the market. Indeed, a major factor accounting for the shrinking pool of marriageable African-American males is their high rate of joblessness (Coontz 1992; Wilson and Neckerman 1986). Potential marriage partners, pregnant or not, are unlikely to formalize a union when the prospective mate is unemployed (Wilson and Neckerman 1986). Cliff Johnson and Andrew Sum (1987) found that the total decrease in marriage rates for young African-American males was directly related to loss of wages.

Some researchers (Glenn 1987; Popenoe 1993) cite the rise of individualism and the decline in social ties to account for the later age at which men are now marrying. Others, such as Edward L. Kain (1990), provide evidence that the current age at first marriage (especially for men) is similar to that at the turn of the twentieth century. Still others, such as Johnson and Sum (1987), indicate that the delay is related to economic factors. One study found that men aged twenty to twenty-four with earnings above the poverty level are three to four times more likely to wed than are men at or below poverty level. According to Coontz (1992), the chances for marriage are slim for the 40 percent of American men who have not obtained a stable permanent occupation by age twenty-

nine. One major reason for this dilemma is that half of the jobs created in the 1980s paid wages lower than the poverty level for a family of four. A related factor is that a high proportion of newly created positions were part-time (part-time positions pay about 60 percent of what full-time jobs pay, and fewer than one-quarter are covered by employer health insurance). In fact, the number of involuntary part-time employees has grown since the 1970s, and part-time employment is not conducive to either family formation or family stability.

Despite the economic challenges facing Americans, most want to marry—90 percent of men and women eventually marry (Coontz 1992), and most plan to have children (Popenoe 1993). A study of high school seniors found that 93 percent of the female students and 95 percent of the males thought it likely that they would want to have children (Goldscheider and Waite 1991). In support of this, Coontz (1992) reports that despite the overall decline in fertility, the rate of childlessness is lower than it was at the end of the nineteenth century.

Conclusion

The family is not a stable, unchanging, nuclear entity. It never has been. The family is a social construct, a social creation influenced by social forces that alter conjugal and parental relationships at all times and in all places. Family values, like the family, are social constructs, societally created and affected by institutional and systemic forces.

The statistics provided in this entry do not suggest a decline in family values; they indicate a rational response to financial uncertainty. The drop in men's earnings is forcing a delay in marriage, women's marketplace participation is increasingly necessary to keep the family out of poverty, and fewer and fewer couples can afford to care for more than one child. The decisions individuals and families make have less to do with values and more to do with survival. Yet individuals continue to meet, marry, and care for the young as families have done for centuries—often within a nonsupportive political, economic, and social environment.

(See also: ADOLESCENT SEXUALITY; DIVORCE: EMOTIONAL AND SOCIAL ASPECTS; HISTORY OF THE FAMILY; MASS MEDIA; POVERTY; RELIGION; SEXUALITY IN THE LIFE CYCLE; TEENAGE PARENTING; UNEMPLOYMENT; WORK AND FAMILY)

BIBLIOGRAPHY

Baca-Zinn, M. (1992). "Family, Race, and Poverty in the Eighties." In Rethinking the Family: Some Feminist

Questions, ed. B. Thorne and M. Yalom. Boston: Northeastern University Press.

Becker, G. S. (1973). "A Theory of Marriage." In *Economics of the Family: Marriage, Children, and Human Capital*, ed. T. W. Schultz. Chicago: University of Chicago Press.

Collier, J.; Rosaldo, M. Z.; and Yanagisako, S. (1992). "Is There a Family? New Anthropological Views." In *Rethinking the Family: Some Feminist Questions*, ed. B. Thorne and M. Yalom. Boston: Northeastern University Press.

Collins, R. (1975). *Conflict Sociology*. New York: Academic Press.

Coontz, S. (1992). *The Way We Never Were*. New York: Basic Books.

Glenn, N. D. (1987). "Tentatively Concerned View of American Marriages." *Journal of Family Issues* 8:350–354.

Goldscheider, F. K., and Waite, L. J. (1991). *New Families, No Families?: The Transformation of the American Home*. Berkeley: University of California Press.

Johnson, C., and Sum, A. (1987). *Declining Earnings of Young Men: Their Relationship to Poverty, Teen Pregnancy, and Family Formation*. Washington, DC: Adolescent Pregnancy Prevention Clearinghouse.

Kain, E. L. (1990). *The Myth of Family Decline: Understanding Families in a World of Rapid Social Change*. Lexington, MA: Lexington Books.

Larkin, J. (1988). *The Reshaping of Everyday Life*, 1790–1840. New York: Harper & Row.

Popenoe, D. (1993). "American Family Decline, 1960–1990: A Review and Appraisal." *Journal of Marriage and the Family* 55:527–542.

Scanzoni, J. (1987). "Families in the 1980s: Time to Refocus Our Thinking." *Journal of Family Issues* 4:394–421.

Stacey, J. (1992). "Backward Toward the Postmodern Family: Reflections on Gender, Kinship, and Class in the Silicon Valley." In *Rethinking the Family: Some Feminist Questions*, ed. B. Thorne and M. Yalom. Boston: Northeastern University Press.

Stacey, J. (1993). "Good Riddance to 'The Family': A Response to David Popenoe." *Journal of Marriage and the Family* 55:545–547.

"Trying to Redefine Debate, Quayle Denounces Hollywood, Praises Single Mothers." (1992). *The Washington Post*, September 3, p. A15.

Wilson, W. J., and Neckerman, K. (1986). "Poverty and Family Structure." In *Fighting Poverty: What Works and What Doesn't*, ed. S. Danziger and D. Weinberg. Cambridge, MA: Harvard University Press.

BARBARA A. ARRIGHI

FAMILY VIOLENCE

The latter decades of the twentieth century brought increasing evidence that the family does not always conform to a peaceful, loving ideal. Instead, violence and neglect characterize many family relationships. In fact, people are more likely to be killed by members of their own families than by strangers (Straus and Gelles 1990).

Violence in families includes child abuse and spouse abuse. According to national surveys in 1975 and 1985, about one in six American marriages, or approximately 8.7 million couples, experienced an incident of physical assault during the year. Physical assaults against children are even more frequent. Almost all young children and about one-third of children aged fifteen to seventeen are hit by their parents; 11 percent of all children are severely beaten, punched, kicked, hit with objects, or threatened with guns or knives (Straus and Gelles 1990).

Child abuse involves physical assaults of children by their parents. Because of the wide use of spanking in American families, there is some controversy over whether this should be considered a form of abuse (Straus, Gelles, and Steinmetz 1980). Spouse abuse includes wife abuse and husband abuse, both of which are prevalent in American marriages. Because of the typically greater size and strength of men, however, abuse of wives tends to be more damaging (Walker 1984).

Other types of family violence include child neglect, sibling violence, sexual abuse, and abuse and neglect of the elderly. Child neglect refers to the failure of parents to provide their children with food, shelter, clothing, and supervision. Such neglect can threaten a young child's life as effectively as direct assaults. Sibling violence, physical assaults among brothers and sisters, is a less recognized form of family violence that involves about 80 percent of all children under eighteen; it is so common that most parents do not consider it a problem (Gelles and Cornell 1990; Straus, Gelles, and Steinmetz 1980). Children may also be victims of sexual assaults by family members, and child sexual abuse has been associated with significant mental health problems in adulthood (Finkelhor and Browne 1988).

With the rise in the number of elderly, neglect and abuse of the elderly have come to the attention of authorities. As people age and become less able to provide for their own needs, they become dependent upon family members to assist them with shopping, food preparation, obtaining medical care, and even fulfilling basic hygiene needs. Elder neglect occurs when this care is not provided. Direct assaults against the elderly, however, constitute elder abuse. Research shows that about 3 percent of the elderly may be victims of some form of elder abuse (Pillemer and Finkelhor 1988). The elderly may be at risk of sexual assaults as well.

The frequent attention given to family violence is sometimes interpreted to mean that such behavior has increased since the 1960s. However, authorities believe that family violence has characterized families throughout history. References to sibling violence, child abuse, and wife abuse can be found in the Bible (Genesis 4:8; 22:9; Judges 19:24–29). Historians also point out that infanticide, child abuse, and wife abuse have existed throughout the history of Western society (Dobash and Dobash 1979; Radbill 1980; Robin 1982). Systematic attention to family violence problems did not develop until the 1960s, however, when physicians first began to recognize symptoms of abuse in children (Kempe et al. 1962). Recognition of spouse abuse, elder abuse, sexual abuse, and other forms followed. The more frequent reports of family violence since that time may be a result of this increased awareness.

The causes of family violence are still unclear. Analysts first suggested that persons who abuse children, spouses, or the elderly must be psychologically abnormal. Subsequent research indicated, however, that the majority of abusers are not mentally ill. There is considerable controversy about whether the use of alcohol and other addictive substances causes family violence. Some authorities suggest that substance abuse is associated with family violence but does not operate as a causal factor (Flanzer 1993; Gelles 1993; Gelles and Cornell 1990).

Other common theories of family violence emphasize the social environment rather than the characteristics of the abuser. The situational stress hypothesis proposes that family violence is linked to the presence of various environmental stresses in the lives of abusers. An early form of this theory suggested that the economic stresses of lower-class life led parents to abuse their children. This has subsequently been expanded to include other environmental stresses, such as marital problems, unemployment, illness, and the stresses of caring for a handicapped child or an incapacitated older person. While such factors have been found to be associated with family violence, this theory does not explain why other families faced with the same stresses do not engage in abusive behavior or why family violence occurs in middle- and upper-income families as well (Gelles and Cornell 1990).

American society has high levels of violence in general; that it permeates the family as well is not surprising. Feminists and advocates for children point out that Western society has, for centuries, viewed women and children as property and as appropriate targets for physical violence. The Bible cautions parents not to "spare the rod" lest they spoil the child,

and English law allowed a man to chastise his wife, provided he used a stick no bigger around than his thumb, from which the term "rule of thumb" is derived. With such a cultural legacy, it is not surprising that parents chastise their children and husbands beat their wives (Dobash and Dobash 1979; Gelles and Cornell 1990; Walker 1984).

Clinical analyses have found that family violence is often perpetuated from one generation to the next, a conclusion that has also been supported by some research. This suggests that the socialization process plays a considerable role in the persistence of family violence. Children who grew up experiencing their parents' violence toward each other and themselves are more likely to establish a violent pattern with their own spouses and children. Violent families also tend to be socially isolated; they have few friends and little contact outside the family. Therefore, they are unlikely to have social support in times of stress or to be influenced by the nonviolent standards of others (Gelles and Cornell 1990). These families need programs developed to teach them how to avoid violence when relating to others.

Suggestions that victims of family violence "enjoy" their victimization are untrue. Most victims are afraid of the abuser, who often threatens retaliation if they report the abuse and pursuit if they leave. They need help to get out of the violent relationship and obtain protection from the abuser. Children and dependent elderly may need removal from the control of the abuser, and abused wives may need protection and assistance in leaving husbands who cannot or will not change their abusive behavior.

(*See also:* CHILD ABUSE AND NEGLECT: SOCIOLOGICAL ASPECTS; CHILD ABUSE AND NEGLECT: EMOTIONAL AND PSYCHOLOGICAL ASPECTS; CHILD ABUSE AND NEGLECT: LEGAL ASPECTS; CONFLICT; DISCIPLINE; ELDER ABUSE; INCEST; INFANTICIDE; RUNAWAY CHILDREN; SPOUSE ABUSE AND NEGLECT; STRESS; SUBSTANCE ABUSE)

BIBLIOGRAPHY

Dobash, R. E., and Dobash, R. (1979). *Violence Against Wives.* New York: Free Press.

Finkelhor, D., and Browne, A. (1988). "Assessing the Long-Term Impact of Child Sexual Abuse." In *Family Abuse and Its Consequences: New Directions in Research,* ed. G. T. Hotaling, D. Finkelhor, J. T. Kirkpatrick, and M. A. Straus. Newbury Park, CA: Sage Publications.

Flanzer, J. P. (1993). "Alcohol and Other Drugs Are Key Causal Agents of Violence." In *Current Controversies on Family Violence,* ed. R. J. Gelles and D. R. Loseke. Newbury Park, CA: Sage Publications.

Gelles, R. J. (1993). "Alcohol and Other Drugs Are Associated with Violence—They Are Not Its Cause." In *Current Controversies on Family Violence*, ed. R. J. Gelles and D. R. Loseke. Newbury Park, CA: Sage Publications.

Gelles, R. J., and Cornell, C. P. (1990). *Intimate Violence in Families*, 3rd edition. Newbury Park, CA: Sage Publications.

Kempe, C. H.; Silverman, F. N.; Steele, B. F.; Droegenmueller, W.; and Silver, H. K. (1962). "The Battered Child Syndrome." *Journal of the American Medical Association* 181:107–112.

Pillemer, K., and Finkelhor, D. (1988). "The Prevalence of Elder Abuse." *Gerontologist* 28:51–57.

Radbill, S. (1980). "A History of Child Abuse and Infanticide." In *The Battered Child*, 3rd edition, ed. R. Helfer and C. Kempe. Chicago: University of Chicago Press.

Robin, M. (1982). "Historical Introduction: Sheltering Arms: The Roots of Child Protection." In *Child Abuse*, ed. E. H. Newberger. Boston: Little, Brown.

Straus, M. A., and Gelles, R. J. (1990). *Physical Violence in American Families*. New Brunswick, NJ: Transaction.

Straus, M. A.; Gelles, R. J.; and Steinmetz, S. K. (1980). *Behind Closed Doors: Violence in the American Family*. Garden City, NY: Doubleday/Anchor.

Walker, L. E. (1984). *The Battered Wife Syndrome*. New York: Springer-Verlag.

MARY C. SENGSTOCK

FATHERS

"Father" is a word derived historically from the Latin term *pater* and is defined by *Webster's* as a man who has engendered a child; a male parent; or a person who takes responsibility for protecting, caring, and rearing. It is only since about the early 1980s that the public and professional focus has been on the more affective use of the term "father"—to protect, care for, and nurture children.

This upsurge of interest in fathers is in part reflective of the interests of Western society at large on families, parenting, and gender roles. This emphasis dates back to the civil rights movement in America during the 1960s, when African Americans demanded equal rights and when the women's movement got under way. As a result, women left home in increasing numbers, entering the work force to seek self-fulfillment and to aid their economic status. One consequence of these trends was that men began to question their own roles in the family. More males began to recognize that it was too confining to serve in only the traditional role of patriarch, and they wanted to live more at the heart rather than the boundaries of their families. Consequently, men began to take on more expressive family roles while becoming less instrumental. Hence, an increased interest in fathers and fatherhood evolved. Until the 1970s, writings and research on this topic were sparse; now, there is a plethora of professional and popular literature on fathers written by a variety of professionals from many perspectives.

Historical Perspectives

At the beginning of American history, fathers were towering figures within families. Their authority was derived from the nature of the agricultural world in which people lived; men served as the family's unquestioned ruler. Their source of power was the ownership and control of all family property, including land, wives, and children. Men were also charged with the moral and spiritual growth of their children and thus with disciplining them. This early father–child relationship has been described as distant, morally instructive, and condescending, as too much affection was believed to lead to parental indulgence, ruining the character of children.

This patriarchal style of fathering continued until the mid-1700s, paving the way for a new concept of parenting that reached America from England. In this emerging view, fathers no longer acted as strict authority figures, but increased their roles as moral teachers. Family life continued to shift during the 1800s, influenced by the Industrial Revolution and the progressive urbanization of the population. Men went to work in factories, while women were left at home during the day, in charge of the children and household. The emergence of modern fatherhood started in the 1800s when mothers became the stable core of families, taking over the role as moral teacher and disciplinarian. Despite the decline of patriarchy and the expanded importance of mothers in nineteenth-century family life, middle-class fathers still had significant roles to play. More than ever before, men were providers for the family, reinforcing their status as heads of households and retaining their place as ultimate disciplinarians of families, but they remained outside the strongest currents of feelings and emotions that ebbed and flowed within and between family members.

During the nineteenth and twentieth centuries, the increased presence of industrialism, bureaucracy, and urbanization helped spread the middle-class phenomenon of emerging modern fatherhood. The separation of the workplace from home life continued to undermine the traditional authority of fathers. This environment spawned two opposing trends or levels of participation, father absence versus father involvement (Rotundo 1985). For some men, the lack of a commanding paternal role in modern families made it possible for them to withdraw psychologically and/or physically from their families without immediate disaster. Alternatively for other men, the traditional formality of patriarchy gave way to their enjoying more warmth, play, and intimacy with children.

Historical scholars assert that the interest in fathering roles since 1900 has not increased but rather fluctuated between fathers as providers (instrumental role) and fathers as nurturers (expressive role) (Atkinson and Blackwelder 1993). An examination of popular magazine articles published from 1900 to 1989 shows that the most predominant changes in the parenthood literature is an increase in material about gender nonspecific parenting. Scholars also suggest that there is a relationship between fertility and the definition of fathering and that this is closely tied to economic conditions. In good economic times, when fathers are able to meet the provider ideal, fertility increases and fathers' provider roles are emphasized. In nonfavorable economic climates, the alternative definition of fathers as nurturers is more prevalent.

The definition of modern fatherhood lies between two sets of opposite poles: father absence versus father involvement and father as provider versus father as nurturer. According to E. Anthony Rotundo (1985), the modern trend of androgynous fatherhood arrived as a result of the women's movement and the subsequent reshaping of gender roles. As part of this movement, more fathers became active participants in everyday child care and involved themselves in more expressive and intimate ways with children. A blurring of distinctions between fatherhood and motherhood was under way. Many modern fathers try to avoid sex-typing children and take interest in the growth and development of children of both genders. The androgynous new age fatherhood is the paradigm in which Americans now live, setting the framework for the future recasting of manhood, womanhood, and family.

Fatherhood and the Family Life Cycle

The genesis of fatherhood varies and influences how men perceive their participation in family life. For example, the couple may or may not be married, conception may be planned or unplanned, and fertilization may be natural or by artificial means, such as in vitro fertilization and/or surrogate parents. Only since the mid-1980s has the role of men in the family

planning process been seriously considered. Janice M. Swanson (1985) first discussed men's reproductive health and stressed the importance of shared contraception and shared pregnancy as the most effective means to secure men's interest in family life.

There is considerable research-based knowledge about the first phase of the family life cycle, the transition to parenthood, which occurs during pregnancy and the birth of the first child (Roopnarine and Miller 1985). Most information is derived from middle-class white men who participate in childbirth education classes with their wives, but prenatal involvement is also becoming more commonplace among other socioeconomic and ethnic groups. Participating in childbirth education classes is not only found to be supportive for pregnant women, but it also enhances men's knowledge of pregnancy and birth, increases their understanding of the father's role, and elevates their self-confidence and self-esteem relative to carrying out the parental role (May and Perrin 1985). Although the short-term effects of this participation are known, it is not yet understood what the long-term lifelong effects of prenatal and perinatal involvement are on marital relationships and subsequent fathering behaviors.

The next phase of fathering as demarked by the family life cycle is during children's infancy. There is much research on this period. While mothers usually provide comfort and security for infants, fathers are more involved in their social play (Lamb 1987). If mothers are not present, fathers also provide comfort and security needs. Infants relate to each parent in different ways (Parke and Tinsley 1981), regarding their mothers mainly as attachment figures and sources of security. However, fathers are also attachment figures and primary sources of affiliative behaviors—playmates and caretakers—as well.

There is little knowledge about fathers and their school-age children. It is known that fathers of children in this age range frequently feel inadequate in the execution of their father role because their occupational demands limit the amount of time spent with their children. Most fathers of school-age children practice instrumental rather than expressive roles. Moreover, they participate in instrumental activities, such as Scouting and sports, more frequently with sons than with daughters. Relationships with daughters during this period are often less close, ostensibly because of the increased difficulty men have identifying with the special needs of their daughters (Bradley 1985; Giveans and Robinson 1985).

During the adolescence phase of the family life cycle, the essence of the father–child relationship centers around identity issues (Martin 1985). Fathers struggle with the troublesome midlife identity crisis, while adolescents struggle with the difficulties of their emergent identity. Relationships with adolescent children may be explosive for no apparent reason. This is often a time of conflict and not just petty disputes (Benson 1985). Typically, fathers spend little time with their adolescent children, since the fathers are tired at the end of the workday and their children are busy with their peers, homework, or other independent projects. What time is spent together is usually spent in passive activities or on parallel activities such as watching television.

Little research has been done on the parent–child relationship during the time span when children leave home to begin their lives as independent adults, referred to as the postparental transition. Fathers gradually develop collegiality and mutuality with their children. Fathers are less authoritarian and directive, and children are more receptive to their father's suggestions. Sharing and negotiating emerge as the primary characteristics of their relationship. Eventually, most children get married and start families of their own, creating for their fathers the role of grandfather (Roberts and Zuengler 1985).

Relatively little research has been conducted on the last stage of fathering, grandfatherhood, and virtually none has been done on great-grandfatherhood. A crucial element of the grandparent–grandchild relationship is that it is mediated by the children's parents, the in-between generation. These parents determine the frequency and possibly even the quality of the grandparent–grandchild relationship. If parents feel negative toward their own fathers, the grandfather–grandchild relationship may be discouraged. The majority of grandfathers derive satisfaction from being a grandfather, and they indulge their grandchildren, since they do not feel as responsible for their grandchildren becoming socially acceptable adults. Traditionally, grandfathers' conversations have usually been more male-centered, making clear distinctions between men's and women's roles and focusing most often on the parental line. Therefore, the strongest bond with grandchildren was likely to be with the sons of a son.

However, as men's roles become more androgynous and men's and women's roles become more egalitarian, grandfathers in the future may not make such clear gender distinctions, and granddaughters may get more of their grandfather's attention. Grandfatherhood is usually the last developmental stage of fathering in the family life cycle (Baranowski 1985).

Contextual Dimensions of Fatherhood

There are many variations of fathering that differ according to the social contexts in which men find themselves (Hanson 1985a). The two-parent traditional family structure is still common, but there are increasing numbers of gay fathers, stepfathers, househusband fathers, fathers in dual-earner families, single custodial and noncustodial fathers, military fathers, adolescent fathers, and widowed fathers.

The most common deviation from the traditional nuclear family is the dual-earner family (Benokraitis 1985). Much research has been done on this family type, but the findings are equivocal at best. For example, women with higher-educated husbands receive more help with household labor than with child care; the opposite is true for families with lower-educated fathers. Other investigators report that fathers in dual-earner families assume little responsibility for either child care or housework, thus leaving their work and career schedules essentially unaffected by the outside working careers of their wives. What appears to be happening is that fathers' roles remain focused and limited, while mother's roles have expanded from that of full-time wives, mothers, and homemakers to include earning wages.

A second variation of fathering occurs when single custodial fathers serve as primary custodians of their children after divorce (Hanson 1985b) or widowhood (Burgess 1985). In America, 26 percent of all families are headed by single parents, 12 percent of these by males. Research on this family form indicates that these men and their families function fairly well. Adaptation to the role of primary parent is initially difficult, especially in organizing household tasks, learning to plan and prepare meals, and budgeting time and money. However, once fathers develop routines and children adjust to fathers being the sole parent, family life usually proceeds smoothly. Initially after divorce or death, children experience adjustment difficulties exemplified in diminished school performance or behavior problems. As children learn to accept the inevitable, these problems gradually subside, especially if fathers foster open communication of feelings. Sometimes short-term counseling is necessary to assist fathers and children in venting their feelings over the loss of the intact family. Adjustment occurs with greater ease after divorce when fathers actively seek custody rather than passively consenting to it.

Unwed teenage fathering is a third contextual variation (Barrett and Robinson 1985a). In America, 29 percent of births to white teenagers and 83 percent to

African-American teenagers occur outside of marriage. Findings showed that most teenage males are unprepared to assume the role of parent and provider. Compared to more mature fathers, teens have unrealistic expectations, lack knowledge about human growth and development, and are more likely to resort to child abuse. Adolescent fathers often have problems fulfilling their paternal responsibilities. Many leave school, assume low-paying jobs, and live a marginal existence. They report feeling isolated and have few friends with whom they can share their experiences. They are often intimidated by their girlfriends' families.

Researchers have found that there is no clear-cut role or pattern of experience for teenage fathers, but there is growing evidence that some of these males are deeply involved in what is happening to them, their girlfriends, and their babies (Barret and Robinson 1985a). The stereotypic notion that all teenage fathers are irresponsible, uncaring, and unconcerned about the mother or the infant should be reexamined. Historically, teenage fathers had no legal rights regarding the children they fathered, but the availability of legal recourse is changing (Walters and Elam 1985).

Culture and Fatherhood

Culture is a broad concept that includes multiple factors that surround and influence parents and families. Cultural variations and constraints that promote or inhibit men's involvement with families is a relatively recent focus of research. Father involvement is often determined by differences in ethnicity, nationality, occupation, and social class. Religion, physical environment (rural/urban residence), and internal family processes or dynamics also affect enactment of the father role (see Bozett and Hanson 1991). Only three aspects of cultural effects on fatherhood will be summarized here: ethnicity, environment (urban or rural residence), and social class. In terms of ethnicity, four groups are recognized as major minority groups in the United States: African American, Latino, Asian American, and Native American (Mirande 1991). However, comments here are limited to African-American and Latino fathers.

The persistent image of African-American fathers is one of an invisible figure who is absent from or at best peripheral to day-to-day family functioning. This view is challenged by research that finds that African-American fathers are neither absent nor uninvolved in family life, but play essential roles within families (McAdoo 1988; Staples 1988). What distinguishes the emerging scholarship on African-American families is

its emphasis on family unity, stability, and adaptability. Studies of middle-class African-American fathers have found that they are very involved in the rearing of their sons; that they maintain warm, interpersonal relations with them; and that generally their sons are well adjusted and motivated. John Lewis McAdoo (1988) found that the predominant verbal interaction pattern among African-American fathers and their children is characterized by warmth and nurturance. Another study found that 75 percent of African-American fathers believed that direct contact with their children is needed every day and that 90 percent wanted to spend more time with their offspring (Hyde and Texidor 1988). Therefore, research focusing on fatherhood in African-American families supports the view that many African-American fathers play an integral role in the family, and rather than being absent or overly permissive, they are present and typically assume an authoritative role.

Hispanic or Latino men have been depicted as visible, dominant, authoritarian figures who rule their families with an iron hand (Mirande 1991). There has been little research on the role of males in Hispanic families, but what there is calls into question the notion of Latino fathers as cold and distant authority figures. In the traditional view, fathers made all major decisions and were masters of the household. Fathers were thought to avoid family intimacy, maintain respect by instilling fear in their wives and children, and punish their children severely. Research suggests that the power of males may be less absolute than once believed and that Latino families are not as rigidly structured along age and gender lines. Latino fathers are found to be warm and affectionate with children and to have significant influence on their children's development (Bronstein 1988). Hence, Hispanic fathers do not conform to traditional stereotypical portrayals commonly found in the literature.

Even though these ethnic families and fathers do not deviate much from Anglo-American families and fathers, they still should not be judged by white-middle-class standards. Ethnic minority families are incredibly diverse, and there is no single monolithic ethnic family structure among or within them. Internal variation within major ethnic groups prohibits generalization.

Physical Environment and Fatherhood

There are differences between urban and rural cultures that influence fathers' enactment of their parental roles. One way in which environment influences fathering is in the inculcation of values. In rural areas, where families are more isolated, strong family ties are crucial for survival. Family members are strongly dependent on one another to provide basic needs such as love and nurturance, physical and emotional support, and economic sustenance. Fathers are frequently visible, exerting great influence on all family members. In contrast, because of the multiplicity and variety of activities and people in urban settings, it is more difficult to instill in children the importance of family solidarity. Since many urban area fathers frequently work a considerable distance from home, often with travel that takes them away overnight, physical proximity and direct face-to-face interaction between urban fathers and their children may be considerably limited. Decreased personal contact makes it more difficult for urban fathers to instill values such as the importance of family cohesion (DeFrain, LeMasters, and Schroff 1991).

Because the urban environment is more diverse, children learn about varieties of races, religions, sexual orientations, social classes, and other differences between and among people. Children learn about these differences whether or not they are of value to parents. Parents may find this information threatening, particularly if they themselves have come from a rural area or a different country. In contrast, in rural or less heterogeneous settings, fathers have been found to have more control over what values children are taught and experience. Exposure to persons of different races or religions may be limited in rural settings, and because fathers have a greater presence, they exert greater control over what their children experience. Moreover, because urban children live in close proximity to one another, and because they have more leisure time and fewer work-related chores than their rural counterparts, the pressure of peers is greater and more influential (DeFrain, LeMasters, and Schroff 1991). Again, these influences may be contrary to parental values, creating conflicts between fathers and their children.

Urban children, who are exposed to a great variety of differences, often develop values that are dissimilar from their parents and ancestry (DeFrain, LeMasters, and Schroff 1991). This may lead to parent–child conflicts, which are less pronounced in the rural setting. In sum, strong family ties are easier to instill and maintain in rural settings as compared to more complex urban settings.

Social Class and Fatherhood

Social class, determined primarily by education and income, also influences men's enactment of the father role (Erickson and Gecas 1991). The United States has three major socioeconomic classes: upper, middle, and lower. Middle-class fathers are more likely to view their roles as involving support and encouragement of children, whereas lower-class men are more apt to view paternal roles as enforcing discipline and exercising control. Also, middle-class fathers seem more inclined to involve themselves in child rearing, whereas working-class fathers typically have less of a desire to do so. These differences occur because middle-class families emphasize more role sharing and an egalitarian division of labor, whereas lower-class families tend toward role segregation, with women primarily responsible for child care and socialization.

There also appears to be a positive relationship between social class and parental support (Erickson and Gecas 1991). Middle-class fathers are more likely to show nurturance and affection toward their children than their lower-class counterparts and are more likely to use inductive control, such as reasoning, with children. In contrast, lower-class fathers exhibit authoritarian behavior and coercive control. Likewise, occupation, education, and income, all of which are measures of social class, influence men's attitudes and values toward parenting. Education is found to be positively related to the development of egalitarian attitudes and more favorable attitudes toward paternal involvement in child rearing, although these attitudes do not necessarily translate into significant increases in actual child caregiving behaviors. For upper-class fathers, income can have a negative or a positive effect on increased child caregiving behaviors, depending on the occupational characteristic observed. For example, the demands and the nature of the fathers' occupations (travel, hours of work, proximity of workplace, etc.) can facilitate or prohibit their daily involvement in child care. Finally, increased maternal education, income, and employment appear to influence paternal involvement positively, as women may serve as gatekeepers to the level and quality of the father–child relationship.

The influence of social class on fatherhood is pervasive and complex, and more needs to be learned about the impact of this variable on parenting. This is especially important because many other cultural determinants influence father behavior, including religion, history, law, work environments, and families' own internal processes.

Future of Fatherhood

Fatherhood is changing. However, two distinct bipolar trends—father absence versus father involvement and father provider versus father nurturer—are still evident in modern fatherhood (Atkinson and Blackwelder 1993; Rotundo 1985). An extreme form of father absence, resulting from divorce and abandonment, has become such a problem that the government is intervening through child support enforcement agencies to force men to provide financially for their children. On the other hand, there are increased numbers of younger middle-class men moving in the direction of more involvement and nurturance in child care and family life, as found in family forms such as househusband fathers and single adoptive fathers. This newer androgynous style fits best with changing goals and with the emerging broader economic and social realities. It is believed that these trends will continue despite a negative attitude by some people toward the blurring of gender roles. The future will offer fathers multiple options rather than stereotypic roles. With fewer parental prescriptions, modern men are and will continue to be freer to choose their own degree of involvement in child rearing and family life. Men (as do women) will have a broader range of parenthood possibilities from which they can choose the most appropriate fatherhood model for themselves and their circumstances.

There is a great need for further research on fathers, fatherhood, and men in families. Although much of what is known was obtained from mothers, more researchers are now obtaining information from fathers themselves. The majority of father–child family research has focused on the early part of the family life cycle—that is, pregnancy, birth, and infancy. There is a great need for further investigations during other developmental periods. It is also important to study fatherhood in different social contexts. Scholars need to make finer distinctions between male and female parenting roles and the impact of each gender on the growth and development of children. Examples of questions that need to be answered are: If society values males as parents, how can males be socialized earlier in life to become more nurturing and caregiving with children? What needs to happen to social, economic, legal, educational, and health-care systems that would enhance men's effective parenting and positive family relationships? Opportunities need to be created for the investigation of these important topics.

(See also: CHILD CUSTODY; CHILD SUPPORT; DUAL-EARNER FAMILIES; ETHNICITY; FAMILY GENDER ROLES; GAY AND LESBIAN PARENTS; GRANDPARENTHOOD; HISTORY OF THE FAMILY; MOTHERS; SINGLE PARENTS; STEPPARENTING; TEENAGE PARENTING)

BIBLIOGRAPHY

Atkinson, M. P., and Blackwelder, S. P. (1993). "Fathering in the 20th Century." *Journal of Marriage and the Family* 55:975–986.

Baranowski, J. (1985). "Men as Grandfathers." In *Dimensions of Fatherhood*, ed. S. M. H. Hanson and F. W. Bozett. Newbury Park, CA: Sage Publications.

Barret, R. L., and Robinson, B. E. (1985a). "The Adolescent Father." In *Dimensions of Fatherhood*, ed. S. M. H. Hanson and F. W. Bozett. Newbury Park, CA: Sage Publications.

Barret, R. L., and Robinson, B. E., eds. (1985b). *Fatherhood*. New York: Guilford.

Benokraitis, N. (1985). "Fathers in the Dual-Earner Family." In *Dimensions of Fatherhood*, ed. S. M. H. Hanson and F. W. Bozett. Newbury Park, CA: Sage Publications.

Benson, L. (1985). "Theoretical Perspectives." *American Behavioral Scientist* 29:25–41.

Biller, H. B. (1993). *Father and Families: Paternal Factors in Child Development*. Westport, CT: Auburn House.

Bozett, F. W., and Hanson, S. M. H., eds. (1991). *Fatherhood and Families in Cultural Context*. New York: Springer-Verlag.

Bradley, R. (1985). "Fathers and the School-Age Child." In *Dimensions of Fatherhood*, ed. S. M. H. Hanson and F. W. Bozett. Newbury Park, CA: Sage Publications.

Bronstein, P., and Cowan, C. P., eds. (1988). *Fatherhood Today: Men's Changing Role in the Family*. New York: Wiley.

Burgess, J. K. (1985). "Widowers as Fathers." In *Dimensions of Fatherhood*, ed. S. M. H. Hanson and F. W. Bozett. Newbury Park, CA: Sage Publications.

Cath, S. H.; Gurwitt, A. R.; and Gunsberg, L., eds. (1989). *Fathers and Their Families*. Hillsdale, NJ: Lawrence Erlbaum.

DeFrain, J.; LeMasters, E. E.; and Schroff, J. A. (1991). "Environment and Fatherhood: Rural and Urban Influences." In *Fatherhood and Families in Cultural Context*, ed. F. W. Bozett and S. M. H. Hanson. New York: Springer-Verlag.

Erickson, R. J., and Gecas, V. (1991). "Social Class and Fatherhood." In *Fatherhood and Families in Cultural Context*, ed. F. W. Bozett and S. M. H. Hanson. New York: Springer-Verlag.

Giveans, D. L., and Robinson, M. K. (1985). "Fathers and the Preschool-Age Child." In *Dimensions of Fatherhood*, ed. S. M. H. Hanson and F. W. Bozett. Newbury Park, CA: Sage Publications.

Griswold, R. L. (1993). *Fatherhood in America: A History*. New York: Basic Books.

Hanson, S. M. H. (1985a). "Fatherhood: Contextual Variations." *American Behavioral Scientist* 29:55–77.

Hanson, S. M. H. (1985b). "Single Custodial Fathers." In *Dimensions of Fatherhood*, ed. S. M. H. Hanson and F. W. Bozett. Newbury Park, CA: Sage Publications.

Hanson, S. M. H., and Bozett, F. W., eds. (1985a). *Dimensions of Fatherhood*. Newbury Park, CA: Sage Publications.

Hanson, S. M. H., and Bozett, F. W. (1985b). "Fatherhood: A Library." *Marriage and Family Review* 9:229–253.

Hanson, S. M. H., and Bozett, F. W. (1987). "Fatherhood: A Review and Resources." *Family Relations* 36:333–340.

Hyde, B. L., and Texidor, M. S. (1988). "A Description of the Fathering Experience Among Black Fathers." *Journal of Black Nurses Association* 2:67–78.

Klinman, D., and Kohl, R. (1984). *Fatherhood USA*. New York: Garland.

Lamb, M. E. (1981). "The Development of Father–Infant Relationships." In *The Role of the Father in Child Development*, ed. M. E. Lamb. New York: Wiley.

Lamb, M. E., ed. (1987). *The Father's Role: Cross Cultural Perspectives*. Hillsdale, NJ: Lawrence Erlbaum.

LaRossa, R., and Reitzes, D. C. (1993). "Continuity and Change in Middle-Class Fatherhood." *Journal of Marriage and the Family* 55:455–468.

Lewis, R. A., and Salt, R. E., eds. (1985). *Men in Families*. Newbury Park, CA: Sage Publications.

Martin, D. H. (1985). "Fathers and Adolescents." In *Dimensions of Fatherhood*, ed. S. M. H. Hanson and F. W. Bozett. Newbury Park, CA: Sage Publications.

May, K. A., and Perrin, S. P. (1985). "Prelude: Pregnancy and Birth." In *Dimensions of Fatherhood*, ed. S. M. H. Hanson and F. W. Bozett. Newbury Park, CA: Sage Publications.

McAdoo, J. L. (1988). "Changing Perspectives on the Role of the Black Father." In *Fatherhood Today: Men's Changing Role in the Family*, ed. P. Bronstein and C. P. Cowan. New York: Wiley.

Mirande, A. (1991). "Ethnicity and Fatherhood." In *Fatherhood and Families in Cultural Context*, ed. F. W. Bozett and S. M. H. Hanson. New York: Springer-Verlag.

Parke, R. D., and Tinsley, B. R. (1981). "The Father's Role in Infancy: Determinants of Involvement in Caregiving and Play." In *The Role of the Father in Child Development*, ed. M. E. Lamb. New York: Wiley.

Roberts, C. L., and Zuengler, K. L. (1985). "The Postparental Transition and Beyond." In *Dimensions of Fatherhood*, ed. S. M. H. Hanson and F. W. Bozett. Newbury Park, CA: Sage Publications.

Roopnarine, J. L., and Miller, B. C. (1985). "Transitions to Fatherhood." In *Dimensions of Fatherhood*, ed. S. M. H. Hanson and F. W. Bozett. Newbury Park, CA: Sage Publications.

Rotundo, E. A. (1985). "American Fatherhood: A Historical Perspective." *American Behavioral Scientist* 29:7–24.

Staples, R. (1988). "The Black American Family." In *Ethnic Families in America: Patterns and Variations*, ed. C. H. Mindel, R. W. Habenstein, and R. W. Wright, Jr. New York: Elsevier.

Swanson, J. M. (1985). "Men and Family Planning." In *Dimensions of Fatherhood*, ed. S. M. H. Hanson and F. W. Bozett. Newbury Park, CA: Sage Publications.

Walters, L. H., and Elam, A. W. (1985). "The Father and the Law." *American Behavioral Scientist* 29:78–112.

SHIRLEY M. H. HANSON

FICTIVE KINSHIP

The social universe established by kinship cannot be defined solely in terms of biology and marriage alone. Indeed, kinship establishes the base, but not the totality, of what individuals think of as family. The roles that family plays in a society are not complete without the inclusion of fictive kin relationships. They are fictive in the sense that these ties have a basis different from bonds of blood and marriage, not in the sense that these relationships are any less important. In many societies, fictive ties are as important as or more important than comparable relationships created by blood, marriage, or adoption.

Briefly defined, fictive kinship involves the extension of kinship obligations and relationships to individuals specifically not otherwise included in the kinship universe. Godparenthood (or coparenthood), in its many manifestations, is the most commonly cited illustration, but there are numerous other examples. In many societies, people have "aunts" or "uncles" who are merely their parents' closest friends. Members of religious movements may refer to each other as "brother" or "sister" while observing the rules and prohibitions attached to those statuses. Crime networks and youth gangs employ kinship bonds and ideas of "blood brotherhood" as organizing principles. Nontraditional family forms such as gay and lesbian unions may be defined in traditional kinship terms.

Nonetheless, all fictive kin relationships have one element in common: They are defined by criteria distinct from those establishing blood or marriage relationships. Fictive relationships may mimic the ties they copy, but they are defined in their own terms. These terms may have a religious or economic component, be predicated on existing social networks, or manipulate reality to fill gaps in real kinship networks. Fictive relationships serve to broaden mutual support networks, create a sense of community, and enhance social control. In essence, fictive kin ties elaborate social networks and regularize interactions with people otherwise outside the boundaries of family. Unlike true kinship bonds, fictive kin ties are usually voluntary and require the consent of both parties in establishing the bond. The idea that you cannot pick your relatives does not apply to fictive kin.

The concept of godparenthood (sometimes referred to as coparenthood) is certainly the best documented example of a fictive kin relationship. *Compadrazgo*, as it occurs throughout Mexico and Latin America, is an elaboration of the Catholic concept of baptismal sponsorship blended with precolonial religious beliefs. However, it is less a relationship between godparents and godchild than a tie between the parents and the godparents. By linking nonrelated families, *compadrazgo* extends formalized social networks. Individuals often seek to establish ties with wealthier families, establishing a sponsorship and providing the possibility of upward social mobility for the child (Foster 1967; Kemper 1982). Similar relationships exist in many other societies, including *dharma atmyo* in Bangladesh (Sarker 1980), *kumstvo* in the former Yugoslavia (Halpern 1967; Hammel 1968), and *kivrelik* in Turkey (Magnarella and Turkdogan 1973).

Another common form of fictive kinship involves the extension of brotherhood roles and obligations between unrelated males of the same generation. Among the Azande in Africa, for example, the concept of blood brotherhood was well established (Evans-Pritchard 1963). In its strictest sense, blood brotherhood ties are sealed by ingestion or some other "mixing" of each other's blood, but this need not always be the case. Among the Serbs in Europe, for example, blood brotherhoods (*pobratimstvo*) were traditionally established when a person was seriously ill or believed himself to be near death. The ceremony, performed at a grave site, involved no exchange of blood. *Pobratim* were supposed to behave toward one another as brothers for life, and their children were prohibited from marrying each other (Halpern 1967). Other forms of less rigid brotherhood extension are also common and are better described as partnerships. Among the Netsilik of North America, such partnerships (*niqaitorvigit*) defined an elaborate pattern of sharing relationships. These sharing relationships were a permanent way of distributing meat and helped spread the risk generated by unpredictable food resources (Balikci 1970).

Many important social relationships are established through marriage. In some instances, a tie established through marriage may be crucial to inheritance (providing continuity to a descent group) or maintenance of social bonds. In cases where families do not have children to marry, fictive marriage may serve as a substitute. Among the Kwakiutl of North America, status was passed from grandfather to grandson through the son-in-law. A man without daughters might "marry" a son to another man to create this important link. If he had no children, the marriage tie might be created to a body part as, for example, a marriage between a son-in-law and his father-in-law's leg (Boas 1897). The Nuer of North Africa "marry" a woman to a man who has died without producing heirs (ghost marriage). The woman is actually married to the ghost through a living male relative, and any children resulting from the bond belong to the ghost father and inherit his property (Evans-Pritchard 1951). Another traditional form of fictive marriage existed among the American Plains Indians in the institution of the *berdache*. In the *berdache*, a man might assume both the dress and the role of a woman, often "marrying" another man.

In postindustrial societies, it is possible to argue that fictive kinship ties have taken on increased importance. Social and geographic mobility, soaring divorce rates, and nontraditional family forms have produced social networks based more on voluntary ties than on traditional bonds of blood and marriage. There is, for example, a growing body of literature describing the importance of fictive kin ties in U.S. African-American urban communities and their effects on everything from child care to educational achievement (Fordham 1986; Johnson and Barer 1990). Some researchers have gone so far as to describe ethnicity as being an elaborated form of fictive kinship (Yelvington and Bentley 1991). At the same time, nontraditional families, such as gay or lesbian couples in which children may have two fathers or mothers, can also be characterized as having elements of fictive kinship. Gerontologists and social workers have also emphasized the importance of fictive kin networks to medical treatment and mental health as individuals seek to fill gaps in their existing support networks (Gubrium and Buckholdt 1982; Wentowski 1981).

(*See also:* ETHNICITY; EXTENDED FAMILY; GANGS; GAY AND LESBIAN PARENTS; INHERITANCE; KINSHIP; RELIGION)

BIBLIOGRAPHY

Balikci, A. (1970). *The Netsilik Eskimo.* Garden City, NY: Natural History Press.

Boas, F. (1897). *Social Organization and Secret Societies of the Kwakiutl Indians.* U.S. National Museum Annual Report, 1895. Washington, DC.

Evans-Pritchard, E. E. (1951). *Kinship and Marriage Among the Nuer.* Oxford: Clarendon Press.

Evans-Pritchard, E. E. (1963). *Essays in Social Anthropology.* New York: Free Press.

Fordham, S. (1986). "Black Students' School Success: Coping with the 'Burden of "Acting White." ' " *Urban Review* 18:176–206.

Foster, G. M. (1967). *Tzintzuntzan: Mexican Peasants in a Changing World.* Boston: Little, Brown.

Gubrium, J. F., and Buckholdt, D. R. (1982). "Fictive Family: Everyday Usage, Analytic, and Human Service Considerations." *American Anthropologist* 84:878–885.

Halpern, J. M. (1967). *A Serbian Village.* New York: Harper & Row.

Hammel, E. A. (1968). *Alternative Social Structures and Ritual Relations in the Balkans.* Englewood Cliffs, NJ: Prentice Hall.

Johnson, C. L., and Barer, B. M. (1990). "Families and Networks Among Older Inner-City Blacks." *Gerontologist* 30:726–733.

Kemper, R. V. (1982). "The *Compadrazgo* in Urban Mexico." *Anthropological Quarterly* 55:17–30.

Magnarella, P. J., and Turkdogan, O. (1973). "Descent, Affinity, and Ritual Relations in Eastern Turkey." *American Anthropologist* 75:1626–1633.

Sarker, P. C. (1980). "Dharma-Atmyo: Fictive Kin Relationship in Rural Bangladesh." *Eastern Anthropologist* 33:55–61.

Sofola, J. A. (1983). "The *Onyenualagu* (Godparent) in Traditional and Modern African Communities: Implications for Juvenile Delinquency." *Journal of Black Studies* 14:21–70.

Wentowski, G. J. (1981). "Reciprocity and the Coping Strategies of Older People: Cultural Dimensions of Network Building." *Gerontologist* 21:600–609.

Yelvington, K. A., and Bentley, G. C. (1991). "Ethnicity as Practice? A Comment on Bentley." *Comparative Studies in Society and History* 33:158–168.

RICHARD A. WAGNER

FILIAL RESPONSIBILITY

Filial responsibility refers to grown children's responsibility or duty to provide aged parents with protection, care, or financial support when needed. This duty is primarily supported by values, attitudes, and customs, but in some cases legal requirements apply.

It is commonly believed that at some time in the United States' past, grown children strongly endorsed an obligation to provide for their parents, even to live with them if necessary, but that modern-day children feel no such obligation. However, decades of research have refuted this myth by showing that feelings of family responsibility to the elderly are firmly rooted in American society and that twentieth-century families are providing extensive care and support for elderly parents. Furthermore, the need for care by elderly parents in the past is not comparable to the much greater need of the late twentieth century when the elderly account for a significantly larger percentage of the United States' population.

Historical Trends in the United States

The American colonies adopted many aspects of the Elizabethan Poor Laws, which held each town responsible for its destitute, but which also held that children had primary responsibility for helping needy parents and that the community was not responsible until the children had made their maximum effort (Schorr 1980). However, such requirements had little effect due to the limited life expectancy and considerable economic power of parents in preindustrial times. As late as 1900, life expectancy in America was only forty-seven years, fewer than one in ten Americans was age fifty-five or older, and only one in twenty-five was age sixty-five or older (U.S. Senate Special Committee on Aging 1991). Furthermore, in preindustrial times the older generation owned the land and equipment necessary to earn an income, so they were not likely to become dependent on their children for support. In fact, grown children were unlikely to achieve financial independence until they inherited property from their parents (Schorr 1980).

It was not until the twentieth century that the concept of filial responsibility as a duty became an issue. With financial independence tied to wages in an industrial society, and with growth in the population of older people, support for the aged became a societal concern. At the turn of the century, older people who were unable to continue in the labor force and lacked sufficient private resources had few options beyond turning to their children for support.

Legal Requirements

Many states have had filial support statutes on the books since the time of their admission to the Union, but these laws have rarely been enforced. Legislation requiring grown children to provide support for aged parents was developed primarily as a means for states to recover public funds spent on services for an older person, rather than as a way to ensure that older people receive support. At one point, among the fifty states and the District of Columbia, twenty-one regions required a contribution from grown children but paid assistance even when the children did not contribute, fourteen required contributions and reduced the assistance paid by the required amount whether or not it was contributed, and sixteen had no requirements for grown children to provide support (Schorr 1980).

A 1988 survey of state statutes on filial responsibility found that thirty states had some type of law regarding family responsibility for support of elderly persons (Bulcroft, Van Leynseele, and Borgatta 1989). However, the laws varied as to who was the first source of support and who else shared responsibility, what sort of support and how much was required, and how such regulations would be enforced. Most states only required support for parents from children "of sufficient ability," but they did not clearly define this qualification. Filial responsibility laws have had only limited enforcement and have rarely been tested in court, probably because of their vagueness and because of social norms that find state intervention in family matters distasteful.

Attitudes and Expectations

When asked, the majority of American adults report feeling considerable responsibility to take care of aging parents, including adjusting their family schedules to provide care and assisting parents financially (Blieszner and Hamon 1992; Brody, Johnsen, and Fulcomer 1984). However, some research has found that the expectations adult children have as to the level of help they should provide to parents are higher than parents' expectations of the amount of help children should provide (Hamon and Blieszner 1990). In general, parents prefer to maintain their independence as they age and do not want or expect direct assistance from their grown children, except in situations of extreme need (Mancini and Blieszner 1989).

In fact, many families may not give much thought to issues of caregiving until a crisis arises. For example, one study of families in which caregivers were caring for their elderly parents in their own homes found that while 93 percent of the caregivers said they believed that care of frail elderly relatives was their legitimate responsibility, 46 percent said they had not expected to be caring for their parents this way nor had they made any plans in advance for providing this care, and approximately 67 percent of the elderly parents who were receiving help had not expected to need assistance from their children (Cox, Parsons, and Kimboko 1988).

However, not all grown children are called on to provide help to aging parents. Many older parents remain self-sufficient until the end of their lives, and others who live far from their children rely on friends, neighbors, or paid helpers. Furthermore, many older parents still provide their grown children with various types of support, such as financial assistance, child care, advice, and emotional support.

Filial Responsible Behavior

Although not legally required to do so, many grown children do respond to their parents' needs, often at great personal sacrifice. In fact, families are the United States' primary resource for providing help to older people who need assistance. Family members provide 80 percent to 90 percent of the help older people need with household tasks, transportation, managing finances, shopping, and personal care (Brody 1985; Older Women's League 1989).

Factors that predict which children are most likely to take on the primary caregiving role for a parent who needs care include gender, geography, and being an only child (Brody 1990). Daughters and daughters-in-law are more likely to take on this role than are sons or sons-in-law. Daughters are also more likely than sons to incorporate regular assistance to parents into their daily activities, to provide hands-on personal care, and to help with daily household chores. Sons are more likely to limit their help to specific tasks, such as assisting with financial management or transportation (Matthews and Rosner 1988; Montgomery and Kamo 1989). However, some research suggests that sons become more involved when parents' needs escalate due to declining health (Hamon 1992).

Although geographic distance between grown children and their parents does not seem to affect their emotional closeness, children who live geographically closer to their parents visit more often and provide more help with tasks such as household chores and personal care (Moss, Moss, and Moles 1985). At least one study has found that geographically distant daughters of widowed elderly mothers report feelings of guilt and strain related to not being able to do more to help (Schoonover et al. 1988).

An extensive body of research literature documents the high costs to millions of grown children who are providing care to frail or disabled elderly parents (AARP 1988; Older Women's League 1989; U.S. House Select Committee on Aging 1987). The majority of these caregivers provide ongoing assistance with household and/or personal tasks such as shopping, banking, housekeeping, meal preparation, bathing, and dressing.

A large survey that collected data from a random sample of U.S. households (AARP 1988) found that approximately 3.7 million households contained current caregivers, the majority of whom were women providing care to a parent or grandparent. On average, these caregivers had been providing care twelve hours per week for the past two years. Personal costs these caregivers reported included spending less time on leisure activities (51%), spending less time with their own families (34%), paying less attention to their own health (33%), being unable to take a vacation (28%), and losing time from their jobs (38%).

The emotional stresses and burdens family caregivers experience are often severe. Caregivers report feelings of depression, anxiety, emotional exhaustion, guilt, and hostility related to their various caregiving responsibilities.

Motivations for Filial Responsibility

Although many American adults clearly feel responsibility for their aging parents and do provide them with care and support, no single theory has emerged to explain their motivations for doing so. One explanation for grown children's motives in taking responsibility for parents is the idea that accepting responsibility for one's parents is a normal developmental life stage that adults must complete to move on to meet the challenges of their own aging successfully (Blenkner 1965). This view sees dependency as a normal stage in old age and caring for dependent parents as part of the maturation process of middle-age children.

Probably the most widely used explanation for adult children's acceptance of responsibility for their aging parents is social exchange theory. This theory suggests that people strive for a balance of costs and rewards in their relationships with others and tend to reciprocate favors received by helping those who help them (Nye 1979). Thus, many adult children feel that they should reciprocate the care they received from their parents while growing up by providing care to their parents when the parents need help. This motivation may lead grown children to take on high levels of burden in caring for parents and to feel guilty that they cannot do even more, because they believe they can never truly reciprocate for all their parents have done for them (Brody 1985).

Some theorists suggest that anticipation of future rewards also enters into the exchange when adult children provide care for aging parents. Grown children may see filial responsible behavior as a family duty that future generations will then provide for them if needed, or they may expect future rewards from their parents through inheritance (Sussman 1985).

Other explanations for filial responsibility include feelings of affection and emotional closeness between grown children and their parents; the influence of social norms that assume adult children, especially daughters, will care for parents who need help; and endorsement of religious or other moral beliefs that require this behavior (Blieszner and Hamon 1992; Thompson 1989).

Some research indicates that many adult daughters who provide care to dependent elderly mothers report that they do so from choice rather than obligation and that they see their mothers as making important contributions in return, by offering love, information, advice, or money (Walker, Pratt, and Oppy 1992; Walker et al. 1990). This research also suggests that better relationships exist between mothers and their caregiving daughters when the mothers believe their daughters are providing care as a choice rather than as a duty.

While both generations seem to prefer that adult children who take on responsibility for aging parents do so primarily because of feelings of affection for their parents, feelings of obligation are also an important motivator. Furthermore, the burden of providing care to a sick or dependent older parent can introduce severe strain into the parent–child relationship. The idea that affection is a necessary motive for adults to provide care to their parents can be confusing for both generations and distressing for children who accept the responsibility primarily as a duty.

Issues for the Future

The aging of the population of the United States raises important questions about who will help the increasing numbers of older people when they can no longer take care of themselves completely. According to the 1990 census, 12.5 percent of the population of the United States is aged sixty-five or over (U.S. Bureau of the Census 1992a). The population of Americans over age sixty-five is growing faster than the total population. The most rapidly growing age group is people age eighty-five or over, who are the group of older persons most likely to need personal assistance. Between 1950 and 1980, the portion of the population age sixty-five or over increased 108 percent and that of the population age eighty-five or over increased 288 percent, while the increase for the rest of the population was only 50 percent (U.S. Bureau of the Census 1983). Between 1980 and 1991, the percentage of the population over age sixty-five increased by 24 percent, more than twice the 11 percent increase for the total population (U.S. Bureau of the Census 1992b).

This means that the elderly dependency ratio, which refers to the number of people over age sixty-five for every 100 people of working age, is increasing in the United States. In one way or another, younger generations will increasingly be required to meet the needs of older Americans.

Most older people report that they do not want to become dependent on their grown children for care, nor do they want to move in with their children. A national housing survey found that the majority of people over age sixty-five own their own homes and want to remain in those homes as they age. However, many of them will need help with chores and daily tasks as they grow older. Others will suffer acute illnesses or chronic disabling conditions that require extensive care (AARP 1990).

Policymakers in society disagree about how to provide elderly citizens with the help they need. Some argue that traditional religious and family values require that families of elderly persons assume primary responsibility for whatever care they need. Others maintain that the public sector should provide elderly Americans with care when they need it, because distributing the burden of care across society is a more equitable solution than leaving the responsibility to individual families.

In a major lecture in 1984, Elaine Brody, a noted gerontologist, raised issues that were even more crucially important ten years later. She contended that it is important to question the values that underlie beliefs about what adult children should do for their dependent elderly parents; she challenged society's standards of individual filial responsibility; and she suggested that society has a collective filial responsibility to provide dependent elderly persons with the formal support services they need (Brody 1985).

The question of whether responsibility for older people belongs to individual families or to the society at large remains highly controversial. As the population continues to age and pressure for family assistance increases, debate regarding the extent of grown children's responsibility for their parents is likely to intensify.

(*See also:* ELDER ABUSE; ELDERS; EXCHANGE THEORY; FAMILY GENDER ROLES; INHERITANCE; INTERGENERATIONAL RELATIONS; RETIREMENT; WIDOWHOOD)

BIBLIOGRAPHY

American Association of Retired Persons (AARP). (1988). *A National Survey of Caregivers*. Washington, DC: AARP Health Advocacy Services Section.

American Association of Retired Persons (AARP). (1990). *Understanding Senior Housing in the 1990s*. Washington, DC: AARP Health Advocacy Services Section.

Blenkner, M. (1965). "Social Work and Family Relationships in Later Life With Some Thoughts on Filial Maturity." In *Social Structure and the Family: Generational Relations*, ed. E. Shanas and G. Streib. Englewood Cliffs, NJ: Prentice Hall.

Blieszner, R., and Hamon, R. R. (1992). "Filial Responsibility: Attitudes, Motivators, and Behaviors." In *Gender, Families, and Elder Care*, ed. J. W. Dwyer and R. T. Coward. Newbury Park, CA: Sage Publications.

Brody, E. M. (1985). "Parent Care as a Normative Family Stress." *Gerontologist* 25:19–29.

Brody, E. M. (1990). *Women in the Middle*. New York: Springer-Verlag.

Brody, E. M.; Johnsen, P. T.; and Fulcomer, M. C. (1984). "What Should Adult Children Do for Elderly Parents? Opinions and Preferences of Three Generations of Women." *Journal of Gerontology* 39:736–746.

Bulcroft, K.; Van Leynseele, J.; and Borgatta, E. F. (1989). "Filial Responsibility Laws." *Research on Aging* 11:374–393.

Cox, E. O.; Parsons, R. J.; and Kimboko, P. J. (1988). "Social Services and the Intergenerational Caregivers: Issues for Social Work." *Social Work* 33:430–434.

Hamon, R. R. (1992). "Filial Role Enactment by Adult Children." *Family Relations* 41:91–96.

Hamon, R. R., and Blieszner, R. (1990). "Filial Responsibility Expectations Among Adult Child–Older Parent Pairs." *Journal of Gerontology:* 45:110–112.

Mancini, J. A., and Blieszner, R. (1989). "Aging Parents and Adult Children: Research Themes in Intergenerational Relations." *Journal of Marriage and the Family* 51:275–290.

Matthews, S. H., and Rosner, T. T. (1988). "Shared Filial Responsibility: The Family as the Primary Caregiver." *Journal of Marriage and the Family* 50:185–195.

Montgomery, R. J. V., and Kamo, Y. (1989). "Parent Care by Sons and Daughters." In *Aging Parents and Adult Children*, ed. J. A. Mancini. Lexington, MA: Lexington Books.

Moss, M. S.; Moss, S. Z.; and Moles, E. L. (1985). "The Quality of Relationships Between Elderly Parents and Their Out-of-Town Children." *Gerontologist* 25:134–140.

Nye, F. I. (1979). "Choice, Exchange, and the Family." In *Contemporary Theories About the Family*, Vol. II, ed. W. R. Burr, R. Hill, F. I. Nye, and I. L. Reiss. New York: Free Press.

Older Women's League. (1989). *Failing America's Caregivers: A Status Report on Women Who Care*. Washington, DC: Older Women's League.

Schoonover, C. B.; Brody, E. M.; Hoffman, C.; and Kleban, M. H. (1988). "Parent Care and Geographically Distant Children." *Research on Aging* 10:472–492.

Schorr, A. L. (1980). *"Thy Father and Thy Mother": A Second Look at Filial Responsibility and Family Policy*. Washington, DC: Social Security Administration.

Sussman, M. B. (1985). "The Family Life of Old People." In *Handbook of Aging and the Social Sciences*, ed. R. H. Binstock and E. Shanas. New York: Van Nostrand-Reinhold.

Thompson, L. (1989). "Contextual and Relational Morality: Intergenerational Responsibility in Later Life." In *Aging*

Parents and Adult Children, ed. J. A. Mancini. Lexington, MA: Lexington Books.

U.S. Bureau of the Census. (1983). *America in Transition: An Aging Society*. Washington, DC: U.S. Government Printing Office.

U.S. Bureau of the Census. (1992a). *Sixty-Five Plus in America*. Washington, DC: U.S. Government Printing Office.

U.S. Bureau of the Census. (1992b). *Statistical Abstract of the United States, 1992*. Washington, DC: U.S. Government Printing Office.

U.S. House Select Committee on Aging. (1987). *Exploding the Myths: Caregiving in America*. Washington, DC: U.S. Government Printing Office.

U.S. Senate Special Committee on Aging. (1991). *Aging America: Trends and Projections*. Washington, DC: U.S. Government Printing Office.

Walker, A. J.; Pratt, C. C.; and Oppy, N. C. (1992). "Perceived Reciprocity in Family Caregiving." *Family Relations* 41:82–85.

Walker, A. J.; Pratt, C. C.; Shin, H.-Y.; and Oppy, N. C. (1990). "Motives for Parental Caregiving and Relationship Quality." *Family Relations* 39:51–56.

LYNN B. OSTERKAMP

FOSTER PARENTING

Foster parenting is the temporary provision of parenting services, in a family home, to children whose birth parents cannot or will not provide adequate care for them. Government child welfare agencies in each state license foster parents, who then may work directly for the state or under the umbrella of a private child welfare agency that contracts with the state. States pay foster parents to care for the foster children, based on the age of the child. The base, monthly maintenance rate for a two-year-old foster child in 1992 averaged $310.25, with a high of $588.00 in Alaska to a low of $161.00 in West Virginia. For a sixteen-year-old foster child the monthly rate averaged $385.90, with a high of $621.00 in Alaska and a low of $234.00 in Alabama.

Foster parenting in the United States dates to the mid-1800s, when Charles Brace and the New York Children's Aid Society began a program of placing children from cities with rural families in the South, West, and Midwest. These families were not paid in dollars for the care of the child; instead, the child's labor was exchanged for his or her care. Under this program as many as 100,000 children were transported on "orphan trains" to new families between 1854 to 1929 (Bremer 1971).

The number of foster families in the United States has been declining. Estimates place the number in 1991 at 100,000, down from 125,000 in 1988 and 142,000 in 1978. According to some estimates, as many as 70 percent of children in state custody, nationwide, are cared for by foster parents in foster family homes. The remainder of these children are placed with relatives (kinship care), in group homes that employ professional staff and houseparents, or in institutions such as state hospitals and juvenile correctional facilities.

Foster parenting is recognized as a difficult and challenging undertaking. The children often exhibit behavioral and emotional problems due to a number of possible factors, including previous abuse and neglect they may have experienced, personality disorders, drug and alcohol problems, and difficulty adjusting to the new setting because of the trauma of separation. Birth parents may intrude and undermine the foster parents' efforts, and financial and service support by the state agency may be minimal. Effective foster parents are believed to possess the following characteristics: the ability and willingness to learn and accept help from outside agencies, warmth and the ability to understand and accept children, a high frustration tolerance, good communication skills, good physical and emotional health, and a sense of humor (Jordan and Rodway 1984).

Issues in foster parenting reflect problems and developments in the larger system (Pecora, Whittaker, and Maluccio 1992). In the 1970s, researchers, practitioners, and policymakers expressed growing concerns about the system. Although foster care was designed to be temporary, children stayed too long in foster care to the extent that it had become a permanent status for many children. Children "drifted" from one placement to another, with little stability or continuity. Children came into custody too easily, with little attempt to preserve them in their family of origin. These concerns coalesced into the "permanency planning movement" whose philosophy and goals emphasized the vital importance of providing lifelong, continuous, family relationships.

In 1980, the federal government passed the Adoption Assistance and Child Welfare Act, whose purpose was to change the foster care system by promoting permanency planning. The law required that "reasonable efforts" be made to prevent the unnecessary separation of children and their parents. If out-of-home placement was required, the law then mandated that a permanency goal be established, with first priority given to reunification with the family and second priority given to adoption. Long-term foster care was discouraged. Because of the permanency planning movement, the number of children in foster care declined by 50 percent in five years, from more than 500,000 in 1977 to 243,000 in 1982. During this time fewer young children were placed in care, more children were reunited with their families, and more children with special needs were adopted.

Since 1982, however, the number of children in foster care at any one time has continued to rise, to about 400,000 in 1990. Experts attribute this rise to many factors, including decreasing social supports to families in the 1980s, rising unemployment, deteriorating housing, increasing substance abuse, and the failure of both the federal and state governments to appropriate sufficient funds to carry out the permanency planning provisions of the Adoption Assistance and Child Welfare Act.

While the number of children in foster care increased, the number of foster families declined, as noted previously, from 142,000 in 1978 to 100,000 in 1991. Numerous factors account for this decline. Foster parents work twenty-four hours a day, often with inadequate training and support. Since reimbursement rates typically do not cover the costs of providing care, foster parents must subsidize the system out of their own pockets. The types of children in foster care have changed and are generally regarded as more difficult to care for (children with HIV infection; crack-addicted and drug-exposed infants; children from multiproblem and substance-abusing families; and adolescents with serious behavioral and emotional problems). The lifestyle of the American family has also changed so that more women, who have traditionally been the primary caregivers in foster care, now are employed full-time outside the home.

Another important factor in the decline of foster parenting is the role confusion that was engendered in the movement toward permanency planning. With the permanency planning emphasis on reunification and adoption, the role of the foster parent is conflicted. Foster parents can serve a useful function in helping children reunite with their birth parents by encouraging visitation and by serving as role models for birth parents. However, studies have also shown that foster parents are one of the best adoption resources for foster children (Barth and Berry 1988). If foster parents view themselves as an adoption resource, can they in good conscience promote and participate actively in reunification? If social workers ask that foster parents focus on reunification, and not consider themselves as adoption resources, will this hurt the child's chances for successful adoption if reunification efforts fail? If the foster parent role is

defined in a more neutral fashion, as providing temporary care only, is not this wasting a potent reunification or adoption resource? Foster parents are understandably confused about their place in the system of care.

To address these issues, many foster parents and professionals are advocating the professionalization of foster parents. Professionalization would involve enhancing the status and compensation of foster parents so that they are viewed as essential members of the professional service team. They would receive ongoing, intensive training, supervision, and support, including respite care and quick access to social workers. Professionalism could involve a degree of specialization in which foster parents and their training would be matched to specific types of children. A career ladder could also be established, with recognition of highly qualified and effective foster parents as "master" foster parents.

Implementation of professional foster parenting has been confined principally to pilot programs providing "therapeutic foster care" to youths with serious behavioral and emotional problems. The greatest obstacle to widespread implementation appears to be inadequate fiscal resources for sufficient compensation, lower social work caseloads, training, and other support services. If resources are not allocated to enhance the attractiveness of foster parenting, then the availability of foster family homes can only be expected to continue to decline. This decline would mean that increasingly higher numbers of foster children would be living in group homes and institutions, further undermining the principle of family relationships that is the hallmark of permanency planning.

(*See also:* ADOPTION; CHILD CUSTODY; ENTITLEMENTS; GUARDIANSHIP; SUBSTITUTE CAREGIVERS)

BIBLIOGRAPHY

Barth, R. P., and Berry, M. (1988). *Adoption and Disruption: Risks, Rates, and Responses.* Hawthorne, NY: Aldine.

Bremer, R., ed. (1971). *Children and Youth in America: A Documentary History, 1865–1965*, Vol. 2. Cambridge, MA: Harvard University Press.

Jordan, A., and Rodway, M. R. (1984). "Correlates of Effective Foster Parenting." *Social Work Research and Abstracts* 20:27–31.

Pecora, P. J.; Whittaker, J. K.; and Maluccio, A. N. (1992). *The Child Welfare Challenge: Policy, Practice, Research.* Hawthorne, NY: Aldine.

CHRISTOPHER G. PETR

FRIENDSHIP

Friendship is a relationship with broad, ambiguous, and even shifting boundaries. The terms "friend" and "friendship" mean different things to different people and different things to the same person at different times. To think and communicate effectively about the topic, people find it necessary to use distinctions such as true friends, best friends, good friends, casual friends, work friends, social friends, and friendly acquaintances. In spite of this vague and seemingly intangible quality, friendships contribute in important ways to psychological development during childhood and adolescence and to emotional health and well-being throughout various phases of adulthood.

Social and behavioral scientists devoted little attention to friendship prior to the late 1960s. Since that time, however, the number of researchers concentrating on friendship has gradually increased until it is now one of the more favored topics among relationship scholars. Although scholars from different social sciences use different approaches to friendship, they have arrived at a remarkable degree of agreement in clarifying its meaning and importance.

Definition and Characteristics

Unlike other important relationships, friendship is not defined by kinship, legal ties, or formal social obligations. Normally, there are no ceremonies surrounding the formation of a friendship. In fact, friendships rarely begin with two people jointly declaring that, "from this day forward, we will be friends." Rather, friendships develop gradually and often unwittingly as the partners begin doing "friendship things" together. Once formed, friendships are largely free of clear social norms or expectations that dictate when the partners should get together and how they should interact when they do. When friendships end, they rarely do so as a result of an announced decision by one or both parties. They merely fade away as the partners cease doing the friendship things that gave the relationship its meaning.

This lack of social definition gives friendship its vague and intangible character. And yet, it is a relationship that seems to exist in a recognizable form in most (but not all) cultures. This combination of factors led Robert Paine (1969) to describe friendship as an "institutionalized non-institution." What, then, verifies a friendship? A friendship exists in the fact that the partners commit time to interaction with one another apart from outside pressures or constraints. In friendship, the partners' lives are interdependent on a voluntary basis. In more structured relationships, such as marriage, the partners' lives are also interdependent, but much of the interdependence is based on social norms and expectations obligating them to relate to one another in prescribed ways. Thus, many behavioral scientists in fields ranging from anthropology to sociology to psychology characterize friendship as a voluntary relationship.

A second key aspect of friendship is what Gerald Suttles (1970) called the "person-qua-person" factor. That is, friends respond to one another as unique, genuine, and irreplaceable individuals. They do not see one another as mere role occupants or representatives of particular groups or statuses. Friends express this focus on individuality as a personalized interest and concern. Combining these two characteristics provides the following definition: Friendship is a relationship in which the partners respond to one another with a personalized interest and concern and commit time to one another in the absence of constraints toward interaction that are external to the relationship itself. The more these two factors are in evidence, the stronger the friendship.

According to this definition, friendship is a matter of degree rather than an all-or-none proposition. Perhaps it would be more accurate, even if awkward, to speak of degrees of "friendness" rather than friendship versus nonfriendship. Evidence suggests that forms of relating following this pattern exist in most cultures.

Benefits of Friendship

As part of their unconstrained and personalized interaction, friends benefit one another in innumerable ways. They listen, encourage, give advice, help with chores, loan money, have fun, exchange trivia, share confidences, and simply "are there" for one another. The specifics vary from time to time and from one friendship to another.

Although several scholars have suggested ways of grouping these various benefits into a manageable number of classes, many researchers consider just two classes of rewards adequate for most purposes. These two classes are most often labeled as instrumental and expressive. Instrumental rewards involve receiving tangible resources, such as goods or money, and obtaining assistance in completing tasks or reaching specific goals. Expressive rewards involve receiving personal advice, encouragement, and emotional support from an understanding confidant.

Although this two-fold classification is adequate for many purposes, people sometimes find it useful to consider specific rewards that are (or are not) present in a friendship or that are present in one friendship but not another. Some researchers have developed more detailed sets of rewards for exploring such nuances. Paul H. Wright (1978, 1985), for example, identified five interpersonal rewards or "friendship values": utility (providing material resources or helping with tasks), stimulation (suggesting new ideas or activities), ego support (providing encouragement by downplaying setbacks and emphasizing successes), self-affirmation (behaving in ways that reinforce valued self-characteristics), and security (providing a feeling of safety and unquestioned trust).

Robert B. Hays (1984) formulated a list of four rewarding "friendship behaviors": companionship (sharing activities or one another's company), consideration (helpfulness, utility, support), communication (discussing information about one's self, exchanging ideas and confidences), and affection (expressing sentiments felt toward one's partner).

How Universal and How Voluntary?

Just how universal is friendship? Given the voluntary and preferential nature of friendship, there are undoubtedly cultures in which such relationships cannot thrive. There are a few known cultures, for instance, where personal relationships are closely formulated in terms of status and kinship (DuBois 1974) or where speaking taboos are confining and rigidly enforced. In these cultures, friendships are rare or nonexistent. So far, however, evidence concerning societies lacking friendships has been confined to small, enclosed cultures that appear to be exceptions that prove the rule.

In contrast, some anthropologists suggest that the human inclination to form friendships is often strong enough to overcome cultural restrictions. Sarah Uhl (1991), for example, observed that some women in the Andalusian region of Spain bypassed explicit prohibitions against forming friendships. They developed voluntary and personalized nonkin bonds under the guise of interaction required by their daily domestic chores. The point remains, however, that friendships are embedded in differing cultural contexts. Researchers studying the nature and significance of friendship at different points in the life cycle have concentrated mostly on complex Western societies, especially the United States. Therefore, their findings may not apply in the same ways to friendships in other cultures.

Is friendship truly voluntary and free of social regulation, even within a given culture? This question deserves careful consideration. Studies indicate that the voluntary and unconstrained nature of friendship gives it special significance as an influence on the individual at different periods of life. If friendship is not, in fact, voluntary and unconstrained, how is one to interpret this special significance? Sociologists Rosemary Blieszner and Rebecca Adams (1992) note that friendships are likely to form on the basis of one's membership in a number of social categories. That is, people tend to choose friends similar to themselves in age, race, geographic area, sex, religion, and status levels. Moreover, people generally agree upon expectations about what friendships should be like.

How, then, can one say that friendship is "voluntary" and that it lacks social definition or "institutionalization"? This point, while well taken, refers to the predictability of friendship patterns based on opportunity and preference due to one's social circumstances. It does not refer to control based on explicit norms and enforced expectations. In the latter respect, friendships are significantly less regulated by external social forces than other relationships such as engagement and marriage (Wright 1985). They are, therefore, sufficiently voluntary and unconstrained in relative terms to give them a unique status as a personal and social relationship.

Friendships Throughout Childhood

From an adult perspective, friendship involves voluntary interaction between two persons who respond to one another on a personal and individualized basis. As such, friendship is an achievement that is beyond the capacity of most children until about the age of ten to twelve. Prior to that time, however, children experience friendship in less complete but increasingly sophisticated ways, beginning with a rudimentary conception at about three years of age (Rubin 1980).

William K. Rawlins (1992) divides children's friendships from toddlerhood through preadolescence into four phases. Following Robert L. Selman (1981), he describes friends in the first phase (ages three to seven years) as "momentary physicalistic playmates." The children respond to age-mates they meet at, for example, day care or the playground on the basis of physical characteristics or possessions. The children are "friends" as long as they are participating jointly in some enjoyable activity. They are often inclusive of one another and exclusive of "outsiders" when other children attempt to join them. This exclusiveness is transitory, however, as the children often lose interest in one activity and pick up another with different partners or new "friends." Brief quarrels, usually over toys or space, are common. Although short in duration, these quarrels involve expressing emotions, sometimes having one's way, and sometimes being compelled to "give in." They often lead to shifts in playmates. During this period, children start developing some of the social skills necessary for forming more enduring friendships. They begin learning, for instance, to take turns and manage their emotions. Moreover, as they become familiar and comfortable with the children they meet repeatedly, they start showing some degree of consistency in their preferred playmates.

Friendships of children from about six to nine years of age follow a pattern that Rawlins (1992) describes as "opportunity and activity." The friends usually live close to one another and are similar in sex, age, social status, and physical maturity. They spend most of their time together in physical activities (skating, biking, running, sports), make-believe games related to domestic or work situations, fantasized athletic exploits, and "adventures" that are modeled after their favorite fictional heroes.

Children at this age still tend to describe their friends according to physical characteristics and possessions, but sometimes they think of them in more social and relational terms, such as showing liking and supportiveness (Furman and Bierman 1983). While they realize that different people may see and respond to the same situation in different ways, they usually feel that friends should share points of view. Thus, one child is likely to see another as a friend only during times when their ideas coincide and when they like doing the same things. When they do not, they are not friends. During their "friendship times," they exchange benefits on a tit-for-tat basis. In sum, at this stage, friendships are on-and-off relationships that are largely self-oriented and opportunistic.

Between the ages of roughly nine and twelve years, children increasingly respond to others in terms of internal characteristics (attitudes, beliefs, values). They learn to infer these characteristics by observing the ongoing acts of others, and they are aware that others can, in turn, infer internal characteristics in the same way. With this cognitive ability, a child can "step outside" of the self and take the perspective of the other, including the perceptions the other has of the child. This enables them to form friendships that Rawlins (1992) labels "reciprocal and equal."

At this stage, children usually choose friends whose beliefs agree with their own. Such agreement confirms the correctness of their emerging views, thereby providing what psychiatrist Harry Stack Sullivan

(1953) called "consensual validation." To the degree that their perspectives differ, however, friends at this age are able to accommodate some of their differences and arrive at a shared outlook. Although these children still tend to be self-oriented and opportunistic, they realize that their friends are equal to them in the sense of being entitled to benefits from the relationship. Therefore, the exchange of rewards tends to be normative and reciprocal. That is, the child provides benefits when the friend has a need for them because that is what friends are supposed to do. That friend, of course, is expected to return the benefits for the same reasons. Thus, friends are people who share ideas, interests, and feelings and who provide rewards on a broadly reciprocal basis. In the "reciprocity and equality" phase, then, children are on the fringes of a conception of friendship as a relatively stable relationship that transcends occasional disagreements and periods of separation.

At preadolescence (about ten to fourteen years of age), children acquire the ability and inclination to respond to other children in terms of personality traits and styles (nice, easy-going, mean, selfish) and special interests and abilities, as well as set beliefs and attitudes. They sometimes see these characteristics as combining to make the other person uniquely admirable and attractive. This sets the stage for what Rawlins (1992) calls the periods of "mutuality and understanding" in children's friendships.

According to Sullivan (1953), preadolescent children experience a need for interpersonal closeness in an especially poignant way, and express this need as a strong desire to establish a same-sex "chumship." Research generally confirms the nature of these chumships and the importance Sullivan attaches to them.

As two children come to recognize uniquely attractive qualities in one another, they are likely to become "real" friends. Such friends consider one another intrinsically worthwhile. They are loyal to one another and provide rewards, not with the expectation of reciprocation, but simply because the partner is deserving. Preadolescent friends share common day-to-day experiences to which they often react with an intensity and immediacy that either puzzles or amuses important adults, such as their parents and teachers. Therefore, chums are especially capable of providing empathy and understanding. At this stage, friendships not only build each child's self-esteem, they provide a context for expressing and "trying out" personal thoughts and feelings in a free and unguarded manner. Such freedom is possible because friendships, while close and caring, lack the socially mandated responsibilities and inequalities present in many relationships, such as that between parents and children.

In sum, children approaching adolescence begin to experience friendship in its full-blown form, that is, as an enduring relationship involving voluntary interdependence and a mutual personalized interest and concern. Through these friendships, they experience and practice empathy, altruism, unselfishness, and loyalty. There is, however, a darker side to preadolescent friendships. Because they are intense and exclusive, they often encourage cliquishness and animosity between sets of friends. At times, too, the friends themselves disagree, become jealous, become competitive, and have an occasional falling-out. At this point, however, the partners have a conception of friendship as a relationship that usually persists in spite of episodic difficulties.

Throughout these phases, children are strongly inclined to select friends of their own sex. Furthermore, girls' and boys' friendships differ, on the average, in several ways. Girls' friendships, for example, are more exclusively pair-oriented, whereas boys' are more group- or gang-oriented. Girls tend to talk, "gossip," and exchange secrets more than boys, who concentrate on games, "projects," and shared activities (Buhrmester and Furman 1987). These basic contrasts foreshadow overall gender differences that appear in adolescence and persist through adulthood.

Friendships Throughout Adolescence

Adolescence extends from the onset of puberty until the individual begins young adult life by entering the work force or undertaking postsecondary education. Because of the developmental tasks characteristic of this period, the meaning and values that close friendships acquired during preadolescence continue and expand. Throughout this time, the typical adolescent encounters differing ideologies and values, a variety of activities to pursue or forego, and potential lifestyles to consider. The adolescent's twofold "task" is to discover which options can and should be committed to and to integrate them gradually into a personal identity.

Although parents normally remain an important source of guidance and support, part of the adolescent's struggle is to work toward independence from them. Thus, adolescents continue to rely on their parents for material support and instrumental rewards, normally respecting their ideals and values as sources of continuity and stability. They are less likely, however, to see their parents as helpful in developing their views on present and future issues. For their part, parents generally feel an obligation to socialize their adolescents "properly" and, hence, tend to be judgmental as their adolescent children explore different directions. Therefore, close friendships, because they involve nonjudgmental yet caring equals, help the adolescent develop a sense of identity by offering "a climate of growth and self-knowledge that the family is not equipped to offer" (Douvan and Adelson 1966, p. 174).

As they carry out their friendships on a day-to-day basis, girls are more likely than boys to emphasize expressive rather than instrumental rewards. As in preadolescence, both girls and boys usually form friendships with members of their own sex. Even so, cross-gender friendships are somewhat more common in adolescence, and most adolescents attempt to make careful distinctions between opposite-sex partners who are friends and those who are romantic or dating partners. Boys, especially, find these cross-gender friendships advantageous because they provide expressive rewards that are not as readily available in their friendships with other boys.

Friendships Throughout Adulthood

Close friendships are possible and, in fact, common at all stages of adulthood. Also, regardless of whether they involve women, men, or cross-gender pairs, close friendships provide benefits that are similar in kind and degree. There are, however, circumstances at young, middle, and later adulthood that affect typical friendship patterns.

Young adulthood starts with the individual's loosening emotional ties with parents and family, while beginning to explore stable work opportunities or pursue further education. This development includes changes in commitments and activities, and often changes in residence. Such changes usually disrupt the individual's network of nonkin associates, creating the opportunity, if not the necessity, of forming new friendships. Indeed, young adults who succeed in forging new friendships report being happier, less lonely, and better adjusted than those who do not (Cutrona 1982; Shaver, Furman, and Buhrmester 1985). Individuals at this stage are relatively free of obligations and social roles (e.g., professional advancement, marriage, and parenthood) that might conflict with forming friendships. Consequently, single young adults report more friendships, including cross-gender friendships, than adults at any other stage.

Gender differences in friendships are as much in evidence during young adulthood as at any other time.

That is, women are, on the average, more expressive and personally oriented in their friendships than men. Moreover, the friendships of women are generally stronger than those of men with respect to both voluntary interaction and the person-qua-person factor (Duck and Wright 1993). As in adolescence, males find that their cross-gender friendships provide expressive rewards to a greater degree than do their same-gender friendships.

With such life events as marriage, parenthood, and accelerated career development, young adulthood merges into middle adulthood. Following marriage, both women and men report having fewer cross-gender friends. One obvious reason for this is suspicion and jealousy, but there are other factors. Men, for example, tend to rely on female friends as confidants. When they marry, their wives often meet their expressive needs by becoming live-in confidants, that is, "friends" (Tognoli 1980). For women, marriage more often means quitting or curtailing vocational pursuits. This, of course, reduces the number of potential male friends a woman might meet through routine daily activities.

Also during middle adulthood, men show a drop in the number and intensity of same- as well as cross-gender friendships. This is partly because their preoccupation with career development leaves them little time to cultivate anything but superficial friendships. In addition, men most often meet other men in work settings. Because of this, many of their potential friends are people with whom they compete for raises or advancement, or with whom they are involved as supervisors or subordinates. Neither of these conditions is conducive to the openness, equality, and personalized concern necessary for the development of a close friendship. When friendships do develop between male work associates, they are likely to center around shared activities and camaraderie rather than personal self-disclosure and expressiveness.

The "friendship situation" for women in middle adulthood is rather complex. Prior to the arrival of children, marriage has little impact on the number, strength, or expressive character of their friendships. With the arrival of children, however, women report a decrease in their number of friendships. This is probably due to women's traditionally greater responsibility for the home and family. The fact that many women also work outside the home further limits the time and energy they have to pursue friendships. Even so, the friendships they are able to maintain retain their expressive and highly personalized character. Later in middle adulthood, presumably as their children become more independent, women report in-

creasing numbers of friends. Women, like men, often form friendships in work settings. However, they are likely to consider such relationships as acquaintanceships rather than friendships. They commonly make distinctions among work friends, activity friends, and "real" friends (Gouldner and Strong 1987).

But what about the friendships of adults who never marry? One often hears anecdotally that such never-marrieds cultivate more friendships and treat their friends as a special "family." Research, however, does not bear out this "friends as family" trend. Rather, findings suggest that most unmarried adults increase their contacts with relatives rather than forming more or different kinds of friendships.

Older adulthood is marked by two kinds of changes that affect friendships. On the one hand, increasing health concerns, reduced mobility, and declining vigor reduce both opportunities for contact with friends and the energy the individual has to devote to them. On the other hand, retirement and reduced social and family obligations increase the free and uncommitted time the individual has to nurture old friendships and develop new ones. Not surprisingly, these factors have a different impact on the friendships of older women than those of older men.

For women, the increasing flexibility of middle adulthood continues into older adulthood. Older women are thus able to sustain established friendships and to form new ones as friends die or relocate. Throughout life, women's friendships tend to be more intense and expressive than those of men. In older adulthood, then, they have both the inclination and the social skills to continue this pattern. Moreover, women are more likely than men to face the prospect of widowhood and to fill the relationship void by emphasizing their friendships. Whereas widows rely on adult children, especially daughters, for material and practical support, they rely mainly on same age friends to meet their expressive needs and maintain their morale.

Because men's friendships are centered mostly around work affiliations and shared activities, when men retire and curtail their activities they often lose their friendships as well. Men are less likely than women to form new friendships to replace the ones they lose. Even so, most men retain their primary source of personal and emotional support, that is, their wives. In the relatively rare case in which an older man outlives his wife, he is likely to remarry rather than seek out new friends. With the loss of friends, however, older men do lose the stimulation, fun, and camaraderie that goes along with shared interests and activities. Therefore, men who depart from the average and maintain close same-gender friendships throughout life are likely to lead fuller and more satisfying lives in their older adult years.

Conclusion

Friendship is, in many respects, a "comfortable" love relationship. Friendships involve as little or as much intimacy as the partners are inclined to express at any given time. Friends are not formally obligated to exchange benefits, but do so in ways that are often so natural as to be unwitting. The ties that bind them are by unfettered mutual consent. In spite of its being so comfortable, in fact because of it, friendship contributes in unique ways to personal development and well-being.

(*See also:* ATTACHMENT; ATTRACTIVENESS; INTIMACY; LONELINESS; LOVE; PEER PRESSURE; PERSONALITY DEVELOPMENT; PERSONAL RELATIONSHIPS; TRUST)

BIBLIOGRAPHY

Adams, R. G., and Blieszner, R., eds. (1989). *Older Adult Friendships: Structure and Process.* Newbury Park, CA: Sage Publications.

Blieszner, R., and Adams, R. G. (1992). *Adult Friendships.* Newbury Park, CA: Sage Publications.

Buhrmester, D., and Furman, W. (1987). "The Development of Companionship and Intimacy." *Child Development* 58:1101–1113.

Cutrona, C. E. (1982). "Transition to College: Loneliness and the Process of Social Adjustment." In *Loneliness: A Sourcebook of Current Theory, Research, and Therapy,* ed. L. A. Peplau and D. Perlman. New York: Wiley.

Douvan, E., and Adelson, J. (1966). *The Adolescent Experience.* New York: Wiley.

DuBois, C. (1974). "The Gratuitous Act: An Introduction to the Comparative Study of Friendship Patterns." In *The Compact: Selected Dimensions of Friendship,* ed. E. Leyton. St. John's, Newfoundland, Canada: Institute of Social and Economic Research.

Duck, S., and Gilmour, R., eds. (1981). *Personal Relationships:* Vol. 2, *Developing Personal Relationships.* New York: Academic Press.

Duck S., and Wright, P. H. (1993). "Reexamining Gender Differences in Same-Gender Friendships: A Close Look at Two Kinds of Data." *Sex Roles* 28:709–727.

Furman, W., and Bierman, K. L. (1983). "Developmental Changes in Children's Conceptions of Friendship." *Child Development* 54:594–556.

Gouldner, H., and Strong, M. S. (1987). *Speaking of Friendship.* New York: Greenwood Press.

Hays, R. B. (1984). "The Development and Maintenance of Friendship." *Journal of Social and Personal Relationships* 1:75–98.

Nardi, P. M. (1992). *Men's Friendships.* Newbury Park, CA: Sage Publications.

O'Connor, P. (1992). *Friendship Between Women: A Critical Review.* New York: Guilford.

Paine, R. (1969). "In Search of Friendship: An Exploratory Analysis in 'Middle-Class' Culture." *Man* 4:505–524.

Rawlins, W. K. (1992). *Friendship Matters.* New York: Aldine.

Rizzo, T. A. (1989). *Friendship Development Among School Children.* Norwood, NJ: Ablex.

Rubin, Z. (1980). *Children's Friendships.* Cambridge, Eng.: Cambridge University Press.

Selman, R. L. (1981). "The Child as a Friendship Philosopher." In *The Development of Children's Friendships,* ed. S. R. Asher and J. M. Gottman. Cambridge, Eng.: Cambridge University Press.

Shaver, P.; Furman, W.; and Buhrmester, D. (1985). "Transition to College: Network Changes, Social Skills, and Loneliness." In *Understanding Personal Relationships: An Interdisciplinary Approach,* ed. S. Duck and D. Perlman. Newbury Park, CA: Sage Publications.

Sullivan, H. S. (1953). *Interpersonal Theory of Psychiatry.* New York: W. W. Norton.

Suttles, G. D. (1970). "Friendship as a Social Institution." In *Social Relationships,* ed. G. J. McCall. New York: Aldine.

Tognoli, J. (1980). "Male Friendships and Intimacy Across the Lifespan." *Family Relations* 29:273–279.

Uhl, S. (1991). "Forbidden Friends: Cultural Veils of Female Friendship in Andalusia." *American Ethnologist* 18:90–105.

Winstead, B. J. (1986). "Sex Differences in Same-Sex Friendships." In *Friendship and Social Interaction,* ed. V. J. Derlega and B. J. Winstead. New York: Springer-Verlag.

Wright, P. H. (1978). "Toward a Theory of Friendship Based on a Conception of Self." *Journal of Human Communication Research* 4:196–207.

Wright, P. H. (1985). "The Acquaintance Description Form." In *Understanding Personal Relationships: An Interdisciplinary Approach,* ed. S. Duck and D. Perlman. Newbury Park, CA: Sage Publications.

PAUL H. WRIGHT

GANGS

Youth gangs have been prominent features of urban life in the United States since late in the nineteenth century. Their importance has grown significantly, as has the attention paid to them by news media, legal authorities, and academia. These gangs originated as by-products of poor immigrant populations' attempts to cope with the conditions they encountered in American cities, confined as they were by both economics and social discrimination to the most run-down neighborhoods, deteriorating housing, and poorly paid jobs. As wave after wave of immigrants from different areas in Europe entered eastern and midwestern cities, the ethnicity and cultural details of youth gangs changed, but many structural similarities continued to characterize the various gangs. By the middle of the twentieth century this condition held true as African-American migrants from the rural South and Puerto Rican migrants succeeded the European immigrants. In addition, gangs also had emerged, in the 1940s, in the Mexican immigrant *barrios* (neighborhoods) in Southern California.

Repeatedly, then, generations of poor newcomers to urban areas have had to adapt to often severe economic conditions and to institutionalized hostile attitudes toward them. Remarkably, most families in each wave of new urban residents were able to function productively and managed to raise their children to be even better prepared to cope with life's problems. Unfortunately, if not unexpectedly, a considerable number of families were, instead, overwhelmed by the magnitude and complexity of the problems they faced. The children in these families received inadequate supervision and socialization at home, and the schools to which they were sent proved inadequate for inculcating relevant strategies for coping with urban poverty and discrimination. With family and school failing them, generations of such children turned to their peers and the older youths they encountered in the streets for guidance. Thus the debate on the existence and persistence of the underclass (segments of the poor who have suffered prolonged and concentrated poverty and in response have routinized patterns of behavior greatly at odds with predominant mores) emanates from within the roots of the gang problem.

Family stress or strain, or what others have referred to as family dysfunction, is one of the ripple effects of such social and economic maladies as unemployment, underemployment, low education levels, lack of skills and training, and so on. This is especially the case when these factors are joined by discriminatory attitudes and behavior. Among the most common family difficulties is the inability of parents to dedicate energies to child-rearing and caretaking duties. Single-parent, usually mother-centered, households tend to reflect this problem, but they are not alone in this. Often both parents in a two-parent household have fallen on bad times and have been shorn of their coping skills, resulting in part in a lack of supervision and guidance of their children. Parenting is doubly difficult in such an environment because household earners and caretakers must operate under conditions of intense culture change and stress.

Ethnicity, Socialization, and Gang Variations

Crowded living conditions and attenuated parental supervision in many poverty-stricken areas have resulted in pushing children out of the home and onto the streets. In this crucible of the city streets, the idea of the gang begins to brew. When home socialization comes up short, street socialization assumes command of the training and preparation of the youths for future life. The void in appropriate socialization in the home is now exacerbated by a similarly missed opportunity to gain solid school socialization. In particular, schools and school personnel confronted with troubled youths from stressed families have been unable to address the problems of many of these inner-city, ethnic minority children successfully. In large part, the streets are filled by similarly disaffected and untethered youths; in effect, a youth who is new to the street encounters same-age peers as well as older, more experienced role models who set the tone and direction for the novitiate.

Since the 1960s, Mexican immigrants as well as Puerto Rican and African-American migrants and their offspring have made up the bulk of the new street gangs and have dominated American cities' street life. Asian-American gangs have also grown rapidly since the 1980s. As was true for earlier generations, some gangs are conflict-oriented, often engaging in rumbles and fights, while others are more oriented to profitable criminal pursuits. By the middle of the twentieth century, drug use and abuse had become a factor, establishing the "retreatist" gangs and the more dedicated, entrepreneurial gangs that are better organized for drug trafficking or other criminal activities. These drug-dealing gangs also reflect a steady increase in gang-related violence since the 1980s. One form of street gang, which some experts have labeled "scavenger," seems to exist primarily to fight aimlessly any youths they encounter. The largest apparent increase is among gangs that get into and stay in conflict with other rival gangs. There is even a noted increase in "wannabes"—individuals who desire to be gang members in the absence of positive role models, even though they hardly share the background, personal situations, and attributes of the typical gang member.

The increase in violent activities has led to variations in levels of participation among gang members. The resultant "hard-core/fringe" dichotomy in levels of participation over the years has evolved into finer shades of attitudinal and behavioral characteristics. These characteristics, in turn, place a gang member into such categories as regular, peripheral, temporary, or situational. The regular gang member has had the most problematic early life and is consequently oriented to street life at a very early age. The peripheral member is as intensely involved as the regular, but because of a less troublesome beginning will more often retain the option of pursuing a conventional life. Temporary and situational members are simply what the words suggest, and as a result, they are less apt to develop deep-rooted gang affiliations.

The Gang as Family

Ethnographic research on gang issues and gangs' interrelationships with family life, either real or re-created, shows that both an insider and an outsider point of view helps understanding. Some authorities suggest that social scientists studying youth gangs should systematically shift from outsider to insider perspectives, and then back, to cross-check the validity of their findings. Learning the rules and regulations of gang behavior in different settings directly from the participants' actions and words is important. Hearing gang youths talk about helping one another out and showing consideration and attention provides color and depth. However, the outsider perspective, which relies on taxonomic principles and the evidentiary rules of science, broadens and contextualizes the meanings within universal patterns. Thus both views are necessary, because the details that show that the gang has become a surrogate family are understood within the context of a wider world that has failed them, including families that have broken down under intense social, economic, and cultural pressures. Gang youths may not comprehend why the gang has become such an important source for identification and support, for they are too close to the reality.

In the context of the streets, where fear, anxiety, and the unknown often dominate one's concerns, youngsters seek protection, friendship, assurance, acceptance, support, and especially sources of identity wherever they can. Street children have to deal with pervasive fears with which their parents and other authorities cannot help them. These children's ties with family, schools, and police have by now become strained. Many of them will have dropped out of school in junior high school, and most of the others will not complete high school. In this context, street socialization introduces new and heretofore unexpected activities. While gang members spend large amounts of time doing the things that most American adolescents do—joke, play, date, and celebrate—they must also learn to participate in specific gang-sanctioned behaviors. All of these new experiences operate in shaping an identity. In time, individuals become the street culture carriers and street socializers. At this point, group psychology begins to make its contribution to the gang reality. The introduction of signs, symbols, rituals, ceremonies, and other group features marks this phase. In general they function to incorporate a youth into the group as a wholehearted participant.

For large numbers of such youths, the gang thus has become a surrogate family and caretaker, a type of fictive kinship network. Among Mexican-American, other Latino, and African-American gang networks, it often is stressed that the unit operates as a family. Members often call one another "brother" or refer to each other by other kinship terms, professing a familial form of love for fellow gang members. In addition to the emotional support and nurturance they find in daily common intractions, gang members regularly maintain that when trouble of whatever kind is afoot, they turn to close confidants within the gang. It is clear that the gang has emerged as a competing force to family and school because of the failure of those caretaking units. Often, the support includes providing transportation; lending money; sharing resources; and, at its most extreme, laying down one's life for a friend. When a fellow gang member is slain, it is quite common for the other members and their affiliates to raise money through car washes, collections, and whatnot, to pay for the funeral expenses, as if they were "family."

Conversely, the establishment of a gang subculture over many decades has tended to create a feedback effect into family life in ways that have reshaped what *barrio* or ghetto families are like and what they must readapt to. Studies show that the existence of a street gang in the neighborhood alters how low-income families raise their children, either in ways calculated to help their children avoid gang members or in other precautions that interfere with normal child-rearing methods. Various types of *cholo* (marginalized) and gang families have resulted from this readjustment. As each generation repeats the living and working conditions that have created gangs, the gang becomes a fixture and a strong socializing agent in the family's external world. For instance, in increasing numbers of families, an older male family member who is gang-affiliated is a household regular and perhaps one of the most important sources of role modeling for the younger children; sometimes one or both parents might be gang members. In older gang neighborhoods, there are family households with two or even three generations represented by gang members.

Immigration and the Gang Lifestyle

Also significant is how this gang subcultural force has affected immigrants or other newcomers. In previous eras of immigration, as noted, people had to adjust to both economic and social hardships. Today the processes and directions of acculturation and assimilation have been sharply reformulated. The presence, example, and pressure of the street gang have worked to undermine immigrant adaptation further,

especially for children who wish to be Americans and who view the gangs as part of this cultural reality. Both parents and children, in neighborhoods where the street gang has a prominent presence, must come to some sort of *modus vivendi* (working relationship) with the gang. This situation often simultaneously weakens parental authority and increases the gang's attractiveness to youths.

When the street gang becomes the strongest force in a youth's life, there are ways to dress, talk, walk, and so on that must be learned, and these customs and habits are acquired from a "multiple-age peer group" rather than one's parents. How he or she associates with and integrates into the group is part of the experience. Clique formation and allegiance organize different age sets of cohorts so that levels of leadership are established and avenues of succession marked out. Gang (or neighborhood or *barrio*) names and personal nicknames are acquired for identification. To ensure that everyone knows what these affiliations and designations are, gang graffiti, in the form of spray paint scrawls on public and private surfaces, and personal graffiti, or tattoos, advertise the gang and personal nickname for all to see.

Perhaps the most significant transformation under the auspices of the group occurs with the rite of passage for gang newcomers. Known as "jumping in" or "counting in," this ordeal involves a usually pro forma beating by other gang members who are already established. As an integral part of this ritual, and in the absence of a household-based and/or -sanctioned role model, the event serves to clarify one's gender and age and thus expedite a certain masculine and disciplined behavior. Gang initiations with such emphases address any ambiguities in gender identity that young males raised in fatherless or ineffective-father households may have developed. The gang initiation also symbolizes the fact that membership is a hard-won status. For this reason, youngsters who have not yet demonstrated their worthiness as fighters, or in some other valued role, may find the pro forma beating to be much more than that. The ordeal simultaneously makes membership "hard-won" and demonstrates that the newcomer "can take it."

By aiding the individual to become group-oriented, the gang provides certain services (e.g., friendship and protection from street threats) but also, in return, expects to receive the loyalty and devotion of the new gang member. The latter is an addition to the mystique and power that is the gang, and it ensures that new members are readied for combat and defense of neighborhood turf when rivals approach. One interesting and destructive activity that the group as a gang inspires and admires is the ability to act crazy and carry out daring and violent acts, referred to as *locura* (playing with quasi-controlled insanity). A person who acts *loco* at appropriate opportunities gains prestige and status in the eyes of other gang members. Another person who does the same on a regular basis, with deep, aggressive convictions born of trauma and anxiety, is looked upon another way: a *loco* actor to be feared, respected, and avoided. Indeed, one advantage of gang membership may be to interpose the gang's familylike mutual respect between oneself and a *loco* member of the same gang.

Conclusion

The relationship between street gangs and the family is complex and fraught with difficulties. Stemming, in part, from the stresses and strains experienced by immigrants, the gang has come to partially supplant the family and the school as socializing agents. In gang neighborhoods, families headed by gang members or former gang members are increasingly common, and gang signs and symbols in the form of graffiti now cover nearly every available surface. However, other disaffected youths have also taken to spraying similar, though not gang-related, messages and symbols on walls. Dress and music styles popularized in gang circles have also diffused throughout much of the youth subculture in America. Thus, the gang has become an influence with which families in most American cities must contend, whatever their station in life.

(*See also:* ADOLESCENCE; ETHNICITY; JUVENILE DELINQUENCY; PEER PRESSURE; POVERTY; TRUANCY)

BIBLIOGRAPHY

Cummings, S., and Monti, D. J., ed. (1993). *Gangs: The Origins and Impact of Contemporary Youth Gangs in the United States.* Albany: State University of New York Press.
Fagan, J., and Wexler, S. (1987). "Family Origins of Violent Delinquents." *Criminology* 25:643–669.
Farrington, D. P. (1978). "Family Backgrounds of Aggressive Youths." In *Aggressive and Antisocial Behavior in Childhood and Adolescence,* ed. L. Hersov, M. Berger, and D. Shaffer. Oxford, Eng.: Pergamon.
Goldstein, A. P., and Huff, C. R., ed. (1993). *The Gang Intervention Handbook.* Champaign, IL: Research Press.
Heath, S. B., and McLaughlin, M. W., ed. (1993). *Identity and Inner-City Youth: Beyond Ethnicity and Gender.* New York: Teachers College Press.
Huff, C. R., ed. (1990). *Gangs in America.* Newbury Park, CA: Sage Publications.
Loeber, R., and Stoutamer-Loeber, M. (1986). "Models and Meta-Analysis of the Relationship Between Family Variables and Juvenile Conduct Problems and Delinquency." In *Crime and Justice: An Annual Review of Research,* Vol. 7, ed. N. Morris and M. Tonry. Chicago: University of Chicago Press.
Moore, J. W. (1991). *Going Down to the Barrio: Homeboys and Homegirls in Change.* Philadelphia: Temple University Press.
Padilla, F. M. (1992). *The Gang as an American Enterprise.* New Brunswick, NJ: Rutgers University Press.
Patterson, G. R., and Dishion, T. J. (1985). "Contributions of Families and Peers to Delinquency." *Criminology* 23: 63–80.
Rosen, L. (1986). "Family and Delinquency: Structure or Function?" *Criminology* 23:553–573.
Vigil, J. D. (1988). *Barrio Gangs: Street Life and Identity in Southern California.* Austin: University of Texas Press.

JAMES DIEGO VIGIL

GAY AND LESBIAN PARENTS

Homosexuality has always been recognized as an aspect of human nature and sexuality (Bozett and Sussman 1989). However, homosexuality has been labeled most negatively throughout history in those cultures having a strong Judeo-Christian heritage. Heterosexism, or the cultural precedence given to heterosexuality at the expense of other sexual lifestyles, is so ingrained as a social tenet that many individuals are not even aware that this is a prejudicial belief system found throughout Western civilization and in the United States in particular (Herek 1984). Heterosexuality is assumed to be the only acceptable sexual orientation, and individuals are held to be heterosexual unless they contradict the assumption. Heterosexism is supported by another prejudicial belief system known as homophobia: prejudicial, hateful, and fearful views about homosexuals and homosexuality that often lead to potentially abusive and violent acts of discrimination (Weinberg 1972).

Because such beliefs are so pervasive, many people are surprised to learn that homosexual men and women form families that include children. In fact, nontraditional families, such as those formed by adult homosexuals, are part of the increasing diversity of family structures found in American society (Bigner 1994a). All sexual minorities are among the most despised and misunderstood social groups in most Western cultures. While there can be much speculation about how homosexual families are targeted by homophobic and heterosexist attitudes as a means of oppression, the prejudicial manifestations of these attitudes are experienced in various ways (Pharr 1988). Homosexual families, although they resemble traditional heterosexual families, experience added burdens not usually faced by other family systems. Their unique identity often is known only by a small group, leading to social isolation. This tendency for homosexual families to be socially isolated serves as a protective mechanism against outside prejudice and discrimination. However, it also serves to perpetuate myths, misconceptions, and misunderstandings about gay and lesbian parents.

For many years, researchers as well as lay individuals have believed that the very best home environment for children was one in which there were two middle-class, opposite-sex adults with the woman providing full-time care for the children and the man working full-time outside of the home. However, as alternative family structures, such as single-parent families, have become more visible, attitudes as well as research information have provided insights into the effects of such environments on child growth and development, parental effectiveness, and other related issues.

Because homosexual families differ on an important aspect from the standard, accepted model (the sex of the adults), it has been assumed by many agents in society that the environment provided by such families is detrimental to children's healthy growth and development. For example, gay and lesbian parents have had difficulty in gaining sole or joint custody of children because the judicial system judged homosexuals to be unfit parents. Objections have also been raised to efforts by homosexuals to adopt children because many people consider homosexuality to be immoral. They also believe gays and lesbians are unacceptable role models for children. However, new research findings and changes in attitudes about homosexuality and gay and lesbian parenting indicate a reversal in this trend.

Gay Fathers

The gay father is a newly emergent figure in homosexual culture, and there is a growing body of knowledge in this area. There is a controversy regarding the exact percentage of homosexuals in the population, with some estimates as low as 2 percent and others as high as 10 percent to 12 percent. Regardless, the group of gay men who also are fathers clearly constitutes a minority within a minority; researchers estimate that about 20 percent to 25 percent of self-identified male

homosexuals are also fathers (Bell and Weinberg 1978; Bozett and Sussman 1989). It is doubtful if a more accurate estimate of gay fathers can be obtained since some gay men are married to a woman or conceal their sexual orientation for other reasons.

A homosexual man who also is a father is a social enigma; even the term "gay father" is a contradiction known as an oxymoron. Gay connotes homosexuality and an antifamily stereotype; father connotes heterosexuality and a strong interest in sexual reproduction. Gay fathers, thus, are faced with resolving a dilemma of having a divided identity as reflected by having a psychological "foot" in two different and disparate social worlds (Barret and Robinson 1990; Bigner and Bozett 1989; Bozett 1981a, 1981b, 1985, 1987; Bozett and Sussman 1989). More precisely, these men are described initially in resolving this dilemma as socially marginal, challenged by having ties to the cultural worlds of both gays and nongays.

The conflict is resolved as a gay father reconciles these two extremes. Each identity (homosexual and heterosexual) essentially is unacceptable in the other culture. Hence, the solution for a gay father is to integrate both identities into a cognitive concept by the same name, "gay father." The process by which this occurs is known as integrative sanctioning (Bozett 1981a, 1981b, 1985, 1987; Bozett and Sussman 1989). This takes place when the man discloses his gay sexual orientation and identity to nongays and his father identity to gays. Close liaisons are then formed with those who accept and support both identities in both cultural worlds. Inevitably, this also involves distancing himself from those who do not accept nor support his identity as a gay father.

Why a man who is homosexual in orientation becomes involved in the heterosexual activity of being a father is not completely understood. However, research findings have suggested several explanations (Barret and Robinson 1990; Bigner and Bozett 1989; Bigner and Jacobsen 1989a, 1989b; Bozett 1987; Bozett and Sussman 1989):

1. Some men have extreme difficulty accepting their homosexual attractions to other men and find the stereotypical homosexual lifestyle to be unacceptable for a number of reasons. These men pursue a heterosexual relationship and marriage during which children are produced, perhaps as an effort to deny and hide their authentic sexual orientation. Inevitably, it becomes more and more difficult to maintain the facade of heterosexuality, and a divorce takes place, allowing the man to pursue his homosexual identity.

2. Sometimes a gay man chooses to become a father as part of a liaison established between himself and a lesbian when both want to become parents. In such instances, reproduction usually occurs via artificial insemination. The lesbian mother typically retains physical custody of the child while the gay father has joint custody or visitation rights. Such means of assuming parenthood require carefully researched and negotiated legal agreements.

3. Some gay or bisexual men enter into heterosexual marriage with both partners knowing the man's sexual orientation and the implications of this on the marriage and parenthood. Such marriages often remain intact for many years.

4. Other gay men become fathers for diverse reasons, including a genuine desire to nurture children, wanting to escape undesirable aspects of their lifestyle, wanting the assumed security that children may provide in old age, and other related reasons.

Gay fathers cite reasons for having children that generally are similar to those of nongay fathers, but with some significant differences (Bigner and Jacobsen 1989a). First, nongay fathers appear to desire children for traditional reasons, such as continuing a family name. Gay fathers seem to place greater emphasis on the fact that parenthood is perceived to confer adult, mature individual status to people. For this reason, those who marry heterosexually may find fatherhood to be important as a means for initially avoiding the negative social stigmas associated with homosexuality.

These men typically marry heterosexually because they find it impossible or undesirable at a time in early adulthood to accept their homosexual orientation for various reasons. However, many of them eventually come to terms with their sexual orientation, often with the approach of middle age and the experience of the mid-life transition. They gain the courage or create the necessity to disclose their orientation to their wives, who typically react to this news in various ways that often are upsetting and disruptive (Barret and Robinson 1990; Hays and Samuels 1989). Few marriages remain intact following this disclosure, since the men usually wish to pursue the delayed development of their true homosexual orientation instead of continuing in a relationship they describe as deceptive, dishonest, and unfulfilling. It is estimated that the majority of gay fathers fall into this category (Bigner 1994b).

Adjustment of gay fathers following divorce is not well documented by research studies. However, while the process may differ in length and experiences, many gay fathers commonly find this period to be difficult or problematic at times in various ways. When a successful relationship is established with another gay man, however, few people may know that children are a part of these men's lives. Some gay fathers, on the other hand, have sole custody of their children. In either circumstance, many consider themselves to have established a gay stepfamily upon establishing a relationship with a male partner.

Lesbian Mothers

Research activity and interest have focused more on gay fathers than lesbian mothers. In general, the experiences of lesbian mothers resemble those of gay fathers. However, researchers have noted differences in their family dynamics and situations.

Lesbian mothers differ from gay fathers in how they become involved in parenthood. While some are similar to gay men who disclose their homosexual orientation after years of heterosexual marriage, many others use artificial insemination from a male donor, unknown or known, as a means for achieving parenthood. Adoption also may occur more frequently among lesbian women than gay men (Pies 1989), involving a number of legal and social challenges men do not usually have to face.

The families formed by lesbians that include children resemble those of heterosexual stepfamilies. In addition, the problems experienced by both types of families are similar. However, because many more lesbian mothers than gay fathers hold custody of their children, they experience distinct challenges not often faced by other families. Three characteristics appear to be unique to lesbian family systems: (1) they experience a lack of legitimacy by not being recognized as families by most communities, causing a variety of problems, such as how to handle parent–teacher conferences; (2) they are confronted more consistently with problems associated with homosexuality that are not experienced to the same extent by gay fathers with joint custody or visitation rights, such as maintaining a family secret regarding the adult women's sexual orientation, generally unhealthy but often a necessity in preventing evictions from rental units or being terminated from employment; and (3) relations between lesbian mothers and ex-spouses and ex-in-laws may be especially strained due to the sexual orientation issues that can serve to threaten the custody arrangements of the lesbian mothers (Pies 1989).

Children of Gay and Lesbian Parents

Researchers have examined a variety of issues in studying the effects on children who grow up with gay or lesbian parents. A consistent and extremely significant finding reported by a number of researchers is that there is no hard empirical evidence proving that having a homosexual parent is detrimental to the healthy growth and development of children (Bigner 1994b).

Children of lesbian mothers and gay fathers experience no difficulties or problems relating to acceptance of their own gender identity. They also fail to show any gender- or sex-role disturbances (Patterson 1992).

A common fear among the lay public is that children of homosexual parents also will become homosexual in orientation as a result of having been raised by these parents. The consensus of research about this issue is that the origins and causes of an individual's sexual orientation are not known, although it does not seem that sexual orientation is transmitted from parents with a particular orientation to the children they rear. The parents of most homosexual individuals are heterosexual. If sexual orientation were transmitted via biological heterosexual parentage, then theoretically there would not be any homosexual children.

Children of homosexual parents are no different in comparison with others in the general population with respect to incidence of psychiatric disturbances and mental illnesses, behavior problems, personality traits, and level of self-esteem.

Research findings fail to support the notion that children of homosexual parents experience greater difficulties in their personal development than children of nongay parents. Having a homosexual parent apparently causes no greater personal difficulty for children than having a nongay parent.

There is a common belief that children of gay and lesbian parents experience greater difficulties with peers because of the negative stigmas associated with homosexuality in general. Researchers report that these children have normal social relationships with peers and that their relationships with same- and opposite-sex adults are also satisfactory. In this regard, findings suggest that children whose lesbian mothers hold sole custody have more frequent interactions with their nongay fathers than children whose divorced mothers are heterosexual (Patterson 1992).

Another myth about children of gay and lesbian parents is that they are more likely to experience sexual abuse than children of heterosexual parents. On the contrary, the consistent finding of researchers is that the overwhelming number of perpetrators of sexual abuse of children are heterosexual males who are family members—fathers, stepfathers, uncles, and cousins (Patterson 1992). There is no evidence to support the belief that children are at a higher risk of sexual abuse by gay men or lesbian women.

Research reports that children of homosexual parents may experience greater strides in healthy growth and development when the parents have accepted their own sexual orientation, made healthy personal adjustments related to their sexual orientation issues, and have established a stable, committed, live-in relationship with a partner (Patterson 1992).

Some evidence suggests that children make better adjustments and become more accepting of their homosexual parent's orientation when the disclosure occurs prior to puberty rather than during adolescence (Patterson 1992). This might be attributed to the additional stresses incurred by the disclosure at a time when an adolescent is endeavoring to establish a personal sexual identity.

Children of homosexual parents apparently have more successful adjustment when they live in environments where the sexual orientation of their parents is accepted by other significant adults and in which they have contact with other children of gay and lesbian parents.

Many children of homosexual parents accept and experience few difficulties with having a parent who is different from other children's parents.

Most children have positive relationships with their homosexual parents. For instance, gay fathers are reported to make more serious attempts to maintain contact with their children following divorce and to create stable home lives for them than do divorced nongay fathers (Patterson 1992).

Children of homosexual parents tend to experience more strict, nontraditional styles of parenting than children of nongay parents (Patterson 1992). Gay fathers, for example, tend to be more responsive to children's needs and to provide more explanations for rules than nongay fathers.

Conclusion

Families formed by homosexual parents are not significantly different from other family units, although they do experience some unique challenges and problems. Even among homosexual families, experiences in parenting children are similar for gay fathers and lesbian mothers. Homosexuality per se does not prevent or hinder someone from being an effective parent. Gay men and lesbian women even become parents for a number of reasons that closely resemble those of nongay individuals. Furthermore, research has consistently failed to support common assertions and beliefs that homosexual families create an unhealthy environment for children. Therefore, the issue of a parent's homosexual orientation has become less prominent in considering the welfare and custodial arrangements of the children involved.

(*See also:* ADOPTION; CHILD CARE; FATHERS; MOTHERS; SEXUAL ORIENTATION; SINGLE PARENTS)

BIBLIOGRAPHY

Barrett, R. L., and Robinson, B. E. (1990). *Gay Fathers.* Lexington, MA: D. C. Heath.

Bell, A. P., and Weinberg, M. S. (1978). *Homosexualities: A Study of Diversity Among Men and Women.* New York: Simon & Schuster.

Bigner, J. J. (1994a). *Individual and Family Development: An Interdisciplinary Lifespan Approach.* Englewood Cliffs, NJ: Prentice Hall.

Bigner, J. J. (1994b). *Parent–Child Relations: An Introduction to Parenting,* 4th edition. New York: Macmillan.

Bigner, J. J., and Bozett, F. W. (1989). "Parenting by Gay Fathers." *Marriage and Family Review* 14:155–176.

Bigner, J. J., and Jacobsen, R. B. (1989a). "The Value of Children to Gay and Heterosexual Fathers." *Journal of Homosexuality* 18:163–172.

Bigner, J. J., and Jacobsen, R. B. (1989b). "Parenting Behaviors of Homosexual and Heterosexual Fathers." *Journal of Homosexuality* 18:173–186.

Boswell, J. (1980). *Christianity, Intolerance, and Homosexuality.* Chicago: University of Chicago Press.

Bozett, F. W. (1980). "Gay Fathers: How and Why They Disclose Their Homosexuality to Their Children." *Family Relations* 29:173–179.

Bozett, F. W. (1981a). "Gay Father: Evolution of the Gay Father Identity." *American Journal of Orthopsychiatry* 51:552–559.

Bozett, F. W. (1981b). "Gay Fathers: Identity Conflict Resolution Through Integrative Sanctioning." *Alternative Lifestyles* 4:90–107.

Bozett, F. W. (1985). "Gay Men as Fathers." In *Dimensions of Fatherhood,* ed. S. Hanson and F. W. Bozett. Newbury Park, CA: Sage Publications.

Bozett, F. W. (1987). "Gay Fathers." In *Gay and Lesbian Parents,* ed. F. W. Bozett. New York: Praeger.

Bozett, F. W., and Sussman, M. B. (1989). "Homosexuality and Family Relations: Views and Research Issues." In *Homosexuality and Family Relations,* ed. F. W. Bozett and M. B. Sussman. New York: Harrington Park Press.

Clark, D. (1987). *Loving Someone Gay,* revised and updated. Berkeley, CA: Celestial Arts.

Eichberg, R. (1990). *Coming Out: An Act of Love.* New York: Penguin Books.

Golombok, S.; Spencer, A.; and Rutter, M. (1983). "Children in Lesbian and Single-Parent Households: Psychosexual and Psychiatric Appraisal." *Journal of Child Psychology and Psychiatry* 135:692–697.

Hays, D. H., and Samuels, A. (1989). "Heterosexual Women's Perceptions of Their Marriages to Bisexual or Homosexual Men." *Journal of Homosexuality* 18:81–100.

Herek, G. M. (1984). "Beyond Homophobia: A Social Psychological Perspective on Attitudes toward Lesbians and Gay Men." *Journal of Homosexuality* 10:1–22.

Lamb, M. E., ed. (1982). *Nontraditional Families: Parenting and Child Development.* Hillsdale, NJ: Lawrence Erlbaum.

Miller, J. A.; Jacobsen, R. B.; and Bigner, J. J. (1981). "The Child's Home Environment for Lesbian vs. Heterosexual Mothers: A Neglected Area of Research." *Journal of Homosexuality* 7:49–56.

Patterson, C. J. (1992). "Children of Lesbian and Gay Parents." *Child Development* 63:1025–1042.

Pennington, S. (1987). "Children of Lesbian Mothers." In *Gay and Lesbian Parents,* ed. F. W. Bozett. New York: Praeger.

Pharr, S. (1988). *Homophobia: A Weapon of Sexism.* Inverness, CA: Chardon Press.

Pies, C. A. (1989). "Lesbians and the Choice to Parent." *Marriage and Family Review* 14:137–154.

Robinson, B. E., and Barret, R. L. (1986). "Gay Fathers." In *The Developing Father: Emerging Roles in Contemporary Society,* ed. B. E. Robinson and R. L. Barret. New York: Guilford.

Weinberg, G. (1972). *Society and the Healthy Homosexual.* Boston: Alyson.

JERRY J. BIGNER

GENDER

Gender is a fundamental principle of social organization. All human societies make distinctions between females and males, and these distinctions form the basis for differences in how each group is treated and what others expect. Of course, gender is not the only important social category—distinctions based on social class, ethnicity, race, age, and religion can also be consequential for a society and its members. Nevertheless, gender is a significant social category that shapes individuals, their interaction patterns and relationships, and the institutions they create and in which they participate. Because gender distinctions are, in the words of Candace West and Sarah Fenstermaker (1993), "potentially omnirelevant to social life," the sociology of gender encompasses a vast range of topics.

Alternative Conceptions of Gender

What is gender? Sociologists have provided diverse answers to this question, and these answers have changed significantly over time. In simplest terms, gender can be defined as "patterned, socially produced distinctions between male and female, feminine and masculine" (Acker 1992). However, this broad definition incorporates two distinct emphases. Specifically, conceptions of gender can be divided into those treating it as an individual property and those viewing it as an emergent feature of social interaction (Thompson 1993; Ferree 1990; West and Fenstermaker 1993). The former approaches thus are concerned with individual characteristics that differentiate women from men, while the latter views emphasize characteristics of the situation or setting where action occurs.

When conceived as an individual property, gender is viewed as sets of traits, preferences, and capabilities that are possessed in different degrees by women and men (Deaux 1984). These characteristics are seen as relatively stable attributes of individuals that gain expression in women's and men's beliefs and actions. A primary goal of researchers who adopt this view is to identify and explore areas of gender difference. The early research addressing these issues is summarized in Eleanor Maccoby and Carol Nagy Jacklin's (1974) important book, *The Psychology of Sex Differences*. After reviewing approximately 1,600 studies concerned primarily with psychological gender differences, these authors find conclusive evidence for differences between women and men in only four areas: verbal abilities, mathematical abilities, visual–spatial skills, and aggression. With the exception of Jeanne Block (1976), who argues that gender differences are more pervasive than Maccoby and Jacklin admit, most assessments of the psychological literature conclude that differences between women and men are smaller than previously believed (Deaux 1984).

Like psychologists, sociologists who view gender as an individual characteristic are also interested in uncovering differences between women and men. However, while psychologists are primarily interested in gender differences in mental processes and rely heavily on laboratory experiments as a data source,

sociologists employ diverse methodologies to explore gender differences in a wide range of behaviors and beliefs, as well as in various aspects of psychological and economic well-being (for a review, see Stockard and Johnson 1992). These studies have uncovered gender differences in many aspects of life.

Despite a shared conception of gender as an individual attribute, social scientists who adopt this approach constitute a diverse group. As noted, these differences pertain to methodology as well as to differences in substantive focus. The relative emphasis placed on biology or environment as the source of gender differences is another line of demarcation among researchers. Conceptions of gender as an individual property typically distinguish between "sex," or the genetic and physical aspects of femaleness and maleness, and "gender," which refers to the social and cultural components of these identities. The influence sex exerts on gender continues to be widely debated, with some arguing that biological factors have consequential influences upon gender (Rossi 1977). Although the relations between "sex" and "gender" may be more complicated than previously assumed, most sociologists nevertheless believe that the social environment is an important (though perhaps not the only) source of the attributes presumed to differentiate women from men.

Some use the concept of "role" to describe the social origins of gender differences (Parsons and Bales 1955). In this view, gender differentiation arises from the fact that women and men have internalized different expectations for their behavior. Gender roles (or sex roles, as they were originally called) therefore represent those beliefs and behaviors socially defined as appropriate for one's gender. These roles are learned as part of the socialization process in families and are reinforced by other social institutions, such as schools and media.

Despite differences in methodology and emphasis, psychological and sociological research on gender differences shares a view of gender as an individual attribute. Although this research has yielded important findings, approaches that treat gender as a property of individuals have come under increasing criticism (Stacey and Thorne 1985; Thompson 1993). Critics argue that these approaches fail to examine similarities between gender categories and divergence within them, are unable to address questions of gender inequality and power, and ignore the roles situational and institutional characteristics play in shaping gender relations. For these reasons, many sociologists have abandoned a view of gender as a set of internalized "roles" or personality traits for an approach emphasizing the social construction of gender relations (West and Fenstermaker 1993).

In West and Fenstermaker's (1993, p. 155) words, "Gender is . . . accomplished through interaction with others." This view treats gender as an emergent feature of social interaction, rather than a stable property of individuals. Greater attention is devoted to exploring the processes through which gender is constructed and maintained than toward identifying gender differences (Ferree 1990). In addition, from this perspective, situational characteristics are of greater research interest than individual ones (Kessler and McKenna 1978). West and Don Zimmerman's (1987) claim that gender is not merely something that people "are," but is also a set of activities that they "do," best captures this point of view.

Many who view gender as an emergent feature of social interaction embrace an ethnomethodological perspective. Ethnomethodologists examine taken-for-granted and hence "objective" aspects of social life to discover the processes through which these are achieved (West and Zimmerman 1987). With respect to gender, as Suzanne Kessler and Wendy McKenna (1978, p. 3) explain, the question becomes "How is a world where there are two, and only two, genders constructed?" Researchers answer this question by examining the interactions of people in particular social situations (e.g., households or workplaces), and the ways these interactions give rise to gendered conceptions of self and others. In this view, situations provide resources and constraints for "doing gender" and therefore are integral to the analysis. For example, in her study of table servers, Elaine Hall (1993) explores how aspects of restaurant work organization (e.g., job titles and uniforms) help maintain gendered styles of service. Even when women and men are performing the same job in the same restaurant, different meanings are assigned to their work. Hall (1993, p. 331) describes the difference between her approach and one treating gender as an individual attribute in this way: "Instead of assuming that workers 'bring' gender to their jobs, I assume workers 'do gender,' performing their jobs in certain ways because their jobs are structured to demand gender displays."

Others who view gender as emergent in social interaction focus attention on variations within gender categories. These researchers explore how gender identities are constructed through relations with others in a variety of settings, such as friendships, the workplace, and sport (Connell 1992; Messner 1992). Researchers use the terms "masculinities" and "femininities" rather than the singular forms of these words. This reflects their view that women and men

are not homogeneous categories, but instead are internally diverse groups. Because the contexts within which gender is constructed vary by participants' social class, race, ethnicity, and sexual orientation, the notion of a single male or female "gender role" is thus inappropriate.

While most social scientists agree that gender involves socially patterned distinctions between female and male, they disagree over how best to conceptualize these patterns. For some, gender is a personal attribute, meaning that it is attached to people as a set of personality traits or behavioral predispositions. For others, gender is a product of social interactions and takes its meaning from features of the contexts where it is produced. Both approaches have inspired important research. Studies of gender differences are valuable in identifying areas of convergence and divergence in women's and men's experiences, while studies of the processes through which gender is constructed yield insights into how and why gender distinctions are maintained.

Theories of Socialization

What is the process through which people learn how to be feminine and masculine? How does a society's messages about what are appropriate behaviors for women and men get transmitted to its members? How, more important, is it that societal members come to use gender as a basis for organizing and assimilating information? Answers to these questions are supplied by various theories of gender socialization. The two views of gender previously described place different importance on the socialization process. This process plays a central role in approaches that treat gender as an individual property, while socialization receives less attention from those who view gender as an emergent process.

There are three major theories of socialization (Bem 1983; Stockard and Johnson 1992). Two theories, social learning and cognitive development, are general learning theories that are also applicable to gender-role acquisition, while the third perspective, identification theory, was developed specifically to explain gender. Social learning theory asserts that gender roles are learned through reinforcements—both rewards and punishments—that children receive for engaging in gender-appropriate and gender-inappropriate behavior (Mischel 1970). This perspective also acknowledges that learning takes place through observation and modeling (Bandura and Walters 1963). According to social learning theorists, reinforcements, whether experienced directly in the form of rewards and punishments or vicariously experienced through observation, are the primary means through which children take on gender-appropriate behaviors. Differential treatment by parents and other socializing agents thus results in gender-differentiated children.

Although reinforcement may be one mechanism through which gender roles are acquired, this theory fails to provide a complete account of this process (Stockard and Johnson 1992; Bem 1983). Evidence suggests that children, especially boys, may persist in gender-appropriate behaviors even when they are not reinforced for these activities, or even when they are negatively reinforced (Stockard and Johnson 1992). More generally, Sandra Lipsitz Bem (1983) argues that children are more actively involved in their own socialization than social learning theorists acknowledge. Regarding social learning theory, she observes: "This view of the passive child is inconsistent with the common observation that children themselves frequently construct and enforce their own version of society's gender rules" (Bem 1983, p. 600).

This assessment leads some to endorse cognitive development theory. Most closely associated with psychologist Lawrence Kohlberg, cognitive development theorists adopt a more active view of children than proponents of social learning. These theorists argue that gender-role learning can be explained using the principles of cognitive development. According to this perspective, once children have labeled themselves as female or male, and recognize this as stable over time and situations, they are motivated to seek out gender-appropriate behaviors. In addition, children attach greater value to these behaviors and experience them as being more positively reinforcing than gender-inappropriate behaviors. With age, children's abilities to interpret gender cues become more sophisticated and flexible, a pattern cognitive development theorists argue parallels intellectual development more generally.

This perspective views children as, in important respects, socializing themselves. It implies that gender distinctions are salient to children and that gender is, because of this, used to organize and process information from the environment. Although this theory receives empirical support, some critics are skeptical of its claim that gender-role learning takes place only after children have labeled themselves as female or male. In addition, Bem (1983) argues that cognitive development theorists fail to explain why and how children come to employ gender, rather than some other attribute (e.g., race), as a cognitive organizing principle.

Identification theory, the third major theory of socialization, differs from the previous two perspectives in significant ways. First, unlike social learning and cognitive development approaches, identification theory is explicitly concerned with gender, gender identity, and sexuality (Stockard and Johnson 1992). More important, however, this perspective rejects claims that gender-appropriate behavior is learned through reinforcement, imitation, or a conscious intent to behave a particular way. Instead, drawing from the ideas of Sigmund Freud and his followers, identification theorists assert that at least some aspects of gender result from unconscious psychological processes (Chodorow 1978; Williams 1989).

Nancy Chodorow's (1978) object-relations approach to gender is the most influential expression of this theory, although she is not the only one to explore the gender implications of Freud's views. Chodorow argues that the organization of family life, and particularly women's responsibility for children, is key to understanding the development of femininity and masculinity. Because young children typically receive their earliest care from their mother, both females and males first identify psychologically with her. To develop a masculine gender identity, however, males must later separate from the mother and forgo this initial attachment. This process is made more difficult by fathers' lesser availability as models to their sons. In contrast, because females are cared for by other females, the development of a feminine gender identity is less problematic for them than for males.

According to Chodorow (1978), these different paths to gender identification are responsible for gender-differentiated female and male personalities. Men learn that masculinity requires the denial of affective ties and connection, while women learn to define femininity in terms of relatedness to others. More important, identification theorists argue that "gender means different things for men and women" (Williams 1989, p. 134). Men have a greater emotional investment than women in the maintenance of gender distinctions, a pattern identification theorists trace to women's and men's earliest experiences with female parenting.

This perspective has been criticized on the grounds that it is empirically unverifiable. Others have challenged Chodorow's failure to consider race and social-class variations in the patterns she describes. At the same time, however, this perspective has informed gender theory and research on many topics, including the workplace, family relations, and morality. Despite its origins in Freudian psychology, identification theory has been more influential among sociologists than psychologists (Bem 1983).

Although social learning, cognitive development, and identification theory constitute the major theories of socialization, there have been efforts to develop synthetic approaches that draw on two or more of these perspectives. For example, Jean Stockard and Miriam Johnson's (1992) cognitive learning theory combines aspects of social learning and cognitive development, as does Bem's (1983) gender schema theory. Gender schema theory aims to explain why and how children learn to process information in gendered ways. Bem argues that in cultures where gender is an important social category children learn to use this category to organize and assimilate new information. Gender schemas thus are cognitive structures that help impose order on perception.

Although they differ in important ways, these theories all attempt to explain how women and men acquire gender-appropriate behaviors and beliefs. Because theories of socialization address how people become gendered, these perspectives are of greater significance to those who view gender as an individual property than those treating gender as emergent. While studies of gender differences often view these differences as the result of gender socialization, those treating gender as an emergent feature of social interaction are skeptical that socialization has such effects. These latter researchers do not deny that socialization takes place, but they do question its capacity to explain adult women's and men's behavior fully (Epstein 1988; Gerson 1985; Ferree 1990).

Consistent with the previously described developments in how gender is conceived, recent years have seen a reconsideration of socialization's role in explaining gender distinctions. Kathleen Gerson (1985) argues that socialization theories falsely create a view of women and men as homogeneous groups, possessing internally consistent and unchanging motives and behavioral dispositions. Instead, her research shows that early childhood experiences and socialization are poor predictors of adult women's work and family decisions. Gerson found that women whose early lives prepared them for domesticity sometimes pursued careers, while some women who anticipated careers became full-time wives and mothers. She argues that women's choices are best viewed as "an interaction between socially structured opportunities and constraints and active attempts to make sense of and respond to these structures" (Gerson 1985, p. 192).

Theories of socialization focus on the processes through which individuals acquire gender-appropriate behavioral orientations and personalities. Because most consider gender distinctions as primarily social rather than biological in origin, researchers view socialization as an important process to understand. However, as conceptions of gender have expanded, researchers have begun to view socialization as only one part of the explanation for gender distinctions. Instead, many believe that situational characteristics interact with, and sometimes offset, internalized personality attributes and behavioral dispositions to create gendered outcomes.

Household Division of Labor

The conceptual and theoretical debates can be more clearly illustrated through a focus on a particular research area in the sociology of gender. The household division of labor is among the topics most studied by gender researchers interested in marriage and family. In the 1950s and 1960s, Talcott Parsons (Parsons 1964; Parsons and Bales 1955) used the gender division of labor in the family as the basis for his conception of female and male "sex roles." In his view, a division of labor whereby men are responsible for the instrumental tasks associated with being a wage earner, while women perform the expressive tasks of caring for children and providing emotional support, is functional for both family solidarity and the larger society.

Along with other aspects of the functionalist perspective from which it emerged, this view of the family has been highly criticized (Stacey and Thorne 1985). Critics charge that Parsons's view of gender relations is inherently conservative and oriented toward prescription rather than description of family behavior. In addition, Parsons's critics suggest that his instrumental/expressive distinction reifies gender stereotypes and prevents consideration of women's work in the home. Finally, the critics argue that Parsons ignores husbands' power over wives (Stacey and Thorne 1985; Stockard and Johnson 1992).

More recent discussions of the household division of labor explore these problematic aspects of Parsons's analysis, and they identify new issues for examination. Much effort has been devoted to describing the kinds of activities women and men perform in the family. Myra Marx Ferree (1990) divides studies into those focusing on the physical labor of housework and those concerned with the symbolic meaning of these activities. Researchers who conceive of household work as physical labor are typically concerned with identifying gender differences in the amount and type of work performed and, hence, tend toward a view of gender as an individual property. By contrast, researchers interested in the symbolic meanings associated with household work are more likely to view gender as an emergent feature of social interaction.

According to Sampson Lee Blair and Michael P. Johnson (1992, p. 570), "Virtually every study investigating the division of household labor has come to two basic conclusions: Women perform approximately twice as much labor as men; and women perform qualitatively different types of chores than men." Arlie Hochschild (1989) reviews some of the many studies of women's and men's performance of housework and child care. She concludes that women spend roughly fifteen hours per week longer than men at these tasks, resulting in women working an extra month of twenty-four-hour days per year (Hochschild 1989). Other estimates of time spent in housework are consistent with these data. For instance, Blair and Johnson (1992) found that women devote approximately thirty-three hours per week to household tasks and men contribute only fourteen hours per week to household tasks.

Women and men also perform different kinds of activities in the home. Household work, like paid work, therefore, is gender-segregated, with women and men each performing tasks typically associated with their gender (e.g., men perform outdoor tasks, such as mowing the lawn or working on the car, while women do cleaning and care for children) (Blair and Lichter 1991; Berk 1985). The tasks typically performed by women and men diverge in other respects as well. Household tasks performed by men involve greater personal discretion than those women perform, are more likely to have a fixed beginning and end, and are more likely to involve a leisure component (Hochschild 1989). In contrast to Parsons's view of the household as an expressive realm, these studies thus indicate that household members perform a significant amount of "instrumental" family work—cleaning, cooking meals, shopping, and so forth. Although the total number of hours devoted to household work has declined over time, these tasks continue to be performed primarily by women (England and Farkas 1986).

Other studies extend this research by examining the factors that influence women's and men's participation in housework. Specifically, they explore the conditions associated with more egalitarian household divisions of labor. Some theorists argue that the relative resources of husband and wife explain the amount of time each devotes to household work (England and Farkas 1986). Because earnings are one important resource in marriage, this perspective sug-

gests that husbands' performance of household work should respond to changes in wives' relative wages. Studies have not found much support for this argument, however (England and Farkas 1986). Even when their wife's wage is equal to or greater than their own, men perform significantly less housework than women (Hochschild 1989). Others argue that situational constraints, such as the presence of children or time demands associated with a job, explain gender differences in the household division of labor. In support of this view, studies suggest that the hours both spouses spend performing housework are influenced by wives' employment demands and having young children. Researchers thus conclude that men's participation in housework increases when their wives are unavailable to perform such work.

Other explanations for gender differences in the household division of labor focus on women's and men's gender ideologies. These studies explore how women's and, to a lesser extent, men's gender attitudes influence the type and amount of household work each performs. The results of this research are mixed. While some conclude that gender ideologies are unrelated to husbands' and wives' performance of household work, others find greater support for this argument (England and Farkas 1986). Hochschild (1989) offers a more complex perspective of the relations between gender ideologies and the household division of labor. She suggests that while gender ideologies shape women's and men's conceptions of their family roles and the "gender strategies" they pursue to enact those roles, there may be an inconsistency between the form each spouse believes the division of labor "should" take and its actual expression. Couples may develop what she calls "family myths" to manage this tension between their gender ideologies and the realities of the household division of labor.

In addition to this research on housework as physical labor, other studies explore the symbolic meanings associated with doing household work. These investigators take issue with those viewing marriage and housework as strictly economic arrangements, arguing instead that the meanings associated with these relations and activities must be explored (Ferree 1990). In this view, the performance of household work results in both the production of goods and services (e.g., meals, clean laundry) and the production of gender (Berk 1985; West and Fenstermaker 1993). In West and Fenstermaker's (1993, p. 162) words, "Our claim is not simply that household labor is regarded as women's work, but that for a woman to do it and a man not to do it draws on and affirms what people conceive to be the essential nature of each."

In her study of "feeding the family," Marjorie L. DeVault (1991) draws on these ideas to explore how family activities related to caregiving, such as cooking and preparing family meals, are constructed as women's work. Women's participation in these activities cannot be understood in strictly instrumental terms using the framework of paid work, nor should it be viewed as a natural expression of women's essential caring natures. Instead, DeVault (1991) argues that the social organization of family life and the cultural meanings associated with women's place in the family give rise to a conception of caring as a gendered activity. On a more general level, Scott Coltrane (1989, p. 473) explores how women's and men's performance of household labor "provides the opportunity for expressing, confirming, and sometimes transforming the meaning of gender." He shows that parents in families where household work and child care are shared are more likely to embrace an ideology of gender similarity than those in households with less equitable arrangements. For Coltrane (1989), however, family members' conceptions of gender are the product, rather than the source, of the household division of labor. In other words, participation in the everyday activities associated with household work produces family members' beliefs about women and men.

Like other areas of gender research, studies of the household division of labor draw on diverse conceptions of gender and hence pursue different objectives. While some seek to identify gender differences in the type and amount of women's and men's household work, others aim to uncover the meanings associated with these activities and the processes through which these meanings are produced. In addition to these efforts are other studies exploring the implications and consequences of the household division of labor. For example, some examine women's and men's perceptions of the division of labor, particularly with respect to its perceived fairness. Others examine the relations between women's performance of household work and their experiences in the labor market (Crosby 1987), while still others assess the implications of the household division of labor for husbands' and wives' marital and psychological well-being (Ross, Mirowsky, and Huber 1983). Finally, there has been an effort to expand the kinds of activities involved in studies of housework to include "emotion work" and "kin work."

Changing Attitudes

One important contribution gender researchers have made to studies of families and marriage is to demonstrate the connections between these entities and the larger society (Ferree 1990). In Hochschild's (1989, p. 11) words, "Each marriage bears the footprints of economic and cultural trends which originate far outside marriage." This suggests that the household division of labor is shaped by more than family members' individual characteristics. These activities are also influenced by larger societal developments that provide the context within which families operate. The societal factors shaping family and marriage are numerous and diverse, as they include economic developments, demographic patterns, political events, and cultural trends.

Efforts to track change and stability in attitudes toward gender represent one kind of attempt to capture the effects of these various societal-level factors on individuals. Longitudinal studies of gender attitudes, or those comparing cross-sectional studies from multiple time periods, attempt to identify change in gender attitudes over time. Studies analyzing data from the 1960s or 1970s to the early 1990s show that both women and men have become less traditional in their gender-related attitudes and values during this time period (Spence, Deaux, and Helmreich 1985; Wilkie 1993; Glass 1992). A greater acceptance of employment for married women, more egalitarian attitudes about women's and men's roles in the family, and greater support for equal opportunities for women in education and employment are examples of how this change has been expressed. Research further suggests that these changes "have been more pronounced among those who are younger, female, and better-educated" (Glass 1992, p. 560).

In addition to longitudinal analyses, other research on gender attitudes employs a cross-sectional design, whereby researchers examine how different groups within society perceive various gender-related issues. Researchers have been most interested in exploring women's and men's perceptions of gender inequalities, and identifying the factors shaping these perceptions. Studies of gender differences in support of gender equality are inconclusive, with some suggesting that women are more supportive of efforts to reduce gender inequality than men and others showing no gender difference (Davis and Robinson 1991).

Research conducted in the United States on women's perceptions of gender inequalities shows that employment, particularly full-time employment, is an important predictor of support for women's rights (Smith 1985). Full-time homemakers are less supportive than employed women of efforts to reduce gender inequalities. These differences can be traced to several factors. For instance, employed women may be more likely than homemakers to experience gender discrimination and, hence, more supportive of efforts to reduce it. Differences between these groups may also reflect other differences in life experience. Glass (1992) found that employed wives have become increasingly different from nonemployed wives in terms of age, education, number of children, and household income. These demographic differences may also help explain differences between full-time homemakers and employed women. Not all researchers agree with these findings, however, and there is some evidence that the factors influencing American women's perceptions of gender inequality differ from those influencing the attitudes of European women (Davis and Robinson 1991).

Conclusion

Research on gender has flourished as sociologists have come to consider gender an important principle of social organization. At the same time, conceptions of what gender is have become more varied.

Gender has long been a topic of interest among family and marriage researchers, who have found that women's and men's work and family practices, as well as their demographic characteristics and the historical era in which they live, have profound influences on their perceptions of gender and gender inequality.

While gender is an important social category, it does not exist in isolation from other aspects of social organization, such as those relating to race, ethnicity, social class, sexuality, age, and religion. Because most gender research concentrates on the white heterosexual middle class, an important task for gender scholars in the years ahead is to broaden their focus to examine other groups. These studies would help to further illuminate the diversity of gender and its expressions in social life.

(*See also:* DIVISION OF LABOR; FAMILY GENDER ROLES; GENDER IDENTITY; PERSONALITY DEVELOPMENT)

BIBLIOGRAPHY

Acker, J. (1992). "Gendering Organizational Theory." In *Gendering Organizational Analysis*, ed. A. J. Mills and P. Tancred. Newbury Park, CA: Sage Publications.

Bandura, A., and Walters, R. H. (1963). *Social Learning and Personality Development*. New York: Holt, Rinehart and Winston.

Bem, S. L. (1983). "Gender Schema Theory and Its Implications for Child Development: Raising Gender-Aschematic Children in a Gender-Schematic Society." *Signs* 8:598–616.

Berk, S. (Fenstermaker). (1985). *The Gender Factory: The Apportionment of Work in American Households*. New York: Plenum.

Blair, S. L., and Johnson, M. P. (1992). "Wives' Perceptions of the Fairness of the Division of Household Labor: The Intersection of Housework and Ideology." *Journal of Marriage and the Family* 54:570–581.

Blair, S. L., and Lichter, D. T. (1991). "Measuring the Division of Household Labor: Gender Segregation of Housework Among American Couples." *Journal of Family Issues* 12:91–113.

Block, J. H. (1976). "Issues, Problems, and Pitfalls in Assessing Sex Differences: A Critical Review of *The Psychology of Sex Differences*." *Merrill-Palmer Quarterly* 22:283–308.

Chodorow, N. (1978). *The Reproduction of Mothering: Psychoanalysis and the Sociology of Gender*. Berkeley: University of California Press.

Coltrane, S. (1989). "Household Labor and the Routine Production of Gender." *Social Problems* 36:473–490.

Connell, R. W. (1992). "A Very Straight Gay: Masculinity, Homosexual Experience, and Gender." *American Sociological Review* 57:735–751.

Crosby, F. J., ed. (1987). *Spouse, Parent, Worker: On Gender and Multiple Roles*. New Haven, CT: Yale University Press.

Davis, N. J., and Robinson, R. V. (1991). "Men's and Women's Consciousness of Gender Inequality." *American Sociological Review* 56:72–84.

Deaux, K. (1984). "From Individual Differences to Social Categories: Analysis of a Decade's Research on Gender." *American Psychologist* 39:105–116.

DeVault, M. L. (1991). *Feeding the Family: The Social Organization of Caring as Gendered Work*. Chicago: University of Chicago Press.

England, P., and Farkas, G. (1986). *Households, Employment, and Gender: A Social, Economic, and Demographic View*. New York: Aldine.

Epstein, C. (1988). *Deceptive Distinctions: Sex, Gender, and the Social Order*. New York: Russell Sage Foundation.

Erickson, R. J. (1993). "Reconceptualizing Family Work: The Effect of Emotion Work on Perceptions of Marital Quality." *Journal of Marriage and the Family* 55:888–900.

Ferree, M. M. (1990). "Beyond Separate Spheres: Feminism and Family Research." *Journal of Marriage and the Family* 52:866–884.

Gerson, K. (1985). *Hard Choices: How Women Decide About Work, Career, and Motherhood*. Berkeley: University of California Press.

Gerstel, N., and Gallagher, S. K. (1993). "Kinkeeping and Distress: Gender, Recipients of Care, and Work-Family Conflict." *Journal of Marriage and the Family* 55:598–607.

Glass, J. (1992). "Housewives and Employed Wives: Demographic and Attitudinal Change, 1972–1986." *Journal of Marriage and the Family* 54:559–569.

Hall, E. J. (1993). "Waitering/Waitressing: Engendering the Work of Table Servers." *Gender and Society* 7:329–346.

Hochschild, A. (1989). *The Second Shift: Working Parents and the Revolution at Home.* New York: Viking Penguin.

Johnson, M. M. (1988). *Strong Mothers, Weak Wives: The Search for Gender Equality.* Berkeley: University of California Press.

Kessler, S. J., and McKenna, W. (1978). *Gender: An Ethnomethodological Approach.* Chicago: University of Chicago Press.

Maccoby, E. E., and Jacklin, C. N. (1974). *The Psychology of Sex Differences.* Stanford, CA: Stanford University Press.

Messner, M. A. (1992). *Power at Play: Sports and the Problem of Masculinity.* Boston: Beacon Press.

Mischel, W. (1970). "Sex-Typing and Socialization." In *Carmichael's Manual of Child Psychology*, 3rd edition, ed. P. H. Mussen. New York: Wiley.

Parsons, T. (1964). *Essays in Sociological Theory.* New York: Free Press.

Parsons, T., and Bales, R. F. (1955). *Family, Socialization, and Interaction Process.* New York: Free Press.

Ross, C. E.; Mirowsky, J.; and Huber, J. (1983). "Dividing Work, Sharing Work, and In-Between: Marriage Patterns and Depression." *American Sociological Review* 48:809–823.

Rossi, A. S. (1977). "A Biosocial Perspective on Parenting." *Daedalus* 106:1–31.

Smith, T. W. (1985). "Working Wives and Women's Rights: The Connection Between the Employment Status of Wives and the Feminist Attitudes of Husbands." *Sex Roles* 12:501–508.

Spence, J. T.; Deaux, K.; and Helmreich, R. L. (1985). "Sex Roles in Contemporary American Society." In *Handbook of Social Psychology*, Vol. 2, ed. G. Lindzey and E. Aronson. New York: Random House.

Stacey, J., and Thorne, B. (1985). "The Missing Feminist Revolution in Sociology." *Social Problems* 32:301–316.

Stockard, J., and Johnson, M. M. (1992). *Sex and Gender in Society.* Englewood Cliffs, NJ: Prentice Hall.

Thompson, L. (1993). "Conceptualizing Gender in Marriage: The Case of Marital Care." *Journal of Marriage and the Family* 55:557–569.

West, C., and Fenstermaker, S. (1993). "Power, Inequality, and the Accomplishment of Gender: An Ethnomethodological View." In *Theory on Gender*, ed. P. England. New York: Aldine.

West, C., and Zimmerman, D. H. (1991). "Doing Gender." In *The Social Construction of Gender*, ed. J. Lorber and S. A. Farrell. Newbury Park, CA: Sage Publications.

Wilkie, J. R. (1993). "Changes in U.S. Men's Attitudes Toward the Family Provider Role, 1972–1989." *Gender and Society* 7:261–279.

Williams, C. (1989). *Gender Differences at Work.* Berkeley: University of California Press.

AMY S. WHARTON

GENDER IDENTITY

Gender identity is the private experience of being male or female. Gender role is the public expression of gender, everything a person says or does that indicates a status as male or female. Gender role includes social and legal identification. Usually gender identity and gender role correspond like two sides of the same coin, with a unity of gender identity/role.

Gender is a psychological and cultural concept, in contrast to sex, which is a biological term. Sex refers to the physical appearance of the genitals and reproductive organs (gonadal sex or sex phenotype), or in some cases the chromosomes (genotype). Sex is divided into two classes: male or female. However, some individuals are born with physical intersex conditions, such as a hermaphrodite, whose genitalia are unfinished or ambiguous at birth so the person cannot readily be typified as one sex or the other. Usually, these persons are assigned to one sex for rearing. In some societies they may be assigned and reared as hermaphrodites. Two examples of this are the "turnim man" in New Guinea and the "guevodoces" in the Dominican Republic.

The word "gender" was used only to refer to classes of nouns in languages until psychologist John Money adopted the term in 1955 to refer to sexual attributes of people. He first introduced the term "gender role" to discuss whether hermaphrodites socially disclosed themselves as male or female. Some were reared as boys, others as girls. In most cases their gender role corresponded to their assigned sex of rearing, rather than their gonads or chromosomes. The term "gender identity" was popularized by Money's naming in 1966 of the Gender Identity Clinic at the Johns Hopkins Hospital, which pioneered in evaluation of transsexuals and sex reassignment. Robert Stoller, at UCLA, also promoted the use of the term "gender" to refer to psychological status as distinct from sex.

Since the 1970s, the use of the term "gender" has captured the public imagination in contexts that go far beyond hermaphroditism and transsexualism. "Gender" has evolved as the term, particularly in feminist usage, to represent the social and cultural characteristics of the sexes as distinct from the biological differences between males and females. Thus "gender" is used to imply what is acquired or learned by the sexes, while "sex" is used to refer to what is thought to be biological and unchangeable. In this framework, sex represents intractable nature, and gender represents malleable nurture. This is a reversal in connotation for the term "gender," which Money had used to describe individuals whose physical sex was hormonally and surgically altered to correspond to their immutable psychological gender identity.

Development of Gender Identity

Gender identity develops through a process of differentiation: interactions of biological, social, and cognitive-learning factors that occur over time. Differentiation means that a basically similar structure develops differently, depending on the influence of other factors. Female and male human fetuses are undifferentiated (have the same physical form) until after the second month of prenatal development. As development progresses, various influences increase the difference between the sexes. Changes in sexual and gender development occur (or do not occur) at specific times or critical periods, and thereafter may be permanent. The process begins prenatally with the sex-determining chromosomes, the development of fetal gonads, and the influence of hormones on the fetus, including influence on the brain. The basic model is female, and something extra has to be added to differentiate a male.

At birth almost all infants are socially labeled as either a girl or a boy, based on the appearance of the external genitals. Others may treat the child differently, depending on the labeled sex. The child begins

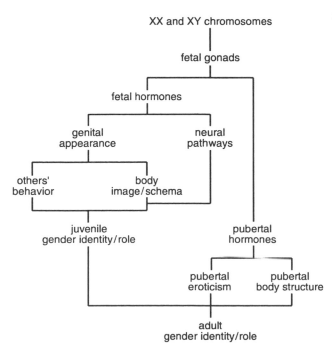

Figure 1 Diagram to illustrate the sequential and interactional components of gender-identity differentiation (Money 1993; reprinted by permission of the author).

to develop a body image of the self as a girl or a boy. After language is acquired, by eighteen months to two years, the child can label the self as "girl" or "boy." This is the early expression of gender identity.

Gender identity is developed through two learning processes: identification and complementation. Some of the learning is based on biological characteristics or physical similarities or differences between the sexes. Identification is the learning process of becoming like someone: The child identifies with the gender characteristics of individuals of the same sex. Complementation is the process of learning by contrary example what not to do: The child complements the gender characteristics of individuals of the other sex. Like learning to dance, the child learns to follow the example of a same-sex model and to mirror the movements of the other-sex partner. The child thus develops mental schemas for both feminine and masculine characteristics. One schema is considered the gender identity of the self, and the other schema is considered to belong to people of the other sex. Some of this learning occurs at biologically determined critical periods of time; once learned, it is imprinted and extremely difficult to alter.

All societies partition some aspects of human existence into two distinct roles of male and female. The specific content of these gender roles varies among different societies. These characteristics may or may not be closely related to the biological functional differences between females and males: Females have a vagina and may bear children; males have a penis and may impregnate. The difficulty that children face in this learning process is determining which characteristics of others are gender-linked and which are not.

Children develop gender identity constancy by five to six years of age. Gender constancy is the concept that if a child is a girl, she will always be female and will grow up to be a woman; if a child is a boy, he will always be male and will grow up to be a man. These continuities are not obvious but must be learned. Before puberty, girls and boys are more like each other than either are like adult women and men. Juvenile gender identity is consolidated through social experiences of exploring sexual and gender characteristics, including games such as "show me" and "playing doctor" and sexual rehearsal play.

The hormones of puberty introduce changes in the sexual characteristics of the body. Usually these changes are consistent with the gender identity and gender role. Sometimes they are not, as when boys develop breasts, or when the physical changes are delayed or do not meet expectations. These physical changes must be incorporated into the gender identity. Standards of feminine or masculine physical attractiveness change from childhood, as do other aspects of gender roles. Social pressures intensify for conformity to female and male gender roles. In addition, the sex hormones fuel romantic and sexual interests. Sexual orientation as heterosexual, bisexual, or homosexual also becomes part of an adult gender identity and role.

Gender identity is usually stable from early childhood through adulthood. The conceptualization of the self as male or female is a basic part of human identity and does not readily change. Only in a few societies or situations is another gender identity possible: the idea of an intersex or transsexual, such as the Native American "berdache" or the "hijra" of India. Although gender identity as man or woman is stable, some of the content of an individual's gender role may change over a lifetime because of changing social norms or a move to another society.

Implications

Many children are raised in households without men. These children spend much of their time with women, including caregivers and teachers. They may not spend much time interacting with adults of both sexes. What effect may their limited access to male role models have on their development of gender identity and roles?

If gender learning were based only on same-sex identification, then children might have difficulty developing gender identities if they grew up in an environment where they primarily interacted with adults of one sex. However, the learning principle of complementation says that children can learn both gender roles even if their adult models are mostly of one sex. Boys complement themselves to women and girls; girls complement themselves to men and boys. Therefore, children are able to differentiate the gender identity appropriate to themselves, even if their caregivers are primarily of one sex. One difficulty of learning about gender roles primarily from one sex is that the child may think that more human characteristics are gender-specific than is the case. Some children with limited models of both sexes may become more sex-role stereotyped, since they have limited opportunities to see both sexes engaging in similar behaviors. Representations of both sexes, and their interactions, in the media can be helpful. Also, peers teach each other about the content of gender roles—although they often are more stereotyped than adults.

There is growing interest in decreasing sex role stereotyping in the family and society. Even in the traditional two-parent family, distinctions between appropriate tasks, roles, and occupations for women and men are changing. Styles of personal grooming and dress are becoming less differentiated, particularly among younger people. How could this affect individuals' gender identities?

There is no precedent for a human society without a distinction between males and females; no society is sexless or gender-neutral. However, societies vary in the content of different sex roles and in the number of characteristics that are sexually differentiated. The irreducible distinction is having a penis or having a vagina. When social differences between males and females are minimized, as in some tribal societies, children are usually exposed to nudity of both sexes. These children can develop gender identities based on physical differences between the sexes and not the social conventions of styles of grooming, dress, or social tasks and roles.

Social learning of new content of gender roles can be as difficult as learning a new language. Changes in the social content of gender roles may be threatening for individuals who developed their gender identities based on superficial gender characteristics.

In marriage and other social relations, interaction and communication are facilitated by a shared sense of gender roles. An individual's own gender identity presupposes a complementary schema for the gender-related behavior of the spouse and individuals of the other sex. Insofar as people do not share the same complementary schema for gender roles, there can be conflict and misunderstood communication. For example, accurate interpretation of the verbal or nonverbal sexual communication of wife and husband presupposes that they each have similar mental schemas for male and female behavior.

Variations, Problems, and Disorders

Some children exhibit many of the gender characteristics of the other sex. This has mostly been studied in Western cultures. "Sissy" boys may prefer girls for playmates, may avoid rough-and-tumble play and team sports with peer boys, and may identify with female characters and prefer feminine roles in play. Such boys may express dissatisfaction with their male sex and express a desire to be the other sex. Despite considerable rejection and teasing from peers, they persist in their "sissy" behavior. "Tomboy" girls may excel in sports and athletics and prefer to engage in these activities with boys. They may avoid domestic play with girls and refuse to wear dresses or skirts. Some also express dissatisfaction with their sex and say they want to be male when they grow up. "Tomboyish" girls are subject to peer pressure to be more feminine but are not usually teased as much as "sissy" boys.

Extreme manifestations of these characteristics are symptoms of gender identity disorders in children. Parents, teachers, and other professionals may be concerned that these children want to change their sex. However, almost none of these children seek sex reassignment when they grow up. Many of the sissy boys turn out to be homosexuals, as do some of the tomboyish girls. Treatment does not seem to influence this outcome.

Homosexuality is a sexual orientation that is also a variation in gender identity and role. Lesbians and gay men fall in love and are sexually attracted to people of the same sex instead of the other sex. This aspect of a person's gender identity is usually revealed in sexual fantasies in adolescence or young adulthood. This variation may come as a surprise to some; to others it explains the incongruity of gender identity that was present from earlier childhood but not understood as sexual orientation. Individuals go through a process of adjusting to this newly revealed component of their gender identity, which is sometimes confusing and upsetting.

Transsexualism represents a severe problem of gender identity and role. People with a gender identity disorder (transsexuals) know which sex corresponds to their body and the gender in which they were raised. Instead of being comfortable with this gender identity and role, however, they experience discomfort, called gender dysphoria. They believe that the other gender role is more appropriate and consistent with how they feel about themselves, their gender identity. This leads them to seek out procedures to alter their bodies and social presentation to correspond with their gender identities.

Variations in gender identity can cause difficulties of acceptance within families of origin or marriage. In these cases, the traditional gender-role expectations of others have been disappointed. In the end, the individual usually strives to live according to her or his gender identity.

Society is sometimes hostile to variations in gender identity and roles. However, changes in social gender roles have little immediate impact on the gender identities of members of that society. Gender identity, once established, is remarkably stable and resistant to change.

(*See also:* FAMILY GENDER ROLES; GENDER; PERSONALITY DEVELOPMENT; SEXUAL ORIENTATION)

BIBLIOGRAPHY

Green, R. (1987). *The "Sissy Boy Syndrome" and the Development of Homosexuality.* New Haven, CT: Yale University Press.

Money, J. (1988). *Gay, Straight, and In-Between: The Sexology of Erotic Orientation.* New York: Oxford University Press.

Money, J. (1993). *The Adam Principle: Genes, Genitals, Hormones, and Gender.* New York: Prometheus.

Money, J., and Ehrhardt, A. (1972). *Man and Woman, Boy and Girl: The Differentiation and Dimorphism of Gender Identity from Conception to Maturity.* Baltimore: Johns Hopkins University Press.

Reinisch, J.; Rosenblum, L.; and Saunders, S., eds. (1987). *Masculinity/Femininity: Basic Perspectives.* New York: Oxford University Press.

Stoller, R. (1974). *Sex and Gender: The Development of Masculinity and Femininity.* New York: Jason Aronson.

GREGORY K. LEHNE

GENDER ROLES *See* FAMILY GENDER ROLES; GENDER; GENDER IDENTITY

GENEALOGY

Genealogy is traditionally defined as the study of a person's ancestry or the study of one's parental lines going back as far as possible in history. Probably the first recorded "genealogy" is that found in the Book of Numbers in the Bible. During the nineteenth century in the United States, genealogy became associated with membership in particular lineage societies. Only those who could prove they were descended from a particular group of people (e.g., Mayflower passengers, participants in the American Revolution) were eligible for membership in specialized societies.

The first genealogical society with membership open to anyone who wished to search for their ancestry, the New England Genealogical Society in Boston, was formed in 1845 and is still in existence. The National Genealogical Society, located in Arlington, Virginia, formed in 1903 with a national focus in its library collection, publications, and conferences. The National Archives, in Washington, D.C., and its branch record centers throughout the United States hold the federally generated records for public research. By the late twentieth century, many state and local genealogical societies were established where extensive library collections were made available to anyone who wished to research, sometimes for a small membership fee.

After the first U.S. centennial celebration in 1876, the number of published genealogies (often compiled by sources within a family and not always documented by public records) increased. By 1900, Gilbert Cope in Pennsylvania, Colonel Lemuel Chester and Henry F. Waters from New England, and Donald Lines Jacobus in Connecticut began to set a more professional standard for the study of one's family. The study and publication of family histories increasingly involved the use of original documents, evaluation of evidence such as that used in a court of law, standards for documenting sources, local history, and the areas of sociology, economics, and psychology. No longer was the study of genealogy only associated with exclusive organizations.

The study of genealogy has greatly expanded beyond an interest in only parental lines to include relatives who descend from all family members—brothers, sisters, aunts, uncles—across many generations of a family. The general genealogical principle in tracing one's family is to begin with present and work backward, one generation at a time, collecting information from all living relatives and learning about the locations in and conditions under which they lived. Once that part of the search is completed, the research turns to a vast array of original source material, such as vital, census, land, probate, court, war, church, cemetery, social security, and employment records in the public domain and printed sources.

The U.S. bicentennial celebration and Alex Haley's *Roots* (1976), the saga of an American family with both African slave and Irish immigrant roots, have been credited with the burgeoning interest in family history. Genealogy has become an extremely popular hobby, as well as a growing profession in the United States. Genetic research and computer programs to store, retrieve, and analyze information on multiple generations of a family are both growing aspects of genealogical research.

Standard forms for collecting and documenting the family's history include an ancestral chart tracing paternal lines only, a family group sheet that documents all the details of each nuclear family, and the genogram or family chart diagramming a family's structure and process through multiple generations.

Home-study courses are offered by the National Genealogical Society, which also sponsors an annual conference in various locations around the country. Open to the general public, the conferences provide opportunities for beginning, intermediate, and advanced researchers to learn how to do personal research and use various source materials. College courses on researching genealogy are often offered at the community-college level in larger metropolitan areas. A handful of universities, including Brigham Young University, Vermont College of Norwich University, and New College of the University of Alabama, offer degree-granting programs specializing in family or local history.

By far, the single largest collection of original source material for researching families is that held by the Family History Library (FHL), owned and operated by the Church of Jesus Christ of Latter-Day Saints (the Mormons) in Salt Lake City. The FHL's collection, open to the general public, includes printed and microfilm material from all parts of the world. Hundreds of branch libraries of the FHL are attached to local stakes of the church and provide access to the holdings of the main FHL collection.

Other publicly and privately owned research facilities with large printed and microfilm holdings exist in every region of the country to assist researchers in locating materials of relevance to their families.

The Association of Professional Genealogists, located in Washington, D.C., is the membership organization for professional researchers. Two organizations grant certification or accreditation to professional researchers in the United States: the FHL and the Board for Certification of Genealogists, located in Falmouth, Virginia.

(*See also:* INHERITANCE; KINSHIP)

BIBLIOGRAPHY

Bentley, E. P. (1994). *The Genealogist's Address Book*, 3rd edition. Baltimore: Genealogical Publishing.

Doane, G. H. (1992). *Searching for Your Ancestors: The How and Why of Genealogy*, 6th edition. Minneapolis: University of Minnesota Press.

Eakle, A., and Cerny, J., eds. (1984). *The Source: A Guidebook of American Genealogy*. Salt Lake City: Ancestry Publishing.

Eichholz, A., ed. (1992). *Ancestry's Red Book: American State, County, and Town Sources*, revised edition. Salt Lake City: Ancestry Publishing.

Greenwood, V. (1990). *The Researcher's Guide to American Genealogy*, 2nd edition. Baltimore: Genealogical Publishing.

Jacobus, D. L. (1968). *Genealogy as Pastime and Profession*, 2nd edition. Baltimore: Genealogical Publishing.

Kemp, T. K. (1990). *International Vital Records Handbook*. Baltimore: Genealogical Publishing.

ALICE EICHHOLZ

GENETIC COUNSELING

Genetic counseling is the process in which a specially trained professional communicates with a person, couple, or family about the occurrence, or chance of occurrence, of a birth defect or genetic condition. Genetic counselors, who have training in both human genetics and counseling, may have an M.D., Ph.D., R.N., or M.S. degree. While many genetic counselors work in university medical centers, others work with private hospitals, state or federal health departments, diagnostic laboratories, or in private practice.

Many individuals, in a variety of situations, may benefit from genetic counseling. Examples of common circumstances in which genetic counseling might be sought are as follows:

1. A forty-five-year-old pregnant woman and her partner are concerned because her obstetrician has informed them that their pregnancy is at increased risk for Down syndrome and other chromosomal abnormalities because of her age.

2. A twenty-three-year-old woman has just given birth to a baby with a birth defect called spina bifida, which can cause some paralysis in the lower limbs and may affect bowel and bladder control. She is concerned about a possible genetic contribution to this condition.

3. A couple in their late twenties is concerned about their two-year-old son's behavior. He is hyperactive and has not yet begun to talk. Their pediatrician recommends a special blood test for the child, which reveals that he has a genetic condition called fragile X syndrome.

4. A couple in their forties has just learned that the husband's mother has been diagnosed with Huntington's disease, a late-onset, degenerative disorder that is hereditary. They are confused about what this means for the mother, for them, and for their three children.

5. Sarah and her boyfriend are moving closer to marriage. She is reluctant to be married until she can discover whether the muscular dystrophy that affected her brother and her uncle may be passed along to her own children.

These scenarios illustrate a few of the situations in which people pursue genetic counseling. Although the specific information discussed in each session varies, the genetic counseling process has some common characteristics. A family history is usually taken, and a "family tree" is drawn. Medical information, such as the precise diagnosis, prognosis, and management of the condition, is reviewed in nonmedical, easily understood terms. The way in which heredity contributes to the condition is also discussed. Specialized tests, and their risks and benefits, are described. This is the science-oriented aspect of the practice of genetic counseling.

Just as important to the process are the active listening and counseling skills practiced by the genetic counselor. He or she pays careful attention to words and gestures and notices the way clients interact. The genetic counselor attempts to create an environment in which people feel entirely comfortable expressing the variety of feelings related to having a birth defect or genetic condition, either in themselves or in a family member. These emotions include, among others, anger, sadness, fear, shame, and guilt. By facilitating this type of communication, the genetic counselor assists the clients in adjusting to the condition.

The cornerstone of the practice of genetic counseling is that it is nondirective. The autonomy of the client, and the right of the individual to make decisions based on his or her own values and beliefs, is paramount. Therefore, a genetic counselor must be willing to work with the client to find the path that seems best from the *client's* point of view.

The demand for genetic counseling has grown as knowledge about the human genome has increased. For a growing number of conditions, a person's DNA can be examined to determine whether a malfunctioning gene is present. DNA testing might reveal that someone who is now perfectly healthy will later become affected by a genetic condition, such as Huntington's disease (see example 4), or it might be determined that a healthy woman is a carrier of a gene that may cause a genetic disease in her children (such as in example 5).

DNA technology holds remarkable power. Prior to its development, those with a family history of a genetic condition made major life decisions, such as whether to have a child, based on a statistical analysis of the chance that the condition would be passed along. Now, for many conditions, an at-risk person can be tested and can know for sure whether he or she has the gene. Prenatal diagnosis, through methods such as chorionic villus sampling and amniocentesis, allows DNA to be obtained from the fetus to determine whether a pregnancy is affected with a genetic disease. Individuals who learn that they may pass along a genetic condition might choose to avoid this risk by conceiving using artificial insemination or in vitro fertilization with a donor egg. They may, on the other hand, choose to adopt a child. Those who decide to have their own biological children can now do so with a better understanding of their risks and can have the opportunity to prepare for the birth of a child with an inherited condition or a birth defect.

This technology, while increasing the amount of information and the number of options an individual has, can lead to other dilemmas. An issue fraught with ethical, moral, and religious overtones is the question of aborting a pregnancy affected with a genetic condition or birth defect. In this situation and many others, genetic counselors provide information and support for the individuals to make their own decisions concerning these difficult issues.

Although the day of determining the entire genetic code for any person remains in the future, the field of genetics is providing an ever-increasing number of people with a higher level of understanding and a greater array of choices. It is the role of genetic counseling to assist people as they grapple with these increasingly complex situations.

(*See also:* ABORTION: MEDICAL AND SOCIAL ASPECTS; BIRTH CONTROL: LEGAL ASPECTS; CONCEPTION: LEGAL ASPECTS; PREGNANCY AND BIRTH)

BIBLIOGRAPHY

Applebaum, E. G., and Firestein, S. K. (1983). *A Genetic Counseling Casebook.* New York: Free Press.

Ferrell, J. (1992). "Genetic Counseling." *Vogue*, February, pp. 150–153.

Kelly, P. T. (1977). *Dealing with Dilemma: A Manual for Genetic Counselors.* New York: Springer-Verlag.

Kessler, S., ed. (1979). *Genetic Counseling: Psychological Dimensions.* New York: Academic Press.

Otten, A. L. (1989). "Parental Agony: How Counselors Guide Couples When Science Spots Genetic Risks." *The Wall Street Journal*, March 8, pp. A1, A8.

ALICIA CRAFFEY

GODPARENTS   *See* FICTIVE KINSHIP

GRANDPARENTHOOD

Since the mid-1970s, there has been an enormous increase in scholarly interest in grandparenthood. This increase is largely due to the greater prevalence of grandparents and an increase in the number of years that people experience in the grandparent role.

Prevalence and Increasing Interest

Increases in life expectancy have made grandparenthood more prevalent. Although only about 37 percent of all males and 42 percent of all females born in 1870 survived to age sixty-five, projections for those born in 1930 were 63 percent for males and 77 percent for females (Cherlin and Furstenberg 1986). Of children born in 1900, only one in four had all four grandparents alive, and by the time they became fifteen years old, only one in fifty still had all four grandparents alive. In comparison, one in six of those who were fifteen years old in 1976 had all four grandparents alive, and almost 90 percent had at least two grandparents alive (Cherlin and Furstenberg 1986).

Longer life expectancy has also led to a longer period of grandparenthood. Once someone becomes a grandparent, he or she will occupy that status for a much longer time than a few generations ago. It is common for one to become a grandparent in his or her early forties, and some people, particularly women, become grandparents in their thirties (Burton and Bengtson 1985). Once someone becomes a grandparent, he or she is most likely to retain that status until death; some people may be grandparents for several decades. Thus grandparenthood has become a more meaningful stage in one's life course.

An increase in the number of single-parent households, resulting from either divorce or birth out of wedlock, has made the role some grandparents fulfill in rearing children more important than it had been previously. Instead of playing merely a supportive role for grandchildren, many grandparents now play a very active role in rearing and socializing their grandchildren. For example, many grandparents perform the role of surrogate father for children in single-mother households.

Grandparenting Styles

Because having all of one's grandparents alive was a rare event in the past, today's grandparents often lack role models. In addition, it is possible for today's grandparents to be as young as in their thirties and for some grandchildren to be as old as retirement age. As a result, despite a clearly defined status of grandparenthood, there is not a clearly defined role of grandparenthood. Therefore, Irving Rosow (1985) has described grandparenthood as a "'tenuous" role. Without good role models or clearly defined social roles, today's grandparents tend to interact with their grandchildren in a more flexible manner, relatively unconstrained by rules and expectations (Johnson 1988).

Traditional literature on grandparenthood focused on how grandparents interact with their grandchildren. Bernice L. Neugarten and Karol K. Weinstein's (1964) pioneering study examined whether grandparents engage in a formal, fun-seeking, or distant-figure style of grandparenting. A formal style of grandparenting follows its traditional norms, which are clearly distinct from those of parents. A fun-seeking style is characterized by informality and playfulness, while a distant-figure style is characterized by infrequent contacts, mostly on ritual occasions. Some literature reports that older grandparents tend to adopt the formal style while younger grandparents tend to adopt the fun-seeking style. This age differentiation may be a result of cohort effect (due to the time of birth of grandparents) or maturational age effect (Bengtson 1985), but no study has been done to examine this issue.

Using different criteria, Andrew J. Cherlin and Frank F. Furstenberg, Jr., (1985) classified styles of grandparenting into five groups: detached, passive, supportive, authoritative, and influential. Although both detached and passive grandparents have little interaction with their grandchildren, the detached do not see their grandchildren often while the passive do. Cherlin and Furstenberg report that detached and passive grandparents tend to be older and psychologically not close to their children. Of those who have substantial interactions with grandchildren, the supportive type refers to those who had interactions involving helping each other and running errands or chores for each other. The authoritative type refers to those who had high scores on parentlike behaviors such as disciplining, giving advice, discussing problems, correcting behavior, and being asked for advice by grandchildren. Finally, the influential type refers to those who had high scores for both supportive and authoritative dimensions. Influential grandparents tend to be younger and see grandchildren more often. Another notable point is that African-American grandparents are much more likely to be either authoritative or influential than their white counterparts, suggesting a prevalence of parent-like behaviors among African-American grandparents.

According to Colleen L. Johnson (1988), most grandmothers have a clear expectation of what kind of grandmothers they want to be, tied to social and emotional rather than instrumental functions. They prefer a relationship more like a friendship than a hierarchical one.

As for cultural norms about grandparenthood, Johnson (1988) states that there are more "should nots" than "shoulds" on enacting a grandmother's role. Grandmothers should not interfere, should not give too much advice, and should not discipline grandchildren. According to these cultural norms, grandparents should not overpower, spoil, or buy love from grandchildren. They should not nag or be judgmental, and should not be disappointed if the grandchildren do not return the favors. On the other hand, they should be fun to be with, should be loving, and should make it easier for parents by providing such services as baby-sitting. Other than baby-sitting activities, these "shoulds" are not well delineated.

Quality of Relationship

Quality of relationships between grandparents and young adult grandchildren was assessed by Gregory E. Kennedy (1992). He claims that five elements of the relationship are important to evaluate the quality from the grandchildren's viewpoint. They are senses of closeness, being known, knowing grandparents, being positively influenced, and having an authentic relationship independent of the parents. In general, the quality of the relationship is better with grandmothers than with grandfathers. The quality is also generally better when grandparents live nearby, when they are in frequent contact, when the parents experience either divorce or single motherhood, and/or when the grandchild is an only child or a firstborn child.

None of Kennedy's five elements of relationship quality is related to the content of grandparent–grandchild interactions. Past literature has not found that particular activities in the relationship (e.g., spending time together or grandparents giving advice to grandchildren) are important to the quality of the grandparent–grandchild relationship. In fact, grandparents seem to do very little in the grandparent–grandchild relationship, and what they do has little effect on grandchildren. Nonetheless, the presence of grandparents has been found to be very important for psychological and behavioral development of small children (Tinsley and Parke 1984). In other words, having grandparents itself, or the fact that grandparents are simply there, seems to be important.

In their review article, Thomas E. Denham and Craig W. Smith (1989) categorize the nature of grandparental influence into three kinds: indirect, direct, and symbolic. Indirect influence refers to factors that affect grandchildren only through the effects on the middle-generation parents, such as psychological or financial support and/or stress. Direct influence refers to face-to-face grandparent–grandchild interaction. Grandparents may baby-sit grandchildren. They may joke, watch TV, and go out with grandchildren, providing fun. They may give grandchildren advice, teach them skills and games, and even discipline them. They often give grandchildren money and presents. By telling grandchildren what it was like growing up themselves, grandparents serve as observational models for grandchildren. In some cases, grandparents work as "arbitrators" between their children and their grandchildren in confrontations between two different values and personalities.

Symbolic influence, on the other hand, refers to the effect of grandparents just being there without necessarily performing concrete functions. Grandchildren feel good to have grandparents as a "stress buffer," whom they can go to in case of conflict among family members. Grandparents give grandchildren a sense of family continuity from the past to the present to the future by offering roots for the family. Grandparents may be considered "family watchdogs" who are there to keep an eye on the family members (Troll 1983). Of the three kinds of influences, symbolic influence seems to be the most important. Although grandparents may be backstage most of the time, they are the backbone of the extended family, and they will be available for help if necessary.

Gender and Relationships

The grandfather role and the grandmother role are differentiated from each other by gender, just as various other social roles are. Grandfathers often play a "head of the family" or "minister of state" role (Bengtson 1985), and grandmothers play a "secretary of the interior" role characterized by such activities as child care, "emotion work," and "kinkeeping." Considering the way in which most grandparents were raised, strong gender differentiation of grandparental roles is to be expected.

Since many more women than men survive into grandparenthood, it is more common for children to have contact with grandmothers than grandfathers. When the differences in the availability of grandmothers and grandfathers are taken into account, studies report that grandchildren have regular contact with grandmothers and grandfathers relatively equally (Eisenberg 1988; Roberto and Stroes 1992). Grandchildren, however, are more influenced by grandmothers than grandfathers in their value development and report a higher degree of psychological closeness with their grandmothers (Hodgson 1992). Grandmothers are also more satisfied with their relationships with grandchildren, while grandfathers are more likely to indulge grandchildren (Thomas 1989).

In the past, American grandfathers adopted either formal, passive, or authoritative styles when dealing with grandchildren, contributing to differences between grandfathers and grandmothers in the intergenerational relationship. Over time, however, more grandfathers seem to have begun adopting fun-seeking and supportive styles. This seems to have decreased, if not completely negated, the differences between the grandchild's relationships with grandfathers and grandmothers.

Alice S. Rossi and Peter H. Rossi (1990) reported that percentages of adults who stated that "[Target grandparent] was very important while I grew up" are different not only between grandmothers and grandfathers but also between the mother's parents and the father's parents. The gender of the middle-generation person is also important for grandparent–grandchild relationships, possibly because women in the middle generation are more likely than men to assume "kinkeeping" roles and to maintain affectionally close intergenerational relationships. In fact, it was reported that grandchildren are most likely to identify maternal grandmothers as their favorite grandparents (Eisenberg 1988; Hodgson 1992).

Demographic Changes and Grandparenthood

The age at retirement has increased and more women are in the labor force than before; thus many grandparents are employed. This contradicts the image of retired grandparents in rocking chairs or in the kitchen baking cookies, with all of their time available for family members, including grandchildren. Better health conditions have made today's grandparents physically much younger than those in traditional images. They are much more active in social life. Better health and financial conditions than in the past for elderly people have also made them less dependent on subsequent generations. Due to a prolonged life expectancy, grandparents are also likely to be caregivers of their own parents.

Increases in the number of teenage mothers have produced a large number of young grandmothers, some of them even in their twenties (Burton and Bengtson 1985). Due to the strains of various roles (grandmother, mother, daughter, granddaughter, employee, and girlfriend) and reluctance to accept grandmotherhood, which symbolizes old age, "off-time grandmothers" tend to be unhappy with their grandmotherhood (Burton and Bengtson 1985). "On-time grandmothers" seem to cope with this new role relatively better. This pattern also may be due to the prevalent "age norm" or "a prescriptive timetable for the ordering of major life events," including becoming a grandparent (Neugarten, Moore, and Lowe 1965). It was reported that about 80 percent of people between forty and seventy years of age responded to the question "When do you think most people should become grandparents?" with answers ranging from forty-five to fifty years old (Neugarten, Moore, and Lowe 1965). Becoming a grandparent earlier is a violation against this age norm and may cause embarrassment. These structural changes have created different and more ambiguous roles for both the grandparents and the grandchildren.

Due to the increased divorce rate, the lower prevalence of remarriage, and the increase in single motherhood, many households lack a parent, and grandparents often play a surrogate parent's role. Although grandparents playing parental roles are discouraged in white middle-class families, this seems to be more condoned and/or more commonly practiced among minority families and working-class families, especially when the middle-generation people are single parents. The most typical scenario is a single mother, either divorced or never married, living with her children and her mother, which is particularly common among African Americans. Grandmothers usually serve as surrogate parents in place of father figures in these single-mother households. This racial difference seems to be attributed not only to a larger proportion of single mothers among African Americans, but also to their cultural preferences, including stronger intergenerational relationships (Cherlin and Furstenberg 1986; Kivett 1991).

When a couple with children divorces, custody of the children becomes an issue not only for the parents but also for the grandparents. Non-custodial grandparents tend to see the grandchildren less often than custodial grandparents (Cherlin and Furstenberg 1986). Because custody is generally awarded to mothers upon divorce, relationships between the children and their maternal grandparents are not hurt as much as those involving their paternal grandparents. To maintain grandparent–grandchild relationships, grandparents, often paternal ones, may make a special arrangement with grandchildren. To avoid confusion for grandchildren who must rotate through many houses on a visit, paternal and maternal grandparents may form a coalition and plan a joint holiday dinner, often including both of the divorced parents (Johnson 1985). More commonly, paternal grandparents form a coalition with their former daughters-in-law for the best interest of the grandchildren, often drawing objections from their sons (Johnson 1988).

Even before the divorce, conflicts between the parents affect the quality of grandparent–grandchildren relationships. It was reported that marital conflicts weaken children's ties to parents and eventually those to grandparents (Rossi and Rossi 1990). This effect was particularly strong for the grandsons, but the granddaughter–grandmother relationship was little affected by the parents' marital discord, probably due to a greater degree of independence.

Conclusion

Grandparenthood has received more scholarly attention due to important demographic changes, and differences based on race and gender have been observed in studies of grandparenthood. Overall, the importance of the grandparent–grandchild relationship lies in the symbolic rather than the functional sense. As the family structure changes, however, this relative importance seems to change in some segments of the population.

(*See also:* ELDERS; FILIAL RESPONSIBILITY; INTERGENERATIONAL RELATIONS; KINSHIP; RETIREMENT; WIDOWHOOD)

BIBLIOGRAPHY

Bengtson, V. L. (1985). "Diversity and Symbolism in Grandparental Roles." In *Grandparenthood*, ed. V. L. Bengtson and J. F. Robertson. Newbury Park, CA: Sage Publications.

Burton, L. M., and Bengtson, V. L. (1985). "Black Grandmothers: Issues of Timing and Continuity of Roles." In *Grandparenthood*, ed. V. L. Bengtson and J. F. Robertson. Newbury Park, CA: Sage Publications.

Cherlin, A. J., and Furstenberg, F. F., Jr. (1985). "Styles and Strategies of Grandparenting." In *Grandparenthood*, ed. V. L. Bengtson and J. F. Robertson. Newbury Park, CA: Sage Publications.

Cherlin, A. J., and Furstenberg, F. F., Jr. (1986). *The New American Grandparenthood: A Place in the Family, a Life Apart.* New York: Basic Books.

Denham, T. E., and Smith, C. W. (1989). "The Influence of Grandparents on Grandchildren: A Review of the Literature and Resources." *Family Relations* 38:345–350.

Eisenberg, A. R. (1988). "Grandchildren's Perspectives on Relationships with Grandparents: The Influence of Gender Across Generations." *Sex Roles* 19:205–217.

Hodgson, L. G. (1992). "Adult Grandchildren and Their Grandparents: The Enduring Bond." *International Journal of Aging and Human Development* 34:209–225.

Johnson, C. L. (1985). "Grandparenting Options in Divorcing Families: An Anthropological Perspective." In *Grandparenthood*, ed. V. L. Bengtson and J. F. Robertson. Newbury Park, CA: Sage Publications.

Johnson, C. L. (1988). *Ex Familia: Grandparents, Parents, and Children Adjust to Divorce.* New Brunswick, NJ: Rutgers University Press.

Kennedy, G. E. (1992). "Quality in Grandparent/Grandchild Relationship." *International Journal of Aging and Human Development* 35:83–98.

Kivett, V. R. (1991). "Centrality of the Grandfather Role Among Older Rural Black and White Men." *Journal of Gerontology* 46:S250–S258.

Neugarten, B. L.; Moore, J. W.; and Lowe, J. C. (1965). "Age Norms, Age Constraints, and Adult Socialization." *American Journal of Sociology* 70:710–717.

Neugarten, B. L., and Weinstein, K. K. (1964). "The Changing American Grandparent." *Journal of Marriage and the Family* 26:199–204.

Roberto, K. A., and Stroes, J. (1992). "Grandchildren and Grandparents." *International Journal of Aging and Human Development* 34:227–239.

Rosow, I. (1985). "Status and Role Change Through the Life Cycle." In *Handbook of Aging and the Social Sciences*, 2nd edition, ed. R. H. Binstock and E. Shanas. New York: Van Nostrand-Reinhold.

Rossi, A. S., and Rossi, P. H. (1990). *On Human Bonding.* New York: Aldine.

Thomas, J. L. (1989). "Gender and Perceptions of Grandparenthood." *International Journal of Aging and Human Development* 29:269–282.

Tinsley, B. R., and Parke, R. D. (1984). "Grandparents as Support and Socialization Agents." In *Beyond the Dyad*, ed. M. Lewis. New York: Plenum.

Troll, L. E. (1983). "Grandparents: The Family Watchdogs." In *Family Relationships in Late Life*, ed. T. Brubaker. Newbury Park, CA: Sage Publications.

YOSHINORI KAMO

GUARDIANSHIP

Guardianship is a legal process that transfers the decision-making authority over an individual deemed incapable of managing his or her personal or financial affairs (a "ward") to another person (the "guardian"). Guardians may be appointed for both minors and adults.

Modern guardianship has its roots in English common law, which was brought to America in Colonial times. Under English common law, the doctrine of *parens patriae* (parent of the country) allowed the courts to assume control of and appoint guardians for "infants" (minors) and "incompetents" (incapacitated adults).

In the United States today, the appointment of guardians is controlled by state law, and guardians are appointed by state courts. Because each state is free to enact its own laws, state guardianship laws vary, even on basic terminology. Under the Uniform Probate Code, a model act in effect in about a quarter of the states, a "guardian" makes personal care decisions, while a "conservator" manages property. But in many other states, the court-appointed manager is referred to as either a "guardian of the person" or a "guardian of the property."

States also vary on procedures for appointment of guardians. Procedures for appointment of a guardian of a minor are different from and generally less detailed than procedures for an adult appointment. Procedures for minors are less detailed because the incapacity of a minor is presumed, while the incapacity of an adult must be proved.

There are numerous alternatives to guardianship, although many relate only to adults and not to minors. Advising individuals on these alternatives is a major function for professionals such as attorneys and social workers, who counsel individuals on planning for possible incapacity.

Types of Guardianship

There are several types of guardianship. Under a plenary or full guardianship, the guardian is granted comprehensive decision-making authority over an individual's personal care, property, or both. Under a limited guardianship, as its name implies, the guardian is granted only limited and specified powers regarding an individual's personal care or property.

A guardian of the person makes decisions with respect to the ward's personal care. For example, the guardian will determine where the ward will live and will arrange for the ward's medical care. The guardian of the property manages the ward's finances. The guardian will disburse funds for the ward's care, will handle the ward's investments, and will determine which assets must be sold.

Guardians are typically appointed for an extended period—until a minor attains the age of majority, for example, or until an adult individual's death or recovery of capacity. Under a temporary or emergency guardianship, however, the guardianship lasts for only a short period of days or months. Because temporary or emergency guardians are appointed for only a short term and often on an emergency basis, the procedures for appointment are usually simpler and more expedited than for a regular, longer-term appointment. Limited and temporary or emergency guardianships are the exception, not the rule, however. The term "guardianship," without qualification, usually is intended to refer to a plenary or full guardianship.

Guardianship, which requires a proceeding before a court before an appointment may be made, must be distinguished from other uses of the term. It is sometimes said that parents, by virtue of their custodial rights, are the natural guardians of their minor children, although this term is falling into disuse. Also, the role of a guardian is very different from that of a guardian ad litem. A guardian ad litem is an individual, usually an attorney, appointed to represent another in a particular court proceeding, such as in a dispute over the validity of a will. It is a narrow, single-purpose function. A guardian ad litem is not otherwise empowered to make decisions about personal care or property.

Guardianship of Minors

Minors do not have the legal right to manage property nor to make many major life decisions, such as to determine their place of residence or to decide what school they will attend. For most minors this lack of legal capacity is not an issue; most minors do not own significant assets. Also, until a minor reaches the age of majority (age eighteen in most states), marries, or is otherwise emancipated, a minor's parents are legally responsible for the minor's custody and care.

Guardianship of a minor's property becomes an issue if the minor acquires significant assets, due to an inheritance or personal injury settlement, for example. A minor's parents do not have the legal right to manage their child's property. For them to do so, they must be appointed as the minor's guardians by a court.

Guardianship of a minor's person becomes an issue whenever there is need for someone other than the parents to assume the child's custody. Guardians must be appointed following the death of both parents, for example, unless an adoption can be arranged. This guardian will usually be a close family member. Guardians are also appointed following termination of the parents' parental rights, which may occur due to a finding of abuse or other unfitness. Termination of parental rights permanently severs the parent–child relationship, including the parents' right to the child's custody. In some cases guardians are appointed without termination of parental rights. Although the court-appointed guardian has legal custody, the parents may be allowed to maintain at least some relationship with the child. This may include the right to visit and a continuation of the obligation to support the child.

This maintenance of a relationship is also frequent if the guardian is appointed with the parents' consent.

The child, for example, may be residing with another family member, and appointment of that family member as guardian may be necessary to qualify the child for public school attendance. Or upon the death of a divorced parent who had custody of the child, it may be decided, with the consent of the other parent, that it is best that the child continue to reside with a stepparent appointed as guardian.

Guardianship is a concern of many parents with minor children. They are concerned about who will take custody of their children in the event of their death. They are also concerned about how property the children may inherit from them will be managed. Many of these concerns can be addressed in the parents' wills. While wills are primarily directed at the disposition of property after death, they may also be used to nominate guardians for minor children, both for the minor's care and for management of the minor's property. In some states a parental nominee has an automatic right to be appointed guardian upon the parents' death. In other states, a court must approve the parents' choice, although this approval is usually automatic. Also, in many states a parental nomination is ineffective if a minor age fourteen or older objects. In those states, a minor age fourteen or older has the right to nominate his or her own guardian.

While parents may nominate guardians to manage the minor's property, guardianship of a minor's property may not be the preferred option. Guardianship of a minor's property terminates when the minor reaches the age of majority, an age at which many parents believe the young adult does not yet have sufficient maturity to manage significant wealth. Creation of a trust is a commonly selected alternative. Under this legal device, which is usually created under the parents' wills, a trustee is named to manage property that would otherwise be placed under guardianship. The responsibilities of the trustee are specified in the will or other trust document. The major advantages of a trust over a guardianship is that court proceedings are avoided and the parents may designate any age for distribution of the assets to the child.

Guardianship of Adults

Appointment of a guardian for an adult is very different from appointment of a guardian for a minor. A minor, by legal definition, lacks the capacity to manage his or her own personal or financial affairs. An adult, however, is presumed to have such capacity. Before a guardian may be appointed for an adult, it must be established to a court's satisfaction that the adult individual lacks capacity to make his or her own decisions. The procedures for the appointment of a guardian of an adult are therefore more detailed than the procedures for a minor's appointment.

Guardianship of adults is an issue of growing importance. The reason for this is changing demographics. Approximately 80 percent of adult guardianship appointments are made for individuals age sixty or older. This segment of the population is rapidly increasing. In 1987, there were 29.8 million Americans age sixty-five or older. By the year 2020, the number is projected to exceed 52 million. Guardians are also frequently appointed for individuals with developmental disabilities; approximately 3.9 million individuals fall within this group. Other population groups for whom guardianship may become a concern include individuals with mental illness and individuals with severe health problems.

Guardians may be appointed only for adults who are determined to lack capacity. Capacity is a legal standard, not a clinical one. Professionals such as physicians, psychologists, and social workers may be asked to provide evidence concerning the individual's medical condition and ability to perform certain tasks, but the determination of whether an individual lacks legal capacity to make his or her own decisions must be made by a court.

The definition of incapacity was traditionally based on a categorical approach: Did the individual have a specified impairment such as mental deficiency, mental retardation, or infirmity of advanced age? In most states, however, the definitions have moved away from such labels and conclusory statements. The growing trend is to focus on the individual's ability to make decisions with respect to self-care and management of property. If the individual is unable to make such decisions, then a guardian may be appointed if the individual's needs cannot be met by any less restrictive means.

Guardianship of an adult is initiated by filing a written petition with a court, requesting that a guardian be appointed. The petition may request the appointment of a guardian of the person, a guardian of the property, or both. The same person may be appointed as guardian of the person and guardian of the property, or different persons may be appointed. The individual for whom guardianship is sought (the "respondent") must be given notice of the petition and has the right to contest the requested appointment. In many states an attorney must be appointed to represent the respondent. The court may also appoint a "visitor" to make an independent investigation on whether guardianship is appropriate or order that

the respondent be examined by a physician, psychologist, or other qualified professional.

The procedure for appointment of a guardian concludes with a formal hearing before a court. At the hearing, the judge considers the evidence and either makes the appointment, rejects the appointment, or orders that the respondent's needs be met by other means. In some states the respondent may request that this determination by made by a jury. As is the case with minors, the guardian will usually be a close family member. Before making the selection, however, the court will usually consider the ward's preferences.

The role of the appointed guardian has traditionally been to act in the ward's best interests. Under this model, the guardian must make an objective determination of what is best for the ward and act accordingly. Whether this determination conflicts with the ward's current or prior expressed wishes is not a factor in this situation.

However, other approaches have become increasingly important. Under the least restrictive alternative model, the guardian may exercise authority only to the extent necessitated by the ward's limitations. The guardian must select the alternative least restrictive of the ward's independence and freedom. The guardian must also encourage the ward to participate in making decisions. A third approach is the substituted judgment model. The guardian must make the decision the ward would have made had the ward still had capacity. Under this approach, the ward's prior expressed wishes and personal values are important factors to be considered.

Many adult guardianships will continue for the ward's lifetime and be terminated only by death. Upon the ward's death, the court will discharge the guardian, and the ward's assets will be distributed under the ward's will or to the ward's heirs. Guardianships are not necessarily lifelong, however. The ward may recover capacity, in whole or in part, or other changed circumstances may suggest that guardianship is no longer needed. In all states, a ward may request termination of the guardianship. To protect this right, many states provide that the ward's request need not be made by a formal petition but may be made by informal letter.

The decision to seek guardianship of an adult should never be made lightly. The position of guardian is a heavy responsibility. The ward, because he or she has been found to lack legal capacity, may lose many basic rights, including the right to vote, to travel, to decide where to live, to divorce or marry, to keep and care for children, and even to drive a car.

Alternatives to Guardianship

There are numerous alternatives to guardianship. Many require prior planning, planning that should be done well before the individual's capacity becomes an issue. Perhaps the most important of these alternatives is a durable power of attorney. Under a durable power of attorney, an individual designates another as agent to make decisions when or should the individual no longer be able to do so. Durable powers of attorney may be used for property management and for making health and personal care decisions.

Another planned alternative is a revocable trust, often referred to as a "living trust." Under this device an individual transfers his or her assets to a trustee, who holds and administers them as provided in the trust document. Most commonly the individual will act as his or her own trustee until such time as he or she is no longer able to manage the property, at which time a designated successor trustee will assume the responsibility.

A number of alternatives do not require prior planning. A representative payee may be named to manage Social Security benefits. Many states have enacted health-care consent statutes allowing family members to make medical decisions for an incapacitated relative. A variety of social services, including assisted living, respite care, and financial counseling may be available to lessen an individual's need to have someone else make decisions. Before initiating the detailed procedure required to secure appointment of a guardian, all alternatives should be explored.

(*See also:* CHILD ABUSE AND NEGLECT: LEGAL ASPECTS; CHILD CUSTODY; CHILDREN'S RIGHTS; CHRONIC ILLNESS; DISABILITIES; ELDERS; INHERITANCE; PSYCHIATRIC DISORDERS)

BIBLIOGRAPHY

Anderer, S. J. (1990). *Determining Competency in Guardianship Proceedings*. Washington, DC: American Bar Association.

Committee on Legal Incapacity. (1980). "Limited Guardianship: Survey of Implementation Considerations." *Real Property Probate and Trust Journal* 15:544–556.

Commission on the Mentally Disabled/Commission on Legal Problems of the Elderly. (1989). *Guardianship: An Agenda for Reform*. Washington, DC: American Bar Association.

Frolik, L. (1981). "Plenary Guardianship: An Analysis, a Critique, and a Proposal for Reform." *Arizona Law Review* 23:599–660.

Grisso, T. (1986). *Evaluating Competencies: Forensic Assessments and Instruments*. New York: Plenum.

Horstman, P. M. (1975). "Protective Services for the Elderly: The Limits of Parens Patriae." *Missouri Law Review* 40:215–278.

Kindred, M. (1976). "Guardianship and Limitations upon Capacity." In *The Mentally Retarded Citizen and the Law*, ed. M. Kindred, J. Cohen, D. Penrod, and T. Shaffer. New York: Free Press.

Krasik, M. K. (1989). "The Lights of Science and Experience: Historical Perspectives on Legal Attitudes Toward the Role of Medical Expertise in Guardianship of the Elderly." *American Journal of Legal History* 33:201–240.

Parry, J. (1985). "Incompetency, Guardianship, and Restoration." In *The Mentally Disabled and the Law*, ed. S. J. Brakel, J. Parry, and B. A. Weiner. Chicago: The American Bar Foundation.

Regan, J. J. (1981). "Protecting the Elderly: The New Paternalism." *Hastings Law Journal* 32:1111–1132.

Rein, J. E. (1992). "Preserving Dignity and Self-Determination of the Elderly in the Face of Competing Interests and Grim Alternatives." *George Washington Law Review* 60:1818–1887.

Ross, A. E. (1981). "Stability in Child–Parent Relations: Modifying Guardianship Law." *Stanford Law Review* 33:905–916.

Schmidt, W. C. (1990). "Quantitative Information About the Quality of the Guardianship System: Toward the Next Generation of Guardianship Research." *Probate Law Journal* 10:61–80.

U.S. Senate Committee on Aging. (1988). *Aging America: Trends and Projections*. Washington, DC: U.S. Department of Health and Human Services.

DAVID M. ENGLISH

HEALTH AND THE FAMILY

The biomedical model has been predominant in the science and practice of medicine. Based on this model, clinicians take an organic approach in the diagnosis and treatment of illness or disease. For example, an illness or disease is the result of a virus, bacteria, or some other organic cause (e.g., diabetes, mellitus, cancer, or cardiovascular disease). The diagnosis and treatment focus on the patient and often involve surgery, administration of medication, or some other medical intervention. This is sometimes simply referred to as the one-cause, one-disease, one-treatment approach. The biomedical approach takes an authoritarian style to patient care: Clinicians know best, and the patient is supposed to follow the doctor's orders (Doherty and Campbell 1988).

Only since the 1970s has there been explicit acknowledgment that illness, or more broadly health, may not be entirely organic in its cause. George L. Engel (1977) proposed a comprehensive model of medicine that includes biological, psychological, and social dimensions. This model argues that humans are thinking organisms: Mind affects body, and body affects mind. Moreover, humans exist in families and other social groupings that provide context for individuals and for understanding individuals. In this sense, families affect the health of the individuals who compose them, and the health of the individuals affects the family. Similarly, families often define for their members whether certain symptoms constitute an illness or necessitate medical attention. Families are often instrumental in carrying out treatment regimens for members who have been treated, which can include lifestyle or behavioral adjustments. In other cases they may be primarily responsible for the noncompliance of the patient (e.g., by not changing the diet of the family to counteract the high blood pressure of the patient).

How families relate to their physical and social environments reflects their "family paradigm" (Reiss 1981). Family members are usually influenced by the same health experiences. For example, a family in which one member has had meningitis may be more likely to seek medical treatment every time that family member has a headache. Thus they have a shared basic understanding of and experience with certain illnesses and diseases. They are likely to react to situations not on the basis of each individual's knowledge, but on the meaning the family places on certain symptoms in certain contexts. Family context, therefore, has importance for family members and health professionals in that it gives additional understanding of the "causes" and meaning of illness and disease. A family member who has recurring bouts of strep, for example, may be thought to have an immune deficiency. However, when the health professional (or the family) takes into account the fact that there is abnormally high stress in the family (e.g., a divorce or separation), the illness may be seen instead as having a different cause—located, at least in part, in the social environment of the patient.

There is evidence that family members have similar risks for many diseases and illnesses, and there are several reasons for this. First, family members influence each other—they have the same diets, including fat and salt, they have similar orientations to exercise; children of smokers are more likely to smoke, and even if they do not smoke, the secondary smoke from their parents will affect the children. A second factor is genetics. Parents and their children share genetic characteristics. Certain propensities for health problems may be the result of these characteristics.

Diagnosis of health problems begins within the family, not with the clinical health professional (Doherty and Campbell 1988). In the ideal model of health care, families evaluate objective criteria of health and illness (e.g., fever) and decide whether a visit to a doctor is warranted. In fact, very few symptoms or illnesses reach the attention of physicians. Individuals tend to discuss their health conditions with family members or close friends. Only when symptoms are of a certain kind or severity is it likely that the individual will choose to see a physician.

There is usually a central family member who is influential in health appraisal. This person, traditionally the wife/mother, sometimes a grandmother or a relative who is a health professional, is viewed by other family members to be the "family health expert" (Doherty and Baird 1983). The family health expert evaluates the family member's symptoms and often decides if the patient should see a physician. The family health expert, the key contact between the physician and the patient and family, can be a key person with whom the doctor will work out a treatment plan. Therefore, the family health expert has considerable power because he or she may ultimately decide whether to send the family member to a physician or (having consulted a doctor) whether to follow the prescribed treatment regimen. Whether intentional or not, the family health expert's actions affect the health of family members, the functioning of the family, and the general success of the family's health practices.

Families and health professionals have very different foci in assessing health and illness. First, health professionals tend to focus on objective criteria of health and illness, such as temperature, blood pressure, or blood counts. Families and individuals, on the other hand, focus on subjective conditions, such as pain or discomfort. Often, families will react with concern to objective conditions, such as low-grade fever, while a physician may not see this as an indicator of serious illness.

A second difference in families' and physicians' foci is in their explanations and understanding of the causes, origins, and prevalence of disease. Health professionals look at symptoms in the context of other symptoms or indicators and in terms of those symptoms being associated with diseases that are rare or common—that is, they use an epidemiological explanation. Moreover, some symptoms, such as fever, are associated with a variety of bacterial and viral infections. Their onset, severity, and duration provide clues to the physician as to the illness and its treatment. For families, a different set of explanations is often used, based on their own interpersonal experiences. Families look to the health and illness experiences of those in their close, interpersonal networks

as guides for understanding symptoms and disease. For example, a husband may report to his wife that the doctor found that he has high blood pressure. The wife might respond that high blood pressure does not run in his family. Consequently, she may not modify the family's diet as recommended by the physician. In this case, a meeting between the physician and the couple may have provided the wife with the opportunity to ask about causes of high blood pressure, the risks, and the potential outcomes of treatment or no treatment.

While families generally want their members to be healthy, and health professionals want to make their patients well, there is inherent conflict in the family's and clinician's approaches. As noted, the biomedical approach is an authoritarian one. In contrast, the biopsychosocial model emphasizes sharing decision-making power among the clinician, the patient, and the family. Interventions are based on understanding that families influence some health conditions in family members, and to improve the health of the patient, the family (not just the patient) must be the focus. Thus diagnosis is a shared opinion about a disease and its symptoms. Treatment takes the form of a social contract involving the patient, the immediate family, the physician, other health-care professionals, and sometimes a wider network of friends and family.

(*See also:* AIDS; CHRONIC ILLNESS; DISABILITIES; EATING DISORDERS; GENETIC COUNSELING; MENOPAUSE; PSYCHIATRIC DISORDERS; SEXUALLY TRANSMITTED DISEASES; SUBSTANCE ABUSE)

BIBLIOGRAPHY

Doherty, W. J., and Baird, M. A. (1983). *Family Therapy and Family Medicine.* New York: Guilford.

Doherty, W. J., and Campbell, T. L. (1988). *Families and Health.* Newbury Park, CA: Sage Publications.

Engel, G. L. (1977). "The Need for a New Medical Model: A Challenge for Biomedicine." *Science* 196:129–136.

Reiss, D. (1981). *The Family's Construction of Reality.* Cambridge, MA: Harvard University Press.

DONALD E. STULL

HISTORY OF THE FAMILY

Generalizations about "the" history of "the" family require extreme caution, since family forms, relationships, values, and even definitions have varied tremendously across cultures and over time. In the ancient Mediterranean world, households and groupings of relatives were so diverse that no single unit of measurement or definition could encompass them. By the late fourteenth century, the word "family" had emerged to designate all those who lived under the authority of a household head. This definition, which included live-in servants, apprentices, and boarders, was common in Europe and America up through the eighteenth century. Among the European aristocracy, however, an alternative definition of family encompassed the larger descent group from which claims to privilege and property derived. From the late seventeenth century, yet another use of the word referred exclusively to a man's offspring, as in the phrase "his family and wife." Not until the nineteenth century did the conventional understanding of family focus on the parent–child group, distinguished sharply from other household residents or more distant kin. By the end of the nineteenth century, the restriction of the word to the immediate, coresidential family was so prevalent that the adjective "extended" had to be added when people wished to include related kin beyond the household.

Family Patterns

Large, coresidential extended families have never been common in European history, but the nuclear family has not been historically invariant. In some parts of Western Europe until the mid-sixteenth century, and as late as the nineteenth century in Eastern Europe, peasant households often included coresidence of brothers and their spouses. In other regions, many families experienced a developmental cycle that moved from extended to nuclear to extended. In the stem family, for example, a young couple spent the first years after marriage living with the man's parents, later becoming a nuclear family until their own eldest son married and brought his wife into the home. Due to the lower lifespans of the elderly, a substantial majority of such households would have been nuclear at any given time, but most of them would have passed through an extended stage.

During the late fifteenth century, most regions in Western Europe developed a distinctive family pattern that differed from practices elsewhere in three ways. The "Western pattern" involved neolocalism (establishment of a new household upon marriage), households based on a single nuclear family (with extra labor needs met by adding servants or apprentices rather than kin), and comparatively late marriage (with a significant proportion of the population never marrying at all). This Western form, especially

in England, was associated with a high degree of independence in the way that a household head could dispose of land, labor, or other resources, and with the relatively weak concept of lineage or corporate family property. English family patterns, then, showed early differences with those of other preindustrial societies, with fewer constraints on the choices and behavior of separate nuclear families. There is much debate over the extent to which these family patterns were the cause or the result of the early development of commodity production and wage labor in Western Europe, especially England.

It is a mistake, however, to read too much continuity into these families. It is true that mean household size remained fairly constant from the sixteenth through the nineteenth centuries, averaging about 4.75, and that even the largest households contained relatively few kin (Laslett and Wall 1972). But such averages obscure a characteristic preindustrial pattern where a few large, socially central households were surrounded by many smaller ones; poor families were truncated and split up, sending their members to live and work in the households of wealthy property-owning families. In contrast to later periods, the majority of people did not live in the average-size household. Furthermore, many English and American families in the sixteenth and seventeenth centuries had a modified extended structure, where a father settled his sons on land that he continued to own, thereby severely limiting the independence of the nuclear unit.

By the late seventeenth century, many of the variations among households had diminished, leading to the increased prevalence of nuclear families throughout the population. This trend was not unilinear, however. The proportion of extended families actually *increased* in industrial towns in England and America during the mid-nineteenth century. Indeed, the shorter lifespans of the elderly meant the number of multigenerational households that actually existed in the late nineteenth century represented a very high proportion of all such families that *might* exist. By the late twentieth century, however, only a small minority of potential multigenerational households actually existed (Ruggles 1994).

Economy and the Family

Louise Tilly and Joan Scott (1987) identify three stages of a family economy in Western Europe since the late Middle Ages: the preindustrial economy of household production, where household members worked within the home or property holding to produce goods for subsistence and local trade; the early wage-labor economy, where seasonal work and children's wage labor on other people's property supplemented the household production or wage work of the household head; and later the consumer economy of full-blown industrialization, where wives increasingly replaced children in the work force and parent–child relations became focused on reproduction and consumption rather than wages and work. This model is also broadly descriptive of changes in American families.

It is important, though, not to be too schematic about such transitions. The family economy of small masters, which used servants and apprentices to supplement the family work force, was not a prior stage to wage work, but depended on a wage economy among poorer villagers. Even modern "consumer" families in one segment of society may depend on a family wage economy or on "preindustrial" household production elsewhere, often in less developed countries, to provide them with cheap consumer goods or services (Heyman 1991).

Changing Dynamics of the Family System

Starting around the seventeenth century in England, and at a slightly later date in America, broadly similar trends in family life emerged. Historians disagree about how much marital love and parent–child intimacy existed in premodern families, but most authorities hold that there has been a long-range trend toward increasing independence of the nuclear unit, individualization of marital choices, the sentimentalization of childhood, and an expectation that marriage will include, or even be based on, romantic love. (This stands in striking contrast to the early tradition of courtly love, for example, which assumed that romantic love could exist only outside of marriage.) There has also been a marked, though by no means uninterrupted, decline in patriarchal authority and coercive power, of men over women and parents over children.

Since the Industrial Revolution, there has been an increased separation of sex and reproduction, accompanied by a general tendency for fertility to fall. Movements and laws to prevent child abuse have set limits on parental rights over children, while freedom of marital dissolution has steadily expanded. In the twentieth century, in both Europe and America, child labor declined sharply, married women steadily increased their participation in paid work outside of the home, the proportion of elderly in the population rose, and parents spent an increasing proportion of their lives without children in the home.

Before these trends in the United States are considered, it is worth noting the many pitfalls that must be avoided in generalizing about family history. Families and family systems are clearly shaped by larger systems of production, exchange, political control, and cultural meanings, yet families are not passive objects of such change. Families actively participate in the historical process and their decisions or behaviors may redirect socioeconomic trends and institutions. Thus, in some kinship societies, family and marital systems that allowed male household heads to mobilize the labor of wives and children for redistribution ceremonies served as starting mechanisms for the emergence of power and property inequalities that eventually led to new political and economic institutions, undermining kinship as an organizing principle of society. In late eighteenth-century America, family strategies designed to maximize household self-sufficiency helped create the very dependence on wage labor and large-scale markets that transformed the preindustrial household economy (Clark 1990).

Many historians advocate the study of the life cycle or life course, which examines the "intersection" between individual life histories, family needs or strategies, and historical forces (Hareven 1978). Yet the notion of family needs or strategies should not imply that the family is an organic, harmonious decision-making body without its own internal differences by age or sex. The struggles and accommodations *within* families over roles, resources, power, and autonomy must be studied.

The interaction, conflicts, and mutual dependencies *among* families must also be explored. Often, a family form that is defined as ideal by the dominant culture depends for its existence on the perpetuation of other family forms defined as deviant or abnormal. When middle-class white families of the early nineteenth century reorganized their internal relations to keep children at home longer and to divert the bulk of maternal attention from production of clothes and food to child care, they were enabled to do so only by the foreshortening of childhood among other sectors of the population—slave families that provided cotton to the new textile mills, working-class women and children who provided the cheap factory labor that made consumer goods affordable for the middle class, and the Irish or free African-American mothers and daughters who left their own homes to work brutally long hours.

Once the interdependence of different kinds of families and the multistranded linkages between family forms and changing socioeconomic conditions are understood, simplistic pronouncements about unilineal trends, having unitary effects, can be avoided. Dire predictions about the imminent collapse of "the traditional family" (Popenoe 1988) are no more helpful than equally cataclysmic denunciations of past family life as "a nightmare from which we have only recently begun to awaken" (de Mause 1974, p. 1). It is better to examine the changing dynamics and contradictions of distinctive family systems, situated in and shaped by a particular, historically specific articulation of economic, political, and cultural forces and conflicts.

American Family Types

In America, there have been four such broad constellations of family types. An ideal family stood at the center of each constellation, sanctioned by law and enshrined in the dominant ideology; but the ideal was often held in place only by the gravitational push and pull of the very different families that orbited around each other. Each family system was part of the larger universe of social reproduction and each brought the genders and age groups into characteristic relations of production and distribution, both in and out of the family; but gender and age relations, like family orbits, varied among different economic and political subgroups.

The first family system in America was that of the native peoples. This was actually a kinship system rather than a family system, for despite the wide variety of marital, sexual, and genealogical customs found in several hundred different cultures, most early Native-American groups subsumed the nuclear family and even the lineage in a much larger network of kin and marital alliances. Kinship rules regulated an individual's place in the overall production and distribution of goods, services, knowledge, and justice. Exogamy, the requirement that a person marry out of his or her natal group into a different clan or section, made each individual a member of intersecting kin groups, with special obligations and rights toward each category of relatives.

This system was severely disrupted by European colonization of North America. Massive epidemics decimated kin networks, disrupting social continuity. Heightened warfare elevated the role of young male leaders at the expense of elders and women. The influence of traders, colonial political officials, and Christian missionaries fostered a growing independence of the nuclear family vis-à-vis the extended household, kinship, and community group in which it had traditionally been embedded. Economic inequities, legislation, and racial discrimination ensured that such independence led more often to downward than upward mobility for these newly isolated families.

The European families that colonized America had conceptions of wealth, private profit, state authority over families, sexuality, and power relations within families that differed sharply from Native-American patterns. Although there were considerable variations among the colonies by region, and the Spanish colonies had a particularly distinctive mix of caste, family, and gender hierarchies (Gutierrez 1991), certain generalizations can be made. Colonial families had far more extensive property and inheritance rights than Native-American families, but they were also subject to more extensive controls by state and church institutions. The redistribution duties of wealthy families, however, were more narrow than those of Native Americans, so there were substantial differences in wealth and resources among colonial families right from the beginning.

Colonial families operated within a corporate system of agrarian household production sustained by a patriarchal, hierarchical political and ideological structure. The propertied conjugal family was the basis of this household order, but poor people without property tended to concentrate in wealthier households as apprentices, slaves, servants, or temporary lodgers, and the nuclear family did not occupy a privileged emotional or physical site in such households.

The propertied household, revolving around a single conjugal family, was the central unit of production, distribution, and authority. Thus, production and reproduction were tightly linked. The household head exercised paternal rights of discipline, including corporal punishment, over all household members; he was responsible for the education, religious instruction, and general behavior of his children, servants, and apprentices. Journals reveal the relative fluidity of household composition; as one or another member lived elsewhere for a while, servants came and went, and distant relatives spent short stays. Yet the need for preservation of the family property demanded a strict hierarchy that left little room for independent reproductive and marital decisions.

Slaves, of course, did not experience this unity of family, work, production, sexuality, and reproduction. Slave families existed only at the discretion of the master, and traditional African kin ties were sundered by the processes of enslavement and sale. African slaves and their descendants, however, strove with considerable success to preserve or recreate kinship networks and obligations through fictive kin ties, ritual coparenting or godparenting, complex naming patterns designed to authenticate extended kin connections, and adoption of orphans.

By the last third of the eighteenth century, many economic, political, and religious forces had begun to undermine the colonial patriarchal, corporate order. Households gained more independence from neighbors and old social hierarchies; the tight bond between reproduction and production was loosened as land shortages disrupted old succession patterns; and the authority of fathers diminished, as witnessed by an erosion of parental control over marriage, an increase in out-of-wedlock births, and a new concept of childhood that stressed the importance of molding the child's character rather than breaking the child's will.

In the early nineteenth century, the gradual separation of home and work, market production and household reproduction, along with the emergence of newly specialized occupations, paved the way for a changing relationship between family activities and economic production, a growing distinction between private and public life, and a new conception of male and female roles that stressed their complementary but sharply divided responsibilities and capacities. This has become known as the doctrine of separate spheres.

Class Distinctions

The family system that emerged in the middle class, and was increasingly adopted by entrepreneurs as well as skilled workers, was based on a highly idealized division of labor between husband and wife. The cult of domesticity gave men responsibility for economic and political tasks and women responsibility for morality, child rearing, and emotional ties. Though this was formulated as a public/private split, in which women were protected from "contamination" by the market, both spheres were tightly linked to the wage-labor system and an increasingly standardized market. The so-called relegation of women to the private sphere in the middle class was not so much a separation of work and home as a family strategy designed to facilitate the emergence of a male career (Ryan 1981). Women's expanded child-rearing duties, as well as their activities in moral reform associations, were critical in preparing their husbands and sons to enter new occupations. Men also became involved in the family in new ways, since fertility restriction was an important component of the middle-class strategy. This strategy involved the concentration of resources on fewer children; lengthened coresidence of parents and children; the use of peer groups to bind middle-

class persons together when outside the family; investment in schooling; and the development of maternal socialization methods designed to inculcate sexual restraint, temperance, family solidarity, conservative business habits, diligence, prolonged education, and delayed marriage.

Within the working class, the withdrawal of wives from paid employment also did not mean a real split between work and family, despite the ideological insistence on such a distinction. Children went out to work, contributing their wages to a family pool, while wives participated in the family economy by processing unfinished consumer goods, scavenging, bartering, peddling, and doing unreported work such as taking in boarders (Boydston 1990). In doing so, they often added more to the family's level of living than they could have earned in wages. The withholding of wives' labor from employers may also have been designed to further the demand for a family wage.

After the Civil War, the pace of industrialization, immigration, and urbanization quickened. As American families adapted to the demands of an industrializing and diverse society, different groups behaved in ways that created some average trends, often lumped together as general characteristics of "modernization." Average family size became smaller; families revolved more tightly around the nuclear core, putting greater distance between themselves and servants or boarders; parents became more emotionally involved in child rearing and for a longer period; couples oriented more toward companionate marriage; and the separation between home and market activities, both physically and conceptually, was sharpened. Yet many pronouncements about the relationship of industrialization to "the modern family" remain suspect, for they ignore important local, chronological, and class variations.

Despite growing agreement about the proper organization of "the family," for example, class distinctions in home furnishings, food, and household labor *widened* in the second half of the nineteenth century. While fertility fell by nearly 40 percent between 1855 and 1915, the birthrates of some unskilled and semi-skilled workers actually *rose* during this period, and the long-term trend toward nuclearity was slowed down between 1870 and 1890 as a number of groups experienced an increase in boarding or temporary coresidence with other kin (Coontz 1988).

Two trends that characterized all classes in the late nineteenth century but ran counter to twentieth-century developments were the withdrawal of wives from paid labor and the increasing length of time that young people lived at home. Again, this experience differed by social class and by gender. Working-class youths tended to get jobs while living at home; middle-class ones tended to go to school. But in the middle class, boys tended to stay in school longer than girls and girls tended to get jobs at a younger age, while working-class daughters stayed in school longer than working-class sons. Both of these trends were reversed in the early 1900s. African Americans were the only nineteenth-century group to anticipate twentieth-century trends in female employment. In the late nineteenth century, while only 4 percent of married white women worked for wages, 20 percent of married black women did so (Pleck 1979). Black families, however, were more likely than other working-class families to keep their children in school than to send them out to work at an early age.

The "Modern" Family

The changes that helped produce more "modern" family forms started in different classes and ethnic groups, meant different things to families occupying different positions in the industrial order, and did not proceed unilinearly. Family "modernization" was less the result of some functional evolution of "the" family than the dialectical outcome of *diverging* responses that occurred in different areas and classes at various times, eventually interacting to produce the trends now associated with industrialization.

By the late nineteenth century, both external and internal challenges to the domestic family and the concept of separate spheres had appeared. Victorian sexual mores clashed with the growing use of birth control and abortion, as well as with the opportunities for nonmarital sex associated with increased urbanization and changing work patterns for youths. Prostitution, once a safety valve for Victorian marriage, became a highly visible big business. A women's rights movement combined campaigns for seemingly conventional goals such as social purity and temperance with attacks on the double standard and demands for expanded legal rights for women. Debates and conflicts over sexuality became increasingly public.

By the turn of the century, these changes in sexual behavior and gender roles—interacting with the transition to mass production, a new corporate economy in which the role of family firms and personal reputation counted for less, and the rise of more centralized government institutions—had produced a new constellation of family types. Many of the direct, class-specific family strategies aimed at preparing children for work, maximizing family security, and coping with

illness, unemployment, or old age were obviated by new hiring and promotion patterns, the advent of unions, compulsory education, new patterns of housing segregation, the rise of specialized health and welfare institutions, and suburbanization. As families relied less on local, particularistic institutions such as craft associations, ethnic organizations, religious institutions, and urban political machines, they related instead to more formal, centralized institutions of education, job recruitment and training, social services, and distribution. Personal ties and intensities that had been dispersed among several complementary institutions, and personal networks that mediated between the individual and the larger society, were increasingly concentrated in the family. New notions of family privacy developed, along with heightened expectations of romance and individual fulfillment in marriage. A youth culture began to reorganize older family-centered courtship patterns into dating rituals that eroded the intense same-sex friendships and mother–child bonds of earlier years.

The new family shifted its axis from the mother–child relationship to the couple relationship and put forward the nuclear family unit as a place for qualitatively different relationships than those to be found with kin or friends. It also assumed a different relation to the state, simultaneously claiming an expanded sphere of private life and becoming more dependent on state subsidies or government institutions. At the same time, the emergence of a public policy aimed at establishing a family wage led to new ideas about family self-sufficiency and to condemnation of "promiscuous" families that pooled resources or shared housing beyond the nuclear unit.

Tensions and contradictions were associated with the new consumer family from the beginning. Peer groups were necessary for romantic love and heterosexual dating, but they conflicted with parental supervision and older sexual mores; elevation of the couple relationship to the primary center of all emotional and sensual satisfactions made an unhappy union seem intolerable, leading to a sharp rise in divorce rates. The emphasis on personal fulfillment opened up potential conflicts between the sacrifices necessary in families and the consumer satisfactions that romantic fantasies promised.

These conflicts began to surface in the 1920s, which experienced a generation gap, sexual revolution, and sense of family crisis that was every bit as disturbing to contemporaries as later rearrangements of family life and sexual behavior have been. Following the stock market crash of 1929, however, such anxieties took a backseat to the exigencies of the Great Depression, followed by World War II. After the family conflicts, separations, and hardships of depression and war, Americans set aside their earlier reservations and wholeheartedly embraced the innovations of the 1920s' family ideal, attaching it to the leap in single-family home ownership and personal consumption made possible by an unprecedented rise in real wages and government subsidization.

The ideal family of the 1950s, portrayed in countless television sitcoms, is now frequently mistaken as "traditional." In fact, the family of the 1950s was a historical blip. For the first time in 100 years, the age for marriage and motherhood fell, fertility increased, divorce rates declined from a 1945 high when one in every three marriages ended in divorce (Cherlin 1981), and women's increasing educational parity with men reversed itself. In a period of less than ten years, the proportion of never-married persons declined by as much as it had during the entire previous half-century.

The young nuclear families that dominated America's cultural landscape in the 1950s were not as idyllic as nostalgia makes them (Coontz 1992). The percentage of American children who were poor was higher during the 1950s than during the early 1990s, and much higher than during the period from 1965 to 1978. A high percentage of African-American two-parent families lived below the poverty line. Social workers and prosecutors failed to act decisively against incest, child abuse, or wife battering, and pervasive discrimination against women led many housewives to report that they felt trapped. Alcohol abuse was widespread.

Even the most successful families of the time, moreover, adopted practices that undermined the ideal of the 1950s. The growing idealization and commercialization of youth and sexuality paved the way for the generational conflicts of the 1960s and 1970s. Family planning became routine. Wives went to work in record numbers, while the concentration of childbearing in early marriage meant that mothers were more free to resume work once their children were in school.

Since the mid-1960s, the pace of change in family life has accelerated immensely (Coontz 1992). More than three-fourths of eighteen-to-twenty-four-year-old men and women have never been married. Almost four times as many Americans between the ages of thirty-five and forty-four live alone, compared to those living alone in 1970. About 50 percent of first marriages, and 60 percent of second ones, can be expected to end in divorce before the couple's fortieth anniversary (although the rise in divorce rates has been roughly balanced by the decline in death rates, so that a couple that marries today is more likely to

reach that fortieth anniversary than at any time prior to the 1960s).

Conclusion

Combined with the weakening correlation between the age at which individuals exit school, enter work, leave home, marry, and bear children (along with growing acceptance of divorce, unwed parents, and gay and lesbian unions), these changes have substantially diversified family forms. Household formation no longer centers around a nuclear family unit, and even two-parent nuclear families have transformed their child-rearing practices and values as mothers have increasingly gone to work outside the home.

Such changes have sparked intense debate over how much to try to strengthen "traditional" families and how much to adjust work, politics, school schedules, child care institutions, and personal value systems to the new diversity.

(*See also:* CHILDHOOD; DEMOGRAPHY; EXTENDED FAMILY; FAMILY VALUES; KINSHIP; NUCLEAR FAMILY; WORK AND FAMILY)

BIBLIOGRAPHY

Abbott, M. (1993). *Family Ties: English Families, 1540–1920.* New York: Routledge.

Boydston, J. (1990). *Home and Work: Housework, Wages, and the Ideology of Love in the Early Republic.* New York: Oxford University Press.

Cherlin, A. J. (1981). *Marriage, Divorce, Remarriage.* Cambridge, MA: Harvard University Press.

Clark, C. (1990). *The Roots of Rural Capitalism: Western Massachusetts, 1780–1860.* Ithaca, NY: Cornell University Press.

Coontz, S. (1988). *The Social Origins of Private Life: A History of American Families, 1600–1900.* New York: Verso.

Coontz, S. (1992). *The Way We Never Were: American Families and the Nostalgia Trap.* New York: Basic Books.

Davidoff, L., and Hall, C. (1990). *Family Fortunes: Men and Women of the English Middle Class, 1780–1850.* Chicago: University of Chicago Press.

de Mause, L., ed. (1974). *The History of Childhood.* New York: Psychohistory Press.

Elder, G.; Modell, J.; and Parke, R., eds. (1993). *Children in Time and Place: Developmental and Historical Insights.* New York: Cambridge University Press.

Goody, J. (1983). *The Development of Marriage and the Family in Europe.* Cambridge, Eng.: Cambridge University Press.

Gordon, M., ed. (1978). *The American Family in Social-Historical Perspective.* New York: St. Martin's Press.

Gutierrez, R. (1991). *When Jesus Came, the Corn Mothers Went Away: Marriage, Sexuality, and Power in New Mexico, 1500–1846.* Stanford, CA: Stanford University Press.

Hareven, T., ed. (1978). *Transitions: The Family and the Life Course in Historical Perspective*. New York: Academic Press.

Hernandez, D. (1993). *America's Children: Resources from Family, Government, and the Economy*. New York: Russell Sage Foundation.

Heyman, J. (1991). *Life and Labor on the Border: Working People of Northeastern Sonora, Mexico, 1886–1986*. Tucson: University of Arizona Press.

Kain, E. (1990). *The Myth of Family Decline: Understanding Families in a World of Rapid Social Change*. New York: Free Press.

Laslett, P., and Wall, R., eds. (1972). *Household and Family in Past Time*. Cambridge, Eng.: Cambridge University Press.

Mintz, S., and Kellogg, S. (1988). *Domestic Revolutions: A Social History of American Family Life*. New York: Free Press.

Modell, J. (1989). *Into One's Own: From Youth to Adulthood in the United States, 1920–1975*. Berkeley: University of California Press.

Pleck, E. (1979). "A Mother's Wages." In *A Heritage of Her Own*, ed. N. Cott and E. Pleck. New York: Simon & Schuster.

Pollock, L. (1987). *A Lasting Relationship: Parents and Children over Three Centuries*. Hanover, NH: University Press of New England.

Popenoe, D. (1988). *Disturbing the Nest: Family Change and Decline in Modern Societies*. New York: Aldine.

Ruggles, S. (1994). "The Transformation of American Family Structure." *American Historical Review* 99:103–128.

Ryan, M. (1981). *Cradle of the Middle Class: The Family in Oneida County, New York, 1790–1865*. New York: Cambridge University Press.

Seccombe, W. (1993). *Weathering the Storm: Working-Class Families from the Industrial Revolution to the Fertility Decline*. London: Verso.

Skolnick, A. (1991). *Embattled Paradise: The American Family in an Age of Uncertainty*. New York: Basic Books.

Stone, L. (1977). *The Family, Sex, and Marriage in England, 1500–1800*. New York: Harper & Row.

Tilly, L., and Scott, J. (1987). *Women, Work, and Family*. New York: Routledge.

Zinn, M. B., and Eitzen, S. (1987). *Diversity in American Families*. New York: Harper & Row.

STEPHANIE COONTZ

HOMELESS FAMILIES

Homeless families are those that either lack shelter or have shelter that is so inadequate, temporary, or insecure that the social, psychological, or physical health of the family is threatened. Homeless families are a departure from the classic homeless image of the single male, detached from society and disaffiliated from kin, friends, and work. In the United States, homeless families have a certain invisibility because they do not conform to this common media image and because the possible removal of the children drives many homeless families into hiding.

Causes of Homelessness

A major cause of family homelessness in the urban centers of North America and Western Europe is the shortage of affordable housing. This shortage is a part of the larger process of postindustrialization. Cities are transformed from manufacturing to service-based economies, and low-rent housing is replaced by offices, retail complexes, and luxury high-rise apartments. A widely used word for this loss of affordable housing is "gentrification," a term introduced by Ruth Glass (1964), who described the process whereby the "gentry" of Britain began to buy up and renovate old buildings in the 1960s.

In the United States, homelessness among families has been caused by a combination of gentrification, the withdrawal of government funding for new low-cost housing, the rise in single-parent households, loss of jobs, reduction in public assistance, and drug and alcohol abuse. Tension exists between those advocates and scholars who emphasize the importance of structural problems (e.g., the reduction in the number of affordable units and the loss of jobs) and those who emphasize the role of personal pathologies (e.g., drug abuse, alcoholism, and mental illness). However, the evidence suggests that the deinstitutionalization of mental patients from psychiatric hospitals has *not* been a contributing factor in homelessness among families.

In the developing world, explanations for homelessness center on rural-to-urban migration, severe unemployment and underemployment, and the existence of large numbers of refugees and victims of disasters (see Bascom 1993).

Numbers of Homeless Families

It is extremely difficult to ascertain the numbers of homeless families because few countries systematically enumerate the homeless in their national censuses. Even those countries that try to include a homeless count in their census have a difficult time isolating the homeless families within the larger homeless population.

In the United States, 190,406 persons were located in emergency shelters during the 1990 census (U.S. Bureau of the Census 1992). However, it is impossible to know how many families this figure included. Furthermore, it is not known how many families were doubled up, sleeping in vacant buildings, or split up due to lack of housing. An approximation of the extent of homelessness in the world was undertaken by the United Nations Centre for Human Settlement (1990). Based on reports from 144 countries, the United Nations estimates that one billion people live in conditions of inadequate shelter or literal homelessness. Most of the reports focused on families living in squatter settlements.

Research of Family Homelessness

The majority of the past research has been devoted to describing homeless families, concentrating on the most visible families (those in shelters, welfare hotels, or squatter settlements). Often missing are descriptions of the same families who are not represented in census reports.

Interest in homeless families in the United States began with studies of families living in shelters. In 1986, 80 homeless mothers and their 151 children were interviewed in 14 family shelters in the state of Massachusetts to assess the reasons for their homelessness and the housing, health, and psychological problems they faced (Bassuk, Rubin, and Lauriat 1986). The interviews revealed a great deal of housing instability among the families. In the previous five years, 85 percent had been doubled up in housing with other families and 50 percent had been in other emergency housing. More than 40 percent had come to the shelter from overcrowded, shared (doubled-up) housing arrangements. Not surprisingly, a high percentage of the mothers and children evidenced psychological stress as well as school-related problems. However, the most disturbed and disruptive families, who often do not seek help from the shelters or are turned away, were not included in the sample.

One issue to emerge from the pervasive use of shelters is whether or not families would deliberately enter a shelter, thereby defining themselves as "homeless," in order to receive preferential treatment in obtaining decent housing. In New York City, there are an estimated 200,000 ill-housed welfare families (Dugger 1992). To prevent many of them from entering the shelter system, shelters began keeping people for a long time before they got housing, as a deterrent to other doubled-up families that might want to leave their situations.

In addition to homeless shelters, hotels have been used as emergency shelter. In his book, *Rachel and Her Children* (1988), Jonathan Kozol vividly describes the plight of families housed in welfare hotels

in New York City. In England and the United States, there is evidence of a wide range of health and safety issues linked to conditions in welfare hotels (bed and breakfasts in England). These conditions include inadequate cooking, toilet, and laundry facilities (Murie and Forrest 1988, pp. 140–141). In New York City, the practice of using hotels for emergency housing had significantly decreased by the early 1990s.

Knowledge of homeless families has been enhanced by studies comparing the homeless with poor but housed families. In a study of social relationships, 677 homeless mothers and 495 poor-but-housed mothers were interviewed in New York City (Shinn, Knickman, and Weitzman 1991). The homeless families were interviewed at the time of their request for shelter to avoid confusing characteristics caused by residence in the shelter with characteristics of the families themselves. A surprising finding was that the *homeless* respondents in fact were in greater touch with their social networks than their housed counterparts. However, the homeless respondents were less able to stay with relatives and friends, in large part because they had already "worn out their welcome" by having stayed with them previously.

Another study comparing the homeless with the poor but housed in Los Angeles found that many of the homeless families had lost their housing because of a discontinuance of Aid to Families with Dependent Children (AFDC) for administrative reasons (Wood et al. 1990). In this study, both groups were spending or had spent two-thirds of their monthly income on rent and utilities, indicating that any loss of income could easily push the housed group into homelessness.

Much of the focus on homelessness in the developing world is on the hundreds of thousands of people living in or around squatter settlements. Squatting, as a generic term, refers to building a shelter of easily found materials on property to which one has no legal claim. These settlements are known by many terms, including *bidonvilles* (tin cities) in Africa, *favelas* in Brazil, and *pueblos jovénes* (young towns) in Peru. The harsh realities of living in a Brazilian *favela* were documented by Carolina Maria De Jesus in *Child of the Dark* (1963), one of the few such first-person accounts.

The name most closely associated with research and advocacy regarding squatter settlements is John Turner, whose book, *Housing by People: Towards Autonomy in Building Environments* (1976), was the seminal presentation of the potential of squatter settlements. These squatter settlements were intially seen as temporary, makeshift arrangements for new but "unintegrated" rural migrants to urban areas. The settlements were seen as marginal to the life of the city. By the late 1960s, squatter settlements were seen as rational alternatives to the housing shortage for low-income people (Moser 1987). Some governments shifted from a policy of demolishing the settlements to projects bringing the settlements clean water, sanitation, electricity, and security of tenure. Critics of governmental encouragement of self-help point out that this absolves governments from committing significant amounts of money to housing their population and that it also reduces the wage requirements of workers by giving them access to low-cost housing.

In addition to living in squatter settlements, families may live on the pavement. In Bombay, for example, Indian families construct dwellings using the side of a building and a tarpaulin supported by bamboo poles. The entire place is generally six feet by four feet and can be dismantled within ten minutes when there is a raid (Ramchandaran 1972). In Calcutta, the majority of the pavement dwellers are migrants from the rural areas of West Bengal or Bangladesh; they could not support themselves in their native villages.

In an overview of the relationship between shelter and health, Robert E. Novick (1987) of the World Health Organization discusses the health consequences of the squatter-settlement conditions, which often include a lack of adequate water supply for drinking and personal cleanliness, inadequate removal or disposal of excreta, insect and rodent infestations, unsupervised food markets, and excessive air and noise pollution. These conditions lead to disease, malnutrition, and undernourishment (which further weakens the body's resistance to disease). Children especially are subject to diarrhea, which leads to dehydration. It is estimated that one-third of all deaths of children under five years of age occur because of diarrheal disease (Novick 1987).

However, squatting is not confined to the Third World. In Philadelphia, the squatter movement occurred during the late 1970s as a community organizer for the North Philadelphia Block Development Corporation began placing homeless families in vacant buildings owned by Housing and Urban Development (HUD). The group screened out alcoholics, drug addicts, and other high-risk people. At the same time, a nationwide advocacy group, ACORN, was mobilizing families to move into city-owned property, and the city was urged to expand its Gift Property Program. By 1982, Philadelphia's city council passed legislation for the deeding of abandoned tax-delinquent properties to squatters, if they agreed to

make repairs that would bring the properties up to minimum standards (Adams 1986).

In an in-depth study of the squatters of vacant Habitations de Loyer Modéréis (HLM) in and around Paris, similar to public housing in the United States, Guy Boudimbou (1992) of the Centre de Recherche sur l'Habitat in Nanterre, France, found that most of the squatters were Northern and West African immigrants and their children. Because of significant discrimination by both privately owned housing as well as HLM housing, the ability to secure housing for the African immigrant has been severely restricted. In some of the deteriorated public-housing units, a network of squatters moves from one vacant building to another. There are also unscrupulous "managers" who draw up a file of vacant apartments, helping the family to break down the door and get installed.

Programs and Policies for Homeless Families

Programs that address family homelessness either increase the number of units of affordable housing, increase the person's ability to rent/own such housing, prevent the loss of housing, or generally advocate for the right for all people to have housing.

One approach to helping homeless families become and stay housed is transitional housing, as it is known in the United States. Transitional housing is generally a multifamily residency program that includes a variety of support services for low-income women and their children. It is sometimes called second-stage housing to distinguish it from emergency shelter for the homeless. Programs may take women in from homeless shelters, doubled-up housing, or other high-risk situations, such as women coming out of prisons. The residency period has a variable but finite duration, generally from six months to two years. Transitional housing provides a bridge for women to self-sufficiency and permanent housing (Women's Institute for Housing and Economic Development 1986).

To help families keep their housing, programs are needed to curtail evictions, one of the causes of homelessness in the United States. One such program is the Tenancy Settlement/Mediation Program in Passaic County, New Jersey, an area with a declining amount of residential housing, a deteriorating economic base, and high rates of poverty and public assistance. The program is staffed by social workers trained in mediation. The settlement/mediation program serves sixteen municipalities with a combined population of 500,000 people. In 1990, approximately 1,300 tenancy disputes were successfully settled, an 89.5 percent success rate (Curcio 1992).

In northwest Nova Scotia, the Hearth Home Project has increased the number of affordable rentals for farmers (some of whom had been living in old truck and bus bodies) through a building project that was congruent with the farmers' culture. Since the families spend most of their time in the kitchen (cooking, eating, and socializing), most did not want the standard National Housing agency-approved home. By 1990, fifty-three homes, renting at $350 per month, were built. They were made of wood and featured a large eat-in kitchen, two bedrooms, a living room, and a bath. The total cost of each house was $44,000, paid for with a mortgage through the Nova Scotia Department of Housing (Daly 1990).

Throughout the Third World, there are programs that enable squatter settlements to upgrade their housing, bring in essential services (potable water, sanitation, electricity), and secure the individual's right to remain in the housing. Nongovernmental agencies (NGOs) as well as governmental agencies have been involved in this effort. The World Bank is one of the leaders in the lending of money for sites and services projects and squatter upgrading projects, which usually feature a strong self-help component. In some parts of the world, households get together to build each other's houses; in others, the household hires people to work for them; in still others, the household builds the house on its own (Keare and Parris 1982).

One successful example of squatter upgrading has been the Kampung Improvement Programme in Jakarta, Indonesia. A kampung is a village, but in Jakarta it refers to urban settlements on swampy land, subject to serious flooding. A survey in 1969 found that out of 4.5 million people in Jakarta, 65 percent had no toilets and 80 percent had no electricity (Oliver 1987). The Kampung Improvement Programme provided 87 kampungs (more than one million people) with clean water, canals to mitigate flooding, improved roads and concrete paths, communal sanitation, and a system of garbage disposal. A World Bank Loan in 1974 added schools and health clinics. One major finding of this project was that bringing these services to the community inspired individual householders to improve their dwellings on their own (Oliver 1987).

The Undugu (Brotherhood in Kiswahili) Society of Nairobi, Kenya, is another example of a community organization that helps shantytown dwellers gain access to land and permission to build a dwelling them-

selves out of materials that can be purchased or found. The society has helped build 1,068 houses in three squatter communities in Nairobi; people there had been living in "igloo" huts of cardboard and plastic—which were subject to frequent fires—under the constant threat of eviction (Settlements Information Network Africa 1986). The program stressed community participation in the planning and building of the new houses, utilizing the skills and resources of the communities' young people, women, and elderly.

Conclusion

Examination of homeless families presents a tremendously diverse picture of the face of homelessness. Families in shelters and hotels, as well as squatters and pavement dwellers, lack the necessary tools to protect themselves from the outside world. They are also unable to nurture and educate their children adequately. Under these circumstances homeless families may eventually lose their ability to function as a family. Therefore, adequate and secure housing is essential in keeping families together; it is the anchor that underlies the very concept of family.

(*See also:* DEMOGRAPHY; ENTITLEMENTS; HOUSING; POVERTY; RESOURCE MANAGEMENT)

BIBLIOGRAPHY

Adams, C. T. (1986). "Homelessness in the Postindustrial City: Views from London and Philadelphia." *Urban Affairs Quarterly* 21:527–549.

Bascom, J. (1993). " 'Internal Refugees': The Case of the Displaced in Khartoum." In *Geography and Refugees: Patterns and Processes for Change*, ed. R. Black and V. Robinson. London: Belhaven Press.

Bassuk, E.; Rubin, L.; and Lauriat, A. (1986). "Characteristics of Sheltered Homeless Families." *American Journal of Public Health* 76:1097–1101.

Boudimbou, G. (1992). "Les Immigrés Africains et le Squatt des Logements Sociaux dans la Région Parisienne." Paper presented at the Fifth International Research Conference on Housing, Montreal.

Curcio, W. (1992). "Mediation and Homelessness." *Public Welfare* (Spring):34–39.

Daly, G. (1990). "Programs Dealing with Homelessness in the United States, Canada, and Britain." In *Homelessness in the United States: Data and Issues*, ed. J. Momeni. New York: Praeger.

De Jesus, C. M. (1963). *Child of the Dark: The Diary of Carolina Maria De Jesus.* Translated from the Portuguese. New York: New American Library.

Dugger, C. W. (1992). "Memo to Democrats: Housing Won't Solve Homelessness." *New York Times.* July 12, p. E9.

Fitchen, J. (1992). "On the Edge of Homelessness: Rural Poverty and Housing Insecurity." *Rural Sociology* 57:173–193.

Glass, R. (1964). *London: Aspects of Change.* London: Centre for Urban Studies and MacGillion & Kee.

Glasser, I. (1994). *Homelessness in Global Perspective.* New York: G. K. Hall.

Hardoy, J. E., and Satterthwaite, D. (1989). *Squatter Citizen: Life in the Urban Third World.* London: Earthscan.

Keare, D. H., and Parris, S. (1982). *Evaluation of Shelter Programs of the Urban Poor: Principal Findings.* World Bank Staff Working Papers No. 547. Washington, DC: World Bank.

Kozol, J. (1988). *Rachel and Her Children.* New York: Crown.

Moser, C. O. N., and Peake, L., eds. (1987). *Women, Human Settlements, and Housing.* London: Tavistock.

Murie, A., and Forrest, R. (1988). "The New Homeless in Britain." In *Affordable Housing and the Homeless,* ed. J. Friedrichs. Berlin: Walter de Gruyter.

Novick, R. E. (1987). "Shelter and Health." *World Health* (July):6–9.

Oliver, P. (1987). *Dwellings: The House Across the World.* Austin: University of Texas Press.

Ramchandaran, P. (1972). *Pavement Dwellers in Bombay City.* Series 26. Bombay: Tata Institute of Social Science.

Settlements Information Network Africa. (1986). "Case Study on Undugu Society Squatter Upgrading in Nairobi." Nairobi: Mazingira Institute.

Shinn, M.; Knickman, J. R.; and Weitzman, B. C. (1991). "Social Relationships and Vulnerability to Becoming Homeless Among Poor Families." *American Psychologist* 46:1180–1187.

Turner, J. (1976). *Housing by People: Towards Autonomy in Building Environments.* London: Marion Boyars.

United Nations Centre for Human Settlements. (1990). *Shelter: From Projects to National Strategies.* Nairobi: Author.

U.S. Bureau of the Census. (1992). *Statistical Abstract of the United States,* 112th edition. Washington, DC: U.S. Government Printing Office.

Women's Institute for Housing and Economic Development, Inc. (1986). *A Manual on Transitional Housing.* Boston: Author.

Wood, D.; Valdez, B.; Hayashi, T.; and Shew, A. (1990). "Homeless and Housed Families in Los Angeles: A Study Comparing Demographic, Economic, and Family Function Characteristics." *American Journal of Public Health* 80:1049–1052.

IRENE GLASSER

HOME SCHOOLING

Home schooling, an educational alternative in which parents assume the primary responsibility for the education of their children, has become a national movement. This movement to educate children in the home is continuing to grow, fueled by a dramatic decline in legal barriers to the practice. In addition, an aggressive home-school lobby has succeeded in bringing public schools and home-school advocates closer together. All fifty states now allow some kind of home schooling. Four states (Oregon, Washington, Vermont, and Iowa) allow home-schooled children to take part in public school extracurricular activities, and one California district provides funds to home-schooling families to purchase textbooks (Natale 1992). However, home educators face a conglomeration of regulations, statutes, and other laws.

Individual states regulate home schools by using existing laws that apply to home schooling, by passing specific home schooling legislation, and by passing legislation that indirectly affects home schooling. Under these conditions, parents with the responsibility of providing most of their children's education may feel the need for some support. A key form of support is available via support group membership. Additionally, because each state has its own set of statutes and other laws, the support group may also function as a repository for and a dispenser of home-schooling information. Structured curricula, subject area studies, and games and equipment are available to parent teachers. Costs of these materials are nearly always borne by the parents, and expenses can range from less than one hundred to several hundred dollars. Suitability of educational materials is at times determined by the child's needs, by the circumstances of parents, and by state requirements. Because support groups are like people—each has a personality of its own and offers different services and activities—a group should be found that best suits a family's particular needs.

Approaches to home schooling vary greatly among participants. Many curriculum materials are supplied by religious publishers, but families not using prepackaged curricula learn to compensate by drawing on outside resources for curriculum content. Such outside resources might include 4-H clubs and environmental organizations.

Home schooling is small and diverse. The exact number of home-schooled students is difficult to determine; however, it is assumed that only 1 percent of the total student population remain at home for their education (Lines 1987). Although specific reasons for home schooling are as diverse as the families themselves, home schoolers appear to share one thing: the firm belief that parents can and should be deeply involved in the education and development of their own children.

Home schooling is the earliest form of education, as old as the family itself. However, the movement began to intensify during the late 1960s as John Holt, "the father of the modern home school movement," encouraged parents to leave the public school system (Litcher and Schmidt 1991). Continuing to challenge the public system, Ray and Dorothy Moore suggest that parents nurture the child at home until eight or nine years of age (Litcher and Schmidt 1991).

Studies suggest that home-schooled students do as well as or better than their public school peers on national standardized tests (Frost and Morris 1988; Ray 1988). Perhaps more important is that anecdotal evidence suggests that many children schooled at home are independent and inquisitive learners. Approximately 50 percent of home-schooled students attend college, about the same rate as their public school counterparts (Frost and Morris 1988).

Home schooling is not for everyone. Personality differences, financial constraints, or personal preferences eliminate home schooling as an option for most families. Those who choose it are generally aware of the demands and difficulties involved. The decision to home-school requires a commitment of a great deal of time and energy by family members, but all home schoolers seem to share a belief that education is integral to family life.

(*See also:* SCHOOL)

BIBLIOGRAPHY

Frost, E. A., and Morris, R. C. (1988). "Does Home-Schooling Work? Some Insights for Academic Success." *Contemporary Education* 59:223–227.

Knowles, J. G. (1991). "Parents' Rationale for Operating Home Schools." *Journal of Contemporary Ethnography* 20:203–230.

Lines, P. M. (1987). "An Overview of Home Instruction." *Phi Delta Kappan* 68:510–517.

Litcher, J. H., and Schmidt, S. J. (1991). "Social Studies in Home School." *Social Education* 55:239–241.

Natale, J. A. (1992). "Understanding Home Schooling." *American School Board Journal* 179:26–27, 29.

Ray, B. D. (1988). "Home Schools: A Synthesis of Research on Characteristics and Learner Outcomes." *Education and Urban Society* 21:16–31.

VIRGINIA ERION

HOMOSEXUALITY   *See* GAY AND LESBIAN PARENTS; GENDER; SEXUAL ORIENTATION

HOUSING

Housing is a topic that has been studied from the viewpoint of nearly all the scientific and humanistic fields. There are aspects of housing best understood through physics and engineering, such as how certain air contaminants can enter a dwelling, and other aspects are best understood through aesthetics and artistic expression, such as the effects on human beings of pleasant environments. The housing of families can also be understood in social and psychological terms.

Housing, Family, and Society

The focus of this entry is the process by which family households obtain and utilize their housing, a process that is conducted by families in the context of the cultural and social milieu. This includes two subprocesses: adjustment and adaptation. Adjustment is the routine meeting of the family's housing needs. Adaptation refers to changes the family would make in its own makeup, including demographic composition and psychological orientations, when adjustment could not produce satisfactory housing conditions.

Analysis of the literature on adjustment and adaptation processes leads to the following conclusions:

1. There are social pressures on households that notify them of the kinds of housing that are culturally appropriate.
2. There are social conditions that determine the kind of housing households actually live in.
3. The relationship between the characteristics of housing and the family's requirements in the context of the culture produces a degree of satisfaction/dissatisfaction.
4. Satisfaction or dissatisfaction affects the motivation to move or alter the present dwelling (adjustment).
5. The motivation affects the occurrence of the actual adjustment behavior (Morris et al. 1990; Morris and Winter 1975, 1978).
6. There are constraining factors that prevent the implementation of adjustment behaviors (Foote et al. 1960).

If the family is unable to complete adjustment behavior and thereby meet its housing needs, it would consider adaptation, which would entail making changes in itself rather than in its housing.

Households engage in a process of adjusting their housing to fit their needs over the life cycle while being constrained by the availability of household resources and the economic, social, and cultural environments. The constraints are the mechanisms that facilitate or hinder housing adjustment and at times make adaptation necessary.

Housing Adjustment

There are eight basic concepts in housing adjustment theory: norms, both cultural and household, used to evaluate current housing conditions; current housing conditions; normative deficits that result when housing conditions do not meet the norms; satisfaction/dissatisfaction with current housing conditions; intentions to engage in adjustment behavior; actual adjustment behavior; constraints that inhibit or facilitate adjustment; values that are used to choose among various characteristics of housing and to evaluate housing with respect to other goods and services the household may need.

Norms. Housing norms are defined as social pressures in the form of rules for behavior and life conditions that are accompanied with related sanctions (Dillman, Tremblay, and Dillman 1979; Morris and Winter 1975). An important consideration when discussing norms is to be sure to differentiate them from behavior. Norms should not be thought of as average behavior. Behavior is what individuals do. Norms are ideas about what individuals *should* do.

The housing norms that have been most extensively studied include those for home ownership, single-family dwellings, bedroom space, and private outdoor space. There are other norms that are less widely shared as well, but these represent the core norms relevant to families. The idea that a family should, if possible, own its home, which should be a single-family dwelling with sufficient bedrooms to allow comfortable sleeping arrangements and some amount of private yard space, is deeply ingrained in American culture and in many other cultures around the world.

These norms apply with particular strength to intact families with children. Exemptions from the norms occur for households with severe constraints such as low income. Nevertheless, the norms themselves apply to families in nearly all ethnic and racial groupings and at all income levels. Numerous researchers have shown that when asked about what kind of housing a family should be able to live in, members of African-American, Hispanic-American,

and European-American families give nearly identical answers. Poor, rich, and middle-income families give the same answers. What differ are the actual housing conditions and behaviors, not the norms.

The norms that are applied in given situations by households are a weighted average of the various norms that may impinge on the family. These include societywide norms, but there may be special group norms depending on the household's background. The family itself may also develop its own unique set of housing norms.

Current housing conditions. The housing conditions of interest are conditions that are prescribed by the norms. Conditions are appropriate for study to the extent that they relate to society's and the household's housing norms. The conditions most often studied are those to which norms are applied: ownership, type of dwelling, bedroom space, and outdoor space.

Normative deficits. The deficits represent unmet needs. A difference between a housing condition prescribed by a norm and the actual condition represents a deficit (Beyer 1949; Nickell et al. 1951; Morris et al. 1990; Morris and Winter 1975, 1978; Rossi 1955). For example, if a household has five bedrooms but the norms prescribe six, the household has a deficit of one bedroom.

The deficits that are most relevant in analysis of family housing are the ones related to the norms and conditions, including home ownership (renters have deficits), single-family dwellings (people living in multiple-family dwellings have deficits), bedroom space (e.g., those with too few bedrooms to permit separation of boys and girls into separate bedrooms when they reach a certain age have deficits), and outdoor private space (those who have no yard or a very tiny yard for children to play in have deficits).

Satisfaction/dissatisfaction. Family satisfaction is a measure of the household's affective state with respect to the degree to which the current housing meets the norms. Two approaches have been used in the research that has been done. In some studies a general measure of overall satisfaction with the dwelling is used; in others, satisfaction with specific characteristics of the housing is used (Coveney and Rudd 1986; Morris, Winter, and Crull 1980; Speare 1974). Those are sometimes combined into a scale of general satisfaction and sometimes are used separately as measures of specific satisfactions. In the latter case the tendency would be to use satisfaction items that match the norms, conditions, and deficits being studied. Therefore, there might be a set of questions asked about whether the family is satisfied with its tenure, type of dwelling, and amount of indoor and outdoor space. These could be considered separately or combined into an average satisfaction indicator.

Behavior and behavior intentions. Because there are two adjustment behaviors—altering the current dwelling or moving—there are two behavior intention concepts: intentions for alterations/additions and intentions for mobility. The point of the intentions concepts is that seldom does adjustment behavior occur without a prior state of motivation or intention to perform the behavior. The obvious exception is the case of involuntary behavior, such as being evicted by a landlord, which is not encompassed within the adjustment processes. A different set of concepts is needed to explain why landlords choose to evict particular tenants.

Constraints. There are five basic classes of constraints: resource constraints, including money, information, skills, and the like; market constraints, including prices and supplies of housing, materials, land, and financing; household organizational constraints, including the ability to marshal resources as well as make and implement decisions; predispositions or psychological dimensions of the household similar to the personality of the individual (e.g., apathy, achievement motivation, and the like); discrimination (Morris et al. 1990; Morris and Winter 1985).

A sixth type of constraint, needed to refer to the effects of the culture, is used in cross-cultural and international comparisons of housing adjustment. It is based on the idea that family housing adjustment concepts are defined in terms of the norms, values, and conditions of particular cultures and that the specific definitions of these concepts may differ from one cultural background to another (Khil 1991).

Values. It is important to recognize the priority of some other concerns (e.g., food) over housing. Expenditure on housing often is postponed during times of scarce resources when most of the household's resources are used for food. Then, in better times, a portion will be diverted to housing improvement. Therefore, competing needs serve as an additional set of constraints on housing behavior. The choice of which of those competing needs to fill is where the concept of values enters the analysis. Households differ in the importance of housing relative to other life domains (Beyer, Mackesey, and Montgomery 1955; Cutler 1947; Goulart 1981) and in the threshold at which resources are diverted to and from housing (Morris and Winter 1978).

Another point at which values enter the analysis is in balancing the various housing characteristics to meet the pattern of specific needs of the household at a specific life cycle stage (Goulart 1981; Morris et al.

1990). For example, large households with limited income must balance their need for space with their desire for a high-quality dwelling. They usually trade quality for space.

In general, the basic concepts of housing adjustment fit together as follows:

1. If a family has a housing deficit, it is likely to become dissatisfied with its housing.
2. If the family is dissatisfied it is likely to develop intentions to correct the deficit.
3. If it has the intention to do something about the deficit, it is likely to do so.

However, many families are stalled somewhere in the adjustment process. The causes are the constraints. A family may have a deficit but not become dissatisfied because of some psychological predisposition. It may be dissatisfied but not motivated to reduce its dissatisfaction because of an ineffective family organization. It may intend to engage in adjustment behavior but be unable to do so because of a market or resource constraint.

Adaptation

There are two basic concepts in adaptation: adaptation that involves needs reduction and adaptation that involves constraint reduction. The preferred method of dealing with housing problems or deficits would be adjustment behavior through which deficits are removed. Because of the severity of the constraints, some families are unable to adjust. They are forced to consider one or both forms of adaptation.

Needs reduction. A popular slogan says "When all else fails, lower your standards." That is the essence of one form of needs reduction. When faced with severe constraints, the family can decide not to try to meet the norms, choosing instead to develop a modified version that is easier to meet. Another method of needs reduction is to change the composition of the family. If the family is getting crowded, perhaps an older child can be encouraged to move into an apartment to release some space for the younger children. If the house is too big and expensive, perhaps another family could be encouraged to move in, and by doubling up, the two families could share the housing expenses.

Constraint reduction. Of the basic types of constraints, only a few are susceptible to change by the individual family. Discrimination, for example, is not really under the control of the victim family. The prices and supplies of housing and related goods and services are not within the ability of individual families to control. The constraints that are possible to change include the resource constraints, which could be removed by investing in training or education to improve income. The household organizational constraint could be reduced by reorganizing the household. Sometimes the member of the family who handles the money and makes economic decisions is not the most able member. If they are having trouble obtaining satisfactory housing, such a household could reorganize and put someone else in charge of money and perhaps remove housing deficits by more effective management.

Conclusion

A summary of social scientific knowledge on housing and its effect on family life depends on the context of the research and analysis that are available and the limitations under which that research was done. There might be interest in finding the answers to questions such as "What effect does a particular arrangement of rooms have on the quality of family life?" The policy implications of answers to such questions would be that by knowing the effects of particular housing arrangements, such effects could be either fostered or inhibited by housing design. However, good answers to such questions do not exist because of the amazing flexibility of individuals and families forced to live under less than desirable conditions. If the layout of a dwelling is not well suited to the resident family, the family may either make changes in the dwelling or compensate for the dwelling by making changes in other aspects of family life. Therefore, limited policies have been developed to guide housing design decisions on other than aesthetic grounds.

One of the reasons for the lack of knowledge about the effects of physical characteristics of housing is that, many scholars have concluded, the wrong questions are being asked. The main direction of influence is from the social and psychological characteristics of individuals and families to the nature of housing rather than the reverse. Winston Churchill's statement to the effect that people determine the form of their buildings and then the buildings shape the people's development as human beings does not represent a symmetrical relationship between humans and their housing. In fact, the dominant forces come from human beings and their social and cultural arrangements to determine the form and use of dwellings.

Because of the forces released in the process of adjustment and adaptation, families' responses feed back to the society, and policies can be developed to help families house themselves in ways that foster high-quality family life and support the social development of the children. There are constraints such as budgets deficits that inhibit the ability of the society to meet the needs of all families completely. Nevertheless, suggestions can now be made about how social policy could best assist families with their housing. Policies that help families with constraint removal or reduction are desirable. Policies that force families to reduce their standards or force them to double up are not desirable.

(*See also:* HOMELESS FAMILIES; RESOURCE MANAGEMENT)

BIBLIOGRAPHY

Beyer, G. H. (1949). *Farm Housing in the Northeast.* Ithaca, NY: Cornell University Press.

Beyer, G. H.; Mackesey, T. W.; and Montgomery, J. E. (1955). *Houses Are for People: A Study of Home Buyer Motivations.* Ithaca, NY: Cornell University Housing Research Center.

Coveney, A. R., and Rudd, N. M. (1986). "Determinants of Housing Satisfaction of Low-Income, Rural, Male, Family Heads." *Housing and Society* 13:3–18.

Cutler, V. (1947). *Personal and Family Values in the Choice of a Home.* Ithaca, NY: New York Agricultural Experiment Station, Cornell University.

Dillman, D. A.; Tremblay, K. R.; and Dillman, J. J. (1979). "Influence of Housing Norms and Personal Characteristics on Stated Housing Preferences." *Housing and Society* 6:2–19.

Foote, N. N.; Abu-Lughod, J.; Foley, M. M.; and Winnick, L. (1960). *Housing Choices and Constraints.* New York: McGraw-Hill.

Goulart, L. X. (1981). "The Effect of the Concordance Between Housing Values and Housing Conditions on Housing Satisfaction." Master's thesis. Ames: Iowa State University.

Khil, S. Y. (1991). "A Cross-Cultural Study of Housing Adjustment Among Korean, Mexican, and American Households." Ph.D. diss. Ames: Iowa State University.

Morris, E. W., and Winter, M. (1975). "A Theory of Family Housing Adjustment." *Journal of Marriage and the Family* 37:79–88.

Morris, E. W., and Winter, M. (1978). *Housing, Family, and Society.* New York: Wiley.

Morris, E. W.; Winter, M.; and Crull, S. R. (1980). "Transformation and Weighting of Items in the Measurement of Satisfaction." In *Refining Concepts and Measures of Consumer Satisfaction and Complaining Behavior,* ed. H. K. Hunt and R. L. Day. Bloomington: Indiana University School of Business.

Morris, E. W.; Winter, M.; Whiteford, M. B.; and Randall, D. C. (1990). "Adjustment, Adaptation, Regeneration, and the Impact of Disasters on Housing and Households." *Housing and Society* 17:1–29.

Nickell, P.; Budolfson, M.; Liston, M.; and Willis, E. (1951). *Farm Family Housing Needs and Preferences in the North Central Region.* Ames: Iowa State University Press.

Riemer, S. (1943). "Sociological Theory of Home Adjustment." *American Sociological Review* 8:272–278.

Rossi, P. H. (1955). *Why Families Move.* New York: Free Press.

Speare, A., Jr. (1974). "Residential Satisfaction as an Intervening Variable in Residential Mobility." *Demography* 11:173–188.

EARL W. MORRIS
MARY WINTER